# UTAH
# HANDBOOK

# UTAH
## HANDBOOK

### BILL WEIR

**MOON**
PUBLICATIONS, INC.

# UTAH HANDBOOK

Please send all comments, corrections, additions, amendments, and critiques to:

**BILL WEIR**
**c/o MOON PUBLICATIONS, INC.**
**722 WALL STREET**
**CHICO, CA 95928, USA**

*Published by*
Moon Publications, Inc.
722 Wall Street
Chico, California 95928, USA
tel. (916) 345-5473

*Printed by*
Colorcraft Ltd., Hong Kong

PRINTING HISTORY

First Edition
1988
Reprinted August 1989
**Second Edition**
**February 1991**

*Library of Congress Cataloging in Publication Data*

Weir, Bill, 1951-
   Utah handbook / Bill Weir. — 2nd ed.
      p. cm.
   Includes bibliographical references and index.
      1. Utah—Description and travel—1981—Guide-books.   I. Title.
F824.3.W44   1991
917.9204'33—dc20                                                      90-49710
                                                                              CIP

   ISBN 0-918373-46-8 : $12.95

Printed in Hong Kong

Cover photo: Canyonlands National Park and distant Abajos from Dead Horse Point State Park; photo courtesy of Tom Till.

Although the author and publisher have made every effort to ensure that the information was correct at the time of going to press, the author and publisher do not assume and hereby disclaim any liability to any party for any loss or damage caused by errors, omissions, or any potential travel disruption due to labor or financial difficulty, whether such errors or omissions result from negligence, accident, or any other cause.

WARNING: Nothing in this book is intended to be used for navigation. Boaters are advised to consult official sailing directions and nautical charts.

# CONTENTS

# LIST OF CHARTS

# LIST OF MAPS

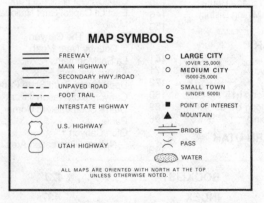

## MAP SYMBOLS

| | |
|---|---|
| ═══════ FREEWAY | O  **LARGE CITY** (OVER 25,000) |
| ─────── MAIN HIGHWAY | O  **MEDIUM CITY** (5000-25,000) |
| ─────── SECONDARY HWY./ROAD | o  SMALL TOWN (UNDER 5000) |
| ─ ─ ─ ─ UNPAVED ROAD | ■  POINT OF INTEREST |
| ─ ·─ ·─ FOOT TRAIL | ▲  MOUNTAIN |
| INTERSTATE HIGHWAY | BRIDGE |
| U.S. HIGHWAY | PASS |
| UTAH HIGHWAY | WATER |

ALL MAPS ARE ORIENTED WITH NORTH AT THE TOP
UNLESS OTHERWISE NOTED.

# PHOTO CREDITS

# ILLUSTRATION CREDITS

# ABBREVIATIONS

| | |
|---|---|
| ATV—all-terrain vehicle | mph—miles per hour |
| AZ—Arizona | NM—New Mexico |
| C.—century | NV—Nevada |
| ca.—*circa,* about | ORV—off-road vehicle |
| CA—California | OW—one way |
| CO—Colorado | pop.—population |
| d—double | RV—recreational vehicle |
| elev.—elevation | s—single |
| F—Fahrenheit | tel.—telephone |
| ft.—feet | UT—Utah |
| jct.—junction | WY—Wyoming |

# ACKNOWLEDGEMENTS

Many thanks go to the hundreds of people who assisted in making *Utah Handbook* as complete and accurate as it is. I am especially indebted to people of the National Park Service, U.S. Forest Service, Bureau of Land Management, and Utah State Parks, whose high standards help make Utah such a wonderful place to visit. Tourist offices, from the tiniest communities to the big cities, supplied valuable maps, ideas, and advice. Super thanks go to Doreen Maxfield of the Salt Lake Convention & Visitors Bureau for her far-above-the-call-of-duty help with this second edition. The wonderful historic photos appear due to the assistance of friendly librarians Bill Slaughter of the LDS Historical Department and Susan Whetstone of the Utah State Historical Society. Extra special thanks go to Sheri Griffith, the wonderful lady of Sheri Griffith Expeditions in Moab, for allowing me to work my way down the Green and Colorado rivers!

**Meet The Moon Crew**
The dedicated group at Moon Publications helped turn computer printouts and illustrations into this book. Not content with just writing the words, the author also pioneered the use of desktop publishing at Moon with the *Utah Handbook*. He used Ventura software on an IBM clone. Asha Johnson typeset the charts for both editions and helped with the typesetting of this edition. Louise Foote put her pen to work for drawings of the Utah wildlife and flowers that grace these pages, then drew most of the maps. Dave Hurst helped with the maps and applied his magic touch to the book's design. Bob Race polished up the cartography for the second edition and did the new Great Western Trail map. All patiently endured suggestions from a fussy author. The *Utah Handbook* manuscript showed substantial improvements from the first drafts to the last, thanks to the enthusiasm and editorial skills of Mark Morris. Mark also proofed the second edition. My mom, Doris Weir, had an equal hand in the editing. Much of the credit for getting this book to you goes to Sales Manager Donna Galassi, Publicist Virginia Michaels, Financial Wizard Cindy Fahey, and Mail-room Manager Rick Johnson. And lastly, appreciation is due my publisher, Bill Dalton, who helped bring this project to a successful completion.

# IS THIS BOOK OUT OF DATE?

Nothing stays the same, it seems. Although this book has been carefully researched, Utah will continue to grow and change. New sights and places to stay and eat will open while others change hands or close. Your comments and ideas for improving *Utah Handbook* will be highly valued. If you find something new or discontinued or changed, or perhaps a map or worthwhile place to visit that has been overlooked, please let me know so that I can include it in the next edition. All contributions (letters, maps, and photos) will be carefully saved, checked, and acknowledged. If we use your photos or artwork, you will be mentioned in the credits and receive a free copy of the book. Be aware, however, that the author and publisher are not responsible for unsolicited manuscripts, photos, or artwork and, in most cases, cannot undertake to return them unless you include a self-addressed, stamped envelope. Address your letters to:

Bill Weir
c/o Moon Publications, Inc.
722 Wall St.
Chico, CA 95928, USA

NORMAN H. BANGERTER

GOVERNOR

STATE OF UTAH
OFFICE OF THE GOVERNOR
SALT LAKE CITY
84114

Welcome to Utah!

I extend a personal invitation to discover the natural beauty, history and great people that make Utah a special place. From the urban excitement of the Wasatch Front to tranquil desert solitude, the Beehive State offers a variety of travel choices and recreational activities unmatched by any state.

As you travel through Utah, the unique qualities that make our state outstanding become evident. From the red rock canyons, mountains, deserts, lakes and cities, Utah offers something for everyone. Discover the freedom of the outdoors at one of the state's many national parks and national monuments or get off the beaten path and enjoy the beauty of our scenic route system. Meet the challenge of skiing the "greatest snow on earth" or hike to the summit of an alpine peak. Enrich your day at our festivals and carnivals, or capture a glimpse of the pioneer past at our many museums and historic landmarks.

Utah represents the heart of an unparalleled vacationland that offers escape, relaxation and sanctuary -- for a day, a week or a lifetime. Whatever your destination, take some extra time to discover Utah's greatest asset--its people. You'll find us friendly and willing to make your visit to Utah memorable and pleasant.

We Utahns want to extend an invitation for you to visit this exceptional state through this book, the Utah Handbook.

Sincerely,

Norman H. Bangerter
Governor

# INTRODUCTION

Few places in the world combine such spectacular terrain and an unusual history as does Utah. The state lies in the heart of the American West, with the majestic splendor of the Rocky Mountains, the colorful canyonlands of the Colorado Plateau, and the remote desert ranges of the Great Basin. This region beckoned as the "Promised Land" to members of the struggling Mormon Church in the 1800s— a place where the faithful could survive and prosper. Not since Moses led the Israelites out of Egypt has there been an exodus of the magnitude of the Mormons' migration from the Midwest to Utah. Utah's museums and historic sites help you to appreciate the accomplishments of the Mormons and other

pioneers of this rugged land.

Today you can comfortably enjoy the scenic splendor of Utah, much of it little changed since the first pioneers arrived in 1847. Salt Lake City in the north and the 5 national parks in the south rank at the top of most visitors' lists, but many other beautiful and intriguing places remain to be discovered. Incredibly varied canyon country, rugged mountain ranges, glistening salt flats, historic sites, Indian reservations, old mining towns, and bright city lights—the *Utah Handbook* will help you discover these and many more attractions. Practical information is given for everyone, including the oft-neglected low-budget traveler.

## THE LAND

Utah's 84,990 square miles places it 11th in size among the 50 states. You could fit Maine, Vermont, New Hampshire, Connecticut, Massachusetts, New Jersey, and Maryland within its borders and still have room for Rhode Island. The varied landscape has been divided into 3 major physiographic provinces: the **Basin and Range Province** of the west-

ern part; the **Middle Rocky Mountain Province** of the soaring Uinta, Wasatch, and Bear River ranges in the north and northeast; and the **Colorado Plateau Province** of canyons, mountains, and plateaus in the southeast. Some physiographers also designate a fourth province, the **Basin and Range-Colorado Plateau Transition.** This area, also known as

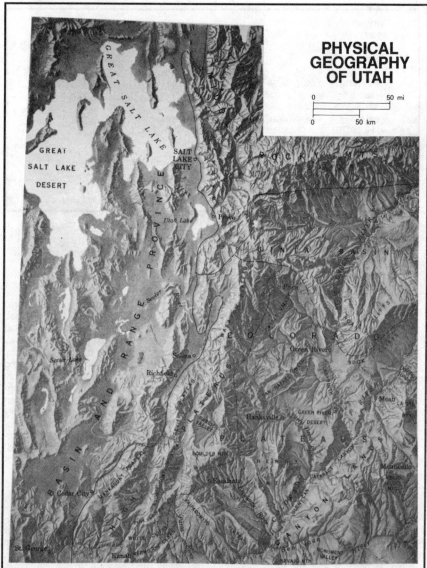

**PHYSICAL
GEOGRAPHY
OF UTAH**

From "Geology and Geography of the Henry Mountains Region, Utah" by Charles B. Hunt;
U.S. Geological Survey Professional Paper 228, GPO 1953.

the "High Plateaus," stretches from the Wasatch Range south into Arizona. Mountains and plateaus in the Transition Province share structural features such as faults with both neighboring provinces.

## Basin And Range Province
Rows of fault-block mountain ranges follow a north-south alignment in this province, located in the Great Basin west of the Wasatch Range and the High Plateaus. Erosion has worn down many of the ranges and has formed large alluvial fans in adjacent basins. Many of these broad valleys lack outside drainage; none have outlets to the ocean. Terraces marking shorelines of prehistoric Lake Bonneville, which once covered most of this province, can be seen on hillsides. Few perennial streams originate in these rocky mountains. Rivers from ranges to the east end their voyages in the Great Salt Lake, Sevier Lake, or barren silt-filled valleys. Most of the province lies between 4,000 and 5,000 feet. Peaks in the Stansbury and Deep Creek mountains rise more than 11,000 feet above sea level, creating "biological islands" inhabited by cool-climate plants and animals.

## Middle Rocky Mountains Province
The Wasatch Range and the Uinta Mountains that form this province provide some of the most dramatic alpine scenery in the state. In both mountainous areas, you'll find cirques, arêtes, horns, and glacial troughs carved by massive rivers of ice during past periods of glaciation. Structurally, however, the ranges have little in common. The narrow Wasatch, one of the most rugged ranges in the country, runs north-south for about 200 miles between the Idaho border and central Utah. Slippage along the still-active Wasatch Fault has resulted in a towering western face with almost no foothills. Most of Utah's ski resorts lie within the Wasatch Range. The Uinta Mountains in the northeast corner of the state are a broad uplifted area about 150 miles long from west to east and some 30 miles across. Twenty-four peaks exceed 13,000 feet, and Kings Peak (elev. 13,528 ft.) is the highest in Utah.

An estimated 1,400 tiny lakes dot glacial moraines of the Uintas.

## Colorado Plateau Province
World-famous for its scenery and geology, the Colorado Plateau covers nearly half of Utah. Elevations lie mostly between 3,000 and 6,000 feet, and some mountain peaks reach nearly 13,000 feet. The Uinta Basin forms the northern part of this vast complex of plateaus; it's bordered on the north by the Uinta Mountains and on the south by the Roan Cliffs. Although most of the basin is gently rolling, the Green River and its tributaries have carved some spectacular canyons into the Roan and Book cliffs. Farther south, the Green and Colorado rivers have sculpted remarkable landscapes of deep canyons, buttes, mesas, arches, and badlands in the "Canyonlands" of southeastern Utah. Uplifts and foldings have formed such features as the San Rafael Swell, Waterpocket Fold, and Circle Cliffs. Exposures of ancient igneous intrusions make up the rounded Abajo, Henry, La Sal, and Navajo mountains. The High Plateaus in southcentral Utah drop in a series of steps known as the

"Grand Staircase." Exposed layers range from the relatively young rocks of the Black Cliffs (lava flows) in the north to the increasingly older Pink Cliffs (Wasatch Formation), Gray Cliffs (Mancos Shale), White Cliffs (Navajo Sandstone), and Vermilion Cliffs (Chinle and Wingate formations) toward the south.

## CLIMATE

Each season has its advantages. Summer draws the largest crowds for festivals, pageants, water sports, and family vacations; wildflowers bloom in the mountains while desert areas turn brown under the hot sun. Autumn brings fine weather to all elevations until the snowline begins to creep down the mountain slopes. Winter snowfalls provide excellent skiing and add beauty to the landscape, but many mountain roads close and you'll need chains or snow tires for those that don't. Spring tends to be unpredictable—wet and windy one day, sunny and calm the next; the deserts are at their greenest then.

Utah's mid-continent location causes wide temperature variations between the seasons. Only a small part of the south experiences winter temperatures that average above freezing. State records include a high of 116° F at St. George in 1892 and a low of -50° F at Woodruff in 1899 and at Strawberry East Portal in 1913.

### Precipitation

Most of Utah is dry—evaporation exceeds precipitation. In fact, among the 50 states, only Nevada receives less moisture annually than Utah's 13 inches. Precipitation varies greatly from place to place due to local topography and the irregularities of storm patterns. Deserts cover about 33% of the state; the driest places are in the Great Basin and Uinta Basin and on the Colorado Plateau, where annual precipitation is usually 5-10 inches. At the other extreme, the highest peaks of the Wasatch Range receive more than 50 inches of annual precipitation, most of it as snow; some 24% of Utah has a highland climate. About 40% of the state, classified as steppeland, receives 8-14 inches of annual precipitation and supports grasslands suitable for ranching. Only 3% of the state's land is humid continental, ideal for agriculture. This strip lies along the Wasatch Front and is heavily populated. Utah enjoys a high percentage of possible sunshine; storm systems usually interrupt the typically sunny weather for just a short time.

### Winter And Spring Weather Patterns (October To April)

Periods of high-pressure systems broken by Pacific storm fronts shape most of Utah's winter weather. The high-pressure systems cause inversions when cold dense air flows down the snow-covered mountain slopes into the valleys, where it traps moisture and smoke. The blanket of fog or smog maintains even temperatures, but is the bane of the Salt Lake City area. Skiers, however, enjoy bright sunny days and cold nights in the clear air of the mountain peaks. The blankets of stagnant air in the valleys are cleaned out when cold fronts roll in from the Pacific. When skies clear, the daily temperature range is much greater until the inversion process sets in again. Most winter precipitation arrives as snow, which all regions of the state can expect. Fronts originating over the Gulf of Alaska typically arrive every 6-7 days and trigger most of Utah's snowfall. These storms occur most frequently from winter to early spring.

### Summer And Autumn Weather Patterns (May To September)

During summer, the valleys still experience inversions of cold air on clear dry nights, but the effect is much less pronounced than in winter. The canyon country in the south has higher daytime temperatures than do equivalent mountain-slope elevations, because there's no source of cold air in the canyons to replace the rising heated air; also, canyon walls act as an oven by reflecting and trapping heat. Thunderstorms are most common in summer, when warm moist air rises in billowing clouds. The storms, though they can produce heavy rains and hail, tend to be erratic and highly localized in areas less than 3 miles across. Southeastern Utah sees the first thunderstorms of the season, often in mid-June. By mid-July, these storms have spread across the entire state. They lose energy as autumn approaches, and by Oct. they have

# UTAH VEGETATION ZONES

ELEV. IN METERS

4,000

3,000

2,000

1,000

500

PRECIPITATION

WET MOIST DRY

TEMPERATURE

COLD WARM HOT

GRASS AND SHRUB
SPRUCE
FIR
ASPEN
DOUGLAS FIR
PONDEROSA PINE
MOUNTAIN BRUSH
PINYON PINE
JUNIPER
SAGEBRUSH
SHADSCALE
YUCCA
JOSHUA TREE
CREOSOTE BUSH

TREELINE

ALPINE TUNDRA LIFE ZONE

HUDSONIAN LIFE ZONE

CANADIAN LIFE ZONE

TRANSITION LIFE ZONE

SONORAN LIFE ZONES

ELEV. IN FEET

14,000
13,000
12,000
11,000
10,000
9,000
8,000
7,000
6,000
5,000
4,000
3,000
2,000
1,000

HIGHEST POINT IN UTAH
13,528 FEET AT KINGS PEAK

LOWEST POINT IN UTAH
2,350 FEET AT BEAVER DAM WASH

been supplanted by lows aloft (low-pressure systems at high altitudes) and Pacific storm fronts. Lows aloft move in erratic patterns, but can cause long periods of heavy precipitation. They're often the main source of weather disturbances during Oct., late April, and May. Surprisingly, most of Utah's moisture originates in the Gulf of California or the Gulf of Mexico. The Pacific fronts often lose most of their moisture by the time they reach Utah, yet their cold air can produce heavy precipitation when it meets warm moist air from the south. Hikers need to be aware that the highest mountain peaks can receive snow even in midsummer.

**Storm Hazards**
Rainwater runs quickly off the rocky desert surfaces and into gullies and canyons. Flash floods can form and sweep away anything in their path, including boulders, cars, and campsites. Take care not to camp or park in potential flash-flood areas. If you come to a section of flooded roadway, a common occurrence on desert roads after storms, just wait until the water goes down, usually after only a short time. Summer lightning causes forest and brush fires, and poses a danger to hikers foolish enough to climb mountains when storms threaten.

# FLORA AND FAUNA

A wide variety of plants and animals find a home within Utah's great range of elevations (more than 11,000 ft.). To help simplify and understand the different environments of Utah, some scientists use the Merriam system of life zones followed here, which will give you a general idea of what kind of vegetation and animal life to expect. Because plants rely on rainfall, which is determined largely by elevation, each life zone can be expected to occur within a certain range of elevations. These ranges are not exact—south-facing mountain slopes receive more sun and lose more moisture to evaporation than north-facing slopes at the same level. Canyons and unusual rainfall patterns can also play havoc with the classifications.

**Lower Sonoran Life Zone**
**(Below 3,500 Feet)**
This zone is found in the Mohave Desert, which extends into the southwest corner of the state. Annual precipitation here is usually less than 8 inches. Creosote bush dominates the plant life, though you're also likely to see grasses, rabbit brush, snakeweed, blackbrush, saltbush, yucca, and cacti. Joshua trees grow on some of the higher gravel benches. Flowering plants tend to bloom either after the winter rains (the Sonoran or Mexican species) or after the summer rains (the Mohave or Californian species).

Most desert animals retreat to a den or burrow during the heat of the day, when ground temperatures can reach 130° F! Look for wildlife in early morning, late afternoon, or at night. You may see kangaroo rat, several kinds of squirrels and mice, desert cottontail, black-tailed jack rabbit, striped and spotted skunks, kit fox, ringtail cat, coyote, bobcat, and mountain lion. Birds include the native Gambel's quail, roadrunner, red-tailed hawk, great horned owl, cactus wren, black-chinned and broad-tailed hummingbirds, and rufous-sided towhee. The endangered desert tortoise lives here too, but it faces extinction in a losing battle with livestock. The rare Gila monster, identified by beadlike skin with black and yellow patterns, is the only poisonous lizard in the United States and is found in Utah only in the southwest corner. It's slow and nonaggressive, but it has powerful jaws. Sidewinder, Great Basin, and western rattlesnakes are occasionally seen. Also watch for other poisonous creatures; scorpions, spiders, and centipedes can inflict painful stings or bites. It's a good idea when camping to check for unwanted guests in shoes and other items left outside.

**Upper Sonoran Life Zone**
**(3,500-5,500 Feet)**
Most of Utah lies in this zone. Shadscale, a plant resistant to both salt and drought, grows

on the valley floors and lower slopes of the Great Basin, Uinta Basin, and Canyon lands. Commonly growing with shadscale are grasses, annuals, Mormon tea, budsage, gray molley, and winterfat. In salty soils, more likely companions are greasewood, saltgrass, and iodine bush. Nonalkaline soils, on the other hand, may have blackbrush as the dominant plant. Sagebrush, the most common shrub of Utah, thrives in the higher terraces and alluvial fans of of nonalkaline soil. Grasses are commonly found mixed with sagebrush and may even dominate. Pinyon pine and juniper, small trees often found together, can grow only if there's 12 inches or more of annual precipitation; the lower limit of their growth is sometimes called the "arid timberline." In the Wasatch Range, a scrub oak-juniper association is common.

Many of the same animals live here as in the Lower Sonoran Zone. You might also see Utah prairie dog, beaver, muskrat, black bear, desert bighorn sheep, desert mule deer, and the antelope-like pronghorn. Marshes of the Great Basin have an abundance of food and cover that attract waterfowl; species include whistling swan, Great Basin Canada goose, lesser snow goose, great blue heron, seagull (Utah's state bird), common mallard, gadwall, and American common merganser. Chukar partridge (from desert lands in Asia similar to Utah's) and the Hungarian partridge (from eastern Europe and western Asia) thrive under the cover of sagebrush in dry-farm areas. Sage and sharp-tailed grouse also prefer the open country. Rattlesnakes and other reptiles like the Upper Sonoran Zone best.

## Transition Life Zone
### (5,500-8,000 Feet)
Ponderosa pine and chaparral often take over above the Sonoran zones. The chaparral association includes oak, maple, mountain mahogany, and sagebrush. The Transition Zone is best developed on the High Plateaus and the Uinta Mountains, less so in the Great Basin and the Wasatch Range. Gambel oak, juniper, and Douglas fir are commonly found among the ponderosa.

Squirrels and chipmunks rely on pine cones for food; other animals living here include Nuttall's cottontail, black-tailed jack rabbit, spotted and striped skunks, red fox, coyote, mule deer, Rocky Mountain elk (Utah's state mammal), moose, black bear, and mountain lion. Moose arrived in the state only during the 1940s, when they crossed over from Wyoming; they now live in northern and central Utah. Merriam's wild turkey, originally from Colorado, is found in oak and ponderosa pine forests of central and southern Utah. Other birds of the Transition Zone include Steller's jay, blue and ruffed grouse, poor-will, great horned owl, black-chinned and broad-tailed humming birds, gray-headed and Oregon juncos, white-throated swift, and the common raven. Most snakes, such as the gopher, hognosed, and garter, are harmless, but you could also come across a western rattler.

## Canadian Life Zone
### (8,000-10,000 Feet)
You'll find Douglas fir the most common tree within this zone in the Wasatch Range, High Plateaus, and northern slopes of the Great Basin ranges. In the Uintas, however, lodgepole pine is the dominant tree. Other trees of the Canadian Zone include ponderosa pine, limber pine, white fir, blue spruce (Utah's state tree), and aspen. Deer and Rocky Mountain elk graze in this zone but rarely higher. Smaller animals of the high mountains include northern flying squirrel, snowshoe rabbit, pocket gopher, yellow belly marmot, pika, chipmunk, and mice.

## Hudsonian Life Zone
### (10,000-11,000 Feet)
Strong winds and a growing season less than 120 days long prevent trees from reaching their full size. This zone receives twice as much snow as the Canadian Zone just below. Often gnarled and twisted, Engelmann spruce and subalpine fir grow in the cold heights over large areas of the Uintas and Wasatches. Limber and bristlecone pines live in the zone also. Lakes and lush subalpine meadows are common. On a bright summer day, the trees, grasses, and tiny flowering alpine plants are abuzz with insects, rodents, and visiting birds, but come winter, most animals will have moved to lower and more protected areas.

**Arctic-alpine Tundra Life Zone
(Above 11,000 Feet)**
Grasses, mosses, sedges, and annuals withstand the rugged conditions atop Utah's highest ranges. Freezing temperatures and snow can blast the mountain slopes even in midsummer. White-tailed ptarmigan, recently introduced to Utah, live in the tundra of the Uinta Mountains.

# THE PEOPLE

Eighty percent of Utah's 1,678,000 citizens live along the Wasatch Front, a magnificent backdrop formed by the Wasatch Range in the northern part of the state. The Mormon pioneers who arrived here in 1847 left a strong heritage of industriousness, self-reliance, and religious faith for their descendants. A relatively young population, combined with the Mormons' emphasis on family life and clean living, has resulted in Utah having one of the highest birth rates and lowest death rates in the country. Racially, the state largely reflects the British and northern European origins of Mormon pioneers; smaller numbers of southern and eastern Europeans, many attracted by mining industries, also arrived during Utah's early years. Minorities form less than 7% of the state's population and include Hispanics (3.9%), American Indians (1.3%), Asians (0.9%), and Blacks (0.6%). Agriculture, pioneered by the Mormons, and mining, pioneered by the gentiles (non-Mormons), remain important to the state's economy. Manufacturing, however, has grown rapidly in recent decades to become the most economically significant. Tourism has increased in importance as more people discover the state's exceptional scenery and outdoor recreation.

## UTAH'S INDIANS

The size of prehistoric Indian populations has varied greatly in Utah. There were probably few inhabitants during the Archaic period (before A.D. 500), but many more during the time of the Anasazi and Fremont cultures (A.D. 500-1250), rising to a peak of perhaps 500,000. New tribes moving into Utah before the historic period may have been a factor in the disappearance of the Fremont and the

Handcart Immigration 1851 *by A. Rosenfeld*

departure of the Anasazi. Numic (Shoshoni-speaking) tribes likely came from the southwestern Great Basin; they settled in much of western and northern Utah between A.D. 1100 and 1300. Navajo, probably from the northern Great Plains, are thought to have entered Utah from the Four Corners area in about 1600. Numic and Navajo tribes first had a nomadic hunting-and-gathering lifestyle. Only later did they begin to cultivate corn and other crops to supplement wild foods. Except for the Athapascan-speaking Navajo, all of Utah's historic tribes spoke Shoshonian languages and had similar cultures.

## Shoshoni

Nomadic bands of Shoshoni once occupied much of northern Utah, southern Idaho, and western Wyoming. Horses obtained from the Spanish via plains Indians allowed hunting parties to cover a large range. The great chief Washakie led his people for 50 years and negotiated the tribe's treaties with the federal government. The Washakie Indian Reserva-

tion in far northern Utah, near Plymouth, belongs to the Northwestern Band of Shoshoni, though few Indians live there now. Tribal headquarters are in Rock Springs, Wyoming, south of the large Wind River Indian Reservation.

## Goshute (or Gosiute)

This branch of Western Shoshoni, more isolated than other Utah tribes, lived in the harsh Great Basin. They survived through intricate knowledge of the land and use of temporary shelters. These peaceful hunters and gatherers ate almost everything that they found—plants, birds, rodents, crickets, and other insects. Because the Indians had to dig for much of their food, early travelers called the tribe "Digger Indians." White men could hardly believe that these Indians survived in such a barren land of alkaline flats and sagebrush. Also known as the Newe, the tribe now lives on the Skull Valley Indian Reservation in Tooele County and on the Goshute Indian Reservation along the Utah-Nevada border.

## Ute

Several bands of Utes, or Núuci, ranged over large areas of central and eastern Utah and adjacent Colorado. They were first hunter-gatherers, but about 1800 they acquired horses and became skilled raiders. Customs adopted from plains Indians included the use of rawhide, tipis, and the travois (a sled used to carry goods). The discovery of gold in southern Colorado and the pressures of farmers there and in Utah forced the Utes to move and renegotiate treaties many times. They now have the large Uintah and Ouray Indian Reservation in northeast Utah, the small White Mesa Indian Reservation in southeast Utah, and the Ute Mountain Indian Reservation in southwest Colorado and northwest New Mexico.

## Southern Paiute

Six of the 19 major bands of the Southern Paiute, or Nuwuvi, lived along the Santa Clara, Beaver, and Virgin rivers and in other parts of southwest Utah. Extended families hunted and gathered food together. Fishing and cultivation of corn, beans, squash, and sunflowers supplemented the diet of most of

*Ute Indian mother and papoose*

the bands. Today, Utah's Paiutes have a tribal headquarters in Cedar City and scattered small parcels of reservation land. Southern Paiutes also live in southern Nevada and northern Arizona.

### Navajo

Calling themselves "Diné," the Navajo moved into the San Juan River area about 1600. The tribe has proved exceptionally adaptable in learning new skills from other cultures: many Navajo crafts, clothing, and religious practices have come from their Indian, Spanish, and Anglo neighbors. After the raising of sheep (obtained from the Spanish) became their major occupation, the tribe relied less on their former nomadic habits of hunting and gathering. The Navajo have become one of the largest and most progressive Indian groups in the country. They occupy 16 million acres of exceptionally scenic land in southeast Utah and adjacent Arizona and New Mexico; tribal headquarters is at Window Rock in Arizona.

## MEET THE MORMONS

If you're new to the "Beehive State," you'll find plenty of opportunities to learn about Mormon history and religion. At least half of Utah's population actively participate in the Mormon Church, and they'll be happy to explain their religion to you. Temple Square in Salt Lake City offers excellent tours and exhibits about the church. You'll also find many other visitor centers and historic sites scattered around the state.

The Church of Jesus Christ of Latter-day Saints, headquartered in Salt Lake City, has a worldwide membership of 7,500,000 (1990), due largely to a vigorous missionary program.

Members usually call themselves "LDS" (Latter-day Saints) for short. The word "Saint" simply refers to their being a Christian, as the apostle Paul used it in writing to members of the early Christian church. Nonmembers commonly use the nickname "Mormon" because of the emphasis put on the *Book of Mormon* by the church. Despite earnest efforts by missionaries, LDS beliefs remain widely misunderstood. Church members believe that God's prophets have restored teachings of the true Christian Church to the world "in these latter days." Thus, although the LDS Church is a Christian denomination, Mormons don't classify themselves as being either Catholic or Protestant. They believe their church presidents, beginning with Joseph Smith, to be prophets of God, and they hold both the Bible and the *Book of Mormon* as the sacred word of God. The *Book of Mormon,* revealed to and translated by Joseph Smith from 1823 to 1830, tells of 3 migrations from the Eastern Hemisphere to the New World and the history of the people who lived in the Americas from about 2200 B.C. to A.D. 421. This remarkable book contains 239 chapters that include teachings given by Christ in the Americas, prophecy, doctrines, and epic tales of the rise and fall of nations. It's regarded as a valuable addition to the Bible—not as a replacement. Membership in the Mormon Church requires faith, a willingness to serve, tithing, and obedience to church authorities. People of the LDS faith feel secure because they have a modern-day prophet to provide guidance and a belief that their families can remain together forever. Sacred rituals in temples reinforce their faith. Even from an outsider's perspective, the Mormon Church emphasizes many good qualities, such as healthful living, good moral conduct, secure family relationships, and a thoughtful approach to social services.

### The Early Church

At the time of his revelations, Joseph Smith was a farmer in New York State. In 1830, he and his followers founded the new church and published the *Book of Mormon.* But Smith's revelations had evoked fear and anger in many of his neighbors, and in 1831 members of the new church moved to Kirtland, Ohio. They set to work to build a temple for sacred ordinances, to develop a missionary program, and to gain new followers. Mormons also settled farther west in Missouri and made plans for a temple and a community of Zion there. Persecution by nonbelievers continued to mount in both Ohio and Missouri. Many perceived the Mormons as a dire threat to existing political, economic, and religious systems. Missourians also disliked the Mormons' anti-slavery views. Violence by gangs of armed men eventually forced church members to flee for their lives. The dark winter of 1838-39 saw Joseph Smith in jail on false charges and many of the members without homes or legal protection. The Missouri Mormons made their way east to Illinois, not knowing where else to go. Brigham Young, a member of the Council of the Twelve Apostles, directed this exodus, foreshadowing a much longer migration that he would lead 8 years later.

## Nauvoo The Beautiful

The Mormons managed to purchase a large tract of swampy land along the Mississippi River in Illinois, then set to work draining swamps and building a city. Joseph Smith, allowed to escape from the Missouri jail,

named the Mormons' new home Nauvoo—a Hebrew word for "the beautiful location." Despite severe poverty and inability to secure reparations for losses suffered in Missouri, the Mormons managed to build an attractive city rivaling Chicago. A magnificent temple, begun in 1841, rose above Nauvoo. Despite their success here, however, the Mormons continued to face virulent opposition from those who wanted to destroy their religion. Smith, who had withstood tarring and feathering and many other abuses, finally met his death in 1844 at Carthage, Illinois. He had voluntarily surrendered to the authorities to stand trial for treason, but a mob stormed the jail and killed both Joseph and his brother Hyrum in a hail of bullets. Opponents thought that the Mormons would disband on the death of their leader. When they did not, their crops and houses were destroyed and their livestock driven off. Brigham Young, who succeeded Smith, realized that the Mormons would never find peace in Illinois. Young and other leaders began looking toward the vastness of the West. They hoped that the remote Rocky Mountains would provide a sanctuary from mobs and prejudiced politicians. Plans for departure from their fair city of Nauvoo began in the autumn of 1845.

*Joseph Smith preaching to Indians in the Midwest*

The Great Westward Exodus—1846 *by A. Rosenfeld*

## The Mormon Exodus

Attacks against Nauvoo's citizens made life so difficult that an evacuation had to begin the following Feb., despite the severe winter weather. Homes, businesses, temple, and most possessions had to be left behind as they crossed the Mississippi into Iowa. (Mobs later took over the town and desecrated the temple; not a single stone of the structure stands in its original position today.) The Mormons slowly pushed westward through the snow and mud. Faith, a spirit of sharing, and skillful leadership enabled them to survive. Brigham Young thought it best not to press on all the way to the Rocky Mountains in that first year, so the group spent a second winter on the plains. Dugouts and log cabins housed more than 3,500 people at Winter Quarters, near present-day Omaha. By early spring of 1847, the leadership had worked out plans for the rest of the journey. The Salt Lake Valley, an uninhabited and isolated region, would be their goal. Mountain men encountered on the journey gave discouraging descriptions of this place as a site for a major settlement. Samuel Brannan, a Mormon who had settled on the West Coast, rode east to meet Brigham Young and to present glowing reports of California. But Young wouldn't be swayed from his original goal. On July 24, 1847, Young arrived at the edge of the Salt Lake Valley and announced, "This is the right place." (See "History" in the Salt Lake City section, pp. 25-27, for an account of the growth of the Mormon empire in Utah.)

# EVENTS

Utah has a full schedule of rodeos, parades, art festivals, historical celebrations, gem and mineral shows, and sporting events. Stop at a tourist office or chamber of commerce to see what's coming up. The offices should also have the annual *Utah! Travel Guide,* which lists many events.

**Major Holidays**
Many museums, recreation areas, and other tourist attractions close on Thanksgiving, Christmas, New Year's, and other holidays. These closings are not always mentioned in the text, so call ahead to check.
*New Year's Day:* January 1
*Martin Luther King, Jr.'s, Birthday (Civil Rights Day):* January 15; usually observed third Mon. in January
*Presidents' Day* (honors Washington and Lincoln): third Mon. in February
*Easter Sunday:* late March or early April
*Memorial Day* (honors veterans of all wars): last Mon. in May
*Independence Day:* July 4
*Pioneer Day:* July 24
*Labor Day:* first Mon. in September
*Columbus Day:* second Mon. in October
*Veterans Day:* November 11
*Thanksgiving Day:* fourth Thurs. in November
*Christmas Day:* December 25

# TRANSPORT

## TOURS

See your travel agent for the latest on package tours to Utah. Within the state, local operators offer everything from tours of city sights to rafting trips. You can also take flightseeing trips from many airports; the 5 national parks are the most popular destinations. "Transport" sections in each chapter list tour operators; also ask local chambers of commerce.

## BY CAR

Public transport serves the cities and some towns but very few of the scenic, historic, and recreational areas. Unless on a tour, you really need your own transport. Most people choose cars as the most convenient and economical way to get around; they're easily rented in any large town. Salt Lake City offers by far the largest selection. Four-wheel-drive vehicles can be rented too, and they'll be very handy if you plan extensive travel on back roads. Most tourist offices carry the Utah road map published by the Utah Department of Transportation; it's one of the best available and is free.

**Driveaways**
These are autos to be delivered to another city. If it's a place you're headed for, a driveaway can be like a free car rental. To sign up, you have to be at least 21 years old and make a refundable deposit of $75-150. There will be time and mileage limits. Ask for an economy car if that's a consideration. Look in the yellow pages under "Automobile Transporters & Driveaway Companies."

**Hitchhiking**
Opinions and experiences vary on hitching. It can be a great way to meet people despite the dangers and long waits. Offer to buy lunch or help with gas money to repay the driver's favor. Highway police tolerate hitchhiking as long as it doesn't create a hazard or take place on an interstate or freeway. They do routinely check IDs, however. Often rides can be arranged with fellow travelers at youth hostels.

Bulletin boards at universities and colleges list rides both available and wanted.

## BY BUS

Greyhound bus line offers frequent service in Utah on their transcontinental routes across Utah and along I-15. Greyhound often features special deals on bus passes and one-way "anywhere" tickets. Outside North America, overseas residents may purchase a Greyhound *Ameripass* at additional discounts. Local bus services come in handy at Salt Lake City, Provo, and Ogden. Service in other towns is usually nonexistent or too infrequent to be useful for the traveler. Always have exact change ready when taking local buses.

## BY TRAIN

Amtrak has 3 luxury train lines across Utah; all stop in Salt Lake City. The *California Zephyr* runs between Oakland and Chicago; the *Desert Wind* goes southwest from Salt Lake City to Las Vegas and Los Angeles; and the *Pioneer* connects Salt Lake City with Portland and Seattle. Amtrak charges more than Greyhound for one-way tickets but has far roomier seating, as well as parlor cars and sleepers. Special fares and roundtrip discounts often make train travel a good value and competitive with the bus. For information and reservations see a travel agent or call Amtrak toll-free (800) 872-7245 anywhere in the country. A *USA Railpass* is sold by travel agents outside North America.

## BY AIR

More than a dozen major airlines connect with Salt Lake City, which has the only major air terminal in the state. Fares and schedules tend to change frequently—a travel agent can help find the best flights. Big-city newspapers usually have advertisements of discount fares and tours in their Sunday travel section. You'll have the best chance of getting low fares by planning at least a week ahead. Regional airlines connect Salt Lake City with other communities in the state; see the "Air" section under Salt Lake City "Transport" for sample destinations and fares. The cost per mile of these short hops is high but you'll often have excellent views!

## BY BICYCLE

Touring on a bicycle is to be fully alive to the land, skies, sounds, plants, and birds of Utah. The experiences of gliding across the desert or topping out on a mountain pass go beyond words. Some effort, a lightweight touring or mountain bicycle, touring gear, and awareness of what's going on around you are all that's needed. Start with short rides if you're new to bicycle touring, then work up to longer cross-country trips. By learning to maintain and repair your steed, you'll seldom have trouble on the road. An extra-low gear of 30 inches or less will take the strain out of long mountain grades. Utah has almost every kind of terrain and road condition imaginable; mountain bicyclists find the Moab area in the southeast especially challenging and scenic. Note that designated wilderness areas are closed to cycling. Bookstores and bicycle shops have good publications on bicycle touring. *Bicycle Touring in Utah* by Dennis Coello contains general information and details on short and long rides within the state. *The Mountain Bike Manual,* also by Coello, has details on this aspect of the sport. As when hiking, always have rain and wind gear and carry plenty of water. Also, don't forget to wear a bicycling helmet. Cyclists with a competitive spirit can test themselves in a series of U.S. Cycling Federation-sanctioned races in the northern part of the state; local bicycle shops have schedules of races and training events.

# MONEY, MEASUREMENTS, AND COMMUNICATIONS

Prices of all services mentioned in this book were current at press time. Whenever possible, taxes have been included in the stated cost given in the text. (Chart listings, however, don't include taxes.) You're sure to find seasonal and long-term price changes, so *please* don't use what's listed here to argue with staff at a motel, campground, museum, airline, or other office!

## Measurements

If you ask a rancher how many kilometers to the next town, you'll probably be out of luck. Most Utahns haven't a clue to what the metric units mean, so foreign visitors need to know the "olde English" system:

|         |   |                   |
|---------|---|-------------------|
| 1 inch  | = | 2.54 centimeters  |
| 1 foot  | = | 0.31 meter        |
| 1 mile  | = | 1.61 kilometers   |
| 1 sq. mile | = | 2.59 sq. kilometers |
| 1 acre  | = | 0.40 hectare      |
| 1 pound (lb.) | = | 0.45 kilogram  |

To figure centigrade temperatures, subtract 32 from the Fahrenheit temperature and divide by 1.8.

## Time Zones

Travelers in Utah should remember that the state is in the Mountain Time Zone and goes on Daylight Savings Time (advanced one hour) from May to October. Nevada is in the Pacific Time Zone (one hour earlier). All other states bordering Utah are in the Mountain Time Zone. An odd exception is Arizona, which stays on Mountain Standard Time all year, except for the Navajo Reservation, which goes on Daylight Savings Time (add one hour May to Oct.) to keep up with its Utah and New Mexico sections. Note that the Hopi Reservation, completely surrounded by the Navajo, stays on standard time year-round with the rest of Arizona.

## Postal And Telephone Services

Normal post office hours are Mon. to Fri. 8:30 a.m.-5 p.m. and sometimes Sat. 8:30 a.m.-noon. All telephone numbers within Utah have an **801** area code (use only when calling from outside Utah). Toll-free numbers in the U.S. have an **800** area code. To obtain a number within the state, dial 1-411; for another state, dial 1, the area code, then 555-1212. Many airlines and motel chains offer a toll-free 800 number; if you don't have it, just dial 1-800-555-1212.

# HEALTH AND HELP

## Medical Services

In emergencies, use the emergency number listed on most telephones or dial a zero for an operator. Emergency rooms of hospitals offer the quickest help, but cost more than a visit to a doctor's office or clinic. Hospital care is very expensive—medical insurance is recommended.

## WILDERNESS TRAVEL

### Keeping The "Wild" In Wilderness

As more people seek relief from the confusion and stress of urban life, the use of wilderness areas increases. Fortunately, Utah has an abundance of this fragile and precious resource. The many designated wilderness areas have been closed to mechanized vehicles (including mountain bicycles) to protect both the environment and the experience of solitude. Most designated areas lie within national forest or Bureau of Land Management lands, and you're normally free to visit them anytime without a permit. The national parks and monuments require backcountry permits for overnight stays. The following are suggestions for backcountry travel and camping:

- Before heading into the backcountry, check with a ranger about weather, water sources, fire danger, trail conditions, and regulations.

- Tell a ranger or other reliable person where you are going and when you expect to return.

- Travel in small groups for the best experience (group size may also be regulated).

- Try not to camp on meadows, as the grass is easily damaged.

- Use a portable stove to avoid leaving fire scars.

- Avoid digging tent trenches or cutting vegetation.

- Help preserve old Indian and historic ruins.

- Camp at least 300 feet away from springs, creeks, and trails. Camp at least ¼ mile from a *sole* water source to avoid scaring away wildlife and livestock.

- Don't drink water directly from streams or lakes, no matter how clean the water appears; it may contain the parasitic protozoan *Giardia lamblia,* which causes the unpleasant disease giardiasis. Boiling your water for several minutes will kill giardia as well as most other bacterial or viral pathogens. Chemical treatments usually work too, although they're not as reliable as boiling.

- Wash away from lakes, streams, and springs.

- Bring a trowel for personal sanitation; dig 4-6 inches deep.

- Bring plenty of feed for horses and mules.

- Leave dogs at home if possible; they may disturb wildlife and other hikers and foul campsites. If you do bring a dog, please keep it under physical control at all times.

- Take home all your trash so animals can't dig it up and scatter it.

- If lost, *realize it,* then find shelter and stay in one place. If you're sure of a way to civilization and plan to walk out, leave a note of your departure time and planned route.

### Know Before You Go

Some of the most spectacular and memorable hiking and camping await the prepared outdoorsperson. But because Utah's deserts and canyons are very different from most other parts of the country, even expert hikers can get into trouble. If you're new to these outdoors, read up on hiking conditions and talk to rangers and local hikers. Backpacking stores are good sources of information too. Start with easy trips, then work up gradually.

## Hypothermia

The greatest danger outdoors is one that can sneak up and kill with very little warning. Hypothermia, a lowering of the body's temperature below 95° F, causes disorientation, uncontrollable shivering, slurred speech, and drowsiness. The victim may not even realize what's wrong. Unless corrective action is taken immediately, hypothermia can lead to death. This is why hikers should travel with companions and always carry wind and rain protection. (Close-fitting rain gear works far better than ponchos.) Remember that temperatures can plummet rapidly in Utah's dry climate—a drop of 40° F between day and night is common. Be especially careful at high elevations, where summer sunshine can quickly change into freezing rain or a blizzard. Simply falling into a mountain stream while fishing can also lead to hypothermia and death unless proper action is taken. If cold and tired, don't waste time! Seek shelter and build a fire; also change into dry clothes and drink warm liquids. If a victim isn't fully conscious, warm him by skin-to-skin contact in a sleeping bag. Try to keep him awake and drinking warm liquids.

## DRIVING HAZARDS

Summer heat in the desert puts an extra strain on both cars and drivers. It's worth double-checking to make sure the cooling system, engine oil, transmission fluid, fan belts, and tires are in top condition. Carry several gallons of water in case of breakdown or radiator trouble. Never leave children or pets in a parked car during warm weather—temperatures inside can cause fatal heat stroke in just

minutes. At times the desert has *too much* water, when late-summer storms frequently flood low spots in the road. Wait for the water to go down before crossing. Dust storms also tend to be short-lived but can completely block visibility. During such storms, the best thing to do is to pull completely off the road and stop; turn off your lights so as not to confuse other drivers. Radio stations carry frequent weather updates when weather hazards exist. Continuous weather forecasts can be received on a VHF radio (162.4 or 162.55 MHz) in the Salt Lake City area (Wasatch Front), Logan (Cache Valley), Vernal (Uinta Basin), Cedar City, Glen Canyon N.R.A., and Las Vegas (NV) areas.

If stranded, whether on the desert or in the mountains, stay with the vehicle unless you're *positive* of where to go for help; then leave a note telling route and departure time. Airplanes can easily spot an obviously stranded car (tie a piece of cloth to your antenna), but a person trying to walk out is difficult to see. It's best to carry emergency supplies: blankets or sleeping bags, first-aid kit, tools, jumper cables, shovel, traction mats or chains, flashlight, rain gear, water, and food (w/can opener).

## FREE INFORMATION

General tourist literature and maps are available from the **Utah Travel Council,** Council Hall/Capitol Hill, Salt Lake City, UT 84114; tel. 538-1030. The many chambers of commerce in the state also have this material and are happy to help with travel suggestions in their areas; see "Information" under each community described in this book. Listed with them are national forest offices and other government agencies that know about outdoor recreation in their areas.

*Great Salt Lake Desert*

# NORTHERN UTAH

## INTRODUCTION

Northern Utah offers a great diversity of sights, recreation, and terrain. The cities have bright lights, art exhibits, concerts, festivals, museums, and amusement parks. Or you can leave civilization behind and head east into the Wasatch Range for skiing and hiking among splendid peaks. Camping, fishing, and boating also bring many visitors into the higher country. West of the cities lie the Western Hemisphere's largest inland body of salt water, lonely salt flats, and little-known mountain ranges.

### THE LAND

Even for Utah, contrasts between barren and luxuriant are especially great in the north. A collision of the earth's plates has pushed up rugged mountains and plateaus in northeast Utah while leaving vast expanses of lower-lying valleys and desert ranges to the west. The Great Salt Lake dominates the low country and seems to cast its spell across the sterile salt flats and rocky ranges west toward Nevada. Yet to the east, the northern Wasatch

Range towers in verdant splendor. Though other mountains rise higher into Utah skies, none match the sheer beauty of these glacier-carved peaks and their sharp drops to the valleys far below. The highest summits reach over 10,000 feet, with Mt. Nebo crowning the range at 11,928 feet. The mountains bring life to northern Utah. Rivers coursing down the slopes turn desert valleys into lush pastures and productive farmland. Salt Lake City and its populous neighbors hug the base of the Wasatches in a long north-south line known as the Wasatch Front.

You'll see large terraces or benches left behind by prehistoric Lake Bonneville. Two terrace levels stand out most clearly, the Bonneville, and the Provo, 400 feet lower. Lake Bonneville gradually shrank to a few remnants, but the largest of these, the Great Salt Lake, is still immense—up to 92 miles long and 48 miles wide. Much of the water comes from the Bear River, originating on the north slopes of the Uinta Mountains and making a long loop through Wyoming, Idaho, and northern Utah. Waterfowl and other wildlife thrive in marshes and lakes where the river meets the

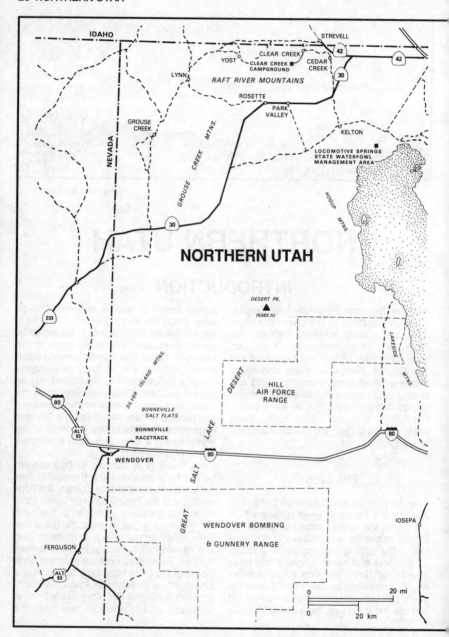

IDAHO

STREVELL

42

42

YOST

CLEAR CREEK

CEDAR CREEK

CLEAR CREEK CAMPGROUND

30

LYNN

RAFT RIVER MOUNTAINS

ROSETTE

PARK VALLEY

KELTON

GROUSE CREEK

LOCOMOTIVE SPRINGS STATE WATERFOWL MANAGEMENT AREA

30

NEVADA

GROUSE CREEK MTNS.

HOGUP MTNS.

NORTHERN UTAH

233

DESERT PK. (6985 ft)

DESERT

HILL AIR FORCE RANGE

SILVER ISLAND MTNS.

LAKESIDE MTNS.

80

ALT 93

BONNEVILLE SALT FLATS

BONNEVILLE RACETRACK

SALT LAKE

80

WENDOVER

80

ALT 93

GREAT SALT LAKE

WENDOVER BOMBING & GUNNERY RANGE

IOSEPA

FERGUSON

ALT 93

0          20 mi

0          20 km

lake. Other rivers, such as the Weber, Ogden, Provo, and Spanish Fork, have cut through the Wasatch Range to empty into the Great Salt Lake or into Utah Lake, a large freshwater lake upstream connected to the Great Salt by the Jordan River.

## Climate

Northern Utah experiences 4 seasons: warm to hot summers, cold and snowy winters, and unpredictable weather in spring and autumn. Spring tends to be the wettest time, and summer the driest. The high mountains stay cool and moist even in summer, when the plains bake under a relentless sun. Semidesert country west of the Great Salt Lake receives as little as 7 inches of annual precipitation and withstands great temperature differences between day and night. Precipitation increases closer to the mountains, typically 14-15 inches beside the Wasatch Range. The high mountains act as a barrier to moisture-laden winds from the west and can get 40 inches or more of precipitation, most in the form of snow. Alta, in the mountains southeast of Salt Lake City, holds the state records for snowfall in one season (52 feet in the winter of 1951-52) and for greatest accumulation from a single storm (105 inches in late Jan. 1965). Winter fronts usually arrive in cycles of 6-7 days from storms originating over the Gulf of Alaska. Low winter temperatures combined with low humidity produce a powder snow ideal for skiing. Utah rightfully claims to have some of the best "white stuff" in the world.

## Flora And Fauna

Water usually attracts abundant wildlife, but the Great Salt Lake has limited appeal. Only certain species of brine shrimp, brine flies, algae, bacteria, and protozoa normally live in the lake, which can be up to 8 times saltier than the ocean. Birds find the freshwater marshes around the Great Salt Lake an ideal place to stop over on migrations in spring and autumn. Birdwatchers have spotted 257 species, of which 117 were nesting. Commonly seen birds include the American white pelican, Canada and snow geese, whistling swan, at least 9 species of ducks, eared and western grebes, great blue heron, white-faced ibis,

California and Franklin's gulls, marsh wren, red-winged and yellow-headed blackbirds, and several species of swallows. The Great Salt Lake Desert to the west, broken here and there by small mountain ranges, has such poor soil and scarce water that almost no vegetation or wildlife can survive. Only salt- and drought-resistant plants like shadscale, greasewood, saltgrass, and iodine bush grow here. In higher ranges near the desert, such as the Raft River Mountains to the north and Deep Creeks to the south, grasslands and forests support such wildlife as mule deer, pronghorn, coyote, cottontail, chukar partridge, and mourning dove.

The Wasatch Range east of the Great Salt Lake has diverse and extensive habitats. Grasses, sagebrush, scrub oak, maple, juniper, and pinyon pine cover the lower slopes to about 7,500 feet. Higher are dense forests of aspen, Douglas fir, ponderosa pine, limber pine, white fir, blue spruce, Engelmann spruce, and subalpine fir. Above timberline (about 11,000 ft.) only grasses, mosses, sedges, and annuals withstand the cold, strong winds. More than 100 wildflower species brighten the mountain country in summer. Wildlife you might see here are mule deer, pronghorn, Rocky Mountain elk, mountain goat (transplanted), bighorn sheep, mountain lion, black bear, ringtail cat, coyote, badger, red and kit foxes, short-tailed and long-tailed weasels, mink, beaver, pika, snowshoe hare, pygmy rabbit, white-tailed and black-tailed jack rabbits, Uinta and golden-mantled ground squirrels, northern flying squirrel, and many species of birds.

# HISTORY

## Indians

The story of man in northern Utah begins long before the founding of Salt Lake City. Archaeologists have evidence that Paleo-Indians hunted big game and gathered plant foods about 15,000 years ago. The early tribes continued their primitive hunting and gathering despite climate changes and the extinction of many big-game species about 10,000 years ago. By A.D. 550 the Fremont culture ap-

*Shoshoni village*

peared with new tools and pottery-making skills, some agriculture, and the bow and arrow, yet had disappeared by A.D. 1300. About the same time, perhaps by coincidence, nomadic Shoshoni moved in. The modern Ute and Goshute tribes likely descended from this Shoshoni group. None of the tribes proved a match for the white men, who eventually drove the Indians from the most desirable lands.

## Mountain Men

Adventurous mountain men seeking beaver pelts and other furs entered northern Utah in the mid-1820s. They explored the mountain ranges, rivers, and the Great Salt Lake, and blazed most of the trails later used by wagon trains, Pony Express, telegraph lines, and railroads. By 1830 most of the mountain men had moved on to better trapping areas and left the land to the Indians. Some did return to guide government explorers and groups of pioneer settlers. The names of several mountain men are remembered on maps today: Peter Skene Ogden (city of Ogden), Etienne Provost (city of Provo), Jim Bridger (Bridgerland is the nickname of Cache and Rich counties), John H.

Weber (Weber River and County), and William Ashley (Ashley National Forest).

## Explorers

Joseph Walker, under Capt. Benjamin Bonneville, crossed the northwest corner of Utah in 1833 on a trip to California. He reported such difficult conditions that no one else attempted the route for the rest of the decade. California-bound wagon trains took heed and followed a more northerly path through Idaho on the Oregon Trail. An exception was the Bartleson-Bidwell wagon train, which turned south into Utah in 1841 and skirted the northern edges of the Great Salt Lake and Great Salt Lake Desert. Though they suffered immense hardships and later had to abandon their wagons, they eventually made it across. The group was the first to take wagons across Utah and included the first white women known to have crossed Utah and Nevada to California. In 1843 John C. Fremont led one of his several government-sponsored scientific expeditions into Utah. Fremont determined the salinity of the Great Salt Lake and laid to rest speculation that a river drained the lake into the Pacific Ocean. Two years later, he led a well-prepared group across the heart of the dreaded Great Salt Lake Desert, despite the warnings from Indians that no one had crossed it and survived. His accounts of the region described not only the salty lake and barren deserts, but also the fertile valleys near the Wasatch Range. Mormon leaders planning a westward migration from Nauvoo, Illinois, carefully studied Fremont's reports.

Langsford Hastings, an ambitious politician, seized the opportunity to promote Fremont's desert route as a shortcut to California. Hastings had made the trip on horseback but failed to realize the problems a wagon train would have. In 1846, the Donner-Reed wagon train on this route so bogged down in the salt mud that many wagons had to be abandoned. Moreover, an 80-mile stretch between waterholes proved too far for many of the oxen, which went crazy from thirst and died. Today motorists can speed in comfort along I-80 on a similar route between Salt Lake City and Wendover.

# SALT LAKE CITY

In 1847 the Mormon prophet Brigham Young proclaimed this site the "right place" for a new settlement. Today many residents and visitors would still agree. Salt Lake City offers an appealing mix of cultural activities, historic sites, varied architecture, shopping, sophisticated hotels, and elegant restaurants. About 163,000 citizens live in the city, by far the largest and most important in Utah. More than half a million more people reside close by in sprawling suburbs. Utah's political life centers on the stately Capitol, which overlooks the city from a hill just north of downtown. The University of Utah serves a major role in education and research on its 1,500-acre campus in the foothills east of the city. Some 7½ million members of the Church of Jesus Christ of Latter-day Saints (Mormons) look to Salt Lake City as their world headquarters. You can't miss seeing the Mormons' splendid temple and soaring office tower in the heart of downtown. Free tours on Temple Square provide a look at the vigorous faith of the "Saints" and their unique history.

## The Setting

Salt Lake City lies on the broad valley floor and terraces once occupied by prehistoric Lake Bonneville. The Great Salt Lake, largest remnant of that ancient inland sea, has state parks on its southern shore and on Antelope Island. The Jordan River winds through the valley, connecting Utah Lake with the Great Salt Lake much as its biblical namesake carries the outflow from the freshwater Sea of Galilee to the salty Dead Sea. Rugged mountain ranges, snowcapped much of the year, nearly surround Salt Lake City. In the Wasatch Range, beginning on the eastern edge of the city, many peaks exceed 11,000 feet. In just minutes, you can be up on the slopes skiing on some of the world's best powder in winter, or hiking among wildflowers in summer. On the other side of the valley, Lewiston Peak (elev. 10,626 ft.) crowns the Oquirrh (pronounced "oaker") Mountains. No ski resorts here yet, but workings of the world's largest open-pit copper mine can be seen on the mountainside.

## Climate

The city experiences a full range of seasons at its 4,300-foot elevation. Rapidly moving storms can bring rain. or snow one day and warm sunshine the next. Average temperatures range from highs in the upper 30s F in Jan. to the lower 90s in July. Total precipitation averages 15.3 inches through the year. Most of the winter moisture arrives as fluffy white flakes; average annual snowfall is 54 inches in town and considerably more in the mountains.

## HISTORY

### The Vision

Salt Lake City began as a dream—a utopia in which the persecuted Mormons would have the freedom to create a Kingdom of God on earth. Their prophet, Brigham Young, led the first group of 143 men, 3 women, and 2 children to the valley of the Great Salt Lake in July 1847. Only great faith could have supported the followers when they saw the wasteland that Young pronounced as "the right place." The bleak valley, covered with sagebrush and inhabited mainly by lizards, could best be described as the land nobody wanted. Even the Indians seldom camped here. Many of the settlers wanted to continue under Young's leadership to the rich lands of California. But Young saw the value in staying; he knew that only a determined people could live here, and that the land's remoteness would protect them against enemies.

### Settlement

The pioneers put their doubts aside and immediately set to work digging irrigation canals, planting crops, constructing a small fort, and laying out a city. Nearly 2,000 more immigrants arrived that same summer. After having endured 17 years of mob attacks and great sacrifices in the Midwest, the Mormons had reached their promised land. From the beginning, church leaders carefully directed the migrations and settlement. The "Saints" acted not as individuals, but as a disciplined and highly motivated group under capable leadership. Brigham Young and other leaders designated a site for the temple and determined land use. Church members shared their resources and eagerly took up tasks assigned by committees. Married men received city lots and farmlands, but these could be taken back if the land was not productively used. Similarly, the community shared streams, forests, and canyons.

By necessity, early citizens had to be self-sufficient—the nearest outposts of civilization lay 1,000 miles distant. Also, Brigham Young had declared that the Kingdom of God should be independent of the "Gentile" (non-Mormon) nations. Through trial and error, farmers learned techniques of irrigating and farming the desert land. Tanneries, flour mills, blacksmith shops, stores, and other enterprises sprang up under church direction. Then disaster struck. A plague of "crickets" descended from the hills to the east and began devouring the crops of the 1848 harvest, nearly ending chances for the community's survival. But flocks of California seagulls appeared out of the west to feed on the insects. Thought a miracle, the seagull intervention saved part of the crops and gave the pioneers hope that life in the Great Salt Lake Valley would eventually be fruitful.

## Success

The "city of Zion" came admirably close to its goal of being a community devoted to God. Nearly all aspects of political, economic, and family life came under the influence of the church during the first 20 years. Immigrants from Europe and the eastern U.S. poured in, many under the sponsorship of the Perpetual Emigrating Fund Company. Colonization of the surrounding country proceeded at a rapid pace. Of all the social experiments ever tried in the United States, the Mormon settlements had the greatest success.

## The Utah War

Mistrust and suspicion from outside Utah flared up just 10 years after the city's founding. The Utah War never really happened, but rumors of a Mormon rebellion caused President James Buchanan to dispatch the largest peacetime army ever assembled in the United States. Mormon "guerrillas" managed to delay the troops by driving off livestock and cutting supply lines. Meanwhile, nearly the entire population of the city staged an orderly evacuation southward. When columns of soldiers marched down the deserted streets in June 1858, they found only a handful of men ready to "torch" the houses and buildings in case the U.S. Army chose to occupy the city. Peace prevailed and residents soon returned.

## Coming Of The Gentiles

The isolation that had shielded Salt Lake City from outside influences began to fade about 1870. Completion of the transcontinental railroad through Utah in the previous year encouraged non-Mormon politicians and businessmen to seek new opportunities in the territory. Also, with cheap transportation close at hand, mining became highly profitable. Virtually no mixing took place between the Mormons and Gentiles—each group developed its own social and political organizations and its own schools. Political life had been very dull during the first decades, when only a single set of church-appointed candidates appeared on the ballots. Voters had a choice of voting "no," but knew that their numbered ballots could be traced. The church discouraged political parties, believing they would lead to corruption and disharmony; civil government should simply be a branch of the church. Still, with the rising power of the Gentile population in the 1870s, the church founded the People's Party to counter the anti-church Liberal Party. Salt Lake City's 2 major newspapers date from this time, with the *Deseret News* stating Mormon views, and the *Salt Lake Tribune* representing the Gentiles. Such fine shades of political views as Republican or Democrat rarely entered the picture. The Mormons steadily lost control of their city; from having a 93% majority population in 1867, they slipped to only 50% by 1891. In 1889 the first non-Mormons were elected to city offices.

## An American City

The church leadership lost its all-embracing grasp on Salt Lake City during the legal battles over polygamy in the 1880s. Embarking on a new course, the church ended plural marriages, dissolved its People's Party, and sold off most of its businesses. Even the famed ZCMI, thought to be the first department store in America, became a private profit-making concern. The end of the 19th C. saw Salt Lake making the transition from a Mormon village to an American city.

## The 20th Century

Wealth from successful mining operations fueled much of the development in Salt Lake City's business district, located in the blocks south of Temple Square. As a rule, the blocks nearest the temple had affiliations with the church and those farther south belonged to non-Mormons. In the early 1900s, skyscrapers began sprouting high above East Temple St.—rechristened Main Street. Exchange Place became the non-Mormon financial center, much like New York City's Wall Street. Though growth in the city has been modest since WW II, a profusion of surrounding towns and expressways has sprung up. Like any major metropolitan area, Salt Lake City suffers its share of air pollution and traffic congestion. On the brighter side, a new interest in conservation has preserved many graceful mansions, ornate churches, and stately office towers. A drive or walk through downtown will reveal the city's unique heritage.

*Zion's Co-operative Mercantile Institution, ca. 1888*

DOWNTOWN
SALT LAKE CITY

# SALT LAKE CITY SIGHTS

## TEMPLE SQUARE

Easily Salt Lake City's most famous attraction, this complex has a special meaning for members of the Church of Jesus Christ of Latter-day Saints, often referred to as the Mormons. Brigham Young chose this spot for a temple in July 1847, just 4 days after arriving in the valley. Though far from the nearest railhead or city, the settlers took their few tools and began construction of a temple and tabernacle. You're welcome to see these buildings, along with the Assembly Hall, exhibits in the North and South visitor centers, and historic monuments—all of which provide an excellent introduction to the Mormon religion and Utah's early history. Only church members in good standing may enter the sacred temple itself; others can learn about temple activities and see photos of interior rooms in the South Visitor Center. Enthusiastic guides offer several tours in Temple Square. To see all the Mormon exhibits on Temple Square and adjacent blocks could easily take more than a day. Flowers and beautiful landscaping on the square give a feeling of peace despite the hustle and bustle outside the walls. Temple Square is open daily 9 a.m.-9 p.m., extended in summer to 8 a.m.-10 p.m.; all tours, exhibits, and concerts are free. Foreign-language tours are available too—ask at the North Visitor Center. Signs request visitors to refrain from smoking on the grounds.

Something's happening every day. Check the bulletin boards as you enter Temple Square, ask any of the guides, or call 240-2534/2535 for programs and times. Organists demonstrate the sounds and versatility of the tabernacle's famous instrument in 25-minute recitals, held daily. The equally well-known Mormon Tabernacle Choir sings on Sun. mornings and rehearses on Thurs. evenings and early Sun. mornings. Occasionally, when the choir is on tour, a youth choir, youth symphony, or other group replaces it. A concert series presents programs on Fri. and Sat. evenings through the year in Assembly Hall or in the tabernacle. Concerts range from soloists to small ensembles to full orchestras. Except for a few special events, you won't need tickets to attend Temple Square performances.

Temple Square takes up an entire city block in the heart of Salt Lake City. The square sits just north of the downtown business district and close to bus and train stations. It's bound-

## DOWNTOWN SALT LAKE CITY

1. Utah Heritage Foundation (Quail House)
2. Pioneer Memorial Museum
3. Utah Travel Council (Council Hall)
4. Union Pacific Depot
5. Triad Center
6. Greyhound Bus Station
7. Museum of Church History and Art
8. Family History Library
9. LDS Office Building
10. Hotel Utah
11. Beehive House
12. Cathedral of the Madeleine
13. First Presbyterian Church
14. Kearns Mansion
15. Symphony Hall
16. Salt Lake Art Center
17. Crossroads Plaza Shopping Center
18. ZCMI Shopping Center
19. Hansen Planetarium
20. Salt Palace
21. Salt Lake Convention & Visitors Bureau
22. Capitol Theatre
23. Promised Valley Playhouse
24. Utah State History Museum and Amtrak Station (Denver & Rio Grande Depot)
25. City and County Building
26. City Library
27. Trolley Corners

be scheduled in advance. Points of interest, which you can also see on your own, include the Seagull Monument (commemorating the miracle of seagulls that devoured a plague of "crickets" in 1848), a bell from the abandoned Nauvoo Temple, sculptures of Christ, church leaders, and handcart pioneers, an astronomy observation site, and a meridian marker (outside the walls at Main and S. Temple) from which surveyors mapped out Utah.

### The Salt Lake Temple

This majestic temple is the best known of nearly 50 Mormon temples found around the world now. Mormons believe that they must have temples within which to hold sacred rites and fulfill God's commandments. According to the Mormon faith, baptisms, marriages, and family-sealing ceremonies taking place inside can last beyond death and into eternity. Prior to entering the temple, members prepare for a spiritual experience by dressing in white clothing representing purity. The temple serves only for special functions; normal Sun. services take place in local stake or ward buildings—in fact the temple is closed on Sundays.

ed by Main, N. Temple, W. Temple, and S. Temple streets. Park at meters around the square, at pay lots on N. Temple St., or for free on streets farther north. A 15-foot-high wall surrounds the square's 10 acres; enter through wrought-iron gates on the south, west, or north sides. Not all of the church buildings could fit on Temple Square. Across the street to the east are the LDS Office Tower and Brigham Young's restored Beehive House, each offering tours. Head west across the street from the square to see the Museum of Church History and Art and the Family History Library.

### Temple Square Historical Tour

Meet a guide near the flagpole in the center of the square to learn about Salt Lake City's Mormon pioneers, temple, tabernacle, Assembly Hall, and historic monuments. The 40-minute tours begin every 10 minutes during the summer season and every 15 minutes the rest of the year. Custom group tours can

The plan of Salt Lake City's temple first came as a vision to Brigham Young when he still lived in Illinois. Young later worked with church architect Truman O. Angell during the actual planning and building. Construction of the monumental project began in 1853. Forty years were needed to chisel granite blocks from Little Cottonwood Canyon, 20 miles southeast of the city, then haul them by oxen and later by railroad for final shaping at the temple site. The foundation alone required 7,478 tons of stone. Walls measure 9 feet thick at the base and taper to 6 feet on the second story. The highest of the 6 slender spires stands 210 feet, topped by a glittering statue of the angel Moroni with trumpet in hand. The 12½-foot statue is made of hammered copper covered with gold leaf. As with all Mormon temples, the interior was open to the public for a short time after completion. Dedication took place on April 6, 1893, 40 years to the day after work began. It wouldn't do for tourists to go tramping through the temple, but you can learn something of what goes on inside at the South Visitor Center.

## The Tabernacle

Pioneers labored from 1863 to 1867 to construct this unique dome-shaped building. Brigham Young desired a meeting hall capable of holding thousands of people in an interior free of supports that would block vision and sound. His design, drawn up by bridge-builder Henry Grow, took the form of massive latticed wooden beams resting on 44 supports of red sandstone. Wooden pegs and rawhide strips hold the structure together. Because Utah lacked many of the building supplies familiar to the workers, they often had to make substitutions. The large organ pipes resemble metal, balcony pillars appear to be marble, and the benches look like oak, yet all are pine wood painted to simulate those materials. The tabernacle has earned fame both for the phenomenal acoustics of the smooth arched ceiling and the tabernacle organ, regarded as one of the finest ever created. From 700 pipes when constructed in 1867, the organ has grown to about 12,000 pipes, 5 manuals, and one pedal keyboard. Daily recitals demonstrate the instrument's capabilities. Temple Square tours include a stop in the tabernacle for a short presentation on the history of the famed building; an acoustic demonstration

*Tabernacle under construction ca. 1867*

shows that a dropped pin can be heard even in the back rows 170 feet away!

Important church conferences take place in the tabernacle every spring and autumn, but the seating capacity of about 6,500—considered huge when built—is now far too small, despite the addition of a balcony. Hundreds of thousands watch the proceedings on TV via a church satellite network. The renowned Mormon Tabernacle Choir, 320 voices strong, sings on Sun. mornings over a national radio (CBS) and regional TV network. The choir's radio broadcast, which dates back to 1929, is the longest continuous broadcast in the world. Visitors may also attend choir rehearsals Thurs. evenings and early Sun. mornings. Families with infants can sit in a glassed-in room at the rear without fear of disturbing other listeners.

## Assembly Hall

Thrifty craftsmen built this smaller Gothic-revival structure in 1877-82, using granite left over from temple construction. The truncated spires, reaching as high as 130 feet, once functioned as chimneys. Inside the hall, there's seating for 1,500 people and a choir of 100. The baroque-style organ, installed in 1983, has 3,500 pipes and 3 manuals; note the organ's horizontal pipes (trumpets). Initially, the Salt Lake Stake congregation met here; now the building serves as a concert hall and for a variety of church functions.

## North Visitor Center

Wander around on your own, or ask help from the ever-present tour guides. Beautiful murals on the lower floor show Old Testament prophets; head upstairs to see paintings of the life of Christ. A spiraling ramp leads to the upper level where the Cristus, an 11-foot replica of a sculpture by Bertel Thorvaldsen, stands in a circular room whose wall mural depicts the universe. An international video theater, near the bottom of the ramp, presents church productions in English and foreign languages. Downstairs display areas and theaters have other offerings, which change periodically.

## South Visitor Center

Two 30-minute tours begin here: **Book of Mormon** and **Purpose of Temples.** Things to see on the main level are paintings of prophets and church history, a baptismal font supported by 12 life-size oxen (representing the 12 tribes of Israel) as used in temples, photos of the Salt Lake Temple interior, and a scale model of Solomon's Temple. Downstairs are replicas of the famed metal plates inscribed with the *Book of Mormon* and revealed to Joseph Smith in 1823. To back up the claim that the plates are genuine, ancient plates of Old World civilizations and stone boxes from the Americas are exhibited too. Mormon literature can be obtained at a desk near the entrance.

# VICINITY OF TEMPLE SQUARE

## Museum Of Church History And Art

Brigham Young encouraged the preserving of church history, especially when he saw that Salt Lake City's pioneering era was drawing to a close. The collection of church artifacts, begun by the Deseret Museum in 1869, includes the plow that cut the first furrows in the Salt Lake Valley. Exhibits honor each of the past church presidents—from Joseph Smith to the present—with paintings, photos, documents, and personal belongings. Art exhibits illustrate many styles of 19th and 20th C. paintings and sculpture. Perhaps the most striking piece is the gilded 11½-foot statue of Moroni which crowned a Washington, D.C., chapel from 1933 to 1976. Temporary exhibits also display Mormon artistry in photography, abstract art, textiles, furniture, and woodworking. Work by American Indians and foreign artists shows the diverse backgrounds of church members. A theater downstairs presents programs about the museum's work and other topics. The museum store sells prints, books, recordings, postcards, and other souvenirs.

Step outside to see the 1847 log cabin, one of only 2 surviving from Salt Lake City's beginnings. The interior has been furnished as it might have been during the first winter here. The Museum of Church History and Art is open (April to Dec.) Mon. to Fri. 9 a.m.-9 p.m. and Sat., Sun., and holidays 10 a.m.-7 p.m.; winter hours (Jan. to March) are daily 10 a.m.-7 p.m. (extended until 9 p.m. Mon. and Wed.); free; tel. 240-3310. It's located just west of Temple Square at 45 N. West Temple.

## Family History Library

This new building houses the largest collection of genealogical information in the world. Library workers have made extensive travels to many countries to microfilm documents and books. More than 500 employees, assisted by over 400 volunteers, keep track of the records. The Mormon Church has gone to this effort to enable members to trace their ancestors, who can then be baptized by proxy. In this way, according to Mormon belief, the ancestors will be sealed in the family and church for eternity. However, the spirits for whom these baptisms are performed have a choice of accepting or rejecting the baptism.

Anyone may use the library. If you'd like to research your family tree, bring what information you have and get the library's *A Guide to Research* booklet. A brief slide presentation explains what types of records are kept and how to get started. Staff will answer questions. In most cases the files won't have information about living persons because of rights to privacy. The Mormon Church leaves nothing to chance in preserving its genealogical records and history—master copies on microfilm rest in vaults deep within the mountains southeast of Salt Lake City. The Family History Library is open Mon. to Sat. at 7:30 a.m., closing Mon. at 6 p.m., Tues. to Fri. at 10 p.m., and Sat. at 5 p.m.; closed Sun. and some holidays. Visitor presentations and the information counter are open Mon. to Sat. at 8 a.m., closing Mon. at 6 p.m., Tues. to Fri. at 9 p.m., and Sat. at 5 p.m.; tel. 240-2331. Located just west of Temple Square at 35 N. West Temple.

## LDS Office Building

Day-to-day running of the massive church organization focuses on the 28-story tower east of Temple Square. On any weekday you'll see earnest church workers busily engaged in leadership, educational, and missionary roles.

*Beehive House and Eagle Gate, ca. 1869*

Such a volume of correspondence takes place that the building has its own zip code. Free tours beginning in the main lobby explain a bit about the work here, but the big attraction is a visit to the 26th-floor observation deck. You'll see Temple Square and all the city spread out below like a map. Weather permitting, the valley, Great Salt Lake, and surrounding mountains stand out clearly. Tours last about 30 minutes, depending on how long you want to take in the panorama. The main lobby has some noteworthy artwork, including a giant 66-by-16-foot mural of Christ appearing to his apostles 40 days after the resurrection and just prior to his ascension. Gardens and fountains grace a small park behind the building. You can take tours Mon. to Fri. (and Sat. from April to Oct.) 9 a.m.-4:30 p.m.; closed Sun. and holidays. Address is 50 E. North Temple.

### Beehive House

This former house of Brigham Young was built in 1854 and occupied by him until his death in 1877. The adobe-brick structure stood out as one of the most ornate houses of early Salt Lake City. Free tours lasting 30-40 minutes take visitors through the house and tell of family life within the walls. The interior has been meticulously restored with many original furnishings. A beehive symbol, representing industry, caps the top of the house and appears in decorative motifs inside. Brigham Young had about 27 wives, but only one stayed in this house at a time. Downstairs,

Young's children gathered in the sitting room for evenings of prayer, talks, and music. Upstairs, he entertained guests and dignitaries in a lavish reception room called the Long Hall. Other rooms to see include the kitchen, family store, bedrooms, playroom, and the "fairy castle," where small children could peer through a window at grown-ups in the hallway below. Tours leave Mon. to Sat. 9:30 a.m.-4:30 p.m. (with extended summer hours Mon. to Fri.) and Sun. 10 a.m.-1 p.m.; closed on Thanksgiving, Christmas, and New Year's Day; open other holidays but may close early (call); tel. 240-2671. Beehive House is on the corner of South Temple and State, in the same block as the LDS Office Tower. The **Lion House** next door was built in 1855-56 of stuccoed adobe; a stone lion guards the entrance. Brigham Young used the dwelling as a supplementary house for his large family. No tours are offered.

### Brigham Young Cemetery

Church president, founder of Utah, colonizer, and territorial governor, Brigham Young rests here with 5 of his wives and his eldest son. Several monuments on the grounds honor the pioneers and Young's family. From State St. near Beehive House, go one-half block east on 1st Avenue.

### Eagle Gate

This modern replacement of the original 1859 gate spans State St. just north of S. Temple. It once marked the entrance to Brigham

Young's property, which included City Creek Canyon. The bronze eagle has a 20-foot wingspan and weighs 2 tons. The present gate, designed by Brigham Young's grandson, architect George Cannon Young, was dedicated in 1963.

## Hansen Planetarium

The heavens come to Earth in multimedia star shows using a sophisticated Digistar computer projection system. Laser/music shows, science shows, and children's programs are also scheduled regularly. Museum exhibits include the planetarium's original Spitz star projector, meteorites, Apollo displays, a rock from the moon, a Foucault pendulum, and hands-on displays. Exhibit halls have free admission; open Mon. to Sat. about 9 a.m.-9 p.m. Shows cost $4-5.50 adult ($3-4 for children 12 and under and seniors) depending on the program; tel. 538-2098 (recording), 363-0559 (laser concerts), or 538-2104 (office). For upcoming astronomical events and telescope viewings, call 532-STAR. A gift shop sells astronomy posters, books, postcards, and other gift items. Hansen Planetarium is in a classic-style building at 15 S. State St. (just east of ZCMI Center) downtown.

## Brigham Young Monument

You'll want to be sure to miss this monument—it stands right in the middle of the busy intersection at Main and S. Temple streets! Brigham Young, in bronze, stands atop a granite pedestal with figures below representing an Indian, a fur trapper, and a pioneer family. Unveiled on July 24, 1897, it celebrates the first 50 years of settlement in Salt Lake City. A plaque lists the names of the first group of 148 Mormon pioneers.

## Hotel Utah

Step inside the lobby to admire the ornate interior. Built of white terra-cotta brick in a Modern Italian Renaissance style, it opened in 1911 as a first-class hotel for church and business leaders. Massive marble columns, chandeliers, and a stained-glass ceiling cre-ate an opulent atmosphere. The LDS Church, owners of the hotel, converted the venerable structure into an office building in 1987 despite pleas from the community.

## Symphony Hall

Easily the most striking modern building in Salt Lake City, Symphony Hall glitters with gold leaf, crystal chandeliers, and more than a mile of brass railing. A glass wall 43 feet high and 135 feet long forms one side of the lobby. Extensive use of oak adds to the warmth inside. Great care with acoustic design has paid off with one of the best concert halls in the world. Construction took 3 years and $12 million before the Utah Symphony Orchestra could inaugurate its new home in 1979. An illuminated fountain plays outside on the plaza during concerts. Tours lasting about 30 min-

*Symphony Hall*

utes take you through the building and explain details of its construction; held weekday afternoons in 'summer and Tues. and Thurs. in winter; free; call the box office for tour times and concert dates: 533-6407/6683. On the southwest corner of S. Temple and W. Temple streets.

### Salt Lake Art Center
Several exhibitions are usually held simultaneously at this busy place. Paintings, photographs, sculptures, ceramics, and some very hard-to-categorize art forms could be shown. Diverse art classes and work shops are scheduled along with films, lectures, poetry readings, music concerts, and theater. A sales shop offers art books, posters, crafts, and artworks. Open Mon. to Sat. 10 a.m.-5 p.m. (until 9 p.m. on Fri.) and Sun. 1-5 p.m.; donation; tel. 328-4201. Located at 20 S. West Temple between Symphony Hall and the Salt Palace; parking validation is given for Crossroads Plaza across the street.

### Utah State History Museum
The Denver and Rio Grande Railroad built this grand terminal in 1910 while in keen competition with the Union Pacific, whose depot lay 2 blocks to the north. Steam whistles no longer blow outside, but Amtrak trains now stop here. The spacious lobby is worth a visit to see changing exhibits on Utah's history; the museum is open Mon. to Fri. and possibly Sat.; free. The Utah State Historical Society has a bookstore just off the lobby with an excellent selection of Utah history and travel books. Upstairs, the society offers a research library containing thousands of books and photos about Utah's past. Call 533-5755 for current hours of museum, bookstore, and library. Located at the west end of 300 South at 455 West.

## NORTH OF DOWNTOWN

### Pioneer Memorial Museum
Descendants of Utah's Mormon pioneers have packed all 4 levels of the museum with a huge collection of pioneer portraits and memorabilia. These artifacts tell the story of persecuted families who fled Nauvoo, Illinois, and trekked 2,000 miles west to Utah to build their city of Zion. It helps to have some knowledge of Mormon history to appreciate the exhibits fully. A video program, shown on request, introduces the collection.

The present museum, built in 1950, is a replica of the old Salt Lake Theatre, used from 1862 until torn down in 1928. Theatrical exhibits on the main floor include printed programs, props, musical instruments, and seats. The main floor also has paintings, photos, and personal effects of Brigham Young and his First Counselor, Heber C. Kimball. A manuscript room in the back is full of proclamations, religious books, maps, scrapbooks, and photos. A family tree shows how Samuel Rose Parkinson (1831-1919) and his 3 wives produced a total of 221 children, grandchildren, and great grandchildren during his lifetime. Indian exhibits scattered around the museum contain some exotic items like an Inca god and a Maori bride's skirt. The second floor has a medical/midwifery display, a pioneer kitchen, clothing, a large doll collection, and chinaware. Third floor has displays of clocks, Utah silk production, furniture, quilts, and lots of bric-a-brac. Go downstairs to the basement for exhibits of spinning and weaving, railroading, mining, and guns. The 2-story Carriage House, connected to the basement by a short tunnel, has saddles and harnesses, a mule-drawn street car, stagecoaches, steam fire pumper, a blacksmith shop, and the wagon in which Brigham Young is believed to have arrived in the Salt Lake Valley. A small gift shop just inside the museum's entrance sells books, postcards, slides, and other souvenirs of Utah's history. The Pioneer Memorial Museum is open Mon. to Sat. 9 a.m.-5 p.m.; also Sun. 1-5 p.m. in summer; closed major holidays; donation appreciated; tel. 538-1050. Located at 300 N. Main St. near the State Capitol; there's free parking at a lot between the museum and State Capitol.

### Utah State Capitol
Utah's Capitol occupies a prominent spot on a hill just north of downtown. Shortages of

funds during the early statehood years left the legislators without a permanent home from 1896 until completion of this building in 1915. If the architectural style looks familiar, that's because the building was patterned after the national Capitol. Utah granite makes up the outside. The interior, with its Ionic columns, is of polished marble from Georgia. Murals depict early explorers and pioneers. Smaller paintings show all the territorial and state governors. Statues, busts, and plaques also honor prominent Utah figures of the past. The Gold Room, used for receiving dignitaries, has a formal setting graced by chandeliers, wall tapestries, elegant furniture, and cherubs on the ceiling. The chambers of the House of Representatives, Senate, and Supreme Court are entered from the mezzanine. Hallways on the lowest floor have photo exhibits of the state's scenic and historic spots, beehive memorabilia, Utah gravestone art, mining, and agriculture. Neatest of all is the Mormon Meteor racing car once driven by native Utahn Ab Jenkins. He used it in the late 1940s and early 1950s to set some of his more than 1,500 American and world records at Bonneville Salt Flats.

Forty acres of park lands with historic statues and monuments surround the Capitol. The heroic Indian statue *Massasoit* in front of the Capitol is a bronze replica by Utah sculptor Cyrus E. Dallin. From this spot you can look out over Salt Lake City and straight down State St., which runs south about 28 miles without a curve. The Mormon Battalion Monument, a large bronze and granite memorial in the southeast corner of the Capitol grounds, commemorates the 549 Mormon soldiers who marched 2,000 miles from Council Bluffs, Iowa, to San Diego, California, to assist in the Mexican War of 1846. Except for an attack by wild animals in the "Battle of the Bulls," the group saw no action. Steps lead down into a small canyon east of the Capitol to **Memory Grove.** Monuments and relics honor Utah's war dead from WW I to the present.

The Capitol is open daily 8 a.m.-6 p.m., extended in summer to daily 8 a.m.-8 p.m. Free tours in summer depart Mon. to Fri. 9 a.m.-3 p.m. every half hour; meet at the large map on the first floor; tel. 538-3000. Visitors are welcome to use the circular cafeteria (open Mon. to Fri. 7 a.m.-4 p.m.) behind the Capitol. Annual legislative sessions begin in Jan. and last about 45 days. The Utah State Capitol is at 300 North and State streets.

**Council Hall**

South across the street from the Capitol lies the venerable Council Hall. Dedicated in 1866, the brick building served as city hall and a meeting place for the territorial and early state legislatures. Many historic decisions were made within its walls. Council Hall used to be downtown at 120 E. 100 South before

*Jenkin's
Mormon Meteor*

being moved here in 1963. Several rooms have been restored and furnished as they were in Utah's early decades. The **Utah Travel Council** occupies the other rooms; drop in for information on sights, services, and events in the state. Council Hall and the Utah Travel Council are open Mon. to Fri. 8 a.m.-5 p.m. (also summer weekends and holidays 9 a.m.-4 p.m.); tel. 538-1030. The 1883 Gothic-Revival-building just to the east was also moved here to make way for a new building. Formerly the 18th Ward Chapel of the LDS Church, it's now the **White Memorial Chapel** and is used for community events.

### Historic Houses

Streets in the **Marmalade District** on the hillside west of the Capitol have names of fruit trees—hence the term "marmalade." Many residences date from the 19th century. The **Utah Heritage Foundation,** located at 355 Quince St. in the 1880s Quayle House, has information and self-guided tour brochures about Salt Lake City's historic districts. Walking tours for groups can be arranged with at least one week's notice; tel. 533-0858. The **McCune Mansion** at 200 N. Main is one of the city's most eye-catching old houses. The turn-of-the-century turreted structure has a tiled roof and exceptional interior woodwork; it's now used for offices and wedding receptions.

### Children's Museum Of Utah

None of the exhibits here have DO NOT TOUCH signs! Kids get to explore by operating a TV station, excavating a saber-toothed tiger, piloting a 727 jet trainer, implanting an artificial heart in a dummy, "shopping," "banking," trying art projects, and using computers to draw. Everything is great fun; just don't say anything to the kids about the exhibits being educational! Handicap-awareness simulations let a youngster experience what life is like for others by entering a blind room or by taking a wheelchair over an obstacle course. Kids also participate in a performance theater.

The building housing the museum used to be known as the Wasatch Plunge or Wasatch

Springs Municipal Baths. Mormon pioneers discovered the sulfurous springs soon after arriving and built a bathhouse. The spot served as a bathing resort until the early 1970s, when the baths closed and the springs were capped. People had lost interest in "taking the waters" for their health and turned instead to jogging and other sports. The Children's Museum is open Mon. to Sat. 9:30 a.m.-5 p.m.; $3 adult, $2.50 children 3-12; tel. 328-3383. Located north of downtown at 840 N. 300 West (US 89). The adjacent city park offers picnic tables, playground and tennis courts.

### Bountiful-Davis Art Center

Exhibits by Utah artists and art classes take place at this gallery 8 miles north of Salt Lake City. Open Mon. 5-9 p.m., Tues. to Fri. 10 a.m.-6 p.m., Sat. and Sun. 2-5 p.m.; closed holidays; free; tel. 292-0367. A gift shop is open during gallery hours. Located at 2175 S. Main in Bountiful (84010); take I-15 North Salt Lake/Woods Cross Exit 318, go east 0.3 mile on 2600 South to 500 West (which becomes Main St.), then turn left (north) 0.2 mile.

## Lagoon Amusement Park And Pioneer Village

History, recreation, and thrilling rides come together in this attractively landscaped park, 16 miles north of Salt Lake City (or 16 miles south of Ogden). Lagoon traces its own history back to 1887, when bathers came to Lake Park on the shores of the Great Salt Lake, 2 miles to the west of its present location. The vast **Lagoon Amusement Park** area includes 5 roller coaster rides, a Ferris wheel, Tilt-a-Whirl, Flying Carpet, Mother Goose Land, Dracula's Castle, Sky Fighter, Fun House, a log flume ride, a steam train ride, and many arcade games. Musical events you might catch include Music USA (song and dance), Country Side (country, pop, and gospel), a Broadway musical in the Lagoon Opera House, and performances by the marching Show Band. Other things to do are picnicking or playing a round of miniature golf (extra charge). **Lagoon A Beach** provides thrilling water slides and landscaped pools; owners claim this to be "Utah's most spectacular water Park." **Pioneer Village** brings the past to life with authentic 19th C. buildings, stagecoach and steam train rides, a Ute Indian museum, a carriage museum, a gun collection, and many other exhibits. Almost every kind of shop or office you'd expect to find in a Utah town of 100 years ago will be here (except no saloon—sorry!). Wild West shootouts take place several times daily. Food booths are scattered throughout the park or you can dine at the Gaslight Restaurant near the Opera House. Lagoon, Lagoon A Beach, and Pioneer Village open at 11 a.m. and close 8-11 p.m. (depending on crowds): Sat. and Sun. from early April to Memorial Day weekend, daily from Memorial to Labor day weekends, then Sat. and Sun. through Sept.; tel. 451-0101. An all-day

ride pass (the best deal as individual rides cost $1.50-2.25) is $15.95 adult, less for children and seniors. Lagoon A Beach costs $10.50, or $20.95 with a Lagoon ride pass. An additional $3 is charged for parking. Take I-15 to Lagoon Exit 327 (Farmington) and follow signs.

**Pioneer Village Campground,** on the south side of the amusement park, offers showers, store, laundry, and discounts for rides; sites for tents or RVs cost $13.10 without hookups, $14.74-16.92 w/hookups; open April 1 to Sept. 30; tel. 451-2812.

## Utah Botanical Gardens

Thousands of brightly colored flowers make this a lovely spot in season. The landscaped grounds include a rose garden, groups of annuals and perennials, herbs, lilies, lilacs, an iris walk, garden vegetables, a native landscape garden, shrubs, and trees. Plant species come from Utah and other temperate regions of the world. Utah State University (Logan) uses the gardens for research and as a demonstration area. The gardens are a pleasant place for a stroll and an opportunity for local gardeners to see what will grow well in this area. Labels identify each type of plant. The staff schedule flower shows, workshops, and gardening classes, as well as answer gardening questions. Public tours are offered Wed. at 10 a.m. from May to September. The grounds are open daily during daylight hours all year; office hours are Mon. to Fri. 8:30 a.m.-4:30 p.m.; tel. 451-3204. Located at 1817 N. Main in Farmington (at the junction of US 89 and UT 272). Take I-15 Exit 327 and go north 2 miles on US 89, then turn right just past the gardens to the entrance.

## · EAST OF DOWNTOWN

### South Temple Street

Probably the most prestigious street address in all of early Utah. Many religious and business leaders had stately mansions along South Temple, once known as Brigham Street. The book *Brigham Street* by Margaret Lester details the history of the people who lived here and their magnificent buildings. The Utah Heritage Foundation sells a self-guided tour booklet, *Historic Buildings Along South Temple Street*. Several buildings dating from the early 1900s are open to the public.

Twin towers and gargoyles festoon the imposing Catholic **Church of the Madeleine**, constructed of sandstone in a Roman Gothic style; open daily 6 a.m.-6 p.m. all year; tel. 328-8941; at 331 E. South Temple. The **First Presbyterian Church** is in an English Gothic Revival style; open daily (check at office if front doors are closed); tel. 363-3889; at 347 E. South Temple. The palatial **Kearns Mansion** at 603 E. South Temple is now the official governor's residence. Thomas Kearns, noted for his silver-mining wealth, became a U.S. senator and publisher of the *Salt Lake Tribune*. He spared no expense to make the 28 rooms as elegant and lavish as possible. Tours of the Kearns Mansion can be arranged early May to early Dec. on Tues. and Thurs. 2-4 p.m.; free; tel. 538-1005.

### University Of Utah

Mormon pioneers placed a high value on education. They had established a university in their short-lived town of Nauvoo, Illinois, and brought its books with them to Utah. The University of Deseret opened in 1850, just 2½ years after the first colonizers reached the Salt Lake Valley. Lack of funds forced the school to close after 2 years, as church educators concentrated their efforts on primary classes. Dr. John R. Park brought the university back to life as a business academy in 1867. It took the name University of Utah in 1892 and moved to its present site on a terrace east of town in 1900. The state-assisted institution now sprawls across a 1,500-acre campus. A giant "U" on the hillside lights up during sporting events; if the university team wins, the lights flash.

About 30,000 students and a faculty of 3,500 take part in a wide range of fields, including the liberal arts, business, medicine, science, engineering, and architecture— some 15 colleges and schools altogether. The university operates on a 4-quarter system. An adjacent Research Park is a partnership of university and private enterprise involving many students and faculty. A center of culture, the U of U offers the Utah Museum of Natural History, Utah Museum of Fine Arts, symphony, bands, dance, theater, and choral groups. Visitors are welcome at the cultural and sporting events, libraries, bookstore, movie theater, and Olpin Union food services. You'll have to attach yourself to someone with a university card to get into most recreational facilities, however. For a campus map, list of scheduled events, and other information, drop by the Park Building (at the top of President's Circle; tel. 581-6515) or the Olpin Union (tel. 581-5888). On-campus parking is available at scattered metered spaces and pay lots next to the Olpin Union and the Marriott Library;

*Kearns Mansion*

free parking can be found off campus on residential streets.

## Utah Museum Of Natural History

This large and varied collection of geology, biology, and anthropology tells the story of Utah before the pioneers arrived. A reproduction of the huge Barrier Canyon Mural picto-graph shows the art of prehistoric Indians. Exhibits display artifacts and trace the development of the early cultures and their replacement by modern tribes, such as the Ute and Navajo. Other exhibits illustrate Utah's colorful mining history and feature beautiful specimens of the state's more than 600 minerals. Impressive natural history specimens

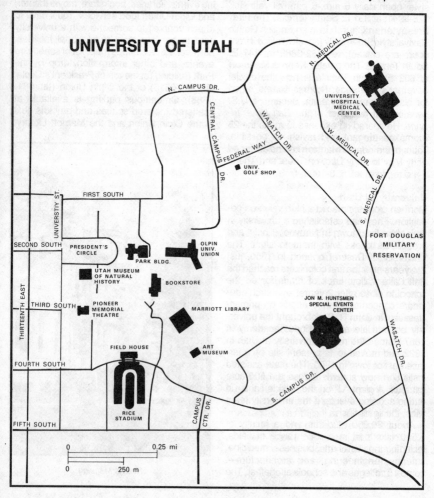

include dinosaurs and early mammals, as well as the varied wildlife of the present day. Also, in the main lobby, look for the exhibit of California gulls *(Larus californicus)* devouring a plague of Mormon crickets (actually a flightless grasshopper, *Anabrus simplex)*. Visiting exhibits may be on display too. A gift shop sells animal souvenirs for the kids, fossil and mineral specimens, a good selection of Utah and natural history books, and posters. The museum is open Mon. to Sat. 9:30 a.m.-5:30 p.m., Sun. and holidays noon-5 p.m.; $2 adult, $1 children 3-14 (special exhibits may cost more); tel. 581-4303. Located on the University of Utah campus on President's Circle; turn in off University St. (1350 East) between 200 and 300 South streets. Free validated parking is available in front.

### Utah Museum Of Fine Arts
Though of modest size, the museum displays a little of everything, from 5,000-year-old Egyptian art to works by contemporary artists. Permanent exhibits include art of China, India, Southeast Asia, Europe, Africa, pre-Columbia, and the early American West. Three large galleries host visiting exhibitions. Open Mon. to Fri. 10 a.m.-5 p.m., Sat. and Sun. 2-5 p.m.; free; tel. 581-7049. Located just south of the Marriott Library on the university campus. Metered parking is available near the museum or at the library; both are off S. Campus Dr., an extension of 400 South Street.

### State Arboretum Of Utah
The entire University of Utah campus has more than 7,000 trees of about 350 species and varieties. A self-guided tour visits 40 different tree species from Utah and around the world. Pick up a map and brochure at the university information desks, the Utah Museum of Natural History, or the arboretum office. Other highlights include a rose garden; the world's largest Russian olive tree (65 ft. high and 118 inches in girth); and the Red Butte Gardens which display orchids and other tropical exotics, succulents, and cacti (open daily 9 a.m.-9 p.m. in summer and daily 9 a.m.-5 p.m. in winter; located on the northeast

edge of campus). The State Arboretum office is near the east edge of campus in Building 436, room 116; tel. 581-5322. Field trips, tree walks, lectures, and a research library are offered. A **Wildflower Hotline** tells where the best wildflower displays can be found in the state; tel. 581-4969.

### Fort Douglas Museum
Artifacts and many historical photos take the visitor back to the days of the Nauvoo Legion, the Mormon Battalion, and U.S. Army life in Utah from its beginnings to the present. In late 1862, Colonel Patrick Connor marched to this site with his California-Nevada volunteers and built Camp Douglas. Officially the post defended the mail route and kept check on the Indians. Connor also felt it necessary to keep an eye (and cannon) on the Mormons, whom he and other federal officials distrusted. The colonel wasted no time before seeking Indians to fight. In Jan. 1863, just months after his arrival, Connor's troops killed several hundred Shoshoni on the Bear River in northern Cache Valley. The event advanced Connor's career, but historians have criticized the action because of the many women and children slaughtered. Later, in a more peaceable mood, the colonel and some of his soldiers pioneered development of Utah's minerals near Park City and elsewhere in the territory. Fort Douglas Museum's exhibits show the unique histories of Fort Douglas and other military bases in Utah. The most unusual may have been Fort Rawlins, whose only battle was with the townspeople of Provo. Soldiers staged a rambunctious raid on the town after a payday, but Provo's citizens didn't see the humor and had the troops and fort promptly removed. A WW I room includes photos of German POWs interned here, and other rooms illustrate the big military buildup during WW II, when Utah even had a naval base! Military history buffs can learn more in the museum's library. Fort Douglas Museum is open Tues. to Sat. 10 a.m.-noon and 1-4 p.m.; closed on federal holiday weekends; free; tel. 524-4154.

The museum building, officers' row, and some of the other structures at Fort Douglas date from the 1870s and 1880s in an architectural style termed Quartermaster Victorian. Pick up a walking-tour leaflet of the fort at the museum; a map shows the nearby post cemetery, where Colonel Connor, soldiers, and German POWs lie buried. Fort Douglas, now used by the military for administration and recruitment offices, is just east of the University of Utah; turn north on Wasatch Dr. from 500 South and go ½ mile to the museum.

## Pioneer Trail State Park

Brigham Young gazed onto the Salt Lake Valley for the first time from this spot, it's believed, and spoke the famous words, "This is the right place. Drive on." Exactly 100 years later, on July 24, 1947, a crowd gathered to dedicate the massive *This Is the Place* monument. Twelve-foot bronze statues of Brigham Young flanked by Heber C. Kimball and Wilford Woodruff stand atop a central pylon. The monument honors not only the Mormon pioneers but also the missionaries from Spain, fur trappers and traders, government explorers, and California immigrants who contributed to the founding of an empire in "the top of the mountains," as prophesied by Isaiah in the Bible. Sculptures, bas-reliefs, and plaques around the base of the monument illustrate Utah's beginnings. A visitor center contains a mural depicting major events on the migration of the "Saints" from Nauvoo, Illinois, to their promised land. An 8-minute narration recounts the journey; several foreign languages can be requested too. The visitor center is open daily 9 a.m.-4:30 p.m. (extended 10 a.m.-6 p.m. from May 16 to Sept. 16); free admission; books, postcards, and souvenirs are sold; tel. 584-8391 (recording). The park has a pleasant picnic area.

**Old Deseret,** near the monument, re-creates a Utah pioneer village. During the summer it comes alive with farming and craft demonstrations and wagon rides. Most of the more than a dozen buildings that were moved here are original—some of the first in the valley. Some notable structures include Brigham Young's forest farmhouse, the 1847 Levi Riter cabin, and the Charles Rich house, de-

signed in the 1850s for polygamous family living. Tours of the historic park cost $1 adult ($.50 children 6-15) during the season; call for hours at 584-8391. At other times you can walk around on your own to see the exteriors. Pioneer Trail State Park is southeast of the University of Utah near the mouth of Emigration Canyon; from Wasatch Dr., turn east ½ mile on Sunnyside Ave. (850 South).

## Hogle Zoo

Salt Lake City's zoo, an especially popular spot with the kids, is on the eastern edge of town and across from Pioneer Trail State Park. Children like to ride the miniature train (60¢; closed in winter), see exhibits in the Discovery Center, and visit the petting farm. Many of the large-animal enclosures have natural settings; here you'll see the familiar elephants, rhinos, and hippos. Sea lions put on shows in summer, but the apes and monkeys carry on almost all the time. Mornings are best to hear the songs of the white-handed gibbons of Southeast Asia. Also meet Dan the gorilla, Otis the orangutan, and admire the mandrill—most colorful of all primates. Tropical, subtropical, and desert rooms contain deadly cobras and vipers, aardvarks, Australian kookaburras, brightly colored birds in a walk-in aviary, and dozens of other exotic species. The cats include lions, leopards, tigers, and ocelots. Though zoos don't normally display stuffed animals, Hogle Zoo's unusual "liger" can be seen in the cat area. Shasta the Liger was born of a Bengal tigress and an African lion father, the result of a mating that wouldn't happen in nature because the animal's territories don't overlap. Hogle Zoo is open daily in summer 9 a.m.-7:30 p.m. (gates close at 6 p.m.) and daily in winter 9 a.m.-4 p.m. Entrance fees are $4 adult, $2 children 5-14 and seniors 65 and over; tel. 582-1631. Snack bars and strollers are available. Located at 2600 Sunnyside Ave. (½ mile east from Wasatch Dr.).

## Westminster College

This private 4-year college provides a liberal arts background with training in such careers

"OK, Mom, where's dinner?"

as business, computer science, education, and nursing. Post-graduate programs are offered in business and education. Westminster College encourages discussion and interaction among its approximately 1,500 students and 100 faculty members through small class sizes. Two 14-week semesters followed by a one-month May term and a summer session make up the school year. Evening and weekend classes allow older "nontraditional" students to work toward a degree. The Salt Lake Collegiate Institute, founded in 1875 by the Presbyterian Church as a boys' preparatory school, became Westminster College about the turn of the century. By 1944 it had grown to be a 4-year college, and in 1974 it became independent. Converse Hall, constructed in 1906 as the first building on the present campus, is a registered national historic site. Shaw Hall in the center of the campus serves as a student meeting place with snack bar, cafeteria, and a small bookstore. Theater performances, lectures by prominent people, and other cultural activities are open to the public. Westminster College is at 1840 S. 1300 East; tel. 484-7651.

## SOUTH OF DOWNTOWN

### Tracy Aviary

Birds have taken over the southwest corner of Liberty Park. Step into their domain to see majestic golden and bald eagles, showy flamingos and peacocks, the hyacinthine macaw (world's largest parrot), Quaker parakeets, the golden pheasant of China, and hundreds of other feathered friends. The big birds, ostriches from Africa and emus from Australia, prance across their fields while ducks, geese, swans, and other waterfowl keep to the ponds. You'll also get to meet Utah's only native vulture, the turkey vulture. Tracy Aviary is open daily 9 a.m.-6 p.m. in summer and 9 a.m.-4:30 p.m. the rest of the year; tel. 596-5034. In summer, a small admission is charged on Sun. and holidays. Located in Liberty Park at 589 E. 1300 South; enter the aviary from the east side.

*Utah Copper Mill, Bingham Canyon, ca. 1905*

**Wheeler Historic Farm**

Kids enjoy a visit to this working farm to experience rural life of milking cows, gathering eggs, churning butter, and feeding the animals. Hay rides (sleigh rides in winter) take visitors around the farm. Geese and ducks congregate around the ice ponds, a popular spot for fishing (poles available; no license needed). Crafts and snacks are sold in the "Ice House." Henry and Sariah Wheeler started the farm in 1887 and developed it into a prosperous dairy and ice-making operation. Tour guides take you through the Wheeler's restored Victorian house, built 1896-98, the first in the county to have an indoor bathroom. Signs on other farm buildings recount their history and use. The Salt Lake County Recreation Dept. operates the farm and offers special programs for both youngsters and adults; call or write for a schedule; tel. 264-2212. Free admission, though a small charge is made for rides, fishing, tours, and other activities. Birthday parties and family picnics are popular (make advance reservations). The Family Garden Program has garden plots and classes available to the community. Though once on

the outskirts of town, Wheeler Historic Farm is now surrounded by suburbs at 6351 S. 900 East (Salt Lake City, UT 84121).

**Bingham Canyon Copper Mine**

An overlook within the world's largest and oldest open-pit copper mine provides a close look at the nonstop excavation work taking place on the terraced slopes. Signs and an audio program explain the mining process. Prospectors discovered the mineral wealth in 1863, though the Mormon rancher for whom the canyon was named never took part in the mining. Most of the early production concentrated on gold, silver, and lead. Attention shifted to copper in 1906 as mining companies began excavation of an open-pit mine. Today, 5 billion tons of rock later, the pit measures 2½ miles in diameter at its top and ½ mile deep. The "richest hole on earth" has yielded 12 million tons of copper and significant amounts of gold, silver, and molybdenum. Efficient mining, smelting, and refining techniques can make a profit even though Bingham Canyon ore now averages only 0.7% copper. Miners once lived in the town of Bingham Canyon, famed for being one street wide and 7 miles long! Expanding operations gradually destroyed the town in the 1950s; by 1961 nothing remained. See photos and mementos of this unusual mining town in the House of Copper gift shop between Copperton and the mine entrance. Company officials lived in the attractive town of Copperton which still survives.

The mine overlook is in the Oquirrh Mountains 25 miles southwest of Salt Lake City. Because of the distance, it's a good idea to check that it will be open before coming out; call Kennecott Copper (322-8270 or 569-6000) or the Salt Lake Convention & Visitors Bureau (521-2868). The overlook is normally open daily from 8 a.m. until dusk from April 1 to Oct. 31; admission is $2 car, $1 motorcycle. Take I-15 Midvale Exit 301 and follow UT 48 west through Copperton to the mine. Stop at the mine gate for a pass, then follow signs to the overlook. For a bird's-eye view of the mine from the crest of the Oquirrh Mountains, follow the winding unpaved roads from Tooele or the Salt Lake Valley (see "Oquirrh Overlook," p. 134).

### Jordan River Temple
One of the largest Mormon temples, this striking building has an exterior covered with white marble chips. A gilded statue of the angel Moroni stands atop a 200-foot central tower. In 1981, when opened to the public just prior to dedication, 570,000 visitors toured the temple in 35 days. Tours of the temple grounds are available June to September. Jordan River Temple is in the town of South Jordan, 18 miles southwest of downtown Salt Lake City, at 10200 S. 1300 West.

## WEST OF DOWNTOWN

### Welfare Square
A tour through this large operation shows how the Mormon Church tackles social problems of its members, and provides insight into how governments might better aid those in need. An unusual twist to Mormon welfare is the emphasis on giving, rather than getting. Church members commonly volunteer their time at Welfare Square, farms, or other work projects. The unemployed, elderly, and handicapped are expected to contribute according to ability—nobody gets the "dole." The system promotes self-respect and a positive outlook on life. Brigham Young stated that "True charity to a poor family or person consists in placing them in a situation in which they can support themselves." Church members have been helping each other since the earliest days, though the shock of the 1930s Great Depression brought about the highly organized system seen today at Welfare Square. A variety of operations, some of which you'll see on the tour, take place in the dairy plant, cannery, grain elevator, warehouses, Deseret Industries (repair and sales of used clothing and household items), and social services

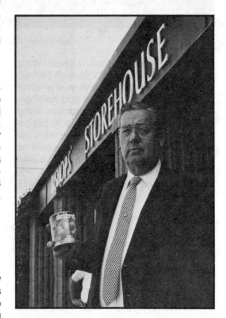

*Bishop Eugene Packer at Welfare Square*

*canning pears at Welfare Square*

(counseling, adoption, foster homes). About 200 people work on the square. A bishop's storehouse, one of 390 around the world, stocks a full range of groceries and clothing—yet nothing is sold or is free for the taking! Those in need receive a bishop's requisition order for essential items before anything can leave the shelves. Tours, lasting about an hour, begin with a short film, *Welfare—Another Perspective.* You're welcome to visit Mon. to Sat. 9 a.m.-4 p.m.; free; tel. 595-1951.

Although Sat. tours are offered, there's usually nothing going on that day. From April to Nov. you can take a shuttle bus from Temple Square; ask at either visitor center there for schedules. Welfare Square is at 751 W. 700 South. Driving here is a bit tricky because the freeway and railroad tracks block 700 South and other streets; 2 suggested routes are west on North Temple, then south on 900 West; or south on West Temple, then west on 800 South.

# SALT LAKE CITY ACCOMMODATIONS

## Youth Hostel

The **Avenues Residential Center,** one mile east of Temple Square, has dorm rooms with use of a kitchen, TV room, and laundry. Information-packed bulletin boards list city sights and goings-on, and you'll meet travelers from all over the world. Year-round rates for the dorm are $9.75 members and $13.11 nonmembers (cost includes sheets). Rooms are $19.67 s, $30.59 d, but lack private baths. Reservations (with first night's deposit) are advised in the busy summer travel and winter ski seasons. The hostel is open during the day (you must check in before 10 p.m.); on the corner of 107 F St. and 2nd Ave., Salt Lake City, UT 84103; tel. 363-8137. From downtown, head east on South Temple St. to F St., then turn north 2 blocks.

## Bed And Breakfasts

These are mostly private homes open to travelers in the European tradition. The degree of luxury varies, but the hosts offer a personal touch not found in the usual motels. Some discourage smoking and pets. Advance reservations are requested. Add 9.25% tax to room rates.

**Brigham Street Inn,** a restored mansion at 1135 E. South Temple, has rooms from $65 s, $95 d; tel. 364-4461. **Anton Boxrud Bed and Breakfast** offers lodging in a 1901 Victorian eclectic brick house at 57 S. 600 East; $35-55 s, $39-59 d; tel. 363-8035. **Saltair Bed & Breakfast,** at 164 S. 900 East, costs $34 s, $49-69 d; tel. 533-8184. **National Historic Bed & Breakfast** is in an 1891 Victorian mansion at 936 E. 1700 South; $37 s, $47 d; tel. 485-3535. The Spruces Bed & Breakfast is a 1903 Gothic Victorian house at 6151 S. 900 East (just north of Wheeler Historic Farm); rooms run $50-100 s or d; tel. 268-8762. **Pinecrest Bed & Breakfast Inn** is on the eastern edge of the city at 6211 Emigration Canyon Rd.; rooms are $65-160 s or d; tel. 583-6663.

## MOTELS AND HOTELS

Salt Lake City has the best selection of accommodations in Utah. An estimated 100 motels and hotels offer more than 10,000 rooms ranging from spartan to posh. Downtown Salt Lake City has the advantage of being close to Temple Square and most other visitor attractions; from here the airport, University of Utah, and ski areas are just a short drive away. Rates listed apply in summer and may be slightly lower the rest of the year. Reservations are most likely to be needed in the summer tourist and winter ski seasons. The listing in the following chart is just a sample. You'll also find many motels and hotels listed in free publications from the Salt Lake Convention & Visitors Bureau, 180 S. West Temple; tel. 521-2868; and at their booth in Terminal 2 of the airport.

## COMMERCIAL CAMPGROUNDS

**Camp VIP** offers tent and RV sites year-round with showers, swimming pool, game room, playground, store, and laundry. Rates are $15.30 tent or RV without hookups, $20.65 w/hookups; tel. 328-0224. The campground is between downtown and the airport at 1350 W. North Temple. From I-15 northbound, take Exit 311 for I-80, go west 1.3 miles on I-80, exit north 0.5 mile on Redwood Rd. (UT 68), then turn right 0.5 mile on North Temple; from I-15 southbound, take Exit 313 and turn south 1.5 miles on 900 West, then turn right 0.8 mile on North Temple; from I-80 either take the North Temple exit or exit on Redwood Rd. (UT 68) and go north 0.5 mile, then right 0.5 mile on North Temple.

**Salt Lake City KOA** features tent and RV sites open all year with showers, swimming pool, miniature golf, store, and laundry. Rates are $16.63 tent or RV without hookups, $21.80 w/hookups; tel. 355-1192. The camp-

# SALT LAKE CITY ACCOMMODATIONS

Add 9.25% tax to all prices

| MOTEL/HOTEL | ADDRESS | RATES | PHONE | FEATURES |
|---|---|---|---|---|
| **DOWNTOWN** | | | | |
| Carlton Hotel | 140 E. South Temple | $44-49 | 355-3418 | restored 1935 hotel |
| Inn at Temple Square | 71 W. South Temple | $75-190 | 531-1000 or (800) 843-4668 | central location |
| Howard Johnson's Motor Lodge | 122 W. South Temple | $48-150 | 521-0130 or (800) 654-2000 | pool |
| Doubletree Hotel | 235 W. South Temple | $65-109 | 531-7500 or (800) 528-0444 | pool |
| TraveLodge at Temple Square | 144 W. North Temple | $30-54 | 533-8200 or (800) 255-3050 | |
| TraveLodge Salt Palace | 215 W. North Temple | $38-45 | 532-1000 or (800) 255-3050 | pool |
| Covered Wagon Motel | 230 W. North Temple | $20-35 | 533-9100 | |
| Royal Executive Inn | 121 N. 300 West (US 89) | $30-42 | 521-3450 | pool |
| Aquarius Motel | 325 N. 300 West (US 89) | $19-49 | 521-9525 | kitchenettes |
| Ken-Dell Motel | 667 N. 300 West (US 89) | $20-50 | 355-0293 | kitchenettes |
| Marriott Hotel | 75 S. West Temple | $69-149 | 531-0800 or (800) 228-9290 | pool, sauna |
| Shilo Inn | 206 S. West Temple | $54-67 | 521-9500 or (800) 222-2244 | pool, sauna |
| Red Lion Hotel | 255 S. West Temple | $99-175 | 328-2000 or (800) 547-8010 | pool, sauna |
| Peery Hotel | 110 W. 300 South | $70-90 | 521-4300 | historic 1910 hotel |
| Stratford Hotel | 169 E. 200 South | $13-18 | 328-4089 | old-style hotel |
| Orleans Inn Hotel | 352 S. 300 East | $49-79 | 521-3790 | kitchenettes, pool |
| Emerald Inn | 476 S. State | $34-45 | 533-9300 | pool |
| Little America Hotel | 500 S. Main St. | $59-99 | 363-6781, (800) 662-5888 in UT, or (800) 453-5888 out of state | pools, sauna |
| Deseret Inn | 50 W. 500 South | $29-37 | 532-2900 | pool |

# SALT LAKE CITY ACCOMMODATIONS (CONT.)

Add 9.25% tax to all prices

| MOTEL/HOTEL | ADDRESS | RATES | PHONE | FEATURES |
|---|---|---|---|---|
| Salt Lake Hilton | 150 W. 500 South | $79-122 | 532-3344 or (800) 445-8667 | pool |
| TraveLodge Downtown | 524 S. West Temple | $38-45 | 531-7100 or (800) 255-3050 | pool |
| Embassy Suites | 600 S. West Temple | $85-95 | 359-7800 or (800) 362-2779 | pool, sauna |
| Quality Inn City Center | 154 W. 600 South | $61-67 | 521-2930 or (800) 221-2222 | pool |
| Olympus Hotel (Best Western) | 161 W. 600 South | $49-59 | 521-7373 or (800) 528-1234 | pool |
| Motel 6 Downtown | 176 W. 600 South | $26-45 | 531-1252 | pool |
| Holiday Inn Downtown | 230 W. 600 South | $59-71 | 532-7000 or (800) 465-4329 | pool, sauna |
| Super 8 Motel | 616 S. 200 West | $55-88 | 534-0808 or (800) 843-1991 | |
| Clarion Hotel and Suites | 999 South Main | $59-79 | 359-8600 or (800) 252-7466 | pool, weight room |
| The Residence Inn | 765 E. 400 South | $95-117 | 532-5511 | kitchenettes, pool |
| Lake City Motel | 925 E. 400 South | $16-31 | 535-8239 | near Univ. of Utah |
| Scenic Motel | 1345 Foothill Dr. | $29-38 | 582-1527 | east edge of SLC |
| **WEST DOWNTOWN TO AIRPORT** | | | | |
| Se Rancho Motor Hotel | 640 W. North Temple | $25-45 | 532-3300 | kitchenettes, pool |
| Econolodge | 715 W. North Temple | $36-45 | 363-0062 | pool |
| Scotty's Travel Motor Hotel | 754 W. North Temple | $19-40 | 531-7300 | kitchenettes, pool |
| Continental Motel | 819 W. North Temple | $24-40 | 363-4546 | pool |
| Regal Inn | 1025 N. 900 West | $23-37 | 364-6591 | |
| Overniter Motor Inn | 1500 W. North Temple | $22-38 | 533-8300 | pool |
| Holiday Inn Airport | 1659 W. North Temple | $54-84 | 533-9000 or (800) 465-4329 | pool |
| Days Inn | 1900 W. North Temple | $29-37 | 539-8538 or (800) 325-2525 | |

# SALT LAKE CITY ACCOMMODATIONS (CONT.)

Add 9.25% tax to all prices

| MOTEL/HOTEL | ADDRESS | RATES | PHONE | FEATURES |
|---|---|---|---|---|
| Motel 6-Airport | 1990 W. North Temple | $25-43 | 364-1053 | pool |
| Chateau Motel & Trailer Court | 1999 W. North Temple | $21-28 | 596-7240 | |
| Nendel's Inn Airport | 2080 W. North Temple | $42-48 | 355-0088 or (800) 547-0106 | pool |
| Airport Inn | 2333 W. North Temple | $39-80 | 539-0438 | pool |
| Airport Hilton | 5151 Wiley Post Way | $59-225 | 539-1515 or (800) 445-8667 | pool |
| Quality Inn Airport | 5575 W. Amelia Earhart Dr. | $60-69 | 537-7020 or (800) 228-5151 | pool |

ground is between downtown and the airport at 1400 W. North Temple; follow same directions as for Camp VIP, above.

**Oquirrh Motor Inn** (21 miles west of Salt Lake City) offers inexpensive RV spaces from March 1 to Oct. 31; $8.56 w/hookups but no showers (no tents); tel. 250-0118; located just south of I-80 Tooele Exit 99.

**Hidden Haven Campground** (18 miles east of Salt Lake City) has showers, store, and a trout stream. Tent and RV sites are open all year; $10.63 no hookups, $13.90 w/hookups; tel. 649-8935. Take I-80 Exit 143, then go east 1.6 miles on the north frontage road (or take Park City Exit 145 and go west one mile on the north frontage road).

**Pioneer Village Campground** (16 miles north of Salt Lake City) at Lagoon Amusement Park is open April 1 to Sept. 30 with showers, store, laundry, and discounts for rides; tent and RV sites cost $13.10 no hookups, $14.74-16.92 w/hookups; tel. 451-2812. Take I-15 Lagoon/Farmington Exit 327 and follow signs.

**Cherry Hill Recreation Park** (18 miles north of Salt Lake City) features a water slide, inner tube ride, swimming pool, miniature golf, and a variety of games, as well as a large campground with showers, store, and laundry. Season lasts about mid-April to mid-Oct.,

though some activities operate only from Memorial to Labor day weekends. Tent or RV sites cost $13.08 no hookups, $17.44 w/hookups; tel. 451-5379. Take I-15 Lagoon/Farmington Exit 327 and go north 2 miles on US 89.

## FOREST SERVICE CAMPGROUNDS

There are 2 campgrounds in Big Cottonwood Canyon, whose mouth is about 15 miles southeast of downtown Salt Lake City. Both have drinking water. **Spruces Campground** (elev. 7,400 ft.) is open from early June to mid-Oct.; $8; it's 9.8 miles up the canyon. The season at **Redman Campground** (elev. 8,300 ft.) is from mid-June to early Oct.; $7; it's located between Solitude and Brighton, 13 miles up the canyon.

Little Cottonwood Canyon, whose mouth is about 19 miles southeast of downtown Salt Lake City, also has 2 campgrounds with drinking water. **Tanners Flat Campground** (elev. 7,200 ft.) is open from mid-May to mid-Oct.; $7; it's 4.3 miles up the canyon. **Albion Basin Campground** lies high in the mountains (elev. 9,500 ft.) and opens from early July to late Sept.; $6; go 11 miles up the canyon (the last 2.5 miles are gravel).

# SALT LAKE CITY RESTAURANTS

Nowhere else in Utah will you find so many places to eat and so varied a selection. The following are just some of the possibilities. The free *Salt Lake Visitors Guide* by the Salt Lake Convention & Visitors Bureau and the magazine *Utah Holiday* also describe dining opportunities. Restaurants in private clubs require purchase of a temporary membership (even if you're not drinking!) unless the club is in the hotel where you're staying. Dinner reservations are advisable at the more expensive restaurants; also check to see if coat and tie are required for the men.

Restaurant prices (for dinner) are marked $ = Inexpensive (to $8); $$ = Moderate ($8-15); $$$ = Expensive ($15 and up).

## AMERICAN

**$ Bill and Nada's Cafe:** An especially good place for breakfast, which is served anytime. At 479 S. 600 East; tel. 359-6984. Open daily 24 hours.

**$ to $$ Cafe Central:** The "New American" menu includes pasta dishes, beef, veal, and fish entrees, sandwiches, and salads. In Trolley Square at 500 South and 700 East; tel. 531-0895. Open daily for lunch and dinner; brunch on Sunday.

**$ to $$ Coyote Bill's:** Western atmosphere for steaks, barbecued ribs, burgers, and seafood. At Shilo Inn, 206 S. West Temple; tel. 355-8106. Open 24 hours (except closed Sun. after 10 p.m.) for breakfast, lunch, and dinner.

**$ Dee's Family Restaurants:** American favorites at 143 W. North Temple (tel. 359-4414), 855 W. North Temple (359-3916), 515 E. 400 South (322-3811), and other locations. Open daily for breakfast, lunch, and dinner.

**$ to $$ The Dodo:** Paintings of giant dodos cover a wall of this popular cafe. At 680 S. 900 East; tel. 328-9348. Open Mon. to Fri. for lunch and dinner, Sun for brunch.

**$ to $$ E.I.B.O.'s:** Chefs grill steak, chicken, shrimp, oysters, scallops, and fish over mesquite charcoal fires. The menu also offers sandwiches, salads, and soups. At Trolley Square, 500 South and 700 East; tel. 531-7788. Open daily for lunch and dinner.

**$$ Harvey's:** Private club serving prime rib, steak, seafood, and chicken specialties. A piano or small jazz combo entertains nightly. At Shilo Inn, 206 S. West Temple; tel. 322-3262. Open Mon. to Fri. for lunch and daily for dinner.

**$ Honey's Restaurant:** Family dining with popular American fare. At the Travelodge on North Temple and 200 West; tel. 532-1444. Open daily for breakfast, lunch, and dinner.

**$ JB's:** American favorites at Howard Johnson's Motor Lodge (102 W. South Temple; tel. 328-8344) and in Crossroads Plaza (South Temple; tel. 355-2100). Open daily for breakfast, lunch, and dinner.

**$$ Lamb's:** Claiming to be Utah's oldest restaurant, Lamb's started in Logan in 1919 and moved to Salt Lake City in 1939. You can still enjoy the 1930s atmosphere as well as the fine food. Offerings include seafood, steaks, chops, chicken, and sandwiches. Downtown at 169 S. Main; tel. 364-7166. Open daily except Sun. for breakfast, lunch, and dinner.

**$$ Little America:** The restaurant at this large hotel is especially noted for its lavish Sunday brunch. Just south of downtown at 500 South Main; tel. 363-6781. Open daily for breakfast, lunch, and dinner.

**$$ to $$$ Mulboon's:** Elegant dining with steak, prime rib, and seafood. In Trolley Corners (across from Trolley Square) at 515 S.

700 East (tel. 363-9653) and in Midvale at 6950 S. State (tel. 562-5147). Open Mon. to Fri. for lunch, daily for dinner, and Sun. for brunch.

**$$ Old Salt City Jail Restaurant:** Dine on steak, prime rib, or seafood in an authentic Old West jail house. Guitar or fiddle players add lively Western music. The Jail is 2 blocks east of Trolley Square and near the University of Utah at 460 S. 1000 East; tel. 355-2422. Open daily for dinner.

**$$ to $$$ Room at the Top:** Enjoy panoramic views of the city while dining on steak, prime rib, and seafood. Live piano music provides entertainment nightly. Atop the Salt Lake Hilton at 150 W. 500 South; tel. 532-3344. Open Mon. to Fri. for lunch and daily for dinner.

**$$ The Shed:** Chow down Texas style with steak, jumbo Gulf prawns, Alaskan halibut, and chicken. Informal Western atmosphere (entertainment on weekends); 1063 E. 2100 South (behind the Pine Cone Restaurant); tel. 467-1442. Open Mon. to Sat. for dinner only.

**$$ Shenanigans Restaurant:** Excellent selection of American, Mexican, and Continental fare—seafood, steak, chicken, sandwiches, and salads. Cartoon-filled menus start the dining off on a humorous note. In the Peery Hotel at 274 S. West Temple; tel. 364-3663. Open daily for lunch and dinner.

**$ Training Table Restaurants:** A great place to come for hamburgers (17 different kinds), sandwiches, salads, and soups. In Salt Lake City at 809 E. 400 South (tel. 355-7523); in Holladay at 4828 Highland Dr. (tel. 272-7398); and in Midvale at 6957 S. State St. (tel. 566-1911). Open daily for lunch and dinner.

## CHINESE

**$ to $$ China Village Restaurant** You'll have a big choice of Cantonese, Szechuan, other Chinese, and American selections.

Downtown at 338 S. Main; tel. 364-6000. Open daily for lunch and dinner.

**$$ Fong Ling:** One of the city's finest restaurants for Cantonese, Szechuan, and Mandarin dining. Located near the mouth of Big Cottonwood Canyon at 3698 E. 7000 South; tel. 943-8199. Open daily for dinner only.

**$ to $$ Great Wall Restaurant:** Good variety of Chinese (Cantonese, Mandarin, and Szechuan) and Korean specialties. Downtown at 238 S. Main; tel. 531-0980. Open daily for lunch and dinner. The buffet lunches offered Mon. to Fri. are an excellent value.

**$ to $$ Hunan Restaurant:** Mandarin and Szechuan cuisine. Located downtown in Arrow Press Square at 165 S. West Temple; tel. 531-6677. Open Mon. to Fri. for lunch, daily for dinner.

**$ King Joy:** Chinese-American cafe with popular Cantonese food. Downtown at 264 S. Main; tel. 355-5243. Open Mon. to Sat. for lunch and dinner.

**$$ Panda Restaurant:** Choose your meats and vegetables to be grilled Mongolian style. Or order from the list of Mandarin and American foods. South of downtown at 1701 S. State; tel. 485-3226. Open Mon. to Sat. for lunch and dinner.

## CONTINENTAL

**$$ Bird's Cafe:** Meat, fish, and pasta specialties. Across from Sugarhouse Park at 1355 E. 2100 South; tel. 466-1051. Open Sun. for brunch, Mon. to Fri. for lunch, and Mon. to Sat. for dinner.

**$$ to $$$ Finn's:** Generous servings of Continental and American food served in an elegant setting. Enjoy live piano music Fri. and Sat. evenings. Selections include New York steak, prime rib, lamb chops, wienerschnitzel, king crab, and halibut. Located southeast of downtown at 2675 Parley's Way; tel. 466-4682. Open daily except Sun. for dinner only.

**$$ to $$$ L'Abeille:** Fine dining with meat and seafood prepared in French and other European styles. In the Marriott Hotel, 75 S. West Temple; tel. 531-0800. Open daily for dinner.

**$$$ La Caille at Quail Run:** You'll feel like you've journeyed to 18th C. rural France at this exceptional restaurant. Vineyards, gardens, ponds, and manicured lawns surround the recreated French chateau. Antique furnishings grace the dining rooms and halls. Once seated inside or on the patio, you can choose from the menu's superb pastry, crêpe, egg, seafood, and meat dishes. Expect to pay $29-39/person for dinner. Dress is semi-formal; reservations advised. Located near the mouth of Little Cottonwood Canyon at 9565 Wasatch Blvd.; tel. 942-1751. Dinner is served Mon. to Sat.; brunch and a Basque-style dinner are served on Sunday.

La Caille at Quail Run

**$$ La Fleur de Lys:** French cuisine with seafood, veal, beef, fowl, lamb, and vegetable entrees. Downtown in Arrow Press Square at 165 S. West Temple; tel. 359-5753. Open Mon. to Sat. for dinner.

**$ to $$ Le Parisien:** A choice of French and Italian specialties at modest prices. Located at 417 S. 300 East; tel. 364-5223. Open Mon. to Sat. for lunch and dinner, Sun. for dinner only.

**$ to $$ Peery Pub and Cafe:** Enjoy fine Continental and other cuisines at cafe prices. Downtown in Peery Hotel at 110 W. 300 South; tel. 521-8919. Open Mon. to Sat. for lunch, Tues. to Sat. for dinner.

**$ to $$ Ristorante Della Fontana:** Fine Italian food, available as 6-course dinners or a la carte, in an old church building. Specialties include spaghetti, lasagna, fettucine, chicken cacciatore, and tenderloin alla griglia. Located at 336 S. 400 East; tel. 328-4243. Open Mon. to Sat. for lunch and dinner.

## DELIS

**$ Marianne's Delicatessen:** Many tempting German foods: sausage, cold cuts, sauerkraut, cheese, breads, and chocolates. Downtown at 149 W. 200 South; tel. 364-0513. Open Tues. to Saturday.

**$ Robert's Deli and Market:** Falafel, taboule, yero, and many other tasty items from Greek, Armenian, and Lebanese cuisines. Both vegetarian and meat foods are offered. At 1071 E. 900 South; tel. 355-8141. Open Mon. to Saturday.

**$ Siegfried's Delicatessen:** Great selection of German sausages, cold cuts, breads, pastries, and cheese. Downtown at 69 W. 300 South; tel. 355-3891. Open Mon. to Saturday.

## GREEK

**$ to $$ Dionysus:** A family restaurant with Greek and American food; try gyros (grilled meat), shish kabob, dolmathes (stuffed grape leaves), steaks, and seafood. Located at 369

S. 400 East; tel. 355-6688. Open daily for breakfast, lunch, and dinner.

## JAPANESE

**$$ Benihana of Tokyo:** Seafood and meats cooked at your hibachi table. Downtown in Arrow Press Square at 165 S. West Temple; tel. 322-2421. Open Mon. to Fri. for lunch and daily for dinner.

**$$ 47 Samurai:** The chef prepares meat and seafood in teppanyaki, sukiyaki, tempura, and other styles. In Trolley Square at 500 South and 700 East; tel. 363-7294. Open Mon. to Fri. for lunch and daily for dinner.

**$$ Hibachi:** Chefs prepare hibachi and suki-yaki steak or seafood at your table. Downtown at 238 E. South Temple; tel. 364-5456. Open Mon. to Fri. for lunch and Mon. to Sat. for dinner.

**$$ Kyoto:** Chefs and waitresses take pride in the authentic food and atmosphere. Try their sukiyaki, teriyaki, and other styles. Located at 1080 E. 1300 South; tel. 487-3525; dinner reservations requested. Open Tues. to Fri. for lunch and Tues. to Sun. for dinner.

**$$ Mikado:** Specialties include steak teriyaki and shrimp tempura. Has a sushi bar. Downtown at 67 W. 100 South; tel. 328-0929; reservations recommended. Open Mon. to Sat. for dinner only.

## MEXICAN

**$$ to $$$ Cordova's El Rancho:** Authentic food in the city's oldest Mexican restaurant. Located at 543 W. 400 North; tel. 355-1914. Open Wed. to Sat. for dinner only.

**$ El Mercado:** Not much atmosphere but good freshly prepared food at low prices. Located at 778 S. West Temple; tel. 531-6331. Open Mon. to Fri. for lunch and dinner; Sat. for lunch only.

**$ La Frontera Cafe:** Enjoy burritos, enchi-ladas, tacos, huevos rancheros, and other Mexican favorites here. Two locations in town: 1236 W. 400 South (tel. 532-3158) and 1434 S. 700 West (tel. 974-0172). Open daily for breakfast, lunch, and dinner.

**$ Rio Grande Cafe:** Good food in the nostal-gic old Rio Grande train station. Downtown at 455 W. 300 South; tel. 364-3302. Open Mon. to Sat. for lunch and daily for dinner.

## MIDDLE EAST

**$$ to $$$ Cedars of Lebanon:** Exotic Medi-terranean flavors from Lebanon, Morocco, Ar-menia, Greece, and Israel. Many vegetarian items too. Belly dancers enliven the scene on weekends. Downtown at 152 E. 200 South; tel. 364-4096. Open Mon. to Sat. for lunch and dinner.

## NATURAL FOODS

**$ New Frontiers Market and Cafe:** Whole-foods cuisine using only the freshest ingre-dients. A health-food store offers meats, sea-food, produce, deli items, and bulk foods. Two locations: 1026 2nd Ave. (open Mon. to Sat. for lunch and dinner; tel. 355-7401) and at 2454 S. 700 East (open Mon. to Sat. for lunch and dinner, Sun. for brunch; tel. 359-7913).

## PIZZA

**$ Gepetto's:** Presenting pizza, lasagna, sandwiches, and salads. Live entertainment is offered Thurs. to Sat. evenings. Near the University of Utah at 230 S. 1300 East; tel. 583-1013. Open Mon. to Sat. for lunch and dinner.

**$ Godfather's Pizza:** Stop here for pizza (also by the slice), Italian sandwiches, and a salad bar. Trolley Square, 500 South and 700 East; tel. 538-0115; and at 1615 Foothill Dr.; tel. 582-0240. Open daily for lunch and dinner.

$ **The Pie Pizzeria:** The Pizzeria offers New York-style hand-thrown pizza near the University of Utah. Live music Thurs. to Sun. evenings. Located downstairs of the University Pharmacy, 1320 E. 200 South; tel. 582-0193. Open daily for lunch and dinner.

## SEAFOOD

$$ to $$$ **Market Street Broiler:** The Broiler specializes in fresh seafood which you can enjoy in the dining room, pick up at the take-out counter, or purchase at the fresh fish market. An in-house bakery creates tempting pastries. Located at 258 S. 1300 East; tel. 583-8808. Open Mon. to Sat. for lunch, daily for dinner.

$$ to $$$ **Market Street Grill:** The Grill features fresh seafood plus steak, prime rib, chops, chicken, and pasta. The Market Street Oyster Bar (private club) is next door with a similar menu and prices. Downtown at 50 Post Office Place (near Main and Broadway); tel. 322-4668. Open daily for breakfast, lunch, and dinner; brunch on Sunday.

$$ **Oceans Restaurant and Oyster Cafe:** On the banks of Big Cottonwood Creek, but you might think you're on the ocean. Excellent selection of seafood includes trout from Utah's mountain streams and fish from the Atlantic, Gulf, and Pacific. The Oyster Cafe offers appetizers and lighter meals. Located at 4760 S. 900 East; tel. 261-0115. Restaurant and cafe are open Mon. to Fri. for lunch and dinner; restaurant is also open Sat. and Sun. for dinner only.

$$ to $$$ **Woody's Wharf:** Private club offering seafood specialties, some Cajun items, and steaks. A lakeside setting adds to the nautical decor. Woody's is near the Airport Hilton in the International Center, 5205 Wiley Post Way; tel. 537-7070. Open Mon. to Fri. for lunch and dinner, Sat. for dinner only.

## THAI

$ to $$ **Sala Siam:** Spicy Thai cuisine with a variety of meat, seafood, and vegetarian dishes. Located at 1371 S. State; tel. 466-8156. Open Mon. to Fri. for lunch (except in summer) and daily for dinner.

## VIETNAMESE

$ **Cafe Trang:** A top-rated restaurant with wonderful food, though don't expect much in the way of decor. Just south of downtown at 818 S. Main; tel. 539-1638. Open Tues. to Sun. for lunch and dinner.

$ to $$ **The Orient:** Expertly prepared and seasoned Vietnamese food. Located southwest of downtown at 4768 Redwood Rd.; tel. 966-3659. Open Mon. to Sat. for lunch and daily for dinner.

# SALT LAKE CITY ENTERTAINMENT

Check local publications to find out what's going on in town. *The Event* newspaper, published every 2 weeks, gives the most detailed coverage of local films, concerts, theater, dance, art exhibits, art classes, and nightspots. Other good sources include *Salt Lake Visitors Guide* (available free at the Salt Lake Convention & Visitors Bureau), *Utah Holiday* magazine (monthly), and *Junction City News* (monthly paper). The daily papers, *Deseret News* and *Salt Lake Tribune,* each have listings in their Fri. "weekend" and Sun. "art and entertainment" sections.

## CONCERTS

**Temple Square**
The **Concert Series** at Temple Square presents hundreds of performances a year for the public—and all are free. The LDS Church

*Robert Cundick at the Tabernacle Organ*

sponsors the varied musical fare with the wish to provide a common meeting ground of great music for people of all faiths. You might hear chamber music, a symphony, operatic selections, religious choral works, piano solos, organ works, a brass band, or a percussion ensemble. Programs last about an hour and usually take place Fri. and Sat. evenings at 7:30 p.m. in either the Assembly Hall or the Tabernacle. Organists present 25-minute **Organ Recitals** in the Tabernacle Mon. to Fri. at noon (also at 4 p.m. in summer) and Sat. and Sun. at 4 p.m. The **Mormon Tabernacle Choir** sings in the Tabernacle on Sun. mornings at 9:30 a.m. (be seated 15 minutes before) for a 30-minute radio broadcast. You're also welcome to attend rehearsals by the Mormon Tabernacle Choir and the Mormon Symphony Chorus. Schedules are posted in Temple Square; tel. 240-2534/2535.

**Utah Symphony Orchestra**
From its modest beginnings in 1940, the Utah Symphony has grown to be one of the best in the country. Each season, the symphony performs in the glittering Symphony Hall at the Salt Palace in Salt Lake City, and travels to Snowbird, Deer Valley, Ogden, Provo, Logan, and other cities. Symphony Hall and ticket offices are at 123 W. South Temple; tel. 533-6407.

**Utah Opera Company**
The company, founded in 1978, stages several operas during its Oct. to May season. Ticket offices and performances are in the restored Capitol Theatre, downtown at 50 W. 200 South; tel. 533-6494. The Capitol Theatre opened in 1913 as the Orpheum, one of Salt Lake City's most flamboyant movie houses. The Italian Renaissance facade has a host of cherubs, theatrical masks, and floral designs.

**University Of Utah**
The University Symphony Orchestra, University Chamber Orchestra, jazz ensembles, op-

Lightning Express,
*Salt Lake Theatre,*
*ca. 1900*

era, bands, ballet, dance, and choral groups present regular concerts on and off campus; season runs Sept. to May. Call the university's Public Relations office (tel. 581-6773) or the Department of Music (tel. 581-6762).

## THEATER

### Promised Valley Playhouse
Musicals and dramas entertain during summer and the Christmas season. Promised Valley Playhouse is downtown at 132 S. State; tel. 364-5696. Originally, vaudeville troupes performed here after the theater was completed in 1905. Later it became a movie palace, and finally a playhouse in 1972.

### Pioneer Memorial Theatre
A wide variety of theatrical performances takes place at this theater on the University of Utah campus. Professional and amateur actors present musicals and plays on Lees Main Stage. University students and faculty stage productions in the Babcock Theatre downstairs. Plays by students in the Young People's Theatre group entertain children. In Sept. and Oct. the university sponsors the Classic Theatre Festival, a program of Greek dramas at

various locations; tel. 581-6448. Pioneer Memorial Theatre is near the corner of 300 South and University St.; tel. 581-6961.

## DANCE

### Ballet West
This versatile group's repertory includes classical, modern, and foreign works. Ballet West began in Salt Lake City in 1963 as the Utah Civic Ballet, but as the group gained fame and began traveling widely, they chose their present name to reflect their regional status. Most Utah performances take place at the Capitol Theatre from Sept. to April. Capitol Theatre and box office are at 50 W. 200 South; tel. 533-5555.

### Ririe-Woodbury Dance Company
This professional company has one of the most active programs outside New York City. The varied repertory includes mixed media, eye-catching choreography, and humor. The group also shares their expertise in teaching production and dance skills to students and professionals. Ririe-Woodbury Dance Company is based at the Capitol Theatre, 50 W. 200 South; tel. 328-1062.

*bareback riding event at the Utah State Fair*

**Repertory Dance Theatre**
A professional company focusing on classical American and contemporary dance. Performances take place year-round in the Capitol Theatre and other locations; tel. 581-6702.

## MOVIES

Newspapers list the latest flicks. For old movie classics, foreign films, and other special films, call: **Avalon Theatre,** 3605 S. State (5.5 miles south of downtown; tel. 266-0258); **Salt Lake City Library,** 209 E. 500 South (tel. 363-5733); **Utah Media Center,** 20 S. West Temple (Salt Lake Art Center; tel. 534-1158); **Cinema In Your Face,** 45 W. 300 South (tel. 364-3647); and **University of Utah** (Olpin Union; tel. 581-5547).

## SPORTS

**Pro Sports**
Utah sports fans cheer on their **Utah Jazz** basketball, **Golden Eagles** hockey, and **Salt Lake Trappers** baseball teams. Basketball and hockey take place at the Salt Palace in downtown Salt Lake City (100 S. West Temple); Jazz tel. 355-DUNK; Golden Eagles tel.

521-6120. Other sporting events, concerts, and special events are held at the Salt Palace too; tel. 534-6660 (schedules) and tel. 363-7681 or (800) 888-SHOW (box office). Dierks Field hosts the baseball games at 1301 S. West Temple; for the Trappers call 484-9901/9900.

**University Of Utah**
University athletic teams compete in football, basketball, baseball, softball, tennis, track and field, gymnastics, swimming, golf, skiing, and other sports. Contact the Special Events Center, on campus near 400 South and 2000 East; tel. 581-6641.

**Bonneville Raceway Park**
For roaring engines, smoking tires, and checkered flags, visit the raceway during its April to Oct. season. Located in West Valley City at 6555 W. 2100 South; tel. 250-2600.

## EVENTS

Concerts, festivals, shows, and other special events happen nearly every day, and the Salt Lake Convention & Visitors Bureau can tell you what's going on, 180 S. West Temple; tel. 521-2822. Also check their *Salt Lake Visitors*

*Guide.* Some of the best-known annual happenings:

**March:** Citizens deck out in green for the St. Patrick's Day Parade downtown. Takes place on the Sat. nearest March 17.

**April:** Semi-annual Conference of the Church of Jesus Christ of Latter-day Saints is held during a weekend at Temple Square. The church president, believed to be a prophet of God, and other church leaders give guidance to members throughout the world. Non-Mormons are welcome to attend too. Expect large crowds. Contact the Temple Square visitor centers for more info; tel. 240-2534/2535.

**June:** Utah Pageant of the Arts brings the world's art masterpieces to life—literally—using actors to stage the scene; this amazing spectacle takes place in American Fork, 32 miles south of Salt Lake City; tel. 756-3505. The Utah Scottish Association Highland Games has lively contests, bagpipe music and dancing, and ethnic food; held in Salt Lake City. Utah Arts Festival features artists' and craftsmen's booths, video art, music concerts, and dance performances; in Salt Lake City. Strawberry Days is a community celebration with rodeos, games, and entertainment in Pleasant Grove, 35 miles south of Salt Lake City; tel. 785-4523. Cowboys show their skills at the Lehi Round-up and Rodeo in Lehi, 30 miles south of Salt Lake City.

**July:** Utah Pageant of the Arts continues. Western Stampede and Rodeo (near the 4th of July) takes place in West Jordan, 12 miles southwest of Salt Lake City. Steel Days is a community celebration in American Fork, 32 miles south of Salt Lake City; tel. 374-8687. Days of '47 Celebration commemorates pioneers arriving here on July 24, 1847; Salt Lake City has a big rodeo at the Salt Palace, parades, fireworks, and other festivities; tel. 533-5759.

**September:** Pioneer Harvest Days recreates early farm life at Pioneer Trail State Park. The Greek Festival celebrates Greek culture with food, music, folk dancing, and tours of the historic Holy Trinity Greek Orthodox Cathedral; tel. 328-9681. Utah State Fair features entertainment, rodeo, horse show, contests, art and craft exhibits, and livestock judging at the fairgrounds, North Temple and 1000 West; tel. 533-5858. Oktoberfest takes place every weekend during Sept. at the Snowbird resort in Little Cottonwood Canyon, southeast of Salt Lake City.

**October:** Second part of semi-annual Conference of the Church of Jesus Christ of Latter-day Saints; see April description above.

**December:** Temple Square Christmas Lighting. The Square blazes with 250,000 lights from late Nov. through New Year's Day.

# SALT LAKE CITY RECREATION

## PARKS

The many parks in Salt Lake City offer golf, tennis, swimming, picnicking, and space to enjoy the outdoors. Special attractions include Tracy Aviary in Liberty Park, the International Peace Gardens, and the canoe trip down the Jordan River. Contact the Salt Lake City Parks and Recreation Department for details on facilities and programs at 1965 W. 500 South, Salt Lake City, UT 84104; tel. 972-7800. For info on touring the Jordan River by canoe, ask at the Jordan River State Park, 1084 N. Redwood Rd., Salt Lake City, UT 84116; tel. 533-4496.

### Liberty Park

Tracy Aviary, historic buildings, children's play areas, a small amusement park, a swimming pool, a tennis center, and acres of grass and shady trees make this large park a popular destination for residents and visitors. Tracy Aviary, with its hundreds of birds, lies in the southwest corner (see p. 43). The Children's Garden playground, amusement park, snack bar, and a large pond with rental boats are in the southeast corner of the park (all closed in winter). The Chase Mill, just north of the aviary entrance, was built by Isaac Chase in 1852. It's one of the oldest buildings in the valley. Free flour from the mill saved many families during the famine of 1856-57. The interior is closed to the public, but you can view the exterior and an old millstone. Formal gardens lie north of the mill. Chase's adobe brick house (built 1853-54), farther to the north, has been restored. Go inside to see exhibits of the Folk Arts Program, sponsored by the Utah Arts Council; open daily noon-5 p.m. from mid-April to mid-Oct.; free; tel. 533-5760. You'll find horseshoe pits to the north of the Chase house. The tennis center on the western side of the park offers 16 lighted courts and instruction; tel. 596-5036. The outdoor swimming pool adjacent to the tennis center is open in summer; tel. 532-9441. Liberty Park is southeast of downtown and bordered by 900 and 1300 South and by 500 and 700 East.

### Sugarhouse Park

Expanses of rolling grassland in the 113-acre park are ideal for picnics, strolling, and jogging. A lake attracts seagulls and other birds. Sweet smells rise from the Memorial Rose Garden in the northeast corner. The park has a playground and fields for baseball, soccer, and football. In winter, the rolling hills provide good sledding and tubing. Mormon pioneers manufactured beet sugar here beginning in 1851; the venture later proved unprofitable and was abandoned. Sugarhouse Park is on the southeast edge of Salt Lake City at 1300 East and 2100 South (access is from 2100 South).

### International Peace Gardens

With wishes for world peace, the Salt Lake Council of Women created this unusual garden next to Jordan Park. Landscaping, vegetation, and monuments represent 18 nations of the world. Open 8 a.m. to sunset from mid-May to late Nov.; free. Located near 900 West and 1000 South.

### Jordan River State Park

A canoe trip down the Jordan reveals birds and other wildlife in a peaceful setting that you wouldn't expect so close to downtown Salt Lake City. A green canopy of willow, Russian olive, and Siberian elm overhangs the river for much of its length. Canoeists can stop at the International Peace Gardens and other parks along the way. The state park office can advise on boating conditions and places to rent canoes, paddles, and life jackets. Park rangers enforce the rule that each boater must have a Coast Guard-approved life jacket; anyone under 12 must wear his or her jacket at all times. Put-in is at 1200 W. 1700 South (across from

Raging Waters) and take-out at 1000 N. 1525 West; allow at least 2½ hours (without stops) for the 6-mile route. This is the only section of river open to boats. You'll need 2 cars or someone to pick you up at trip's end. Jordan River State Park office is at 1084 N. Redwood Rd., Salt Lake City, UT 84116; tel. 533-4496 (open Mon. to Fri. 8 a.m.-5 p.m.). It's a good idea to call the park before a trip to check on possible river obstructions. Off-season boating isn't recommended because of the greater likelihood of hazards blocking the way.

Attractions along the Jordan River include Raging Waters (a private water park with wave pool at 1200 W. 1700 South; tel. 973-9900), International Peace Gardens, jogging and exercise areas, 4 golf courses, a bicycle moto-cross track, an equestrian trail, a wheelchair exercise course (take bridge across river from 350 N. Redwood Rd.), a model airplane field ($3 per vehicle, $3 adult walk-in day-use fee) and various parks. A map available from the state park office shows the locations.

## SKIING

Utah's "Greatest Snow on Earth" lies close at hand. Within an hour's drive from Salt Lake City you can be at one of 7 downhill areas in the Wasatch Range, each with its own character and a distinctive combination of skiing terrain. Cross-country skiers can ski on maintained trails at Mountain Dell (Parleys Canyon) and Park City. The snow season runs from about mid-Nov. to April or May; call 521-8102 for Utah snow conditions. Be sure to get the free *Utah Ski Vacation Planner* publication from Ski Utah, Inc. (307 W. 200 South, Suite 1003, Salt Lake City, UT 84101; tel. 534-1907) or from most tourist offices in Utah. It lists most Utah resorts with diagrams of the lifts and runs, lift ticket rates, and detailed info on lodging. Public buses (UTA) will take you to the 4 resorts on the west side of the Wasatch Range: Solitude and Brighton in Big Cottonwood Canyon and Snowbird and Alta in Little Cottonwood Canyon; you can get on the buses at the airport, downtown, University of

Utah, or at the bottoms of the canyons; tel. 287-4636. Lewis Brothers Stages head to the 3 resorts on the other side of the range: Park-West, Park City, and Deer Valley; they also have a shuttle between Park City and Snowbird, Alta, Brighton, Solitude, and Sundance; tel. 359-8347.

The ski areas near Salt Lake City actually lie close together as the crow flies. **Interconnect Adventure Tours** provides a guide service for extensive touring among them. Skiers should be experienced and in good condition because of the high elevations (around 10,000 ft.) and the need for some walking and traversing. Touring is with downhill equipment. Trips include Snowbird-Alta-Brighton-Solitude ($80) and Park City-Brighton-Solitude-Alta-Snowbird ($95). For details, contact Ski Utah, Inc., 307 W. 200 South, Suite 1003, Salt Lake City, UT 84101; tel. 534-1907.

### Solitude Ski Area

Skiers come here for the wide variety of runs—some highly challenging for experts, and others ideal for beginners and intermediate skiers. Honeycomb Canyon, on the back side of the resort, contains 500 acres of ungroomed powder skiing. Seven lifts (one quad, 2 triple chair, and 4 double chair) service the 60 named runs and bowls. Skiers enjoy a vertical drop of 2,000 feet from the top of the highest lift. One run makes a loop with nearby Brighton Ski Area for even more skiing. Solitude has a ski school, Moonbeam Learning Center, rentals, ski shops, and 6 restaurants. Adult lift tickets cost $24 ($18 half day) and $35 for skiing both Solitude and Brighton. Lift tickets for children (12 and under) and beginners cost $15. Kids under 48 inches can use the Link Lift for the Easy Street run free of charge. Contact Solitude at Box 21350, Salt Lake City, UT 84121-0350; tel. 534-1400. The ski area is 12 miles up Big Cottonwood Canyon and only a 23-mile drive southeast of downtown Salt Lake City. Nearest accommodations are in Brighton (see below) 2 miles up the canyon or at Silver Fork Lodge ($52.32 s, $65.40 d), 1.5 miles down the canyon; tel. 649-9551. Solitude Ski Area plans to open a series of hotels beginning in the 91-92 season.

## Solitude Nordic Ski Center

Plenty of snow and groomed tracks make this one of the best places in Utah for cross-country skiers. The 10 miles or so of trails range from easy level loops to varied rolling terrain. Most trails have both compacted snow for skating and set tracks. The center is based in the Alpinist shop (first building on the left on the one-way loop in Brighton); open daily 9 a.m.-4:30 p.m. from mid-Nov. to mid-April. Trail fee is $6 ($5 after 12:30 p.m.), $3 children 8-12, and free for children under 8 and seniors 65 and over. Staff at the shop offer rentals (touring, racing, telemark, and snowshoes), sales, instruction, day and overnight (stay in a yurt) ski tours, and advice on back-country touring and avalanche hazards. Tickets can also be purchased at Solitude Ski Area. For more info, contact Box 21350, Salt Lake City, UT 84121-0350; tel. 272-7613.

## Brighton Ski Area

A favorite with local families for the excellent skiing and friendly, unpretentious atmosphere. While 26% of the runs are beginner and 44% intermediate, Brighton does offer some difficult powder-bowl skiing and steep runs as well. A triple chairlift and 4 double chairs climb as high as 10,200 feet for a 1,445-foot vertical descent to the base. Hop on the Sol Bright run to visit Solitude Ski Area; a lift there will put you back on a trail to Brighton. Night skiing is offered Mon. to Sat., too. Brighton has a ski school with a learn-to-ski package, rentals, 2 shops, and 3 cafeterias. Adults ski for $20 day, $15 afternoon, $8 night, $10 beginner's lift, and $35 for skiing both Brighton and Solitude. Children 7-12 go at $10 day or half day, $5 night; kids 6 and under go free with paying adult. The adjacent Brighton Lodge offers accommodations with a heated outdoor pool and jacuzzi at $49.16 dorm, $81.93 s, $109.25 d. Contact the ski area and lodge at Brighton, UT 84121; tel. 532-4731 or (800) 873-5512. Brighton is at road's end, 2 miles past Solitude, in Big Cot-

tonwood Canyon. Cabins can be arranged through Brighton Chalets ($115-328; 2750 E. 9800 South, Sandy, UT 84092; tel. 942-8824) and the Brighton Village Store ($963 per week; Brighton, UT 84121; tel. 649-9156). The Brighton Village Store also has a small cafe serving American food (open daily for breakfast, lunch, and dinner) and the Blind Miner Restaurant featuring Continental cuisine (open Thurs. to Sat. for dinner; reservations suggested).

## Snowbird Ski Area

This highly developed resort lies in Little Cottonwood Canyon on the west side of the Wasatch Range. Snowbird had a difficult time getting started back in the early '70s—not everyone wanted to see high-rise hotels among the mountains. Today, the complete resort facilities, excellent snow conditions, varied terrain, and large lift capacity (8,810 people per hour) entice many skiers. Twenty percent of the runs are classed beginner, 30% intermediate, and 50% advanced. Plenty of ungroomed areas lie in the backcountry too. Snowbird's ski school and separate "bunny hill" make it a good place to learn, too. Seven double chairlifts and a large aerial tram serve the 40 named runs. The longest run is 3½ miles and drops 3,100 feet. Nonskiers can also enjoy the heights aboard the tram as it climbs 2,900 vertical feet to the summit of Hidden Peak (elev. 11,000 ft.) for a fantastic panorama of the Wasatches, surrounding valleys, and the distant Uinta Mountains. Wear a warm jacket and hat for this round trip; $7 adult, $4.50 children under 12. The exceptionally long season at Snowbird continues to mid-May or mid-June, though most lifts close by early May. Adult lift tickets cost $35 ($28 half day) including tram and $28 ($22 half day) chairlifts only. Seniors (62+) and children (12 and under) ski for $20 ($15 half day) including tram and $15 ($13 half day) chairlifts only. All skiers can use the beginners' Chickadee Chairlift free of charge. Guided ski tours of about 2 hours (free with lift purchase) introduce new customers to the resort's skiing; groups divide up according to ability. Advanced skiers may take the Snowbird Mountain Experience ($65 plus cost of lift ticket), a 5-hour guided tour on steeper, more challenging terrain, including powder and off-trail skiing. Helicopter skiing provided by Wasatch Powderbird Guides at the resort also has powder and off trail. In addition to its ski school, Snowbird offers rentals, a wide selection of shops, restaurants, snack bars, 4 lodges, swimming pools, health spa, and child-care services. Accommodation costs vary according to early/late, value, and peak seasons. Some sample nightly rates: dormitory ($26-44), lodge room ($75-171), studio w/fireplace and kitchen ($156-359), 2-bedroom suites w/fireplace and kitchen ($231-533). For reservations and information on the skiing and year-round resort facilities, contact Snowbird Ski Resort, Snowbird, UT 84092; tel. 742-2222 (snow conditions), 532-1700 or (800) 453-3000 (reservations). Snowbird is 6 miles up Little Cottonwood Canyon and 25 miles southeast of downtown Salt Lake City.

### Alta Ski Area
Famed for its deep powder, wide-open terrain, and luxurious accommodations, Alta is probably the best known of Utah's ski resorts. In 1937, when some skiers decided to try the revolutionary concept of using ski lifts, detractors complained that the $2.50/day lift tickets reserved the sport just for the rich. Some of the original Collins single chairs are still around; look for them at the bus stop beside Goldminer's Daughter Lodge and in the Shallow Shaft Steak House. Today Alta offers 8 double chairlifts serving 35 named runs of which 25% are rated beginner, 40% intermediate, and 35% advanced. The longest run is 3½ miles and drops 2,500 feet. Beginners can use the free rope tow beside Alta Lodge or the 3 beginners' lifts. Lift tickets cost $21 ($16 half day) or $15 ($10 half day) for the beginners' lifts. Alta offers a ski school, rentals, shops, child-care services, and restaurants (2 are on the slopes). You can choose from 5 lodges and 3 condominiums, but all are expensive—even for dormitory space. The lodges operate only on the MAP plan, with 2 or 3 meals

*skiing on Hidden Peak, at Snowbird Ski Resort*

included or added to the price. Expect to pay upward of $62 dormitory, $118 s, $194 d for a room; skiers on a lower budget can base themselves in Salt Lake City. The *Utah Ski Vacation Planner* lists facilities, prices, and package plans. For more info, contact Alta Ski Resort, Alta, UT 84092; tel. 742-3333 (office), 572-3939 (snow conditions), 942-0404 (lodging reservations). Alta is 7 miles up Little Cottonwood Canyon in an old silver mining area.

### Alta Cross-country Skiing
Both beginning and experienced skiers enjoy cross-country skiing at Alta. No groomed tracks, but you can head up the unplowed summer road to Albion Basin. Snow cats often pack the snow. The road begins from the upper end of the Albion parking lot, then climbs gently to the top of Albion Lift, where skiers can continue to Albion Basin. Intermediate and advanced skiers also ski to Cather-

ine Pass and Twin Lakes Pass. Cross-country skiers may ski the beginner (green) Alta trails. Those heading for the back country should have proper equipment and experience; the Alta ski school office at the Albion ticket building can advise on avalanche hazards. There's no charge for skiing at Alta unless you use the lifts. Rent track and telemark cross-country skis at the Albion Day Lodge near the trailhead.

## ParkWest Ski Area

One of 3 ski areas near Park City, ParkWest is the first one you'll reach if coming from Salt Lake City. The slopes look deceptively easy from the lodge at the base, but tucked into 3 mountains lie machine-groomed slopes, open bowls, and challenging moguls. Seven double chairs serve 50 designated runs. Ski trails are rated 22% beginner and lower intermediate, 30% intermediate, 48% advanced and expert. Longest run is 2½ miles and drops 2,200 feet. Adult lift tickets cost $24 ($12 half day) or $15 for full-day beginner lifts. Children 12 and under pay $12 full day, $8 half day, or $8 full-day beginner lifts. The Kids Central facility offers day care, supervised lunches, ski lessons, and rentals for the younger set. ParkWest includes a ski school, rental and sales shop, 4 restaurants (2 mid-slope), helicopter skiing nearby (Utah Powderbird Guides), and a free shuttle service from lodges in Park City. For skiing info, contact ParkWest at 4000 Park West Dr., Park City, UT 84060; tel. 649-5400. ParkWest is 27 miles east of Salt Lake City via I-80 and UT 224.

## Park City Ski Area

Utah's biggest ski area is located in the historic silver mining town of Park City. A gondola, 2 quad chairs, 5 triple chairs, and 5 double chairs carry skiers high onto the eastern slope of the Wasatch Range. The 83 trails range in length from ¼ to 3½ miles (17% easier, 49% more difficult, 34% most difficult). Also, experienced skiers can enjoy the powder in 5 open bowls near the top of the mountain—a total of 650 acres. The longest run drops 3,100 feet in elevation from the top of Jupiter Bowl

to the resort center. Park City Ski Area and the adjacent village offer night skiing, a ski school, rentals, ski shops, ice skating, and restaurants (3 are on the slopes). A Town Lift and 2 runs allow skiers staying in downtown Park City to connect directly with the ski area. Visitors without skis can enjoy the mountains on a 23-minute ride in the gondola to the Summit House, which has a restaurant; $6. Adult lift tickets cost $37 all day, $25 afternoon, or $8 night skiing. Contact Park City at Box 39, Park City, UT 84060; tel. 649-8111 (office), 649-9571 (snow report), 649-0493 or (800) 222-PARK (lodging reservations). You'll find accommodations right at the ski center and many more places close by in town; see the *Utah Ski Vacation Planner* or *Park City Winter Vacation Planner* for details. Park City is 31 miles east of Salt Lake City via I-80 and UT 224.

## Deer Valley Ski Resort

The crème de la crème of Utah ski areas. Here you'll find good uncrowded skiing with all the extras of posh accommodations, gourmet dining, attentive service, and polished brass everywhere. Attendants meet you in the parking lot to assist in unloading your skis and guide you; help is never far away. Video programs in the ski rental shop show how to put on and use your gear. Don't look for "men's" or "women's" restrooms at Deer Valley—here it's "Gentlemen's Lounge" and "Ladies' Lounge." One quad chair, 9 triple chairs and one double chair carry skiers to the top of Bald Eagle Mountain, Bald Mountain, and Flagstaff Mountain, providing 55 runs, 3 bowls, and a vertical drop of 2,200 feet. Longest run is 1.4 miles. Fifteen percent of the skiing is rated easier, 50% more difficult, and 35% most difficult. The majestic Snow Park Lodge (elev. 7,200 ft.) contains the ski school, rentals, ski shop, child-care service, gift shop, and a restaurant. You can drive 1,000 feet higher to Silver Lake Lodge, which offers 2 more restaurants. Adult lift tickets cost $39 full day or $29 afternoon. Deer Valley will reserve accommodations, lift tickets, restaurants, flights, and local transportation for you. Contact Deer

Valley Central Reservations, Box 3149, Park City, UT 84060; tel. 649-1000 (skiing info and reservations), 649-2000 (snow report), or (800) 424-DEER (reservations). Deer Valley is 1.5 miles south of downtown Park City (33 miles east of Salt Lake City).

### White Pine Touring
Park City's cross-country ski center offers rentals, instruction, and guided tours. It has a touring center and 10 km of groomed trails at the Park City Golf Course (Park Ave. and Thaynes Canyon Dr.) during the winter; tel. 649-8701. Season runs about mid-Nov. to early April. Trail fee is only $1; kids under 12 and seniors 65 and up ski free. Year-round office is at 363 Main St. in Park City; tel. 649-8710.

## OTHER SPORTS

### Swimming Pools And Gymnasiums
For an outdoor swim, try **Liberty Park** (1300 South and 700 East.; tel. 532-9441) or **Fairmont Park** (2361 S. 900 East; tel. 483-5441). For a bigger splash, **Raging Waters** features more than 40 aquatic attractions, including 15 waterslides and the Wild Wave pool. The children's area has waterfalls, geysers, and a small wave pool. Located at 1200 W. 1700 South; tel. 973-9900.

**Deseret Gymnasium** has a variety of facilities for both men and women, including 2 indoor swimming pools, weight and exercise rooms, racquetball, handball, squash, volleyball, badminton, table tennis, and a golf practice range. The gymnasium, run by the LDS Church, is open to the public for a daily fee or by membership. Classes are offered in swimming, racquetball, golf, and exercise. Located ½ block north of Temple Square at 161 N. Main St., Salt Lake City, UT 84103; tel. 359-3911.

The **Y.M.C.A.** Rotary Central Branch offers an indoor pool, racquetball, handball, squash, outdoor running track, and a variety of youth and family programs. Open to the public for a daily fee or by membership. The Y.M.C.A. facility is east of downtown at 737 E. 200

South; Salt Lake City, UT 84102; tel. 533-YMCA.

### Tennis
Seventeen city parks have one or more courts; call the Salt Lake City Parks and Recreation Dept. for the one nearest you; tel. 972-7800. **Liberty Park** offers a pro shop, instruction, and 16 courts at 1300 South and 500 East.; tel. 596-5036.

### Golf
Salt Lake City has plenty of places to tee off. The following lie close to town and are open to the public. (See the telephone yellow pages for golf courses in neighboring towns.) **Bonneville** is an 18-hole/72-par course east of downtown at 954 Connor St. (2130 East off Sunnyside Ave. near the Hogle Zoo); tel. 596-5041. **University** is a 9-hole/34-par course on the University of Utah campus at 100 S. 1900 East; tel. 581-6511. **Mountain Dell** is an 18-hole/72-par course east in Parleys Canyon; take I-80 East Canyon/Emigration Canyon Exit 134; tel. 582-3812. **Forest Dale** is a 9-hole/36-par course at 2375 S. 900 East (near Sugarhouse Park); tel. 483-5420. **Nibley Park** is a 9-hole/33-par course at 2780 S. 700 East; tel. 483-5418. **Glendale** is an 18-hole/72-par course at 1630 W. 2100 South; tel. 974-2403. **Rose Park** is an 18-hole/72-par course northwest of downtown at 1386 N. Redwood Rd.; tel. 596-5030.

### Horseback Riding
**Valley View Riding Stables** offers instruction and trail rides in the Wasatch Range; at 13800 S. 1300 East in Draper (20 miles south of Salt Lake City); tel. 572-9088. **East Canyon Outfitters** lead hourly, day, breakfast, sunset, and overnight rides on the Mormon Pioneer Trail and other areas in the Wasatch Range east of Salt Lake City; located 20 miles from Salt Lake City via I-80 and UT 65 (several miles south of East Canyon Reservoir); tel. 355-3460.

### Skating
**Cottonwood Heights Community Recreation Center** offers year-round ice skating and

lessons, indoor and outdoor pools, racquetball courts, and weight room at 7500 S. 2700 East; tel. 943-3190. Roll with **Roller Towne USA** (The 49th Street Galleria, 4998 S. 360 West in Murray; tel. 265-3866) and **Classic Roller Skating Centers** (2774 S. 625 West in Bountiful; tel. 295-8301; and at 9151 S. 255 West in Sandy; tel. 561-1791).

# OTHER PRACTICALITIES IN SALT LAKE CITY

## SHOPPING

### Trolley Square

Salt Lake City's most unusual shopping center came about when developers cleverly converted the old trolley barn. Railroad magnate E.H. Harriman built the barn in 1908 as a center for the city's extensive trolley system. The vehicles stopped rolling in 1945, but their memory lives on in Trolley Square. Inside you'll see several trolleys, a large stained-glass dome, salvaged sections of old mansions and churches, and many antiques worked into the decor. More than 100 shops and restaurants call this gigantic barn their home. Watch movies at Trolley Theatres (4 screens; tel. 521-8181) and The Flick (2 screens; tel. 466-6266). Trolley Square is open daily, including Sun. afternoons, at the corner of 500 South and 700 East; tel. 521-9877. **Trolley Corners** across the street at 515 S. 700 East is a smaller shopping area with shops, restaurants, and Trolley Corners Theatres (tel. 364-6183).

### Crossroads Plaza

In the heart of downtown, this modern shopping center on 4 levels has more than 100 shops, fast-food restaurants, banks, and Crossroads Cinemas (3 screens; tel. 355-3883). Waldenbooks on the main floor and B. Dalton Bookseller on the second level have good selections of Utah books. Crossroads Plaza is open daily, including Sun. afternoons; tel. 531-1799 or 363-1558. Located on South Temple across from Temple Square.

### ZCMI Mall

What may be America's oldest department store, Zion's Cooperative Mercantile Institution, began in 1869 as a church-owned operation. The old facade graces the Main St. side, but the more than 90 shops and restaurants inside are new. Deseret Book Co. specializes in LDS literature and has many books on Utah's history. ZCMI Mall is open Mon. to Sat.; tel. 321-6000. Downtown at the corner of South Temple and State streets.

### Arrow Press Square

Restaurants and shops have taken over the picturesque old buildings in what used to be Salt Lake City's printing district. Downtown at 165 S. West Temple; tel. 531-9700.

### Mormon Handicrafts

Purchase lovingly made quilts, teddy bears, Raggedy Anns, doll houses, baby apparel, dresses, lace, porcelain figures, and other creations. Or, if you'd rather do it yourself, buy supplies and patterns for making quilts, counted cross stitch, and other crafts. Open Mon. to Sat.; tel. 355-2141. Located across from Temple Square at the corner of Main and North Temple streets.

### TP Gallery

Crafts and art by native Americans are featured here. Look for beadwork and leather items (Ute Indians), jewelry (Navajo, Hopi, and Zuni tribes), pottery (Hopi and New Mexico pueblo tribes), kachina dolls (Hopi), baskets (Papago), sandpaintings, books, and cassettes. Open Mon. to Sat.; tel. 364-2961. Located downtown at 252 S. Main Street.

### Recreational Equipment, Inc. (REI)

This large store has an outstanding array of outdoor recreation gear for hiking, camping, bicycling, skiing, river running, rock climbing, and travel. Gear can be rented too. The book section is a good place to look for regional outdoor guides. Topo maps sold cover the most popular hiking areas of Utah. REI memberships (optional) allow you to receive annual dividends on your purchases; tel. 486-2100. Open Mon. to Sat. and sometimes on Sunday. Located southeast of downtown in The Brickyard Plaza (1100 East and 3150 South); from downtown drive south on 1300 East to the traffic light at 3130 South (Brickyard Rd.) and turn right. Many other stores in the Salt Lake City cater to outdoor activities too; see the telephone yellow pages.

## SERVICES

The main **downtown post office** is at 230 W. 200 South; tel. 530-5902. Pioneer branch is on the first floor of the Federal Bldg., 125 S. State. The University of Utah has a post office in the bookstore.

**Change foreign currency** at Zions First National Bank downtown at Main and South Temple (tel. 524-4873) or at the airport (tel. 524-4775). Morris Travel also changes money at the airport; tel. 487-9731.

Minor medical emergencies can be treated by **InstaCare,** just west of downtown at 55 N. Redwood Rd., and at 5 other area locations; tel. 321-2490. Hospitals with 24-hour emergency care include: **Holy Cross Hospital** (1045 E. 100 South; tel. 350-4111), **LDS Hospital** (8th Ave. and C St.; tel. 321-1100), **St. Mark's Hospital** (1200 E. 3900 South; tel. 268-7074), and **University Hospital** (50 N. Medical Dr. [1800 East]; tel. 581-2121). For a physician referral, contact one of the hospitals or the Utah State Medical Assoc.; tel. 355-7477.

**Salt Lake Community Education** can tell you about classes in art, astronomy, business, computers, dance, languages, sports, writing, yoga, and other subjects; some classes are for children too; 233 W. 200 North, Salt Lake City, UT 84103; tel. 363-4601.

The **Salt Lake Art Center School** offers classes in ceramics, drawing, painting, sculpture, photography, and crafts; 20 S. West Temple; Salt Lake City, UT 84101; tel. 328-4201.

Low on dough? **Salt Lake Job Service Center** offers free services, 1234 S. Main; tel. 533-2400.

## PHONE NUMBERS

Emergencies (fire, police, medical): 911.
Police (Salt Lake City): 799-3000.
Sheriff (Salt Lake County): 535-5441.
Road Conditions (local): 964-6000.
Road Conditions (statewide):
   (800) 492-2400.
Weather Forecast: 575-7669.
Salt Lake Convention & Visitors Bureau
   (local travel info): 521-2868.
Utah Travel Council (statewide travel info):
   538-1030.
Utah Recreation/Ski Report: 521-8102.
Utah State Parks: 538-7220.
Utah Division of Wildlife Resources:
   538-4700.
Community Information & Referral Service:
   487-4716.
Lawyer Referral Service (Utah State Bar
   Assoc.): 531-9075.
Physician Referral Service (Utah State
   Medical Assoc.): 355-7477.
Utah Transit Authority (UTA): 287-4636.

## INFORMATION

**Tourist Offices**
**Salt Lake Convention & Visitors Bureau** will tell you about the sights, facilities, and goings-on in town. The office also has many helpful magazines and brochures. Open Mon. to Fri. 8 a.m.-5:30 p.m. (to 7 p.m. in summer), Sat. 9 a.m.-4 p.m., and Sun. 10 a.m.-4 p.m.; tel.

521-2868. Located downtown at the corner of West Temple and 200 South (180 S. West Temple, Salt Lake City, UT 84101-1493); you can park in spaces behind the office. The Visitors Bureau has a branch office in Terminal 2 at the airport; open daily 9 a.m.-10 p.m.; tel. 575-2800. The chamber of commerce downtown has little visitor info; their main work is business promotion.

The **Utah Travel Council** publishes a well-illustrated *Utah Travel Guide,* travel maps (series of 5 covering the state), and other helpful literature. You can usually find these publications at the Salt Lake Convention & Visitors Bureau and at local chambers of commerce. Or stop by the Utah Travel Council offices in historic Council Hall, across the street from the Capitol; (write: Council Hall/ Capitol Hill, Salt Lake City, UT 84114). Open Mon. to Fri. 8 a.m.-5 p.m. (also summer weekends and holidays 9 a.m.-4 p.m.); tel. 538-1030. While you're at Council Hall, be sure to see the restored rooms. They look as they did a century ago when Utah's early leaders met in them.

## Wasatch-Cache National Forest

The supervisor's office has general information and forest maps for all the national forests in Utah, some forest and wilderness maps of Nevada, Idaho, and Wyoming, and regional books. Open Mon. to Fri. 7:30 a.m.-5 p.m.; tel. 524-5030. Located downtown on the eighth floor of the Federal Bldg., 125 S. State St., Salt Lake City, UT 84138.

For detailed information on hiking and camping in the nearby Wasatch Range, visit the Salt Lake Ranger District office. The district includes the popular Mill, Big Cottonwood, and Little Cottonwood canyons in the Wasatch Range, the Wasatch Range east of Bountiful and Farmington, and the Stansbury Mountains west of Tooele. Large reference books cover nearly every recreational activity and trail. The foresters here will likely have personal knowledge of the area you're heading to. Open Mon. to Fri. 8 a.m.-4:30 p.m.; tel. 524-5042. The office is a few blocks west of the mouth of Big Cottonwood Canyon at 6944 S. 3000 East, Salt Lake City, UT 84121.

## U.S. Geological Survey

Topo maps for Utah, adjacent states, and Montana can be purchased here. Other publications include geologic maps, national park maps, a satellite photo of the Great Salt Lake, specialized books of regional geology, and free brochures on earth science topics. Open Mon. to Fri. 8 a.m.-4:15 p.m.; tel. 524-5652. Downtown in Room 8105, Federal Bldg., 125 S. State St., Salt Lake City, UT 84138.

## Bureau Of Land Management

The state office has general information on BLM areas in Utah and sells recreation and land status maps of the state. Open Mon. to Fri. 7:45 a.m.-4 p.m.; tel. 539-4001. Downtown on the fourth floor at 324 S. State St., Salt Lake City, UT 84111-2303.

## Utah Division of Parks and Recreation

Obtain literature and the latest information for all of Utah's state parks. Reservations for campgrounds and some other services can be made at tel. 322-3770 or (800) 322-3770; a reservation fee of $5 family or $10 group applies. If you're planning a lot of state park visits, ask about the $50 annual park pass. Open Mon. to Fri. 8 a.m.-5 p.m.; tel. 538-7220 (general information). West of downtown at 1636 W. North Temple, Salt Lake City, UT 84116.

## Utah Division Of Wildlife Resources

Staff issue fishing and hunting licenses and information. Fishermen may want to purchase the book, *Fishes of Utah,* and a series of 10 booklets, *Lakes of the High Uintas.* Open Mon. to Fri. 8 a.m.-5 p.m.; tel. 538-4700. Located at 1596 W. North Temple, Salt Lake City, UT 84116.

## Libraries

The large **City Library** contains a wealth of varied reading material, a children's library, records, and audio and video tapes. Special collections include Western Americana and Mormon history. Movie buffs will enjoy the foreign film series presented in spring and autumn by the library, usually shown Thurs. evenings. The Atrium Gallery hosts art exhibits. Puppet shows and story hours entertain the kids. Large bulletin boards on the main floor list upcoming art shows, entertainment, local events, classes, volunteer opportunities, and bus routes. Open Mon. to Fri. 9 a.m.-9 p.m., Sat. 9 a.m.-6 p.m., and Sun. (Oct. to April only) 1-5 p.m.; tel. 363-5733. The main library is at 209 E. 500 South. Call for locations of the 5 branch libraries.

The **Marriott Library** at the University of Utah ranks as one of the leading research libraries of the region. You'll find more than 2 million volumes and over 14,000 periodical titles inside. Special collections include the Middle East, United Nations, Western Americana, and Utah manuscripts. The large map collection has topo maps of all 50 states as well as maps and atlases of distant lands. Hikers can photocopy maps of those areas they plan to visit. The public is welcome to use the library; a Library Permit Card can be purchased to use materials outside of the library. Open Mon. to Thurs. 7 a.m.-10 p.m., Fri. 7 a.m.-5 p.m., and Sat. 9 a.m.-5 p.m.; shorter hours during summer and breaks; tel. 581-6085 (hours) or 581-6273 (information).

### Newspapers And Magazines

The *Salt Lake Tribune* morning daily reflects the liberal views of the city. *Deseret News* comes out daily in the afternoon with a conservative viewpoint and greater coverage of Mormon Church news. The monthly *Utah Holiday* magazine reports on the politics, personalities, recreation, cultural events, restaurants, and other aspects of life in Utah. *The Event* (every 2 weeks) paper describes the latest on art, entertainment, events, and social spots. *Sports Guide* appears monthly with articles and event listings for bicycling, running, kayaking, rafting, canoeing, and other sports; available free at sporting goods stores and newsstands.

### Book Stores

**Cosmic Aeroplane Books & Records** has an excellent and varied selection on most any subject; this is a good place to look for travel, alternative, small-press, used, and out-of-print titles. Recordings run the gamut from classical to rock; a bulletin board lists local events and classes. At 258 E. 100 South; tel. 533-9409. **Sam Weller's Zion Book Store** claims to be one of the West's largest, with more than half a million new and used books covering many topics; 254 S. Main; tel. 328-2586. **Waldenbooks** has a good selection of general reading and Utah books in the Crossroads Plaza (50 S. Main; tel. 363-1271) and in The Brickyard Plaza (1100 East at 3300 South; tel. 486-0943). The **B. Dalton Bookseller** stores are also a good source for general reading and Utah books, at Crossroads Plaza (50 S. Main; tel. 355-7906) and in Trolley Square (500 South and 700 East; tel. 532-7107). **Deseret Book Co.** specializes in LDS literature, but it also has many general reading and Utah books; 36 S. State (ZCMI Mall); tel. 328-8191. **Waking Owl Books** features literature and fiction; 208 S. 1300 East; tel. 582-7323. The **University of Utah's Bookstore** has a varied selection of books on many subjects; tel. 581-6325. **The Magazine Shop** claims to have "something for everyone" among their paperbacks, magazines, and newspapers (out-of-state and foreign too); 267 S. Main; tel. 359-3295.

## TRANSPORT

### Tours

The **Gray Line** offers a 2½-hour city tour in the morning (afternoons too in summer) for $12 adult, $6 age 5-12. A 4-hour Utah Copper Mine & Great Salt Lake tour visits the Bingham Canyon open-pit mine and a beach on the Great Salt Lake for $22 adult, $11 age 5-12. Both tours can be combined for a small discount. Three-day tours head south to Bryce, Zion, and Grand Canyon national parks ($355 s, $275 d, $240 children under 12) or northeast to Yellowstone and Grand Teton national parks ($345 s, $260 d, $215 children under 12); 553 W. 100 South, Salt Lake City, UT 84101; tel. 521-7060.

**Interwest Jet Center** will show you any part of this scenic state, including the Salt Lake City area (1 hour, 25 minutes), the Uinta Range, Flaming Gorge, and Dinosaur National Monument (2 hours, 20 minutes), Canyonlands and Arches national parks (3 hours), Capitol Reef, Bryce Canyon, Lake Powell, and Monument Valley (4 hours, 20 minutes), and Zion, Grand Canyon, and Bryce Canyon (4 hours, 30 minutes); write Interwest Jet Center, AMF 22063 International Airport, Salt Lake City, UT 84122; tel. 359-2085 or (800) 752-5382 out of state.

**Classic Helicopter Service** has flights to and between ski areas, helicopter skiing, and tours of the Salt Lake City area; tel. 580-1694/3232 or (800) 444-9223.

## Local Bus

**Utah Transit Authority (UTA)** provides inexpensive bus service in town and to the airport, University of Utah, and surrounding communities. Buses go as far north as Ogden and as far south as Provo. No charge is made for travel downtown within the "No-Fare Square" (area bounded by North Temple and 400 South and from West Temple to 200 East). During the winter ski season, skiers can hop on the Ski Bus Service to Solitude, Brighton, Snowbird, and Alta ski areas from the airport, downtown, University of Utah, and other locations. A bus route map and individual schedules are available from the ground transport info desk at the airport, the Salt Lake Convention & Visitors Bureau downtown, Temple Square visitor centers, Crossroads Mall, and ZCMI Mall. Or call UTA at 287-4636 (BUS-INFO) Mon. to Sat. 6 a.m.-7 p.m. Free transfers are given when the fare is paid, if asked for. On Sun., only the airport, Ogden, and a few other destinations are served. UTA shuts down on holidays.

The distinctive **Brigham Street Trolleys** connect Temple Square and other downtown areas with Trolley Square. The rubber-tired trolleys roll by every 10-20 minutes from about 10 a.m.-10 p.m. Mon. to Sat.; 50¢; tel. 287-4636.

**Lewis Brothers Stages** has a Red Horse Express service during the ski season to Park City from the Salt Lake City airport ($10 one way) and downtown ($5 one way). A shuttle during the ski season connects Alta and Snowbird ski areas with those at Park City ($8

one way). Reservations 2 days in advance are advised for these trips; tel. 359-8677 (Salt Lake City), 649-2256 (Park City), or toll free (800) 826-5844.

## Long-distance Bus

**Greyhound** goes to the Utah towns of Brigham City (6X daily, $5.70), Logan (2X daily, $8.71), Provo (2X daily, $8.88), Cedar City (2X daily, $36.70), St. George (2X daily, $41.44), and other places along I-15. Out-of-state destinations include Portland (4X daily, $110), Seattle (4X daily, $90), Vancouver (4X daily, $133), San Francisco (4X daily, $80), Los Angeles (2X daily, $90), Las Vegas (2X daily, $44), Yellowstone (summer only, 1X daily, $64), and Denver (4X daily, $55). The Greyhound station is downtown at 160 W. South Temple; tel. 355-4684.

## Auto Rentals

You'll find all the major companies and many local outfits eager to rent a set of wheels. See the telephone yellow pages for names. In winter you can find "skierized" vehicles with snow tires and ski racks ready to head for the slopes. Many agencies have an office or delivery service at the airport.

## Taxis

Rates for all the companies in Salt Lake City are fixed at about 95¢ flag up, then $1.30/mile. The following have 24-hour service: City Cab (tel. 363-5014), Ute Cab (tel. 359-7788), and Yellow Cab (tel. 521-2100).

## Train

Three **Amtrak** trains stop at the cavernous Denver and Rio Grande Depot. A partial list of destinations and one-way fares: *The California Zephyr* heads west to Reno ($103) and Oakland ($133) and east to Denver ($100) and Chicago ($196); *The Desert Wind* goes southwest to Las Vegas ($82) and Los Angeles ($129); and *The Pioneer* rolls west to Portland ($123) and Seattle ($142). Amtrak has many special discount fares for regional round trips, families, and to certain destinations; call for details. Amtrak office hours

*stained-glass window in the
Union Pacific Station*

(timed to meet the trains) are irregular, so call first; tel. (800) 872-7245 (info and reservations), 364-8562 (local office). The station lobby is worth a visit to see the changing exhibits of the Utah State History Museum. Located near downtown at 320 S. Rio Grande (300 South and 455 West).

## Air

Salt Lake City International Airport is conveniently located 7 miles west of downtown; take North Temple or I-80 to reach it. Many airlines fly here, and in fact, this is the only Utah airport served by the major carriers. Two regional airlines serve other towns in the state; destinations and one-way fares (ask about roundtrip discounts and other special fares):

**SkyWest Airlines** flies at least once daily to Vernal ($81), Cedar City ($104-119), St. George ($108-127), and towns in adjacent states; tel. 532-7123 (Salt Lake City) or (800) 453-9417.

**Alpine Air** flies most days to Price ($45), Vernal ($50), Moab ($69-109), Monticello ($74-114), Blanding ($79-119), Salina ($45), and Richfield ($45); tel. 575-2839 (Salt Lake City office information), 373-1508 (reservation office in Provo).

The **airport** has 2 terminals; in each you'll find a ground transport info desk, cafeteria, motel/hotel courtesy phones, auto rentals (Hertz, Avis, National, Budget, and Dollar), Morris Travel office (has currency exchange), and a ski rental shop. Terminal 1 also houses Zions First National Bank (has currency exchange), an ice-cream parlor, and gift shops. The Utah Information Center (Salt Lake Convention & Visitors Bureau) is upstairs in Terminal 2; hours are daily 9 a.m.-10 p.m.; tel. 575-2800. Staff at the ground transport info desks will know the bus schedules into town and limousine services direct to Park City, Sundance, Provo, Ogden, Brigham City, Logan, and other communities. UTA Bus #50 is the cheapest way into town. It leaves the airport daily except holidays every hour from about 6:30 a.m. to midnight.

Saltaire Resort, ca. 1900

# VICINITY OF SALT LAKE CITY

## THE GREAT SALT LAKE

Since its discovery by fur trappers in the 1820s, the lake has both mystified and entranced visitors. Early explorers guessed that it must be connected to the ocean, without realizing that they had come across a body of water far saltier. Only the Dead Sea has a higher salt content. When Mormon pioneers first tried evaporating the lake water, they found the residue bitter tasting, because it's only 84% sodium chloride (table salt); the remaining 16% is sulfates and chlorides of magnesium, calcium, and potassium. Mining companies have extracted salt, magnesium, lithium, chlorine, gypsum, potassium sulfate, and sodium sulfate from the water, which yields up to 27% solids. The lake's northern arm, isolated by a railroad causeway, contains the highest mineral concentrations—about twice those of the southern arm. Lowest salt levels occur on the south and east sides at river inlets. Bacteria grow in such numbers that they sometimes give a red tint to water in the northern arm, as do reddish-orange algae

*(Dunaliella salina).* The blue-green algae *(Dunaliella viridis)* occasionally give their own hue to the lake's southern arm. A tiny brine shrimp *(Artemia salina),* and 2 species of brine fly *(Ephydra sp.)* live in the lake too. The harmless flies emerge from the lake near the end of their life cycle to lay eggs, then die several days later. Until recently, no fish had ever been found alive in the Great Salt Lake. By the spring of 1986, however, unusually heavy runoff from tributaries had diluted the lake so that small rain water killifish could survive.

The lake has always been changing—rising with spring snowmelt, then falling due to evaporation that peaks in late summer and autumn. These annual variations result in differences in lake levels of 6 to as much as 18 inches. Long-term changes have affected the lake too: climate variations and diversion of river water for irrigation have caused a 21-foot difference between record low and high levels. Because the lake lies in a very shallow basin, its area has varied dramatically between 900 square miles at the lowest water level to 2,500 square miles at the highest. The record low surface elevation of 4,191 feet was reached in 1963, and the "experts" thought the lake might shrivel to nothing. Unfortunately, at that time much construction was going on near the shore without thought that the waters could rise. The lake's previous record high had occurred in 1873, causing concern to Brigham Young and other church leaders. They devised a plan to pump lake water into the desert to the west, but receding levels eliminated need for the pumping project.

Present-day Utahns haven't been so lucky. In just 5 years, from 1982 to 1987, the lake rose 12 feet to record-setting elevations. The spreading waters threatened to inundate parts of Salt Lake City, nearby towns and farms, the airport, rail lines, and I-80. High levels also upset the lake's ecology and ruined much of the surrounding marshland. Seven of the state's 9 bird refuges flooded, including world-famous Bear River Migratory Bird Refuge. An emergency session of the Utah Legislature in May 1986 authorized a pumping project with an initial price tag of $60 million to transfer water to the West Pond site, located in the Great Salt Lake Desert. From a peak elevation of 4,212 ft. in Jan. 1987, the lake level subsided, soon eliminating the need for pumping. The Great Salt Lake continues to confound the experts. Will the lake continue to rise? Will pumping into the 320,000-acre West Pond create a "lake effect," increasing fog, rain, and snow? How should lake-shore development be controlled?

### Antelope Island State Park

Though just a short distance offshore from Salt Lake City, Antelope Island seems a world away. Its rocky slopes, rolling grasslands, marshes, sand dunes, and lake views instill a sense of remoteness and rugged beauty. An extension of the Oquirrh Mountains, Antelope Island is the largest of the lake's 8 islands. It measures 15 miles long and 5 miles wide; Frary Peak (elev. 6,596 ft.) rises in the center. Archaeologists have found prehistoric sites showing that Indians came here long ago, perhaps on a land bridge during times of low lake level. In 1843, explorers John Fremont and Kit Carson rode their horses across a sand bar to the island and named it after

antelope (pronghorn) herds that the party hunted for food. In 1849, Brigham Young established a ranch here for church herds of cattle, sheep, and horses. Ranching has continued to be a major activity, though the Mormons lost ownership of the island in 1884. Today the entire island is a state park. Buffalo, deer, and other wildlife roam free here. Before 1984 you could drive to the island on a 7-mile causeway, but that's now under water! At press time, Antelope Island was closed to visitors. Call the state park office (tel. 533-5127) to check if it has been opened and how to get there.

### Great Salt Lake State Park

Bathers have enjoyed hopping into the lake ever since the 1847 arrival of Mormon pioneers. Extreme buoyancy in the dense water makes it impossible for a bather to sink—no swimming ability is needed! But anyone who puts his head underwater quickly realizes that the salty water causes great irritation to the eyes, throat, and nose.

Beginning in the 1880s, several resorts grew up along the lake's east and south shores. Besides bathing, guests could enjoy lake cruises, dances, concerts, bowling, arcade games, and roller-coaster rides. Saltair Resort stood as the last and grandest of the old resorts. Completed in 1893, the Moorish structure rose 5 stories and contained a huge dance floor where as many as 1,000 couples could enjoy the orchestra's rhythms. A rail line from Salt Lake City ran out on a 4,000-foot pier to the resort, which stood over the water on pilings. After 1930, low water levels, the Great Depression, fires, and fewer visitors gradually brought an end to Saltair. Its buildings burned for the second and last time in 1970 and nothing remains today. A developer recently built a smaller replica of Saltair Resort on the southern shore near I-80, but rising lake waters soon inundated the first floor.

The adjacent **Great Salt Lake State Park beaches** suffered a similar fate, but have since been restored; $3/vehicle; tel. 533-4080. Concessions near Saltair Resort sell snacks and souvenirs; open daily in summer and possibly off season too. Stop in at the nearby **Great Salt Lake Visitor Center** to see a video and exhibits about the lake; free; a good selection of local travel info is available too; open daily year-round; tel. 533-4083. From Salt Lake City, drive west 9 miles on I-80, take Exit 111 (7200 West), and follow the north frontage road west to the beaches; or take I-80 Exit 104 (Magna) and turn east on the north frontage road. If water levels permit, beaches west of Exit 104 will also be restored.

## WASATCH RANGE AND CANYONS

Spectacular mountains and canyons of the Wasatch Range begin right at the edge of Salt Lake City. The name Wasatch comes from an Indian word meaning "high mountain pass," of which the range has a great abundance. The range is about 200 miles long, extending from Mount Nebo in central Utah to the Bear River in southern Idaho. Geologic forces over the last 20 million years have uplifted and twisted these block-faulted mountains into a confusing jumble of rock layers. Intrusions of molten granitic rock and volcanic eruptions then added to the complexity. Massive rivers of ice carved knife-edge ridges and U-shaped valleys during at least 3 major periods of glaciation in the last 500,000 years. None of the glaciers remain, though some snowfields persist through years of heavy precipitation.

City Creek, Mill Creek, Big Cottonwood, and Little Cottonwood canyons beginning on the edge of Salt Lake City have a special attraction for visitors. Paved roads lead up each canyon to idyllic picnic spots and trailheads for dozens of hiking paths. Brilliant autumn colors of maple, aspen, and oak trees decorate hillsides from mid-Sept. to early October. Big and Little Cottonwood canyons also have campgrounds, lodges, and ski resorts (see "Salt Lake City Recreation" pp. 61-65 for descriptions of ski areas). Canyon streams and alpine lakes harbor elusive trout. Hikers will find detailed trail descriptions in *Hiking the Wasatch* by John Veranth (trails and major routes) and in 2 pocket-sized books published by the Wasatch Hiking Club: *Wasatch Trails,*

*Volume One* describes 37 trips for beginner to intermediate hikers; *Wasatch Trails, Volume Two* has 32 trails and routes, most for intermediate to advanced hikers. Other good books with Wasatch hikes include *The Hiker's Guide to Utah* by Dave Hall and *Utah Mountaineering Guide* by Michael Kelsey. For first-hand information on recreation in the range, contact the **Salt Lake Ranger District** office of the Wasatch-Cache National Forest. The office is near the mouth of Big Cottonwood Canyon at 6944 S. 3000 East; open Mon. to Fri. 8 a.m.-4:30 p.m.; tel. 524-5042. Camping is allowed only at designated sites or in the back country. Camps must be at least 200 feet from trails and water sources and ¼ mile from the trailhead, but because of the steep terrain, nearly all camping is near the top of the trail. Dogs are prohibited in City Creek, Big Cottonwood, and Little Cottonwood canyons to protect drinking-water sources. Don't forget to bring

Red Pine Lake Trail in Little Cottonwood Canyon

wind and rain gear in case a sudden storm appears; hypothermia is a serious danger in the mountains. Poison ivy, with its shiny leaves in groups of 3, grows along streams at lower elevations. Rattlesnakes live in many areas as high as 8,000 feet; look for them before reaching or stepping over rocks and logs.

## SKYLINE DRIVE

This 28-mile scenic drive north of Salt Lake City climbs nearly 5,000 feet for impressive views west across the Great Salt Lake and east over the Weber River Valley; allow 2-3 hours. **Bountiful Peak Overlook,** just below the peak's 9,259-foot summit, has the most sweeping panorama. The forest road is narrow and mostly unpaved; it's not recommended with trailers or for those who fear heights. Begin the drive either in Bountiful or Farmington; see the Wasatch-Cache National Forest map. From Bountiful (I-15 Exit 321), go east 2 miles on 400 North, turn left (north) 2 blocks on 1300 East, turn right (east) on 600 North, then right on 1375 East (Skyline Drive) to Ward Canyon; look closely for the switchback below the giant "B"—don't take the road past a large gravel pit. From Farmington (I-15 Exit 327), go east one mile on State, then turn left (north) on 100 East into Farmington Canyon. See map on p. 37.

**Bountiful Peak Campground** (elev. 7,500 ft.) is north of the overlook and 8.5 miles up Farmington Canyon; open mid-June to early Oct. with drinking water; free. **Sunset Campground** (elev. 6,400 ft.) is 5.3 miles up Farmington Canyon; open early May to mid-Oct.; no water or charge; a hiking trail climbs to Sunset Point. The Francis Peak Rd. turns off near Bountiful Peak Campground to an overlook 8 miles away with more good views.

## CITY CREEK CANYON

This pretty canyon begins just east of the State Capitol, then winds northeast into the Wasatch Range. Since pioneer days, people have obtained precious water here and en-joyed the diverse vegetation, wildlife, and scenery. Because City Creek is still a watershed, regulations prohibit dogs, horses, and overnight camping. A paved road through City Creek Canyon extends 6 miles past picnic areas to a trailhead. Hikers and joggers may travel on the road every day; bicyclists may enter only on odd calendar days, motorized vehicles may drive up only on even calendar days; a gate at the bottom controls entry. A $2 charge applies if you drive through to the trailhead at the upper end (no reservation needed). The big attraction for many visitors is a stop at one of the picnic areas along the road. Picnickers *must* reserve sites with the Water Dept.; obtain the required receipt at least a day ahead by visiting the accounting office in the Public Utilities Bldg. at 1530 S. West Temple (Salt Lake City, UT 84115). Allow 2 weeks or more to obtain reservations by mail and mark envelope "attn. City Creek Reservations"; tel. 483-6797. Picnic permits cost $2.50 and up depending on size of group. The entrance to City Creek Canyon is reached by Bonneville Blvd., a one-way road. From downtown Salt Lake City, head east on North Temple (which becomes 2nd Ave. after crossing State St.), then turn left (north) 1.3 miles on "B" St. (which becomes Bonneville Blvd. after 11th Ave.) to City Creek Canyon Road. Returning from the canyon, you have to turn right on Bonneville Blvd. to the State Capitol. Bicyclists and joggers may approach City Creek Canyon from either direction.

A popular hiking destination from the trailhead at road's end (elev. 6,050 ft.) is City Creek Meadows, 4 miles away and 2,000 feet higher. After 1½ miles, you'll pass Cottonwood Gulch on the left; a side trail up the gulch leads to an old mining area. After another ½ mile on the main trail, a spring off to the right in a small meadow is the last reliable source of drinking water. During the next mile, the trail steepens and winds through aspen groves and then passes 2 shallow ponds. The trail becomes indistinct here, but you can continue one mile northeast to City Creek Meadows (elev. 8,000 ft.); a topo map and compass help. For splendid views of the Wasatch Range, climb north ½ mile from the meadows

# CENTRAL WASATCH RANGE

ROCKPORT STATE PARK

ROCKPORT LAKE

TO EAST CANYON STATE PARK

HAILSTONE

HEBER CITY

PARK CITY

DEER VALLEY SKI AREA

PARK CITY SKI AREA

WASATCH MTN. STATE PARK

MIDWAY

PARKWEST SKI AREA

GUARDSMAN PASS

BRIGHTON SKI AREA

RANGE

WASATCH

DESOLATION LAKE

BRIGHTON LAKES TR.

ALBION BASIN C.G.

REDMAN C.G.

ALTA SKI AREA

SPRUCES C.G.

SOLITUDE SKI AREA

*HIDDEN PEAK (11,000 ft.)*

*GOBBLER'S KNOB (10,246 ft.)*

BIG COTTONWOOD CANYON

SNOWBIRD SKI AREA

DESOLATION TRAIL

MINERAL FORK

*TWIN PEAKS (11,330 ft.)*

MILL CREEK CANYON

LITTLE COTTONWOOD CANYON

TANNERS FLAT C.G.

WHITE PINE LAKE

MTN. DELL GOLF COURSE

PARLEYS CANYON

*MT. OLYMPUS (9026 ft.)*

RED PINE LAKE

LAMBS CANYON

*LONE PEAK (11,253 ft.)*

EMIGRATION CANYON

PIONEER ROUTE

THIS IS THE PLACE MONUMENT

UNIV. OF UTAH

CITY CREEK CANYON

STATE CAPITOL

SALT LAKE CITY

WHEELER HISTORIC FARM

MURRAY

MIDVALE

SOUTH JORDAN

RIVERTON

2 mi

2 km

up the ridge to where Davis, Salt Lake, and Morgan counties meet. Hikers also enjoy shorter strolls from the trailhead along the gentle lower section of trail.

## MILL CREEK CANYON

Plentiful picnic areas and many hiking possibilities lie along Mill Creek just outside Salt Lake City. Canyon entrance is at Wasatch Blvd. and Mill Creek Rd. (3800 South). You may bring your dog along too—this is one of the few canyons where pets are welcome. Picnic sites are free and on a first-come, first-served basis; most lack water. The first one, Church Fork Picnic Area, is 3 miles in at an elevation of 5,700 feet; Big Water Picnic Area is the last, 8.8 miles up at an elevation of 7,500 feet. A small usage fee may apply to visitors in Mill Creek Canyon.

**Salt Lake Overlook** on Desolation Trail is a good hiking destination for families. The trail climbs 1,200 feet in 2 miles for views of the Salt Lake Valley. Begin from the lower end of Box Elder Picnic Area (elev. 5,760 ft.) on the south side of the road. Energetic hikers can continue on Desolation Trail beyond the overlook to higher country near timberline and go all the way to Desolation Lake (19 miles). The trail runs near the ridgeline separating Mill and Big Cottonwood canyons, connecting with many trails from both canyons. Much of this high country lies in the Mt. Olympus Wilderness. See Mt. Aire and Park City West 7½-minute topo maps.

**Alexander Basin Trail** winds to a beautiful wooded glacial bowl below Gobblers Knob; the trailhead (elev. 7,080 ft.) is on the south side of the road 8 miles up Mill Creek Canyon, 0.8 mile beyond Clover Springs Picnic Area. The moderately difficult trail begins by paralleling the road to the northwest for a few hundred feet, then turns southwest and switchbacks one mile to the beginning of Alexander Basin (elev. 8,400 ft.). The trail to Bowman and Porter forks turns right here, but continue straight ½ mile for the meadows of the upper basin (elev. 9,000 ft.). The limestone rock here has many fossils, mostly of shellfish.

From the basin it's possible to rockscramble to the summit of Gobblers Knob (elev. 10,246 ft.). The name comes from an attempt by mine owners at raising turkeys after their ores played out; the venture ended when bobcats ate all the birds. See the Mt. Aire topo map.

## BIG COTTONWOOD CANYON

Cliffs towering thousands of feet form the gateway to Big Cottonwood Canyon. Skiers come in season to try the downhill slopes at Solitude and Brighton and to cross-country ski at the Solitude Nordic Ski Center. Enter the canyon from Wasatch Blvd. and 7000 South, about 15 miles southeast of downtown Salt Lake City. The 14-mile drive to Brighton Basin reveals splendid vistas at each turn while climbing to an elevation of 8,700 feet. Guardsman Pass Rd. turns off just before Brighton and winds up to Guardsman Pass (elev. 9,800 ft.) at the crest of the Wasatches, then drops down into either Park City or Heber City on the other side; the mostly unpaved road is usually open late June to mid-October. Eight picnic areas lie along Big Cottonwood Creek. You'll come first to Dogwood Picnic Area (elev. 5,200 ft.), 1.1 miles from the entrance, and finally to Silver Lake Picnic Area (elev. 8,720 ft.) near road's end, 14.5 miles up the canyon. Silver Lake will have handicapped access to fishing and picnic sites. All picnic areas are first-come, first-served except Jordan Pines (8.8 miles from the canyon entrance), which is by reservation only; has water. **Spruces Campground** has family ($8) and group sites 9.8 miles up at an elevation of 7,400 feet; open with water from early June to mid-October. **Redman Campground** lies 13 miles up between Solitude and Brighton at an elevation of 8,300 feet; family sites cost $7; open with water from mid-June to early October.

You can find fancier accommodations at Silver Fork Lodge (about $48 s, $60 d; has a restaurant; tel. 649-9551), 11.3 miles up the canyon, and at Brighton Lodge (summer: $16.39 dorm, $32.78 s, or $43.70 d and up; has heated pool and jacuzzi; tel. 649-2999) in Brighton. Brighton Village Store has cabins

**BRIGHTON AND VICINITY**

TO SALT LAKE CITY

SOLITUDE SKI AREA

152

BIG COTTONWOOD

REDMAN C.G.

CANYON

GUARDSMAN PASS RD.

(9050 ft.)

LAKE SOLITUDE

SILVER LAKE

BRIGHTON

HONEYCOMB CLIFFS

MT. EVERGREEN

(10,479 ft.)

TWIN LAKES RESERVOIR

BRIGHTON SKI AREA

TWIN LAKES-LAKE MARY TRAIL

TO ALTA & SALT LAKE CITY

LAKE MARY

210

MT. MILLICENT (10,452 ft.)

DOG LAKE

LITTLE COTTONWOOD CANYON

LAKE MARTHA

MT. WOLVERINE (10,795 ft.)

BRIGHTON LAKES TR.

LAKE CATHERINE

PIONEER PK.

CATHERINE PASS

ALBION BASIN

ALBION BASIN C.G.

SUNSET PK. (10,648 ft.)

CECRET LAKE TR.

CECRET LAKE

0                    0.5 mi
0              500 m

DEVIL'S CASTLE

from $85. Silver Fork Lodge and Brighton Village Store have restaurants. Visit the Alpinist in Brighton for hiking supplies, rentals, and information on exploring the back country.

**Mineral Fork Trail** follows an old mining road past abandoned mines, cabins, and rusting equipment to a high glacial cirque. Waterfalls, alpine meadows, wildflowers, and abundant birdlife make the steep climb worthwhile. The signed trailhead is on the south side of the road 6 miles up the canyon (0.8 mile past Moss Ledge Picnic Area). You'll climb 2,000 feet in 3 miles to Wasatch Mine, whose mineralized water makes up much of the flow of Mineral Fork Creek. Another 2 miles and 1,400 feet of climbing lead to Regulator Johnson Mine. A loop trip can be made by climbing the ridge west of Regulator Johnson (no trail) and descending Mill B South Fork Trail to Lake Blanche and the main road, coming out 1.5 miles west of the Mineral Fork Trailhead. See Mt. Aire and Dromedary Peak 7½-minute topo maps.

**Brighton Lakes Trail** winds through some of the prettiest lake country in the range. Families enjoy outings on this easy trail, which begins in Brighton behind the Brighton Lodge. The first section follows Big Cottonwood Creek through stands of aspen and evergreens. The trail continues south across meadows filled with wildflowers, then climbs more steeply to Brighton Overlook, one mile from the start. Dog Lake, surrounded by old mine dumps, lies 200 yards to the south. Continue on the main trail ½ mile to Lake Mary, a large deep lake below Mt. Millicent. Lake Martha is another ½ mile up the trail. Another mile of climbing takes you to Lake Catherine, bordered by a pretty alpine meadow on the north and steep talus slopes of Sunset and Pioneer peaks on the south. Total elevation gain for the 3-mile hike to Lake Catherine is 1,200 feet. Hikers can also go another ½ mile to Catherine Pass and descend 1½ miles to Albion Basin in Little Cottonwood Canyon. Sunset Peak (elev. 10,648 ft.) can be climbed by following a ½-mile trail from the pass. See the Brighton 7½-minute topo map.

## LITTLE COTTONWOOD CANYON

The road through this nearly straight glacial valley ascends 5,500 feet in 11 miles. Splendid peaks rise to more than 11,000 feet on both sides. In winter and spring, challenging terrain attracts skiers to Snowbird and Alta ski areas. Enter Little Cottonwood Canyon from the junction of UT 209 and UT 210, 4 miles south of the entrance to Big Cottonwood Canyon. Granite rock for the Salt Lake Temple came from quarries one mile up the canyon on the left. Here too are the Granite Mountain Record Vaults, containing genealogical and historical records of the LDS Church, stored on millions of rolls of microfilm. Neither site is open to the public. There aren't any picnic areas in the canyon, but the U.S. Forest Service offers 2 places to camp. **Tanners Flat Campground** is 4.3 miles up at an elevation of 7,200 feet; sites cost $7 and have water from mid-May to early Sept., then no water or fee to mid-October. **Albion Basin Campground** lies 11 miles up near the head of the canyon at an elevation of 9,500 feet (the last 2.5 miles are gravel road); sites cost $7 and have water from early July to early Sept., then no water or fee to late Sept./early October.

**Snowbird Resort,** 7 miles up the canyon on the right, offers luxury accommodations, a good selection of restaurants, a varied calendar of concert and dance performances, sports facilities, and a tram ride to the heights. Lodging rates range from $75-152. The tram ride to the 11,000-foot summit of Hidden Peak gives you sweeping panoramas from the crest of the Wasatch Range; the tram operates 11 a.m.-8 p.m. from mid-May to mid-Oct.; $6 adult, $3.50 children 6-16 and seniors 62 and over, or $16 family up to 4 kids. The Mountaineering Center (Level 3) rents mountain bicycles, packs, and child carriers and offers tours for hiking, climbing, backpacking, and mountain bicycling; tel. extension 4147. A hiking map available at the Mountaineering Center shows local trails and jogging loops. A spa is located atop the Cliff Lodge; tel. extension

5900. Contact the resort at Snowbird, UT 84092; tel. 521-6040 (Salt Lake City), 742-2222 (local), or (800) 453-3000 (lodging reservations only).

**Alta's** original reputation lay in the rich silver veins of the hills and the rip-roaring saloon life in town. Mining started in 1865 with the opening of the great Emma Mine and peaked in 1872, when Alta had a population of 5,000 served by 26 saloons and 6 breweries. Crashing silver prices the following year and a succession of deadly avalanches ended the boom. A few diehards continued to work the hills but the town faded away. Little remains from the old days except abandoned mine shafts, a few shacks, and the cemetery. Ski enthusiasts brought Alta to life again with ski jumping in 1930 and the introduction of ski lifts in 1937. **Alta Lodge** offers summer accommodations at $55-84 and limited restaurant service; tel. 742-3500 or 322-4631. Alta

lies 8 miles up the canyon (one mile beyond Snowbird).

**White Pine, Red Pine, and Maybird Gulch trails** lead to pretty alpine lakes. Red Pine and Maybird Gulch lie in the Lone Peak Wilderness. All 3 trails begin from the same trailhead, then diverge into separate valleys. On any one, you'll enjoy wildflowers and superb high-country scenery. Start from White Pine Trailhead (elev. 7,700 ft.), 5.3 miles up the canyon and one mile beyond Tanners Flat Campground. The trail crosses a bridge over Little Cottonwood Creek and contours west, then southwest to White Pine Fork. The effects of several avalanches can be seen along this section. The trails divide after one mile, just before crossing White Pine Fork; turn sharply left for White Pine Lake or continue straight across the stream for Red Pine Lake and Maybird Gulch. Red Pine Trail contours around a ridge, then parallels Red Pine Fork

*Alta City during its early years*

## WHITE PINE, RED PINE, AND MAYBIRD GULCH TRAILS

TO SNOWBIRD & ALTA

210

WHITE PINE TRAILHEAD

TO SALT LAKE CITY

TANNERS FLAT C.G.

LITTLE COTTONWOOD CR.

RED PINE FORK

MAYBIRD GULCH

WHITE PINE FORK

(10,121 ft.)

(9,947 ft.)

MAYBIRD LAKES

(10,516 ft.)

RED PINE LAKE

(10,718 ft.)

WHITE PINE LAKE

(11,171 ft.)

(10,897 ft.)

0       0.5 mi

0     500 m

to the lake (elev. 9,680 ft.), a beautiful deep pool ringed by conifers and alpine meadows. Energetic hikers can rockscramble along the stream another ½ mile (no trail) to Upper Red Pine Lake. The upper lake sits in a glacial cirque devoid of trees. Trout lurk in the waters, though the lake may remain frozen until late June. Maybird Gulch Trail begins 2 miles up Red Pine Trail from White Pine Fork and leads to tiny Maybird Lakes. From the trailhead, White Pine Lake is 3½ miles (2,300-foot elevation gain), Red Pine Lake is 3½ miles (1,920-foot elevation gain), and Maybird Lakes are 4½ miles (2,060-foot elevation gain). See the Dromedary Peak 7½-minute topo map. This whole area receives heavy use from hikers, so greater care with the environment is needed than usual. Please follow the Forest Service regulation that prohibits wood fires within one mile of the lakes.

**Peruvian Gulch-Hidden Peak Trail** gives you the advantage of hiking just one way from either the top or bottom by using the Snowbird tram. From the top of Hidden Peak (elev. 11,000 ft.), the trail crosses open rocky country on the upper slopes, spruce- and aspen-covered ridges lower down, then follows an old mining road down Peruvian Gulch. Elevation change along the 3½-mile trail is 2,900 feet. Dromedary Peak 7½-minute topo map covers this area.

**Cecret Lake Trail** begins from the west side of Albion Basin Campground and climbs glacier-scarred granite slopes to a pretty alpine lake (elev. 9,880 ft.) below Sugarloaf Mountain. Wildflowers put on colorful summer displays along the way. The trail is just one mile long and makes a good family hike; elevation gain is 360 feet. Continue another mile for fine views south to Mt. Timpanogos from Germania Pass. It's no secret that early miners had trouble spelling Cecret Lake; you'll see both versions on maps!

TO
PARKWEST
SKI AREA (4 mi)
SALT LAKE CITY (31 mi)
(80) (6 mi)

PARK AVE.

HOLIDAY
RANCH
LOOP RD.

LUCKY
JOHN DR.

PARK
MEADOWS
GOLF
COURSE

MEADOWS DR.

PAYDAY DR.

LITTLE KATE RD.

MONITOR DR.

KEARNS BLVD.

(248)

TO
U.S. 40 (2 mi)
& HEBER CITY (20 mi)

THAYNES CANYON DR.

(224)

KEARNS BLVD.

SIDEWINDER DR.

THREE KINGS DR.

PARK CITY
GOLF COURSE

HOMESTAKE RD.

PROSPECTOR AVE.

1

EMPIRE
AVE.

IRON HORSE DR.

DEER VALLEY DR.

BONANZA DR.

SILVER
KING
DR.

14th ST.

PARK CITY
SKI AREA

2

13th ST.
12th ST.
11th ST.
10th ST.
9th ST.

AERIE DR.

MELLOW MTN. RD.

**PARK CITY**

LOWELL AVE.

EMPIRE AVE.

NORFOLK AVE.

WOODSIDE AVE.

8th ST.

3

DEER VALLEY DR.

DEER VALLEY DR.
NORTH

TOWN LIFT

HEBER AVE.

MAIN ST.

DEER VALLEY DR.

4

DEER VALLEY
DR. SOUTH

5

5th ST.

ONTARIO AVE.

DEER VALLEY
DR. EAST

4th ST.

6

NORFOLK AVE.

HILLSIDE AVE.

DALY AVE.

ROYAL ST.

SNOW PARK
LODGE
DEER VALLEY
SKI AREA

ONTARIO CANYON

(224)

1. Holiday Village Mall
2. library and city park
3. Kimball Art Center
4. Park City Museum and
   Visitor Infomation Center
5. post office
6. Egyptian Theatre

0                    0.5 mi

0              500 m

DEER VALLEY SKI AREA

ROYAL ST. WEST

STERLING

ROYAL ST. EAST

TO BRIGHTON &
GUARDSMAN'S
PASS

SILVER LAKE LODGE

# PARK CITY

Approaching this old silver mining town, you might think the name should be changed to "Condo City," but keep going to the picturesque downtown area. Turn-of-the-century buildings along Main Street and on the hillsides recall Park City's colorful and energetic past. Here you'll find a historic museum, art galleries, specialty shops, and fine restaurants. A busy year-round schedule of festivals, concerts, and sporting events help make Park City a lively place. Instead of digging for silver, today's visitors head for the slopes to mine the light and dry powder snow in winter and to enjoy the verdant mountain scenery in summer. Three ski areas—ParkWest, Park City, and Deer Valley—offer varied terrain and luxurious accommodations; see "Salt Lake City Skiing," pp. 64-65. The U.S. Ski Team liked the town so well that it based its headquarters here. Park City lies in a mountain valley at an elevation of 7,000 feet on the eastern side of the Wasatch Range. From Salt Lake City, drive 31 miles east via I-80 and UT 224.

## History

In Oct. 1868, with winter fast approaching, 3 off-duty soldiers from Fort Douglas discovered a promising outcrop of ore on a hillside 2 miles south of the present townsite. Their sample assayed at 96 ounces of silver per ton, with lesser values of lead and gold. Two years later, the Flagstaff Mine began operations at that first discovery and development of one of the West's richest mining districts took off. What had been a peaceful valley with grazing cattle now swarmed with hordes of fortune hunters and rang to the sound of pick axes. The famed Ontario Mine and dozens of other strikes soon followed. Silver from the Ontario, as much as 400 ounces in a ton, started the fortunes of U.S. Senator Thomas J. Kearns of Salt Lake City and George Hearst, father of publisher William Randolph Hearst. By 1880, Park City had grown to be a substantial town with a population of 3,500 of many nationalities. The *Park Mining Record,* later the *Park Record,* began weekly publication that continues to the present. Scandinavian miners introduced skiing to the community, though the heavy 10-foot boards used then have little in common with today's equipment. A lively red-light entertainment district sprang up in Deer Valley Gulch, but it's long gone today.

The great hotel fire of 1898 nearly brought an end to the young city. The fire raced along Main St. reducing 200 businesses and houses to ashes and leaving much of the population homeless. Determined citizens immediately set to work rebuilding and had a new downtown within 3 months. Many of the businesses you see along Main St. date from that time. In the early 1900s, Park City's mining economy began seeing more depressions than upswings. Mine flooding, labor troubles, and a big drop in metal prices during the Great Depression caused many residents to leave. By the early 1960s the town looked ready to fold up, but then the big skiing and resort boom brought it to life again!

## SIGHTS

### Park City Museum

Drop in to see historic exhibits of the mining, skiing, colorful personalities, and other aspects of early Park City. The museum is at 528 Main St. in the old City Hall Building, built in 1885 and rebuilt after the 1898 fire. Go downstairs to see the original jail, known as the "dungeon." Open Mon. to Sat. 10 a.m.-7 p.m., Sun. noon-6 p.m.; hours in May and Oct. change to daily noon-5 p.m.; free admission; tel. 649-6104. The **Visitor Information Center** is here too during the same hours; staff can answer your questions and provide literature on the area. Ask for a historic walking tour leaflet. Guided walking tours are scheduled too.

### Kimball Art Center

This large art gallery exhibits works of noted artists and sponsors classes and workshops. Galleries on the main floor and downstairs

# PARK CITY ACCOMMODATIONS

Add 10.25% tax to all prices; W = winter, S = summer

| LODGING | ADDRESS | RATE RANGE | PHONE | FEATURES |
|---|---|---|---|---|
| Alpine Prospector Lodge | 151 Main St. Box 4155 (84060) | $39-69 (W) $20-40 (S) | 649-9975 or 649-3483 | restored miners' boardinghouse |
| Blue Church Lodge & Townhouses | 424 Park Ave. Box 1720 (84060) | $60-380 (W) (S: closed) | 649-8009 | kitchens |
| Budget Lodging & Reservations | 1940 ProspectorAve. Box 3868 (84060) | $65-900 (W) $35-400 (S) | 649-2526 or (800) 522-7669 | kitchens, pool |
| Chateau Aprés Lodge | 1299 Norfolk Ave. Box 579 (84060) | $46 (W) $27 (S) | 649-9372 | dormitories available |
| Coalition Condos | 1300 Park Ave. Box 75 (84060) | $60-275 (W) $30-150 (S) | 649-8221 or (800) 829-9191 | kitchens |
| Condominium Rentals of Park City/IML | 2000 Prospector Ave. Box 2909 (84060) | $85-210 (W) $34-80 (S) | 649-2687 or (800) 221-0933 | kitchens |
| Deer Valley Lodging | 1375 Deer Valley Box 3000 (84060) | $250-1300 (W) $103-545 (S) | 649-4040 or (800) 453-3833 out of state | kitchens, pool |
| Edelweiss Haus | 1482 Empire Ave. Box 495 (84060) | $80-285 (W) $29-75 (S) | 649-9342 or (800) 438-3855 | kitchens, pool |
| Goldener Hirsch Inn | Silver Lake Village Box 859 (84060) | $205-350 (W) $98-198 (S) | 649-7770 or (800) 252-3373 | Austrian Inn; hot tub, sauna |
| Imperial Hotel | 231 Main St. Box 1628 (84060) | $75-125 (W) $40-75 (S) | 649-1904 | bed & breakfast inn (1904 boarding house) |
| The Innsbruck | 1201 Norfolk Box 222 (84060) | $110-152 (W) $40-60 (S) | 649-9829 | chalets, pool |
| Landmark Inn (Best Western) | 6560 N. Landmark Dr. (I-80 Park City exit) | $64-84 (W) $39-50 (S) | 649-7300 or (800) 548-8824 | pool |
| Old Miners' Lodge Bed & Breakfast Inn | 615 Woodside Ave. Box 2639 (84060) | $80-150 (W) $40-80 (S) | 645-8068 or (800) 648-8068 | historic 1893 bldg. |
| Olympia Resort Hotel & Convention Center | 1895 Sidewinder Dr. Box 4439 (84060) | $109-230 (W) $55-130 (S) | 649-2900 or (800) 234-9003 | indoor pool, fitness room |
| Park City Reservations | 1790 Bonanza Dr. Box 680128 (84068) | $75-750 (W) $40-375 (S) | 649-9598 or (800) 453-5789 | condominiums |
| Park Plaza Resort | 2060 Sidewinder Dr. Box 3988 (84060) | $95-210 (W) $65-175 (S) | 649-0870 | kitchens, pool |
| Park Station Condominium Hotel | 950 Park Ave. Box 1360 (84060) | $50-350 (W) $50-110 (S) | 649-7717 or (800) 367-1056 | kitchens, pool |

# PARK CITY ACCOMMODATIONS (CONTINUED)

Add 10.25% tax to all prices; W = winter, S = summer

| LODGING | ADDRESS | RATE RANGE | PHONE | FEATURES |
|---------|---------|------------|-------|----------|
| ParkWest Village | 3819 W. Village Round Dr. Box 1655 (84060) | $45-165 (W) $35-85 (S) | 649-8023 or (800) 421-5056 out of state | kitchens; at ParkWest Ski Area |
| Prospector Square Hotel & Conference Center | 2200 Sidewinder Dr. Box 1698 (84060) | $98-245 (W) $55-125 (S) | 649-7100, 322-3123 SLC, or (800) 453-3812 out of state | athletic club with indoor pool |
| Radisson Inn Park City | 2346 Park Ave. Box 1778 (84060) | $75-200 (W) $60-150 (S) | 649-5000 or (800) 345-5076 | indoor/outdoor pool |
| Silver King Hotel | 1485 Empire Ave. Box 2818 (84060) | $180-420 (W) $80-175 (S) | 649-5500, 322-5155 SLC, or (800) 331-8652 | kitchens, year-round pool |
| Star Hotel | 227 Main St. Box 777 (84060) | $41/person (W) $30 (S) | 649-8333 | family style lodging |
| Stein Eriksen Lodge | Deer Valley Resort Box 3177 (84060) | $265-1435 (W) $120-590 (S) | 649-3700 or (800) 453-1302 out of state | kitchens, pool |
| Tramway Lodge | 1475 Park Ave. Box 9 (84060) | $75 (W) $40 (S) | 649-8443 | hot tub, sauna |
| Washington School Inn | 543 Park Ave. Box 536 (84060) | $145-225 (W) $75-120 (S) | 649-3800 or (800) 824-1672 | bed & breakfast, in historic schoolhouse |
| The Yarrow Hotel | 1800 Park Ave. Box 1840 (84060) | $79-299 (W) $79-199 (S) | 649-7000 or (800) 327-2332 | outdoor pool |

display paintings, prints, sculptures, ceramics, photography, and other media. Exhibits change every 4 weeks. The gift shop has many items for sale. Open Sun. noon-6 p.m. and Mon. to Sat. 10 a.m.-6 p.m.; tel. 649-8882. Located at the corner of Heber and Park near the bottom of Main Street. Look for other art galleries along Main St. too.

## ACCOMMODATIONS

Park City offers more than 70 places to stay. Guest capacity far exceeds the town's permanent population! Rates peak during the ski season, when accommodations may be hard to find. Off season, prices can drop as much as 50% at the more expensive places. See the *Vacation Planner* published by the Park City Area Chamber/Bureau for detailed listings of accommodations (Box 1630, Park City, UT 84060). Skiers will also want to check accommodation and ski package listings in the *Utah Ski Vacation Planner* (Ski Utah, Inc., 307 W. 200 South, Suite 5005, Salt Lake City, UT 84101). Lodging reservations services include **A-Vermeers Reservations** (tel. 649-1103), **Deer Valley Central Reservations** (includes Park City; 649-1000), **Park City Ski Holidays** (649-0493), **Park City Travel and Lodging** (645-8200), and **Reservations Network** (649-1592).

## Campgrounds

**Hidden Haven** offers tent and RV sites all year with showers; guests may cast for trout in a stream running beside the campground; $10.63 no hookups, $13.90 w/hookups; tel. 649-8935; drive to I-80 Park City Exit 145 (5 miles north of town on UT 224) and turn west one mile on the north frontage road.

# RESTAURANTS

## American

**Barking Frog Grill** features contemporary Southwest cuisine; open daily except Tues. for lunch and dinner at 368 Main St.; tel. 649-6222. **The Riverhorse Cafe** has a variety of seafood and pasta dishes; open daily except Wed. for lunch and dinner (open daily in winter for dinner only); in the old Masonic building at 540 Main St.; tel. 649-3536. **Brand X Cattle Company** serves up steaks, prime rib, local trout, and seafood with a large salad bar; open daily for dinner at 1064 Park Ave.; tel. 649-2346. **Cafe Mariposa** prepares "classic and current" cuisine; open daily in ski season for lunch and dinner at Deer Valley Resort (Silver Lake Lodge, mid-mountain); tel. 649-1005 (reservations suggested). **The Claimjumper** features steaks, prime rib, and seafood; open daily for dinner at 573 Main St.; tel. 649-8051. **The Eating Establishment** is a favorite place for breakfast, served all day; lunch and dinner are served too; open daily at 317 Main St.; tel. 649-8284. **Grub Steak Restaurant** rustles up steak, prime rib, seafood, and has a large salad bar; open Sun. for brunch, Mon. to Sat. for breakfast, Mon. to Fri. for lunch, and daily for dinner at the Prospector Square Hotel (Kearns Blvd. and Sidewinder Ave.); tel. 649-8060. The **Huggery** creates outstanding buffets during the ski season, daily for breakfast and lunch and Tues. to Sat. for dinner (seafood buffet); open in summer Tues. to Sat. for dinner; at Snow Park Lodge in Deer Valley Resort; tel. 649-1007. **The Stew Pot** serves stews, chicken, seafood, sandwiches, and salads; open daily for lunch and Mon. to Sat. for dinner in Deer Valley Plaza; tel. 645-STEW. **Texas Red's Pit Bar-** becue dishes out ribs, beef, pork, chicken, 2-alarm chili, and catfish in a Western setting; open daily for lunch and dinner at 440 Main St.; also has take-out; tel. 649-7337.

## Continental Cuisine

**Adolph's** varied international menu features lamb, veal, chicken, and seafood dishes; open daily for lunch and dinner at Park City Golf Course (corner Park Ave. and Thaynes Canyon Dr.); tel. 649-7177 (reservations suggested). **Cisero's Italian Ristorante** serves pasta, veal, chicken, and seafood; open daily for lunch and dinner at 306 Main St.; tel. 649-5044. **Mid-Mountain Restaurant** offers such Continental delights as Swiss-style veal bratwurst, chicken Wellington, and roast loin of lamb; open daily during the ski season for lunch in an old miners' mess hall on the Webster run (Pioneer lift) in the Park City Ski Area; tel. 649-3044. **Mileti's** Italian restaurant uses homemade pasta in their traditional and modern dishes; open daily for dinner at 412 Main St.; tel. 649-8211. **Philippe's Restaurant** offers a variety of European cuisines; open daily for dinner (also breakfast and lunch during the ski season) at Stag Lodge in Deer Valley (8200 Royal St. East); tel. 649-2421 (reservations recommended). **Scrooge's** has a festive decor for its varied menu of chicken cacciatore, duck, poached salmon, and other specialties; open daily for dinner at 402 Main St.; tel. 649-9627. Chefs prepare German and other specialties at **The Depot**; open Wed. to Sun. for breakfast and daily for lunch and dinner at 660 Main (bottom of hill); has a piano bar; tel. 649-2102. The **Glitretind** offers fine European cuisine in elegant surroundings; open daily for breakfast, lunch, and dinner in the Stein Eriksen Lodge at Deer Valley Resort; tel. 649-3700 (reservations recommended).

## Chinese

**Szechuan Chinese Restaurant** offers spicy and mild dishes; open daily for lunch and dinner at 438 Main St.; tel. 649-0957. **Yen-Jing Restaurant** features Mandarin and Szechuan cuisines; open daily for lunch and dinner next to the ice rink at the Park City Ski Area; tel. 649-7800.

**Japanese**
**Ichiban Sushi** prepares sushi, sashimi, tempura, teriyaki, and other styles; open daily for dinner at 424 Main St.; tel. 649-2865.

**Mexican**
The **Baja Cantina** serves favorite south-of-the-border items plus steaks and seafood; open daily for lunch and dinner at the Resort Center (Park City Ski Area); tel. 649-2252. The **Irish Camel,** despite its name, serves good Mexican food; open daily for lunch and dinner at 434 Main St.; tel. 649-6645. **Utah Coal and Lumber** has become a Mexican restaurant, though the old sign remains; open daily for lunch and dinner at 201 Heber Ave. (bottom of Main St.); tel. 649-9930.

**Pizza And Sandwiches**
**Davanza's Pizza** fixes pizza, subs, burgers, and salads; take-outs too; open daily for lunch and dinner at the Holiday Village Mall; tel. 649-2222. **Park City Pizza Company** prepares pizza, hot sandwiches, pasta dishes, and salads for sit-down or take-out; open daily for lunch and dinner at 430 Main St.; tel. 649-1591. **Red Banjo Pizza Parlour** offers pizza, spaghetti, sandwiches, and salads; open daily for lunch and dinner at 322 Main St.; tel. 649-9901.

## OTHER PRACTICALITIES

**Entertainment And Events**
Catch movies at **Holiday Village Cinemas III** in Holiday Village Mall, 1776 Park Ave. (north edge of town); tel. 649-6541. **Park City Performances** put on plays, musicals, films, and children's programs in the historic Egyptian Theatre, 328 Main St.; tel. 649-9371. Contact the Park City Area Chamber/Bureau for the latest news on happenings around town; tel. 649-6100. Major annual events include:

**January:** United States Film Festival (screenings and seminars of the best American cinema projects). Senators' Ski Cup (U.S. senators compete in a charity fundraiser). Utah Winter Games (alpine and nordic skiing and ice skating). Steve Garvey Celebrity Ski Classic (local and national celebrities ski in a charity fundraiser).

**February:** Snow Sculpture Contest and Winterfest by Park City High School.

**March:** Utah Special Winter Olympics (handicapped people compete in winter sports). Para-Ski Meet at ParkWest (one day of parachuting and one day of skiing competition).

**April:** Easter Egg Hunt at Park City and ParkWest ski areas.

**June:** Blast to the Past (concerts, personalities, and car show of the 1950s). Concert Series at ParkWest. Savor the Summit is a food festival presented by area restaurants; takes place at the Resort Center. Writers at Work (readings and seminars by nationally known writers and poets).

**July:** Old-Fashioned Fourth of July Celebration with a parade and fireworks. Shakespeare Festival (3 plays are presented Thurs. to Sat. evenings during July and Aug.). Utah Symphony Summer Series (weekly concerts at Deer Valley in July and Aug.). Oakley Rodeo (Thurs. to Sat. on the July fourth weekend; 15 miles east of Park City). Utah Cycling Festival (major bicycle event with road race, criterium, and time trial stages).

**August:** Shakespeare Festival continues. Utah Symphony Summer Series continues. Deer Valley Chamber Music Festival. Art Festival (about 200 artists exhibit their work on Main St.). Shootout at Jeremy Ranch (senior PGA golf tournament).

**September:** Deer Valley Bluegrass Festival. Miners' Day Celebration (parade and mucking and drilling contests held on Labor Day weekend). Autumn Aloft Hot-Air Balloon Festival (dozens of balloons take flight over Park City, 2 weeks after Labor Day weekend). Rugby Challenge Cup (2 weeks after Labor Day weekend).

**November:** Ski areas open!

**December:** Christmas in the Park (lighting of community tree, carols, and a visit by Santa). Christmas Eve Torchlight Parade (skiers descend the slopes with torches at Park City Ski Area). Santa Claus on the Mountain (Santa takes to skis to give treats to the kids at Park

City Ski Area). New Year's Eve Fireworks at ParkWest ring in the new year with a bang; check before coming out.

**Recreation**

**Winter sports** draw the most visitors to Park City! Because the ski areas near Salt Lake City and here are so close together; all have been listed with each other under "Salt Lake City Skiing," pp. 61-65.

The **Alpine Slide** gives the thrill of a toboggan ride for summer visitors. A chairlift takes you to the start of a 3,000-foot track that twists and winds down the hillside. No special skills are needed to ride the sled. Open late May to mid-Sept.: weekdays noon-10 p.m., weekends 10 a.m.-10 p.m.; located at Park City Ski Area; tel. 649-7150. Play the **Silver Putt Miniature Golf Course** at Park City Ski Area; open same hours as the Alpine Slide; tel. 649-7150. Ride the **Gondola** up the mountains on a 22-minute ride to the Summit House Restaurant, elev. 9,300 ft.; runs Fri. to Mon. and holidays 11 a.m.-5 p.m. through the summer; Park City Ski Area; tel. 649-8111.

Golfers have a choice of three 18-hole courses. **Park City Municipal Golf Course** is at Park Ave. and Thaynes Canyon Dr.; tel. 649-8701. **Park Meadows Golf Club's** course, designed by Jack Nicklaus, is the longest in the state at 7,340 yards; 2000 Meadows Dr.; tel. 649-2460. **Jeremy Ranch Golf Course** was designed by Arnold Palmer; players must be members or guests of members; located 8 miles north of Park City on the I-80 frontage road; tel. 649-2088.

Though expensive, a flight aboard a hot-air balloon is an exhilarating experience. Balloons take off in the early morning year-round, weather permitting. Typical costs are $75/30 minutes, $135/one hour with **Balloon the Rockies** (tel. 645-7433), **Balloon Adventures** (tel. 645-8787), **Balloon Affaire** (tel. 649-1217), **Balloon Biz** (Park Meadows; tel. 278-7208), **Moon's Balloons** (tel. 645-9092), and **Sunrise Fantasy Balloon** (tel. 645-7499).

The **city park** next to the library has picnic tables, playground, volleyball, basketball, and ball fields. **Park City Recreation Dept.** organizes classes in art, music, folk dancing, gymnastics, aerobics, karate, and a variety of sports; tel. 649-9321. The **Norwegian School of Nature Life** is a nonprofit organization offering cross-country ski tours and instruction, snowshoeing, hiking, backpacking, canoeing, and mountain-bike treks for people of all ages; tel. 649-5322.

**Prospector Athletic Club** has an indoor pool, racquetball and tennis courts, gym,

*Park City looking south ca. 1900*

weight room, saunas, jacuzzi, and classes; open daily at the Prospector Square Hotel, 2200 Sidewinder Dr.; tel. 649-6670. **Park City Racquet Club** features an outdoor pool, racquetball and tennis courts, and saunas at 1200 Little Kate Rd.; tel. 649-8080.

## Services

The **post office** is downtown at 450 Main St.; tel. 649-9191. **Park City Family Health and Emergency Center** provides care 24 hours a day; located in the Holiday Village Mall, 1800 Park Ave.; tel. 649-7640. For **emergencies** (police, fire, or medical) dial 911.

Bicycles (mountain and road), camping gear, and cross-country skis can be purchased and rented at **White Pine Touring;** tours on cross-country skis and mountain bicycles can be arranged too; 363 Main St.; tel. 649-8710. **Herman's World of Sporting Goods** has skiing, hiking, camping, fishing, and other outdoor gear in Holiday Village Mall, 1780 Park Ave.; tel. 649-6922. **Recreation Rental** rents snowmobiles in winter and Honda 4-wheelers in summer; located near Guardsman Pass (a shuttle service is provided from town in winter); tel. 649-FUNN. **Park City Adventure Center** serves as a reservation center for many of Park City's activities; 514 Main St.; tel. 649-1217 or (800) 648-1217.

## Information

**Park City Area Chamber/Bureau** has excellent vacation planners and other free literature; staff know of upcoming events and will answer your questions. Stop by the Visitor Information Center at the Park City Museum, 528 Main St. (Box 1630, Park City, UT 84060); tel. 649-6100, (800) 640-6420 in Utah, or (800) 453-1360 out of state. The main office is in Prospector Square at 1910 Prospector Ave.; staff here provide help for convention planning and for new residents; open Mon. to Fri. 8 a.m.-5 p.m. (same phone numbers and mailing address). Park City's **public library** is in a historic brick building, originally dedicated in 1904 as a miners' hospital; it has a good collection of regional books and maps; open Sun. noon-4 p.m., Mon. to Thurs. 10 a.m.-9 p.m, and Fri. and Sat. 10 a.m.-6 p.m.; at 1354 Park Ave.; tel. 649-8118. **Dolly's Book Store** has a selection of regional and general reading books and topo maps at 510 Main St.; tel. 649-8062.

## Transport

During the ski season, **Park City Transit** operates a trolley bus up and down Main St. (about every 10 minutes from 10 a.m. to 11 p.m. daily) and has several bus routes to other parts of town, including Park City and Deer Valley ski areas (about every 10-20 minutes from 7:30 a.m. to 12:30 a.m. daily). Services may also be available in summer with shorter hours. All buses are free; pick up a transit guide from the Visitor Information Center or any of the buses or call Park City Transit; tel. 649-6660. **ParkWest** runs a free shuttle to their ski area during the ski season from lodges at the other ski resorts; tel. 649-5400. **Park City Transportation** provides year-round services to Salt Lake City downtown ($15 one way) and airport ($15 one way); ski shuttles in the winter ($20 round trip) go to Brighton, Solitude, Snowbird, Alta, or Sundance ski areas; call 2 days in advance for reservations and to check if a passenger minimum applies; tel. 649-8567 (Park City), 539-7944 (Salt Lake City), or (800) 637-3803 (out of state). **Lewis Bros. Stages** has a scheduled express service during the ski season with downtown Salt Lake City ($7 one way, $12 roundtrip) and airport ($13 one way, $24 roundtrip); a ski shuttle also connects Park City with Solitude, Brighton, Snowbird, Alta, or Sundance ski areas during the winter ($10 one way, $17 roundtrip); tel. 649-2256 (Park City), 359-8347 (Salt Lake City), or (800) 826-5844; reservations are recommended 2 days in advance for these trips.

Rent cars from **Avis** (tel. 649-7419), **Budget** (tel. 649-7554), **General** (tel. 645-7740/8582), **Hertz** (tel. 649-5022), **Park City Rent-A-Car** (tel. 649-5499), or **Summit Car & Truck Rental** (tel. 649-9140). For a taxi, call **Deer Valley Transit** (tel. 649-TAXI), **Park City Taxi** (tel. 649-8515), or **Snow Park Taxi** (tel. 649-5499/8515).

# VICINITY OF PARK CITY

Enjoying the outdoors comes naturally to visitors and residents of Park City. The invigorating climate and surrounding mountains encourage exploration of the high forests and tundra, with wildflowers in summer and endless views in any season. Relics of the mining past lie scattered about. You're likely to come across miners' cabins in all states of decay, hoist buildings, aerial tramway towers, rusting machinery, and great piles of mine tailings. Unlike other parts of the Wasatch Range, most of the land here belongs to mining companies and other private owners. Visitors need to keep a distance from mine shafts, which can be hundreds of feet deep, and respect "no trespassing" signs. *Park City Trails* by Raye Ringholz describes many hiking and ski touring possibilities in the area, along with a history and walking tour of Park City.

# COALVILLE AND VICINITY

In 1858, when William Smith noticed that wheat spilled here from wagons grew to maturity, he decided that this area would be a good place to settle. Smith returned the following spring with several families to begin farming. Coal mines discovered by the pioneers provided additional income and gave the community its name. Today coal has lost importance, but a large oil and gas field discovered in the 1970s holds future promise. Coalville (pop. 1,100), the Summit County seat, lies 40 miles east of Salt Lake City on I-80 near the confluence of Chalk Creek and the Weber (pronounced "WEE-ber") River. The nearby Rockport and Echo reservoirs attract fishermen and boaters.

## Practicalities

Stay at **A Country Inn/Blonquist Motel** (99 S. Main; tel. 336-2451; $22-40) or **Moore's Motel** (90 S. Main; tel. 336-5991; $25.07 s, $30.52 d). **Flying W RV Resort** offers tent sites ($7.63) and RV sites ($7.63 no hookups; $14.17 w/hookups) year-round; has showers and store; tel. 336-2969; located just off I-80 Coalville Exit 164. **Dean's Coffee Shop,** 53 S. Main, and a couple of fast-food places offer meals. A big **Fishing Derby** is held in June at Echo Reservoir, 3.5 miles to the north. In August, the **Summit County Fair** features a parade, rodeo, horse show, roping, demolition derby, entertainment, and exhibits. The **city park** has picnicking, playground, and tennis courts, 4 blocks east of the junction of Main and Center. For visitor information, stop by the **city hall** at 8 N. Main; tel. 336-5981. **Coalville Health Center** provides medical care, 82 N. 50 East; tel. 336-4403.

## Rockport State Park

Rockport Reservoir (1,189 surface acres) is tucked in the Weber River Valley 13 miles south of Coalville. Visitors enjoy fishing, water skiing, sailing, windsurfing, and swimming. Fishermen come to reel in rainbow, cutthroat, and German brown trout and smallmouth bass. The Weber River above and below the lake also has good fishing for trout and whitefish. During freeze-up, from Dec. to April, fishermen try their luck through the lake ice. Like most high-country lakes, Rockport (elev. 6,100 ft.) is usually calm in the mornings and evenings, but windy in the afternoons. The state park facilities are along the eastern shore with a paved boat ramp, docks, 3 picnic areas with covered tables, 8 primitive campgrounds, and the modern Juniper Campground (with showers). In summer, the marina has a store, snack bar, boat rentals, and boat storage. Windsurfing instruction and rentals at the lake are offered too. Cabin rentals may be available. Reservations are recommended for Juniper Campground on summer weekends, though there's usually plenty of space in the primitive campgrounds. The main season runs April to Oct., but a camping area is kept open for winter visitors. Entrance fees are $3 day use, $5 primitive camping, and $8 for Juniper Campground. Fishermen may park in highway pullouts on the lake's west side without charge. Contact the park at 9040 North, State Hwy. 302, Rockport, UT 84036; tel. 336-2241 (ranger), 538-7221 (Salt Lake City), or (800) 322-3770 (reservations). Rockport

State Park is 45 miles east of Salt Lake City; take I-80 Wanship Exit 156 and go south 5 miles on US 189.

### Echo Reservoir
This privately owned reservoir between Coalville and Echo averages about 1,000 surface acres. **Echo Park Resort,** in a grove of large cottonwood trees on the eastern shore, has a paved boat ramp, picnicking and camping, and a snack bar. Fishing, mostly for rainbow and brown trout and channel catfish, is fair to good. Water skiing and sailing are the most popular lake activities. Open early May through Sept.; fees are $3 parking, $4 boat launch, $6.75 tent or RV camping w/hookups; tel. 336-9894/2247. Take I-80 Coalville Exit 164 and go north 3.5 miles (or take I-80 Echo Exit 169 and go south 2 miles).

### Echo
An old railroad town at the junction of I-80 and I-84, 5 miles north of Coalville. The **Kozy Cafe and Motel** (tel. 336-5641) and the **Echo Cafe** serve travelers. I-80 enters Echo Canyon east of here, following the route used by Indians, fur trappers, Mormon pioneers, and the first transcontinental railroad.

## MORGAN AND VICINITY

Mormons settled here along the Weber River in 1852 and named their community after one of its members. The town (pop. 2,100) is the Morgan County seat and a center for farming, livestock raising, and dairying. Morgan lies 21 miles southeast of Ogden and just a few miles east of the Wasatch Range. Nearby attractions include Devil's Slide, Lost Creek Reservoir, and East Canyon Reservoir. Look for **Devil's Slide** 7.5 miles east of Morgan on the south side of I-84; the natural rock formation resembles a giant playground slide; view areas allow a stop for a better look.

### Practicalities
The old **Como Springs Resort** has a restaurant (open daily for lunch and dinner); follow Commercial St. east past the fairgrounds and across a bridge; tel. 829-3489. Morgan also

has the **Spring Chicken Inn Cafe** (open daily for breakfast, lunch, and dinner; 4 N. State; tel. 829-6062) and several fast-food places. Rodeo action takes place during **Morgala Days** in late June and at the **Morgan County Fair** in August. **Round Valley Golf & Country Club** maintains a 9-hole golf course, tennis courts, and a campground ($5; showers available) at 1875 E. Round Valley Rd. (go east 2.8 miles on 100 South); tel. 829-3796. The county clerk's office knows about events and services of the area, 48 W. Young St. (across from Spring Chicken Inn Cafe); tel. 829-6811.

### Lost Creek State Park
Steep hillsides covered with grass, sage, and groves of evergreens surround the 365-acre reservoir. Picnicking and camping are primitive; there are outhouses but no established sites, tables, or drinking water. The east arm has a paved boat ramp. Fishermen catch mostly rainbow trout. No entrance or camping fees; for info contact East Canyon State Park; tel. 829-6866 (538-7221 in Salt Lake City).

*yellowbelly marmot* (Marmota flaviventris)

The graveled access road is normally open to vehicles from mid-May to mid-Oct.; elevation at the lake is 6,000 feet. Snowmobilers may come in winter to ice fish. Take I-84 Devil's Slide/Croydon Exit 111, go northeast 2 miles past a cement plant to the small farming town of Croydon, then turn left 13 miles to Lost Creek Reservoir. Or take I-84 Henefer Exit 115 and turn northwest 4.5 miles to Croydon, then right 13 miles to the reservoir.

### East Canyon State Park

East Canyon Reservoir is one of the closest mountain lakes to Salt Lake City (38 miles). It's also close to Ogden (33 miles) and Morgan (12 miles). The 600-acre lake is about 6 miles long and 1½ miles wide; elevation is 5,700 feet. Power boating, water skiing, and angling are the most popular activities. Fishing is good for kokanee salmon and rainbow trout in the lake and in East Canyon Creek. You'll find a marina and most of the state park facilities at the lake's north end. The marina is open from late May to mid-Sept. with a store, snack bar, boat storage, slips, and boat rentals (fishing boats with or without motors, canoes, jet skis, paddle boats, and ski boats); tel. 829-3498. A beach east of the marina is popular with swimmers and picnickers. The state park is open all year; facilities at the north end of the lake include a paved boat ramp, picnic area, and campground (water but no showers). Parking areas with outhouses are along the east side and at the south end. Camping reservations are recommended for summer weekends. The park office can be reached at Box 97, Morgan, UT 84050; tel. 829-6866 (538-7221 in Salt Lake City), or (800) 322-3770 (reservations). Entrance fees are $3 for day use at the recreation area and at the south end of the lake, $5 for camping at the 5 primitive areas, and $6 for developed camping at the north end. **East Canyon Resort,** ¼ mile south of the reservoir, has a restaurant open to the public. For the most scenic way in from Salt Lake City, go east on the road through Emigration Canyon, then turn left on UT 65 over the Wasatch Range at Big Mountain Pass (elev. 7,420 ft.); forests of aspen, maple, and oak near the pass blaze with colors in autumn. A faster route is east on I-80 to Exit 134, then UT 65 over Big Mountain Pass. Northern approaches are I-84 Morgan Exit 103 or 104, then south on UT 66 (best route in winter) or I-84 Henefer Exit 113 or 115, then south on UT 65.

**East Canyon Outfitters** offers a variety of horseback rides along the Mormon Trail and other areas in the Wasatch Range. The stables are south of East Canyon State Park on UT 65; tel. 355-3460.

*porcupine*
(Erethizon dorsatum)

# OGDEN

Travelers enjoy a stop here to see the museums, historic sites, and scenic spots. Ogden Canyon, beginning on the east edge of town, is the gateway to lakes, campgrounds, hiking trails, and 3 downhill ski areas in the Wasatch Range. Ogden lies 35 miles north of Salt Lake City at the foot of the Wasatch Range.

## History

Tribes of nomadic Shoshoni Indians chose the confluence of the Weber and Ogden rivers as a winter camp because of the relatively mild climate, good fishing and hunting, and plentiful grass for their horses. This same location, the site of present-day Ogden, was also used in the winter of 1825-26 by a group of American fur trappers with their Indian wives and children. The Shoshoni maintained friendly relations with the new Americans and continued to camp in the area. Peter Skene Ogden of the British Hudson's Bay Co. explored and trapped in the upper reaches of the Ogden and Weber valleys, but he never descended to the site of the city that bears his name. In 1846, Miles Goodyear established an out-of-the-way trading post and stockade here, one of the first permanent settlements in Utah, and named it Fort Buenaventura. When Mormons arrived at the site of Salt Lake City in 1847, Goodyear, a former mountain man, felt too crowded. He sold out to the Mormons and left for California. Captain James Brown of the Mormon Battalion, who negotiated the purchase, moved in with his family. In 1849, Brigham Young visited the site, then known as Brownsville, and thought it favorable for settlement. The following year he sent 100 families to found the town of Ogden. The pioneer community suffered floods, drought, early frosts, insects, cholera, and Indian attacks, but managed to get by. At times residents had to supplement their meager harvests with roots of sego lilies, thistles, and other wild plants. Arrival of the transcontinental railroad in 1869 changed Ogden forever. Although the Golden Spike had been driven at Promontory Summit, 55 miles northwest, Ogden earned the title "Junction City" as lines branched from it through Utah and into surrounding states. New industries and an expanding non-Mormon population transformed the sleepy farm town into a bustling city. Today, Ogden (pop.

69,000) serves as a major administrative, manufacturing, and livestock center for the intermountain West.

Mormon pioneers laid out the city in their typically neat fashion, but adopted a different street-naming system. Streets running east-west are numbered beginning with 1st St. in the north of town to 47th St. in the south; streets running north-south commemorate U.S. presidents and other historical figures. The intersection of 25th St. and Washington Blvd. is usually considered the city's center.

## SIGHTS

### Union Station Museums

Travelers thronged into this cavernous building during the grand old days of railroading. Completed in 1924, it saw more than 120 trains stopping daily during the peak WW II

---

# OGDEN

1. Ogden Nature Center
2. Fort Buenaventura
3. Union Station (museums and tourist office)
4. Marshall White Center (pool)
5. bus station (Greyhound)
6. Egyptian Theatre
7. Ogden City Mall
8. Temple Square (Mormon Temple and Tabernacle, Pioneer Museum, and Miles Goodyear Cabin)
9. Municipal Gardens and local bus information booth
10. post office (downtown branch)
11. U.S. Forest Service (Ogden Ranger District)
12. Eccles Community Art Center
13. Weber County Library
14. Lorin Farr Park (pool)
15. Ben Lomond Community Pool
16. El Monte Golf Course
17. Ogden Community Pool
18. Mount Ogden Park and Golf Course
19. Weber State College (entrance and information booth)
20. McKay-Dee Hospital
21. Dee Events Center

---

years. Now, though, Union Station echoes mostly with memories. Visit the main lobby to see murals done in 1978 when the city restored the station to its former glory. The South Mural shows workers of the Central Pacific building the first transcontinental railroad from Sacramento (note the many Chinese laborers); the North Mural pictures the Union Pacific laying their line from Omaha. Special shows and performances occasionally take place in the lobby or at the M.S. Browning Theatre. The Golden Spike Empire Information Center office off the lobby supplies local travel information; open Mon. to Sat. 8 a.m.-8 p.m. and Sun. 10 a.m.-6 p.m.; tel. 399-8288 or (800) ALL-UTAH out of state. Union Station also houses shops that sell train, antique, and gift items. The museums and a small art gallery in the station are well worth a visit. A single ticket gives admission to all exhibits; purchase it from the gift shop in the lobby: $2 adult, $1 children 12 and under, and $1.50 age 65 and over. Open Mon. to Sat. 10 a.m.-6 p.m. (also Sun. 1-5 p.m. in summer); tel. 629-8444. Union Station is at 25th St. and Wall Avenue.

**Browning-Kimball Car Museum** displays a glittering collection of about a dozen antique autos, ranging from a one-cylinder 1901 Oldsmobile to a 16-cylinder 1930 Cadillac sport sedan. Chicago gangsters once owned the 1931 Pierce Arrow—probably the museum's most famous car; note the built-in gun holster. The Utah license plate exhibit shows every tag from 1915, when they were first issued, to the present.

**Wattis-Dumke Railroad Museum** uses highly detailed dioramas to illustrate railroad scenes and construction feats. Eight model trains (HO scale) roll through the Ogden rail yard, wind through the Sierra and Humboldt Palisades, cross the Great Salt Lake on the Lucin Cutoff, and descend Weber Canyon. Exhibits and photos show railroading history and great trains, such as the "Big Boys" that weighed more than one million pounds and pulled heavy freights up the mountain ranges. A documentary film about the first transcontinental railroad is shown on request. Outside, just to the south of the station, you can visit giant diesel locomotives and some cabooses; ask for tour times.

The **Natural History Museum** displays beautiful rocks, minerals, and gemstones. Fossils reveal dinosaurs and other life forms of long ago. Indian artifacts and crafts can be seen too.

**Browning Firearms Museum** (upstairs) contains the gun shop and many examples of firearms invented by the Browning family. John M. Browning (1855-1926), a genius in his field, held 75 major gun patents. He developed the world's first successful automatic firearms, which used gases from the bullet to expel the old shell, load a new one, and cock the mechanism. The skillfully done exhibits have both military and civilian handguns, automatic weapons, rifles, and shotguns. A 17-minute slide show illustrates the Browning family's story and their advancement of firearms design.

**Myra Powell Art Gallery** (also upstairs) displays paintings, sculpture, and photography in a former pigeon roost. Exhibits rotate monthly.

### Historic 25th Street
The 2 blocks of 25th St. in front of Union Station still have many buildings from Ogden's early years. The Mormons, followed by new immigrants of many nationalities, built their grocery and hardware stores, blacksmith shops, livery stables, hotels, and restaurants here. The historic district is slowly being restored. Pick up a brochure detailing histories of many of these buildings from the Golden Spike Empire tourist office in Union Station.

### Egyptian Theatre
You can't miss the unusual facade of this venerable building! The interior of this "atmospheric theater" has a sun that moves across the ceiling, floating clouds, and glittering stars. Restoration is currently taking place. When done, it will be open as a performing arts theater. Contact the Golden Spike Information Center for opening dates.

### Pioneer Museum And The Miles Goodyear Cabin
Drop in to examine the furnishings, clothes, and crafts of the Mormon pioneers. Walk behind the museum to see the Goodyear cabin, probably the oldest non-Indian structure in Utah. It was built in about 1845 of cottonwood logs and later moved here from its original site near the Weber River. The cabin can be seen even when the museum is closed. Pioneer Museum is open Mon. to Sat. 10 a.m.-5 p.m. from May 15 to Sept. 15; free; tel. 393-4460. The former Weber Stake Relief Society building (1902) that houses the museum is on Grant Ave. between 21st and 22nd in Tabernacle Square.

### Ogden Temple And Tabernacle
The modern temple of white cast stone and reflective glass has a central gold spire much like the Provo Temple. In fact, both temples were designed by the same architect and completed about the same time. Dedicated in Jan. 1972, the Ogden Temple contains 283 rooms on 4 levels, efficiently accommodating many people while retaining a reverent atmosphere. Only Mormons engaged in sacred ordinance work may enter. The white-steepled Ogden Tabernacle, completed in 1956, sits just to the north. Visitors are welcome inside the tabernacle; exhibits and short video programs about the Mormon faith may be available; 2133 Washington Blvd. on Tabernacle Square; tel. 627-1627.

### Fort Buenaventura State Park
Miles Goodyear built the original Fort Buenaventura in 1846 to serve as a trading post and way station for travelers crossing the remote Great Basin region. Now a replica of the tiny fort provides a link with Utah's mountain-man past. Researchers excavated the original site and pored through historical documents so that reconstruction would be authentic. The location, dimensions, and materials used for the stockade and 3 cabins inside closely follow the originals. Volunteers often have displays and presentations inside the cabins daily in the summer and weekends in spring and autumn. Special programs are scheduled too. Weekly summer events include bluegrass jam sessions, music presentations, and melodramas. You might also catch the mountainman rendezvous each Easter weekend or the crafts fair held on July 24. Check program schedules with the Golden Spike Empire of-

fice (tel. 399-8288) or the park office (tel. 621-4808). Trees and grass surrounding the fort provide a peaceful setting near downtown. The park has a picnic area and a pond, popular for canoeing in summer and ice skating in winter. Groups of 20 or more can reserve a campground. Open daily in summer 8 a.m.-9 p.m. (reduced hours the rest of the year); $3/vehicle or $1/person walk in. From downtown Ogden, take 24th St. west across the rail yard and Weber River, turn left on "A" Ave., and follow signs to 2450 A Ave. (Ogden, UT 84401).

### Eccles Community Art Center
Exhibits display the best regional paintings, sculpture, photography, and other media. Shows change monthly. The ornate mansion that houses the art center is an attraction in itself. Turrets, cut glass, and carved woodwork decorate the brick and sandstone structure, built in 1893 in a Richardsonian Romanesque style. The carriage house in back contains a sales gallery. Open Mon. to Fri. 9 a.m.-5 p.m. and Sat. 10 a.m.-4 p.m.; 2580 Jefferson Ave.; tel. 392-6935.

### Ogden Nature Center
The 127 acres of wildlife sanctuary on the outskirts of Ogden provide a place for children and adults to learn about nature. Trails lead through woods, wetlands, and open fields. Deer, porcupines, muskrats, rabbits, snakes, and about 130 species of birds have been spotted here. Ecology exhibits in the pioneer farmhouse include a see-through beehive and displays of local creatures and plants. Animals not ready to be released into the wild can be seen in cages outside. Visitors are welcome to use the picnic area. Call for information on summer camps and other children's programs or to arrange a tour. Open Mon. to Sat. 10 a.m.-4 p.m.; $1 age 4 and up; tel. 621-7595. Located northwest of downtown at 966 W. 12th St. (Ogden, UT 84404).

### Hill Air Force Base Museum And Park
Construction of Hill Field began in 1940, just in time to serve the aircraft maintenance and storage needs of the military during the hectic WW II years. The decades since have seen a parade of nearly every type of bomber, fighter, helicopter, and missile belonging to the U.S. Air Force. More than 30 of these can be seen close up in outdoor and indoor exhibits at Hill AFB Museum. A B-17 and B-29 represent the distinguished bombers of WW II, while jet fighters and bombers trace the development of modern aircraft. Several helicopters show the varied shapes and sizes that have flown. The R4B helicopter indoors dates from WW II. Other exhibits inside include flight simulators,

*B-29 at Hill AFB Musuem*

missiles, a Norden bombsight, uniforms, aircraft art, and models. The gift shop sells posters, books, T-shirts, models, and other souvenirs. Groups can sometimes arrange tours by calling in advance. Chances are you'll see jets from the adjacent air force base streaking overhead on training missions. Open all year Tues. to Fri. 9 a.m.-3 p.m., Sat. 9 a.m.-5 p.m., and Sun. 11 a.m.-5 p.m.; hours and exhibits will expand when the new museum building opens; donation; tel. 777-6818/8623. Located 5 miles south of Ogden on I-15; take Roy Exit 341 and follow signs east 0.2 mile.

# WEBER STATE UNIVERSITY

Weber (WEE-ber) State University emphasizes undergraduate education, though the 4-year school also has a few graduate programs in education and business. The school began in 1889 as Weber Stake Academy under the Mormon Church, then became a state-supported junior college in 1933, Weber State College in 1963, and Weber State University in 1991. It now operates on a 4-quarter system with a student population of about 11,000 and faculty and staff of 1,000. The institution serves largely as a community college for the Ogden area. Visitors are welcome on campus for the natural history museum, art gallery, library, recreational facilities, and a variety of cultural and sporting events. Obtain a free parking permit and map at the information

booth along the main entrance road off 3750 Harrison Blvd.; tel. 626-6975. Tours can be arranged too; tel. 626-6348. A clock tower at the center of campus makes a handy landmark, so it's hard to get lost. Weber State University is southeast of downtown on a bench of prehistoric Lake Bonneville; the Wasatch Range rises steeply behind. Mailing address is Ogden, UT 85508.

## Natural History Museum
This small museum has a little of everything: dioramas of native wildlife in realistic habitats, a fierce allosaurus skeleton, geology exhibits, and more. A Foucault pendulum swings in a hallway. Open weekdays 8 a.m.-5 p.m. during school terms; free. Located on the main floor of the circular Lind Lecture Hall; tel. 626-6160. The Layton Ott Planetarium presents star shows on Wed. evenings from Sept. to May; tel. 626-6160.

## Collett Art Gallery
Almost anything could be on display in the Collett Art Building during the late Sept. to early June season. Open Mon. to Thurs. 8 a.m.-10 p.m. and Fri. 8 a.m.-4 p.m.; tel. 626-6455.

## Shepherd Union Building
The social center of campus. On the first floor are the post office and bookstore (good selection of general reading, art supplies, WSC clothing and souvenirs, and topo maps of the area). On the second floor you'll find an information desk, movie theater, bowling alley, game room, and snack bar. Head to the third floor for the cafeteria and another level up for fine dining in the Sky Room (lunch and dinner).

## Recreation, Sports, And Events
Swenson Gymnasium offers swimming, racquetball, tennis, basketball, indoor track, and weight room facilities to the public; south end of campus; tel. 626-6466. Wilderness Recreation Center rents bicycles, white-water kayaks, rafts, cross-country skis, camping gear, and other sports equipment; located next to Swenson Gymnasium; open year-round Mon. to Fri. 9 a.m.-5 p.m., Sat. 8 a.m.-5 p.m., and

Sun. 2-5 p.m.; tel. 626-6373. Weber State University belongs to the Big Sky Athletic Conference for men's athletics and the Mountain West Athletic Conference for women. Basketball, football, and popular concerts take place in the 12,000-seat Dee Events Center; tel. 626-8500. Concerts, theater, opera, and ballet performances usually take place in the Val A. Browning Center (tel. 626-7000).

## ACCOMMODATIONS

### Motels And Hotels
See the chart on page 100.

### Campgrounds
**Century Mobile Home and RV Park** has showers, swimming pool, game room, store, and laundry. Sites are open all year: $13.11 tent or RV without hookups, $17.75 w/hookups; tel. 731-3800. Located at 1399 W. 21st St. (I-15 Exit 346, then one block west on Wilson Lane). Nearby campgrounds are described under "Salt Lake City Campgrounds" (pp. 47, 50), "East of Ogden" (pp. 103-105), and "Willard Bay State Park" (pp. 106).

## FOOD

### American
**Chick's Cafe** is a favorite breakfast spot; open Mon. to Sat. for breakfast, lunch, and dinner at 319 24th St.; tel. 621-9159. **Graycliff Lodge** serves steak and seafood in a romantic setting; open Sun. brunch and Tues. to Sun. for dinner at 508 Ogden Canyon (5 miles up Ogden Canyon on the left); tel. 392-6775. The **Oak Tree Restaurant** has steak and other American favorites; also a private club and country-western dancing; open Sun. to Fri. for lunch and Wed., Fri., and Sat. for dinner at 460 W. 12th St.; tel. 393-8616. **Prairie Schooner** fixes steak, prime rib, and shrimp in an informal Western atmosphere (dine in a covered wagon!); open daily for dinner at 445 Park Blvd.; tel. 392-2712. **Tamarack Restaurant** is open 24 hours daily and has live country music Tues. to Sat. nights at 1254 W. 21st St. (near I-15 21st St. Exit); tel. 393-8691. **Timber Mine** serves steak and seafood in a

rustic mine decor; open daily for dinner at 1701 Park Blvd.; tel. 393-2155. **Ye Lion's Den** has steak, prime rib, and seafood in an old English atmosphere; open daily for lunch and dinner at 3607 Washington Blvd.; tel. 399-5804. **Zito's Fireside Supper Club & Steak House** features steak and seafood in an elegant setting; open Mon. to Sat. for dinner at 7695 S. US 89 (mouth of Weber Canyon at Uinta); tel. 479-4640.

### Chinese
**Bamboo Noodle Parlor** features steak, seafood, and noodle dishes; open daily except Tues. for lunch and dinner at 2426 Grant Ave.; tel. 394-6091. **Ho Wah's Restaurant** serves Chinese and American favorites; open daily for lunch and dinner at 2454 Monroe Blvd.; tel. 621-2036. **Kim Wah's** offers Cantonese and American dining; open Mon. and Wed. to Sat. for lunch and daily except Tues. for dinner at 350 37th St.; tel. 392-7761. **Lee's Mongolian Barbecue** prepares Mongolian and Mandarin dishes; open Mon. to Sat. for lunch and dinner at 2866 Washington Blvd.; tel. 621-9120. **Eastern Winds Restaurant** serves Mandarin and Cantonese styles; open Mon.-Sat. for lunch and daily for dinner at 3740 Washington Blvd.; tel. 627-2739. **Star Noodle Parlor** has popular Chinese and American dishes; open daily except Mon. for dinner at 225 Historic 25th St.; tel. 394-6331.

### Continental
**Bavarian Chalet** features German gourmet cooking; open Tues. to Sat. for dinner at 4387 Harrison Blvd. (across from Dee Event Center); tel. 479-7561. **La Ferrovia Ristorante** presents pasta, pizza, sandwiches, and other items; open Tues. to Sat. for lunch and dinner in the south end of Union Station, 2501 Wall Ave.; tel. 394-8628. **Berconi's Pasta House** has a long menu of veal and chicken specialties, pasta dishes, and pizza; open for Sun. brunch, Mon. to Sat. for lunch, and daily for dinner at 4850 Harrison Blvd.; tel. 479-4414. **Paisano's Restaurant** offers Italian-American cuisine including veal parmesan, pasta, pizza, lamb, halibut, and steaks; open Tues. to Sat. for dinner at 3050 Grant Ave.; tel. 392-9701. **Piccolo Brothers** fixes home-style

# OGDEN ACCOMMODATIONS

Add 9.25% tax to all prices

| MOTEL/HOTEL | ADDRESS | RATES | PHONE | FEATURES |
| --- | --- | --- | --- | --- |
| Big Z Motel | 1123 W. 21st St. | $25-34 | 394-6632 | kitchenettes |
| Colonial Motel | 1269 Washington Blvd. | $23-29 | 399-5851 | kitchenettes |
| Flying J Motel (Best Western) | 1206 W. 21st St. | $35-49 | 393-8644 or (800) 528-1234 | pool, 24-hour restaurant |
| High Country Inn (Best Western) | 1335 W. 12th St. | $34-95 | 394-9474 or (800) 528-1234 | pool |
| Holiday Inn Ogden | 3306 Washington Blvd. | $44-59 | 399-5671 or (800) 465-4329 | indoor pool |
| Millstream Motel (Budget Host) | 1450 Washington Blvd. | $24-44 | 394-9425 or (800) 835-7427 | kitchenettes |
| Motel Orleans | 1825 Washington Blvd. | $26-34 | 621-8350 | kitchenettes, pool |
| Motel 6 | 1455 Washington Blvd. | $24-30 | 627-4560 | pool |
| Mt. Lomond Motel | 755 N. Harrisville Rd. | $20-24 | 782-7477 | kitchenettes |
| Ogden Imperial Motel | 1956 Washington Blvd. | $25-28 | 393-8667 | kitchenettes, pool |
| Ogden Park Hotel | 247 24th St. | $69-99 | 627-1190 (800) 367-4939 (UT), (800) 421-7599 (out) | indoor pool |
| Quality Inn | 5000 S. 1500 West | $40-69 | 627-2880 or (800) 221-2222 | pool, tennis |
| Radisson Suite Hotel | 2510 Washington Blvd. | $39-89 | 627-1900 or (800) 228-9822 | suites, health club |
| Super 8 Motel of Ogden | 1508 W. 21st St. | $27-41 | 731-7100 or (800) 848-8888 | |
| TraveLodge Ogden | 2110 Washington Blvd. | $36-48 | 394-4563 or (800) 255-3050 | pool |
| Western Colony Inn | 234 24th St. | $20-49 | 627-1332 | kitchenettes |

Italian pasta dishes and hand-tossed pizza; open daily for dinner at 1303 Washington Blvd.; tel. 399-0618; and at 4553 S. 300 West; tel. 394-3361. The **Radisson Hotel Restaurant** offers veal oscar, prime rib, and other specialties; open daily for breakfast, lunch, and dinner at 2510 Washington Blvd.; tel. 627-1900.

### Japanese
**Windy's Suki-Yaki** has a varied Japanese menu including teppanyaki and tempura cooking; open Tues. to Fri. for lunch, and Mon. to Sat. for dinner at 3809 Riverdale Rd.; tel. 621-4505.

### Mexican
**Casa Diego** is open Mon. to Sat. for lunch and dinner at 4387 Harrison Blvd. (across from Dee Event Center); tel. 479-8620. **El Matador** is open daily for lunch and dinner at 2564 Ogden Ave.; tel. 393-3151. **Fiesta Mexicana** is open daily for lunch and Mon. to Sat. for dinner at 236 24th St.; tel. 394-3310.

## OTHER PRACTICALITIES

### Entertainment And Events
Ogden has a busy calendar of theater, dance, festivals, shows, and sporting events. To find out what's going on, visit the Golden Spike Empire tourist office in Union Station; tel. 399-8288.

**January:** Winterfest/Hof Sister City Festival celebrates winter and Ogden's German sister city Hof with ski and dog-sled races and German food, music, and dancing.

**February:** President's Day ski races at Powder Mountain and Nordic Valley ski areas.

**March:** Golden Spike Gem and Mineral Show. Utah Gun Collectors Show. Home and Garden Show at Dee Events Center. Para-Ski Competition (a day of parachuting followed by a day of skiing) at Nordic Valley Ski Area.

**April:** Antique Show.

**May:** May Tenth Golden Spike Anniversary Celebration at Golden Spike Natl. Historic Site.

**June:** Utah State Railroad Festival in mid-June opens with "Junction Function," a sampling of food from area restaurants, then hand-

car races, entertainment, and a model railroad fair at Union Station. Morgala Days (rodeo and livestock shows) in Morgan. Utah Musical Theatre.

**July:** Pioneer Days (parade, rodeo, and crowning of Miss Rodeo Utah; held 19th-24th excluding Sun.). Corps Encore features competitions among top drum and bugle groups. Vintage Car Show and Swap Meet takes place at Liberty Park. Ogden Street Festival and Chili Cook Off has a 10K run, dog trick contests, sales booths, and chili. North Ogden Cherry Days celebrates North Ogden's favorite crop with a parade, food booths, and contests. Utah Musical Theatre continues.

**August:** Davis County Fair puts on a horse show, horse racing, livestock sale, and exhibits. Morgan County Fair and Rodeo has competing cowboys and cowgirls, horse show, horse racing, livestock sale, and exhibits. Roy Days celebrates with a parade, rodeo, and carnival. Railroaders' Festival at Promontory stages a reenactment of the transcontinental railroad completion with a spike-driving contest, steam engine demonstrations, and speeches at Golden Spike Natl. Historic Site. Utah Musical Theatre continues.

**September:** Autumnfest enlivens the month with entertainment, contests, craft exhibits, and food on the weekend after Labor Day at Union Station. Peach Days celebrates the harvest at Brigham City on the weekend after Labor Day. Golden Spike Bicycle Classic is a road race of about 85 miles from Promontory Summit to Ogden, also on the weekend after Labor Day.

**October:** Greek Festival celebrates Ogden's Greek heritage with food, dancing, and entertainment at the Greek Orthodox Church of the Transfiguration (674 42nd St.).

**November-December:** Christmas Village Lighting Ceremony and Parade enchant kids and adults with visiting Santas, animated figures, and lighted trees at Ogden Municipal Park. Christmas Tree Express has exhibits and charity sales of decorated Christmas trees, holiday foods, and handicrafts at Union Station.

### Recreation
Year-round swimming is offered at **Ben Lomond Community Pool** (1049 7th St.; tel.

629-8690), **Ogden Community Pool** (2875 Tyler Ave.; tel. 629-8693), and **Marshall White Center Pool** (222 28th St.; tel. 629-8646). The outdoor **Lorin Farr Community Pool** is open in summer at 1691 Gramercy Ave.; tel. 629-8691. **Wild Waters Water Slide Park** has still more ways to get wet in summer, 1750 S. 1350 West; tel. 629-8800. **Tennis courts** are located at many parks around the city; call the Ogden Parks Dept. for the one nearest you; tel. 629-8284. The **Ogden City Recreation Dept.** organizes many sports and crafts programs for children and adults; tel. 629-8253. **Classic Skating Center** has a roller-skating rink and waterslides at 4181 Riverdale Rd.; tel. 394-0822.

Enjoy golfing at any of these courses: 18-hole **Ben Lomond** (1600 N. 500 West; tel. 782-7754), 9-hole **El Monte** (1300 Valley Dr. at the mouth of Ogden Canyon; tel. 629-8333), 9-hole **Golf City Family Fun Center** (also has a lighted 18-hole miniature golf course; 1400 E. 5600 South; tel. 479-3410), 18-hole **Mt. Ogden** (30th and Taylor; tel. 629-8700), 9-hole **Nordic Valley** (15 miles east at 3567 Nordic Valley Way in Eden; tel. 745-3511), 18-hole **Schneiter's Riverside** (5460 S. Weber Dr.; tel. 399-4636), 18-hole **Valley View** (2501 E. Gentile in Layton; tel. 546-1630), 18-hole **The Barn** (305 W. Pleasant View Dr. in North Ogden; tel. 782-7320), and 18-hole **Wolf Creek** (15 miles east at 3900 N. Wolf Creek Dr. in Eden; tel. 745-3365).

You'll find good downhill skiing in the Wasatch Range 15-19 miles east of Ogden at Nordic Valley, Snowbasin, and Powder Mountain; see "East Of Ogden" below. **Cross-country skiers** can use the easy set tracks in Mt. Ogden Park and Golf Course at 30th and Taylor or head into the mountains for more challenging terrain. The Ogden Ranger District office of the U.S. Forest Service (25th and Adams Ave.; tel. 625-5112) has a list of popular cross-country and snowshoeing areas. The *Wasatch Ski Touring and Hiking Map #3* by Alpentech details routes near Ogden.

## Shopping

**Ogden City Mall** is a giant indoor shopping area with 5 department stores and more than 100 smaller shops and restaurants; open daily including Sun. afternoons, downtown at 24th and Washington Blvd.; tel. 621-2680. The **Newgate Mall** also has many stores; open daily including Sun. afternoons in the southwest part of town at Wall Ave. and Riverdale Rd.; tel. 621-1161. Outdoor supplies for camping, backpacking, and skiing (and rentals for both downhill and cross-country) can be obtained at **Alpine Sport Shop** (1165 Patterson; tel. 393-0066) and **Herman's World of Sporting Goods** (29th and Washington Blvd.; tel. 621-2263). **Ogden Touring Co.** (1742 Washington Blvd.; tel. 392-0851) specializes in cross-country ski sales and rentals, backpacking, and climbing gear.

## Services

In **emergencies** (police, fire, ambulance/paramedic) dial 911. The downtown **post office** is at 2641 Washington Blvd.; tel. 627-4184. Hospital care and physician referrals are provided by **McKay-Dee Hospital Center** (3939 Harrison Blvd.; tel. 627-2800) and **St. Benedict's Hospital** (5475 S. 500 East; tel. 479-2111). Minor medical problems can be handled at **NowCare,** 335 12th St.; tel. 394-7753.

## Information

The **Golden Spike Empire Information Center** in Union Station can tell you about the sights, facilities, and goings-on for Ogden and surrounding communities, Wall Ave. and 25th St. (Ogden, UT 84401); open Mon. to Sat. 8 a.m.-8 p.m. and Sun. 10 a.m.-6 p.m.; tel. 399-8288 or (800) ALL-UTAH out of state. Visit the **Ogden Ranger District** office of the U.S. Forest Service to find out about local road conditions, camping, hiking, horseback riding, ski touring, snowshoeing, and snowmobiling; the district covers the Wasatch Range from Kaysville to just south of Brigham City; open Mon. to Fri. 8 a.m.-4:30 p.m. at 507 25th St. and Adams Ave. (Ogden, UT 84401); tel. 625-5112.

Weber County's **main library** has good reading; open Mon. to Thurs. 10 a.m.-9 p.m., Fri. and Sat. 10 a.m.-6 p.m., and Sun. (Oct. to May) 1-5 p.m.; 2464 Jefferson Ave.; call for info on the county's 2 branch libraries; tel. 627-6913. Weber State College has the large **Stewart Library**; hikers can make photocopies of topo maps; open Mon. to Thurs. 7:30 a.m.-10 p.m., Fri. 7:30 a.m.-4:30 p.m., Sat. 9 a.m.-5 p.m., and Sun. 1-6 p.m.; shorter hours in summer and school breaks; tel. 626-6415/6403.

**Transport**
**Utah Transit Authority** (UTA) buses serve many areas of Ogden and head south to Salt Lake City and Provo; schedules operate Mon. to Sat. and have some late-night runs; one route goes several times to Salt Lake City on Sunday. UTA has an information booth at its main downtown bus stop in the city park at the corner of 25th and Washington Blvd.; open weekdays noon-5 p.m.; tel. 621-4636. **Greyhound** has long-distance service from the terminal at 25th and Grant Ave.; tel. 394-5573.

**Amtrak** trains depart from Union Station east to Denver and Chicago and northwest to Portland and Seattle; other trains connect in Salt Lake City for San Francisco, Las Vegas, and Los Angeles; tel. (800) 421-8420. Air travelers use the Salt Lake City International Airport, just 35 miles away.

Ogden has many auto rental agencies, both local and national; see the telephone yellow pages. **Yellow Cab** provides 24-hour taxi service; tel. 394-9411.

# VICINITY OF OGDEN

## EAST OF OGDEN

**Ogden Canyon**
Precipitous cliffs rise thousands of feet above the narrow canyon, just barely allowing the highway and Ogden River to squeeze through. Fiery reds of maples and golden hues of oaks add color in autumn. This scenic drive deep within the Wasatch Range begins on the eastern edge of Ogden and, about 6 miles farther, comes out at Pineview Reservoir in the broad Ogden Valley. In winter, skiers turn south from the reservoir to Snowbasin Ski Area and north to Nordic Valley and Powder Mountain ski areas. Summer visitors have a choice of staying at swimming beaches and campgrounds on the shore of Pineview Reservoir or heading to canyons and mountain peaks of the Wasatch. For recreation and road information, contact the Ogden Ranger District office at 507 25th St. and Adams Ave. in Ogden; tel. 625-5112. The canyon is reached from Ogden by heading east on 12th St. (take I-15 Exit 348).

**Pineview Reservoir**
This many-armed lake on the Ogden River provides excellent boating, fishing, water-skiing, and swimming. At an elevation of 4,900 feet, it is about 4 miles long and wide and has a surface area of 2,000 acres. Campgrounds, picnic areas, and marinas ring the shore. **Anderson Cove,** a large campground with a swimming beach on the southern shore, is 8 miles east of Ogden. Camping costs $8 (picnicking is $4); open Memorial Day to Labor Day weekends; sites have drinking water but no showers. Reservations can be made for family and group sites at 6902 E. 900 South, Huntsville, UT 84317; tel. 745-6666. **Jefferson Hunt Campground** is on the South Fork of the Ogden River where it meets Pineview Reservoir, one mile east of Anderson Cove; sites have drinking water and cost $6. **Bluffs Swim Area** offers sandy beaches and shaded picnic areas at Cemetery Point on the lake's east side ($3 vehicle, day use only); a marina with boat ramp, docks, and snack bar is nearby ($3 boat launch); follow UT 39 to the Huntsville turnoff (10.5 miles east of Ogden), then turn west 2 miles. **Middle Inlet** is another beach area 1.5 miles north of Huntsville ($2 vehicle). **Port Ramp** on the lake's western shore has a boat ramp, small store, dock, slips, fuel, and storage ($3 to launch or park); open daily May 1 to Sept. 30; tel. 745-2320.

**Abbey Of Our Lady Of The Holy Trinity**
This community of 30-40 Trappist monks welcomes visitors to its chapel and reception

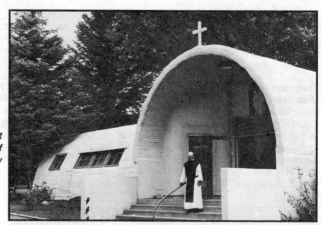

Father David Kinney at Abbey of Our Lady of the Holy Trinity

room. The monks explain the monastery's work and sell locally produced bread, honey, and farm products. Although no tours are given, a slide show illustrates the religious life and work of the community. You may attend the Mass and chants held daily in the chapel. Quonset buildings, originally just temporary, have proved both practical and unique for nearly all the monastery's needs. The founders chose this location for its seclusion and beautiful setting. The reception room is open Mon. to Sat. 8 a.m.-noon and 1-5 p.m.; tel. 745-3784. Located 4 miles southeast of Huntsville at 1250 S. 9500 East; follow signs for "Monastery" from UT 39.

## Ogden Valley Accommodations And Food

**Jackson Fork Inn** has motel rooms ($49-82), a dinner club open for Sun. brunch and daily for dinner, and a convenience store; tel. 745-0051; on UT 39 at Milepost 18 (7345 E. 900 South). Huntsville has a couple of places to eat and Utah's oldest bar—the **Shootin' Star Saloon**—in business since 1879 (at 7350 E. 200 South). **Vue de Valhulla Bed & Breakfast** is on 2787 Nordic Valley Rd. (northwest of Pineview Reservoir in Liberty, UT 84310); rooms cost $38-44; tel. 745-2558. **Wolf Creek Drive Condos/Skinner's Inc.** offers luxury

accommodations ($93-164) with 18-hole and miniature golf, tennis, swimming pools, and horseback riding in summer and skiing in winter; 3720 N. Wolf Creek Dr., Eden, UT 84310; tel. 745-2621 or (800) 345-8824 out of state. Several restaurants are in the Wolf Creek area. Wolf Creek is north of Pineview Reservoir on the road to Powder Mountain Ski Area.

## Other Camping And Picnic Areas

The **Maples Campground** (elev. 6,200 ft.) is nestled among maples and aspen in the mountains near Snowbasin Ski Area; season lasts from late May to early Sept.; no drinking water or charge; drive to the ski area's lower parking lot (signed "Lower Shop"), then turn west 1.5 miles on a gravel road.

**Magpie Campground** (elev. 5,200 ft.) is the first of a series of 8 recreation areas along the South Fork of the Ogden River. Magpie's sites are open from about mid-May to late Oct. with drinking water; $6; located 5.5 miles east of Huntsville on UT 39. **Botts Campground** has been a popular stopping place since pioneer days; open from about mid-May to late Oct. with drinking water; $6; 6 miles east of Huntsville on UT 39. **Hobble Campground** has only 8 sites; open from about mid- May to late Oct.; no drinking water or charge; you can also stay here the rest of the year, but no services are

provided; 7 miles east of Huntsville on UT 39.
**South Fork Campground** is open from about
mid-May to late Sept. with drinking water; $6;
6.5 miles east of Huntsville on UT 39. **Perception Park** offers a campground with family and
group sites and a separate picnic area; open
from about mid-May to late Sept. with drinking
water; $7 (picnic area is free); 3 group sites
can be reserved. Perception was specially
built to accommodate handicapped people;
7.5 miles east of Huntsville on UT 39. **Upper
and Lower Meadows** and **Willows** camp
grounds are open mid-May to late Sept. with
drinking water; $6; all 3 campgrounds lie along
the South Fork of the Ogden River (elev. 5,300
ft.), 7.8 miles east of Huntsville on UT 39.

**Weber County Memorial Park** is one mile
down the paved road to Causey Reservoir, a
narrow crescent-shaped lake in upper South
Fork of the Ogden River. A paved road in the
park crosses the river to individual sites (first
come, first served; free); 3 group sites can be
reserved with Weber County Parks and Recreation; water is available from late May to late
Sept.; tel. 399-8491. Turnoff for Causey Reservoir is one mile east of Willows Campground
on UT 39. **Monte Cristo Campground** sits
high in mountain forests of spruce, fir, and
aspen (elev. 8,400 ft.); sites are open early
July to late Sept. with drinking water; $7 (2
group sites can be reserved); located between
Mileposts 48 and 49, 40 miles east of Ogden
(21 miles west of Woodruff) on UT 39. The
highway summit (elev. 9,008 ft.) near the
campground has great panoramas. Snowmobilers find the terrain and snow in the
Monte Cristo area excellent for their sport; a
snowmobile trail guide can be obtained from
most tourist and state park offices. **Birch
Creek Campground** is a primitive BLM camping area between upper and lower Birch Creek
reservoirs; no drinking water or charge; turnoff
is between Mileposts 61 and 62, 13 miles east
of Monte Cristo Campground (8 miles west of
Woodruff) on UT 39; go north one mile on a
gravel road past the lower reservoir to the
campground. Hike up the earth dam for rainbow trout fishing in the larger upper Birch
Creek Reservoir (can be low in late summer).

# OGDEN AREA SKIING

### Snowbasin Ski Area
Skiers have been gliding down the varied
terrain here since the early 1940s. Four triple
and one double chairlifts serve more than 40
runs, of which 20% are rated beginner, 50%
intermediate, and 30% expert. The longest
run is 3 miles and drops 2,400 feet in elevation. Snowbasin's season usually lasts from
Thanksgiving until mid-April. Adult lift tickets
cost $21 full day, $17 afternoon, $11 beginner
full day, $9 beginner afternoon. Snowbasin
offers a ski school, ski shop, rentals, and a day
lodge. Snowbasin is 17 miles southeast of
Ogden; go through Ogden Canyon, continue
2.5 miles past Pine view Dam, then turn right
on Snowbasin Rd.; Box 348, Huntsville, UT
84317; tel. 399-1135/1136 (main office), 399-
0198 (snow report), 399-4611 (ski school),
and 399-0197 (ski shop).

### Nordic Valley Ski Area
This downhill ski area is the closest to Ogden
and is especially popular with families (Mon.
is family night). Two double chairlifts serve 16
named runs, of which 30% are beginner, 50%
intermediate, and 20% expert. Elevation drop
is 1,000 feet. You can ski at night too—all runs
are under lights Mon. to Sat. until 10 p.m. Day
skiing takes place Fri. to Sun., and all school
holidays. Nordic Valley's season runs early
Dec. to late March. Adult lift tickets cost $12
full day and $10 half day or night. Nordic Valley
has a ski school, ski shop, and a day lodge.
Located 15 miles northeast of Ogden; go
through Ogden Canyon, turn left at Pineview
Dam, and follow signs; Box 478, Eden, UT
84310; tel. 745-3511.

### Powder Mountain Ski Area
Two double and one triple chairlifts, each to a
different peak, serve more than 30 interconnected runs; 10% are beginner, 60% intermediate, and 30% expert. Three surface lifts
supplement the chairlifts. High elevations
(7,600-8,900 ft.) catch plentiful powder snow.

You can ski at night from the Sundown Lift until 10 p.m. Powder Mountain's season lasts from mid-Nov. to late April. Adult lift tickets cost $18 all day, $15 half day, and $8.50 night. Facilities include a ski school, ski shops, rentals, and 3 day lodges. Located 19 miles northeast of Ogden; go through Ogden Canyon, turn left at Pineview Dam, and follow signs; Box 450, Eden, UT 84310; tel. 745-3771.

# NORTH OF OGDEN

### Golden Spike Fruitway
Following the old US 89 highway north to Brigham City, you'll pass many orchards. Fruit stands, open during the July to mid-Sept. season, offer a bountiful supply of cherries, apples, peaches, pears, apricots, plums, berries, and vegetables.

### Willard
This small community (pop. 1,600) is known for its fine pioneer houses. The city park has picnic tables and a playground. Willard lies at the foot of the Wasatch Range 11 miles north of Ogden on US 89 (take I-15 Exit 360).

### Willard Bay State Park
Two separate recreation areas along the eastern shore of Willard Bay provide a variety of water sports, camping, and opportunities for nature study. More than 200 species of birds have been observed near the park; common ones include the white pelican, California gull, snowy egret, western grebe, killdeer, black-necked stilt, and American avocet; ask a park ranger for the *Nature Guide to Willard Bay* brochure. Conditions are great for water skiing and power boating, but only fair for sailing. Fishermen catch channel catfish, crappie, and walleye. Winter visitors find good ice fishing in the bay from mid-Dec. to late February. Only 2 miles of Willard Bay's 15-mile circumference are natural shoreline. Dikes enclose nearly all of the bay to keep out salt water from the Great Salt Lake, just to the west. Canals carry water into the bay during winter and spring, then out for irrigation during the growing season. Park fees are $3 day use, $8 camping. Contact Willard Bay State Park at 900 W. 650 North,

Box A, Willard, UT 84340; tel. 734-9494 (ranger) or (800) 322-3770 (reservations).

**North Marina** features a sandy swimming beach, campground (with showers), boat ramp, and dock. The developed campground's season is normally April 1 to Oct. 31, but an overflow area on the shore stays open all year. Reservations are recommended on summer weekends and holidays. A concession has a snack bar, camping and boating supplies, fuel, and rentals (jet skis, sailboats, sailboards, and fishing boats); open daily Memorial Day to Labor Day weekends; tel. 723-6152. North Marina is just west of I-15 Willard Exit 360.

**South Marina** has a boat ramp, docks, and campground (with showers). The area is set up mostly for day use, as the open grassy areas used for camping lack designated sites. The dikes on this part of the bay prevent beaches and lake views, but you won't be so crowded here on summer weekends and the campground nearly always has room. South Marina is open April 1 to Oct. 31; no reservations are taken here. Access is from I-15 Exit 354, then follow signs west 2.5 miles.

# BRIGHAM CITY

Peaks of the Wasatch Range exceeding 9,000 feet form the backdrop to this city of 20,000 people, 21 miles north of Ogden. Pioneers settled along Box Elder Creek in 1851, naming both the creek and town for the trees growing here. Five years later they renamed their community to honor Mormon Church president Brigham Young. Brigham City serves as Box Elder County seat and a center for surrounding fruit orchards, truck farms, and ranches. Historic displays in the **Brigham City Museum-Gallery** show how residents lived in the 19th C.; the art gallery features changing shows by Utah and local artists; open Tues. to Fri. 11 a.m.-6 p.m. and Sat. 1-5 p.m.; free; 24 N. 300 West; tel. 723-6769. Many people think the Mormon **Box Elder Tabernacle** to be Utah's most beautiful building. Construction took place from 1876-90, then the tabernacle burned 6 years later; the present structure dates from 1897. Gothic

*Box Elder Tabernacle*

arched windows and doors, a soaring white steeple, and 16 smaller spires make the stone and brick structure distinctive. Tours are conducted in the tabernacle daily 9 a.m.-9 p.m. from May 1 to Oct. 31; 251 S. Main St.; tel. 723-5376.

## Practicalities

Main Street, which runs north-south through Brigham City, has half a dozen motels and a variety of restaurants. **Brigham City KOA** offers camping sites for tents and RVs ($13.90 no hookups, $19.08 w/hookups) with showers, pool, store, and laundry; open March 1 to Nov. 15; tel. 723-5503; located 4 miles south of Brigham City on US 89. Other nearby places to camp are at Willard Bay State Park (see above) and Mantua Reservoir (see below). **Maddox Ranch House** is a popular dining spot south of town for steak, chicken, and trout; open Tues. to Sat. for lunch and dinner; tel. 723-8545; located 1.5 miles south on US 89. During **Golden Spike Days** (early June) the city has art exhibits, an antique car show, Golden Spike Marathon, and other festivities. **Peach Days** (weekend after Labor Day) is a community celebration of the harvest with a parade, entertainment, carnival, art show, Peach Queen Pageant, bicycle race, and a foot race. **Box Elder County Fair and Rodeo** (late Aug.) in nearby Tremonton features a parade, rodeo, horse pulling, livestock judging, and varied exhibits.

**Box Elder Natatorium** has an indoor pool, basketball court, and weight room at Box Elder High School, 380 S. 600 West; tel. 723-2622. An outdoor swimming pool is in **Pioneer Park** at 800 W. Forest; tel. 723-2711. **John Adams Park** has picnicking, playground, and tennis courts at 100 North and 500 East. The 18-hole **Eagle Mountain Golf Course** is at 1100 S. Main on the south edge of town; tel. 723-3212. **Brigham City Community Hospital** is at 950 S. 500 West; tel. 734-9471. The **chamber of commerce** will answer your questions about the area; open Mon. to Fri. 9 a.m.-noon and 1-4 p.m.; 6 N. Main St.; tel. 723-3931. The **city library** is at 26 E. Forest; open Mon. to Sat.; tel. 723-5850.

## VICINITY OF BRIGHAM CITY

### Bear River Migratory Bird Refuge

Millions of birds drop in to feed or nest in the freshwater marshes created by the meeting of the Bear River and the Great Salt Lake. About 60 species nest in the refuge. In pioneer days, reports told of flocks of waterfowl that would blacken the sky. Flooding in the late 1980s had closed the area and displaced many birds; receding waters allowed it to reopen in

1990. At press time a 12-mile loop road is open to visitors. Head west about 16 miles on Forest St. from Brigham City. The refuge office has a bird list and information at 862 S. Main in the Breintenbeker Plaza (Brigham City, UT 84302); open Mon. to Fri. 7:30 a.m.-4 p.m.; tel. 723-5887.

## Mantua Reservoir

This 554-acre reservoir beside the town of Mantua is popular for fishing, boating, and picnicking. From Brigham City, follow US 89/91 east 4 miles up Box Elder Canyon. **Box Elder Campground** (U.S. Forest Service) is just west of the reservoir; open with drinking water from mid-May to late Oct.; $6; the adjacent picnic areas are free. **Mount Haven RV Park** has tent ($8.75) and RV ($9.80 no hookups, $11 w/hookups) spaces with showers and a store; open early April to late Sept.; tel. 723-7615/1292; in Mantua at 130 N. Main Street. Visitors are welcome to view the native cutthroat and lake trout at **Mantua Fish Hatchery,** one mile southeast of Mantua; open daily 8 a.m.-5 p.m. Exhibits show how the trout are obtained as eggs at Bear Lake and returned a year later after growing to a 5-inch length. All of the one million trout produced annually go to Bear Lake.

## Inspiration Point

Beginning as Main St. in Mantua, unpaved Forest Route 084 leads south 14 miles to Inspiration Point (elev. 9,422 ft.) and dizzying views across the Great Salt Lake and much of northern Utah; mountains in Nevada, Idaho, and Wyoming can be spotted on a clear day. Limber pine grow near the summit and subalpine fir lower down. The road is rough in spots, though cars with good clearance can make it to the top in dry weather. Keep left at the 3-way fork 2.5 miles from Mantua; see the Wasatch-Cache National Forest map. Dispersed camping can be done in Willard Basin (elev. 9,000 ft.), 2 miles before Inspiration Point; no facilities or designated sites. Skyline Trail begins from Willard Basin and winds south to the summit of Ben Lomond (elev. 9,712 ft.) and other peaks, then to North Ogden Pass and finally Ogden Canyon, 22 miles away. Or you could start hiking from Inspiration Point. Other trails branch off Skyline too; see the Mantua, North Ogden, and Huntsville 7½-minute topo maps. For more info, contact the Ogden Ranger District office at 507 25th St. and Adams Ave. in Ogden; tel. 625-5112.

## Crystal Springs

The water park features hot mineral baths, waterslide rides, and a freshwater swimming pool. You can visit the snack bar (summer weekends only) or bring your own picnic. Crystal Springs stays open all year, summer: daily 10 a.m.-9 or 10 p.m. and winter: Sun. noon-7 p.m., Mon. to Thurs. noon-9 p.m., Fri. noon-10 p.m., and Sat. 10 a.m.-10 p.m.; admission is $4.50 adult, $3.50 children 3-12 and seniors; the waterslide costs an additional

*horse pull (pony class) at the Box Elder Country Fair*

$3.50-4.50; tel. 279-8104. A campground with showers has tent spaces ($9) and RV sites ($9 no hookups, $13 w/hookups); open early May to late September. Crystal Springs is one mile north of Honeyville, so named because this spot reminded settlers of a biblical land flowing with milk and honey. From Brigham City, go north 10 miles on UT 69 or take I-15/84 Honeyville Exit 375.

**Tremonton**

This agricultural center 15 miles northwest of Brigham City was settled in 1888 and named for Tremont, Illinois. **North Box Elder County Museum** has historic exhibits and Indian artifacts; open in summer Mon. to Fri. 8 a.m.-4 p.m., then Mon. to Fri. 9 a.m.-5 p.m. the rest of the year; donation; tel. 257-3371; at 150 S. Tremont. Three motels are in town: **Marble Motel** (116 N. Tremont; tel. 257-3524; $26.16 s, $28.34 d), **Sandman Motel** (585 W. Main; tel. 257-5675; $31.61 s, $34.88 d), and **Western Inn** (2301 W. Main at I-84 Exit 40; tel. 257-3399; $34.88 s, $38.15 d). A selection of restaurants is scattered around town too. **Box Elder County Fair and Rodeo** (late Aug.) features a parade, rodeo, horse pulling, livestock judging, and varied exhibits. **Bear River Valley Hospital** provides medical services at 440 W. 600 North; tel. 257-7441. For information about the area, visit the information desk in the Tremonton Community Center, 150 S. Tremont (Tremonton, UT 84337); tel. 257-3371.

**Belmont Springs**

Hot springs have been developed into a swimming pool and hot tubs, a 9-hole golf course, and a campground. Volleyball and horseshoe equipment are available too. Belmont Springs are 10 miles north of Tremonton and one mile south of Plymouth. The season at this small resort runs early May to early October. Open 9 a.m.-9 p.m.; golf hours are 8:30 a.m. until dark; tel. 458-3200. Admission to the pool and hot tubs is $3 with discounts for children and seniors; camping costs $7.63 no hookups and $10.90 w/hookups (ask about tent rates).

**Corinne**

The location beside the Bear River and along the transcontinental railroad seemed ideal in 1869, when Corinne's founders laid out the town. Banks, freight companies, and mining concerns based themselves at the promising new site. A steamboat service began ferrying ore across the Great Salt Lake to a mill and smelter at Corinne. The population swiftly rose to the 2,000 mark as business boomed. Saloons, dance halls, and "soiled doves" entertained the largely non-Mormon population and prompted Brigham Young to declare the town off limits to his followers. Corinne became the Gentile capital of Utah and a hotbed of political opposition to the Mormon Church. Yet the "curse of Corinne" kept the town from realizing its dreams. Lowering lake levels grounded the steamboat business, a diphtheria epidemic killed many citizens, appeals for political support from the U.S. Congress failed and, finally, the railroads chose the Mormon city of Ogden as their junction point. Today Corinne is a sleepy farm town with a few old buildings from its past. The Methodist church, corner of S. 6th St. and Colorado, dates from 1870 and is believed to be the first non-Mormon church built in Utah. Corinne is 5 miles west of Brigham City on the way to Golden Spike National Historic Site.

## GOLDEN SPIKE NATIONAL HISTORIC SITE

At 12:47 p.m. on May 10, 1869, rails from the East and West met for the first time. People across the country closely followed telegraph reports as dignitaries and railway officials made their speeches and drove the last spikes, then everyone broke out in wild celebration. The joining of rails at this windswept pass in Utah's Promontory Mountains marked a new chapter in the growth of the United States. A transcontinental railroad at last linked both sides of the nation. The far western frontier would be a frontier no more. Swift-moving Army troops would soon put an end to

Indian troubles. Vast resources of timber, mineral wealth, and farmland lay open to development.

## History

This unlikely spot for the final linking came about as a compromise. The Central Pacific and Union Pacific railroads, eager for land grants and bonuses, had been laying track at a furious pace and grading the lines far ahead. So great was the momentum that the grader crews didn't even stop when they met, but laid parallel grades for 225 miles across Utah. Finally Congress decided to join the rails at Promontory Summit and stop the wasteful duplication of effort. A ragged town of tents, box cars, and hastily built wooden shacks sprang up along a single muddy street. Outlaws, crooked gambling houses, and plenty of prostitutes earned Promontory Summit an awful reputation as a real "hell on wheels town." That ended 6 months later when the railroads moved the terminal operations to Ogden. Soon only a depot, round house, helper engines, and other rail facilities remained. The Lucin Cutoff across the Great Salt Lake in 1904 bypassed the long twisting grades of Promontory Summit and dramatically reduced traffic along the old route. The final blow came in 1942 when the rails were torn up for scrap to feed wartime industries.

## Visitor Center

The Golden Spike National Historic Site, authorized by Congress in 1965, recreates the momentous period of railroad history that took place here. The visitor center has excellent exhibits and programs that illustrate the difficulties of building the railroad and portray the officials and workers who made it possible. A short slide show introduces Promontory Summit's history. The 20-minute program, *The Golden Spike,* presents a more detailed account of building the transcontinental railroad.

*Bottles of champagne and ale help celebrate completion.*

119 *and* Jupiter *at Golden Spike N.H.S.*

Other related films are shown too. Rangers give talks several times a day in summer. An exhibit room has changing displays on railroading. Historic markers behind the visitor center indicate the spot where the last spike was driven.

The annual Last Spike Ceremony reenacts the original celebration every May 10th with great fanfare. The Railroaders' Festival in Aug. has special exhibits, a spike-driving contest, reenactments, hand-car races, and entertainment. The visitor center is open daily 8 a.m.-6 p.m. in summer and 8 a.m.-4:30 p.m. the rest of the year; closed Thanksgiving, Christmas, and New Year's Day. Admission is $3 vehicle or $1 adult, whichever is less. A sales counter offers a good selection of books on railroading, Utah history, and natural history, as well as post cards, and souvenirs. Motels and restaurants are in Brigham City and Tremonton. From the I-15 Brigham City Exit 368, head west on UT 13 and UT 83 and follow signs 29 miles. (Mailing address: Box W, Brigham City, UT 84302; tel. 471-2209.)

**The Locomotives**
The 2 locomotives that met here in 1869, Central Pacific's *Jupiter* and Union Pacific's *119,* succumbed to scrapyards around the turn of the century. However, they have been born again as authentic replicas. Every day in summer the trains steam along a short section of track from the Engine House to the historic spot.

**Promontory Trail Auto Tour**
Imagine you're riding the rails across Utah a century ago. This scenic drive follows the old grades past many construction feats of hardworking railway men. You'll see the parallel grades laid by the competing Union Pacific and Central Pacific, clearings for sidings, original rock culverts, and many cuts and fills. Wildflowers, grass-covered hills, and views over the blue Great Salt Lake appear much the same as they did to early train travelers. A booklet available at the visitor center describes the features and history at numbered stops on the drive. Allow about 1¼ hours for the complete tour. If time is short, drive along just the west section (45 minutes) or the east section (30 minutes).

**Big Fill Walk**
An easy 1½-mile round trip at the east end of the driving tour leads farther down a railroad grade to the famous Big Fill and Big Trestle sites. Rugged terrain on this side of the Prom-

ontory Mountains posed some of the greatest construction challenges to either line. The Central Pacific tackled an especially deep ravine here with a massive fill, 170 feet deep and 500 feet long, requiring about 2 months of work by 500 men and 250 teams of animals. The Union Pacific, pressed for time, threw together a temporary trestle over the gorge, paralleling the Big Fill.

## VICINITY OF GOLDEN SPIKE N.H.S.

### Promontory Point

This peninsula that juts into the Great Salt Lake has no connection with the first transcontinental railroad, but it does make a pleasant scenic drive. A paved road follows the eastern shore of the peninsula below the Promontory Mountains for 30 miles, then becomes dirt for the last 7 miles. There are good views of the Great Salt Lake, Wasatch Range, and the Lucin Cutoff railroad causeway. Lake Crystal Salt Co. at road's end was a salt extraction plant (no longer in operation). The Promontory Point road turnoff is 6 miles east of the Golden Spike Visitor Center.

### Thiokol

Many buildings of this giant aerospace corporation lie scattered across the countryside about 6 miles northeast of the historic site. You're not likely to be allowed to tour the facility, but you can see a group of missiles, rocket engines, and a space shuttle booster casing in front of administrative offices. Turn north 2 miles on UT 83 at the junction with the Golden Spike N.H.S. road (8 miles east of the visitor center).

## THE NORTHWEST CORNER

### Raft River Mountains (Sawtooth National Forest)

Few Utahns know about these mountains in the northwest corner of the state, despite their pretty alpine scenery of forests and glacial cirques. Panoramic views from the top take in the Great Salt Lake, barren desert, farmlands, and many mountains of Utah, Nevada, and Idaho. The range runs east-west, something of a rarity in the region. The summit ridge isn't what you'd expect either—it's a long ridge of gently rolling grasslands. Bull Mountain (elev. 9,931 ft.) crowns the range, though it's hard to pick out from all the other grassy knolls! Hikers haven't discovered the range—you'll find pristine forests and canyons but no real trails. Aspen, Douglas fir, subalpine fir, and limber pine thrive in the canyons and northern slopes below the summit ridge. Ranchers run cattle on the top and other meadow areas. A 4WD road climbs the mountains from Yost.

Clear Creek Campground (elev. 6,400 ft.) has sites in a beautiful setting below the north slope of the Raft River Range. Aspen and alders grow in the campground and deer aren't at all shy about dropping in to browse. Hand pumps and springs are in the campground, but it's best to bring your own drinking water; open early June to mid-Oct.; free. Located 35 miles west of Snowville; take I-84 Exit 5 and go west 25 miles on UT 42 to Strevell (just into Idaho), turn left 3.5 miles on the gravel road signed "Yost," then turn left (south) 6 miles on a gravel road to the campground.

Hikers will see the best scenery and forests on the Lake Fork route from the north. Drive to Clear Creek Campground, follow a jeep road from the gate at the end of the campground south about 1¼ miles to a stream ford, then turn right 2½ miles up Lake Fork Canyon. Use a map to make sure you're in the correct canyon; the Park Valley 15-minute topo map is best. Walk along the stream or follow deer trails to a marshy area with some small ponds. Bull Basin Lake lies a short distance upstream in a rugged cirque. To reach Bull Mountain, return to the marsh and look for a small trail climbing the rocky slope to the west. You'll come out on the grassy ridge and meet the jeep road; Bull Mountain is about ½ mile to the southwest. Many other climbing routes are possible too. Nearly all hiking is done from the north; land south of the summit belongs to ranchers who prohibit hikers because the cattle are easily spooked.

**Park Valley**

Travelers can easily cross the lonely country of Utah's northwest corner on paved highways UT 42 and UT 30. Park Valley, south of the Raft River Mountains, has a small store and gas station (closed Sun.), the **Overland Trail Motel** (open all year; $27.25-32.70; tel. 871-4755), and a cafe (closed Sun.).

# LOGAN AND VICINITY

Logan (pop. 32,500) lies surrounded by lush farmlands of the Cache Valley to the west and lofty peaks of the Bear River Range to the east. Terraces mark ancient shorelines of Lake Bonneville in Logan and other places around Cache Valley. Plentiful water from the Logan River, named for the early trapper Ephraim Logan, made this site a good choice for the valley's largest settlement. Travelers enjoy the city because of its many trees, parks, and historic buildings. Utah State University adds considerably to the culture, sports, spirit, and population of the community. The mountains provide abundant year-round recreation, including scenic drives, camping, fishing, hiking, cross-country ski touring, and downhill skiing.

## History
Mountain men tramped through Utah's northernmost lands in search of beaver and other fur-bearing animals as early as 1819. They found good trapping near Cache Valley and

stayed for several seasons, holding one rendezvous here and 2 at nearby Bear Lake. The fur trappers often stored their valuable pelts in a cache, a French word for hiding place, for which the valley was later named. Cold winters and hostile Indians discouraged permanent settlement in the area until 1856, when a small group of Mormons established Maughan's Fort (now Wellsville). Uncertainties caused by the Utah War delayed the founding of Logan and other communities another 3 years. Farms, dairy industries, and livestock raising begun in the early years continue to be an important part of Logan's economy today.

## SIGHTS

### Mormon Temple And Tabernacle
The distinctive castellated temple rises from a prominent hill just east of downtown. After Brigham Young chose this location in 1877, church members labored 7 years to complete the temple. Architect Truman O. Angell, designer of the Salt Lake Temple, oversaw construction. Timber and blocks of limestone came from nearby Logan Canyon. Only Mormons engaged in sacred work may enter the temple, but visitors are welcome on the grounds to view the exterior. Located 2 blocks east of Main St. at 175 N. 300 East.

The tabernacle also stands as a fine example of early Mormon architecture. Construction of the stone structure began in 1865, but other priorities—building the temple and ward meetinghouses—delayed dedication until 1891. The public may enter when it's open; downtown at Main and Center streets.

### Cache Valley Historical Museum
### (Daughters of the Utah Pioneers Museum)
Exhibits give an idea of how Logan's early settlers lived. You'll see their tools, household furnishings, clothing, art, and photographs.

TO SMITHFIELD

LOGAN

TO LOGAN CANYON &
BEAR LAKE

TO
BRIGHAM CITY

TO HYRUM

0      0.5 mi

0      500 m

1. Willow Park and Zoo
2. Cache County Fairgrounds
3. Western Park Campground
4. Bandit's Cove RV Park
5. Community Recreation Center
6. Worthington Park (Logan H.S.)
7. post office
8. Cache Chamber of Commerce
   (Bridgerland Tourist Council)
9. Logan Library
10. Mormon Tabernacle
11. Bicentennial Park
12. Central Park
13. Mormon Temple
14. Mount Logan Middle School

15. Municipool
16. Logana Pool and Waterslide
17. Cache Valley Mall
18. Logan Regional Hospital
19. Romney Stadium (USU)
20. The Spectrum (USU)
21. Parking Terrace (USU)
22. Taggart Student Center (USU)
23. Old Main Building (USU)
24. Merrill Library (USU)
25. Harrison Museum of Art (USU)
26. Logan Ranger District
    (U.S. Forest Service)
27. Logan Golf and Country Club
28. Canyon Entrance Park

More of Logan's history can be seen on a driving or walking tour; ask for *A Guide to Logan, Utah's Historical Homes and Sites* from the Bridgerland Tourist Council office. Call the Tourist Council for museum hours; tel. 752-2161. Free admission; downtown at 160 N. Main.

## Willow Park Zoo

This small zoo displays exotic birds such as the Andean condor, golden pheasant, mitered conure, and the more familiar golden and bald eagles, peacocks, swans, and ducks. Animals you might meet include capuchin monkeys, coatimundi, and black bear. Willow Park also has picnic areas and a playground among its large shady trees. The zoo is open daily all year except some holidays from 8 a.m. until dark; free. Located at 419 W. 700 South.

# UTAH STATE UNIVERSITY

In 1888, a federal land-grant program opened the way for the territorial legislature to establish the Agricultural College of Utah. The school grew to become Utah State University in 1957 and now has 8 colleges, 45 departments, and a graduate school. USU's "Aggies" number more than 14,000 with 2,000 faculty and staff. Classes are held on a 4-quarter system. The university continues its original purpose of agricultural research while diversifying into atmospheric and space sciences, ecology, creative arts, social sciences, and other fields. The campus sits northeast of downtown on a bench left by a northern arm of prehistoric Lake Bonneville. Large maples and other trees shade the grounds. Old Main Building, begun one year after the college was founded, has housed nearly every office and department at one time or another. The high bell tower of Old Main is a campus landmark. Attractions on campus include the art museum, student center, and a large library. A full schedule of concerts, theater, lecture series, art exhibits, and sports competitions fills the calendar. The University Relations Dept. knows of upcoming cultural events and can provide general information and arrange tours; Room 102 in Old Main; tel. 750-1158. Park free along streets off campus or for a small charge at the Parking Terrace on 700 North (between 800 East and 900 East). Try USU's famous Traditional Aggie Ice Cream, available in the student center and other locations.

## Nora Eccles Harrison Museum Of Art

Galleries display ceramics from the museum's permanent collection and changing exhibitions of paintings, sculpture, ceramics, prints, drawings, and photography. Open Tues. to Fri. 10:30 a.m.-4:30 p.m. (to 9 p.m. Wed.), Sat. and Sun. 2-5 p.m.; free; tel. 750-1412. On campus near 1200 East and US 89.

## Taggart Student Center

This popular building offers many services and places to eat. On the lower floor you'll find several snack bars, the book store, ticket office branch, post office, bowling alleys, and a game room. The main floor has an information desk (tel. 750-1710), cafeteria, and movie theater. The Skyroom Garden Restaurant on the fourth floor serves lunch Mon. to Fri.; a dinner menu of steak, prime rib, and seafood is offered Fri. evenings; tel. 750-1767.

## Merrill Library

More than one million bound volumes and 7,000 different periodicals are housed here. Hikers and travelers can plan trips with help from the 51,000 maps on the fourth floor. The special collections are noted for Utah and Western history. Open Mon. to Thurs. 7 a.m.-midnight, Fri. 7 a.m.-9 p.m., Sat. 9 a.m.-6 p.m., and Sun. 1 p.m.-midnight; shorter hours and closed weekends during summer and breaks; tel. 750-2633.

## Cultural And Sports Events

The Convocations program features prominent speakers of many fields; usually held Thursdays at 12:30 p.m.; call University Relations for program and location; tel. 750-1158. The USU Symphony, Chorale, Symphonic Band, Chamber Music Society, Utah State

Theatre, and other university or visiting groups present a wide range of entertainment. Men's and women's teams battle their opponents in USU's active sports programs. For ticket information to sports and performing arts events, call 750-1657.

## PRACTICALITIES

### Accommodations

Places to stay in Logan, listed in order of increasing price, are: **Alta Motel** (51 E. 500 North; tel. 752-6300; $21.89 s, $22.89 d), **Center Street Bed & Breakfast** (169 E. Center; tel. 752-3443; $27.25-103.55), **Super 8 Motel** (865 S. Hwy. 89-91; tel. 753-8883 or 1-800-848-8888; $29.30 s, $33.66 d), **Days Inn** (364 S. Main; tel. 753-5623; $30.52 s, $32.70 d), **Comfort Inn** (447 N. Main; tel. 752-9141 or 800-221-2222; $30.52-39.24 s, $35.97-41.42 d), **Baugh Motel (Best Western)** (153 S. Main; tel. 752-5220 or 800-528-1234; $34.88 s, $41.42 d), and **Weston Inn (Best Western)** (250 N. Main; tel. 752-5700 or 800-528-1234; $34.88 s, $43.60 d).

### Campgrounds

**Riverside RV Park** is just south of town with showers and laundry; $8.72 tent, $13.08 RV w/hookups; turn east on 1700 South from US 89/91. **Western Park Campground** offers basic facilities including showers; $10 tents and RVs no hookups, $12 RVs w/hookups; tel. 752-6424; 350 W. 800 South (signs point the way from S. Main). **Bandit's Cove RV Park** has sites for tents ($8.48) and RVs ($13.08 w/hookups); showers, snack bar, and a miniature golf course are available; tel. 753-0508; 590½ S. Main. **Hyrum State Park** offers camping, swimming, fishing, and boating 7 miles south near the town of Hyrum; see "Hyrum State Park" below. The U.S. Forest Service has many campgrounds beginning 6 miles east of town on US 89 in Logan Canyon; see "Logan Canyon" below.

### Food

Like any college town, Logan has a full array of pizza and fast-food places; you'll find most of them along N. Main. Restaurants serving American fare include: **Angie's Restaurant** (open daily for breakfast, lunch, and dinner; 690 N. Main; tel. 752-9252), **Blue Goose** (open Mon. to Sat. for lunch; 1 N. Main; tel. 752-0619), **Cottage Restaurant** (open Sun. for breakfast and lunch, Mon. to Sat. for breakfast, lunch, and dinner; 51 W. 200 South; tel. 752-5260), **Freeman's Kitchen Cafe** (open Sun. for breakfast and lunch, Mon. to Sat. for breakfast, lunch, and dinner; 633 S. Main; tel. 752-9913), **Frontier Pies Restaurant** (open daily for breakfast, lunch, and dinner; 43 E. 1400 North; tel. 752-9280), **Glauser's Restaurant** (open Mon. to Sat. for breakfast, lunch, and dinner; 25 W. Center; tel. 752-1681), **Golden Corral** (open daily for lunch and dinner; 1114 N. Main; tel. 753-2611).

Steak and seafood top the menu at **The Bluebird** (open Sun. for lunch and dinner, Mon. to Sat. for breakfast, lunch, and dinner; 19 N. Main; tel. 752-3155), **DeVerle's Juniper Inn** (open Tues. to Sat. for lunch and dinner; 4088 N. Main; tel. 563-3622), and the **Sizzler** (open daily for lunch and dinner; 1165 N. Main; tel. 752-2771). **Zanavoo Lodge Restaurant** prepares steak and seafood dinners; open Mon. to Sat. for dinner; 4880 E. Hwy. 89 in Logan Canyon; tel. 752-0085.

**Gia's Restaurant** specializes in fine Italian cuisine; open Wed. to Sun. for lunch, daily for dinner; 119 S. Main; tel. 752-8384. Dine Chinese at **China House** (open daily for lunch and dinner; 1079 N. Main; tel. 752-9969), **Mandarin Garden** (open Mon. to Fri. for lunch and daily for dinner; 432 N. Main; tel. 753-5789), and **New Grand View Cafe** (open daily for lunch and dinner; 25 W. 300 North; tel. 752-5892). For Mexican food, try **Garcia's** (open daily for lunch and dinner; 130 S. Main; tel. 753-0777) and **El Sol** (open daily for lunch and dinner; 871 N. Main; tel. 752-5743). The **Shangri-La** sells a full range of health foods; 438½ N. Main; tel. 752-1315.

### Entertainment

The old **Lyric Theatre** (known as the New Lyric when it opened in 1913) hosts musicals and plays in summer; 28 W. Center; tel. 750-

1657/1500. Watch the movies at **Excellence Theatres** (Cache Valley Mall, 1300 N. Main; tel. 753-3112 recording or 752-7762 office), **Capitol Theatre** (43 S. Main; tel. 752-7521), **Redwood Theatre** (795 N. Main; tel. 752-5098), **Cinema Theatre** (60 W. 100 North; tel. 753-1900), or the **Utah Theatre** (18 W. Center; tel. 752-3072).

## Events

The Cache Chamber of Commerce can fill you in on what's happening in the area; tel. 752-2161. Major annual events include:

**May:** Mendon May Day Festival has a May pole dance and other festivities (11 miles west). Cache Dairy Festival Pageant takes place on the USU campus. Richmond Black and White Days is a Holstein cattle show (13 miles north). University students compete in the USU Intercollegiate Rodeo at Cache County Fairgrounds in Logan. Smithfield Health Days presents a parade, historic tour, crafts, and games (7 miles north).

**June:** Summerfest Art Faire in downtown Logan features works by local artists, concerts, food, and a home tour. Clarkston Pony Express Days is a community celebration (21 miles northwest).

**July:** A big fireworks show takes place on July 3rd at the USU Romney Stadium. Hyrum puts on a July 4th rodeo and parade (7 miles south). Lewiston observes the Fourth with

horse racing, games, and fireworks (19 miles north). Festival of the American West celebrates Western heritage with a historical pageant and Great West Fair: the multimedia pageant presented each evening has a cast of 200 actors, dancers, and musicians; fair exhibits feature traditional pioneer and Indian food, fiddle and banjo music, square dancing, medicine man shows, a mountain man camp, and Indian and pioneer craft demonstrations; events take place on the Utah State University campus and last 8 days, usually starting on the last Fri. in July.

**August:** Festival of the American West continues. Cache County Fair and Rodeo has agricultural and craft exhibits along with PRCA rodeo action at the fairgrounds in Logan. The Martin Harris Pageant recreates pioneer and Mormon history at the Clarkston Amphitheater (21 miles northwest). Providence City Celebration has parades, concerts, games, and food (2 miles south).

**September:** Wellsville Founders Day Celebration on Labor Day commemorates the first pioneers to settle in Cache Valley (7 miles southwest).

**November:** A Christmas Parade starts off the holiday season.

## Recreation

**Willow Park** is a good place for a picnic and has the added attractions of a small zoo,

*rousing finale of the Martin Harris Pageant*

playground, volleyball courts, and a softball field; at 450 W. 700 South. **Bicentennial Park** offers picnic spots downtown at 100 S. Main. Swim year-round at the indoor **Municipool,** 114 E. 1000 North; tel. 752-9323. **Logana Pool & Waterslide** has summertime fun at 410 W. 1400 North; tel. 752-3111. The **Community Recreation Center** features tennis and handball/racquetball courts, basketball, volleyball, weight room, indoor track, table tennis, sauna, and whirlpool at 195 S. 100 West; tel. 752-3221. **Tennis courts** are also at Mount Logan Middle School (875 N. 200 East), Central Park (85 S. 300 East), and Worthington Park (Logan High School, 162 W. 100 South). **Golf** at 18-hole Logan Golf & Country Club (semiprivate, 710 N. 1500 East; tel. 753-6050), 18-hole Birch Creek Golf Course (600 E. Center in Smithfield, 7 miles north; tel. 563-6825), or the 9-hole Sherwood Hills (in Sardine Canyon, 13 miles southwest on US 89/91; tel. 245-6055/4622). Sherwood Hills also offers 2 outdoor and one indoor pools, horseback riding, cross-country ski trails, racquetball, and tennis. **Ice skating** is popular in winter at Central Park, 85 S. 300 East. The Logan Ranger District has lists of hikes and cross-country ski tours in the area; 860 N. 1200 East; tel. 753-2772.

**Beaver Mountain Ski Area** has 3 double chairlifts serving 16 runs, longest of which is 2¼ miles and drops 1,600 vertical feet. A cafeteria, ski shop, rentals, and lessons are available at the day lodge. Open daily 9 a.m.-4 p.m. from early Dec. to Easter; tel. 753-4822 (snow and road conditions), 753-0921 (office, ski school, and lift tickets). Go 28 miles east on US 89, then 1.5 miles north on UT 243.

### Services

The **post office** is at 151 N. 100 West; tel. 752-7246. **Logan Regional Hospital** provides 24-hour emergency care at 1400 N. 500 East; tel. 752-2050, (800) 824-6061 in Utah, or (800) 824-6601 out of state. **Trailhead Sports** has hiking and camping gear, cross-country ski rentals and sales, and topo maps

at 117 N. Main; tel. 753-1541. Outdoor sporting goods are also sold at **Surplus Savers** (140 S. Main; tel. 752-5745), **The Sportsman** (129 N. Main; tel. 752-0211), and **Herman's World of Sporting Goods** (585 N. Main.; tel. 752-4287).

### Telephone Numbers

Emergency (police, fire, or medical): 911.
Utah Highway Patrol: 752-1110.
Cache County Fire/Sheriff: 752-4103.
Logan City Police: 752-8140.
Local road and weather info: 752-0045.
Mountain weather/avalanche hazards/
   forest facts: 752-4146.

### Information

The **Bridgerland Tourist Council/Cache Chamber of Commerce** has maps and travel information for Cache and Rich counties, including Logan and Bear Lake; open Mon. to Fri. 8 a.m.-5 p.m., Sat. 9 a.m.-6 p.m.; located downtown at 160 N. Main (Logan, UT 84321); tel. 752-2161 or (800) 657-5353. To learn more of local history and architecture, ask for the booklet, *A Guide to Logan, Utah's Historical Homes and Sites.* For recreation information and maps of the surrounding mountain country, visit the **Logan Ranger District office;** open Mon. to Fri. 8 a.m.-5 p.m. (and Sat. 8 a.m.-5 p.m. in summer); on the east edge of the USU campus at 860 N. 1200 East (Logan, UT 84321); tel. 753-2772. The district covers Logan Canyon, the Bear River Range, and the Wellsville Mountains. Logan's **public library** is open Mon. to Sat. at 255 N. Main; tel. 752-2365. Good places for regional and general reading include **A Bookstore** (130 N. 100 East; tel. 752-9089) and **The Book Table** (87 N. Main; tel. 752-3055).

### Transport

**Greyhound buses** run daily south to Ogden and Salt Lake City and northeast to Idaho Falls (and West Yellowstone in summer); 18 E. Center; tel. 752-4921. **Logan Cab** provides taxi service; tel. 753-3663. See the telephone yellow pages for auto rentals. No scheduled airlines serve Logan.

## VICINITY OF LOGAN

### Ronald V. Jensen Living Historical Farm

This outdoor museum recreates life on a Mormon family farm in 1917. Workers dress in period clothing to plow the soil, thresh the grain, milk the cows, shear sheep, and butcher hogs much as the early 20th C. farmers did. The men mostly work out in the fields, while women stay closer to home to cook, can, quilt, gather eggs from the hen house, and pick vegetables from the garden. You'll see animals and breeds representative of early farms, a lineup of steam tractors, a giant early gasoline tractor, and many other pieces of farm machinery. Buildings here include an 1875 farmhouse, summer kitchen, root cellar, smoke house, blacksmith shop, horse barn, sheep shed, and a privy or two. Special demonstrations take place all through the year, usually on Sat.; call to have a schedule sent. The farm is open Tues. to Sat. 10 a.m.-4 p.m. during June, July, and Aug.; $2 adult, $.50 children, $5 family, $1 high-school student or senior. Utah State University graduate students work the historical farm, located 6 miles southwest of Logan on US 89/91; tel. 245-4064.

### Hyrum State Park

The Little Bear River feeds this popular 450-acre reservoir beside the town of Hyrum. Boaters come to water ski, sail, or paddle across the waters. There are sandy beaches at several places along the shore (no lifeguards). Fishing for perch and smaller numbers of rainbow and brown trout tends to be only fair, but fishermen sometimes have good luck in the river just below the spillway. Winter visitors fish through the ice, ice skate, and sail ice boats during freeze-up from about mid-Dec. to late March. The state park has 2

*cutting alfalfa at the Ronald V. Jensen Farm*

developed areas on the north shore. The launch and campground area has showers, a group area, picnic grounds, beach, boat ramp, docks, and the ranger office. Most park visitors head for the Day Use Area farther east along the shore for picnicking, lying on the beach, and swimming. It's reached by a ½-mile drive (follow signs) or by a ¾-mile foot trail from the campground. There may be boat rentals at the lake. Groceries and boating and fishing supplies are nearby in Hyrum. The main season at Hyrum Lake (elev. 4,700 ft.) runs mid-April to late Sept.; water and outhouses are available off season at the campground. Day use costs $3, camping $8. Campground reservations are advised on summer weekends. The park makes a good base for exploring the Cache Valley area; rangers can suggest places to go. They also have snowmobiling information. The ranger office, at the main entrance, is open daily 8 a.m.-5 p.m. during the warmer months and 8 a.m.-noon the rest of the year; 405 W. 300 South, Hyrum, UT 84319; tel. 245-6866 (ranger) or (800) 322-3770 (reservations). From Logan, drive south 7 miles on the Hyrum Road, which branches off US 89/91 on the south edge of town, or go southwest 6 miles on US 89/91, then turn east 3 miles on UT 101 and follow signs.

## Hardware Ranch And Blacksmith Fork Canyon

The Utah Division of Wildlife Resources operates this ranch in the midst of the northern Wasatch Range to provide winter feed for herds of elk. In winter, staff sometimes offer sleigh rides for a closer look at the large animals; tel. 245-3131. You're not likely to see elk here in the warmer months, though the drive in is still pretty. The 16-mile paved road from Hyrum east to Hardware Ranch follows the scenic Blacksmith Fork Canyon past fishing spots (for trout and whitefish), **Shenoah Picnic Area,** and **Pioneer Campground.** Pioneer's sites are open late May to late Oct. with water; $6. Two small campgrounds, Friendship and Spring, are to the north along the Left Hand Fork of Blacksmith Canyon; they're open mid-May to late Oct. (no water or fee). An extensive snowmobile trail system

extends from Hardware Ranch as far as Logan Canyon to the north and the Monte Cristo area to the south, with many side trails.

## Cache Valley Dairy

About 100,000 pounds of cheese roll out daily from what's claimed to be one of the world's largest Swiss cheese plants. The dairy makes other types of cheese too, which you can sample or see being made on self-guided tours. The Cheese Chalet sales room is open Mon. to Sat. 8 a.m.-5 p.m.; tel. 563-3281. Cache Valley Dairy is in Amalga at 6351 N. 2150 West. From Logan, follow Main St. (US 91) north 7 miles to Smithfield, then turn left 3 miles at the light.

## Wellsville Mountains Wilderness

Rarely do mountain ranges rise so high from so narrow a base. Steep slopes on each side tower 5,000 feet above the Cache Valley to the east and the Great Salt Lake to the west. Box Elder Peak tops the range at 9,372 feet. A loop hike to the Mendon Peak area offers outstanding views and bird-watching. Carry water as it's a long climb up. Also bring wind and rain gear; the breeze on the ridge is far cooler than temperatures in the valley. See the Honeyville and Wellsville 7½-minute topo maps. Few people backpack here because of the steep terrain on the way up, exposed ridges on top, and scarcity of water.

From the farm community of Mendon (11 miles west of Logan) head west 2 miles on Third North to a parking area on the right. Follow a dirt road, too rough for most vehicles, about ⅓ mile (keep left at the fork) to the trailhead in Deep Canyon. The trail is easy to follow and well graded. Even so, expect a strenuous hike because of the relentless climb. From the trailhead (elev. 5,400 ft.) in woods of oak and box elder, you'll climb 2,700 feet in 3 miles through groves of aspen, mountain ash, and white fir to the ridgeline. Panoramic views take in the Cache Valley, Great Salt Lake, meanders and oxbow lakes of the Bear River, and many mountains of northern Utah and southern Idaho. Mendon Peak (elev. 8,766 ft.) is just to the east, ½ mile away and 660 feet higher; the trail contours to a saddle just past the peak, then switchbacks up the ridge to the summit. Limber pine and wildflowers cling to the slopes. Bird-watchers can turn northwest after first reaching the ridge from Deep Canyon, then go one mile to the "8585" peak—a prime hawk-watching point, especially in fall. Hawks and other birds cavort in the thermals.

To complete the loop (a car shuttle is needed), follow the ridge trail southeast 1¾ miles past Mendon Peak and Scout Peak to Stewart Pass (elev. 8,376 ft.), then drop steeply east into Coldwater Canyon; tiny Coldwater Lake is 1¾ miles away, then it's a more gentle ¾ mile to Coldwater Trailhead. This trailhead is reached by taking Main St. south from Mendon and following signs 3.5 miles for "To National Forest."

## LOGAN CANYON

From its mouth on the east edge of Logan, Logan Canyon winds more than 20 miles into the Bear River Range. These mountains are sometimes considered a northeast extension of the Wasatch Range. Steep slopes on the west rise to rolling plateau country across the top and moderate slopes descend to Bear Lake on the east. Paved US 89 follows the canyon floor past picnic areas, campgrounds, fishing spots, and trailheads before turning away from the Logan River and topping out at an elevation of 7,800 feet at Bear Lake Summit. Beaver Mountain Ski Area offers downhill action near the upper end of Logan Canyon. In autumn, maples of the lower canyon turn a brilliant crimson while aspen of the higher country are transformed to gold. Roadside geologic signs explain features in Logan Canyon. Picnicking is free at picnic areas, though you have to pay to picnic at some campgrounds. Contact the Logan Ranger District office for info on picnicking, camping, fishing, hiking, cross-country skiing, snowmobiling, and road conditions; open Mon. to Fri. 8 a.m.- 5 p.m.; 860 N. 1200 East in Logan; tel. 753-2772. Some campsites can be reserved through MISTIX; tel. (800) 283-CAMP.

## Logan Canyon Scenic Drive

**Mile 0:** Entering Logan Canyon (2.5 miles east of downtown Logan on US 89). Ragged cliffs rise steeply on each side, allowing just enough room for the river and highway to squeeze through.

**Mile 2.7:** Zanavoo Lodge Restaurant on right.

**Mile 2.9:** Bridger Campground (elev. 5,000 ft.) on right. Open early June to mid-Sept. with water; $6.

**Mile 3.9:** Spring Hollow Campground to right across bridge. Open early June to mid-Sept. with water; $6. Riverside Nature Trail goes upstream to Guinavah Campground, 1½ miles away. The easy walk is good for bird watching. From Guinavah, you can loop back to Spring Hollow via the Crimson Trail; this more strenuous trail takes you up the limestone cliffs and down in another 2 miles. It takes its name from the autumn colors visible along the way.

**Mile 4.4:** Dewitt Picnic Area on right.

**Mile 4.6:** (just past Milepost 379) Wind Cave Trailhead on left, parking on right. Wind Cave, with eroded caverns and arches, is one mile and an 1,100-foot climb from the trailhead.

**Mile 4.9:** Malibu and Guinavah campgrounds (elev. 5,200 ft.) on right. Open mid-May to late Sept. with water; $6.

**Mile 6.8:** Card Picnic Area on right.

**Mile 7.5:** Choke Cherry Picnic Area on right.

**Mile 7.8:** Preston Valley Campground (elev. 5,500 ft.) on right. Open mid-May to late Sept. with water; $6.

**Mile 9.0:** Lodge Campground (elev. 5,600 ft.) one mile to right on Forest Route 047. Open late May to mid-Sept. with water; $6.

**Mile 9.8:** China Row Picnic Area on right.

**Mile 10.0:** Wood Camp Campground (elev. 5,600 ft.) on left. Open mid-May to late Oct.; no water or charge. The Jardine Juniper Trail begins nearby, climbing 1,900 feet in 2½ miles to Old Jardine, a venerable Rocky Mountain juniper tree. Still growing after 3,200 years, it measures about 27 feet in circumference and 45 feet high. The name honors a USU alumnus.

**Mile 11.7:** Logan Cave on left. This wild cave, about 2,000 feet long, can easily be explored (have at least 2 lights). Though dissolved from limestone, the cave lacks elaborate formations.

**Mile 15.3:** Rick's Spring on left. Crystal-clear water flows out of a small cave.

**Mile 19.2:** Tony Grove Lake Recreation Area to left. Lewis Turner Campground (elev. 6,300 ft.) is 0.5 mile in from the highway; open early June to late Oct. with water; $6. Tony Grove Lake Campground (elev. 8,100 ft.) is 7 miles in beside an alpine lake; open mid-July to late Sept. with water; $7. Fishermen try for the lake's trout; no boat motors allowed. An easy

*Tony Grove Lake*

self-guided nature trail circles clockwise around Tony Grove Lake; brochures should be in a box at the end of the road. This is also the trailhead for White Pine Trail and Naomi Peak Trail. Naomi Peak (elev. 9,980 ft.) crowns the Mount Naomi Wilderness.

**Mile 20.2:** Red Banks Campground (elev. 6,500 ft.) on left. Open early June to mid-Oct. with water; $6.

**Mile 22.5:** Highway leaves Logan Canyon and climbs along Beaver Creek.

**Mile 25.3:** Beaver Mountain Ski Area 1.5 miles to left on paved UT 243. Sink Hollow Cross-country Ski Trail begins near the turnoff; open about mid-Dec. to late March, depending on snow. Beaver Mountain Ski Area offers 3 double chairlifts serving 16 runs, longest of which is 2¼ miles with a 1,600-foot vertical drop. A cafeteria, ski shop, rentals, and lessons are available at the day lodge. Open daily 9 a.m.-4 p.m. from early Dec. to Easter; tel. 753-4822 (snow and road conditions), 753-0921 (office, ski school, and lift tickets).

**Mile 30.3:** Bear Lake Summit (elev. 7,800 ft.). Limber Pine Nature Trail begins from the parking area on the right and goes to a massive limber pine 25 feet in circumference and 44 feet high. Brochures should be in a box near the start. At one time this tree was thought to be the world's oldest and largest limber pine, but a forestry professor at USU discovered that it is really 5 trees grown together and "only" about 560 years old. The easy self-guided walk takes about an hour; Bear Lake can be seen to the east.

**Mile 31.1:** Sunrise Campground (elev. 7,000 ft.) on right. Open mid-June to mid-Sept. with water; $7.

**Mile 31.3:** Bear Lake Overlook on right. This viewpoint has a sweeping panorama of Bear Lake and surrounding mountains. Signs tell you about this unique lake. The Sawtooth Mountains on the northeast horizon belong to the Salt River Range, a southern extension of the Grand Tetons. The Uinta Mountains to the southeast are the only major range in the "lower 48" states running east-west; Kings Peak, Utah's highest summit, tops the range at 13,528 feet.

**Mile 37.4:** Garden City on the shore of Bear Lake.

## BEAR LAKE

More than 28,000 years ago, faulting of massive blocks of the Earth's crust created a basin here 50 miles long and 12 miles wide. Bear Lake filled the entire valley during the last ice age, but it now has receded to cover an area 20 miles long and 8 miles wide, at an elevation of 5,900 feet. About half the lake lies in Utah and half in Idaho. The turquoise color is thought to be caused by limestone particles suspended in the water. The ecology of Bear Lake has been upset somewhat by canals diverting water from the Bear River in times of surplus and draining water when needed downstream for irrigation. Eight thousand years ago the lake and river were connected, then changing conditions separated the 2 bodies of water until man intervened. Bear Lake National Wildlife Refuge occupies 17,600 acres of marshlands north of the lake, a favored stopping place for sandhill cranes, herons, white pelicans, egrets, and many species of ducks. Four species of fish evolved in Bear Lake that are not found any other place in the world. One of these, the Bonneville cisco, attracts fishermen by the thousands. During spawning in Jan., nets are used to dip the small (6-8 inches long) and tasty fish from the icy water. Fish sought year-round by anglers include the native Bear Lake cutthroat and Bonneville whitefish and the introduced rainbow trout, mackinaw trout, and yellow perch. Keep an eye out for the Bear Lake Monster, a dark dragonlike creature 90 feet long that spouts water!

David McKenzie, an early fur trapper, named the lake after the many black bear once found here. Nomadic Indian tribes and groups of trappers frequented the shores during the 1820s and held 2 large rendezvous here. Mormons arrived beginning in 1863 to start scattered farms and ranches. Thousands of summer cabins have sprouted along the shore and hillsides in recent years to take advantage of the scenery and water sports.

Bear Lake State Park offers a marina and campground on the west shore, a large camping area on the south shore at Rendezvous Beach, and undeveloped campgrounds on the east shore.

### Bear Lake State Park: Marina

The 71,000 acres of Bear Lake give plenty of room to water ski, sail, or fish. The marina has boat slips protected by a breakwater, a boat ramp, swimming area, picnic tables, campground with showers, and ranger offices. Season is year-round; $3 day use, $8 camping; Box 184, Garden City, UT 84028; tel. 946-3343 or (800) 322-3770 (reservations). On busy summer weekends it's a good idea to have reservations for the marina or Rendezvous Beach areas. The marina is one mile north of Garden City on US 89.

### Bear Lake State Park: Rendezvous Beach

A wide sandy beach is the big attraction on the lake's southern shore. The park has a day-use area with a boat-rental concession and several campgrounds with showers. Ask at the entrance station for recommended places to camp; some sites have lake views, some offer hookups, and some are set up mainly for RVs. Open early May to late Sept.; $3 day use, $8 camping, $12 camping w/hookups; Box 184, Garden City, UT 84028; tel. 946-3343 or (800) 322-3770 (reservations). Located 8 miles south of Garden City near Laketown.

### Bear Lake State Park: East Shore

Primitive campgrounds and day-use areas are located on the east side of Bear Lake. From south to north are First Point, Second Point (day-use only), South Eden, East Side (day-use only), Cisco Beach, and Rainbow Cove. Sites stay open all year; outhouses are provided but only South Eden had drinking water at press time; $3 day use, $5 camping. First Point and Rainbow Cove have boat ramps. Scuba divers like the steep underwater drop-offs near Cisco Beach; they sometimes hold a Cisco Disco get-together here in August. Turn north from Laketown.

### Garden City And Vicinity

This small town (year-round pop. 300), on the east shore at the junction of US 89 and UT 30, comes to life in summer. You can learn about the area at a **tourist information cabin** at the highway junction; open Mon. to Sat. 8 a.m.-7 p.m. from May to September. The town celebrates the harvest of its most famous crop during the **Raspberry Festival** on the first weekend in Aug. with a parade, crowning of Miss Raspberry, Little Buckaroo Rodeo, crafts, and entertainment. The **Mountain Man Rendezvous** reenacts the big gatherings of fur trappers and Indians that took place at Bear Lake in the summers of 1826 and 1827; the modern event is held the third weekend of Sept. at Rendezvous Beach, Bear Lake State Park; tel. 946-3343.

**Bear Lake Motor Lodge** is open all year and has a restaurant; rooms cost $38.15-65.40; located just south of the hwy. junction at 50 S. Bear Lake Blvd. (UT 30); tel. 946-3271. **Ideal Beach Resort** offers condo accommodations year-round ($76.30-218 in summer, less off-season), the **South Shore Grill** restaurant (open summer only Tues. to Sat. for dinner; tel. 946-3421), boat rentals, beach, swimming pools, and miniature golf; tel. 946-3364 or (800) 634-1018 in Utah; located at 2144 S. Bear Lake Blvd., 3.3 miles south of Garden City. The nearby 9-hole **Bear Lake Golf Course** is open to the public; tel. 946-8742. **Bear Lake Bed and Breakfast** is open all year off US 89, 2 miles north of the Utah-Idaho border; $40-65 d; tel. (208) 945-2688. **Fay's Trailer Park** is open mid-April to late Sept.; 285 N. Bear Lake Boulevard; tel. 773-2415; $7 tent or RV no hookups, $10 w/hookups; no showers. **Bear Lake KOA** offers a swimming pool, miniature golf, tennis, store, showers, and laundry; open from May 1 to Oct. 30; $13.63 tent, $18 RV w/hookups, $24.53 cabins; tel. 946-3454; 0.8 mile north of Garden City on US 89, near the state park marina. **Bear Lake West** has a steak and seafood restaurant open in summer for Sun. brunch and Thurs. to Sun. for dinner (tel. 208-945-2221) and a 9-hole golf course (tel. 208-945-2222); 4.5 miles north of Garden

City, just across the Idaho border (3 miles south of Fish Haven). **Pickleville Playhouse** features family entertainment during the summer, usually Thurs., Fri., and Sat. evenings; a Western-style cookout precedes the show; tel. 946-2918 (Garden City) or 753-1944 (Logan); 2.8 miles south of Garden City. A water-tube slide provides a splash, 3 miles south on UT 30. A roadside picnic area is near the lake 7 miles south of Garden City and one mile north of Rendezvous Beach.

**Randolph**

Rich County seat, Randolph (pop. 800) is a quiet rural town 19 miles south of Bear Lake. Farming and ranching have been the main activities ever since Randolph H. Stewart led the first settlers here from Idaho in 1870. Rich County Round-Up Days, held in Aug., has a rodeo, parade, and exhibits. No accommodations in town, just one cafe.

*elk* (Cervus canadensis)

*Pavant Butte*

# WESTCENTRAL UTAH

## INTRODUCTION

Utah's Wild West remains nearly as wild as ever. Rugged mountain ranges and barren desert valleys have discouraged all but the most determined individuals. Explorers, pioneers in wagon trains, Pony Express riders, and telegraph linemen crossed the inhospitable land with only the desire to reach the other side. It took the promise of gold and silver to lure large numbers of people into the jagged hills. Fading ghost towns still show the industry of the early miners. Hardy ranchers also braved the isolation to grow hay and run their cattle and sheep. Shortage of water has always been the limiting factor to development. Travelers, however, can enjoy the solitude and the thrill of exploring a land little changed since white men first arrived. Roads provide surprisingly good access for such a remote region. Paved I-80, US 50/6, and UT 21 cross it, while dirt roads branch off in all directions. Driving along the Pony Express and Stage Route from Fairfield to Ibapah might be the most unique driving tour; you experience some of the same unfenced wilderness as did the tough young Pony Express riders. This and many other back roads can be negotiated by car in dry weather. For the adventurous, the wildly beautiful mountain ranges offer countless hiking possibilities—though you'll have to rough it. Hardly any developed trails exist.

### THE LAND

Located in the Great Basin, westcentral Utah has about equal amounts of valley and mountain terrain. Geologic forces have worked here

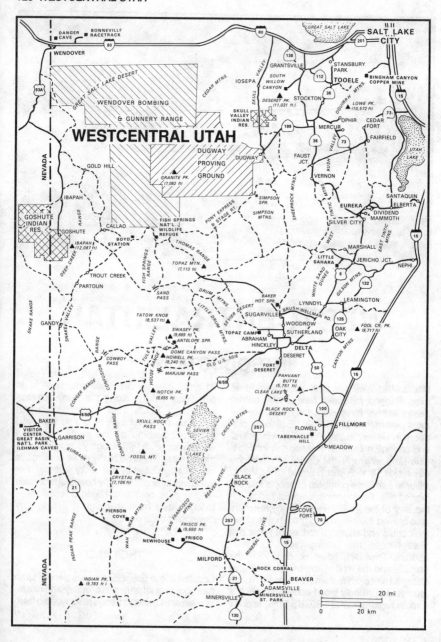

on a grand scale. Great blocks of the earth's crust rising along faults formed the mountains, all of which run north-south. Volcanic activity has left well-preserved craters, cinder cones, and lava flows. The massive sandbars that once lined the southern shore of Lake Bonneville have blown northeastward to form impressive dunes at Little Sahara. Streambeds in westcentral Utah actually drain into several different subbasins; the 2 largest are Great Salt Lake and Sevier Lake.

Clouds moving in from the Pacific Ocean lose much of their moisture to the Sierra Nevada and other towering mountain ranges in California and Nevada. By the time the depleted clouds reach westcentral Utah, only the Deep Creek, Stansbury, and southern Wah Wah mountains reach high enough to gather sufficient rain and snow to support permanent streams. Notable summits of the region include Ibapah (12,087 ft.) and Haystack (12,020 ft.) peaks of the Deep Creek Range, Deseret Peak (11,031 ft.) of the Stansbury Mountains, Swasey (9,669 ft.) and Notch (9,655 ft.) peaks of the House Range, Frisco Peak (9,660 ft.) of the San Francisco Mountains, and Crystal Peak (7,106 ft.) of the Wah Wah Range.

Though westcentral Utah is now one of the driest parts of the Great Basin, a far different scene existed 10,000 years ago. Freshwater Lake Bonneville then covered 20,000 square miles, one-fourth of Utah. Forests blanketed the mountains that poked above the lake waters. With time, the giant inland sea gradually shrank to much smaller remnants such as Great Salt Lake, leaving behind the glistening salt flats of the Great Salt Lake Desert. Rainfall variations in historic time have caused Sevier Lake, southwest of Delta, to fluctuate between being a dry lakebed and the state's third largest body of water.

### Climate
Precipitation averages 8-10 inches annually over most of the region at the lower (4,000- to 6,000-ft.) elevations. The rain and snow that do fall soon disappear because of the low humidity and abundant sunshine. Rainfall

peaks in spring and again during the late summer-early autumn thunderstorm season. In this harsh semi-desert, winter temperatures can drop into the subzeros, but the summer sun can send the thermometer climbing above 100 degrees. Visibility to 70 miles or more in the clean, dry air rewards mountain climbers with incredible views.

## FLORA AND FAUNA

Vegetation in the valleys consists of sparse, low-growing plants such as saltbush, greasewood, black and bud sagebrush, shadscale, little rabbitbrush, Mormon tea, and grasses. Big sagebrush, juniper, and pinyon pine grow higher up. The highest peaks support mountain shrubs, aspen, and a variety of conifers, including the long-lived bristlecone pine.

Availability of water determines the quantity and variety of wildlife. Of the larger animals, mule deer and pronghorn are most widespread. Elk can be found in mountainous areas east of Delta. Rocky Mountain bighorn sheep have been reintroduced in the Deep Creek Range. Herds of wild horses roam the Confusion and House ranges. Other wildlife includes coyote, mountain lion, bobcat, kit fox,

beautiful thistle
(Cirsium pulchellum)

spotted and striped skunks, and black-tailed jack rabbit. Vast numbers of birds visit Fish Springs National Wildlife Refuge and other desert oases. Waterfowl and marsh birds stop over in greatest numbers during their early spring and late autumn migrations. Many smaller birds nest near water sources in late spring and early summer.

## HISTORY

### Indian Peoples

Paleo-Indians entered the region about 15,000 years ago to collect wild plants and to pursue the now-extinct mammoth and other big game. After 5,000 years or so, the drying climate and changing environment caused many of the large animals to disappear. Still nomadic, the Indian groups adapted by relying more on small game and wild plant foods. New technologies of bow and arrow, pottery, and small-scale agriculture distinguished the Fremont people around A.D. 550. When the Fremont culture faded about 1300, perhaps because of drought and depletion of resources, the culturally distinct Shoshoni Indians moved in. These nomadic hunters and gatherers proved well suited to the dry environment. The modern Goshute (or Gosiutes) and Ute Indians likely descended from them.

Within the first decades of Utah's settlement by white men, all the tribes suffered great losses of population and land. Even today the Indians struggle to adapt to modern ways. The Goshutes occupied northwest Utah and adjacent Nevada, and they now live in the Goshute and Skull Valley reservations. The Utes had the greatest range of all Utah's tribes, extending from westcentral Utah into Colorado and New Mexico; they now have reservations in northeast Utah and southwest Colorado.

### Explorers And Overland Trails

Imposing terrain and scarcity of water discouraged early explorers from crossing the Great Basin region. In 1776, the Spanish became the first non-Indians to visit westcentral Utah when members of the Dominguez-Escalante expedition left the Utah Lake area and headed southwest, passing near the present-day towns of Delta and Milford. Most American mountain men of the 1820s also kept to the Great Basin's edge, but not Jedediah Smith. With a party of 17 men, Smith set out in 1826 from northern Utah for Spanish California, searching for new fur-trapping areas. During his return to Utah with 2 companions, the little group nearly perished from deep snows in the Sierra Nevada and from thirst in the desert. Government explorer John C. Fremont named and made the first scientific studies of the Great Basin in 1845, putting to rest myths about the Great Salt Lake's monsters, whirlpools, and subterranean outlets to the Pacific.

In the following year, travelers began crossing the Great Basin as a shortcut to California. Horses and mules made the crossing safely, but the Donner-Reed wagon train met disaster. Mud of the Great Salt Lake Desert slowed the group so much that they ran out of water and lost some of their wagons and oxen. The exhausted and demoralized group reached the Sierra Nevada late in the season, when snowstorms trapped and killed 40 of the 87 emigrants. In 1859, Captain J.S. Simpson surveyed a military road to the south of the treacherous desert to connect Camp Floyd in central Utah with Carson Valley in western Nevada. Swift riders of the Pony Express used the road, known as the South-Central Overland Route, in 1860-61, before the telegraph ended this brief chapter of American history. The Lincoln Highway, America's first designated transcontinental motoring route, included part of this road from 1910 until 1927.

### Gold!

Prospectors began locating placer gold deposits in the early 1860s, though significant production had to wait for arrival of the transcontinental railroad in 1869. Deposits of gold, silver, copper, lead, and zinc were found in quick succession. Major mining districts included Ophir, Mercur, and Tintic to the southwest of Salt Lake City; Gold Hill, Clifton, and

Willow Springs in the far west of Utah; Detroit near Delta; and the San Francisco Mountains near Milford. Active gold mining continues in the Mercur, Tintic, and Detroit districts.

### Bombs Away!

Much of the Great Salt Lake Desert is off-limits to visitors because of military activities. Jet aircraft and helicopters occasionally break the silence in flights above the Wendover Bombing and Gunnery Range. Scientists and engineers at Dugway Proving Grounds work on chemical and biological weapons. The base received some notoriety in 1968 after 6,500 sheep died on neighboring ranches. The military never admitted that they had released toxic warfare chemicals, but they did compensate the ranchers. Just south of Tooele you'll see the neat rows of buildings across the vast Tooele Army Depot, which functions as a storage, maintenance, repair, and training center.

## WENDOVER AND VICINITY

This desert oasis has a split personality—half the town lies in Utah and half in Nevada. On both sides you'll find accommodations and restaurants where you can take a break from long drives on I-80. Several casinos on the Nevada side offer a chance to lose your money in the usual gambling games. Most of the town's visitor facilities line Wendover Blvd., also known as State Hwy., which parallels the interstate. Stop in at the **Nevada-Wendover Welcome Center** for information about the area; open daily 8:30-11:30 a.m. and noon-5 p.m.; located on the Nevada side at 937 Wendover Blvd. (Box 2468, Wendover, NV 89883); look for the WW II memorial capped by a B-29 in front; tel. (702) 664-3414 or toll-free (800) 426-6862. Two major annual events happen near Wendover in August, **Speed Week** (see "Bonneville Salt Flats International Speedway" below) and the **Wendover Air Show**.

Wendover began in 1907 as a watering station during construction of the Western Pacific Railroad. The highway went through in 1925, marking the community's beginnings as a travelers' stop. Wendover Air Force Base got its start in 1940 and soon grew to be one of the world's largest military complexes. During WW II, crews of bombers and other aircraft learned their navigation, formation flying, gunnery, and bombing skills above 3½ million acres of desert belonging to the base. Only after the war ended did the government reveal that one of the bomber groups had been training in preparation for dropping atomic bombs on Japan. Little remains of the base, once a city of nearly 20,000 people. Hill Air Force Base, near Ogden, continues to use the vast military reserve for training air crews.

### Bonneville Speedway Museum

This sizable museum collection represents America's love affair with cars. Photos show the drivers and the sleek machines they used in setting new speed records at Bonneville

*Speed Week at the Bonneville Salt Flats*

Salt Flats. You'll also find a few of the actual cars that were driven. Exhibits rotate; models on display include such antiques as a 1915 Dodge Touring Car, a 1926 Model-T Ford, and classics like the 1955 Mercedes 300 SL Gull Wing and 1962 Sport Roadster Thunderbird. The gift shop sells automobile memorabilia. Open daily in summer (June 1 to Sept. 15) 10 a.m.-6 p.m., then Sat. and Sun. 10 a.m.-6 p.m. the rest of the year; $2 adult, $1 children 6-12; tel. 665-7721. Located on the east edge of town at 1000 Wendover Boulevard.

## Bonneville Salt Flats
## International Speedway
A brilliant white layer of salt left behind by prehistoric Lake Bonneville covers more than 44,000 acres of the Great Salt Lake Desert. For much of the year, a shallow layer of water sits atop the salt flats. Wave action planes the surface almost perfectly level—it's said that the curvature of the earth can be seen here. The hot sun usually dries out the salt flats enough for speed runs in summer and autumn. Cars began running across the salt in 1914 and continue to set faster and faster times. Rocket-powered vehicles have exceeded 600 mph. Exceptionally long and wide courses can be laid out; the main speedway is 10 miles long and 80 feet wide. A small tent city goes up near the course during the annual **Speed Week** in late Aug.; vehicles of an amazing variety of styles and ages take off individually to set new records for their class.

The salt flats, just east of Wendover, can easily be visited. Take I-80 Exit 4 and follow the paved road 5 miles north, then east. Signs and markers indicate if and where you can drive on the salt. Soft spots underlain by mud can trap vehicles venturing off the safe areas. Take care not to be on the track when racing events are being held!

## Danger Cave
Archaeologists from the University of Utah discovered thousands of prehistoric Indian artifacts in this cave. The 5 distinct layers of debris, the oldest dating back at least 10,000 years, have provided much new information on the region's early inhabitants. During field work in the 1950s, a huge piece of the cave's ceiling came crashing down. Nobody was hurt, but "Danger Cave" seemed an appropriate name. The cave is an undeveloped state historic monument. No exhibits or even a sign exist, so there's nothing special to see. If you'd like to come here anyway, take I-80 Exit 4, turn north 0.4 mile, turn left (west) 1.4 miles on a paved road, and turn right (northwest) 1.8 miles on a gravel road (keep left past gravel pits) to the cave. The road curves southwest along the face of the Silver Island Mountains. The cave entrance, easy to locate, lies about 200 feet from the road. Excavation work and the collapsed ceiling can be seen in the large room that once was home to ancient Indians.

# TOOELE

To sound like a native, pronounce the town's name "too-ILL-uh." Origin of the word is uncertain, but it may honor the Goshute Chief Tuilla. The attractive town (pop. 15,200) lies 34 miles southwest of Salt Lake City in the western foothills of the Oquirrh (OH-ker) Mountains. At its 4,900-foot elevation, Tooele enjoys fine views of the Great Salt Lake to the north and Tooele Valley and Stansbury Mountains to the west. Mormon pioneers settled here in 1849 to farm and raise livestock, but today the major industries are the nearby Tooele Army Depot, Dugway Proving Ground, and mining. Visitors wanting to know more about the region's history will enjoy the Tooele County Museum (mining, smelting, and railroading) and DUP Museum (pioneer history) in Tooele and the Donner-Reed Pioneer Museum in nearby Grantsville. Other attractions of the area include a scenic drive and overlook in the Oquirrhs, Ophir ghost town, the restored Benson grist mill, and hiking and camping in South Willow Canyon Recreation Area of the Stansbury Mountains.

## SIGHTS

### Tooele County Museum

A steam locomotive and a varied collection of old railroad cars surround Tooele's original (1909) train station. Inside are the restored station office and old photos showing railway workers, steam engines, and trestle construction. You might also meet and hear stories from retired railway men who volunteer as museum guides. Mining photos and artifacts illustrate life and work in the early days at Ophir, Mercur, Bauer, and other booming communities now faded to ghosts. Much of the old laboratory equipment and many tools on display came from the Tooele Smelter, which was built by International Smelter & Refining Company in 1907-09. It was used to process copper, lead, and zinc until 1972. Ore came over the Oquirrh Mountains by aerial tramway from the Bingham Mine. More than 3,000 people worked here during the hectic WW II years. A highly detailed model shows the modern Carr Fork Mill, built near Tooele but used only 90 days before being dismantled and shipped to a more profitable site in Papua New Guinea. Outside, kids can ride the scale railway (Sat. only), check out a caboose, or explore a simulated mine. Tooele County Museum is open Mon. to Sat. 10 a.m.-4 p.m. from Memorial to Labor Day weekends; donation; tel. 882-2836. Off-season visits can sometimes be arranged by calling 882-3195. From downtown Tooele, go east 0.5 mile on Vine St.; the museum is between Third East and Broadway.

### DUP Museum

Meet Tooele's pioneers in 128 framed pictures and see their clothing and other possessions. The small stone building housing the collec-

*DUP Museum*

tion dates from 1867 and was used as a courthouse for Tooele County. The little log cabin next door, built in 1856, was one of the town's first residences. The DUP Museum is open on request; tel. 882-0653 or 882-5470. Located downtown at 39 E. Vine St., just ½ block east of Main.

## Oquirrh Overlook

A look into the world's largest open-pit copper mine, panoramic views, and canyon scenery reward those who drive to this spot atop the Oquirrh Mountains. Views take in much of northern and western Utah: Great Salt Lake, Wasatch Range, Salt Lake City, Tooele Valley, and the Stansbury Mountains. Intricate patterns of the terraced **Bingham Canyon Copper Mine** lie directly below. To reach the overlook, 10.5 miles from town, head east on Vine St. and enter Middle Canyon. Forests of box elder and maple dominate the lower canyon, with firs and aspen farther up. After 7 miles you'll see a picnic and parking area on the right. The pavement ends here, and vehicles with trailers and large RVs should not go beyond it. The gravel road begins a steep one-mile climb with sharp curves to Butterfield Pass (elev. 8,400 ft.). Turn left at the pass and continue 2.5 miles to the overlook (elev. 9,400 ft.). Ice and snow close the road in winter.

By continuing east at the pass you'll descend on a gravel road through Butterfield Canyon into the Salt Lake Valley; ask about conditions as this road is sometimes closed. After 7 miles, the road meets a bend in a paved highway (this junction may not be signed). Continue straight (east) 11 miles to I-15 (Exits 294 and 295) or turn left (north) 5 miles to UT 48 and the Bingham Canyon Copper Mine entrance.

## Benson Grist Mill

Pioneers constructed this mill, one of the oldest buildings in western Utah, in 1854. Wooden pegs and rawhide strips hold the timbers together. E.T. Benson (the grandfather of LDS president Ezra Taft Benson) supervised its construction for Brigham Young, the mill's first owner. The mill operated until 1960, though it produced only animal feed during the last years. Local people restored the exterior in

1986. Much of the original machinery inside is still intact. To arrange a visit, call Bob or Marilyn Shields at 882-7137. A log cabin and other buildings stand on the grounds to the east, and to the west are ruins of the Utah Wool Pullery, which once removed millions of tons of wool annually from pelts. Future plans include restoration of the grist mill interior and the addition of other buildings to the grounds for a historic park. Benson Grist Mill is one block west of Mills Junction (UT 36 at UT 138); 8 miles north of Tooele, 4 miles south of I-80 Exit 99, and 10 miles east of Grantsville.

# PRACTICALITIES

## Accommodations

All the motels are conveniently along Main St. (UT 36). From north to south are: **Villa Motel** (475 N. Main; tel. 882-4551; $26.87 s or d, $32.10 kitchenette); **Great American Motor Inn** (491 S. Main; tel. 882-6100; free breakfasts, pool; $45.15 s, $48.38 d); and **Valleyview Motel** (585 Canyon Rd.; tel. 882-3235; all kitchenettes $32.50 s or d). No developed campgrounds are in or near town, but campers sometimes head east on Vine St. to Middle Canyon or southeast on Settlement Canyon Rd. (from south edge of town, 0.3 mile south of Valleyview Motel) into Settlement Canyon. Other possibilities are the campgrounds in **South Willow Canyon Recreation Area,** 20 miles west (see "Stansbury Mountains" below).

## Food

For a variety of American food, including steaks, seafood, roast beef, veal, and sandwiches, try the **Glowing Embers Restaurant** at 494 S. Main (across from Great American Motor Inn); open daily for breakfast, lunch, and dinner; tel. 882-0888. **Golden Corral Steakhouse** is an inexpensive family place open daily for lunch and dinner at 411 N. Main; tel. 882-6579. Dine Chinese-American at the **Sun Lok Yuen,** open daily for lunch and dinner at 615 N. Main; tel. 882-3003. Pick up pizza at: **Pizza Hut** (open daily for lunch and dinner at 540 N. Main; tel. 882-3924) or **Tooele Pizza & Restaurant** (also has Greek foods; open Mon. to Sat. for lunch and dinner at 21 E. Vine; tel. 882-8035). For Mexican and American food it's **Casa del Cielo** at 100 N. Main; open daily for breakfast, lunch, and dinner; tel. 882-2000. **Subway Sandwiches** offers deli sandwiches at 124 N. Main; open daily for lunch and dinner; tel. 882-8822.

### Entertainment And Events

Catch movies at the **Ritz,** 111 N. Main; tel. 882-2273. Bowl at **Harris Lanes,** near the corner of Main and Second North; tel. 882-3204. Annual events include the **High School Rodeo** the last weekend in March; **Arts Festival** in June; **Clover Stampede Rodeo** and **Fourth of July parade (fireworks** rotate between here and Grantsville) in July; **Tooele County Fair** in mid-Aug.; **Tooele Gem & Mineral Show** in Sept.; and **Tooele Valley Cutters Race** in November.

### Services

In **emergencies** (police, fire, or paramedic), dial 911. The **post office** is downtown at 65 N. Main; tel. 882-1429. **Tooele Valley Regional Medical Center** has 24-hour emergency services at 211 S. First East; tel. 882-1697. The **city park** offers picnicking, playground, and an indoor swimming pool (open year-round) at the corner of Vine and Second West; tel. 882-3247. **Elton Park** at Second North and Broadway has tennis courts and ball fields. **Middle Canyon** has a picnic area 7 miles from town (head east on Vine St.). **Settlement Canyon** contains a small reservoir (a local fishing and swimming spot) 0.5 mile up and **Legion Park,** a picnic area 1.5 miles up. Play golf at the 9-hole **Oquirrh Hills Golf Course** at Seventh and Edgemont on the east side of town; tel. 882-4220; or at the 18-hole course in **Stansbury Park** 8 miles north on UT 36; tel. 882-4162.

### Information

The **Tooele Chamber of Commerce** can tell you about the sights and services here; its office is at 50 E. 100 North (Box 1112, Tooele, UT 84074; open Mon. to Fri. about 9:30 a.m.-4:30 p.m.; tel. 882-0690. The **public library** is at 47 E. Vine St.; open Tues. to Sat.; tel. 882-2182.

# WEST OF TOOELE

## GRANTSVILLE

Old buildings and tall Lombardy poplars reflect the pioneer heritage of this rural community, first settled in 1851 and named Willow Creek Fort. The museum in town offers a look at local history. Grantsville stretches along UT 138, 9 miles northwest of Tooele. For hiking and camping in the Stansbury Mountains, crowned by 11,031-foot Deseret Peak, head south 10 miles to South Willow Canyon Recreation Area.

### Donner-Reed Pioneer Museum

Early residents built this one-room adobe schoolhouse within the old fort walls in 1861. Today it's a museum honoring the Donner-Reed wagon train of 1846. These pioneers crossed the Great Salt Lake Desert to the west with great difficulty, then became trapped by snow in the Sierra Nevada of California. Only 47 of the 87 who started the trip survived the winter. Museum displays include guns and relics abandoned on the salt flats by the desperate travelers, pottery, arrowheads, and other Indian artifacts, and more. Outside you can try out Grantsville's original iron jail and see an early log cabin, blacksmith shop, and old wagons. Another adobe building across the street served as a church and dates from 1866. The museum is open on request; free. To view the exhibits, visit or call the Grantsville Municipal Building (see "Practicalities" below). From the municipal building, go 2 blocks west on Main to Cooley St., then one block north to the museum.

### Practicalities

The small **Donner Motel** on Main St. has rooms at $21.40 s, $23.60 d; tel. 884-6531. Also on Main St. are **Daisy Mae,** serving

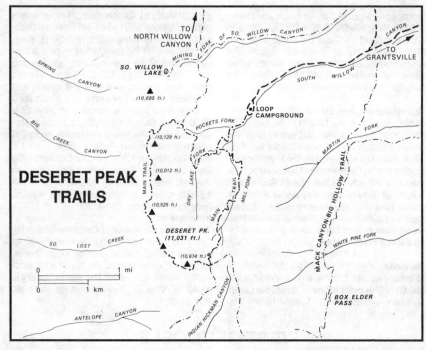

DESERET PEAK TRAILS

standard American fare daily, and 2 drive-ins. The **city park** offers picnicking and a playground; turn south from Main on Quirk (220 East) Street. Local events include the **Old Folks Sociable** (entertainment, dinners, dances) in March, **High School Rodeo** in late April, **July Fourth** parade and fireworks (the show alternates between here and Tooele each year), **Tooele County Stock Show and Rodeo** in July, **Pioneer Day** (parade, dances, entertainment) on July 24, and a **Christmas Parade** the first week in Dec.; contact the Grantsville Municipal Building for details, open Mon. to Fri. 8:30 a.m.-5 p.m. at the corner of 7 Park and Main; tel. 884-3411.

# STANSBURY MOUNTAINS

Not all western Utah is desert, as a visit to this section of Wasatch National Forest will show. Trails lead to Deseret Peak and other good day-hiking and overnight destinations. For more information about the area, contact the Salt Lake Ranger District of the Wasatch-Cache National Forest, 6944 S. 3000 East, Salt Lake City, UT 84121; tel. 524-5042. To reach South Willow Canyon from Salt Lake City, take I-80 to Exit 99, turn south 4 miles on UT 36, turn right (west) 10 miles on UT 138 to Grantsville, turn left (south) 5 miles on South Willow Rd., then right (southwest) 5 miles to the recreation area.

## Campgrounds
**South Willow Canyon Recreation Area,** on the east slope of the range, has 6 small campgrounds along the South Fork of Willow Creek. They are open from early June to mid-Sept.; no drinking water; free. Cottonwood, box elder, Douglas fir, and aspen thrive in the canyon. Elevations range from 6,080 feet at the first campground to 7,400 feet at the last one, at the end of the road. Sites can be crowded on summer weekends.

## Deseret Peak

Hikers enjoy expansive views amidst alpine forests and glacial cirques in the Deseret Peak Wilderness Area, in the central portion of the Stansbury Mountains. The moderately difficult 3,600-foot climb to the summit is 7½ miles roundtrip. Most of the way is easy to follow, though it's recommended that you carry the USGS topo maps Deseret Peak West and Deseret Peak East (7½-minute) or Deseret Peak (15-minute). Trail begins from Loop Campground at the end of the road up South Willow Canyon and connects to make a loop to the summit. After ¾ mile the main summit trail turns left and follows Mill Fork (the trail forking right leads to an alternate summit trail and to North Willow Canyon). The main trail ascends 2 more miles through meadows, aspen, Douglas fir, limber pine, and a glacial cirque to a high ridge at 10,000 feet. Follow the ridge west ¾ mile to Deseret Peak (elev. 11,031 ft.). On a clear day atop the summit you can see much of the Wasatch Range on the eastern horizon, the Great Salt Lake to the north, Pilot Peak in Nevada to the northwest, Great Salt Lake Desert to the west, and countless desert ranges to the southwest. To make a loop, follow the trail along the north ridge about 1½ miles, contouring on the west side of 3 smaller peaks, then drop east ½ mile into Pockets Fork. At the junction with the trail connecting North and South Willow canyons, turn right 1¼ miles back to the trail junction in Mill Fork, ¾ mile from the start. For other trails and access roads in the Stansburys, see the topo and Wasatch-Cache National Forest maps. Only foot and horse travel are permitted in the wilderness area (west of Mack Canyon-Big Hollow Trail, north of Dry Canyon, and south of Pass Canyon).

# SKULL VALLEY

## Iosepa

Now a ghost town with little more than a cemetery, foundations, and a few houses, Iosepa once had a population of 226 Polynesian settlers. Devout Mormon Hawaiians who desired to live in the promised land of Utah began the settlement in 1889. All the good farmland around Salt Lake City had been taken, so the group wound up in this desolate valley west of the Stansbury Mountains. Undaunted by the harsh climate and scarcity of water, the Hawaiians laid out a townsite and named it Iosepa (Joseph) after the sixth president of the LDS Church, Joseph F. Smith. Livestock were raised, crops and trees were planted, and roses bloomed in the new desert home. The islanders celebrated Pioneer Day on Aug. 28, the date they arrived in Skull Valley, with feasts of *poi* and roast pig. Not all harvests produced a profit, however, and life here was hard. Leprosy appeared in 1896 and its several victims were forced to live in a separate building—Utah's only known leper colony. News in 1916 of a Mormon temple to be built in Hawaii brought a wave of homesick-

descending Deseret Peak

ness, and within a year, the struggling settlement disbanded.

Today Iosepa is a large ranch along the road 15 miles south of I-80 Timpie Springs Exit 77. There's no sign at the ranch, but it's the largest in the area, with 4 houses along the road and several farm buildings. The 2 small frame houses belonged to the original Hawaiian settlement; 2 other surviving buildings are farther back. Residents don't mind people visiting the old townsite, but ask first. To see the cemetery, turn east past a group of mailboxes and the northernmost house, go through a gate, then keep left at a fork. The cemetery, marked by 6 flagpoles, is ¾ mile in; the road may be too rough for cars. Time and the elements have reduced the graves to mounds of gravel with just a few marble headstones. Their Hawaiian names seem out of place in this lonely desert valley.

### Skull Valley Indian Reservation

From prehistoric times, Goshute Indians have ranged over this region to hunt and gather wild plant foods. And since the 1860s, they have been ranching and farming. Except for road signs, you wouldn't know you're on a reserva-

tion, as the widely scattered ranches look like any others in the area.

# SOUTH OF TOOELE

## OQUIRRH MOUNTAINS GHOST TOWNS

### Ophir

Picturesque old buildings and log cabins line the bottom of Ophir Canyon, which once boomed with saloons, dance halls, houses of ill repute, hotels, restaurants, and shops. In the 1860s, soldiers under General Patrick Connor heard stories of Indians mining silver and lead for ornaments and bullets. The soldier-prospectors tracked down the Indian mines to this canyon and staked claims. By 1870 a town was born, named after the biblical land of Ophir where King Solomon had his mines. Much of the ore went to General Connor's large smelter at nearby Stockton. Later the St. John & Ophir Railroad entered the canyon to haul away the rich ores of silver,

lead, and zinc, and small amounts of gold and copper. Ophir's population peaked at 6,000, but unlike most other mining towns of the region, Ophir never quite died. People still live here and occasionally prospect in the hills. The city hall and some houses have been restored, but canyon vegetation has claimed the rest.

Paved roads go all the way into town. From Tooele, head south 12 miles on UT 36 through Stockton, turn left 5 miles on UT 73, then left 3.5 miles to Ophir. Tailings and foundations of a flotation mill built in 1930 are near the mouth of Ophir Canyon. The road to Ophir follows an old railroad grade; part of an abandoned passenger car still lies on the right just before the town. A gravel road continues up the canyon beyond Ophir through forests of box elder and aspen before ending 2.5 miles farther. Ophir Creek has to be crossed several times on the way. People sometimes camp here (no facilities). Hikers can continue upstream and ascend Lowe Peak (elev. 10,572 ft.) and other summits of the Oquirrh Mountains.

## Mercur

General Connor's soldiers also discovered silver in the canyon southeast of Ophir during the late 1860s. After a slow start, prospectors made rich strikes and the rush was on. The mining camp of Lewiston boomed in the mid-1870s, then busted by 1880 as the deposits worked out. Arie Pinedo, a prospector from Bavaria, began to poke around the dying camp and located the Mercur Lode of gold and mercury ore. He and other would-be miners became increasingly frustrated when all attempts to extract gold from the ore failed. Then in 1890, a new cyanide process proved effective, and a new boom town with the Golden Gate Mill arose 5 years later. Though fire wiped out the business district in 1902, Mercur rebuilt and had an estimated population of more than 8,000 by 1910. Only 3 years later the town closed up when ore bodies appeared depleted. Mining revived in the 1930s and

again in the 1980s. Barrick Mercur Gold Mines now owns the ghost town site, of which little remains. Current technology allows profitable mining of both the massive old tailing piles and new deposits.

The company has an information center at the entrance gate with artifacts and photos of the early mining days; open in summer. To reach it from the Ophir turnoff, continue southeast 4 miles on UT 73, then turn left 3.5 miles on a paved road. A sign at the junction indicates if the center is open. If it's closed, there's no reason to drive in, as the mining and ghost town site can't be seen without special permission. Tours of the operations can sometimes be arranged; ask at the information center.

## Other Ghost Towns

Stories of several other historic mining sites and the famous Ajax underground store make fascinating reading, but little remains at these sites. Good sources to learn more include *The Historical Guide to Utah Ghost Towns* by Stephen L. Carr and *Some Dreams Die: Utah's Ghost Towns and Lost Treasures* by George A. Thompson.

*Golden Gate Mill at Mercur, ca. 1898*

# PONY EXPRESS AND STAGE ROUTE

In 1860, Pony Express officials put together a line of stations between St. Joseph, Missouri, and Sacramento, California. Relays of frontier-toughened men covered the 1,838-mile distance in 10 days. Riders stopped at stations spaced about 12 miles apart to change horses. Only after changing horses about 6 times did the rider complete his day's work. Despite the hazards of frontier travel, just one mail pouch was ever lost, and Indian wars held up service for only one month. Historians credit the daring enterprise with providing communications vital to keeping California aligned with the Union during the Civil War and proving that the West could be crossed in all kinds of weather—thus convincing skeptical politicians that a transcontinental railroad could be built. The Pony Express operated for only 18 months; completion of the transcontinental telegraph in Oct. 1861 put the riders out of work. The company, which received no government assistance, failed to make a profit for its owners.

Relive some of the Old West by driving the Pony Express route across western Utah. The scenic route goes from spring to spring as it winds through several small mountain ranges and across open plains, skirting the worst of the Great Salt Lake Desert. Interpretive signs and monuments along the way describe how Pony Express riders rode swiftly on horseback to bring the country closer together. The 140 miles between Fairfield in the east and Ibapah near the Nevada border provide a sense of history and appreciation for the land; this sense is lost to motorists speeding along I-80. Allow at least a full day for the drive and bring food, water, and a full tank of gas. The Bureau of Land Management (BLM) has campgrounds at Simpson Springs (water year-round) and south of Callao. No motels or restaurants line the road, but Ibapah has 2 gas station/grocery stores. The well-graded gravel road can be driven by car; just watch for the usual backcountry hazards of wildlife, rocks,

and washouts. Adventurous travelers may want to make side trips for rockhounding, hiking, or visiting old mining sites. Always keep vehicles on existing roads—sand and mud flats can be treacherously deceptive!

You can begin your trip down the historic route from the Stagecoach Inn at Fairfield (from Salt Lake City or Provo, take I-15 to Lehi, then go 21 miles west on UT 73). You could also begin at Faust Junction (30 miles south of Tooele on UT 36) or Ibapah (51 miles south of Wendover on US 50-A). For the latest road conditions and travel info, contact the BLM Salt Lake District Office, 2370 S. 2300 West, Salt Lake City, UT 84119; tel. 977-4300. The following are points of interest along the route.

## Stagecoach Inn At Fairfield

John Carson built this inn for travelers in 1858. Now it's a state park. Inside the restored structure you can see where weary riders slept and sat around tables swapping stories. Stagecoach Inn is 36 miles northwest of Provo; see pp. 171-172.

## Simpson Springs

Indians had long used these excellent springs before the first white men came through. The name honors Capt. J.H. Simpson, who stopped here in 1859 while leading an Army survey across western Utah and Nevada. About the same time George Chorpenning built a mail station here that was later used by the Pony Express and Overland Express companies. A reconstructed stone cabin on the old site shows what the station looked like. Ruins of a nearby cabin built in 1893 contain stones from the first station. Foundations of a Civilian Conservation Corps camp lie across the road. In 1939, the CCC boys built historic markers, improved roads, and worked on conservation projects. The BLM campground higher up on the hillside has water year-round and good views across the desert; a $2/vehicle fee applies March 1 to Oct. 31. Sparse juniper trees grow at the 5,100-foot elevation. Simpson Springs is 25 miles west of Faust Junction and 67 miles east of Callao.

## Fish Springs National Wildlife Refuge

The Pony Express station once located here no longer exists, but you can visit the 10,000 acres of marsh and lake that attract abundant bird and animal life. Waterfowl and marsh birds stop over in greatest numbers during their early spring and late autumn migrations. Many smaller birds nest here in late spring and early summer, though they're difficult to see in the thick vegetation. Opportunistic hawks and other raptors circle overhead. A self-guiding auto tour makes an 11.5-mile loop through the heart of the refuge. Most of the route follows dikes between the man-made lakes and offers good vantage points from which to see ducks, geese, egrets, herons, avocets, and other water birds. Tour route and a picnic area near the entrance are open from sunrise to sunset; no camping is allowed in the refuge. Stop at the information booth near the entrance to pick up a brochure, to see photos of birds found at the refuge, and to read notes on the area's history. Fish Springs National Wildlife Refuge (tel. 831-5353) is 42 miles west of Simpson Springs and 25 miles east of Callao.

## Boyd Pony Express Station

Portions remain of the station's original rock wall. Signs give the history of the station and the Pony Express. Site is 13 miles west of Fish Springs and 12 miles east of Callao.

## Callao

This cluster of ranches dates from 1859-60, when several families decided to take advantage of the desert grasslands and good springs here. The original name of Willow Springs had to be changed when residents applied for a post office—too many other Utah towns had the same name. Then someone suggested Callao (locally pronounced as "CAL-ee-o"), because the Peruvian town of that name has a similar setting of valley backed by high mountains. Residents raise cattle, sheep, and hay. Children go to Callao

*red-tailed hawk*
(Buteo jamaicensis)

elementary school, one of the last one-room schoolhouses in Utah. Local people believe that the Willow Springs Pony Express station site lies off the main road at Bagley Ranch, but a BLM archaeologist contends that the foundation is on the east side of town. Callao is 67 miles west of Simpson Springs and 28 miles east of Ibapah (via Pony Express and Stage Route). A free BLM campground is 4.3 miles south beside Tom's Creek. The high Deep Creek Range rises to the west.

## Canyon Station

(Follow signs for Sixmile Ranch, Overland Canyon, and Clifton Flat between Callao and Ibapah.) The original station used by Pony Express riders was in Overland Canyon, northwest of Canyon Station. However, Indians attacked in July 1863, burned the first station, and killed the Overland agent and 4 soldiers. The new station was built on a more defensible site. You can see its foundation and remnants of a fortification. A signed fork at Clifton Flat points the way to Gold Hill, a photogenic ghost town 6 miles distant; it's described below. Canyon Station is north of the Deep Creek Range, 13 miles northwest of Callao and 15 miles northeast of Ibapah.

### Ibapah
Pronounce it "EYE-buh-paw" to avoid sounding like a tourist! Actually Ibapah is about the same size as Callao—little more than a group of some 20 ranches. The large ranch west of the highway has some old log cabins of the Deep Creek station dating from Pony Express days and **Nicholes General Store** (built in the 1880s). The store has groceries and a lone gas pump (regular). The owner was unsure of the store's future operation at the time of writing. Back on the road and 1.3 miles farther south is **Goshute General Store** with groceries, fuel (regular, unleaded, and diesel), and the post office; it's normally open daily all year.

## VICINITY OF IBAPAH

Continuing south a short way past Goshute General Store, the main road (US 50-A) forks left to Goshute Indian Reservation, while the right fork crosses into Nevada to US 93 (58 miles) on the old Pony Express and Stage Route. From Ibapah you can also go north to Gold Hill ghost town (14 miles) and Wendover (51 miles) on US 50-A and south to US 50/6 near Great Basin National Park via Callao, Trout Creek, and Gandy (90 miles).

### Goshute Indian Reservation
Goshute Indians mastered living in the harsh desert by knowing of every edible seed, root, insect, reptile, bird, and rodent, as well as larger game. Their meager diet and possessions appalled early white settlers, who referred disparagingly to the Indians as "diggers." Loss of land to ranchers and dependence on manufactured food put an end to the old nomadic lifestyle. In recent times the Goshute have gradually been regaining independence by learning to farm and ranch. Several hundred members of the tribe live on the Goshute Indian Reservation, which straddles

the Utah-Nevada border. Most of the reservation is off-limits to nonmembers without special permission. About the only reason to come here would be to hike into the Deep Creek Range from the west side (see "Deep Creek Range" below).

### Gold Hill
Miners had been working the area for 3 years when in 1892 they founded Gold Hill. A whole treasure trove of minerals came out of the ground here—gold, silver, lead, copper, tungsten, arsenic, and bismuth. A smelter along a ridge just west of town processed the ore. But 3 years later Gold Hill's boom ended. Most people lived only in tents anyway, and soon everything but the smelter foundations and tailings was packed up. A rebirth occurred during WW I when the country desperately needed copper, tungsten, and arsenic. Gold Hill grew to a sizable town with 3,000 residents, a railroad line from Wendover, and many substantial buildings. Cheaper foreign

sources of arsenic knocked the bottom out of local mining in 1924, and Gold Hill began to die again. Another frenzied burst of activity occurred in 1944-45 when the country called once more for tungsten and arsenic. The town again sprang to life, only to fade just as quickly after the war ended. Determined prospectors still roam the surrounding countryside awaiting another clamor for the underground riches. Decaying structures in town make a picturesque sight. (Several year-round residents live here; no scavenging allowed.) Visible nearby are the cemetery, mines, railroad bed, and smelter site. The smaller ghost town of **Clifton** lies over the hill to the south but little remains; "No Trespassing" signs make visitors unwelcome. Good roads (partly dirt) approach Gold Hill from Ibapah, Wendover, and Callao.

# DEEP CREEK RANGE

The range soars spectacularly above the Great Salt Lake Desert. Few people seem to know about the Deep Creeks despite their great heights, diverse wildlife, and pristine forests. Ibapah Peak ("EYE-buh-paw"; elev. 12,087 ft.) and Haystack Peak to the north (elev. 12,020 ft.) crown the range. Glacial cirques and other rugged features have been carved into the nearly white granite that makes up most of the summit ridge. Prospectors have found gold, silver, lead, zinc, copper, mercury, beryllium, molybdenum, tungsten, and uranium. You'll occasionally run across mines and old cabins in the range, especially in Goshute Canyon. Of the 8 perennial streams on the east side, Birch and Trout creeks still contain Lake Bonneville cutthroat trout that originated in the prehistoric lake; both creeks were closed to fishing at press time. Wildlife includes Rocky Mountain bighorn sheep (reintroduced), deer, pronghorn, mountain lion, coyote, bobcat, and many birds. Vegetation ranges from grass and sagebrush in the lower foothills to pinyon pine and juniper, then to montane forests of aspen, Engelmann spruce, Douglas fir, white fir, subalpine fir, ponderosa pine, and limber pine.

Bristlecone pine grows on some of the high ridges. Alpine tundra covers the highest peaks. The Deep Creek Range gets plenty of snow in winter, so the climbing season runs from about late June to late October. Aspen and some mountain shrubs put on colorful displays in Sept. and early October. Streams in the range have good water (purify first), but watch for cattle pollution in the lower canyons. Carry water while hiking on the dry ridges.

## Main Climbing Routes

Most of the canyons have roads into their lower reaches. Four-wheel-drive vehicles will be able to get farther up the steep grades than cars before having to park. Usually hikers start up Granite or Indian Farm creeks and head for Ibapah or Haystack peaks. **Granite Creek** is the most popular starting point for Ibapah Peak, about 12 miles roundtrip and a 5,200-foot elevation gain. The road to Granite Creek turns west off Snake Valley Rd. 10.0 miles south of Callao (7.8 miles north of Trout Creek Ranch). Keep left at a junction about one mile in, then follow the most used track. The road enters Granite Canyon after 3 miles and becomes increasingly rough. Four-wheel-drives can push on another 2 miles. Easiest way from here to the summit ridge is to follow the old road and pack trail shown on topo maps. Atop the ridge, you can hike south to Red Mountain or north to Ibapah and Haystack peaks. A more difficult hike is up via the ridge north of Granite Creek, or you can simply go straight up Ibapah from Granite Creek. Impressive panoramas take in the rugged canyons and ridges of the Deep Creek Range below and much of western Utah and eastern Nevada beyond. Remains of a heliograph station sit atop Ibapah. Early mapmakers measured the highest point in the range at 12,101 feet and named it "Haystack." A later survey determined the correct height to be 12,087 feet and renamed the peak "Ibapah"; the second highest peak then got the old Haystack name.

## Other Climbing Routes

The jeep trail to **Toms Creek** leads to a route to the head of the creek, from which Haystack

# DEEP CREEK RANGE

CHOKECHERRY CANYON

TO IBAPAH & WENDOVER

TO IBAPAH

TO GOLD HILL & WENDOVER

PONY EXPRESS & STAGE ROUTE

DEEP CREEK VALLEY

▲ BALD MTN. (9,820 ft.)

RANGE

GOSHUTE CANYON

JEEP TRAIL

Warning: Do not travel past tribal headquarters on the Goshute Indian Reservation without permission.

▲ ROCKY PK. (10,749 ft.)

THE BASIN

BIG CANYON CREEK

CALLAO

PONY EXPRESS & STAGE RT.

TO FISH SPRINGS

■ TRIBAL HEADQUARTERS

STEVES CREEK

JEEP TRAIL

INDIAN

TOMS CREEK

■ BLM CAMPGROUND (OLD C.C.C. SITE)

FIFTEENMILE CREEK

▲ HAYSTACK PEAK (12,020 ft.)

FARM

CR.

WEISS HWY.

▲ IBAPAH PEAK (12,087 ft.)

CREEK

RED CEDAR

CR.

GOSHUTE INDIAN RESERVATION

PACK TRAIL

QUEEN OF SHEBA CANYON

▲ RED MTN. (11,588 ft.)

COTTONWOOD CANYON

JEEP TRAIL

TO TOPAZ MTN. & DELTA

TROUT CREEK JEEP TRAIL

DEEP

GRANITE CREEK

BIRCH CREEK

JEEP TRAIL

TO BOYD PONY EXPRESS STATION RUINS

WOOD CANYON

JEEP TRAIL

TROUT CREEK

0    2 mi

0    2 km

TO US 50/6 & GREAT BASIN NAT'L PARK

PONY EXPRESS AND STAGE ROUTE 145

Peak is about 3 miles south along the crest of the range; turnoff for Toms Canyon is 1.6 miles south of Callao and 8.4 miles north of the Granite Creek turnoff. A more direct route to Haystack Peak goes up through **Indian Farm Canyon.** Turnoff for this canyon is 4.3 miles south of Callao and 5.7 miles north of the Granite Creek turnoff. **Red Cedar Creek** in the heart of the Deep Creeks remains pristine—no trails, roads, or other developments. It's also very rugged; allow a day or two just to hike through one way. What the early ranchers thought was red cedar is actually Rocky Mountain juniper. **Trout Creek** is another good hiking area. A trail goes most of the way up the valley.

Approaches to the peaks from the **Goshute Indian Reservation** have been less used because of travel restrictions. Also, this western slope is much drier. Probably the easiest way up from here is to drive though Goshute village to Fifteen Mile Creek and to hike the pack trail to the ridge between Ibapah Peak and Red Mountain, meeting the trail coming up from Granite Creek. To visit the west side you need to plan ahead and get permission from the Tribal Council, which meets twice a month. Write to them at Box 6104, Ibapah, UT 84034, explaining the purpose of your trip and what you'll be doing, dates, roads and trails to be used, and the organization you're with, if any.

For more information call the tribal chairman at 234-1137 or the administration office at 234-1138.

**Information**

Hikers venturing into this remote range must be experienced in wilderness travel and self-sufficient. Topo maps you'll need are the 7½-minute Ibapah Peak and Indian Farm Creek for the central part of the range, the 7½-minute Goshute and Goshute Canyon for the northern part, and the 15-minute Trout Creek for the southern part. The metric 1:100,000 Fish Springs quad covers the whole area, but with less detail. For firsthand information, contact the BLM House Range Resource Area, 15 E. 500 North, Fillmore, UT 84631; tel. 743-6811. The Sierra Club book *Hiking the Great Basin* by John Hart has detailed trail descriptions.

All approaches to the Deep Creeks involve dirt road travel and generally sizable distances. Some of the ways in (to Granite Creek road junction) are from Wendover via Gold Hill (92 miles), from Provo via the Pony Express and Stage Route (158 miles), from Delta via the Weiss Hwy. (93 miles), and from US 50/6 near the Utah-Nevada border via Gandy and Trout Creek (52 miles). Ibapah has the nearest gas and groceries (38 miles from Granite Creek turnoff).

# EUREKA AND TINTIC MINING DISTRICT

The lucky prospectors who cried "Eureka! I've found it!" had stumbled onto a fabulously rich deposit of silver and other valuable metals. Eureka sprang up to be one of Utah's most important cities and the center of more than a dozen mining communities. Much can still be seen of the district's long history—mine headframes and buildings, shafts and glory holes, old styles of residential and commercial architecture, great piles of ore tailings, and forlorn cemeteries. Exhibits at the Tintic Mining Museum in Eureka show what life was like. Paved highways provide easy access: from I-15 Santaquin Exit 248 (south of Provo) go west 21 miles on US 6; from Delta go northeast 48 miles on US 6; or from Tooele go south 54 miles on UT 36.

## History

Mormon stockherders began moving cattle in here during the early 1850s to take advantage of the good grazing lands. Ute Indians under Chief Tintic, for whom the district was later named, opposed the newcomers but couldn't stop them. Mineral deposits found in the hills remained a secret with the Mormons, as Church policy prohibited members from prospecting for precious metals. In 1869, though, the promising ores were noted by George Rust, a gentile (non-Mormon) cowboy. He had no such qualms and soon the rush was on. Ores assaying up to 10,000 ounces of silver per ton began pouring out of the mines. Silver City, founded in 1870, became the first of many mining camps. New discoveries kept the Tintic District booming. Gold, copper, lead, and zinc added to the riches. By 1910 the district had a population of 8,000 with the end nowhere in sight. The hills shook from underground blasting and the noise of mills, smelters, and railroads. Valuable Tintic properties kept the Salt Lake Stock Exchange busy, while Salt Lake City office buildings and mansions rose with Tintic money. Mining began a slow decline in the 1930s but has continued, sporadically, to the present. Most of the old

Eureka mines, ca. 1900

mining camps have dried up and blown away. Eureka and Mammoth drift on as sleepy towns—monuments to an earlier era. The ghosts of former camps can be worth a visit too, though most require considerable imagination to see them as they were. Do not go near decaying structures or mine shafts.

# EUREKA

Mines and tailing dumps surround weather-beaten buildings. Eureka lacks the orderliness of Mormon towns; the main street snakes through the valley with side streets branching off in every direction. Few recent buildings have been added, so the town retains an authentic atmosphere from earlier in this century. Eureka now has a population of about 750, down from the 3,400 of its peak years.

## Tintic Mining Museum
The varied exhibits of this small museum will give you an appreciation for the district and its mining pioneers. A mineral collection from the Tintic area has many fine specimens. You'll see early mining tools, assay equipment, a mine office, courtroom, blacksmith shop, many historic photos, a kitchen of the 1920s, and displays showing social life in the early days. One room is dedicated to the influence of Jessie Knight, a Mormon financier and philanthropist. Knightsville, now a ghost town site near Eureka, gained fame as one of the few mining towns in Utah without a saloon or gambling hall. Knight also promoted mine safety and closed his mines for a day of rest on Sundays—both radical concepts at the time. Museum galleries are upstairs in the City Hall (built 1899) and next door in the former railroad depot (built 1925). The *Tintic Tour Guide* sold here describes a 35-mile loop to some of the nearby ghost towns and mines. The Tintic Mining Museum is usually open summer weekends and some weekdays, at other times on request; free; tel. 433-6842

## Bullion-Beck Mine
A large timber headframe on the west edge of town beside the highway marks one of the most productive mines in the district. John

Beck arrived in 1871 and began sinking a shaft. At first people called him the "Crazy Dutchman," but the jeers ended when he hit a huge deposit of rich ore 200 feet down. The present 65-foot high headframe dates from about 1890; originally a large wooden building enclosed it.

## Practicalities
The small **Tintic Motel** is downtown on Main St.; $25.07 s, $28.34 d; tel. 433-6311. The **Pit Stop** serves fast food on the east edge of town. Eureka celebrates **Depot Days and Tintic Silver Festival** with a parade, mountain men rendezvous, mine tours, arts and crafts exhibits, a dance, and entertainment; it's held on the third weekend of August.

# VICINITY OF EUREKA

## Dividend
Emil Raddatz bought this property on the east slope of the Tintic Mountains in 1907, believing that the ore deposits mined on the west side of the Tintics also extended to here. Raddatz nearly went broke digging deeper and deeper, but the prized silver and lead ore 1,200 feet below proved him right. After his 1916 discovery, a modern company town grew up complete with hotel, movie theater, golf course, and ice plant. The miners, whose wages had been paid partly in stock certificates, chose the name Dividend because they had been so well rewarded. Mining continued until 1949, producing $19 million in dividends, but today only foundations, mine shafts, and large piles of tailings remain. A loop road east of Eureka will take you to this site and other mining areas. Walking or driving off the road is forbidden because of mine shafts and other hazards. Though the road is paved, some sections are badly potholed and need to be driven slowly. From downtown Eureka, go east 1.5 miles on US 6 and turn right on the Dividend road (0.1 mile east of Milepost 141); the road climbs into hills and passes the Eureka Lily headframe and mine on the left after 2.5 miles; continue 0.3 mile to Tintic Standard #1 shaft on right, then 0.3 mile more to the site of Dividend and the #2 shaft

(signed); the road ends at a junction 0.9 mile farther; turn left 0.7 mile to US 6 (4 miles east of Eureka). The Sunshine Mining Company currently operates the Burgin Mine about one mile east of Dividend.

## Mammoth

Prospectors made a "mammoth" strike over the hill south of Eureka in 1870. The town of Mammoth, more mines, mills, and smelters followed. The eccentric mining engineer George Robinson built a second town, immodestly named after himself, one mile down the valley. Both towns prospered so well that they grew together and people couldn't tell which was which. Eventually the two became just "Mammoth." Nearly 3,000 people lived here when activity peaked in 1900-10. Then came the inevitable decline as the high-grade ores worked out. By the 1930s, Mammoth was well on its way to becoming a ghost. People still live here and have preserved some of the old buildings. The Mammoth glory hole and mine buildings overlook the town at the head of the valley. Ruins of smelters and mines cling to hillsides. From Eureka, go southwest 2.5 miles on US 6, then turn left (east) one mile on a paved road. Upper and lower towns can now be distinguished.

## Silver City

Optimistic prospectors named their little camp for the promising silver ore, but a city it was not to be. The cost of pumping water out of the mines cut too deeply into profit margins, then a 1902 fire nearly put an end to the town. At that point Mormon financier Jessie Knight stepped in to improve the mines and rebuild the town. He also built a smelter and later a mill. Silver City reached its peak about 1908 before declining to ghost town status in the 1930s. You can't miss the giant piles of tailings (light colored) and slag (dark colored) from the smelter and mill at the old townsite. Extensive concrete foundations show the complexity and size of the operations. Sagebrush has reclaimed the rest of the town, of which only debris and foundations survive. Mining and prospecting are still done in the area, though; a new mining operation is currently reprocessing the old smelter waste products. Silver City ghost town site lies 3.3 miles southwest of Eureka (0.8 mile past the Mammoth turnoff) just off US 6.

## Other Tintic Ghost Towns

These towns exist mostly as a memory. Diligent searching through the sagebrush may uncover foundations, tailings piles, broken glass, and neglected cemeteries. Yet behind many of the sites are dramatic stories of attempts to win riches from the earth. History buffs may want to look at the book *Faith, Hope and Prosperity: The Tintic Mining District* by Philip Notarianni, available at the Tintic Mining Museum. Also see *The Historical Guide to Utah Ghost Towns* by Stephen L. Carr and *Some Dreams Die* by George A. Thompson.

# SHEEPROCK MOUNTAINS

Black Crook Peak (elev. 9,275 ft.) tops this little-known range northwest of Eureka. Sheeprock Mountain Trail (Forest Trails #051 and #052) follows the crest of the mountains for most of their length. Several other trails connect from each side. See the Uinta National Forest map and the 7½-minute Erickson Knoll, Dutch Peak, Lookout Pass, and Vernon topo maps. Mining, which peaked in the early 1900s, still continues on a small scale for silver, lead, and zinc. Bald eagles winter here from about Dec. to March; their

*black-tailed jack rabbit* (Lepus californicus)

numbers appear to fluctuate with the rabbit population. Fishermen try for brook and brown trout in Vernon Reservoir and Vernon and Bennion creeks. The small Little Valley Campground is open May to Nov.; no water or charge. Benmore Experimental Pastures, northeast of the mountains, dates from 1933 as a cooperative state and federal program to develop techniques of restoring and managing rangelands. Although the Sheeprock Mountains are in the Wasatch National Forest, the Spanish Fork Ranger District office of the Uinta National Forest manages this area, known as the Vernon Division: 44 W. 400 North, Spanish Fork, UT 84660; tel. 798-3571. Follow UT 36 northwest 17 miles from Eureka (or south 42 miles from Tooele) to a junction signed "Benmore," just east of Vernon; turn south 5 miles to Benmore Guard Station, then left 2.5 miles for Vernon Reservoir. Little Valley Campground is off to the right in a side valley 2.3 miles past the reservoir. A road in via Lofgreen is a bit rough for cars. None of these roads are recommended in wet weather.

## LITTLE SAHARA RECREATION AREA

Sand dunes have made a giant sandbox between Eureka and Delta. Managed by the BLM, the recreation area covers 60,000 acres of free-moving sand dunes, sagebrush flats, and juniper-covered ridges. Elevations range from about 5,000 to 5,700 feet. Varied terrain provides challenges for dune buggies, motorcycles, and 4WD vehicles. While off-road vehicles can range over most of the dunes, areas near White Sands and Jericho campgrounds have been set aside for children. The Rockwell Natural Area in the western part of the dunes protects 9,150 acres for nature study.

The dunes originated 150 miles away as sandbars along the southern shore of Lake Bonneville roughly 10,000 years ago. After the lake receded, prevailing winds pushed the exposed sands on a slow trek northeastward at a rate of about 18 inches per year. Sand Mountain, however, deflected the winds upward, and the sand grains piled up into large dunes downwind. Lizards and kangaroo rats scamper across the sands in search of food and, in turn, are eaten by hawks, bobcats, and coyotes. Pronghorn live here all year and mule deer visit in winter. Juniper, sagebrush, greasewood, saltbush, and grasses are the most common plants. An unusual species of fourwing saltbush *(Atriplex canescens)* grows as high as 12 feet and is restricted to the dunes area.

Three developed campgrounds with water (White Sands, Oasis, and Jericho) and a primitive camping area (Sand Mountain) are open all year. In winter, water is available only at the visitor center on the way in. Visitors to Little Sahara pay a daily $4/vehicle fee (a pickup truck or trailer carrying off-road vehicles count as one vehicle), which includes use of campgrounds. For more information or group camping permits, contact the BLM at 15 E. 500 North, Fillmore, UT 84631; tel. 743-6811. Entrance road is 4 miles west of Jericho Junction; distance from Nephi (I-15 Exits 222 and 228) is 31 miles via UT 132 and Juab County 148. From Eureka head south 17 miles on US 6, then west 4 miles. From Delta go northeast 31 miles, then west 4 miles. Distance from Salt Lake City is 115 miles.

# DELTA AND VICINITY

The barren Pahvant Valley along the lower Sevier River had long been considered a wasteland. Then in 1905, some Fillmore businessmen purchased water rights from Sevier River Reservoir and 10,000 acres of land. The farm and town lots they sold became the center of one of Utah's most productive agricultural areas. Other hopeful homesteaders farther out from Delta weren't so fortunate. Thousands of families bought cheap land in the North Tract but found the going very difficult. Troubles with the irrigation system, poor crop yields, and low market prices forced most to leave by the late 1930s. A few decaying houses and farm buildings mark the sites of once-bustling communities. Farmers near Delta raise alfalfa seed and hay, wheat, corn, barley, mushrooms, and livestock. The giant coal-burning Intermountain Power Project (IPP) and the Brush Wellman beryllium mill have helped boost Delta's population to about 4,000. Miners have been digging into the Drum Mountains northwest of Delta since the 1870s for gold, silver, copper, manganese, and other minerals; some work still goes on there. The beryllium processed near Delta comes from large deposits of bertrandite mined in open pits in the Topaz and Spors mountains, farther to the northwest.

A pioneer log cabin (built 1907-08), now on Main St. in front of Delta's Municipal Building, was the second house and the first post office in Melville, which was later known as Burtner and finally Delta in 1910. Historical markers near the cabin commemorate the Spanish Dominguez-Escalante expedition that passed to the south in 1776 and also the Topaz Camp for Japanese-Americans interned during WW II. For travelers, Delta makes a handy base for visiting the surrounding historic sites, rockhounding, and exploring nearby mountain ranges.

## Rockhounding

Beautiful rock, mineral, and fossil specimens await discovery in the desert surrounding Delta. Sought-after rocks and minerals include topaz, bixbyite, sunstones, geodes, obsidian, muscovite, garnet, pyrite, and agate. Some fossils to look for are trilobites, brachiopods, horn coral, and crinoids. The chamber of commerce in Delta is a good source of local information. Cut and polished gemstones from the area can be seen at Tina's Jewelry & Minerals. Useful publications include *Guide to Rocks and Fossils* available at the chamber of commerce and *Collector's Guide to Mineral and Fossil Localities,* published by the Utah Geological and Mineral Survey (June 1977). A hat and plenty of water will add to comfort and safety when enjoying the outdoors. Always be watchful when hiking to avoid rattlesnakes and mine shafts. Both are occasionally found in caves, where the dim light makes them harder to see.

## Accommodations

All of Delta's motels are on or close to Main Street. Rates below are for summer; most drop a few dollars in winter. From west to east are **Starglo Motor Lodge** (234 W. Main; tel. 864-2041; $24.96 s, $27.13 d); **Killpack Motor Lodge** (201 W. Main; tel. 864-2734; $26.16 s, $28.34 d; also one kitchenette); **Rancher Motel** (171 W. Main; tel. 864-2741; $21.70 s, $23.87 d); **Willden Motel** (127 W. Main; tel. 864-2288; $17 s, $20 d); **Deltan Inn Motel** (347 E. Main; tel. 864-5318; $27.20 s, $32 d); **Cedar Inn Motel** (½ block south of Main on 350 East; tel. 864-4533; $30.52 s or d; also kitchenettes); and **Best Western Plaza Motel** (near jct. of US 50 and US 6 on the east side of town; tel. 864-3882 or (800) 528-1234; $46.87 s, $51.52 d).

## Campgrounds

**B Kitten Klean Trailer Court** is open all year and has showers; $5 s, $7 d tent, $10 RV w/hookups; at 181 E. Main; tel. 864-2614. **Oak Creek Campground** lies in a pretty wooded canyon in the Fishlake National Forest; sites have drinking water late May to early Oct., $4; head east 14 miles on US 50 and UT 125 to Oak City, then turn right 4 miles on a paved road.

### Food

**Tops City Cafe** serves standard American fare daily for breakfast, lunch, and dinner at 313 W. Main; tel. 864-2148. The **Rancher Motel** has a cafe with American and Mexican food and a dining room upstairs serving steak and seafood; open daily for breakfast, lunch, and dinner at 171 W. Main; tel. 864-2741. **Chef's Palace** offers steak, seafood, chicken, and a salad bar; open Mon. to Sat. for dinner only; 225 E. Main; tel. 864-2421. The **Pizza House** features pizza, pasta, barbecued ribs, a long list of sandwiches, and salad bar; open Mon. to Sat. for lunch and dinner; 69 S. 300 East; tel. 864-2207. Several fast-food places and 2 supermarkets are in town too. **Delta Valley Farms** has a family restaurant 2 miles northeast of Delta on US 6; open Mon. to Sat. for lunch; call in advance if you'd like a tour of their cheese-making plant; tel. 864-2725.

### Entertainment And Events

Catch movies at **T&T Twin Theatres** in Pendray Plaza (east end of town just north of US 6 and US 50 jct.); tel. 864-4551. Annual events include the **Renaissance Fair** (entertainment, food, arts and crafts) in June, **July 4th** fireworks and demolition derby, **Pioneer Day** (parade, rodeo, games) on July 24 in Hinckley, and **Millard County Fair** (parade, horse show, games, demolition derby, and street dance) at the fairgrounds near Deseret in early August.

### Recreation And Services

The indoor **West Millard County Swimming Pool** is at the corner of 200 East and 300 North; open all year; tel. 864-3133. A **city park** with picnicking and tennis courts is at the corner of Main and 100 West; restrooms are in the nearby municipal building. **Sunset View Golf Course** offers 9 holes, just northeast of town on US 6; tel. 864-2508. **Gunnison Bend**

**Park** west of town has picnicking, water-skiing, and fishing (catfish and largemouth bass); go west 2.5 miles on US 50/6, then right 2 miles. **Tina's Jewelry & Minerals** offers beautiful gems, some from western Utah, at 305 E. Main; tel. 864-2444. The **post office** is at the corner of 300 East and 100 South; tel. 864-2811. **Delta Community Medical Center** provides emergency care at 126 S. White Sage Ave. (south off US 50 on east side of town); tel. 864-5591. In **emergencies** (police, fire, or medical) call 911.

### Information

**Delta Chamber of Commerce** will tell you about services in town and sights in the surrounding area; the office is in the municipal building at Main and 200 West (80 N. 200 West, Delta, UT 84624); open Mon. to Fri. 10 a.m.-noon and 1-5 p.m.; tel. 864-4316. The **public library**, also in the municipal building, is open Mon. to Sat.; tel. 864-4945.

## NORTH OF DELTA

### Baker Hot Springs

Though Crater Springs Health Resort has closed, local people still come to soak in the hot springs. Easiest way from Delta is to go northeast 11 miles on US 6, turn left (west) 20 miles on the paved Brush Wellman Road, then right (north) 7 miles on a dirt road. Springs are on the left and parking on the right. Hot Plug, a volcanic neck, rises to the west from a field of lava. The 200-foot-high pinnacle of gray and red rock makes a good hiking destination. It's about 6 miles roundtrip (allow 4 hours). In cool weather you may see mist rising from the plug.

## EAST OF DELTA

### Canyon Mountains

Oak Creek Campground lies along the creek amid Gambel oak, cottonwood, maple, and juniper on the west side of the mountains. Canyon walls cut by Oak Creek reveal layers of twisted and upturned rock. This forest service campground (elev. 5,900 ft.) has water from late May to early Oct. ($4 for family sites). Groups can reserve a large area with amphitheater, sports area, and shelter. Oak Creek usually has good fishing for rainbow trout. Much of its flow comes from a spring at the upper end of the campground. From Delta go east 14 miles on US 50 and UT 125 to the small farming town of Oak City, then turn right 4 miles on a paved road. A gravel road continues upcanyon past the campground to other forest roads and hiking trails; see the Fishlake National Forest map. Unpaved roads also provide access to the steeper east side of the Canyon Mountains. Fool Creek Peak tops this small range at 9,717 feet. For more information, contact the Fillmore Ranger District office at 390 S. Main in Fillmore (Box 265, Fillmore, UT 84631); tel. 743-5721.

# SOUTH OF DELTA

## Fort Deseret
A fading piece of pioneer history. Mormon settlers hastily built the adobe-walled fort in only 18 days in 1865 for protection against Indians during the Black Hawk War. The square fort had walls 550 feet long and 10 feet high with gates in the middle of each side. Bastions were located at the northeast and southwest corners. Indians never attacked the fort, though it came in handy to pen up cattle at night. Parts of the wall and stone foundation still stand. From Delta go west 5 miles on US 50/6, then turn left (south) 4.5 miles on UT 257. The site is on the west side of the road near Milepost 65, about 1.5 miles south of the town of Deseret.

## Great Stone Face
A natural rock formation 7 miles southwest of Deseret has a striking resemblance to the Mormon prophet Joseph Smith. To see the profile you have to view the rock from the west. From the town of Deseret, go south 3 miles on UT 257, then turn right (west) 4 miles (should

be signed) on a dirt road. A short hike at road's end leads up a lava flow to the stone face.

## Clear Lake State Waterfowl Management Area
Lakes and marsh country offer ducks, Canada geese, and other birds a refreshing break from the desert. Roads cross Clear Lake on a causeway and lead to smaller lakes and picnic areas to the north. Utah Division of Wildlife Resources manages the area. From the junction of US 50/6 and UT 257 west of Delta, go south 15.5 miles on UT 257, then turn left (east) 7 miles on a good gravel road.

## Pahvant Butte
Locally known as Sugar Loaf Mountain, this extinct volcano rises 1,000 feet above the desert floor. Waters of prehistoric Lake Bonneville leveled off the large terrace about halfway up. Remnants of a crater, now open to the southwest, are on this level. Another terrace line is at the bottom of the butte. Hikers can enjoy the volcanic geology, expansive panoramas, and a visit to curious ruins of a windmill. Construction of the wind-powered electric power station began in 1923 but it was never completed. A large underground room and 2 concentric rings of concrete pylons give an eerie Stonehenge-like atmosphere to the butte.

Easiest way up is an old road on the south side that goes to the windmill site. From Clear Lake (see above), continue east 3.3 miles to the second signed turn on the left for Pahvant Butte; there's a sign here "Pahvant Butte Road: 3 miles, Sugarloaf Well #1: 8 miles"; turn left 3.5 miles at the sign, then turn left 0.5 mile on Pahvant Butte Road. Park before the road begins a steep climb. Daredevils in 4WDs have tried going straight up the slope from here, but the real road turns right and switchbacks 0.7 mile to the windmill site. This last 0.7 mile is hazardous for vehicles because of soft volcanic rock, but it's fine for walking; elevation gain is about 400 feet. Pahvant Butte's highest point is about ½ mile to the north and 265 feet higher; you'll have to find your own way across if headed there. Dirt roads encircle Pahvant Butte and go northeast to US 50 and southeast to Tabernacle Hill and Fillmore. The Tabernacle Hill area provides good examples of volcanic features; see p. 184.

## WEST OF DELTA

### Topaz Camp

Easily Utah's most dispirited ghost town site. Other ghost towns had the promise of precious metals or good land to lure their populations, but those coming to Topaz had no choice—they had the bad fortune to be of the wrong ancestry during the height of WW II hysteria. About 9,000 Japanese, most of whom were American citizens, were brought from the West Coast to this desolate desert plain in 1942. Topaz sprang up in just a few months and included barracks, communal dining halls, post office, hospital, schools, churches, and recreational facilities. Most inmates cooperated with authorities; the few who caused trouble were shipped off to a more secure camp. Barbed wire and watchtowers with armed guards surrounded the small city—Utah's fifth largest for a time. Everyone was released at war's end in 1945 and the camp came down almost as quickly as it had gone up. Salvagers bought and removed equipment, buildings, barbed wire, telephone poles, and even street paving and sewer pipes. An uneasy silence pervades the site today. Little more than the streets, foundations, and piles of rubble remain. You can still walk or drive along the streets of the vast camp, which had 42 neatly laid-out blocks. A concrete memorial stands at the northwest corner of the site.

One way to get here is to go west 6 miles from Delta on US 50/6 to the small town of Hinckley, turn right (north) 4.5 miles on a paved road (some parts are gravel) to its end, turn left (west) 2.5 miles on a paved road to its end in Abraham, turn right (north) 1.5 miles on a gravel road to a stop sign, then turn left 3 miles on a gravel road; Topaz is on the left.

*on their way to Topaz*

### Drum Mountains

Strange subterranean noises can sometimes be heard in these desert mountains; some say the sounds are like thumps or rumblings of a drum. Prospectors began combing the parched hillsides in 1872 but did little mining development. Harry Joy and Charles Howard, mining engineers from Michigan, organized the Detroit Mining District here in 1879. They dug for gold, silver, and copper and built a smelter. Mining centered on the small town of **Joy.** Crumbling foundations are all that remain of the townsite, though dilapidated mine buildings can be found in nearby canyons. Western States Minerals has an active gold mine in the Drums. The mountains can be reached by continuing west from Topaz or from US 6 on the paved Brush Wellman Road.

## HOUSE RANGE

This range about 45 miles west of Delta offers great vistas, scenic drives, wilderness hiking, and world-famous trilobite fossil beds. Swasey Peak (elev. 9,669 ft.) is the highest point.

From a distance, however, Notch Peak's spectacular 2,700-foot face stands out as the most prominent landmark in the region. What the 50-mile-long range lacks in great heights, it makes up for in massive sheer limestone cliffs and rugged canyons. Precipitous drops on the western side contrast with a gentler slope on the east. Hardy vegetation such as juniper, pinyon pine, mountain mahogany, and sagebrush dominates the dry slopes. Bristle-cone pines grow on high ridges of Swasey and Notch peaks; the long-lived trees are identified by inward-curving bristles on the cones and by needles less than 1½ inches long in clusters of 5. Some of the high country also harbors limber pine, ponderosa pine, white fir, Douglas fir, and aspen. Wildlife includes mule deer, pronghorn, chukar partridge, bald and golden eagles, and peregrine falcon. Wild horses roam Sawmill Basin to the northeast of Swasey Peak. Permanent water is found only

*view north from Swasey Peak*

at a few scattered springs in the range. Limestone caves attract spelunkers, especially Antelope Spring Cave near Dome Canyon Pass (ask directions at the BLM office in Fillmore or from the Speleological Society of Utah). Council Cave on Antelope Peak (between Notch and Swasey peaks) has an enormous opening, visible for more than 50 miles.

Mining in the range has a long history. There are stories of finding old Spanish gold mines with iron tools in them that crumbled to the touch. More recent mining, for tungsten and gold, has occurred on the east side of Notch Peak. Outlaws found the range a convenient area to hide out; Tatow Knob (north of Swasey Peak), for example, was a favorite spot for horse thieves. Death Canyon got its name after a group of pioneers became trapped and froze to death; most maps now show it as Dome Canyon.

### Driving In The House Range
The dirt roads here can be surprisingly good. Often you can zip along as if on pavement, but watch for loose gravel, large rocks, flash floods, and deep ruts that sometimes appear on these backcountry stretches. Roads easily passable by car connect to make a 43-mile loop through Marjum and Dome Canyon passes. You'll have good views of the peaks and go through scenic canyons on the west side of both passes. Drivers with high-clearance vehicles can branch off on old mining roads or drive past Antelope Spring to Sinbad Overlook for views and hiking near Swasey Peak. Shale beds near Antelope Spring have given up an amazing quantity and variety of trilobite fossils dating from about 500 million years ago. Professional collectors have leased a trilobite quarry, so you'll have to collect outside. Trilobites can also be found near Swasey Spring and near Marjum Pass. Flat-edged rock hammers work best to split open the shale layers. During WW I, a hermit took a liking to the House Range and built a one-room cabin in a small cave, where he lived until his death. He entertained visitors with a special home brew. You have to walk ¼ mile up a small side canyon from the road

to see the cabin, which is on the right side of the road coming down to the west from Marjum Pass.

Several roads connect US 50/6 with the loop through Marjum and Dome Canyon passes. Going west from Delta on US 50/6, you have the choice of the following turnoffs: after 10 miles, turn right 25 miles at the fork for the unpaved old US 50/6; or after 32 miles, turn right 10 miles on a road signed "Antelope Spring"; or after 42 miles, turn right 16 miles on a road also signed "Antelope Spring"; or after 63 miles (30 miles east of the Utah-Nevada border), turn right 14 miles on a road signed "Painter Spring."

## Hiking In The House Range

Most hiking routes go cross-country through the wilderness. Springs are very far apart and can be polluted, so carry water for the whole trip. Bring topo maps and compass; help can be a long way off if you make a wrong turn. Because of the light precipitation, hiking season at the high elevations can last from late April to late November. Most destinations, including Swasey and Notch peaks, can be visited on a day hike. These peaks have fantastic views over nearly all of westcentral Utah and into Nevada. For more information on the House Range, contact the BLM office at 15 E. 500 North in Fillmore (Box 778, Fillmore, UT 84631); tel. 743-6811.

## Swasey Peak

A good half-day hike usually done as a loop. Total distance for the moderately difficult trip is about 4½ miles with a 1,700-foot elevation gain to the summit (elev. 9,669 ft.). Drive to the Antelope Spring turnoff, 2.5 miles east of Dome Canyon Pass, and follow the well-used Sinbad Overlook road 3.3 miles, passing the spring and trilobite area, up a steep grade to a large meadow below Swasey Peak. Cautiously driven cars might be able to get up this road, though it's safer to park low-clearance vehicles and walk the last 1.5 miles. (Non-hikers with suitable vehicles will enjoy driving to Sinbad Overlook for views at the end of the road.) From the large meadow at the top of the

grade, head northeast on foot up the ridge, avoiding cliffs to the left. After 1¼ miles you'll reach a low summit; continue ½ mile along the ridgeline, curving west toward Swasey Peak. To complete the loop, descend ½ mile to the northwest along a ridge to bypass some cliffs, then head southwest ¾ mile to the end of Sinbad Overlook road. From here it's an easy 1½ miles by road back to the start; Sinbad Spring and a grove of ponderosa pines are about halfway. No signs or trails mark the route, but hikers experienced with maps shouldn't have any trouble. Topo maps for this hike are the 7½-minute Marjum Pass and Swasey Peak. Route-finding is easier when hiking the loop in the direction described. You'll get a close look at the mountain mahogany on Swasey Peak—some thickets of this stout shrub have to be crossed; wear long pants to protect your legs.

## Notch Peak

The 2,700-foot sheer rock wall on the western face of this prominent peak is only 300 feet less than El Capitan in Yosemite. Most hikers prefer the far easier route on the other side via Sawtooth Canyon. This moderately difficult canyon route is about 9 miles roundtrip and has a 1,700-foot elevation gain. Bring water, as no springs are in the area. Like the Drum Mountains, Notch Peak has a reputation for strange underground noises. The 15-minute Notch Peak topo map is needed as much for navigating the roads to the trailhead as for the hiking. First take Antelope Spring Road to the signed turnoff for Miller Canyon; this turnoff is 4.5 miles north of Milepost 46 on US 50/6 (42 miles west of Delta) and 11.5 miles south of old US 50/6 (35 miles west of Delta). Turn west 5.3 miles on Miller Canyon Road, then bear left to Sawtooth Canyon at a road fork. A stone cabin 2.5 miles farther on the right marks the trailhead. The cabin is owned and used by people who mine in the area. Follow a rough jeep road on foot into Sawtooth Canyon. After ¾ mile the canyon widens where 2 tributaries meet; take the left fork in the direction of Notch Peak. A few spots in the dry creekbed require some rock scrambling. Be on the lookout for flash floods if thunderstorms threaten. After about 3 miles the wash becomes less distinct; continue climbing to a saddle visible ahead. Then a short but steep ¼-mile scramble takes you to the top of 9,655-foot Notch Peak and its awesome drop-offs. Other ways up Notch Peak offer challenges for the adventurous. The other fork of Sawtooth Canyon can be used, for example, and a jeep road through Amasa Valley provides a northern approach.

# CONFUSION RANGE

The Confusions lie in a long jumbled mass west of the House Range. The sparse vegetation consists largely of pinyon pine, juniper, sagebrush, shadscale, and cheatgrass. Some Douglas fir grow on the King Top Plateau, the highest area in the Confusion Range, where elevations reach 8,300 feet. Shortages of water and feed allow only small numbers of wild horses, pronghorn, deer, and smaller animals to eke out an existence.

**Fossil Mountain** in the southeast part of the Confusions has an exceptional diversity of marine fossils, many very rare. Thirteen fossil groups of ancient sea creatures have been found in rocks of Early Ordovician age (350-400 million years ago). Fossil Mountain stands 6,685 feet high on the west edge of Blind Valley. A signed road to Blind Valley turns south off US 50/6 between Mileposts 38 and 39 (54 miles west of Delta). Fossil Mountain is about 14 miles south of the highway.

# GREAT BASIN NATIONAL PARK

Lehman Caves and Wheeler Peak lie just across the Nevada border in a brand-new national park. Lehman Caves, a national monument since 1922, has long been known for its beautiful formations. Wheeler Peak (elev. 13,063 ft.), with its glacial features, alpine lakes, forests, and great views, stands as one of the best examples of the Great Basin mountains. Legislation in 1986 joined the caves and peak to form Great Basin National

Park. The 6,200-foot difference in elevation between the upper Sonoran Desert and the alpine tundra on Wheeler Peak encompasses the region's full spectrum of plant and wildlife habitats.

## Lehman Caves

Underground heat long ago turned layers of limestone on the east side of Wheeler Peak into marble. Much later, the caves formed as water containing carbon dioxide slowly worked into cracks and dissolved the rock. After the underground chambers had partly drained, stalactites, stalagmites, and other features typical of limestone caves began to grow. Indians knew about the caves in times past but didn't venture beyond the entrance room. A rancher named Absalom Lehman became the first to explore the wonders within. He had come to the area about 1869 to try his hand at ranching and raising fruit, knowing that nearby mining camps would provide a good market. (Some trees from his orchard still grow in front of the park's visitor center.) Word of the cave system spread quickly after its discovery in 1885 and hundreds of sightseers arrived in the first year. Lehman guided many of the visitors until his death in 1891.

## Visitor Center

Cave entrance, exhibits, and park headquarters are in a pinyon pine and juniper woodland on the east slope of Wheeler Peak. Views at the 6,825-foot elevation look over valleys and ranges of western Utah. A short film and exhibits introduce the geology of Lehman Caves and illustrate cave formations, flora, wildlife, and human history of the park. Books, topo maps, postcards, slides, and other interpretive materials can be purchased. Rhodes Cabin, just north of the visitor center, has additional historical and natural history exhibits. Mountain View Nature Trail begins a ½-mile loop here; pick up a trail guide at the visitor center. In summer, rangers give evening programs nightly in two of the campgrounds; check the posted schedule for locations and times. The visitor center is open daily 8 a.m.-5 p.m. except on New Year's Day, Thanksgiving, and Christmas. The only fees charged are for the cave tour and campsites. From Baker, Nevada (just west of the Utah-Nevada line and 5 miles south of US 50/6), head west 5 miles to the visitor center. The park is about 106 miles west of Delta, Utah. Contact the Great Basin National Park at Baker, NV 89311; tel. (702) 234-7331.

## Cave Tours

Ranger-led tours begin daily (except on the holidays noted above) from the visitor center 8 a.m.-5 p.m. The schedule has frequent departures (hourly or half-hourly) in summer, decreasing to 4 tours a day in winter. In summer you can also take a daily candlelight tour of the cave and see it much as Ab Lehman did. The cave's cool interior (50° F) comes as a welcome relief from desert heat, and a jacket or sweater is recommended. Tours cover 0.6 mile with some stairs and inclines in a leisurely

1½ hours. Cost of tours is $3 adult, $2 children 6-15, and $1.50 with Golden Age cards; no discount for Golden Eagle cards. Don't forget that Nevada is on Pacific Time, one hour earlier than Utah.

## Spelunking Tours

Tours lasting 2½ hours give participants an experience in the sport and science of cave exploring. These trips require considerable crawling and use of caving equipment. You'll see parts of the cave system not normally seen by visitors. Contact the park in advance for information and required reservations. Trips take place on summer weekends; minimum age is 14; $6.

## Wheeler Peak

The 76,800-acre park is centered on this lofty mountain. Glaciers and streams have carved sheer cliffs and rugged canyons in its slopes. A ridge extending north and south from the 13,063-foot summit has many peaks exceeding 11,000 feet. Hikers can climb to the top of Wheeler Peak on trails from Wheeler Peak Campground (elev. 10,000 ft.). The strenuous trip takes 6-8 hours for the 10 miles to the top and back. Wheeler Peak Campground is accessible by car from about late May to Oct. on a 12-mile road beginning near the visitor center. For an easier hike from this campground, another trail makes a 3-mile loop past Stella and Teresa lakes. A 6-mile (roundtrip) spur trail leaves this loop at Teresa Lake and winds through rocky country and a bristlecone pine forest to a snowfield below Wheeler Peak. Trails in other sections of the park lead to highly scenic areas too. Wildflowers bloom in profusion beginning in spring at lower elevations and progressing to the high country by late summer. Maps, trail descriptions, and backcountry permits are available at the visitor center.

## Practicalities

A snack bar and gift shop at the visitor center are open from April to October. Picnic grounds are just a short distance away. Campgrounds in the park, with distances from the visitor center, are: Lower Lehman Creek—2 miles (elev. 7,500 ft.; open all year); Baker Creek—3 miles (elev. 8,000 ft.; open mid-May to mid-Oct.); Upper Lehman Creek—3 miles (7,800 ft.; open mid-May to mid-Oct.); Wheeler Peak—12 miles (10,000 ft.; open early July to mid-Sept.), and Snake Creek—23 miles (7,800 ft.; open mid-May to late Sept.). Lower and Upper Lehman Creek campgrounds have drinking water and a $5 fee; Baker Creek and Wheeler Peak campgrounds have water, but it may need treating; they may have a fee. Snake Creek has no water or charge.

The small town of **Baker** has the **Silver Jack Motel** (tel. 702-234-7323; $27 s, $30.24 d), **The Outlaw Cafe** (lunch and dinner daily), and a service station/grocery store. The **"Y"** has a restaurant (breakfast, lunch, and dinner daily) and RV spaces ($7.56 no hookups, $10.80 w/hookups) open all year; located on US 50/6 at the NV 487 turnoff for Baker; tel. (702) 234-7223. The **Border Inn** straddles the Utah-Nevada line on US 50/6 with motel rooms ($29.43-40.33) in Utah and a restaurant (breakfast, lunch, and dinner daily) in Nevada; also has a gas station; tel. (702) 234-7300.

# WAH WAH MOUNTAINS

The Wah Wah Mountains extend southward about 55 miles in a continuation of the Confusion Range. Elevations range from 6,000 to more than 9,000 feet. The name comes from a Paiute Indian term for salty or alkaline seeps. Sparse sagebrush, juniper, and pinyon pine cover most of the land. Aspen, white fir, ponderosa pine, and bristlecone pine grow in the high country. Mule deer, pronghorn, and smaller animals roam the mountains. Carry water, maps, and compass into this wild country. Few people visit the Wah Wahs despite their pristine ecosystem. A 1986 BLM publication reported an estimated 155 visitor days per year for recreation in the Wah Wah Mountains Wilderness Study Area, which includes the northern and central parts of the range. That's an average of less than half a person per day!

## Crystal Peak
This snow-white pinnacle in the north end of the Wah Wah Mountains stands out as a major landmark. The soft white rock of the peak is tuff, outpourings of an ancient volcano thought to predate the block-faulted Wah Wahs. The best way to climb the peak (elev. 7,106 ft.) is to ascend the ridge just south of it from the east, then follow the ridge northeast up the peak. Be careful of soft crumbly rock. See the 15-minute Crystal Peak topo map.

## Central Section
The heart of the Wah Wahs has some of the best scenery and opportunities for nature study. Rugged cliffs mark the west edge of the range. A good hiking route begins at about 6,600 feet in elevation at the end of a dirt road going up Pierson Cove. Follow the dry wash upstream a short way to a split in the drainage, then take the left fork north through a canyon. After about 2 miles you'll come out of the canyon onto a high plateau. For the best views, turn northwest and continue climbing ¾ mile to the summit of an 8,918-foot peak. See the 15-minute Wah Wah Summit topo map.

# SAN FRANCISCO MOUNTAINS AND GHOST TOWNS

Frisco Peak (elev. 9,660 ft.) crowns this small range northwest of Milford. The Wah Wah Valley and Mountains lie to the west. Silver strikes in the San Francisco Mountains in the 1870s led to the opening of many mines and the founding of the towns of Newhouse and Frisco. By 1920 the best ores had given out and both communities turned to ghosts. A jeep road goes to the summit of Frisco Peak.

## Frisco
The Horn Silver Mine, developed in 1876 at the south end of the San Francisco Mountains, was the first of several prolific silver producers. Smelters, and charcoal ovens to fuel them, sprouted up to process the ore. A wild boom town developed as miners flocked to the new diggings. The railroad reached

Frisco in 1880 and later extended to nearby Newhouse. Frisco's population of 6,000 included quite a few gamblers and other shady characters. Twenty-three saloons labored to serve the thirsty customers. Gunfights became almost a daily ritual for a while, keeping the cemetery growing. Yet all came to an end early in 1885 when rumblings were heard deep within the Horn Silver Mine between shifts. The foreman luckily delayed sending the next crew down, and a few minutes later the whole mine collapsed with a deafening roar that broke windows in Milford 15 miles away. Out of work, most of the miners and business people moved on. More than $60 million of silver and other valuable ores had come out of the ground in the 10 frenzied years. Some mining has been done on and off since, but Frisco has died.

Today Frisco is one of Utah's best-preserved mining ghosts, with about a dozen stone or wood buildings surviving. A headframe and mine buildings, still intact, overlook the town from the hillside. Five beehive-shaped charcoal kilns stand on the east edge of Frisco. You can see the kilns and the townsite if you look north from UT 21, 15 miles west of Milford, between Mileposts 62 and 63. Dirt roads wind their way in. A historical marker for Frisco is at the turnoff for the town; turnoff for the beehive kilns is 0.3 mile east. Hiking off the roads can be very dangerous near the old mines and time-worn buildings.

### Newhouse

Prospectors discovered silver deposits in 1870 on the southwest side of the San Francisco Mountains but lacked the funds to develop them. Mining didn't take off until 1900, when Samuel Newhouse financed operations. A sizable town grew up here as ore worth $3.5 million came out of the Cactus Mine. Citizens maintained a degree of law and order not found in most mining towns. Even the saloon and the working girls had to operate outside the community. Deposits of rich ore ran out only 10 years later and the town's inhabitants departed. The railroad depot was moved to a nearby ranch and other buildings went to Milford. Today Newhouse is a ghostly site with about half a dozen concrete or stone buildings standing in ruin. Foundations of a smelter, mill, other structures, railroad grades, and lots of broken glass remain. A good dirt road turns north 2 miles to the site from UT 21 (between Mileposts 57 and 58), 20 miles west of Milford.

## MILFORD

Miners on their way to Frisco and Newhouse crossed the Beaver River at a ford below a stamp mill, so Milford seemed the logical name for the town that grew up here. Most of Milford's businesses in the early days relied on supplying the mining camps. Today the town serves as a center for the railroad, nearby farms, and a geothermal plant. Steam from wells at the Blundell Geothermal plant, 13 miles northeast of town, produce electricity for Utah Power and Light. Travelers heading west will find Milford their last stop for supplies until the Nevada border. Milford is at the junction of UT 21 and UT 257; Beaver is 32 miles east, Baker (NV) is 96 miles northwest, and Delta is 77 miles north.

### Practicalities

The **Station Motel** has rooms at $26.16 s, $31.61 d and up at the corner of 100 West and 500 South; tel. 387-2481. Its **Station Restaurant** is open daily for breakfast, lunch, and dinner; tel. 387-2804. **Old Hickory Inn** also serves American food; open daily for lunch and dinner; tel. 387-5042. **Hong Kong Cafe** prepares inexpensive Chinese and American food 24 hours daily at 433 S. Main; tel. 387-2251. **Prospector Cafe** serves standard fare for breakfast, lunch, and dinner Mon. to Fri. at 450 S. Main.

The **city park** at 300 South and 200 West has a picnic area. An outdoor pool is behind the high school at 62 N. 300 West. Milford's 5-hole **golf course** is open April 1 to Oct. 31 on the west edge of town (about 1000 South and 700 West); tel. 387-2711. **Post office** is at 458 S. Main. **Milford Valley Memorial Hospital** is at 451 N. Main; tel. 387-2411.

**Milford City Office** will answer questions about the area; open Mon. to Fri. 8 a.m.-3 p.m. at 302 S. Main (Box 69, Milford, UT 84751); tel. 387-2711. The **public library** is open weekday afternoons, 336 S. 100 West; tel. 387-5039.

## MINERSVILLE STATE PARK

The 1,130-acre reservoir has good year-round fishing for rainbow trout (ice fishing in winter). Most people come here to fish, though some visitors go sailing or water-skiing. Park facilities include picnic tables, campsites (some with electric and water hookups), restrooms with showers, paved boat ramp, fish-cleaning station, and dump station. Fees are $3 day use, $10 camping, and $5 overflow sites. Reservations are a good idea on summer holidays. In winter the restrooms and water sources may be closed, but water is available at the ranger residence. For information about the park, write Box 51, Beaver, UT 84713-0051; tel. 438-5472 or (800) 322-3770 (reservations). Minersville Reservoir lies just off UT 21 in a sage-and juniper-covered valley, 18 miles east of Milford and 14 miles west of Beaver.

*coyote*
(Canis latrans)

*Fort Utah (Provo); Timpanogos Peak rises in background*

# CENTRAL UTAH

In many ways, the geography and history of central Utah are extensions from the northern part of the state. The rugged Wasatch Range attains its greatest heights here at Mt. Nebo (elev. 11,928 ft.). Gently rolling alpine country of the Wasatch Plateau extends farther south where the Wasatch Range ends. Mormon pioneers pushed south into the valleys of central Utah in 1849, just 2 years after the founding of Salt Lake City. Farms and quiet Mormon villages occupy much of the lower country today. Mountains entice visitors with scenic drives, hiking, fishing, boating, and winter sports.

## PROVO

Utah's second largest city (pop. 84,000) has a striking setting on the shore of Utah Lake, beneath the west face of the Wasatch Range. Provo is best known as the home of Brigham Young University, a large, dynamic school sponsored by the Mormon Church. Museums and cultural events on the BYU campus make it a popular destination.

### History
In 1776, members of the Dominguez-Escalante expedition visited the Utah Valley, where Provo now is, and gave glowing reports of the fertile soil, plentiful game, and beautiful countryside. The Spanish friars who led the group had hoped to return and establish missions for the local Indians, but faraway political deci-

# CENTRAL UTAH

sions prevented them from doing so. The expedition had friendly relations with the Ute Indians (known here as the "Timpanogotzis"), as did most later mountain men and early Mormon settlers. Fur trappers included Etienne Provot, a French-Canadian who passed through in 1824 and 1825. His Anglicized name was adopted in 1849 when Mormons arrived in the Utah Valley to start their first settlement. Within the next 2 years, the communities of Lehi, Pleasant Grove, American Fork, Springville, and Payson had also sprung up in the valley. Geneva Steel and other major industries established during the WW II years transformed the Provo area from an agrarian landscape to the major urban center it is today. The downtown business district, though, still has many distinctive buildings from the turn of the century and earlier.

## BRIGHAM YOUNG UNIVERSITY

The university had a modest beginning in 1875 as the Brigham Young Academy, established under the direction of Mormon Church President Brigham Young. Like the rest of Provo, BYU's population and size have grown dramatically in recent decades. No ordinary university, BYU is one of the largest church-affiliated schools in the world. The 27,000 students come from every state in the nation and 90 foreign countries. Students aren't required to be Mormons, but about 95% do belong to the LDS Church. High academic standards upheld by the students and the 1,300 full-time faculty have made the university a leader in many fields. BYU offers bachelors degrees in 150 fields, masters in 115, and doctorals in 56. Everyone attending the school must follow a strict dress and grooming code, something you'll notice immediately on a stroll across the modern campus. An honor code requires high moral conduct according to LDS teachings. A giant "Y," another nickname of the university, overlooks the campus from a hillside to the east.

Students pursue a vigorous program in the arts, including performances of classical music, jazz, theater, and folk dancing. Exhibits and concerts are held in the **Harris Fine Arts Center** (just north of the Wilkinson Center) and other locations on campus; tel. 378-7444 (music ticket office), 378-7447 (theater performances). BYU also goes all out to support its Cougars football and other athletic teams. More than half of the students participate in intramurals, which offer a choice of 53 sports. Major sporting events take place in the 65,000-seat Cougar Stadium and the indoor 23,000-seat Marriott Center; tel. 378-5666 (ticket office).

You're welcome to visit the more than 600 acres of BYU's vast campus. The **Hosting Center** provides literature and advice about things to see, events, and facilities open to the public; open Mon. to Fri. 8 a.m.-5 p.m.; on the brow of the hill near Maeser Building, traveling south on Campus Drive; tel. 378-4678. Campus tours, taken in small open-air vehicles, introduce the university; student guides point out features of interest and tell about student life and research work. The free tours last about an hour and depart Mon. to Fri. at 11 a.m. and 2 p.m. from the Hosting Center; groups can schedule tours at other times too. Free parking is available beside the Hosting Center (south side) for those taking guided tours or needing information about the campus. Additional free visitor parking (signed) is near the north end of Campus Drive and near the Wilkinson Center (east across the street).

**Wilkinson Center** serves as the social center for BYU. The main level has a choice of cafeterias and snack bars (open Mon. to Sat. for breakfast, lunch, and dinner), Varsity Theater (current movies), an art gallery, lounge areas, and an information desk. The **Skyroom Restaurant** on the sixth floor offers great views and fine dining (open Mon. to Fri. for lunch and Fri. for dinner); tel. 378-5001. The lower level has **Outdoors Unlimited** (rentals of bicycles and equipment for sports, camping, boating, snowshoeing, cross-country skiing, and downhill skiing; tel. 378-3390) and a **post office**. Some of the other recreation facilities are open only to university staff. The **BYU Bookstore** occupies 3 levels on the west side of the Wilkinson Center with a good selection of general books, textbooks, LDS titles, art supplies, and BYU clothing and souvenirs. The **Harold B. Lee Library,** just west

# PROVO

1. Utah Lake State Park
2. Fort Utah City Park
3. Timpanogos Municipal Golf Course
4. Pioneer Park
5. post office
6. Provo Tabernacle
7. Provo Public Library
8. Uinta Natl. Forest Supervisor's Office
9. Greyhound Bus
10. McCurdy Historical Doll Museum
11. Utah County Conv. & Visitor Bureau
12. North Park and Pioneer Museum
13. Utah Valley Medical Center
14. Provo High School
15. Museum of Peoples and Cultures (BYU)
16. Hosting Center (BYU)
17. Wilkinson Center and bookstore (BYU)
18. Harris Fine Arts Center (BYU)
19. Bean Life Science Museum (BYU)
20. Marriott Center (BYU)
21. Earth Science Museum (BYU)
21. Missionary Training Center
22. Provo Temple

of the bookstore, has an impressive collection of books and maps on 5 levels; the genealogical library on the fourth floor ranks second in size only to the one in Salt Lake City; main collections are open Mon. to Sat. 7 a.m.-midnight; tel. 378-2926.

## BYU MUSEUMS

Small collections on campus include a series of salt- and freshwater aquariums in the basement of the Widtsoe Building, and Earth Science exhibits and a Foucault pendulum in the lobby and hallways of the Eyring Science Center. The Summerhays Planetarium in the Eyring Science Center presents programs to the public; small charge; tel. 378-4361. The university hopes to build a natural history museum complex incorporating the Monte L. Bean Life Science Museum. The Earth Science and Peoples and Cultures museums will be moved here. A museum of fine arts is planned to showcase some of the school's more than 12,000 art objects in a building next to the Harris Fine Arts Center.

### Monte L. Bean Life Science Museum
Mounted animals and dioramas realistically depict wildlife of Utah and distant lands. The exhibits not only identify the many species on display but show how they interact within their environments. The Children's Discovery Room has cages of insects and small animals. Special presentations include movies, talks, workshops, and live-reptile demonstrations; call for the schedule. The research library is open Mon. to Fri. 8 a.m.-5 p.m. Natural history items can be purchased in the gift shop. Museum exhibits are open Mon. 10 a.m.-9 p.m. and Tues. to Sat. 10 a.m.-5 p.m.; free admission; located southeast of the Marriott Center on 1430 North; tel. 378-5051.

### Earth Science Museum
This small museum features excellent exhibits of dinosaurs and early mammals. The popular dinosaur video program both entertains and educates. A viewing window lets you observe researchers cleaning and preparing bones. Open Mon. to Fri. 8 a.m.-5 p.m. and possibly Mon. evenings and Sat.; free admission; 1683 N. Provo Canyon Rd. (across from Cougar Stadium); tel. 378-2232.

### Museum Of Peoples And Cultures
The museum's purpose is to communicate knowledge about both modern and ancient peoples of the world. Exhibits reflect research in the Great Basin in Utah, the American Southwest, Mesoamerica, South America, the Near East, and Polynesia. Open Mon. to Fri. 8 a.m.-5 p.m.; free admission; corner of 700 North and 100 East; tel. 378-6112.

Head Preparator Dee Hall assembling skull of a female Uintatherium, an Eocene herbivore; this prehistoric mammal had an exceptionally small brain in relation to its body size. (BYU Earth Science Museum)

## OTHER PROVO SIGHTS

### McCurdy Historical Doll Museum

Mrs. Laura McCurdy Clark, who started the collection, often used her dolls to teach history to students. The original collection has been expanded until now there are about 4,000 dolls, representing U.S. presidents and their wives, other historical figures, and diverse nationalities. Private parties can be arranged here. The museum shop sells dolls, doll supplies, toys, and books. Open Tues. to Sat. noon-6 p.m (1-5 p.m. Jan. to March); $2 adult, $1 under 12; 246 N. 100 East; tel. 377-9935.

### Provo Tabernacle

Architect William Folsom, who designed the St. George and Manti temples, patterned this English-style structure after a Presbyterian church he had visited in Salt Lake City. Construction, begun in 1883, required 15 years. Members of the LDS Church offer free tours that explain the history, architectural details, and purpose of the building; open Memorial Day weekend to the end of Sept. 10 a.m.-10 p.m.; 375-2011. Organ recitals and other concerts take place here. Located at 100 S. University Avenue.

### Provo Temple

The modern building of white cast stone incorporates floral elements and a central golden spire. It's particularly impressive at night lit up against the sky. Dedication took place in 1972 with 75,000 people in attendance. Church members carry out sacred work within the 283 rooms. Visitors can't go inside, but are welcome to visit the landscaped grounds. Free walking tours explain the Mormon religion and the purpose of temples; a brochure shows views of the temple interior. Weather permitting, tours are offered from late May to early Oct. 9 a.m.-9 p.m.; 2200 N. Temple Dr. (turn east on 2230 North from University Ave. or drive north on 900 East).

### Missionary Training Center

Before a Mormon missionary goes off to serve in a foreign country, he must learn the language. Here it takes only 2 months to complete a course in any of the 32 languages offered. Tours can be arranged, but the center needs at least one week's notice. West of the Provo Temple at 2000 N. 900 East; tel. 378-2602.

### Utah Lake State Park

The largest body of freshwater completely within the state, Utah Lake is 24 miles long (north to south) and 11 miles wide. Average depth is only 9.4 feet. Mountains form the skyline in all directions. Swans, geese, pelicans, ducks and other migratory birds stop by. Best bird-watching is at the south end of the lake and near the Provo airport. The state park provides recreation facilities on the east shore, just a short drive from downtown Provo. Boaters come for water-skiing, windsurfing, and fishing; 4 paved boat ramps, docks, and slips are provided. The swimming beach offers another way to cool off. Fishermen catch white bass, channel catfish, walleye pike, yellow perch, carp, and other warm-water fish during most of the year. The lake usually freezes over by late Dec. and has good ice fishing; trout descend from the mountain rivers during this season. A visitor center has ice skating in winter. The campground is open all year on a first-come first-served basis; it has showers from late April to late October. The park is open year-round at 4400 W. Center, Provo, UT 84601; $3/vehicle day use, $6 or $8/vehicle for camping; tel. 375-0733/0731 or (800) 322-3770 (reservations). Head west 4 miles on Center from downtown Provo or take the I-15 exit for W. Center and go west 3 miles.

### Springville Museum Of Art

The museum began in the early 1900s as a collection of the Springville High School, but when it began to receive gifts of major works from artists Cyrus Dallin and John Hafen, townspeople decided that a special building was needed. They built this fine Spanish-style structure during the Depression years with federal and LDS Church assistance. The town is now also known as "Art City" because of its great interest in the arts. The permanent collection contains 700 American art works, including some of the best by Utah artists from the days of early pioneers and Indians up to the present. Eleven galleries display visiting exhibits (downstairs) and the permanent collection (upstairs). The annual April Salon is a major show of American contemporary artists. The museum is open Sun. 2-5 p.m. and Tues. to Sat. 10 a.m.-5 p.m. (until 9 p.m. on Wed.); closed Mon. and state holidays (also closed for 2 weeks prior to the April Salon); free admission; tel. 489-9434. The museum is at 126 E. 400 South in Springville. From Provo, drive 7 miles south on US 89 (S. State St.).

## PRACTICALITIES

### Campgrounds

**Lakeside RV Campground** has sites for tents ($9.83) and RVs ($14.70 w/hookups) with showers, pool, laundry, store, and canoe rentals; open all year at 4000 W. Center (just

Appeal to the Great Spirit
*Cyrus Dallin (1912)*

before Utah Lake State Park); tel. 373-5267. **Provo KOA Campground** has sites for tents ($11.94) and RVs ($16.55 w/hookups) with showers, pool, laundry, and store; open year-round at 320 N. 2050 West (¼ mile west of I-15 on Center, then one block north); tel. 375-2994. **Silver Fox RV Resort** offers sites for tents and RVs ($10.93 no hookups, $13.66 w/hookups) with showers, pool, and laundry; open all year at 101 W. 1500 South (behind Motel 6); tel. 377-0033. **Frazier Park** lies along the Provo River, 5 miles up Provo Canyon; $5 tent, $10 RV w/hookups; open year-round with showers; tel. 225-5346. **Riverbend Trailer Park** has sites for RVs ($8 w/hookups; no tents) with showers and laundry; open April 15 to Oct. 15; located about 6 miles up Provo Canyon on US 189; tel. 225-1863.

### Food

**Annie's Pantry** offers family dining at 150 S. University Ave.; tel. 373-3900; open daily for breakfast, lunch, and dinner. **Good Earth Natural Foods** has a cafe (open Mon. to Sat. for lunch), bakery, and groceries at 384 W. Center; tel. 375-7444. **Govinda's** features vegetarian cuisine from around the world at 260 N. University Ave.; tel. 375-0404; open Mon. to Sat. for lunch and dinner, except closed Wed. evening. **Magleby's** serves steak, seafood, and chicken in a European atmosphere at 1675 N. 200 West; tel. 374-6249; open Mon. to Fri. for lunch and Mon. to Sat. for dinner. The Excelsior Hotel offers fine dining in **Mingles**, open daily for breakfast, lunch, and dinner; 101 W. 100 North; tel. 377-4700. **The Underground** features American and Mexican specialties and pizza in a Prohibition-era setting; downstairs at 55 N. University Ave.; tel. 377-5044; open Mon. to Sat. for lunch and dinner. The **Sensuous Sandwich** has a great choice of ingredients for their hot and cold sandwiches, sold by the inch from 4 to 24 inches; 163 W. Center; tel. 377-9244; open Mon. to Sat. for lunch and dinner. **Claimjumper Steakhouse** serves up steak, prime rib, and other fare at 834 E. Provo Canyon (about one mile up from the mouth of the canyon); tel. 226-8324; open daily for dinner. **Paris New York Grill** features French, American, and Italian cuisine at moderate

# PROVO ACCOMMODATIONS

Add 9.25% tax to all prices

| MOTEL/HOTEL | ADDRESS | RATES | PHONE | FEATURES |
|---|---|---|---|---|
| City Center Motel | 150 W. 300 South | $24-28 | 373-8489 | kitchenettes, pool |
| Colony Inn | 1380 S. University Ave. | $28-56 | 374-6800 or (800) 524-9999 | kitchenettes, sauna, pool |
| Columbian Motel (Best Western) | 70 E. 300 South | $34-48 | 373-8973 or (800) 528-1234 | pool |
| Comfort Inn | 1555 N. Canyon Rd. | $44-58 | 374-6020 or (800) 221-2222 | indoor pool, spa, and Cont. breakfast |
| Cottontree Inn (Best Western) | 2230 N. University Pkwy. | $40-90 | 373-7044 or (800) 528-1234 | pool |
| Days Inn | 1675 N. 200 West | $38-48 | 375-8600 or (800) 325-2525 | pool |
| East Bay Inn | 1292 S. University Ave. | $23-59 | 374-2500 or (800) 326-0025 | pool, hot tub |
| Excelsior Hotel | 101 W. 100 North | $70-350 | 377-4700 or (800) 824-4193 (UT), (800) 824-3676 (out) | pool, spa, weight room, suites |
| Holiday Inn | 1460 S. University Ave. | $50-54 | 374-9750 or (800) HOLIDAY | pool |
| Hotel Roberts | 192 S. University Ave. | $10-18 | 373-3400 | historic 1882 hotel |
| Motel 6 | 1600 S. University Ave. | $22-28 | 375-5064 | pool |
| Rome Inn (Best Western) | 1200 S. University Ave. | $32-48 | 373-0060 or (800) 528-1234 | kitchenettes, pool |
| Safari Motel | 250 S. University Ave. | $24-38 | 373-9672 | kitchenettes, spa, pool |
| Super 8 Motel | 1288 S. University Ave. | $28-35 | 375-8766 or (800) 848-8888 | |
| TraveLodge | 124 S. University Ave. | $33-39 | 373-1974 or (800) 255-3050 | pool |
| University Western Inn | 40 W. 300 South | $23-30 | 373-0660 or (800) 322-8029 | kitchenettes, pool |
| Uptown Motel | 469 W. Center | $20-36 | 373-8248 | kitchenettes, pool |
| Valley Inn Motel | 1425 S. State | $19-25 | 377-3804 | |

prices; 463 N. University Ave.; tel. 377-4545; open Mon. to Fri. for lunch and Mon. to Sat. for dinner. For Italian pasta, pizza, and baked goods, try **La Dolce Vita** (61 N. 100 East; tel. 373-8482; open Mon. to Sat. for lunch and dinner) or the **Brick Oven** (150 E. 800 North; tel. 374-8800; open Mon. to Sat. for lunch and dinner).

**Four Winds Restaurant's** varied menu includes Chinese, American, and Italian items at 250 W. Center; tel. 374-9323; open Mon. to Sat. for lunch and dinner. **China Chef Cao** has oriental cuisine at 1295 N. State (500 West); tel. 374-1007; open Mon. to Sat. for lunch and dinner. Other places for Chinese food include **Chinatown Restaurant** (330 S. State; tel. 373-7699; open Mon. to Sat. for lunch and dinner); **Panda Cafe** (138 W. Center; tel. 377-3323; open Mon. to Sat. for lunch and dinner); and **South China Restaurant** (1700 N. State; tel. 374-9114; open daily for lunch and dinner). **Cafe Viet Hoa** presents a good variety of Vietnamese food at 278 W. Center; tel. 373-8373; open Mon. to Sat. for lunch and dinner. **Yuli Market** is an oriental grocery store and Japanese fast-food place at 1145 N. 500 West; tel. 375-3789. **Kimo's Luau Hawaiian Restaurant** presents native Hawaiian and many Asian styles at 400 W. 40 North; tel. 377-5278; open Tues. to Sat. for lunch and dinner and take-out.

Flavorful Mexican food is prepared at **Los Hermanos** (16 W. Center; tel. 375-5732; open Mon. to Sat. for lunch and dinner); **Joe Vera's** (250 W. Center; tel. 375-6714; open Mon. to Sat. for lunch and dinner); and **Mi Rancherito** (368 W. Center; tel. 373-1503; open Mon. to Sat. for lunch and dinner). **El Salvador Restaurant** is a small cafe with Salvadoran and Mexican items at 232 W. Center; tel. 377-9411; open Mon. to Sat. for lunch and dinner.

## Entertainment

Catch movies at the **Academy Theatre** (56 N. University Ave.; tel. 373-4470); **Mann 4 Central Square Theatre** (175 W. 200 North; tel. 374-6061); or BYU's **Varsity Theatre** (Wilkinson Center; tel. 378-3311). **SCERA Shell** offers family entertainment movies year-round inside and summer plays and musicals in an outdoor shell at 699 S. State in Orem; tel. 225-2560 (recorded info) or 224-8797 (office). **Brigham Young University** has a busy calendar of cultural and sporting events; tel. 378-7444 (music ticket office), 378-7447 (theater performances); tel. 378-5666 (sporting events).

## Events

For current happenings in Provo and nearby towns, check with the Utah County Convention and Visitor Bureau at 100 E. Center, Room 2400; tel. 370-8393. Major annual events include:

**June:** Utah Pageant of the Arts brings the world's art masterpieces to life—literally—using actors to stage classic paintings and sculptures. Art City Days takes place in Springville. Strawberry Days is a community celebration with rodeos, games, and entertainment in Pleasant Grove. Cowboys show their skills at the Round-up and Rodeo in Lehi.

**July:** Utah Pageant of the Arts continues. Provo celebrates July Fourth with a Freedom Festival parade, entertainment, and fireworks. Steel Days is a community celebration in American Fork. A Pioneer Day parade and entertainment take place on July 24 in Provo and other towns. Fiesta Days in Spanish Fork has a parade, rodeo, and entertainment for 3 days near July 24.

**August:** Utah County Fair presents a rodeo, exhibits, and entertainment in Spanish Fork. The World Folk Festival brings dance groups from many lands to Springville.

## Recreation

**Provo Recreation Center** at Provo High School has an indoor pool, racquetball/wallyball courts, and a weight room at 1155 N. University Ave.; tel. 379-6610. **North Park** has Veterans' Memorial Pool (outdoor; tel. 379-6614), picnic areas, playground, and a **DUP Pioneer Museum** (open Mon. to Fri. 1-4 p.m. in summer, then 1-4 p.m. on the last Thurs. of each month during the rest of the year) at 500 W. 500 North. **Fort Utah City Park** has picnic tables, playground, and a replica of the fort built by Provo's first settlers; from downtown, head west on Center past the I-15 interchange and turn north one block on UT 114 (2050

West). **Pioneer Park** has picnicking and a playground at Center and 500 West. The big **Seven Peaks Resort Water Park** contains thrilling slides, twisting tubes, and a variety of pools to cool off in; guests can also picnic or play such games as volleyball, basketball, softball, and horseshoes; open about late May to early Sept.; admission is $10.57 ($5.84 after 5 p.m.) age 10-64, $8.45 age 4-9, and free for toddlers (age 3 and under) and seniors (65 and over); tel. 377-7717 (recording), 377-4700, or (800) 824-4193; turn east on Center St. to its end and follow signs. **Trafalga Family Fun Center** features a water-tube slide, mini golf, and arcade games at 168 S. 1200 West in Orem (take I-15 Exit 274); tel. 224-7415. Play golf at the 27-hole **East Bay Municipal Golf Course** (turn east on East Bay Blvd. from S. University Ave. near the I-15 interchange; tel. 379-6612) or the 9-hole **Cascade Fairways Public Golf Course** (1313 E. 800 North in Orem; tel. 225-6677). In winter, skiers hit the slopes at **Sundance Ski Area** 14 miles northeast of town; tel. 225-4107. Head out on horseback from **Big Springs Ranch** on one-hour, 2-hour, and half-day rides; hay, sleigh, overnight, and drop-camp trips are offered too; drive up Provo Canyon to the Chalet Cafe in Vivian Park (2 miles past Bridal Veil Falls) and turn in 3.3 miles to the ranch; tel. 225-8589. **Hansen Mountaineering** leads trips and provides instruction in rock climbing, winter camping, and cross-country skiing; 757 N. State, Orem, UT 84057; tel. 226-7498.

## Services

The **post office** is at 95 W. 100 South; tel. 374-2000. For **highway conditions,** call 224-3112. The **U.S. Forest Service** provides avalanche/mountain weather information during the snow season at 374-9770. **Utah Valley Regional Medical Center** is at 1034 N. 500 West; tel. 373-7850 (24-hour Crisis Line is 375-4673). **Primedical** clinic is at 1850 S. Columbia Lane in Orem; tel. 225-7343.

## Information

**Utah County Convention and Visitor Bureau** offers advice on sights and services in Provo and the Utah Valley; open Mon. to Fri. 8 a.m.-5 p.m.; 100 E. Center, Room 2400 (Box 912, Provo, UT 84603); tel. 370-8393 or (800) 222-UTAH out of state. The U.S. Forest Service has 3 offices in the area. That of the **Uinta National Forest Supervisor** has general information about all districts in the forest and some books for sale; open Mon. to Fri. 8 a.m.-5 p.m. at 88 W. 100 North, Provo, UT 84601; tel. 377-5780. Contact the **Pleasant Grove Ranger District** office for specific information about the Alpine Scenic Loop and other areas in the Uinta National Forest north of Provo; open Mon. to Fri. 8 a.m.-5 p.m. (daily 8 a.m.-5 p.m. in summer); 390 N. 100 East, Pleasant Grove, UT 84062; tel. 785-3563. The **Spanish Fork Ranger District** office covers the Uinta National Forest east and southeast of Provo and the Wasatch National Forest, Vernon Division, southwest of town; open Mon. to Fri. 8 a.m.-4:30 p.m. (daily 8 a.m.-5 p.m. in summer); 44 W. 400 North, Spanish Fork, UT 84660; tel. 798-3571. **Provo City Public Library** is open Mon. to Wed. 10 a.m.-9 p.m., Thurs. to Sat. 10 a.m.-6 p.m.; at 425 W. Center; tel. 379-6650. BYU's **Harold B. Lee Library,** just west of the Wilkinson Center, has an impressive collection of books and maps on 5 levels; open Mon. to Sat. 7 a.m.-midnight; tel. 378-2926. The **BYU Bookstore** at the Wilkinson Center has one of the best and largest selections in the state; tel. 378-3584. **Valley Book Center** sells magazines and books downtown at 52 W. Center; tel. 374-6260.

## Transport

**Utah Transit Authority (UTA)** provides local bus service in Provo and connects with Salt Lake City, Ogden, and other towns; buses stay home on Sun. and holidays; tel. 375-4636. **Greyhound Bus** has at least 2 northbound and 2 southbound departures daily; 124 N. 300 West; tel. 373-4211. **Amtrak** trains serve Provo; tel. (800) 872-7245. **Yellow Cab** provides taxi service; tel. 377-7070. Scheduled airline flights leave from the Salt Lake City airport.

# NORTHWEST OF PROVO

### Hutching's Museum Of Natural History

This amazingly diverse collection in the town of Lehi (LEE-high) began as a family museum. Highlights include pioneer rifles, Indian crafts, glittering minerals, ancient fossils, mounted birds of Utah, and colorful tropical shells. Open Mon. to Sat. 9:30 a.m.-5:30 p.m.; $2 adult, $1 children under 12; tel. 768-8710. Located at 685 N. Center St. in Lehi (16 miles northwest of Provo on I-15).

### Saratoga Resort

This family amusement park on the north shore of Utah Lake features 4 swimming pools, a 350-foot long "Kamikazi" water slide, arcade games, Kiddieland rides, miniature golf, boating on the lake, snack bar, picnicking, and camping. Mineral springs emerging from the ground at 111° F feed the pools, which are kept at about 95° (upper pool) and 85° (lower pool). The campground has showers with spaces for tents ($8) and RVs ($10 w/electric hookups). Saratoga's season lasts from about Memorial Day to Labor Day; tel. 768-8206/8205. Costs depend on facilities used; a small parking fee is charged on weekends. From Lehi, drive west 2 miles on UT 73 and turn south 3.3 miles on 9550 West at the sign.

### Camp Floyd Stagecoach Inn State Park

A restored inn, an old U.S. Army building, and a military cemetery preserve a bit of pioneer history at Fairfield, a sleepy village on the other side of Utah Lake from Provo. John Carson, who had been one of the first settlers at the site in 1855, built a family residence and hotel 3 years later. About the same time, troops of the U.S. Army under Colonel Albert Johnston marched in and established Camp Floyd nearby. The soldiers had been sent by President Buchanan to put down a rumored Mormon rebellion. Upon finding that no "Utah War" existed, the colonel led his men to this site so as not to intimidate the major Mormon settlements. Fairfield jumped in size almost overnight to become Utah's third largest city, with a population of about 7,000 including the 3,000 soldiers. Even for the times, it was rowdy—17 saloons served the Army men. The camp (later named Fort Crittenden) served no real purpose, however, and was abandoned in 1861 so troops could return east to fight in the Civil War. Carson's hotel, later known as the Stagecoach Inn, continued to serve travelers on the dusty main road across Utah. Pony Express riders, stagecoach passengers, miners, sheep herders, and every other kind of

*Stagecoach Inn, built by John Carson in 1858*

traveler stopped here for the night until the doors closed in 1947.

Now the inn is a state park, furnished as in the old days and full of exhibits showing frontier life. A shaded picnic area is beside it. The only surviving building of Camp Floyd has been moved across the street and has a diorama of the fort and some excavated artifacts. Camp Floyd's well-kept cemetery is a ¾-mile drive

west and south of Fairfield. The Stagecoach Inn is open daily 11 a.m.-5 p.m. from about Easter weekend to the end of September. The season may be extended depending on visitation; it's a good idea to call ahead, especially if driving out just to see the exhibits. Admission is $1 adult, $.50 children 6-15; tel. 768-8932. From Provo or Salt Lake City, take I-15 to Lehi and turn west 21 miles on UT 73.

# NORTH OF PROVO

## TIMPANOGOS CAVE NATIONAL MONUMENT

Beautiful cave formations reward visitors who hike the trail to the cave entrance on the north side of Mt. Timpanogos. The branching helictites, icicle-like stalactites, rising stalagmites, and graceful flowstone formations appear snow white or in delicate hues of green, yellow, or red. Tunnels connect 3 separate limestone caves, each of which has a different character. The first was discovered by Martin Hansen in 1887 while tracking a mountain lion. Middle and Timpanogos caves weren't reported until 1921-22. Timpanogos Cave so impressed early explorers that a trail, lighting, and national monument protection came soon afterward.

Exhibits and a short slide show in the visitor center introduce the formation, history, and ecology of the caves. Staff provide information on special cave tours and on wildlife and plants of the area. A brochure available here identifies plants and trees along the trail to the caves and illustrates the geology and formation of the caves. Related books, hiking maps, posters, and slides are sold. Be sure to obtain tickets here for the cave tour before starting up the trail. Rangers schedule nature walks on the trail to the caves.

Allow about 3 hours for the complete trip, including 45-60 minutes for the cave tour. The 3-mile roundtrip hike from the visitor center to the caves is moderately difficult; you'll climb 1,065 feet to an elevation of 6,730 feet. Many

points along the way have fine views up and down American Fork Canyon and out onto the Utah Valley. People with breathing, heart, or walking difficulties shouldn't attempt the trail; wheeled vehicles (including strollers) and pets aren't allowed. Rangers enforce safety rules that prohibit running, throwing rocks, or short-cutting; children under 16 must stay with their parents.

Ranger-led tours wind about ½ mile through the caves. Underground temperatures are about 43° F all year, so a sweater or jacket is handy. The caves close during winter because snow and ice make the trail too hazardous. Normal season lasts from mid-May to mid-Oct.; ticket sales (in the visitor center only) are open 9 a.m.-3:30 p.m. (extended to 7 a.m.-4:30 p.m. in the peak summer season). On Sat., Sun. afternoons, holidays, and mid-summer weekdays, you may have a long wait and tours can even sell out. It's a good idea to call ahead to check hours and find out how busy the caves are. Tickets can also be purchased 2 weeks in advance by mail or anytime in person. Admission fees for the cave tours are $3 adult, $2 children 6-15, free for children under 6; Golden Age card holders pay $1.50 but no discount is given with Golden Eagle cards.

A snack bar at the visitor center is open in summer. Picnickers can use tables across the road from the visitor center and at a site ¼ mile west. The U.S. Forest Service has several campgrounds nearby. Contact the monument at Rt. 3, Box 200, American Fork, UT 84003; tel. 756-5238. The visitor center is 2 miles up American Fork Canyon on the Alpine Scenic Loop (UT 92). You can take I-15 American Fork Exit 279 if coming north from Provo or the I-15 Alpine Exit 287 if coming south from Salt Lake City.

## ALPINE SCENIC LOOP

The narrow paved highway twists and winds through some of the most beautiful alpine terrain in Utah. Mount Timpanogos rises to 11,750 feet in the center of the loop and presents sheer cliff faces and jagged ridges in every direction. More than a dozen campgrounds and several picnic areas line the way. Fishermen try for trout in swift clear streams. Timpanogos Cave National Monument, on the north side of the loop, and the Bridal Veil Falls Skytram on the south side are major attractions. Autumn brings brilliant golds of aspen and scarlets of maples. Winter snows close the loop at its higher elevations but attract skiers to Sundance Resort. The most scenic section of the loop lies along American Fork Canyon and its South Fork, Provo Canyon and its North Fork, and a high pass between these drainages. A drive on US 89 or I-15 completes the approximately 40-mile loop. With a few stops, a full day can easily be spent on the drive. If you'd like to see Timpanogos Cave on the way, it's recommended to begin the loop there to avoid waiting in ticket lines, especially on weekend afternoons.

*black-chinned hummingbird*
(Archilocus alexandri)

Most of the picnic areas and campgrounds lie along American Fork Canyon at elevations of 5,400-6,200 feet; their season begins in early May and lasts to late October. Higher recreation areas are Granite Flat Campground (elev. 6,800 ft.), Altamont Group Campground (elev. 6,600 ft.), Timpooneke Campground (elev. 7,400 ft.), Mt. Timpanogos Campground (elev. 6,800 ft.), and Theatre in the Pines Picnic Area (elev. 6,800 ft.); their season runs from about Memorial Day weekend to the third week in September. Nearly all the recreation areas have water and a $7 fee for individual units. Some areas can be reserved through Mistix reservations service; tel. (800) 283-CAMP. **Pleasant Grove Ranger District** office of the Uinta National Forest has information and maps for recreation areas along the Alpine Scenic Loop and for the Lone Peak and Mount Timpanogos wildernesses; open Mon. to Fri. 8 a.m.-5 p.m. (daily 8 a.m.-5 p.m. in summer) at 390 N. 100 East, Pleasant Grove, UT 84062; tel. 785-3563. (You'll pass the office if taking US 89 and UT 146 between Provo/Orem and the mouth of American Fork Canyon.)

### Lone Peak Wilderness

The summit of Lone Peak rises to 11,250 feet on the divide between Little Cottonwood and American Fork canyons. Despite its closeness to Provo and Salt Lake City, the wilderness (30,088 acres) offers good opportunities for solitude. Hikers sometimes spot mountain goats. A climb to the summit is a very strenuous day hike; many people prefer taking 2 days. Some routes have dangerous drop-offs and require mountaineering skills. Lower elevations have fine scenery as well as easier hiking. Lake Hardy (southeast of the summit) is a popular destination. Four main trailheads provide access to the wilderness: Bells Canyon from lower Little Cottonwood Canyon to the north, Draper Ridge to the west, Alpine to the south, and Granite Flat Campground (off American Fork Canyon) to the southeast. Topo maps for the wilderness are the 7½-minute Lehi, Draper, Dromedary Peak, and Timpanogos Cave. Trail descriptions are given in *Wasatch Trails, Volume Two* by Daniel Geery and *The Hiker's Guide to Utah* by Dave Hall. Contact the Salt Lake City Ranger District office for hiking information on the north slope or the Pleasant Grove Ranger District office for the south side.

## Mount Timpanogos Wilderness

Sheer cliffs of Mt. Timpanogos tower 7,000 feet above the Utah Valley and present one of the most dramatic sights of the Wasatch Range. Trails to the heights lead past waterfalls, flower-filled alpine meadows, lakes, and permanent snowfields. One trail continues to the 11,750-foot summit for superb vistas of central Utah. The climb is strenuous, especially the last 3 miles, but requires no special skills. You'll see whole families—from grandchildren to grandparents—on this popular mountain. Even short hikes can be very rewarding. Take care to bring storm gear in case the weather suddenly turns bad. A shelter at Emerald Lake provides a refuge from storms. Hike either the Timpooneke Trail from Timpooneke Campground or Aspen Grove Trail from Theatre in the Pines Picnic Area; both trailheads lie just off the Alpine Scenic Loop. One-way distances to the summit are 9.1 miles on the Timpooneke Trail (4,350-foot elev. gain) and 8.3 miles on the Aspen Grove Trail (4,900-foot elev. gain). A hike on both trails (highly recommended) can be done with a car shuttle. If a trip to the summit sounds too ambitious, you can hike just the 12 miles between the trailheads via Emerald Lake (elev. 10,300 ft.). The Summit Trail branches off west of Emerald Lake, climbs a steep slope to the jagged summit ridge, then follows the ridge southeast to the top. A large snowfield and the deep blue waters of Emerald Lake, which is passed on the Aspen Grove Trail, lie directly below. Chunks of ice break off the snowfield and float in the lake during even the hottest summer days. Local people often refer to the snowfield as a glacier, but technically it's just a snowfield. Some climbers continue southeast along the summit ridge and drop down onto the snowfield and slide or walk to Emerald Lake, but this can be a bit hazardous.

*on the Aspen Grove Trail*

Hiking season is from about mid-July to mid-October. In winter and spring, hikers must be equipped and experienced for snow travel. Topo maps are the 7½-minute Timpanogos Cave and Aspen Grove, though you're not likely to need them unless snow covers the trails. The Pleasant Grove Ranger District office can advise on hiking conditions.

## Cascade Springs

Crystal-clear water emerges amidst lush vegetation and flows down a long series of travertine terraces at this beautiful spot. The springs produce more than 7 million gallons of water daily. Boardwalks and short trails with interpretive signs allow a close look at the stream and pools. Trout can be seen darting through the water (no fishing). Plant life includes maple, oak, aspen, willow, water birch, box elder, cattails, watercress, and wildflowers. The drive to Cascade Springs is also very pretty, either from the Alpine Scenic Loop or from Heber Valley. A paved road (F.R. 114) branches off the Alpine Scenic Loop near its summit (between Mileposts 18 and 19) and winds northeast 7 miles to the springs. An unpaved road, passable by car if the road is dry, begins on the west edge of Heber Valley and climbs high above the valley with good views, then drops down to the springs; turn west 7 miles on UT 220 from UT 113 (between Midway and Charleston) and follow signs.

## Sundance Resort

Since actor/director Robert Redford purchased the land in 1969, he has worked toward obtaining an ideal blend of recreation, the arts, and natural beauty. Musicals and other entertainment of the Sundance Summer Theatre take place outdoors; tickets can be purchased the day of the show or reserved by calling 225-4107. Redford founded the Sundance Institute in 1980 as a laboratory for independent filmmakers; its program is expanding and it may have screening rooms and other facilities open to the public. Sundance Nature Trail leads through forests of maple, oak, and aspen to the base of 600-foot-high Stewart Falls. Signs identify plants and trees and their uses by pioneers and Indians. The pretty valley below the falls was the site of Bear Claw's cabin in the movie *Jeremiah Johnson.* Allow about 2 hours for the 3-mile roundtrip; elevation change is 700 feet. The trail begins behind the lodge; a sign should mark the start. You can also hike to the falls from Theatre in the Pines Picnic Area (4 miles roundtrip; 350-foot elev. change).

Downhill skiing begins in mid-Dec. and lasts into April. Two double chairlifts and 2 triple chairs take skiers high on the southeast slopes of Mt. Timpanogos. The 39 runs provide challenges for people of all abilities; total elevation drop is 2,150 feet. Ski instruction, rentals, accommodations, and restaurants are available at the resort. Adult lift tickets cost $22 full day and $16 half day on weekends and holidays, $15 full day and $12 half day on weekdays, with discounts for children under 12 and for purchases of 3 days or more.

Year-round accommodations in mountain cottages and houses range $90-300 per night. Sundance Grill serves breakfast, lunch, and dinner daily. The Tree Room prepares elegant dinners daily. A barbecue is held prior to performances of the Sundance Summer Theatre. Reservations are recommended for all dining. Contact Sundance at RR #3, Box A-1, Sundance, UT 84604; tel. 225-4107 for skiing information, accommodations, dining, and scheduled events. The resort can be easily reached by taking US 189 from Provo, Orem, or Heber City, then turning 2.5 miles northwest on UT 92 (Alpine Scenic Loop).

## Bridal Veil Falls Skytram

One of the world's steepest trams provides a thrilling ride with good views of Mt. Timpanogos, Provo Canyon, and Utah Valley. You'll also have a close look at the falls, which drop 607 feet in 2 cascades; they're a major tributary of the Provo River. The Swiss-made tramway rises 1,228 feet in a single 1,753-foot span; a pair of 14-ton counterweights provide tension for the track cables. At the top, you can turn right 200 feet to an overlook of the Utah Valley, or turn left ¼ mile to see a smaller set of waterfalls not visible from the bottom. Short hiking trails also begin at the Provo River and go to the base of the lower falls (easy) and the base of the upper falls (more difficult). The Skytram runs daily 9 a.m.-9 p.m. from about mid-May to Labor Day, then 11 a.m.-8 p.m. until mid-Oct., weather permitting; $5.25 adult, $2.65 children 3-12, $4.19 seniors 62 and up; tel. 225-4461. The ticket office has a snack bar and gift shop. Trout swim in the clear pool at the base of the falls; they like to be fed, but you're not allowed to catch them. The falls and Skytram lie 4 miles up from the mouth of Provo Canyon on US 189.

## Squaw Peak Road

This scenic drive follows the Wasatch Range east of Provo and has many fine views over Utah Valley. The road turns south from US 189 in Lower Provo Canyon, then climbs high into the mountains. Pavement ends after 5 miles at the turnoff for **Hope Campground** (has water from late May to mid-Oct.; $5; elev. 6,600 ft.). The road continues south 8 miles to **Rock Canyon Campground** (mainly a group area but has some family sites; may have water) and on to the Left Fork of Hobble Creek, east of Springville, for a total of 26 miles one way. Squaw Peak Road has some rough spots in the middle section, but cars with good clearance can usually be driven through if it's dry. The Pleasant Grove Ranger District office can advise on camping, hiking, and road conditions.

# HEBER CITY

Its setting in a lush agricultural valley surrounded by high mountains has earned Heber City the title "Switzerland of America." Many of its people work at farming, raising livestock, and dairying as their families have done since pioneer days. A massive snowslide blocked passage of the first settlers making their way up Provo Canyon in 1859, but they simply disassembled their wagons and portaged them to the other side. The town's name honors Heber C. Kimball, a counselor to Church President Brigham Young. Heber City (pop. 5,500) makes a handy stop for travelers exploring the nearby Wasatch and Uinta ranges or visiting the large Deer Creek and Strawberry reservoirs. A railroad museum in town has a pioneer village and Utah's largest collection of steam locomotives. The Heber Creeper trains puff out of the depot for scenic excursions into Provo Canyon. Skies over Heber Valley often have excellent thermals; you'll probably see sailplanes soaring overhead and lined up at the local airport. Skiers often take advantage of the less expensive accommodations at Heber City when they're skiing at Park City (18 miles northwest) or Sundance (18 miles southwest).

## Heber Creeper
Hop aboard this historic train for a trip along Deer Creek Reservoir and into the depths of Provo Canyon. From 1899 until 1969, trains carried produce, freight, and passengers between Heber Valley and Provo. Today, the Heber Creeper preserves a bit of railroading past on a section of that run. Trips last 3½ hours, including a ½-hour stop in Vivian Park at the other end of the line. Some of the cars have open sides for unobstructed views of the scenery. Trains depart morning and afternoon, beginning on weekends in mid-May, then daily from Memorial Day weekend to mid-October. Winter runs may be scheduled too. Usually steam engines do the pulling, but diesel locomotives are used on weekdays early and late in the season. Roundtrip fares are $11 adult, $6.75 children 3-12; discounts are given for one-way and diesel trips. Snacks and drinks can be purchased on board. For reservations and the latest schedule, call 654-2900 (Heber City), 531-6022 (Salt Lake City), or 649-9521 (Park City). Eight steam locomotives, half of which still run, are based here. Old and reconstructed buildings form a pioneer village with craft and souvenir shops and a cafe. Trains depart from the depot at 600 W. 100 South (turn west 6 blocks on 100 South from Heber City's only traffic light).

## Midway Fish Hatchery
You're welcome to visit this state-run trout hatchery; open daily 8 a.m.-4:30 p.m.; located one mile south of Midway just off UT 113 (Charleston Road).

## Accommodations
Places in town include **Aloma Motel** (90 N. Main; tel. 654-0231; $25.07 s, $27.25 d and up; also kitchenettes); **Cottage Bed & Breakfast** (830 S. Main; tel. 654-2236; $21.80 s, $27.25-38.15 d); **High Country Inn** (1000 S. Main; tel. 654-0201; $35.97 s, $39.24 d); **Hylander Motel** (425 S. Main; tel. 654-2150; $28.34 s, $38.15 d and up); **Mac's Motel** (670 S. Main; tel. 654-0612; $22.35 s, $25.62 d); **Swiss Alps Inn** (167 S. Main; tel. 654-0722; $26.16 s, $28.34 d and up); and the **Viking Lodge** (989 S. Main; tel. 654-2202; $32.70 s, $39.24 d).

Two hot-spring resorts, 3 miles west of town near Midway, feature mineral baths, swimming, and accommodations. "Hot pots" of natural hot springs dot the surrounding landscape. The spring water is believed to be good for the skin. Spacious grounds and stately buildings of **The Homestead** may remind you of an age long past, but the facilities are modern. A large volcanic-like cone beside the resort is actually composed of travertine deposited by the springs; water once flowed out of the top, but it's now piped to indoor and outdoor pools and hot tubs. Pools are open to the public for a small fee; call for hours. Stables offer horseback and hay rides (sleigh rides in winter) and bicycle rentals; tel. extension 440. Rooms cost $64.31-179.85 and should be reserved well in advance, especially for summer weekends. A restaurant serves breakfast, lunch, and dinner daily; reservations are requested for dinner. The Grill Room offers lighter fare in summer. Open all year at 700 N. Homestead Dr. (Midway, UT 84049); tel. 654-1102 (Midway), 649-2060 (Park City), or (800) 327-7220 (out of state).

**Mountain Spaa Resort** features 2 large swimming pools (indoor and outdoor) of warm mineral water, soaking tubs of hot mineral water, a guest house and cabins ($28.34-49), a cafe with an old-fashioned soda fountain, dining room, RV park ($5.50 tent, $10 RV w/hookups), horseback rides, dance floor (square dances sometimes held), and a picnic area. Open noon-8 p.m. on Sun. and Thurs. and 10 a.m.-10 p.m. the rest of the week; season runs from about early June to mid-Sept.; tel. 654-0721 (in-season), 654-0807 (off-season). The indoor pool is also open weekends before and after the main season. Located at 800 N. Mountain Spaa Lane in Midway; one way to get here is to turn north on Center in Midway, turn right on 600 North, then left on 200 East/Mtn. Spaa Lane.

## Food

**High Country Inn's** restaurant has a varied American menu at 1000 S. Main; tel. 654-2022; open daily for breakfast, lunch, and dinner. Other places for American food are

**Chick's Cafe** (154 S. Main; tel. 654-1771; open daily for breakfast, lunch, and dinner); **Main Street Deli** (98 S. Main; tel. 654-3343; open Mon. to Sat. for breakfast and lunch); and **Wagon Wheel Cafe** (220 N. Main; tel. 654-0251; open daily for breakfast, lunch, and dinner). **Blazing Saddles Restaurant** serves American and Mexican food at 605 W. 100 South (across from the Heber Creeper station); tel. 654-3300; open daily for lunch and dinner. **Hylander Restaurant** is a cafe with American and Chinese items at 410 S. Main; tel. 654-3203; open daily for breakfast, lunch, and dinner. Pick up pizza at **Pizza Hut,** 750 S. Main; tel. 654-3636; open daily for lunch and dinner.

## Events

Horse shows and rodeos take place through the summer in the Heber City area. A Pow Wow in June brings Indians for dances and craft sales. The High School Rodeo is also held in June. Wasatch Fair Days features a parade, rodeo, exhibits, livestock show, entertainment, and demolition derby in early August. Swiss Days are celebrated with a parade, entertainment, food, and flea market, usually the Fri. and Sat. before Labor Day.

## Services

The **city park** at Main and 300 South has picnic tables and a playground. **Wasatch Community Pool** has indoor swimming and racquetball at Wasatch Middle School, 175 E. 800 South (turn east from Main onto 600 South, then right on 200 East); tel. 654-3450. **Tennis courts** are at Wasatch County High School, 600 South and 200 East. **High Valley Aviation** arranges sailplane rides at the airport; tel. 654-5831. The **post office** is at 125 E. 100 North; tel. 654-0881. **Wasatch County Hospital** is at 55 S. 500 East; tel. 654-2500. In **emergencies** (police, fire, paramedic), dial 911.

## Information

The **Heber Valley Chamber of Commerce** has an Information Center at 575 N. Main; (Box 427, Heber City, UT 84032); open Mon.

to Fri. 8 a.m.-5 p.m. (and Sat. June to Sept.); tel. 654-3666. **Heber Ranger District** office manages the Uinta National Forest lands east and southeast of Heber City; staff provide literature and advice for camping, hiking, horseback riding, boating, fishing, cross-country skiing, snowmobiling, and back-road travel; open Mon. to Fri. 8 a.m.-5 p.m. (also Sat. and Sun. from June to Sept.); upstairs at 125 E. 100 North (Box 190, Heber City, UT 84032); tel. 654-0470. **Wasatch County Library** is open Mon. to Sat. at 188 S. Main; tel. 654-1511.

# VICINITY OF HEBER CITY

## Wasatch Mountain State Park
Utah's largest state park encompasses 22,000 acres of valleys and mountains on the east side of the Wasatch Range. An excellent 27-hole golf course in the park has a pro shop and a cafe. Unpaved scenic drives lead north through Pine Creek Canyon to Guardsman Pass Road (turn right for Park City or left over the pass for Brighton), northwest through Snake Creek Canyon to Pole Line Pass and American Fork Canyon, and southwest over Decker Pass to Cascade Springs. No hiking trails have been developed, but you can set out on your own. Winter brings snow depths of 3-6 feet from about mid-Dec. to mid-March. Separate cross-country ski and snowmobile trails begin near the golf course. **Homestead Cross-country Ski Center** provides equipment for both sports; tel. 654-1102.

The large **Pine Creek Campground** has showers and hookups from late April/early May to late Oct.; located just north of the golf course at an elevation of 5,600 feet. **Little Deer Creek Campground** is a smaller, more secluded area in an aspen forest; open with water from June to mid-September. It's also open earlier and later without water; check with the park office first because groups often reserve all the sites. You can get here by driving the 7-mile unpaved road to Cascade Springs, then turning 4 miles north on another unpaved road. The park visitor center, just before the golf course, has an information

desk open all year daily 8 a.m.-5 p.m.; Box 10, Midway, UT 84049; tel. 654-1791 or (800) 322-3770 (reservations). Make golf course reservations at tel. 654-0532/1901. Admission is $3/vehicle day use, $6/vehicle overnight at Little Deer Creek Campground, or $12/vehicle overnight at Pine Creek Campground. From Heber City, drive 3 miles west to Midway, then follow signs north 2 miles.

## Deer Creek State Park
The 7-mile-long Deer Creek Reservoir lies in a very pretty setting below Mt. Timpanogos and other peaks of the Wasatch Range. A developed area near the lower end of the lake has a campground with showers, picnic area, paved boat ramp, dock, and fish-cleaning station; elevation is 5,400 feet. Island Beach Area, 4.5 miles to the northeast, has a gravel swimming beach and a marina (open in summer with a store, snack bar, boat ramp, and rentals of fishing boats, ski boats, and jet skis); ice fishermen can park here in winter. Rainbow trout, perch, largemouth bass, and walleye swim in the lake. Good winds for sailing blow most afternoons. You'll often see a lineup of catamarans at the sailboat beach near the campground and crowds of sailboaders at the Island Beach Area. Deer Creek State Park is open mid-April to late Oct.; Box 257, Midway, UT 84049; tel. 654-0171 or (800) 332-3770 for reservations (advised Memorial Day to Labor Day weekends). Admission fee is $3/vehicle day use (includes Island Beach Area) or $8/vehicle camping at the campground area. The campground is just off US 189, 11 miles southwest of Heber City and 17 miles northeast of Provo.

**Deer Creek Island Resort**, at the Island Beach area, has boat rentals (fishing, ski, sport), parasailing rides, and a snack bar in summer; a restaurant offers fine dining Fri. and Sat. evenings year-round; tel. 654-2155. **Snow's Marina,** on Wallsburg Bay 1.2 miles northeast of the state park campground, has a small store, snack bar, boat ramp ($2), RV park ($7 no hookups, $10 w/hookups; no showers), and fishing-boat rentals (with or without motor); tel. 654-4779. Open daily May to October.

sailboarding off Island
Beach Area, Deer
Creek State Park

## Strawberry Reservoir

This 17,000-acre reservoir lies on a high rolling plateau 23 miles southeast of Heber City. Creation of the original Strawberry Reservoir was begun in 1906 as a federal reclamation project to divert water from the Colorado Basin west to the Utah Valley. Soldier Creek Dam (constructed in 1973) greatly increased the reservoir's size. A section of lake called "The Narrows" separates Strawberry Arm on the west from the smaller Soldier Creek Arm on the east. The water at this 7,600-foot elevation is cold for water-skiing, but hardy souls in wet suits do it. Fishing is good all year (through the ice in winter) for rainbow and cutthroat trout and some brook trout and kokanee salmon. Several winter parking areas along US 40 provide access for cross-country skiing, snowmobiling, and ice fishing. Check with the Heber Ranger District office for information on recreation at the reservoir and in the surrounding Uinta National Forest; tel. 654-0470.

The U.S. Forest Service maintains 3 campgrounds around the lake; all are open with water from late May to late Oct.; $5 ($10 multiple-family units). **Strawberry Bay Recreation Complex,** on the west shore of Strawberry Bay, has a large campground, an overflow campground (group and individual family sites can be reserved), paved boat ramp, several fish-cleaning stations, and Strawberry Bay Marina. The marina has a cafe (open daily for breakfast, lunch, and dinner), store, gas pump, boat rentals (with and without motor), gas dock, and boat storage; open late April/ early May through deer season (the cafe closes weekdays between Labor Day and deer season); tel. 548-2261. **Soldier Creek Recreation Complex** lies on the west shore of Soldier Creek Bay with a large campground, paved boat ramp, several fish-cleaning stations, and Soldier Creek Marina. The marina offers a store, gas pump, boat rentals (with and without motor), gas dock, and boat storage; open in summer; tel. 548-2696. **Aspen Grove Campground** is a smaller area on the southeast side of Soldier Creek Bay. Picnickers can stop at free day-use areas at Strawberry Bay, Chicken Creek, Haw's Point, and Soldier Creek. Haw's Point has handicapped fishing access.

## Other Recreation Areas In The Heber Ranger District

**Whiskey Springs Picnic Area** is near the mouth of Daniels Canyon, 8 miles southeast of Heber City on US 40; water is available in summer; elevation is 6,400 feet; signs along the short Whiskey Springs Nature Trail identify plants. **Lodgepole Campground** lies in upper Daniels Canyon, 16 miles southeast of Heber City on US 40; open late May to late Oct. with water; $7; lodgepole pine and aspen grow at the 7,800-foot elevation.

**Current Creek Reservoir** (elev. 8,000 ft.) has a campground, boat ramp, fish-cleaning station, and handicapped fishing access. Fishermen catch rainbow, cutthroat, and brook trout; ice fishing is good in winter. **Racetrack Campground** (on the southwest shore) is open with water from late May to late Oct.; $7. Currant Creek Nature Trail begins from loop D of the campground and climbs 400 feet in a 1¼-mile loop; signs tell about the ecology. The best way to get here from Heber City is to drive southeast 42 miles on US 40 past Strawberry Reservoir to Currant Creek Lodge (motel and cafe; tel. 548-2373), then turn north-

west 19 miles along Currant Creek on Forest Route 083. Another route in from Heber City goes east 28 miles on Center Street, which becomes Lake Creek/Currant Creek Road (Forest Route 083).

**Mill Hollow Campground** sits on the shore of Mill Hollow Reservoir at an elevation of 8,800 feet in an Engelmann spruce forest, 37 miles from Heber City; open with water from mid-June to late Oct.; $7; the reservoir has trout fishing; take US 189 to Francis (northeast of Heber City), then UT 35 and Forest Route 054.

**Wolf Creek Campground** is in an Engelmann spruce forest at 9,500 feet, 38 miles from Heber City; open with water from early July to late Oct.; take UT 35 east from Francis.

# SOUTH OF PROVO ALONG I-15

## HOBBLE CREEK–
## DIAMOND FORK LOOP

Pleasant canyon and mountain views line this 34-mile scenic drive east of Springville. The road is open from about mid-May to late October and is normally fine for cars; all but about the middle 8 miles are paved. Along the way you'll pass picnic spots, campgrounds, hiking trailheads, and fishing holes. Back roads branch off to Squaw Peak Road, Strawberry Reservoir, and other destinations. Hikers can choose from a trail network totaling about 100 miles. Contact the **Spanish Fork Ranger District** office for maps and recreation information at 44 W. 400 North, Spanish Fork, UT 84660; tel. 798-3571; open Mon. to Fri. 8 a.m.-5 p.m. (also Sat. and Sun. in summer). Family and groups sites at some campgrounds can be reserved through Mistix reservation service; tel. (800) 283-CAMP. To drive the loop from Main St. in Springville (take I-15 Exit 263), head east 3 miles on 400 South to the mouth of Hobble Creek Canyon and follow Forest Routes 058 and 029.

Stops, listed with mileages from the mouth of Hobble Creek Canyon are: **Hobble Creek**

**Golf Course** (2.7 miles; 18 holes, pro shop, and restaurant; tel. 489-6297); **Cherry Picnic Area and Campground** (4.6 miles; open with water from early May to mid-Sept.; free day use; sites can be used for camping if they haven't been reserved; $7; elev. 5,200 ft.); **Balsam Campground** (10 miles; open mid-May to mid-Sept. with water; $7; elev. 6,000 ft.); **Road Summit** with scenic views at pass between Hobble Creek and Diamond Fork drainages (13.8 miles); cold **sulfur springs** can be seen and smelled beside the road (21.2 miles); **Three Forks Trailhead** (24 miles; elev. 5,600 ft.); **Diamond Campground** (28 miles; open early May to late Sept. with water; $5; elev. 5,200 ft.); **Palmyra Campground** (29 miles; open early May to late Sept. with water; $5; elev. 5,200 ft.); and **end of drive** at US 6/89 (34 miles; turn right 12 miles to return to Springville).

## NEBO SCENIC LOOP

This mountain drive loops off I-15 and winds into the heights of the southern Wasatch Range. You'll enjoy alpine forests, fine panoramas of the valleys below, and a close look

**1.** Salt Lake Temple, Salt Lake City; **2.** Logan Temple, Logan; **3.** Box Elder Tabernacle, Brigham City; **4.** LDS Conference (Priesthood Session) in the Tabernacle, Salt Lake City; **5.** inside the Tabernacle Organ, Salt Lake City; **6.** Angel Moroni in Museum of Church History and Art, Salt Lake City (all photos by author)

1. wildflowers and meadows atop the Wasatch Plateau;
2. collared lizard *(Crotaphytus collaris)* of the Colorado Plateau (all photos by author)

**1.** Greenshow of the Utah Shakespearean Festival, Cedar City; **2.** Greek Festival, Salt Lake City; **3.** Wayne County Fair exhibits, Loa; **4.** Conference time at Temple Square, Salt Lake City; **5.** rodeo action at Utah State Fair, Salt Lake City; **6.** rafting through Red Canyon, Flaming Gorge National Recreation Area
(all photos by author)

**MOUNT TIMPANOGOS**
**1.** waterfall in Primrose Cirque; **2.** summit view east to Deer Creek Reservoir and Heber City;
**3.** meadow and wildflowers above Primrose Cirque (all photos by author)

at Mount Nebo—highest peak in the range. The entire 43-mile length from Payson to Nephi is paved; it's open about mid-June to late October. In winter and spring, cross-country skiers and snowmobilers come up to glide across the snow. You can begin the drive from Payson in the north (I-15 Exit 254) or Nephi in the south (take I-15 Exits 222 or 228 and go east 6 miles on UT 132). A partly paved road from Santaquin (I-15 Exit 248) goes southeast 11 miles via Santaquin Canyon to connect with the main drive.

More than 100 miles of trails lead into the backcountry. **Devil's Kitchen Geologic Area** lies at the end of a ¼-mile trail, 28 miles south of Payson; eroded layers of red-tinted river gravel and silt form spires and sharp ridges. **Mount Nebo Wilderness** is west of the drive and can be reached by several trails. Strong hikers can climb the south summit (elev. 11,877 ft.) by trail in a day or overnight trip. The higher north summit (elev. 11,928 ft.) is 2 peaks farther north along a knife-edge ridge (no trail). *The Hiker's Guide to Utah* by Dave Hall has hiking descriptions for Mt. Nebo and Santaquin Peak.

Recreation facilities, trailheads, and overlooks along the Nebo Scenic Loop are provided by the U.S. Forest Service. Contact their **Spanish Fork Ranger District** office for maps and information at 44 W. 400 North, Spanish Fork, UT 84660; tel. 798-3571; open Mon. to Fri. 8 a.m.-5 p.m. (also Sat. and Sun. in summer). If coming from the south, you can stop at the forest service's **Nephi Ranger District** office for info on the Nebo Scenic Loop at 740 S. Main; open Mon. to Fri. 8 a.m.-5 p.m. (also Sat. in summer); tel. 623-2735. Campgrounds and picnic areas, from north to south (with distances from Payson), are **Maple Bench Campground** (7.6 miles; open with water from early May to mid-Sept.; $5; elev. 5,800 ft.; Maple Lake is one mile away); **Payson Lakes Campground** (12 miles; open with water from late May to mid-Sept.; $7; elev. 8,000 ft.; several lakes nearby); **Blackhawk Campground** (16 miles; open with water from late May to mid-Sept.; elev. 8,000 ft.; also has group reservation sites and horse facilities); **Ponderosa Campground** (36 miles; open with water from mid-May to mid-Sept.; $7; elev. 6,200 ft.; along Salt Creek below Mt. Nebo); and **Bear Canyon Picnic Area** (38 miles; open with water from mid-May to mid-Sept.; free day use; elev. 6,800 ft.; 2 miles upstream from Ponderosa Campground). Travelers taking the road from Santaquin can stop at **Trumbolt Picnic Area** (open with water from mid-May to mid-Sept.; free day use; elev. 6,200 ft.) and **Tinney Flat Campground** (open with water from mid-May to mid-Sept.; $5; elev. 7,000 ft.). The private

*Mt. Nebo*

**Nephi KOA Campground** is near the south end of the drive at the junction with UT 132 (6 miles east of Nephi); open mid-May to mid-Oct.; sites cost $13.63 tent or RV no hookups, $16.90 w/hookups; tel. 623-0811.

## NEPHI

This small town (pop. 3,500) serves as the commercial center for the region and as the seat of Juab County. The first settlers arrived in 1851 and named the place for a patriarch in the Book of Mormon. Pleasant scents fill the air at the **Nephi Rose Garden,** one block east of Main on 100 North.

About half a dozen motels and as many restaurants line Main between I-15 Exits 222 and 228. You can't miss the **Whitmore Mansion Bed & Breakfast,** an ornate Eastlake/Queen Anne-style structure built in 1898-1900 at 110 S. Main; tel. 623-2047; $49-70.85; lunches and dinners are served by reservation. Nephi's annual events are the Ute Stampede and Rodeo in July and the Juab County Fair in August. The **city park** has picnic tables, playground, outdoor pool, and a tourist information booth (open in summer) at Main and 500 North. **Canyon Hills Park Golf Course** (9 holes) lies up a canyon at 1200 E. 100 North; tel. 623-9930. **Central Valley Medical Center** is at 549 N. 400 East; tel. 623-1242. The **Nephi Ranger District** office of the Uinta National Forest has information on the Nebo Scenic Loop at 740 S. Main; open Mon. to Fri. 8 a.m.-5 p.m. (also Sat. in summer); tel. 623-2735.

## YUBA STATE PARK

Sevier Bridge Reservoir, 26 miles south of Nephi, is 22 miles long and 11,000 acres when full; elevation is 5,014 feet. Minerals give the lake a turquoise tint that varies with the lighting. There's plenty of space for both water-skiers and fishermen. Windsurfers often find good wind conditions here and warmer water in springtime than at most other Utah lakes.

Fishermen catch yellow perch, walleye, channel catfish, and northern pike; ice fishing, mostly for yellow perch, is done from Jan. to early March. North Sandy Beach (on the main road to the campground) and East Beach (reached from UT 28) have the best swimming; there's also a beach at the campground. For many years the reservoir and state park were known as Yuba Lake, despite the fact that no such thing existed! The name "Yuba" refers to the dam, begun in 1902 and originally named "U.B." Farmers helping to build the dam received water rights from the Deseret Irrigation Company in payment for their labor; if they stopped working they lost their stock, if they kept working they had to do additional work to pay for an assessment. An old song lamented that "U.B. damned if you do and U.B. damned if you don't."

The campground, picnic area, and a paved boat ramp lie on the west shore; take I-15 Exit 202 and follow signs 4.3 miles. North Beach is off to the left 2.2 miles in; a small store here is open on summer weekends. If driving to the campground from the south, you can save 8 miles by taking the I-15 frontage road (west side) from Scipio. East Beach and Painted Rocks Pictograph Site, both on the east shore, can be reached by boat or from UT 28 (an unpaved road from North Beach provides a shortcut to UT 28). Boaters can also use a boat ramp near Painted Rocks Pictograph Site. The park and campground stay open all year, though the campground showers close Nov. to March. It's a good idea to reserve campsites for summer weekends. If the campground is full, ask a ranger about other areas around the lake. Admission fees are $3/vehicle day use, $5/vehicle camping at Painted Rocks (no water), or $8/vehicle camping at the main campground; Box 159, Levan, UT 84639; tel. 758-2611.

## FILLMORE

In 1851, Brigham Young and the Utah Territorial Legislature designated Fillmore as the territorial capital, even before the town was established. They chose this site in the Pah-vant Valley because it lay in the approximate geographic center of the territory. Their plans didn't work out, but Fillmore (pop. 2,430) has become the center of a large agricultural region and the Millard County seat. A state historical museum in the Territorial Statehouse contains a wealth of pioneer history.

## Territorial Statehouse State Park

Completed in 1855, the statehouse is Utah's oldest government building. Architect Truman O. Angell designed the 3-story sandstone structure, originally planned to have 4 wings capped by a large Moorish dome. Only the south wing was completed, though, because antagonism between the U.S. government and the Mormons blocked the appropriation of expected federal funds. Several legislatures met here, but only the fifth session in 1855 stayed for its full length; the sixth and eighth sessions opened here, then quickly adjourned to Salt Lake City's better-suited facilities.

Rooms are furnished to represent a typical pioneer bedroom, parlor, and kitchen. Other exhibits display clothing, tools, and Indian artifacts. Lawbreakers spent time in the jail, one of the many uses to which the building has been put. Historic photos and paintings show leaders of the church and government in early Utah. Open daily 9 a.m.-5 p.m. (to 6 p.m. in summer season); $1 adult, $.50 age 6-15; tel. 743-5316. Guided tours can be arranged with advance notice at no additional charge. A restored 1867 rock school house on the grounds can be opened on request. Rose gardens surround the statehouse, located downtown at 50 W. Capitol Ave. (behind the Millard County Courthouse).

## Accommodations And Campgrounds

Motels, from north to south on the I-15 Business Loop, are **Paradise Inn (Best Western)** (800 N. Main near the I-15 exit; tel. 743-6895 or 800-528-1234; $39.24 s, $41.42 d; has an indoor pool); **Fillmore Motel** (61 N. Main; tel. 743-5454; $20.71 s, $22.89 d); **El Ana Motel** (50 N. Main; tel. 743-5588; $23.98 s, $28.34 d); **Capitol Motel** (40 E. Center; tel. 743-6633; $16.35 s, $23.44 d); and **Spinning Wheel Motel** (65 S. Main; tel. 743-6260; $26.16 s or d; has kitchenettes). **Wagons West RV Campground** is open all year with showers, laundry, and store at 501 N. Main; tel. 743-6188; $9.81 tent or RV no hookups, $13.08 w/hookups.

## Food

The **Truck Stop Cafe** is open daily for breakfast, lunch, and dinner at 590 N. Main; this is also the Greyhound Bus stop; tel. 743-6876. The **Paradise Restaurant** is open daily for breakfast, lunch, and dinner at 800 North Main; tel. 743-5414. A couple of other cafes may be open downtown.

## Events

Quarterhorse racing is held in June. A parade, carnival, and fireworks celebrate July Fourth. Mule Days, patterned after the one in Bishop (CA), features a rodeo, mule competitions, and crowning of the Mule Queen; held Labor Day weekend.

## Services

For **emergencies** (police, fire, paramedic) dial 911. The **city park** in front of the Territorial Statehouse has picnic tables and playground. An indoor **swimming pool** is just west of the statehouse. **North Park** at 500 N. Main offers picnicking and a tourist information booth (open in summer). **Fillmore Community Medical Center** is at 674 S. Hwy. 99; tel. 743-5591.

## Information

An **information booth** is open in summer at North Park, 500 N. Main; you can reach the Fillmore Chamber of Commerce year-round at tel. 743-6121. The **Fillmore Ranger District** office of the Fishlake National Forest has information about camping, fishing, hiking, horseback riding, and back-road travel in the nearby Pahvant Range and Canyon Mountains; open Mon. to Fri. 8 a.m.-5 p.m. at 390 S. Main (Box 265, Fillmore, UT 84631); tel.

743-5721. Visit the office of the **BLM's Warm Springs and House Range resource areas** to learn about the valleys and rugged mountains of westcentral Utah; open Mon. to Fri. 8 a.m.-5 p.m. at 15 E. 500 North (Box 778, Fillmore, UT 84631); tel. 743-6811. The **public library** is at 25 S. 100 West; tel. 743-5314.

## VICINITY OF FILLMORE

### Pahvant Range

These mountains east of Fillmore have 7 summits over 10,000 feet; Mine Camp Peak (elev. 10,222 ft.) is the highest. Elk, deer, and other wildlife live here. A network of trails and forest roads leads into the high country; contact the Fillmore Ranger District office for a Fishlake National Forest map, recreation information, and group campground reservations. Turn east 6 miles on 200 South from downtown Fillmore to reach 4 picnic areas along wooded Chalk Creek; they have water in summer; free; elevations are 5,700-6,100 feet. Fishermen catch rainbow and German brown trout in the creek. **Adelaide Campground** lies along Corn Creek farther south near Kanosh; open with water from late May to early Oct.; $4; cottonwood, pinyon pine, juniper, spruce, and maple grow at the 5,500-foot elevation; from the southernmost east-west street in Kanosh, turn east 5 miles on a gravel road (Forest Route 106). The road continues through pretty country and descends Mud Spring Hollow to I-70. Corn Creek has fishing for rainbow and German brown trout. Two recreation areas are in the northern part of the range: **Maple Hollow Picnic Area,** on the west side, has water from late May to early Oct. (elev. 6,900 ft.); take the I-15 South Holden Exit 174 and go east 6 miles; box elder, maple, oak, and fir trees grow in the hollow. **Maple Grove Campground** is open with water from late May to early Oct. (elev. 6,400 ft.); $4; turn west 4 miles on the signed paved road from US 50 (near Milepost 47 between Scipio and Salina); maple, water birch, oak, pinyon pine, juniper, and aspen grow in the valley; Ivie Creek has fishing for rainbow trout.

### Tabernacle Hill

Volcanic eruptions in the desert 15 miles southwest of Fillmore have covered the land with cinder cones, a tuff ring, a collapsed caldera, spatter cones, pit craters, pressure ridges, and squeeze-ups. When viewed from the north, the tuff ring resembles the Mormon Tabernacle in Salt Lake City. The first eruptions occurred 12,000-24,000 years ago when Lake Bonneville covered the region. Explosive cinder and ash eruptions built a circular ring of tuff 3,000 feet across and 200 feet or more high, rising above the lake waters. In a second period of eruptions 11,000-12,000 years ago, molten lava filled the tuff ring and spilled out to the north, forming a 7-square-mile island of black lava in the receding lake. About two-thirds of the tuff ring survives as Tabernacle Hill. The collapsed caldera inside is 1,000 feet across and 60 feet deep. Two splatter cones near the hill represent the last gasps of the final eruption. A lava-tube cave, most of which lies west of the caldera, can be traced (on the surface) for about a mile. Bats live in some of the cave sections. You can enter the cave where its roof has collapsed, though rock falls commonly block the passages. Watch for Great Basin rattlesnakes when exploring the caves and other features here.

You can visit Tabernacle Hill any time of the year, but in summer, try to visit early in the day. From Fillmore, go west 6 miles on 400 North (UT 100) to Flowell, turn left (south) one mile, turn right 2 miles (pavement ends), turn left (south) 3.5 miles on the less-used road at a junction (the other road continues to cinder pits), continue on the main track toward Tabernacle Hill in the distance; at a major gravel road, turn west, then immediately turn south again on a narrow dirt road; Tabernacle Hill is 2.5 miles farther. You may have to walk the last 2 miles, depending on road conditions. Tabernacle Hill can also be reached from Meadow, 8 miles to the southeast. The BLM office in Fillmore has maps and information helpful in exploring this and other areas of Utah's Great Basin; tel. 743-6811.

*Tabernacle Hill and surrounding lava beds*

### Cove Fort

In 1867, during the Black Hawk War, Church President Brigham Young ordered construction of this fort. Walls of volcanic basalt 100 feet square and 13 feet high enclosed 12 rooms and a spring. Gunports above the 2 entrances and along the upper walls discouraged Indians from ever attacking the fort. The privately owned fort may be open in summer. It's near the junction of I-15 and I-70; take I-15 Exit 135 and go southeast 2 miles or take I-70 Exit 1 and go northwest one mile.

## BEAVER

Mormon pioneers settled near the mouth of Beaver Canyon in 1856 to farm and raise livestock. Large flocks of sheep kept a woolen mill busy. The pastoral tranquility came to an end 4 years later, though, when prospectors discovered silver and gold in the San Francisco Mountains to the west. The incoming flood of rambunctious miners and the staid Mormon community regarded each other with

such mutual distrust that, combined with a fear of Indian attack, both sides called for federal troops. The Army arrived in 1872 and built a fort, later named Fort Cameron, and stayed until 1882. Today, Beaver (pop. 2,100) is a handy travelers' stop just east of I-15. Main Street (the I-15 Business Loop) has a good selection of motels and restaurants. Highway UT 21 (Center St.) goes west to Minersville State Park (fishing and boating) and the desert country of westcentral Utah, a popular region for rockhounding. An entirely different world lies just to the east on UT 153 (200 North St.)—wooded canyons, alpine lakes, and a ski area in Utah's third highest mountain range, the Tushars.

### Historic Buildings

More than 200 historic houses of architectural interest lie scattered around town. You'll see many of them by driving along the side streets. A large stone building remaining from Fort Cameron still stands on the east edge of town across the highway from the golf course. The

**old Beaver County Courthouse,** with an ornate clock tower, represents the architectural splendor of its period. Begun in 1877, the courthouse served Beaver County from 1882 until 1975, and it now houses a historical museum. Drop by Tues. to Sat. 2-8 p.m. in summer (Memorial Day to Labor Day weekends) to see pioneer portraits, historic documents, an 1892 wedding cake, other artifacts, and mineral specimens. Visit the courtroom on the top floor, then head down to the dungeonlike jail cells in the basement (check out the graffiti here). Located on Center one block east of Main.

## Accommodations

Summer rates are listed here; they often drop a few dollars in winter. From north to south on the I-15 Business Loop are **Paradise Inn (Best Western)** (just off I-15 Exit 112; tel. 438-2455 or (800) 528-1234; $41.42 s,

*Beaver County's old courthouse*

$43.60 d; pool); **Country Inn** (just off I-15 Exit 112; tel. 438-2484; $32.70 s, $38.15 d; indoor pool); **Comfort Inn** (645 N. Main; tel. 438-2409; $39.24 s, $45.78 d); **De Lano Motel** (480 N. Main; tel. 438-2418; $28.34 s, $30.52 d); **Thompson Motel** (410 N. Main; tel. 438-2261; $15.26 s, $21.80 d); **Mansfield Motel** (Main and 10 W. Center; tel. 438-2486; $17.44 s, $21.80 d, $27.25 kitchenette); **Granada Inn** (75 S. Main; tel. 438-2292; $21.80 s, $26.16 d); **Paice Inn (Best Western)** (161 S. Main; tel. 438-2438 or (800) 528-1234; $39.24 s, $41.42 d; pool); **Jacks Motel** (255 S. Main; tel. 438-5160; $17.59 s, $21.75 d); **Beaver Lodge Motel** (355 S. Main; tel. 438-2462; $23.98 s, $26.16 d; kitchenettes); **Sleepy Lagoon Motel** (882 S. Main; tel. 438-5681; $41.45 s or d; pool); and **Quality Inn** (1540 S. 450 West near I-15 Exit 109; tel. 438-5426; $39.24 s, $45.78 d).

## Campgrounds

**Beaver KOA Campground** has showers, store, laundry, and pool at the north edge of town (take I-15 Exit 112, go south 0.6 mile on the business loop, then turn left on Manderfield Rd.); sites cost $12.54 tent or RV no hookups, $16.55 w/hookups; open Feb. 1 to Nov. 30; tel. 438-2924. **De Lano Motel's RV park** has showers at 480 N. Main; $9.27 w/hookups (no tents); open all year; tel. 438-2418. **Beaver Canyon Campground** has showers, laundry, and a Mexican cafe on the east side of town at 1149 E. Canyon Road (200 North); $8.79 tent or RV no hookups, $10.90 w/hookups; open May 1 to Nov. 1; tel. 438-5654. **United Beaver Camperland** offers showers, store, laundry, and pool at the south edge of town (near I-15 Exit 109); sites cost $8.67 tents, $10.85 RV no hookups, $14.12 w/hookups; open all year; tel. 438-2808. **Minersville State Park** has a campground 14 miles west on UT 21 (see p. 160). The Tushar Mountains have good camping too (see below).

## Food

**El Bambi Cafe** is open 24 hours daily at a truck stop at 935 N. Main; the Reindeer Room features a fancier decor and a menu including steaks, veal, and seafood; tel. 438-2983. You'll also find American food at **Garden of Eat'n** (at Paradise Inn on north edge of town), **Country Inn** (north edge of town), **Arshel's Cafe** (711 N. Main), **Ponderosa Restaurant** (330 S. Main), and **Timberline Restaurant** (south I-15 interchange). **Korner Bakery** prepares deli sandwiches and baked goods at 1 N. Main; closed Sunday. **Maria's Cocina** serves Mexican food at the Beaver Canyon Campground, 1149 E. Canyon Rd. (200 North); tel. 438-5654; open daily for dinner. **Los Hermanos Restaurant** offers Mexican dining at the south I-15 interchange; tel. 438-2996; open Mon. to Sat. for lunch and dinner.

### Entertainment And Events
**Summer Theater** performances take place from late June to late July in the old Beaver County Courthouse or in the Opera House Civic Center across the street. **Horse races** run through the summer. Beaver celebrates **Pioneer Day** on July 24 with a parade, rodeo, horse racing, and games. The **Beaver County Fair** is held in Aug. at the fairgrounds near Minersville to the west.

### Recreation And Services
**City parks** offer picnic tables and playgrounds at Main and Center and at 400 East and 300 North. This second park also has the indoor **Municipal Swimming Pool**; tel. 438-5066. **Tennis** courts are at the rodeo grounds on the east edge of town. Play golf at the 9-hole **Canyon Breeze Golf Course** on the east edge of town; tel. 438-9601. There's good **rockhounding** in the Mineral Mountains northwest of town and in other areas to the west; a brochure that describes collecting sites is available from the Beaver County Visitor Information Center and many local businesses. The **post office** is at 20 S. Main; tel. 438-2321. **Beaver Valley Hospital** provides medical care at 85 N. 400 East; tel. 438-2416.

### Information And Transport
Foresters at the **Beaver Ranger District** office can tell you about camping, fishing, hiking,

and road conditions in the forest lands of the Tushar Mountains to the east; open Mon. to Fri. 8 a.m.-5 p.m. at the corner of 200 North and 100 East (Box E, Beaver, UT 84713); tel. 438-2436. Drop in at the **Beaver County Visitor Information Center** to learn more about sights and services in the area; open about Mon. to Sat. 10 a.m.-8 p.m. and Sun. noon-6 p.m.; 1419 S. Main (Box 272, Beaver, UT 84713); tel. 438-2975. The **public library** is at 55 W. Center; tel. 438-5274. **Greyhound Bus** stops at Bee Store, 590 S. Main; tel. 438-2450.

## THE TUSHAR MOUNTAINS

Although higher than the Wasatch Range, the Tushars remain relatively unknown and uncrowded. Travelers on surrounding highways get glimpses of their rocky summits, but people who hurry by rarely appreciate their size and height. Delano Peak (elev. 12,169 ft.) crowns the Tushars and is the highest point in central Utah. Highway UT 153 (200 North St.) from Beaver winds into the alpine country of the Fishlake National Forest to a ski area, campgrounds, fishing spots, and hiking trails. (The first 19 miles are paved, followed by 21 miles of dirt.) The road takes you through meadows and forests before making a steep descent to the town of Junction on US 89. Forest Route 137 branches off UT 153 10 miles from Beaver to Kents Lake, Anderson Meadow, and other pretty areas, then returns to the highway to complete a scenic loop (54 miles roundtrip from Beaver). For recreation information and road conditions, visit the Beaver Ranger District office at the corner of 200 North and 100 East in Beaver; tel. 438-2436.

### Camping And Picnicking
From Beaver, the first campground and picnic area reached is **Little Cottonwood,** 6 miles east on UT 153; sites are open with water from late May to early Sept.; $6; elevation is 6,500 feet. **Ponderosa Picnic Area** is 2½ miles farther up Beaver Canyon on UT 153 in a grove of ponderosa pine; it has water in sum-

mer; elevation is 7,000 feet. Little Cottonwood and Ponderosa lie along the rushing Beaver River, which has trout fishing. **Mahogany Cove Campground** overlooks Beaver Canyon 12 miles east of town on UT 153; open with water from late May to early Oct.; $4. Its name comes from the abundant curlleaf mountain mahogany; other trees at the 7,500-foot elevation include ponderosa pine, Gambel oak, juniper, and cottonwood. **Puffer Lake,** 21 miles from town on UT 153, is set among forested hills of spruce, fir, and aspen at 9,700 feet. The lake, privately owned by Puffer Lake Resort on the other side of the highway, has trout fishing, primitive camping ($5), and a primitive boat ramp. The resort offers boat rentals, a small store, and cabins from about May to Oct.; tel. 864-2751.

To reach additional campgrounds or to drive the scenic loop, turn southeast on Forest Route 137 at a junction 10 miles east of town (near Milepost 10 on UT 153). The first 8 miles are on a good gravel road (to Anderson Meadow), then there are 7 miles of dirt road to UT 153; the last half is passable when dry by cars with good clearance, but it can be too rough for RVs. **Little Reservoir Campground** is less than one mile in on Forest Route 137; sites are in a ponderosa pine forest at 7,350 feet; open with water and a $5 fee from late May to early October. The reservoir here covers only 3 acres but often has good trout fishing. **Kents Lake Campground** overlooks Kents Lake, 5 miles in on Forest Route 137; sites are in a forest of spruce, fir, and aspen at 8,800 feet; open with water and a $5 fee from mid-June to early October. The 100-acre lake offers trout fishing; there's a primitive boat ramp. **Tushar Lakeside Campground** is a county-managed group area below Kents Lake. **Anderson Meadow Campground** lies in high forests and meadows overlooking Anderson Meadow Reservoir at 9,500 feet; it's 8 miles in on Forest Route 137; open with water and a $4 fee from mid-June to early October. The reservoir has trout fishing. **La Baron Reservoir** is another popular fishing spot 4 miles farther (12 miles in on Forest Route 137), but it has only primitive

camping; elevation is 9,900 feet. In another 3 miles (15 miles in on Forest Route 137), you'll return to UT 153; turn right for City Creek Campground and the town of Junction or left for Puffer Lake, Elk Meadows Resort, and Beaver.

The gravel and dirt section of UT 153 from the town of Junction on US 89 makes an unrelenting 5-mile climb from the valley to the mountains—you'll need a low gear going up and good brakes coming down; this drive isn't recommended for trailers or RVs. This east side of UT 153 is open from late June until sometime in October. **City Creek Campground** is located near the bottom of the grade; from the turnoff 5 miles northwest of Junction, follow a side road in for one mile; sites lie along City Creek in a diverse forest of cottonwood, aspen, ponderosa pine, pinyon pine, Gambel oak, and juniper at an elevation of 7,600 feet; open with water from Memorial Day to Labor Day weekends; free.

### Hiking
Relatively few hikers have discovered this area, but good trails for hiking and horseback riding lead into the high country. Contact the Beaver Ranger District office in Beaver for details. Three peaks of the Tushars rise above 12,000 feet and make good climbing destinations—Delano Peak (elev. 12,169 ft.), Mt. Belknap (12,139 ft.), and Mt. Baldy (12,082 ft.); each involves an ascent of about 2,000 feet and can be reached on a day hike. (Strong hikers have climbed all 3 in one day!) Delano can be climbed by a route up its southwest slope, Mt. Belknap by a trail up its southeast side, and Mt. Baldy by a route from Blue Lake up its southeast side. All 3 trails are reached from the Big John Flat Road, which turns north from UT 153 between Mileposts 16 and 17. The dirt road is often OK when dry for cars. Other climbing routes are possible too, such as an ascent of Delano Peak from Elk Meadows Resort via the southeast ridge. Topo maps for the peaks are the 15-minute Delano Peak or the 7½-minute Delano Peak, Mt. Brigham, Mt. Belknap, and Shelly Baldy Peak maps.

**Elk Meadows Ski And Summer Resort**
The resort offers skiing and year-round accommodations in the Tushars 18 miles east of Beaver. Ski season normally begins at Thanksgiving and lasts to mid-April. The ski area has a total of 30 runs, up to 2½ miles long with a vertical drop of 1,200 feet; 14% of the runs are rated beginner, 62% intermediate, and 24% advanced. Two double chairs, one triple chair, a poma, and a T-bar serve the slopes. Lift tickets cost $19 adult (all day), $14 adult (morning or afternoon); a beginner's special includes lesson, equipment, and beginner lift ticket for $19.95. Free shuttle buses connect the ski area. The resort offers a ski school, rentals, races, several restaurants, and condominium-style accommodations. Lodging costs run $60-285 depending on room, day of week, and season. Contact Elk Meadows Resort at Box 511, Beaver, UT 8471; tel. 438-5433 or (800) 248-SNOW (out of state in the western U.S.).

# SOUTH OF PROVO ALONG US 89

## SKYLINE DRIVE

This scenic back road, nearly all of which is unpaved, follows the crest of the Wasatch Plateau for about 100 miles between US 6 in the north and I-70 in the south. Few people travel the entire length, however, preferring to do shorter sections reached from the many access roads. Much of the drive lies above 10,000 feet in vast meadows and alpine forests; you'll reach an elevation of 10,897 feet at High Top, the drive's summit (above Ferron Reservoir). Major attractions include the sweeping vistas, fishing, hiking, horseback riding, and winter sports.

Probably the 4 most popular recreation areas on the plateau are **Scofield State Park** (see pp. 235-236), **Huntington Canyon (UT 31)** (see pp. 241-242), **Joes Valley Reservoir** (see p. 243), and **Ferron Reservoir** (see p. 244). Cars can normally reach Skyline Drive from these places when the roads are dry. The easiest access to the drive is paved UT 31 between Fairview on the west and Huntington on the east; the road is kept clear in winter so that cross-country skiers, snowmobilers, and ice fishermen can reach the plateau. Other roads may be too rough for low-clearance vehicles or even occasionally closed to all traffic; it's best to check with the forest service offices when planning a trip. A snowbank on Skyline Drive near Jet Fox Reservoir (east of Manti) often blocks traffic until middle or late July. The rest of the drive can usually be traveled from about mid-June to middle or late October. Unfortunately, the drive may not be signed at either end because of lack of cooperation between the U.S. Forest Service and the state; the north end is off US 6 at a highway rest area near Tucker (between Mileposts 203 and 204); the south end is reached from I-70 Ranch Exit 72. Nearly all of the drive is in the Manti-LaSal National Forest; get recreation information and road conditions from the supervisor's office at 599 W. Price River Dr., Price, UT 84502; tel. 637-2817. District offices are **Price Ranger District** (same address and phone as the supervisor's office) for the northeastern part of the Wasatch Plateau, **Ferron Ranger District** (Box 310, Ferron, UT 84523; tel. 384-2372) for the southeastern part of the plateau, and **Sanpete Ranger District** (150 S. Main, Ephraim, UT 84627; tel. 283-4151) for the west half of the plateau.

## FAIRVIEW

Mormon farmers settled on the grasslands of the upper San Pitch (or Sanpete) River Valley in 1859, giving their community its original name of North Bend. Many pioneer buildings can still be seen in town. The unusual Fairview Museum of History and Art is worth a visit. Fairview (pop. 1,173) lies 42 miles south of Provo on US 89; turn east on UT 31 to reach the alpine lands of the Wasatch Plateau. Stay at the **Skyline Motel**, 236 N. State; tel. 427-

3312; $27.25 s, $32.70 d. A couple of places to eat are in town, too.

## Fairview Museum Of History And Art

Many of the varied exhibits show a sense of humor. You'll see stern-faced pioneer portraits, furniture, clothing, tools, telegraph and telephone equipment, mounted wildlife, Indian crafts, geology displays, and artwork. Noted Utah sculptor Dr. Avard Fairbanks donated much of the art, including *Love and Devotion,* depicting Peter and Celestia Peterson, Fairview residents who were married for 82 years. A large threshing machine and other antique farm equipment are outside. The museum is open from about mid-May to mid-Oct., Mon. to Sat. 10 a.m.-5 p.m.; free; tel. 427-9216. Located in a former elementary school (built in 1900) at 85 N. 100 East; from US 89, turn east one block on 100 North.

# EPHRAIM

The first settlers arrived in 1854 and named their place after a tribe mentioned in the *Book of Mormon.* A fort guarded against Indian attacks during the first 6 years. Pioneer structures dating back more than a century can be seen on Ephraim's side streets. Turkey-raising is big business here and in nearby towns.

## Snow College

One of the nation's leading junior colleges, Snow College began in 1888 as a Mormon academy. Today it's a state school with about 1,800 students and 70 faculty. You're welcome to attend the plays, concerts, and lecture series on campus; tel. 283-4021, ext. 251, for cultural events and general information. Many sports facilities at the Activity Center are open to the public too, including an indoor pool, track, basketball, racquetball, tennis, and fitness center; 300 East and Center; tel. 283-4021, ext. 381. The Badgers football team won the junior college national championships in 1985; call the Activity Center for schedules of their games and other sporting events. Union Building has a snack bar and bookstore at 100 East and Center. The library

is at 250 E. Center; tel. 283-4021, ext. 364. For more information about Snow College, visit or write the Administration Building at 150 E. College Ave., Ephraim, UT 84627.

## Practicalities

Stay at **Iron Horse Motel** (670 N. Main; tel. 283-4223; $27.16 s, $37.10 d) or **Travel Inn Motel** (330 N. Main; tel. 283-4071; $25.07 s, $31.07 d). **Ephraim Homestead Bed & Breakfast** is at 135 W. 100 North; tel. 283-6367; $54.50 d. Several cafes and fast-food places are also downtown. Turn east 8.5 miles on 4th South for **Lake Hill Campground** (open with water about mid-June to early Sept.; $4; elev. 8,400 ft.) and other areas of the Wasatch Plateau; the road continues to Skyline Drive. Ephraim celebrates the **Scandinavian Festival** in May (Memorial Day weekend) with historic town tours, pioneer demonstrations, craft sales, and a fun run. The **post office** is at 45 E. 100 North; tel. 283-4189. **Ephraim Medical Clinic** is at 9 E. 100 North; tel. 283-4076. **Sanpete Ranger District** office has recreation and road information for the western half of the Wasatch Plateau; open Mon. to Fri. 8 a.m.-4:30 p.m. at 150 S. Main, Ephraim, UT 84627; tel. 283-4151.

# MANTI

The town dates to Nov. 1849 and is one of the oldest in Utah. Brigham Young named it for a place mentioned in the *Book of Mormon.* An estimated 100 buildings built before 1880 can be seen on the side streets. Manti (pop. 2,200) is the Sanpete County seat.

## Manti Temple

The temple, on a small hill, has a commanding position over the town. Brigham Young dedicated the site in April 1877, just 3 months before his death. Workers labored 11 years to complete construction, using locally quarried blocks of oolitic limestone. The temple architecture combines several 19th C. styles in a rectangular plan similar to the first Mormon temples in the Midwest.

*Manti Temple*

## Practicalities

**Manti House Inn** provides bed and breakfast accommodations in an 1880 pioneer house; workers who built the temple stayed here in the 1880s; 401 N. Main; rates range from $51.23 to the $92.65 honeymoon suite; tel. 835-0161. Other places to stay are the **Manti Motel** (445 N. Main; tel. 835-8533; $21.80 s or d); **Temple View Lodge** (260 E. 400 North; tel. 835-6663; $26.16 s, $30.52 d); **Brigham House Inn Bed & Breakfast** (123 E. Union; tel. 835-8381; $43.60-70.85 d); and **Yardley's Inn Bed & Breakfast** (190 W. 200 South; tel. 835-1861; $38.15-70.85 d). **Palisade Lodge,** 4.5 miles south of Manti, offers budget, deluxe, and group accommodations starting at $21.80 s, $38.15 d; recreation facilities include a pool, waterslide, racquetball court, weight room, spas, and sauna; tel. 835-5413.

**Yogi Bear's Jellystone Park** has children's activities, pool, store, showers, and laundry on the north edge of town; $14.17 tent, $18.53 RV w/hookups; may close in winter; balloon rides can be arranged at about $50/person for half-hour rides and $95/person for an hour; tel. 835-CAMP or (800) 558-2954. **Manti Community Campground** is in the Manti-LaSal National Forest, 7 miles east on 500 South/ Manti Canyon Road (open with water from mid-June to early Sept.; $4; elev. 7,400 ft.); the road continues 9 miles to Skyline Drive. **Kay's Country Restaurant** (145 N. Main) and a couple of fast-food places are in town.

The **Mormon Miracle Pageant** in July portrays the history of the Book of Mormon and of the pioneers and early church leaders; the very popular production takes place at night on Temple Hill; a large cast provides lots of action. **Sanpete County Fair** is held in August. A **city park** at 300 W. 200 North has picnic tables, playground, and an outdoor pool (tel. 835-4961). The **post office** is at 140 N. Main; tel. 835-5081. **Manti Medical Clinic** is at 159 N. Main; tel. 835-9231. Manti's **public library** is downtown at 2 S. Main; tel. 835-2201.

## VICINITY OF MANTI

### Palisade State Park

People have been enjoying themselves at 70-acre Palisade Lake since 1873. A pleasure resort here once featured a dance hall and a steam excursion boat. Now a state park, the lake lies 6 miles south of Manti, then 2 miles east. Only nonmotorized craft may be used. Canoeing and windsurfing are popular here. Canoes can be rented at the park. Fishermen catch rainbow and cutthroat trout. The swimming beach and fishing conditions are best early in the season, before the water level drops. Cottonwoods shade the picnic area and campground. The campground is open with showers from early April to late Oct.; restrooms close in winter, but self-contained campers can still stay here. Admission fees are $3/vehicle day use, $8/vehicle camping; Box H, Manti, UT 84642; tel. 835-7275. Campground reservations are a good idea on summer weekends.

The 9-hole **Palisade Golf Course,** just beyond the state park entrance, has a clubhouse, pro shop, and driving range; tel. 835-4653. **Cedar Crest's Palisade Country Inn** is on the left about one mile before the state park; it has bed and breakfast accommodations ($39.24 s, $44.69 d) and an elegant restaurant (open Mon. to Sat. for dinner; reservation required); may close Jan. and Feb.; tel. 835-6352.

**Gunnison Reservoir,** 3 miles west of the state park, has good water-skiing and fishing for bass and perch; there are no developed facilities here, though people use the shore to launch boats (west shore is best); ask directions in Manti. **Nine Mile Reservoir** has a fine reputation for rainbow and other trout; the small lake is west of US 89 and 2 miles south of Sterling.

### Gunnison

The name honors Captain John Gunnison, an Army surveyor killed by Indians in 1853 near Sevier Lake. Gunnison (pop. 1,300) is an agricultural center; 2 motels and several places to eat are in town. An information booth is open in summer in the park on N. Main.

### Salina

Salina (suh-LINE-uh) is a Spanish word for "salt," which is mined nearby. The first pioneers arrived in 1863, but Indian troubles forced them to evacuate the site from 1866 to 1872. Today, Salina is a handy travelers' stop, strategically located at the junction of US 89 and I-70. More than half a dozen motels and places to eat can be found downtown and near the I-70 interchange. **Don's Texaco** has RV sites ($8.43 w/hookups and showers; no tents) at 215 W. Main; tel. 529-3531. **Butch Cassidy Campground** offers sites for tents ($5.45 s, $10.90 d) and RVs ($10.90 no hookups, $15.20 w/hookups) with showers, store, and laundry; at 1100 S. State, between I-70 Exit 54 and downtown; tel. 529-7400. **Salina Creek RV Camp,** behind the Texaco Station at 1385 S. State, costs $9.81 RV no hookups and $13.94 RV w/hookups; has showers; tel. 529-3711.

**July Fourth** is the big annual event, celebrated with a rodeo, parades, contests, and fireworks. **Salina Medical Clinic** is at 310 W. Main; tel. 529-7411. An information booth (open in summer) is located downtown on Main.

### Vicinity Of Salina

The **Redmond Clay and Salt Company** operates an open-pit salt mine north of town (3 miles north of Redmond); you're welcome to watch the operations from an overlook, open Mon. to Fri. 8 a.m.-4:30 p.m.; for more information, contact the office at 370 S. State in Redmond; tel. 529-7402.

From I-70 east of Salina, you can turn north on back roads to Skyline Drive and the Wasatch Plateau or head south into the alpine country of the Fish Lake Mountains. The small Gooseberry Campground lies along Gooseberry Creek in an aspen forest of the Fish Lake Mountains; elevation is 7,800 feet. Open with water from late May to early Nov.; free. Take I-70 Gooseberry Road Exit 61 and go south 10 miles (6 miles of pavement, then 4 miles of gravel). Snowmobiling is popular in this area during winter. The road continues south, climbing steadily through forests and meadows to **Niotche-Lost Creek Divide** (elev. 10,320 ft.) in another 10 miles; the road then winds down to Johnson Valley Reservoir, where pavement continues to Fish Lake.

# RICHFIELD

The seat of Sevier County and center of a large agricultural region, Richfield (pop. 6,300) has a dozen motels, a good selection of restaurants, and other services for travelers; most are along the I-70 business route. See some local history in the museum exhibits inside the **Ralph Ramsey House,** on E. 200 North (behind the courthouse); open Tues. to Fri. noon-5 p.m. in summer, then Tues. to Sat. noon-4 p.m. the rest of the year. The stuccoed-adobe structure dates from 1873-74. Before settling in Richfield, Ralph Ramsey carved the original Eagle for the famous gate beside Brigham Young's residence in Salt Lake City.

## Campground
The only campground in town is **Richfield KOA,** open all year with spaces for tents and RVs at 600 S. 600 West; $13.11 no hookups, $16.93 w/hookups; tel. 896-6674.

## Events
Sevier County Fair in Aug. presents entertainment, livestock shows, 4-H exhibits, and a demolition derby. Quarterhorse and Thoroughbred races take place during the summer.

## Services
The **city park** at Main and 300 North (where US 89 makes a bend) has covered picnic tables, playground, tennis courts, and an information booth (open in summer). An indoor/outdoor **swimming pool** is at 600 W. 500 North; tel. 896-8572. **K-C Waterslide** offers another way to get wet on the south edge of town; open in summer; tel. 896-5334. **Cove View Municipal Golf Course** has 9 holes on the southwest edge of town (take S. Airport Rd. from S. Main); tel. 896-9987. The **post office** is at 93 N. Main; tel. 896-6231. **Sevier Valley Hospital** is at 1100 N. Main; tel. 896-8271.

## Information
For travel info, visit the **information booth** in the city park at Main and 400 North (open Mon. to Sat. 10 a.m.-7 p.m. in summer) or the **Richfield Chamber of Commerce** at 15 E. 100 North (Box 327, Richfield, UT 84701); open Mon. to Fri. 10 a.m.-2 p.m.; tel. 896-4241. Contact the **Richfield Ranger District** office of the Fishlake National Forest for recreation and road information of the mountain country south and east of town; maps and books are sold; open Mon. to Fri. 8 a.m.-5 p.m.; 115 E. 900 North (Richfield, UT 84701); tel. 896-4491. The **public library** is open Mon. to Sat. afternoons and evenings in a Carnegie building (built 1913-14) at 83 E. Center; tel. 896-5169.

## VICINITY OF RICHFIELD

### Paiute ATV (All-terrain Vehicle) Trail
ATVers have about 300 miles of scenic trails in 2 loops and side trips through the scenic Pahvant Range, Tushar Mountains, and Monroe Mountain surrounding Richfield. Trail users travel among cool mountains, rugged canyons, and desert country. Access points include Richfield, Fillmore, Fremont Indian State Park, Piute State Park, Marysvale, and Circleville. Information and a brochure are available from the Fishlake National Forest office, see Richfield "Information" above, and local tourist and state park offices.

### Monroe Hot Springs
Steaming mineral water (168° F) from springs on a hillside above Monroe feeds a hot tub (102-110° F) and heats a swimming pool at this resort. The hot tub stays open all year, but the pool is open just in summer. The campground has showers; $9.81 tent or RV no hookups, $11.99 RV w/hookups; may close in winter. Monroe Hot Springs is on the east edge of Monroe, about 10 miles south of Richfield on US 89 and UT 118 or 5 miles east of Joseph on UT 118; signs point the way; tel. 527-4014. From I-70, take Elsinore Exit 31 or Joseph Exit 24.

### Monrovian Park
A paved road leads southeast from Monroe into this park in a pretty canyon. Cottonwood and Gambel oak trees shade picnic areas along gurgling Monroe Creek. Drinking water is usually available in summer. Four trails from the park area wind up onto the high Sevier Plateau above. Most spectacular is the trail that goes up Monroe Creek from the picnic areas, then follows Third Left Hand Fork to Scrub Flat Trail (6 miles one way); you'll have to do some wading. A narrow unpaved road with steep grades also climbs into the mountains. The Richfield Ranger District office in Richfield has detailed information about exploring this area. To reach the park, head

south on Main St. in Monroe and follow signs 4 miles.

# FREMONT INDIAN STATE PARK

The prehistoric Fremont people had lived over much of Utah, yet archaeologists weren't aware of this group's identity until 1931. Artifacts discovered along the Fremont River in central Utah indicated that the Fremont was a distinct culture. The largest known site that has been excavated turned up here in Clear Creek Canyon during construction of I-70 in 1983. Five Finger Ridge Village site probably had more than 150 occupants at its peak around A.D. 1100; more people lived nearby in the canyon. The Fremont farmed in the canyon bottom and sought game and wild plant foods. They lived in pit houses and stored surplus food in carefully constructed granaries. More than 500 rock art panels in the canyon show their religious and hunting life in a cryptic form. Nothing remains at the village site, located across the canyon; workers constructing I-70 cut most of the ridge away to use as fill after the scientific excavations had been completed. Only an experienced eye can spot pit-house villages after nearly 1,000 years of weathering, so there was little to see at this village site anyway.

## Visitor Center

The park's visitor center, dedicated in 1987, has excellent displays of artifacts found during excavations. Many aspects of Fremont life remain a mystery, but exhibits present ideas of how the Indians could have lived here and made the best use of their resources. Children can use a Fremont *mano* and *metate* to grind corn. A 16-minute video program introduces the Fremont, their foods, events that may have caused their departure, and excavation of Five Finger Ridge Village. The exhibit area also has short video programs on the Fremont and on modern Indian tribes of Utah. Models show pit-house construction and how Five Finger Ridge Village may have looked. Full-size replicas of a pit house and granary, outside across the parking area, show how the Fremont built their villages.

Three loop trails begin outside the visitor center; pick up a pamphlet inside for each one. Keyed to numbered stops, the pamphlets provide more insight into Fremont life, partly by using Hopi Indian legends. **Show Me Rock Art Trail** (200 yards) leads past fine petroglyphs; the trail is level and graded and can be used by people with strollers or wheelchairs. **Discovery Trail** (200 yards) goes to more rock art and climbs a short way above the visitor center. **Canyon Overlook Trail** (1¼ miles) ascends about 500 feet above the visitor center for fine views of the canyon and surrounding mountains; this is primarily a nature trail. Rangers lead walks in summer.

You can purchase related books, maps, rock-art posters, petroglyph replicas, Indian crafts, T-shirts, and postcards. Video programs can be seen on request. Park staff will take groups to other sites in the canyon; call or write at least a week in advance; 15500 Clear Creek Canyon Rd., Sevier, UT 84766; tel. 527-4631. Open daily 9 a.m.-6 p.m. in summer and daily 9 a.m.-5 p.m. the rest of the year; closed on winter holidays; $1 adult, $.50 children 6-16, or $3/vehicle (whichever is less). The park is near I-70 Exit 15 in Clear Creek Canyon, 5 miles west of US 89 and 16 miles east of I-15. Two picnic areas are on the frontage road east of the visitor center. You can camp at Castle Rock; see below.

# VICINITY OF FREMONT INDIAN STATE PARK

## Tours

Horseback rides are offered near the park from mid-April to mid-Sept.; trips range from ½ hour to overnight and there's a dinner ride. Hiking and driving tours can be arranged too. Local people lead the tours and know lots of Indian and pioneer lore. Tushar Mountain Village, Box 577, Monroe, UT 84754; tel. 527-3384.

## Castle Rock Campground

Clear Creek cut its canyon through tuff, a soft rock formed of hot volcanic ash from eruptions in the Tushar Mountains area. Erosion has

carved towering buttresses and narrow canyons at Castle Rock, just off the main canyon.
Campsites lie in a cottonwood and oak forest
beside Joe Lott Creek; drinking water is available during the warmer months; $5. (This is
part of the Fishlake National Forest.) Castle
Rock also makes a pleasant place for a picnic.
Take I-70 Fremont Indian State Park Exit 15,
turn onto the south frontage road, and follow
it 1.3 miles.

### Kimberly Scenic Drive
This 16-mile unpaved road climbs to about
10,000 feet on the north slopes of the Tushar
Mountains. You'll enjoy good views and cool
forests of aspen and fir. Old Kimberly, a ghost-
town site and once the center of the Gold
Mountain Mining District, is reached about
halfway. Miners started the town in 1888. Gold
production peaked around the turn of the century, then dropped off after 1907, and production has been only sporadic since. Little remains of the town and its mills except the mine
shafts, tailings, and foundations. Cars with
good clearance can usually negotiate the road
if it's dry; ask locally or at the Beaver Ranger
District office of the Fishlake National Forest
(corner of 190 North and 100 East in Beaver);

tel. 438-2436. Take I-70 Exit 17, turn west on
the north frontage road, and follow it under
I-70; the drive ends at Marysvale on US 89.

### Big Rock Candy Mountain
This multicolored mountain, rising above the
Sevier River, is the site of a small resort. Cold
mineral springs high on the mountainside are
claimed to be very healthful and a cure for
many ailments. The water, usually diluted before drinking, has a slight lemonade tang but
no scent. You can walk behind the cafe for a
closer look at the mountain and its small
spring-fed stream. The resort has a motel
($24.53 s, $38.15 d) and a cafe (open daily for
breakfast, lunch, and dinner); tel. 326-4263.
Mineral water, groceries, and souvenirs can
be purchased. A rock shop is open in summer.
The resort is on US 89, 24 miles south of
Richfield and 6 miles north of Marysvale.

## JUNCTION

This tiny village (pop. 151), near the confluence of the south and east forks of the
Sevier River, is the Piute County seat. The
entire county has only 1,329 inhabitants. It's

*company housing at
Upper Kimberly,
ca. 1900*

one of the smallest and most mountainous in the state, but local people say that if all the mountains were ironed out, the county would be one of Utah's largest! The outlaw Butch Cassidy grew up in this country and learned his first lawless ways here by altering cattle brands. The rustic cabin the Cassidys once called home still stands 2.5 miles south of Circleville (between Mileposts 156 and 157 on US 89). The bright red county courthouse dates from 1902-03; drop in on weekdays for tourist information. **Junction Motel** is on the south edge of town; open April 1 to late Nov.; $18 s or d, $22.35 kitchenettes s or d; tel. 577-2629. **T&L Cafe and RV Park** is one block west from the courthouse; open daily; sites cost $5 tent, $10 RV w/hookups; tel. 577-2672. **City Creek Campground** is 5 miles northwest on UT 153, then right one mile; sites lie along wooded City Creek at an elevation of 7,600 feet; open with water from Memorial Day to Labor Day weekends; free. The **"biggest little rodeo in the world"** is held in July in Marysvale. The **Piute County Fair** takes place in August. Vehicles with stout engines can follow UT 153 up a long grade into the Tushar Mountains to Puffer Lake (18 miles) and other scenic spots, then descend to Beaver (40 miles); pavement ends just outside Junction, then there's 25 miles of dirt road before pavement begins again. See "The Tushar Mountains," pp. 187-189.

## VICINITY OF JUNCTION

### Piute State Park
The 2,500-acre Piute Reservoir is one of the largest in central Utah. It's relatively undeveloped, however, with just an outhouse or 2 and a place to launch boats. Fishermen catch rainbow trout. The lake also has plenty of room for water-skiers. The park has no drinking water, established sites, or fee. Contact Otter Creek State Park (see below) for more information. From the town of Junction, drive north 6 miles on US 89 and turn right 1.4 miles at the sign (near Milepost 172).

### Otter Creek State Park
Otter Creek Lake has some of the best trout fishing in Utah; it's 6½ miles long and ½-¾ mile wide (2,500 acres). Bird-watching is often good, especially in winter for raptors and swans, then in spring for waterfowl and songbirds. Shore fishing can be productive in spring and autumn, but in summer you really need a boat because of moss near the shore and because the fish move to deeper waters. The park stays open all year and offers ice fishing in winter. The campground area at the south end of the lake (elev. 6,400 ft.) has showers, tables with windbreaks, boat ramp, dock, and a fish-cleaning station. Boats with motors can be rented just outside the park. You can make reservations for the developed sites, or you can nearly always find a slot in the adjacent overflow areas. People also camp and fish at Fisherman's Beach and Tamarisk Point on the west shore; no water or charge (BLM land). Entrance fees at the state park are $3/vehicle day use, $8/vehicle camping, or $6/vehicle camping at overflow areas; Box 43, Antimony, UT 84712; tel. 624-3268/3267. From the town of Junction, go 2 miles south on US 89, then turn east 13 miles on UT 62. **Otter Creek RV Park Marina,** across the highway, offers RV sites ($9.79 w/hookups and showers), boat rentals, and fishing supplies; open March 1 to Oct. 1; tel. 624-3292.

# FISH LAKE AND VICINITY

The large lake and surrounding mountain country have great beauty. You'll see expansive vistas, pristine meadows, sparkling streams, and dense forests on drives through the area. Hikers can reach more remote areas, such as the 11,633-foot summit of the Fish Lake Hightop Plateau. Fish Lake formed when a block of the earth's crust dropped along faults. The water that filled the basin created one of Utah's largest natural lakes, 6 miles long and one mile wide. Fishermen angle for lake (mackinaw) and rainbow trout and splake (a hybrid of mackinaw and eastern brook trout). Swimming isn't recommended due to the cold 50° water temperatures. Summers are cool at this 8,800-foot elevation. Heavy winter snows provide recreation for snowmobilers and cross-country skiers. The lake and surrounding country lie in the Loa Ranger District of the Fish Lake National Forest. The **Forest Information Center** in Fish Lake Lodge is open daily in summer about 11 a.m.-8 p.m.; books, maps, and pamphlets are available; tel. 836-2768. You can also contact the district office for the latest camping, fishing, hiking, and road conditions at 138 S. Main, Loa, UT 84747; open all year Mon. to Fri. 8 a.m.-4:30 p.m.; tel. 836-2811. Paved UT 25 branches off UT 24 (30 miles southeast of Richfield) and climbs over a small pass to the lake; the road is usually kept open year-round.

## FISH LAKE CAMPGROUNDS AND RESORTS

Most of the forest service campgrounds lie just off UT 25 along the lake's west shore. Dispersed camping isn't permitted near Fish Lake; you'll have to head farther into the backcountry if you'd like an undeveloped spot. The camping season runs from about late May to late Oct.; all the campgrounds along the lake have water and a $6 fee. Picnic areas are free. Some campsites can be reserved through Mistix; tel. (800) 283-2267. Recreation sites, with distances from the junction of UT 25 and UT 24, are: **Doctor Creek** (7 miles; in an aspen grove on the southwest shore; group areas can be reserved; has a dump station); **Twin Creek Picnic Area** (8.8 miles; day use only; a ranger station is opposite the turnoff); **Mackinaw Campground** (9 miles; in an aspen grove overlooking the lake); **Bowery Creek Campground and Picnic Area** (10 miles; in an aspen grove overlooking the lake); **Joe Bush Fishermen Parking** (10.7 miles); **Pelican Promontory** (12 miles; turn left one mile for a panoramic view; not suitable for low-clearance vehicles); **Frying Pan Campground** (14.5 miles; on the edge of an aspen grove near Johnson Valley Reservoir); **Tasha**

**Equestrian Campground** (14.7 miles, then ½ mile in; for people with horses); and **Piute Parking Area** (14.8 miles; access to the reservoir). At the junction just past the reservoir, you can turn north along Sevenmile Creek on Forest Route 640 to I-70 and Salina (36 miles) or south on Forest Route 036 to a boat ramp on Johnson Valley Reservoir (one mile), Fremont River (3 miles), and Loa (20 miles). Both drives have exceptional scenery and pass many good spots for fishing and primitive camping; the roads are usually OK for cars.

**Fish Lake Lodge** and **Lakeside Resort** each offer accommodations, a store, and a marina on the lake's southwest shore; Fish Lake Resorts operates both areas. The marinas have rentals of fishing and pontoon boats, boat ramps, slips, bait, tackle, and boat gas. **Lakeside Resort** is 7.3 miles in on UT 25, where the highway first meets the lake; cabins cost $21.80-158, some of which are open all year; RV sites cost $13.08-15.26; tel. 836-2700. **Fish Lake Lodge,** 1.2 miles beyond Lakeside Resort, is a huge rambling log structure built in 1932; it has a dining area, dance hall, and a small store. Cabins near the lodge cost $30.52-41.42 and are open Memorial Day weekend to the end of hunting season; newer cabins cost $54.50-261.60 and are available all year; tel. 836-2700. The rustic dining room in the lodge has lake views and is open daily for breakfast and dinner. Showers are available to the public for a small fee. Accommodations can be reserved by calling Lakeside Resort and Fish Lake Lodge from late May to late Oct., or year-round through Fish Lake Resorts, Richfield, UT 84701; tel. 836-2700 or Box 1634, Provo, UT 84603; tel. 377-9750.

**Bowery Haven Resort** lies near Fish Lake about 10 miles in on UT 25. Amenities include a marina (fishing boats, ramp, slips, and supplies), cabins ($22.89 rustic, $43.60 modern), motel rooms ($50.14 s or d), RV park ($10.90 w/hookups); has showers and laundry; no tents; cafe (open daily for breakfast, lunch, and dinner), and a small store. The resort's season lasts from late May to late Oct.; Fish Lake, UT 84701; tel. 836-2788 (in season), 782-7378 (off-season).

# THOUSAND LAKE MOUNTAIN

This high plateau rises above the Fremont River to an elevation of 11,306 feet at Flat Top. Panoramas from the rim take in the wooded valleys surrounding Fish Lake to the west and the colorful rock formations and canyons of Cathedral Valley in Capitol Reef National Park to the east. Roads and trails provide access to viewpoints and fishing lakes on the plateau. Forest roads lead to the heights from UT 72 on the west and from the middle Desert and Cathedral Valley on the east. Actually Thousand Lake Mountain may have been misnamed because its lakes number far fewer than a thousand. Some people think that a mapmaker in the 1800s accidentally switched names between this and Boulder Mountain to the south, which has far more lakes. For more information, contact the Loa Ranger District office in Loa; maps are the 15-minute Torrey topo and the Fishlake National Forest.

## Elkhorn Campground

The small campground makes a good base for hikes to lakes and the Flat Top summit. Open with water from about mid-June to late Sept.; no charge. Meadows and a forest of aspen, fir, and spruce surround the sites; elevation is 9,300 feet. From the north edge of Loa, turn east and north 12 miles on UT 72 to Forest Route 206. The winding mountain road is unpaved, but passable by cars in dry weather; follow it 8 miles to the campground. Desert View Overlook, 3 miles before the campground, has a fantastic view of Cathedral Valley and beyond. The road to Elkhorn Campground can also be approached from I-70 via UT 72; this paved road climbs over Hogan Pass (elev. 8,961 ft.) past meadows, groves of aspen, and fine views of Cathedral Valley and beyond. Vehicles with high clearance (only) can drive up directly from Cathedral Valley via Forest Routes 020 and 022.

# LOA

Pioneers settled here in the mid-1870s. The town's unusual name was suggested by a former Mormon missionary who had served in Hawaii. A commemorative marker (next to the 1897 Loa Tithing House, on Center St. one block west from Main) has a rock from Mauna Loa. The small town (pop. 364) is the Wayne County seat and a handy base for exploring the Fish Lake area to the north. **Wayne County Fair** on the third weekend in Aug. has a parade, rodeo, exhibits, barbecue, and games.

**Road Creek Ranch Inn** is a bed and breakfast ($43.60-70.85); its restaurant features trout, steak, sandwiches, and pizza (open daily for lunch and dinner) at 90 S. Main; tel. 836-2485 or (800) ET-TROUT. **Wayne Wonderland Motel** is at 42 N. Main; tel. 836-9692; $21.80 s, $26.16 d. The **Aspen Country Cafe** serves breakfast, lunch, and dinner daily at 289 N. Main; motel rooms are available at $22.20 s or d; an RV park here costs $10 w/hookups (no tents); tel. 836-2873. **River Inn** has an RV park ($8.50 w/hookups) and a cafe serving lunch and dinner daily except Sun.; located north of Loa just past the town of Fremont; tel. 836-2715. Loa's courthouse and post office are at the junction of Main and Center; step inside the courthouse to see a small rock and mineral collection in the lobby. A tourist information booth is occasionally open on the lawn in front of the courthouse, or you can obtain local information inside; tel. 836-2731 (county clerk). The **Loa Ranger District** office has camping, fishing, hiking, and road condition information for the Fish Lake National Forest lands north and east of town; 138 S. Main, Loa, UT 84747; open Mon. to Fri. 8 a.m.-4:30 p.m.; tel. 836-2811. You can visit the **Loa Fish Hatchery** 2.2 miles north of town; go north on Main and keep straight on the county road where UT 24 curves to the left; open daily 8 a.m.-4:30 p.m.; tel. 836-2858.

# NORTHEASTERN UTAH

## INTRODUCTION

Northeastern Utah has an extremely varied landscape of barren desert, deep canyons, high plateaus, and the lofty Uinta Mountains. Thousands of well-preserved dinosaur bones unearthed in the region tell of a time about 140 million years ago when reptiles large and small roamed a land that looked very different from today. The dinosaurs lived in a relatively moist subtropical climate amid tree ferns, evergreens, and ginkgo trees. You can meet the skeletons of these creatures in excellent museums in Vernal and Price and visit bone excavations at Dinosaur National Monument and Cleveland-Lloyd Dinosaur Quarry. The high country of the Uinta Mountains has some of Utah's loveliest alpine scenery. Kings Peak tops the range at 13,528 feet—the highest point in the state. Fishermen seek trout and arctic grayling in the countless lakes and streams of the Uintas. Trails provide access for hiking and pack trips into the High Uintas Wilderness at the heart of the range. Other popular recreation areas include Flaming Gorge National Recreation Area, Dinosaur National Monument, Wasatch Plateau, and San Rafael Swell. Fishermen and boaters have a choice of many large reservoirs, 6 of which are state parks. River runners enjoy lively rides down the Green River through Red, Lodore, Whirlpool, Split Mountain, Desolation, and Gray canyons. You'll see 2 spellings in this region—Uinta and Uintah—both of which are pronounced "you-INT-ah." Geographical terms have no "h," as in Uinta Mountains and Uinta Basin. Political divisions usually have an "h," as in Uintah County and Uintah and Ouray Indian Reservation.

# NORTHEASTERN UTAH

## Climate

In summer, the valleys have average highs of about 90° F, which drop to the low 50s at night. Valley temperatures plummet in winter to about 30° during the day and 5 degrees at night. The Wasatch Plateau and Uinta Mountains experience cool weather year-round. Above 10,000 feet, summer highs rarely exceed 70 degrees in the day and drop to the 30s and 40s at night; freezing weather is possible at any time of year. In the mountains winter brings highs in the 20s and lows well below zero. Annual precipitation changes dramatically with elevation, from about 8 inches in the desert to 40 inches in the high country. Snowfall is widespread in winter and very heavy in the mountains.

## HISTORY

### Prehistoric Indians

Paleo-Indians wandered across the land beginning at least 15,000 years ago. About A.D. 550, the Fremont culture emerged as a distinct group. The Fremont ranged widely in search of wild foods and places to grow their corn, beans, and squash. By 1300, however, the tribe had mysteriously disappeared, leaving behind village sites, artifacts, and intriguing rock art.

### Ute Indians

Nomadic Ute Indians moved in at about the same time that the Fremont culture faded away, though the Utes seemed to have no knowledge of their more sophisticated predecessors. Utes guided the Spanish Dominguez-Escalante expedition through the Uinta Basin, south of the Uinta Mountains, in 1776, and they were the first Indian group encountered in Utah by the Mormons. Mountain men traded with the tribe during the 1820s and 1830s on beaver-trapping expeditions. Neither the Utes nor the mountain men, however, made permanent homes in the Uinta Basin. White men figured that this land, seemingly short of water and most other resources,

was worthless. Pressures of settlements elsewhere in Utah and Colorado gradually forced more and more Utes from their traditional lands into the Uinta Basin. In 1861, President Lincoln issued an executive order making nearly the entire Uinta Basin into the Uintah Indian Reservation—about 2,287,000 acres. By 1864, the U.S. Army had moved nearly all the state's Utes onto the reservation. The Ouray Indian Reservation was established in 1881, then was merged with the Uintah 5 years later. Whites started having second thoughts, though, when they discovered coal and oil and realized the agricultural potential that irrigation held for the area. Much Indian land was taken back. Heavily promoted homesteading programs beginning in 1905 brought in floods of settlers. The Utes recovered some cash awards for their lost lands during the 1950s and obtained the Hill Creek Extension south of the Uinta Basin. The reservation now covers approximately one million acres in the Uinta Basin, in the foothills of the Uinta Range and Tavaputs Plateau, and in the remote East Tavaputs Plateau.

The Ute Indian Tribe today consists of 3 bands, the Uintah (of Utah), the Whiteriver (moved from Colorado in 1880), and the Uncampahgre (moved from Colorado in 1882). About half of the current 2,830 Utes on the reservation and in nearby towns belong to the Uncampahgre Band; the rest are equally divided between the Uintah and Whiteriver bands. Each band elects 2 members to the Ute tribal government. Tribal headquarters are east of Roosevelt at Fort Duchesne (pronounced "doo-SHAYN"), site of a U.S. Army base from 1886 to 1912. A tribal museum at the nearby Bottle Hollow Resort displays Ute artifacts and historic exhibits; you can also ask at the resort about Indian dances, pow wows, and rodeos. In summer you might be able to see the Sun Dance, an important religious and social ceremony learned from the Wind River Shoshone. Other ceremonies are the Bear Dance (performed in the spring) and the Turkey Dance (held on many social occasions).

## Early White Settlement

In the 1870s and early 1880s, the Mormon Church sent out calls for members to colonize lands east of the Wasatch Plateau. Though at first the land looked harsh and barren, crops and orchards eventually prospered with irrigation. Nevertheless, it took some time for the first families to take a liking to this country. Mrs. Orange Seely of the Castle Dale area is credited with the quote, "The first time I ever swore was when we arrived in Emery County and I said 'Damn a man who would bring a woman to such a God-forsaken country!'" Individual families also came out on their own and started isolated farms and ranches in the Uinta Basin and along the eastern edge of the Wasatch Plateau to the south. Much of the land proved too dry or rugged for any use, and remains in its natural state today. Discoveries of coal in 1877 and oil in 1900 attracted waves of new people to the sleepy Mormon settlements east of the Wasatch Plateau. Immigrant miners fresh from Europe brought a new cultural diversity to the region.

# UINTA MOUNTAINS

This outstanding wilderness area contains lofty peaks, lush grassy meadows, fragrant coniferous forests, crystal-clear streams, and thousands of tiny alpine lakes. The Uintas, unlike most other major ranges of the United States, run west-east. Underground forces pushed rock layers up into a massive dome 150 miles long and 35 miles wide. Ancient Precambrian rocks exposed in the center of the range consist largely of quartzite (metamorphosed sandstone). Outcrops of progressively younger rocks are found away from the center. Glaciers have carved steep ridges and broad basins and left great moraines. Barren rock lies exposed across much of the land, including the peaks and high ridges. Trees, from 10,000 feet to timberline at about 11,000 feet, include limber pine, Engelmann spruce, and subalpine fir. Lower slopes (7,000-10,000 ft.) support dense unbroken forests of lodgepole pine (the most common tree in the Uintas), aspen, Douglas fir, white fir, blue spruce, and scattered stands of ponderosa pine. The remoteness of the Uinta Mountains has protected much of the forests from the ravages of logging industries. The central part received protection in 1931 as a primitive area and in 1984 as the High Uintas Wilderness. Four of Utah's major rivers have their source in these mountains: the Bear and Weber rivers on the north slope and the Provo and Duchesne rivers on the south slope. Despite their great heights, the Uintas have a gentler terrain than the precipitous Wasatch Range. High plateaus and broad valleys among the peaks hold the abundant rain and snowfall in marshes and ponds, supporting large populations of wildlife and fish.

Elk, moose, mule deer, and Rocky Mountain goat (reintroduced) come here to graze in summer. Also foraging for food are black bear, mountain lion, coyote, bobcat, raccoon, porcupine, badger, pine marten, snowshoe hare, marmot, and pika. Fishermen seek out arctic grayling and native cutthroat, Eastern brook, rainbow, German brown, and golden trout. Aerial stocking keeps even the most remote lakes swimming with fish. Your luck at a lake or stream can range from lousy to fantastic, depending on the timing of the last stocking and how many other fishermen have discovered the spot.

## Visiting The Uintas

Highway UT 150 winds over the western end of the range from the town of Kamas to the Wyoming border, with splendid panoramas and access to fishing lakes and hiking trails. On the east, US 191 and UT 44 provide access to the Uintas and Flaming Gorge Reservoir from Vernal. Unpaved roads also lead to trailheads on all sides of the range. Developed and primitive campgrounds can be found along these highways and at other locations, including many of the trailheads.

Most people prefer to visit the Uintas from mid-June to mid-September. Campers should be prepared for cold nights and freezing rain even in the warmest months. Afternoon showers are common in summer. Arm yourself with insect repellent to ward off the mosquitoes, especially in July. Snow stays on the ground until well into June and the meltwater can make trails muddy until early July. The lakes and campgrounds along UT 150 are crowded on summer weekends and holidays, though you can usually get off by yourself on a short hike into the backcountry.

An extensive trail system with about 20 trailheads goes deep into the wilderness and connects with many lakes. A great number of trips are possible, from easy day hikes to rigorous treks lasting weeks. Climbers headed for the summits can take trails to their bases or to a nearby pass, then rockscramble to the top. Kings Peak (elev. 13,528 ft.) attracts the most attention because it's the highest in Utah. The shortest approach is from Henrys Fork Trailhead on the north, requiring 3 days of hiking for the 32-mile roundtrip; elevation gain is about 4,100 feet. Southern approaches from Swift Creek or Uinta trailheads usually take an extra day. More than a dozen other peaks in the Uintas exceed 13,000 feet. No permits are needed for travel in the wilderness area, though it's recommended that you sign registers at the trailheads. The High Uintas Wilderness, about 450,000 acres, is closed to mechanized vehicles (including bicycles). Horses can use nearly all trails in the wilderness area. An exception is Bluebell Pass, which is impassable for them; other passes may be rough going depending on recent storms and trail maintenance. Winter snows close UT 150 and the back roads, at which time snowmobilers and cross-country skiers come out to enjoy the snowy landscapes.

## Information

The U.S. Forest Service manages the Uintas and surrounding forest lands. Northern and western parts are administered by the Wasatch National Forest (8226 Federal Bldg., 125 S. State St., Salt Lake City, UT 84111; tel. 524-5030). Most of the southern and eastern areas are part of the Ashley National Forest (355 N. Vernal Ave., Vernal, UT 84078; tel. 789-1181). For specific information, it's best to contact the district offices directly. In the Wasatch National Forest: **Kamas Ranger District** (Box 68, Kamas, UT 84036; tel. 783-4338) for the western end of the range including the Provo River drainage; **Evanston Ranger District** (Box 1880, Evanston, WY 82930; tel. 801-642-6662 in summer or 307-789-3194 year-round) for the northwestern end including the Bear River and Blacks Fork drainages; and **Mountain View Ranger District** (Box 129, Mountain View, WY 82939; tel. 307-782-6555) for the northern side including Smiths Forks and Henrys Fork drainages. In the Ashley National Forest: **Flaming Gorge Ranger District** (Box 278, Manila, UT 84046; tel. 784-3445/3409) for the northeastern side including Spirit Lake and Sheep Creek; **Vernal Ranger District** (353 N. Vernal Ave., Vernal, UT 84078; tel. 789-1181) for the southeastern end including Whiterocks River; **Roosevelt Ranger District** (244 W. Hwy. 40, Box 33-6, Roosevelt, UT 84066; tel. 722-5018) for the southern end including Lake Fork, Yellowstone, and Uinta drainages; and **Duchesne Ranger District** (Box I, Duchesne, UT 84021; tel. 738-2482) for the southwestern end including Rock Creek and North Fork of Duchesne drainages. All these offices have the forest maps and the High Uintas Wilderness topo map (1:75,000 scale). Hikers will find good trail descriptions in the books *High Uinta Trails* by Mel Davis, *Hiker's Guide to Utah* by Dave Hall, and *Utah Mountaineering Guide* by Michael Kelsey. If you plan to do some serious fishing, a set of 10 booklets, *Lakes of the High Uintas,* published by Utah Division of Wildlife Resources, has detailed descriptions of lakes, kinds of fish stocked, trail access, and camping; each booklet covers different drainages; they're available from the main office at 1596 W. North Temple, Salt Lake City, UT 84116; tel. 538-4700; and from the Vernal office at 152 E. 100 North, Vernal, UT 84078; tel. 789-3103.

# HIGH UINTAS WILDERNESS

## KAMAS AND THE MIRROR LAKE HIGHWAY (UT 150)

### Kamas

Pioneers settled on this spot at the mouth of Beaver Creek Canyon in 1857. Today, Kamas is the start of what is probably Utah's most spectacular alpine drive. The Mirror Lake Highway (UT 150) begins here at an elevation of 6,500 feet and climbs to the crest of the western Uinta Mountains at Bald Mountain Pass (elev. 10,678 ft.) before descending on the other side and continuing to Evanston, Wyoming. Kamas has the **Summit Inn,** a small bed and breakfast at 80 S. Main (tel. 783-4453; $31.61-42.51 s or d), and several cafes. Nearest motels are in Heber City (17 miles southwest) and Park City (19 miles west). The **Kamas Ranger District** office is at 50 E. Center (Box 68, Kamas, UT 84036); open Mon. to Sat. 8 a.m.-4:30 p.m. from July 1 to mid-Sept., and Mon. to Fri. 8 a.m.-4:30 p.m. the rest of the year; tel. 783-4338. The office has forest maps and detailed recreation information; staff can advise on road conditions, campgrounds, hiking, cross-country skiing, and snowmobiling. **Paiute Creek Outfitters,** just north of Kamas, organizes guided pack trips into the Uintas lasting from overnight to 10 days; hourly, half-day, and dinner rides are offered too; 3000 N. 900 East, Kamas, UT 84036; tel. 783-4317 or (800) 225-0218 (outside Utah).

### Mirror Lake Highway

The highway is open from about mid-June to mid-October. In winter it's kept cleared to Soapstone, 15.5 miles from Kamas, to provide access for cross-country skiing and snowmobiling. Five trails used by both skiers and snowmobilers begin along the highway and at Soapstone. Skiers using snowmobile trails will find the most solitude on weekdays. Beaver Creek Ski Touring Trail begins from the Slate Creek Snowplay Area (6 miles east of Kamas) and parallels the highway to Pine Valley Campground, a distance of 5½ miles one way with an elevation gain of 440 feet. This trail is easy; branching off from it are other ski trails rated intermediate and advanced. Obtain information and brochures for these and other skiing areas from the Kamas Ranger District office. People also like the Slate Creek Snowplay Area for sledding and tubing. Mileages given below correspond to mileposts along the highway:

**Mile 0.0:** Heading east on UT 150 from the junction with US 189 in Kamas.
**Mile 0.1:** Kamas Ranger District office on the right.
**Mile 3.3:** Kamas Fish Hatchery on the right; visitors welcome.
**Mile 3.7:** Sign for "Beaver Creek Nudist Ranch" (someone's idea of a practical joke!).
**Mile 6.1:** Entering Wasatch National Forest; Slate Creek Snowplay Area.
**Mile 6.7:** Yellow Pine Campground on the left. Sites are in a forest of ponderosa and lodgepole pines and juniper at 7,200 feet; open late May to late Oct.; no water or fee. Yellow Pine Creek Trail begins just north of the campground and goes up the creek to Lower Yellow Pine Lake (elev. 9,600 ft.; 4 miles one way) and beyond; this is a good hike early in the season.
**Mile 8.2:** Beaver Creek Campground on the right. Sites line both sides of Beaver Creek amid lodgepole pine and willow at 7,300 feet; open from early May to mid-Oct., no water or fee.
**Mile 8.9:** Taylor Fork Campground on the right. Sites are along Beaver Creek in lodgepole pine and aspen at 7,400 feet; water from early June to mid-Sept., $6 fee.
**Mile 9.3:** Shingle Creek Campground and Picnic Area on the right. Sites are in a mixed forest of pine, spruce, and fir at 7,400 feet; water from early June to mid-Sept., $6 fee (no charge for day use).
**Mile 9.9:** Shingle Creek Trail follows the creek upstream to East Shingle Lake (elev. 9,680 ft.; 5½ miles one way) and Upper Setting Trail; this is a good early-season hike. Past the trailhead, the highway climbs over a small pass to the Provo River and follows it upstream.

**Mile 10.5:** Lower Provo River Campground is one mile south on Pine Valley Road. Sites are along the Provo River in a pine and spruce forest at 7,600 feet; water from early June to mid-Sept., $6 fee. The nearby Pine Valley Group Camping Area is the only group reservation area in the Kamas District.

**Mile 15.5:** Soapstone Campground on the right. Sites are along the Provo River amid lodgepole pine at 8,200 feet; water from early June to mid-Sept., $7 fee.

**Mile 17.0:** Shady Dell Campground on the right. Sites lie along the Provo River at 8,200 feet; water from early June to mid-Sept., $7 fee.

**Mile 17.7:** West Portal of Duchesne Tunnel; a sign describes this 6-mile conduit that brings water from the Duchesne River to the Provo River.

**Mile 18.8:** Cobblerest Campground on the right. Sites are near the Provo River in a pine and spruce forest at 8,500 feet; water from mid-June to mid-Sept., $7 fee.

**Mile 22.3:** Slate Gorge Overlook on the right.

**Mile 23.1:** Upper Provo River Bridge Picnic Area on the right; no water.

**Mile 23.9:** Provo River Falls Overlook on the left.

**Mile 25.4:** Trial Lake Campground is ¼ mile to the left on Spring Canyon Road. Sites are on the southeast shore of the lake in a pine and spruce forest at 9,500 feet; water from early July to early Sept., $7 fee. There's a fishermen's parking area near the dam. Spring Canyon Road continues past the dam to Washington and Crystal lakes and Crystal Lake Trailhead. Notch Mountain Trail begins at Crystal Lake Trailhead, goes north past Wall and Twin lakes, through The Notch to Ibantik and Meadow lakes, to the Weber River (elev. 9,000 ft.; 6.5 miles one way), and to Bald Mountain Pass (elev. 10,790 ft.; 10 miles one way). The Lakes Country Trail starts at the Crystal Lake Trailhead and goes west past Long, Island, and other lakes before joining the Smith-Morehouse Trail after 3½ miles.

**Mile 26.4:** Lilly Lake Campground to the right. Sites are in a spruce and fir forest at 9,800 feet; water from early July to early Sept., $7 fee. Lilly, Teapot, and Lost lakes lie within short walking distances.

**Mile 26.7:** Lost Creek Campground to the right. Sites are beside the creek in a spruce and pine forest at 9,800 feet; water from early July to early Sept., $7 fee. Lost Lake is a short walk to the southwest.

**Mile 29.1:** Bald Mountain Pass (elev. 10,678 ft.). Bald Mountain Picnic Area and Trailhead are on the left. The hike up Bald Mountain is 4 miles roundtrip and climbs 1,100 feet; this national recreation trail is a strenuous trip because of the high elevation and steep grades. From the top, weather permitting, you'll enjoy grand views of the High Uintas Wilderness, the Lakes Roadless Area, and the Wasatch Range. Notch Mountain Trail also begins near the picnic area and connects with Trial Lake.

**Mile 30.5:** Moosehorn Campground on the left. Sites are on the east and north shores of Moosehorn Lake in a spruce and fir forest at 10,400 feet; water from early July to early September, $6 fee. Fehr Lake Trail begins ¼ mile south and across the highway; it goes to Fehr Lake (½ mile), Shepard Lake (1¼ miles), and Hoover Lake (1½ miles).

**Mile 31.2:** Mirror Lake Campground and Picnic Area are ½ mile to the right. This is the largest campground (91 sites) on the Mirror Lake Highway. Sites are near the lake in a forest of spruce, fir, and lodgepole pine at 10,200 feet; water from early July to early Sept., $7 fee. The picnic area is free. Fishermen can park at the south end of the lake and at the Mirror Lake Trailhead; boats can be hand launched; no motors at all are permitted

*Uinta chipmunk*
*(Eutamias umbrinus)*

on the lake. Highline and North Fork Duchesne trails lead from the trailhead to the High Uintas Wilderness.

**Mile 32.1:** Pass Lake Trailhead on the left, across the highway from Pass Lake. Lofty Lake and Weber Canyon trails begin here and connect with other trails. Weber Canyon Trail goes to Holiday Park Trailhead (elev. 8,000 ft.; 7 miles one way), reached by road from Oakley.

**Mile 33.9:** Butterfly Lake Campground on the left. Sites are on the south shore of the lake in a spruce, fir, and lodgepole pine forest at 10,300 feet; water from early July to early Sept., $6 fee.

**Mile 34.2:** Hayden Pass (elev. 10,200 ft.). Highline Trailhead is on the right. This is the closest point on the highway to the High Uintas Wilderness. The Highline Trail tends to be muddy, rocky, and heavily used. It winds east from here across the Uintas nearly 100 miles to East Park Reservoir north of Vernal. The highway makes a gradual descent from the pass along Hayden Fork of the Bear River. Contact the Evanston Ranger District offices for camping, hiking, and backroad travel in this area.

**Mile 35.0:** Ruth Lake Trailhead on the left; the lake is an easy ¾-mile hike west.

**Mile 38.9:** Sulphur Campground on the right. Sites lie near the Hayden Fork of Bear River in a forest of lodgepole pine, fir, and spruce at 9,000 feet; water from early June to mid-Sept., $5 fee.

**Mile 41.8:** Beaver View Campground on the right. Sites overlook Hayden Fork of Bear River from a lodgepole pine and aspen forest at 8,900 feet; water from early June to mid-Sept., $5 fee.

**Mile 42.4:** Hayden Fork Campground on the right. Sites lie along Hayden Fork of Bear River in a lodgepole pine and aspen forest at 8,900 feet; water from early June to mid-Sept., $5 fee.

**Mile 45.6:** Stillwater Campground on the right. Sites are in a lodgepole pine and aspen forest at 8,500 feet, near where Hayden Fork and Stillwater Fork meet the Bear River; water from early June to mid-Sept., $5 fee.

*pica*
(Ochotona princeps)

**Mile 45.8:** Christmas Meadow Road goes right 4 miles to Christmas Meadow Campground and Stillwater Trailhead. Sites overlook a large meadow from a forest of lodgepole pine at 9,200 feet; water from early June to mid-Sept., $5 fee. Stillwater Trailhead, near the campground, is the starting point for hikes to lakes in Amethyst, Middle, and West basins to the south.

**Mile 46.5:** Bear River Ranger Station on the right. Stop here for recreation information in the northwestern part of the Uinta Range. The office is open 8 a.m.-noon and 12:30-4:30 p.m. (to 5 p.m. on weekends); season is weekends only mid-May to late May, daily late May to mid-Oct., then weekends only to late Oct.; tel. 642-6662. Off-season, you'll need to contact the Evanston, Wyoming, office (Box 1880, Evanston, WY 82930; tel. 307-789-3194), one mile south of I-80 at 1565 Hwy. 150, Suite A.

**Mile 47.5:** A road turns right 2 miles to Lily Lake.

**Mile 48.2:** Bear River Campground on the left. Sites are along the Bear River just upstream from the East Fork confluence in a lodgepole pine and aspen forest at 8,400 feet; water from early June to mid-Sept., $5 fee.

**Mile 48.3:** East Fork Bear River Campground on the left. Sites are along the Bear River just below the East Fork confluence in a lodgepole pine and aspen forest at 8,400 feet; water from early June to mid-Sept., $5 fee.

**Mile 48.6:** Forest Route 058 goes right about 17 miles to Little Lyman Lake Campground. Sites are near the east shore of the lake in a lodgepole pine forest at 9,200 feet; water from early June to mid-Sept., $5 fee. Lyman Lake is just a short walk away. Meeks Cabin Reservoir and Campground are 2 miles farther on Forest Route 058, then left about 5 miles on Forest Route 073. Sites here are along the southwest shore of the reservoir in a lodgepole pine forest at 8,800 feet; water from early June to mid-Sept., $5 fee.

**Mile 48.7:** Leaving Wasatch National Forest. This is approximately the end of the scenic drive. The valley opens up and supports sagebrush and scattered aspen groves.

**Mile 54.6:** Wyoming border; highway becomes WY 150. Bear Service (gas and groceries) is 0.3 mile farther and Evanston is 23 miles ahead.

# VERNAL

One of the oldest and largest communities in northeastern Utah, Vernal makes a handy base for travels to the many sights of the region. The perennial waters of Ashley Creek, named for mountain man William H. Ashley who passed by in 1825, attracted the first settlers to the valley during the early 1870s. The small community went through a succession of names—Hatchtown, Ashley Center, and Ashley—before residents decided on Vernal in 1893. Rugged terrain and poor roads isolated the area from the rest of Utah for years. In 1916, when a local businessman wanted to order a shipment of bricks from Salt Lake City for the facade of a new bank, he solved the problem of expensive shipping costs by having the bricks sent by parcel post! Freight cost $2.50 per hundred pounds while the postal service charged only $1.05. Other Vernal residents caught on to the post office's bargain rates, and even started parcel-posting crops to market until the postal service changed its regulations. The Bank of Vernal, nicknamed the "Parcel Post Bank," still serves the town at the corner of Main and Vernal. Growth of the oil industry in recent decades has been a mixed blessing because of its boom-and-bust cycles. Vernal is the Uintah County seat and has a population of 7,500.

*portable drilling rig for oil wells, early 1920s*

## SIGHTS

### Utah Field House Of Natural History
Come here to see the dinosaurs. More than a dozen full-size models stalk or fly in the Dinosaur Gardens outside. The natural setting makes the strange creatures seem almost alive. Inside, the Geology and Fossil Hall displays 45-million-year-old skulls of ancient mammals, crocodiles, and alligators that once roamed across Utah. Other exhibits have fossil specimens ranging in size from tiny insects to massive dinosaur bones. A geologic map 36 feet across shows the structure of rock layers in northeastern Utah. Other exhibits trace Utah's Indians from the Desert Culture through Anasazi and Fremont groups to the modern Ute. The Natural History Hall offers a close look at mounted wildlife of the state. The museum dates from 1948 and is now a state park. It's open daily 8 a.m.-9 p.m. from Memo-

rial Day to Labor Day weekends, decreasing to daily 9 a.m.-5 p.m. in winter. Admission is $1 adult, $.50 age 6-15; tel. 789-3799. The gift shop sells dinosaur T-shirts, books, postcards, and other souvenirs. The Vernal Welcome Center in the museum building has area travel information. A city park behind the museum contains a playground and offers a shady spot for a picnic. The Utah Field House of Natural History is at 235 E. Main.

### DUP Pioneer Museum
Get to know Vernal's pioneers here. The many historical photos and carefully labeled exhibits present a good idea of what life was like in the old days. The large collection includes a pioneer kitchen, spinning wheels, farm machinery, a buggy, old organs, clothing, guns, and a model of a Western town. You'll see Dr. Harvey Coe Hullinger's well-stocked medicine chest, last used in 1926 when he was 101 years old. One room of the museum is the stone tithing office, built in 1877. The Daughters of the Utah Pioneers operate the museum, open Mon. to Sat. 1-7 p.m. in summer and at other times by request (ask at the Vernal Welcome Center). Located across the street from the Uintah Stake Tabernacle at the corner of 200 South and 500 West.

### Thorne Museum
This small private museum has a collection of pioneer rifles and pistols and local Indian artifacts, including gaming balls, moccasins, bows and arrows, a mummified burial, and baskets. Open Mon., Tues., Thurs., and Fri. 9:30 a.m.-6 p.m.; free; tel. 789-0392. Downtown in the Thorne Studio, 18 W. Main.

## PRACTICALITIES

### Accommodations
Motels, listed in order of increasing price, include: **Sage Motel** (54 W. Main; tel. 789-1442; $23.98 s, $26.16 d); **Lazy K Motel** (1581 E. Hwy. 40; tel. 789-3277; $27.25 s or d); **Split Mountain Motel** (1015 E. Hwy. 40; tel. 789-9020; $27.25 s, $34.88 d); **Diamond Hills**

Motel (590 W. Main; tel. 789-1754; $27.52 s, $30.41 d); **Econo-Lodge** (311 E. Main; tel. 789-2000 or 1-800-446-6900; $27.70 s, $32.06 d); **Weston Inn** (260 W. Main; tel. 789-1011; $32.70 s, $39.79 d; has a pool); **Weston Lamplighter Inn** (120 E. Main; tel. 789-0312; $35.43 s, $39.79 d; has kitchenettes and a pool); **Antlers Best Western Motel** (423 W. Main; tel. 789-1202 or 1-800-528-1234; $46.87 s or d; has a pool); **Weston Plaza Hotel** (1684 W. Hwy. 40; tel. 789-9550; $52.32 s, $61.04 d; has an indoor pool and jacuzzi); and **Dinosaur Inn (Best Western)** (251 E. Main; tel. 789-2660 or 1-800-528-1234; $54.50 s, $57.77 d; has a pool).

## Campgrounds

**Vernal KOA** is on the west side of town (turn in beside the Weston Plaza Hotel; facilities include a pool, showers, laundry, and playground; $11.45 tent, $12.54 RV no hookups, and $16.90 w/hookups; open May 1 to Sept. 30; tel. 789-8935. **Campground Dina** is on the north side of town at 930 N. Vernal Ave.; has showers, laundry, and miniature golf; $10.90 tent or RV no hookups, $15.21 w/ hookups; open May 1 to Sept. 30; tel. 789-2148. Other campgrounds are north at Steinaker State Park (8 miles from Vernal), at Red Fleet Reservoir (11 miles), and in the Ashley National Forest (about 20 miles) and east in Dinosaur National Monument (23 miles).

## Food

For American fare, try the **Crack'd Pot Restaurant** (1089 E. Hwy. 40; tel. 781-0133; open daily for breakfast, lunch, and dinner); **Sage Restaurant** (56 W. Main; tel. 789-2277; open Mon. to Sat. for breakfast, lunch, and dinner); **Skillet Coffee Shop** (251 E. Main in Dinosaur Inn; tel. 789-3641; open daily for breakfast, lunch, and dinner); **Seven-Eleven Ranch Restaurant** (77 E. Main; tel. 789-1170; open daily except Sun. for breakfast, lunch, and dinner and a Sat. chuckwagon dinner); **Lamplighter Inn Restaurant** (120 E. Main; tel. 789-0312; open daily for breakfast and lunch, also dinner on weekdays); and **JB's Big Boy**

(475 W. Main; tel. 789-4547; open daily for breakfast, lunch, and dinner). The **Golden Corral Family Steakhouse** offers steak and other items in an informal Western atmosphere, 1046 W. Hwy. 40; tel. 789-7268; open daily for lunch and dinner.

**H.R. Weston** in the Weston Plaza Hotel offers a varied menu of Continental and American specialties, 1684 W. Hwy. 40; tel. 789-9550; open daily for breakfast, lunch, and dinner. **Jerry's Steak and Seafood** features fine dining with steak, seafood, and Mexican items, 831 W. Main; tel. 789-2030; open Mon. to Sat. for lunch and dinner. The **Pizza Barn** (part of Jerry's Steak and Seafood; same address and phone) serves pizza and other Italian as well as Mexican food; open Mon. to Sat. for lunch and dinner. **Pizza Hut** is at 1819 W. Hwy. 40; tel. 781-1048; open daily for lunch and dinner. **Diamond Hills Cafe** prepares popular Chinese and American foods, 578 W. Main; tel. 789-3053; open Mon. to Sat. for breakfast, lunch, and dinner. **Casa Rios** specializes in south-of-the-border cuisine, 2015 W. Hwy. 40; tel. 789-0103; open Tues. to Sat. for lunch and dinner.

## Entertainment

See movies at **Tri Cinema** (1400 W. Hwy. 40); **Vernal Theatre** (40 E. Main); or **Sunset Drive-In** (open in summer on W. Hwy. 40). Call the Movie Information Line to find out what's playing at the theaters; tel. 789-6139.

## Events

**May:** The Square Dance Festival sets the town a-jumping. Horse races begin. Governor's Invitational Fishing Derby (Lucerne Valley) brings excitement to Flaming Gorge Reservoir. Manila Fishing Derby also takes place at Flaming Gorge Reservoir. **June:** Junior Livestock Show. Horse racing continues. The Outlaw Trail Festival brings in some wild characters for shooting events, a bank robbery, trail rides on old outlaw paths, musicals, western art competition, oil-painting workshop, and song-writing contest; begins mid-June and lasts through July. Water-skiing competition at Steinaker Reservoir on the last Sat. of June.

**July:** Fireworks on the Fourth. Outlaw Trail Festival continues. Dinosaur Roundup Rodeo (PRCA) pits man against beast and features a parade; country musicians show their stuff in the True Value Country Showdown a few days before the rodeo. A parade celebrates Pioneer Day on the 24th. Dinosaur Triathlon. Water-skiing competition at Steinaker Reservoir on the last Sat. in July.

**August:** Dinosaur Days presents special programs at the Utah Field House and a variety of kids activities around town. The Flaming Gorge Yacht Club organizes a Parade of Lights at Lucerne Bay. Uintah County Fair. Water-skiing competition at Steinaker Reservoir on the last Sat. in August.

**September:** Balloon races.

### Recreation

**Aquanoodle** has water-tube fun in summer at 1155 E. Hwy. 40; tel. 789-5281. Play tennis or baseball at the **city park,** corner of 400 North and 900 West. Golf at the 9-hole **Dinaland Municipal Golf Course,** 675 S. 2000 East; tel. 781-1428.

### Services

In **emergencies** (police, medical, and fire), dial 911. The **post office** is near the corner of Main and 800 West; tel. 789-2393. **Ashley Valley Medical Center** provides hospital care at 151 W. 200 North; tel. 789-3342. Camping and fishing supplies are available at **Murray's Sporting Goods** (39 S. Vernal Ave.; tel. 789-5779); **Basin Sports** (511 W. Main.; tel. 789-2199); and **Gart Bros.** (872 W. Main; tel. 789-0536). The **Plaza Shopping Center** has a K mart and other stores at 1153 W. Hwy. 40.

### Information

Staff at the **Vernal Welcome Center** know about the many attractions of "Dinosaurland" and offer a short video program showing highlights of the region and other parts of Utah; a series of 9 self-guiding tour brochures has maps and mileages of suggested trips. The center is open daily 8 a.m.-8 p.m. in summer, then daily 8 a.m.-5 p.m. the rest of the year;

tel. 789-4002; it's located in the Utah Field House of Natural History at 235 E. Main (Vernal, UT 84078). Foresters at the **Vernal Ranger District** office of the Ashley National Forest can tell you about scenic drives, camping, hiking, cross-country skiing, and snowmobiling in the eastern Uinta Mountains; books and forest maps are sold; travel plans showing vehicle restrictions are free; open Mon. to Fri. 8 a.m.-5 p.m.; tel. 789-1181; 353 N. Vernal Ave. (Vernal, UT 84078). The **Ashley National Forest Supervisor's Office,** next door at 355 N. Vernal Ave. (same phone), has general information about the Flaming Gorge, Roosevelt, and Duchesne districts. The **Bureau of Land Management (BLM)** Vernal District office knows about the John Jarvie Historic Ranch in the northeast corner of the state and areas south of Vernal such as Pelican Lake and the White River; land-use maps and a variety of brochures on recreation areas are available; open Mon. to Fri. 7:45 a.m.-4:30 p.m.; tel. 789-1362; 170 S. 500 East (Vernal, UT 84078). For detailed fishing and hunting information, stop at the **Utah Division of Wildlife Resources;** books on fishing and wildlife are sold; open Mon. to Fri. 8 a.m.-5 p.m.; tel. 789-3103; in the courthouse building, second floor, 152 E. 100 North (Vernal, UT 84078). The **U.S. Fish and Wildlife Service** has information about the Ouray National Wildlife Refuge to the south and Jones Hole National Fish Hatchery to the northeast; open Mon. to Fri. 8 a.m.-noon and 1-5 p.m.; tel. 789-0351; Room 1220 on the second floor, 1680 W. Hwy. 40 (Vernal, UT 84078-4125). The **Uintah County Library** has good reading; you can also see the **Ladies of the White House Doll Collection** here; open Mon. to Sat.; tel. 789-0091; 155 E. Main. **Bitter Creek Books** offers a selection of regional and general titles and topo maps; tel. 789-4742; 672 W. Main.

### Tours

River trips down the Green or Yampa in Dinosaur National Monument provide the excitement of big rapids and the beauty of remote canyons. One-day and longer trips are offered by **Don Hatch River Expeditions** (Box 1150,

Vernal, UT 84078; tel. 789-4316/4715 or 800-342-8243 out of state) and **Adrift Adventures** (summer: Box 192, Jensen, UT 84035; tel. 789-3600; year-round: 1816 Orchard Place, Ft. Collins, CO 80521; tel. 800-824-0150). Expect to pay about $44 for day trips and about $100/day for longer excursions; children usually get discounts. Both companies offer trips on other rivers of the West too.

**Transport**
**Greyhound** buses go at least once daily west to Salt Lake City and east to Denver; tel. 789-0404; 510 E. Main. Rent cars from **Avis** (at the airport; tel. 789-7264) or **Showalter Ford** (100 E. Main; tel. 789-3818). **Skywest Airlines** has daily connections with Salt Lake City ($81 one way), Grand Junction, Rock Springs, Idaho Falls, Las Vegas, Reno, and other regional cities; tel. (800) 453-9417.

# NORTH OF VERNAL

**Drive Through The Ages**
You cross 19 geologic formations going far back in time on the drive between Vernal and Flaming Gorge Reservoir. Uplift of rock layers during the creation of the Uinta Mountains and the erosion that followed have revealed an exceptionally thick geologic layer cake. The 30-mile drive begins 4 miles north of town on US 191; a tour map at a pullout shows the formations that will be seen ahead. *Drive Through the Ages* brochures are available at the Vernal Welcome Center, U.S. Forest Service, and BLM offices. Signs on the drive identify and briefly describe each formation from the Mancos (80 million years old) to the Uinta Mountain Group (1 billion years old). The signs face only northbound traffic.

**Steinaker State Park**
Water sports, camping, and picnicking at the park's 750-acre Steinaker Reservoir make this a popular place in summer. Fishermen catch largemouth bass, rainbow and a few brown trout, bluegill, and green sunfish. Water-skiers have plenty of room on the lake's 2-mile length. Warm weather brings bathers to a swimming beach near the picnic area. Scuba divers find the best conditions from midsummer to late autumn, when visibility is up to 30 feet. In winter, visitors come to ice fish or to cross-country ski on a 6-km trail (easy, with a few hills). The campground (elev. 5,500 ft.) is open with drinking water from about Easter to mid-Oct.; no showers or hookups. The park charges $3/vehicle day use or $6/vehicle camping; tel. 789-4432/0321 or (800) 322-3770 (reservations). From Vernal, go north 6 miles on US 191, then turn left 2 miles.

**Red Fleet State Park**
Colorful cliffs and rock formations, including 3 large outcrops of red sandstone, inspired the name of Red Fleet Reservoir. Fishermen catch largemouth bass, rainbow trout, and some brown trout. Like the larger Steinaker Reservoir, Red Fleet stores valuable water for irrigation and municipal use. A developed area offers covered picnic tables, water, restrooms, fish-cleaning station, and paved boat ramp; charges are $3/vehicle day use or $6/vehicle camping; contact Steinaker State Park for more information. From Vernal, go north 10 miles on US 191 to Milepost 211, then turn right 2 miles on a paved road to its end.

**Jones Hole National Fish Hatchery**
Canyon walls tower 2,000 feet above Jones Hole. Springs supply water for the young trout raised here that will later go to Flaming Gorge Reservoir and other areas. Visitors may view the operation daily 7 a.m.-3:30 p.m. or just the outdoor raceways at any time during the day; tours can be arranged on weekdays with at least one day's notice. The fragile eggs usually aren't on display, but you can see the newly hatched fish swimming in tanks inside the buildings. Young trout spook easily, so they're kept indoors, where they eat better and grow faster. When the trout reach a length of 3 inches they go outside. At an age of 14 months, the trout are 8 inches long and ready to be transplanted to the wild. The hatchery produces about 3 million rainbow, brown, brook, and cutthroat trout annually. Call 789-4481 for information. Jones Hole is 38 miles northeast of Vernal via paved roads; head east on 500 North and follow the signs over

**1.** Deseret Peak hike (Great Salt Lake is visible in background); **2.** Raft River Mountains; **3.** Cedar Creek Canyon in the Deep Creek Mountains; **4.** Red Pine Lake (lower) in Little Cottonwood Canyon, Wasatch Range; **5.** Notch Peak at sunset, House Range; **6.** canyons of the Green River from Harpers Corner Trail, Dinosaur National Monument (all photos by author)

1. Landscape Arch, Arches National Park; 2. alcove along Harris Wash, Escalante River system; 3. Green River sunset from Swasey Beach, near the mouth of Gray Canyon; 4. Golden Throne (center) enveloped by mist, Capitol Reef National Park; 5. Goosenecks of the San Juan River, Goosenecks State Park; 6. foggy morning in Bryce Amphitheater, Bryce Canyon National Park (all photos by author)

**1.** Cedar Breaks National Monument; **2.** Weeping Rock, Zion National Park; **3.** North Fork of Virgin River from Gateway to Narrows Trail, Zion National Park (all photos by author)

**1.** Maze District, Canyonlands National Park; **2.** confluence of Salt Creek and Colorado River in the Needles District, Canyonlands National Park (all photos by author)

Diamond Mountain Plateau. Diamond Mountain is believed to be the site of a hoax played in the 1870s; 2 men salted the area with genuine diamonds, then sold out for a fortune; one culprit was caught, the other escaped. Unpaved roads connect Jones Hole Road with US 191 and Browns Park. Hatchery staff discourage visits from mid-Nov. to mid-March because ice and drifting snow can make driving hazardous; it's best not to come then unless you call ahead, have 4WD, and are prepared for winter camping.

An easy hiking trail begins below the raceways and follows Jones Hole Creek 4 miles to the Green River in Dinosaur National Monument. Hikers enjoy the spectacular canyon scenery, lush vegetation, a chance to see wildlife, and some Fremont Indian pictographs. The creek has good fishing; special regulations (posted) include use of artificial lures and flies only. You may camp midway on the trail near the confluence with Ely Creek by first obtaining a backcountry permit from Dinosaur National Monument. Ely Creek has good places to camp and explore. The trail begins at an elevation of 5,550 feet and descends 500 feet to the Green River in Whirlpool Canyon.

### John Jarvie Ranch
Browns Park, along the Green River in Utah's northeast corner and adjacent to Colorado, has always been remote. The Wild Bunch and other outlaws often used the area as a hangout. John Jarvie settled here in 1880 and stayed until his death in 1909. He ran a store, post office, and ferry, while still having time to take care of the ranch and do some prospecting. A guided tour of the restored ranch takes in the original (1880s) corral, blacksmith shop and tools, farm implements, crude dugout, stone house, and other structures. Jarvie's store has been reconstructed and filled with shelves of canned goods, dried food, pots and pans, tools, harnesses, barbed wire, and other necessities of turn-of-the-century ranch life. Exhibits also show artifacts dug up from the original store site. The John Jarvie Ranch is open daily 8 a.m.-5 p.m. from May to Oct.; free; tel. 885-3307 (or call the BLM office in Vernal; tel. 789-1362). Winter visits are possible too; call first to find out road conditions. Boaters on the Green River can easily stop off to see the ranch; a sign marks where to pull in. Bridge Hollow Recreation Site (¼ mile downstream of the ranch) and Indian Crossing Recreation Site (¼ mile upstream of the ranch) have free campgrounds; you can obtain drinking water at the ranch.

Trucks or cars with good clearance can drive to the ranch on an unpaved road through scenic Crouse Canyon; this route branches off Jones Hole Road 26 miles from Vernal, goes north past Crouse Reservoir and into the canyon, winds west through hills and parallels the Green River (the river is hard to see from the road), crosses a bridge over the swift-flowing Green, and turns left 0.3 mile; distance from Jones Hole Road is 28 miles. Another way in is to go north from Vernal on US 191 to 0.7 mile past the Wyoming border and turn right 22 miles on a gravel road; a steep 14% grade into Browns Park makes climbing back difficult for RVs and other underpowered vehicles. A third approach is from Maybell, Colorado, on CO 318 (paved until the Utah border); this is the best road, especially in winter. Highway CO 318 also provides access to Browns Park National Wildlife Refuge, a stopover point for migratory waterfowl in spring and autumn and a nesting habitat for ducks and Great Basin Canada geese. A gravel tour road goes through the refuge.

### Ashley National Forest (Vernal District)
The southeastern part of the Uinta Mountains has very pleasant mountain country with scenic drives, fishing, hiking, camping, picnicking, and winter sports. Contact the U.S. Forest Service office in Vernal for road conditions and recreation information. Roads at the higher elevations open about the beginning of June and are often passable through October. Most roads to the campgrounds and reservoirs are OK for cars. Some areas may be closed to vehicle use because of wet conditions, wildlife habitat, sheep ranges, or erosion problems. **Lodgepole Campground** offers sites with water from late May to early Sept. at an elevation of 8,100 feet; it's 30 miles north of Vernal on US 191 on the way to Flaming Gorge N.R.A.; $5. **East Park Campground,**

at East Park Reservoir, has water and a $4 fee; go 20 miles north of Vernal on US 191, then 10 miles northwest on forest roads (all but the last mile is paved); elevation is 9,000 feet. **Iron Springs Campground and Picnic Area,** on the Red Cloud Loop Scenic Drive, is mainly a group area; individuals can also use the sites if there's room; a hand pump supplies water. Other campgrounds include **Red Springs, Oaks Park, Paradise Park, Kaler Hollow,** and **Whiterocks.**

Fishermen will find rainbow trout in most of the lakes and streams. Brown trout and native cutthroat trout live in some areas. Most hiking trails are rocky with some steep sections; topo maps should be carried. Trails lead into the High Uintas Wilderness from Chepeta Lake and West Fork of Whiterocks trailheads; road distances to the trailheads are relatively long, then there's a hike of about 6-7 miles to the wilderness boundary. In winter, 3 cross-country ski trails lead west from US 191 into the Grizzly Ridge and Little Brush Creek areas; signed trailheads are about 25 miles north of Vernal. Most of these trails are rated intermediate to advanced, though some sections are good for beginners too. Snowmobilers have an extensive network of trails that mostly follow forest roads.

### Red Cloud Loop Scenic Drive
This 74-mile loop winds through scenic canyons and mountains northwest of Vernal. Allow about half a day for just the drive. Side roads go to East Park and Oaks Park reservoirs, campgrounds, fishing streams, and hiking areas. Aspen trees put on a brilliant display in autumn. About half the drive follows unpaved forest roads, so it's a good idea to check road conditions first with the U.S. Forest Service office in Vernal. Cars with good clearance can usually make the trip if the roads are dry. Drive 20 miles north from Vernal on US 191 (or 15 miles south from the junction of US 191 and UT 44 in Flaming Gorge N.R.A.) and turn west on the paved East Park Reservoir Road at the sign that says "Red Cloud Loop." Signs then show the rest of the way. The Vernal Welcome Center's brochure *Red Cloud Loop* describes points of interest.

# FLAMING GORGE NATIONAL RECREATION AREA

Flaming Gorge Reservoir winds through 91 miles of gentle valleys and fiery red canyons. The rugged land displays spectacular scenery where the Green River cuts into the Uinta Mountains—cliffs rising as high as 1,500 feet, twisted rock formations, and sweeping panoramas. Although much of the lake lies in Wyoming, most of the campgrounds and other visitor facilities, as well as the best scenery, are in Utah. Boating on the clear blue waters of the lake or the river below is one of the best ways to enjoy the sights. Water-skiers have plenty of room on the lake's 66 square miles. Swimming is popular too. Fishermen regularly pull trophy trout and smallmouth bass from the lake and trout from the river. Rafting the lively Green River below the dam offers a thrilling ride that anyone with care and proper safety equipment can take—no special skills or permits are needed. The U.S. Forest Service and private concessions offer boating facilities and about 2 dozen campgrounds in the recreation area. Information centers at Flaming Gorge Dam and Red Canyon Overlook have exhibits, video programs, maps, and literature. Flaming Gorge N.R.A. can be easily reached by heading north 35 miles on US 191 from Vernal. In Wyoming, you can take WY 530 south from the town of Green River or US 191 south from near Rock Springs.

Look for groups of graceful pronghorn in the open country east of the lake at Antelope Flat (north of Dutch John) and in the Lucerne area on the west side. Other wildlife in the area include deer, elk, moose, mountain lion, black bear, bighorn sheep, fox, bobcat, mink, and eagles.

### Flaming Gorge Dam And Visitor Center
Nearly a million cubic yards of concrete went into the dam, completed in 1964. The structure rises 502 feet above bedrock and is 1,285 feet long at the crest. Park at the visitor center on the west end of the dam and walk across to the elevator to begin a self-guided tour.

You'll descend inside for a look at the 3 giant generators in the power-plant room, then go one floor below where a shaft connects the turbine and generator of one of the units. A visit takes about 20 minutes and is free. The dam is open daily 8 a.m.-4 p.m. from the first weekend in April to the last weekend in September. The visitor center has a large 3-D map of the area and a video introduction; books and maps are for sale and staff will answer your questions. Open daily 9:30 a.m.-5 p.m. from Memorial Day to Labor Day weekends. The dam and visitor center are 6.5 miles northeast on US 191 from the junction with UT 44, or 2.8 miles southwest of Dutch John.

### Red Canyon Visitor Center
Sheer cliffs drop 1,360 feet to the lake below. The visitor center and nearby viewpoints have splendid panoramas up and down the canyon and to the lofty Uinta Mountains in the distance. A nature trail connects the overlooks

*Flaming Gorge; view uplake from Red Canyon Overlook*

and has signs about the ecology; the trail is wheelchair accessible. Exhibits inside describe local wildlife and flora, Indian groups that once lived here, and early history and settlement of the area. Books and maps are for sale at an information desk; staff offer a video program and will answer your questions. Open daily 9:30 a.m.-5 p.m. from Memorial Day to Labor Day weekends. Located 3.5 miles west on UT 44 from the junction with US 191, then 3 miles in on a paved road.

### Additional Information
As the 2 visitor centers are open only in summer, you'll need to visit one of the Flaming Gorge Ranger District offices for information during the off-season. Forest Service staff and volunteers can give information for backcountry travel. The Manila Headquarters office is at the junction of UT 44 and UT 43 in the center of Manila; open daily 8 a.m.-4:30 p.m. in summer and Mon. to Fri. 8 a.m.-4:30 p.m. the rest of the year (may also be open Sat. mornings in autumn); forest and topo maps and some books are sold; Box 278, Manila, UT 84046; tel. 784-3445/3409.

### Off-season Visits
Peace, quiet, and snow prevail in winter. Dedicated fishermen still cast their lines into the Green River or fish through the lake ice. Cross-country skiers and snowmobilers make their trails through the woods. Flaming Gorge Lodge, Grubbs Motel (Manila), and Steinaker's Motel (Manila) provide warm places to stay. Campgrounds are closed, though snow campers and hardy RVers can stop for the night in parking areas.

### Sheep Creek Canyon Geological Area
Canyon walls on this scenic loop drive reveal rock layers deformed and turned on end by immense geological forces. The earth's crust broke along the Uinta Crest Fault and the south side rose 15,000 feet relative to the north. Fossils of trilobites, corals, sea urchins, gastropods, and other marine animals show that the ocean once covered this spot before the uplifting and faulting. Fossilized wood and tracks of crocodile-like reptiles are preserved

in rock layers of yet another time. Nongeologists can appreciate and enjoy the drive too. The road through Sheep Creek Canyon is paved but has some narrow and rough places; it's closed in winter. The 13-mile loop branches off UT 44 south of Manila between Mileposts 14 and 15 and rejoins UT 44 at Milepost 22; the loop can be done in either direction. The *Wheels of Time* geology brochure, available at visitor centers and the Manila Headquarters, describes geologic formations at marked stops. Three picnic areas line the drive. Camping in the canyon has been prohibited ever since a flash flood in 1965 killed a family of 7; Palisades Memorial Park marks the site.

## Boating On Flaming Gorge Lake

Watch for strong winds on the lake which can whip up large waves without warning—even on a clear day. Rock reefs may appear and disappear as the lake level changes. Three marinas along the lake's length offer rentals, fuel docks, and supplies. Free paved boat ramps at these and several other locations are maintained by the U.S. Forest Service. **Cedar Springs Marina,** at the lower end of the lake, rents boats (fishing, ski, and pontoon) and fishing gear, and has a fuel dock, slips, store, scenic tours, and guided fishing trips; open April to Oct.; Box 337, Dutch John, UT 84023; tel. 889-3795. Turnoff for the marina is 1.7 miles west of Flaming Gorge Dam on US 191. **Lucerne Valley Marina** provides services on the broad central section of the lake near Manila; the marina has boat rentals (fishing, ski, pontoon, and houseboats), fishing gear rentals, a fuel dock, slips, store, and guided fishing trips; open mid-March to mid-Nov.; Manila, UT 84046; tel. 784-3483/3133. The marina is 8 miles east of Manila on paved roads. **Buckboard Marina** is on the west shore in Wyoming; services include boat rentals (fishing, ski, and pontoon), fishing gear rentals, a fuel dock, slips, store, scenic tours, and guided fishing trips; Star Route 1, Green River, WY 82935; tel. (307) 875-6927. It's 22.5 miles northeast of Manila on UT 43/WY 530, or 23.5 miles south of Green River on WY 530.

## The Green River Below Flaming Gorge Dam

The Green bounces back to life in Red Canyon below the dam and provides enjoyment for boaters, fishermen, and hikers. Anyone in good shape with a raft, life jacket, a paddle (and spare), bailing bucket, and common sense can put in at the launch area just below the dam and float downriver to Little Hole (2½-3 hours for 7 river miles) or to Indian Crossing just above the John Jarvie Historic Ranch (5-8 hours for 14½ river miles). It's also possible to continue 11 miles beyond Indian Crossing to Swallow Canyon take-out or 35 miles to Gates of Lodore; these runs are mostly flat water and have troublesome sandbars at low water. Gates of Lodore marks the beginning of some big rapids in Dinosaur National Monument; you'll need permits and whitewater experience here or you can make prior arrangements to join a commercial river trip.

People with canoes, kayaks, and dories can float all sections of the Green between the dam and Gates of Lodore, though river experience is needed for these craft. No permits are required—just have proper equipment before you get in and go. Raft rentals and shuttle services are provided by Flaming Gorge Lodge (tel. 889-3773), Flaming Gorge Recreation Services at the Dutch John Store (tel. 885-3191), and Flaming Gorge Flying Service at the Dutch John Airport (tel. 885-3338). Rentals typically cost $35/day for a 6-person raft or $50/day for one holding 8; shuttles cost about $25 to Little Hole, $70 to Indian Crossing, and $85 to Swallow Canyon. Drivers can also drop their vehicle off at Little Hole and take an early morning shuttle back to the starting point.

Friday, Saturday, and holidays in summer often see large crowds on the river; you'll need reservations then for raft rentals and shuttles. For solitude, try to come Sunday to Wednesday. Guide services for boating and fishing trips can be contacted through the rental outfits. Life jackets (included with rentals) must be worn by all boaters—the water is too cold (57° F in summer, 40° in winter) to swim in for long. The 10 class-II rapids between the dam and Little Hole lend some excitement to the trip but aren't usually dangerous. Red Creek Rapid below Little Hole is a class-III rapid and can be difficult; scouting before running is recommended. Many groups portage this rapid. Camping is permitted downstream of Little Hole at established primitive sites or dispersed sites. Bring drinking water or obtain some at Little Hole. No motors are allowed between the dam and Indian Crossing. Water flow varies according to power needs; allow more time if the flow is small. Call the Bureau of Reclamation for present conditions; tel. 885-3121.

Trips begin at the end of a 1.4-mile paved road (may not be signed) which turns off US 191 0.3 mile east of the dam. The parking area at the river is small, for unloading boats and passengers only. The main parking areas are 0.7 mile back up the road. Drivers can take either of 2 foot trails which descend from the parking lots to the river. The shuttle to Little Hole is only 8 miles (5 are dirt) via Dutch John. The drive to Indian Crossing is much longer, 38 miles (25 unpaved); go north on US 191 to 0.7 mile beyond the Wyoming state line, then turn east on a gravel road to Browns Park and follow signs; one section of this road has a 14% grade.

**Little Hole Trail** follows the north bank of the Green River through Red Canyon for 7 miles between the main parking area below the dam and Little Hole. Many good fishing spots can be found along the way. No camping, horses, ground fires, or motorized vehicles are allowed. The Green River downstream of the dam has a reputation for some of western America's best river fishing. Trophy catches have included 22-pound rainbow, 18-pound brown, and 14-pound cutthroat trout. Modifications to the dam allow the ideal temperature mix of warmer water near the lake's surface and cold water from the depths. Special regulations apply here to maintain the high-quality fishing (check for current regulations): trout between 13 and 20 inches (the most prolific breeders) must be returned to the water, there's a 3-fish limit (2 under 13 inches, one over 20 inches), and only artificial lures and flies may be used. Fishermen using waders should wear life jackets in case the river level rises unexpectedly; neoprene closed cell foam waders are recommended for their extra flotation and protection against hypothermia.

### Hiking Trails
**Hideout-Carter Creek Trail #002** goes to Hideout Boat Camp on the lake, 10 miles one way with some steep sections; trailhead is on UT 44, 4.5 miles west of the Red Canyon Visitor Center turnoff; the trail has been widened for tractor access so new facilities could be added to the campground at Hideout.

You can save several miles if you start from Dowd Mountain Overlook Road. **Browne Lake** is a popular starting point for hikes outside the recreation area: Trail #005 goes to the **Ute Mountain Fire Lookout Tower,** a national historic site (2 miles one way); Trail #016 goes to **Hacking Lake** (7 miles one way); Trail #012 goes to **Tepee Lakes** (5 miles one way) and **Leidy Peak** (elev. 12,028 ft.; 8 miles one way); and Trail #017 goes to **Spirit Lake** (15 miles one way). Browne Lake is 4.5 miles west on unpaved Forest Route 221 from the Sheep Creek loop drive, then 1.5 miles southeast on the Browne Lake road; see the Ashley National Forest map. Visitor centers and forest service offices have a map of hiking trails. The USGS topo maps are recommended too.

## Campgrounds

The camping season begins with the opening of Lucerne Valley Campground (8 miles east of Manila), usually on Easter Sunday. By Memorial Day, everything should be open. Campgrounds begin closing after Labor Day, though at least one is left open through Oct. for hunters. If you're here early or late in the season, stop by or call the Manila or Dutch John forest service offices to find out what's available. Most campgrounds have water and a $5 base fee. Group sites and single family units in some areas can be reserved through Mistix reservation service; tel. (800) 283-CAMP. Some primitive campgrounds on the lake can be reached only by boat or trail; these include Kingfisher, Island, Gooseneck, Hideout, and Jarvies Canyon.

## Accommodations

**Flaming Gorge Lodge** offers motel rooms all year ($46.87 s, $53.51 d), condos ($79.57 s, $86.11 d), and a restaurant serving breakfast, lunch, and dinner daily from early April to late November. The lodge, store, and raft rentals are 7 miles southwest of Dutch John; tel. 889-3773; Dutch John, UT 84023. **Red Canyon Resort,** closed at press time, sits beside the privately operated Green's Lake a short distance from the Red Canyon Visitor Center; ask at the visitor centers to find out if it has reopened.

## Other Services

**Flaming Gorge Recreation/Dutch John Service** at the turnoff for Dutch John on US 191 has a snackbar (open daily Memorial Day to Labor Day weekends), store (open mid-May to late Oct.), raft rental and shuttle services (spring through autumn), and a gas station (open all year); tel. 885-3191. **Flaming Gorge Flying Service** at Dutch John Airport offers raft rentals, river trips, shuttle service, and showers; tel. 885-3338. Dutch John has always been a government town. It sprang up in 1957-58 to house workers during construction of Flaming Gorge Dam and had a peak population of about 3,000. About 150 current residents work in various state and federal agencies.

The tiny town of Manila, just west of the recreation area, is the seat of Daggett County, smallest and least populated in Utah. Year-round population of Manila totals only 284. The name commemorates Admiral Dewey's capture of Manila in the Philippines, which occurred in 1898 when surveyors were laying out the Utah townsite. Manila is a handy base for travel in the Flaming Gorge area. The town is 63 miles northwest of Vernal and 46 miles south of Green River (WY). Stay at **Grubbs Motel** (in the center of town; tel. 784-3131; $26.16 s, $30.52 d); **Steinaker's Motel** (E. Hwy. 43; tel. 784-3363; $23.98 s, $27.25 d); or **Vacation Inn** (W. Hwy. 43; tel. 784-3259; all kitchenettes: $39.24 s or d, $45.78 for 3 or 4; open April 1 to Oct. 31). **Flaming Gorge KOA** on W. UT 43 is open with showers, laundry, pool, and playground from May 1 to Oct. 1; tel. 784-3239; tent or RV spaces cost $12.54 no hookups, $16.35 w/hookups. Dine at **Grubbs Cafe** (center of town; open daily for breakfast, lunch, and dinner) or **Niki's Place** (W. Hwy. 43; open daily for breakfast, lunch, and dinner). **Crossroads Market & Sandwich Company** has a general store and snackbar in the center of town. The **3M Market** on E. Hwy. 43 has groceries and fishing supplies. **Cow Country Rodeo** in July is the big annual event. The **Flaming Gorge Ranger District** office is in the center of town (see "Additional Information" above).

*loading up for a pack trip at Spirit Lake Lodge*

## Vicinity Of Flaming Gorge N.R.A.

**Browne Lake** has a small campground (elev. 8,200 ft.; no water or fee) and fishing for native cutthroat trout. Several trails start nearby (see "Hiking Trails" above). Browne Lake is 4.5 miles west on unpaved Forest Route 221 from the Sheep Creek loop drive, then 1.5 miles southeast on the Browne Lake road; see the Ashley National Forest map.

**Ute Mountain Fire Lookout Tower** (elev. 8,834 ft.) has a good panorama of surrounding alpine lakes, Flaming Gorge Lake, and the Uintas. The tower has recently been restored as a historic site. Turn west one mile on Forest Route 221 from the Sheep Creek loop drive, then 1.5 miles south on Forest Route 005.

**Spirit Lake** has a beautiful setting in high country of the Uintas. The lake (elev. 10,000 ft.) offers fishing, boating, a campground, and a lodge. Hikers can take trails to nearby lakes (17 are within 3 miles!) and to the High Uintas Wilderness. The campground is in a fir, spruce, and lodgepole pine forest; open early June to early Oct.; $5; obtain water from the nearby Spirit Lake Lodge. **Spirit Lake Lodge** offers cabins ($26 s or d, $32 up to 5, $38 up to 8, $48 up to 14), a cafe (open daily for breakfast, lunch, and dinner), a small store, guided pack trips, trail rides, and rowboat and canoe rentals; open early June to early Oct.; tel. 783-2339; write: 1360 Hallam Rd., Francis, UT 84036. Take unpaved Forest Route 221 west 10.5 miles past the Ute Mountain Fire Lookout Tower and Browne Lake turnoffs to the junction with Forest Route 001, then follow 001 southwest 6.5 miles to Spirit Lake; this last section may have some rocky areas, but is usually passable for cars with good clearance. Spirit Lake is 69.5 miles from Vernal, 41 miles from Flaming Gorge Dam, and 31 miles from Lone Tree (WY).

# EAST OF VERNAL

## DINOSAUR NATIONAL MONUMENT

The monument owes its name and fame to one of the world's most productive sites for dinosaur bones. More than 2,300 bones of 10 different dinosaur species cover a rock face at the quarry. The spectacular canyons of the Green and Yampa rivers form another aspect of the monument. Harpers Corner Scenic Drive winds onto high ridges and canyon viewpoints in the heart of Dinosaur. River running allows a close look at the geology and wildlife within the depths and provides the bonus of thrilling rapids. Dinosaur National Monument straddles the Utah-Colorado border, but dinosaur bones are visible only at the quarry, in the western end of the monument.

### The Land

From the original 80 acres reserved at the quarry in 1915, Dinosaur National Monument has grown to more than 200,000 acres of rivers, canyons, valleys, plateaus, and mountains. Elevations range from 4,750 feet at the Green River near the quarry to 9,006 feet atop Zenobia Peak of Douglas Mountain. The high country is part of the east flank of the Uinta Mountains, whose geology is so graphically revealed in deep canyons of the Green and Yampa rivers. Wildlife inhabiting this rugged terrain includes mule deer, elk, pronghorn, Rocky Mountain bighorn sheep, mountain lion, black bear, coyote, bobcat, red and gray fox, badger, striped and Western spotted skunk, ringtail cat, raccoon, beaver, bats, and many species of rats and mice. Streamside vegetation consists largely of cottonwood, box elder, willow, tamarisk, and some black birch. Desert plants such as sagebrush, greasewood, shadscale, saltbush, and rabbitbrush grow on the slopes at lower elevations. Middle elevations have pinyon pine and juniper trees, serviceberry, buckbrush, and sagebrush.

Douglas fir, aspen, ponderosa pine, spruce, and mountain mahogany thrive on the mountains and in the protective shade of canyon walls. Annual precipitation averages about 9 inches.

### Dinosaurs

A fortunate combination of sand and water preserved the bones of dinosaurs, turtles, crocodiles, and clam shells at this spot about 145 million years ago. River floods washed the carcasses onto a sandbar where they were buried and saved from complete decay. Pressure from thousands of feet of additional sediments above gradually turned the sand to rock, and the bones within it were partially mineralized. Later, uplift of the Rockies and Uintas tilted the sandstone layer nearly on edge and exposed the overlying rocks to erosion.

In 1909, Earl Douglass, of the Carnegie Museum in Pittsburgh, Pennsylvania, suspected that dinosaur bones might be found here because similar rock layers had yielded fine specimens in Colorado and Wyoming. He was right. A discovery of 8 brontosaurus tail bones in their original position the following year became the first of many rewarding finds at the site. Douglass and other workers continued excavations until 1924, removing 350 tons of bones and attached rock that included 22 complete skeletons and parts of hundreds of other specimens. (Some of the best mounted skeletons can be seen at the Carnegie Museum.) After 1924, quarry work shifted emphasis from removing bones to exposing them in relief in their natural positions in the sandstone.

### Dinosaur Quarry

A large enclosure protects the quarry face from the elements and houses laboratories and visitor exhibits. Near the entrance, you'll pass a realistic stegosaurus before climbing a spiral ramp to the quarry observation deck.

Exhibits illustrate the sandbar and Morrison scene and place the quarry in context within the span of geologic time. The rock layer is 8-12 feet thick and dates from the Jurassic Period, about the middle of the Age of Dinosaurs. Roughly three-quarters of the bones that you'll see come from sauropods—giant plant eaters with long necks and tails. All the bones appear in a jumble in the rock, just as they were deposited in the river sands long ago. One skeleton has a number marked on each bone; a diagram lets you figure out which piece is which. Reliefing of bones still takes place in summer; air hammers, hoists, chisels, and other tools lie ready to expose more bones. Models, artwork, and specimens on the lower level depict the variety of dinosaurs found here. Exhibits also show how workers remove bones from the rock and how they learn details about the dinosaurs' size, shape, diet, and muscle structures. Peek through windows of the paleontology lab to see bones under study and the instruments used. In winter, you may see research ers at work here.

Staff will answer questions about the quarry and other places to see in the monument.

*stegosaurus*

Handouts, available on request, include bird and mammal lists and information on back-country roads, hiking, river running, and Fremont rock art. A schedule posted during the main season lists times and places of ranger talks, nature walks, auto tours, children's programs, and campfire programs. A good selection of dinosaur and natural history books, posters, postcards, slides, topo and geologic maps, and film is sold. The Dinosaur Quarry is open daily 8 a.m.-4:30 p.m. (extended to about 7 p.m. in spring and summer); closed Thanksgiving, Christmas, and New Year's Day; tel. (801) 789-2115. Mailing address is Box 210, Dinosaur, CO 81610. From Vernal, drive east 13 miles on US 40 to Jensen, then turn north 7 miles on UT 149. Admission to the quarry is $2 adult ($.50 bus passenger) or $5/vehicle; free for children under 16. Parking space is in short supply during the busy summer season, so a free shuttle operates every 15 minutes between the quarry and a separate parking area. The rest of the year you can drive all the way in.

### Quarry To Josie Morris Cabin Drive

Stop at the Dinosaur Quarry or a roadside pullout for the booklet *Cub Creek Sampler*, which describes points of interest of an auto tour to the Cub Creek area. The drive goes 10 miles past the quarry turnoff to a historic ranch, passing sites of Fremont rock art and the Split Mountain and Green River camp-grounds on the way. A small overhang known as the "Swelter Shelter" contains some petroglyphs; the pullout is one mile beyond the quarry turnoff; a trail leads 200 feet to the cave. Continue 1.7 miles to the Split Mountain Campground turnoff; the side road winds down one mile to the campground at the Green River. Sites stay open all year; in summer they have water and a $5 fee. The Green River emerges from Split Mountain Canyon here after some of the roughest rapids on the whole river. **Red Rock Nature Trail** begins at the campground entrance and makes a 2-mile loop; a trail brochure available near the start describes plants and geology seen along the way; allow 1½-2 hours.

Back on the main road, a Green River overlook is on the left 1.2 miles past the Split Mountain Campground turnoff. The road to Green River Campground is a short way farther on the left; the campground is open only in summer and has water and a $5 fee. Placer Point Picnic Area is 1.1 miles beyond the junction, just before a bridge across the Green River. The main road continues past a private ranch, then pavement ends. A road fork on the right, 2.7 miles past the bridge, goes to Blue Mountain (high-clearance vehicles and good maps needed); keep left for the Josie Morris Cabin. A petroglyph panel is on the left beside the road 0.7 mile beyond the road fork. Continue past this panel 0.2 mile and park in a pullout on the right (may not be signed) for a look at no less than 7 lizard petroglyphs on the cliffs above and to the left; a steep climb up the slope (no trail) allows a closer view of these and other figures. Large shade trees surround the Josie Morris Cabin at the end of the road, 0.9 mile farther. Josie grew up in Browns Park during the 1870s and 1880s and settled here about 1914. She spent much of the next 50 years alone at the ranch, tending the fields, garden, cows, pigs, and chickens. She was in her 90s when she died as a result of a hip broken in a riding accident. You can visit her cabin, outbuildings, orchards, and a nearby box canyon.

## Monument Headquarters

A few exhibits and a 10-minute slide show (shown on request) introduce the monument's history, dinosaurs, and canyons. Staff offer handouts, books, and maps and will answer your questions. Open daily 8 a.m.-4:30 p.m. from Memorial Day to Labor Day weekends, then Mon. to Fri. 8 a.m.-4:30 p.m. the rest of the year; tel. (303) 374-2216; Box 210, Dinosaur, CO 81610. The River Office here handles permits for groups running the Green or Yampa rivers within the monument. A self-guided scenic drive to Harpers Corner begins at the headquarters. Admission to the exhibits and scenic drive is free. You won't see any dinosaur exhibits in this part of the monument—the bones are only at the quarry area. From Vernal, go 35 miles east on US 40 to the Colorado town of Dinosaur, then continue another 2 miles east to the monument headquarters. Dinosaur has a couple of small motels and places to eat.

## Harpers Corner Road

This scenic drive begins at monument headquarters in Colorado and winds north past many scenic overlooks. The road opens in about early May and closes after the first big snowstorm in November. In winter, the road is kept clear to Plug Hat Butte overlook, 4.3 miles in. A booklet available at the Dinosaur Quarry or monument headquarters has good background material on the area and describes the sights at numbered stops along the way. The paved road is 31 miles long (one way); allow about 2 hours for the roundtrip or half a day if you also plan to hike the 2 nature trails. You pass 3 picnic areas along the way, but no water or campgrounds are available. The road climbs a series of ridges with fine views of much of the monument, including Island Park, Echo Park, and canyons of the Green and Yampa. You'll see spectacular faulted and folded rock layers, and a complete range of vegetation, from the cottonwoods along the rivers far below to aspen and firs of the highlands. **Plug Hat Nature Trail** is an easy half-mile loop in a pinyon-juniper forest at a stop 4.3 miles from the beginning of the drive. At Island Park Overlook, about 26 miles along the drive, **Ruple Point Trail** heads west 4 miles (one way) on an old jeep road to an overlook of the Green River in Split Mountain Canyon; carry water. The drive ends at Harpers Corner, a long and narrow peninsula. You can continue one mile on foot to the very tip by taking the **Harpers Corner Trail;** a brochure available at the start describes features visible from numbered stops. Cliffs on each side drop to a bend of the Green River at the beginning of Whirlpool Canyon, about 2,500 feet below. Echo Park, Steamboat Rock, and the sinuous curves of the Yampa River Canyon are visible too. Allow 1½-2 hours for the easy to moderately difficult walk. Binoculars come in handy for a better look at the geology and other features.

## Echo Park

A rough dirt road branches off Harpers Corner Road 25 miles from monument headquarters and winds down more than 2,000 feet in 13 miles to Echo Park. The setting of Echo Park, near the confluence of the Green and Yampa rivers, is one of the prettiest in the monument. The massive sandstone fin of Steamboat Rock looms into the sky across the Green River. Echo Park offers a campground (water in summer; free), river access for boaters (permit needed), and a ranger station (open summer only). Cars with good clearance can often make this side trip, though it's better to have a truck. Like all dirt roads in Dinosaur National Monument, it shouldn't be attempted when wet with any vehicle. The clay surface becomes extremely slick after rains, yet it usually dries out in 2-3 hours. Hikers can follow an unmarked route from Echo Park

*Echo Park, from Harper's Corner Trail*

along the banks of the Yampa River to the mouth of Sand Canyon, go up Sand Canyon until it opens out, cut across benchland to Echo Park Road in lower Pool Creek Canyon, and follow the road back to Echo Park; high water levels of the Yampa can block the route from about late May to late June; you'll need to do some rockscrambling in Sand Canyon. The loop is 6-8 miles long, depending on the route taken.

Drivers with 4WD trucks can also explore the backcountry on Yampa Bench Road, which turns off 8 miles down the Echo Park Road. Yampa Bench Road has views of the Yampa River Canyon and Douglas Mountain to the north and Blue Mountain to the south; allow 4-5 hours to drive the 38 miles between Echo Park Road and US 40. It's always a good idea to get directions and the latest road conditions from a ranger before a backcountry driving trip. Rains occasionally cut off travel, so it's recommended that you carry extra water, food, and camping gear.

## Other Areas

Gates of Lodore, on the Green River, has a campground, a boat launching area for river runners, and a ranger station—all open year-round. The campground has water in summer and is free. **Gates of Lodore Trail** follows the river downstream to the dramatic canyon entrance, an easy 1½-mile roundtrip; get a trail leaflet at the ranger station or the trailhead. Gates of Lodore is 106 miles from monument headquarters via US 40, CO 318, and 10 miles of graded dirt road.

Deerlodge Park Campground at the east end of the monument sits just upstream from the Yampa River Canyon. Camping is primitive, with no designated sites, water, or fee; closed in winter. A ranger station is open in summer. River trips on the Yampa usually begin here. The site is 53 miles from monument headquarters by paved roads.

Rainbow Park and Ruple Ranch are on the west shore of the Green River at opposite ends of Island Park. Both offer primitive campgrounds (no water or fee) and a place to launch or take out river boats. Easiest access is from the quarry area; distances are 26 miles to Rainbow Park and about another 5 miles to Ruple Ranch via the rough and unpaved Island Park Road. Cars with good clearance may be able to drive in, but the road is impassable during wet weather.

## Hiking In The Monument

Any of the trails can easily be done on a day trip. The 2 longest—Jones Hole and Ruple Point trails—are about 8 miles roundtrip and moderately difficult. The Echo Park-Sand Canyon route is also a similar distance. Easier, self-guided nature walks are Red Rock (2 miles roundtrip), Plug Hat (½ mile roundtrip), Harpers Corner (2 miles roundtrip), and Gates of Lodore (1½ miles roundtrip). Each trail is described in the text above (see "North of Vernal," pp. 212-213, for visiting Jones Hole). Overnight trips are possible on the longer trails or on cross-country routes. Off-trail hikers must be able to navigate with map and compass and find (or carry) water, and they should have experience in desert travel over rugged terrain. One possibility is the 3- to 5-day hike from Echo Park to Gates of Lodore; before starting, though, you'll need to find river runners to take you across the Yampa. Obtain the required backcountry permit for overnight hikes from rangers at monument headquarters or at the Dinosaur Quarry.

## River Running

Trips down the Green or Yampa rivers feature outstanding scenery and exciting rapids. All boaters in the monument must have permits or be with a licensed river-running company, even for day trips. A one-day trip on the Green gives a feeling for the river at a modest cost; see "Tours" in the Vernal section, pp. 211-212. The most popular day run begins at Rainbow

*Gates of Lodore*

Park or Ruple Park; you bounce through the rapids of Split Mountain Canyon to take-outs at Split Mountain Campground. Longer trips usually begin on the Green at Gates of Lodore in the north end of the monument. Names of rapids like Upper and Lower Disaster Falls, Harp Rapids, Triplet Falls, and Hells Half Mile in Canyon of Lodore suggest that this isn't a place for inexperienced boatmen. In 1869, John Wesley Powell lost one of his 4 boats and many of the supplies at Disaster Falls on his first expedition. As a result, the rest of the trip was too hurried for making all the scientific studies he had planned. Powell's second trip in 1871 also had trouble when another boat was upset here. Canyon depths reach 3,350 feet, the deepest in the monument. Echo Park marks the end of Canyon of Lodore 19 river miles later. The Yampa River joins the Green here and noticeably increases its size and power. Whirlpool Canyon begins downstream with modest rapids for the next 17 miles, followed by an interlude of slow water at Island Park. The river picks up speed again on entering the warped walls of Split Mountain Canyon and roars through Moonshine, S.O.B., Schoolboy, and Inglesby rapids on the 8 miles to Split Mountain Campground. From here, the Green flows placidly the next 100 miles through open country.

The Yampa remains the last major undammed tributary of the Colorado River system. Snowmelt in the mountains of Colorado and Wyoming swells the Yampa to its highest and best levels from May to mid-July. Most boaters put in at Deerlodge Park at the east end of the monument. The next take-out point is 46 miles downriver at Echo Park. A series of rapids culminates in Warm Springs Rapids, the Yampa's wildest. At times of shallow water, boaters may have difficulties with sandbars and rocks.

Guided river trips are often best for first-time visitors. Contact the monument for a list of river concessioners. Private groups planning a trip on the Green or the Yampa should write far in advance to the River Unit at monument headquarters; the office will let you know about equipment regulations and procedures to obtain the required permits. One-day permits are the easiest to obtain. Contact the River Unit at Box 210, Dinosaur, CO 81610; tel. (303) 374-2468. The *Dinosaur River Guide* by Laura Evans and Buzz Belknap has maps and descriptions of both rivers in the monument.

## VICINITY OF DINOSAUR NATIONAL MONUMENT

### Stewart Lake State Waterfowl Management Area

Birders might want to make a short side trip south of Jensen to visit their feathered friends. Abundant vegetation in the water and on the shore of the shallow lake provides food and shelter for bird life. Take the small paved road south 1.4 miles from Jensen, then keep straight 1.2 miles on a gravel road where the paved road curves right. The road is OK for cars, but is too narrow for large rigs or trailers.

Echo
Park

# SOUTH OF VERNAL

## Ouray National Wildlife Refuge

This desert oasis along the Green River provides a lush habitat for migratory and nesting waterfowl. Other birds and animals also find food and shelter in the brush, grass, marsh, and trees. A list compiled at the refuge names 206 bird species. More than 2,000 pairs of ducks nest in summer. Migratory populations peak in April and again in October. Some mallards and Canada geese winter along the Green River. A self-guided auto tour loops through a variety of habitats on the 11,480-acre refuge. The tour begins at an information booth, which has a brochure and other literature, then follows gravel roads for 9 miles past 12 numbered stops; open daily all year during daylight hours; free; tel. 545-2522 or 789-0351 (Vernal office). An observation tower gives a bird's-eye view of the marshlands. Hiking is permitted (take insect repellent). Some roads may close during spring flooding and autumn hunting; those in the east part of the refuge may require 4WD in wet weather. From Vernal, head southwest 14 miles on US 40, turn south 14 miles on UT 88, then turn into the refuge on a gravel road.

## Pelican Lake

Birds also stop in large numbers at this lake west of Ouray National Wildlife Refuge. The BLM has a campground (no water or fee) and a boat ramp on the south shore. From a junction northwest of the lake, go south on a narrow road (partly paved) that swings around the lake's west side to the campground and boat ramp. The lake has fishing for largemouth bass and bluegill. There's no swimming because of schistosomes (parasitic flatworms) in the water.

## White River

The White has some of the best canoeing in Utah and is good for kayaking and rafting too. The river originates in Colorado's White Mountains and meanders west to meet the Green River near the town of Ouray, Utah. The scenic ride through White River Canyon has only a few rapids, and they're easy. Trips can be a day to a week long, depending on where you put in and take out. Boating provides good opportunities for viewing wildlife. Groves of cottonwoods make pleasant places to camp. The best time to go is during spring runoff, from mid-May to the end of June. No permits are needed—the BLM gives boaters the responsibility of proper boating safety and clean camping. Launch point is at the Bonanza Highway Bridge (40 miles south of Vernal) and take-out is at the Mountain Fuel Bridge, 40 river miles downstream. The shuttle between the 2 bridges is only 20 miles on graded dirt roads. The trip can be extended by putting in at Cowboy Canyon, 9 miles upriver from Bonanza Highway Bridge on a very rough road, or by taking out at the confluence of the White and the Green, 22 miles downriver from the Mountain Fuel Bridge. Both the confluence and Mountain Fuel Bridge take-outs are on Ute Indian land; the tribe requires a permit to park overnight at them or boat through Indian land (below Mountain Fuel Bridge); contact the Ute Indians at Box 190, Fort Duchesne, UT 84026; tel. 722-3941, ext. 308). Bring life jackets, spare paddle, insect repellent, and drinking water. Obtain information and a brochure on this trip from the BLM Vernal District office at 170 S. 500 East, Vernal, UT 84078; tel. 789-1362.

## Other Places

The remote desert country south of Vernal has many sites of geologic or historic interest for those who enjoy exploring back roads. The BLM office in Vernal can suggest places to go. Fantasy Canyon contains eroded sandstone formations; a high-clearance vehicle is needed; contact the BLM for a map. The old Uinta Railway grade from Mack (CO) to the ghost towns of Dragon, Watson, and Rainbow can be driven part way on a rough road. Gilsonite, a natural asphalt mined at these towns, provided the railway with most of its business. The narrow-gauge line operated 1904-39 and had some of the steepest slick track and sharpest curves in the world.

# WEST OF VERNAL

## UINTAH AND OURAY INDIAN RESERVATION

The reservation covers nearly one million acres scattered across the Uinta Basin and south on the East Tavaputs Plateau. A 1987 count of 2,830 tribal members included 3 bands of Ute Indians and some mixed-blood Utes. They guard their lands jealously. Non-members must keep to the main roads on the reservation and purchase permits for most activities. Bottle Hollow Reservoir offers a developed campground, boat ramp, and paved access roads. Camping is also allowed at the backcountry lakes open to fishing; you'll need either a fishing or a camping permit; boats need permits too. Some lakes have boat ramps. A brochure with map and regulations lists fishing areas and fees. Backcountry sites have outhouses and perhaps some tables; bring your own water. Small-game hunting is permitted with a tribal license. You'll need special permission to explore outside the permitted areas. Obtain permits at Bottle Hollow Campground, at sporting goods stores (in Vernal, Price, Salt Lake City, and other towns), or the Ute Indian Tribe Fish & Game Department in Fort Duchesne (Box 190, Fort Duchesne, UT 84026; tel. 722-3941, ext. 308).

### Bottle Hollow Resort

The distinctive architecture of this resort uses triangular elements reminiscent of an Indian teepee. Bottle Hollow Resort includes a tribal museum, motel, restaurant, gift shop, swimming pool, campground, and facilities for boating and fishing. It's located 24 miles southwest of Vernal and 6 miles east of Roosevelt on the south side of US 40. The resort usually closes in winter.

The museum, on the west side of the motel complex, has exhibits of prehistoric artifacts, tribal history, ceremonies, early reservation life, and crafts. Ute crafts on display include moccasins, gloves, beadwork, ceremonial dress, and musical instruments. Open Mon. to Fri. 8:30 a.m.-4 p.m.; donation.

*Ute Indian Chief Sevara and family, ca. 1899*

Motel rooms at the resort cost $25.44 s, $30.74 d; tel. 722-3941, ext. 14. A restaurant serves American food and Indian tacos; open Mon. to Sat. for breakfast, lunch, and dinner. Check the gift shop for Indian art and craft items. **Bottle Hollow Campground** is ½ mile south of the resort on a paved road; sites are usually open March to Nov.; showers and laundry are available. It was closed at press time—you might want to check first with the motel. The campground overlooks 300-acre Bottle Hollow Reservoir, which has fishing for trout and channel catfish; be sure to have tribal fishing and boating permits. There's a boat ramp at the north end.

## Events

The July Fourth **Pow Wow and Rodeo** is the main annual event, with Indian tribes from all over the West participating. Dances, rodeo action, craft displays, and food booths entertain the crowds. Other pow wows, rodeos, and dances happen at different times of the year—ask at Bottle Hollow Resort.

# ROOSEVELT

President Theodore Roosevelt opened the way for settlement of whites on the Uintah and Ouray Indian Reservation by a proclamation in 1902. Three years later, grateful home-steaders named 2 of their new towns in his honor—Theodore (later renamed Duchesne) and Roosevelt. Today Roosevelt (pop. 5,000) is the largest town in Duchesne County and a supply center for surrounding agricultural and oil businesses and for the Ute Indians. Roosevelt offers a good selection of places to stay

and eat along the main highway (200 East and 200 North streets in downtown). The community is 30 miles west of Vernal and 146 miles east of Salt Lake City. Travelers can head north to Moon Lake and the High Uintas Wilderness. A scenic backcountry drive goes south to the many rock art sites in Nine Mile Canyon (see "Nine Mile Canyon" below under "Vicinity of Price").

## Accommodations

In order of increasing price are **Regal Motel** (160 S. 200 East; tel. 722-4878; $20.71 s, $25.07 d); **Western Hills Motel** (737 E. 200 North; tel. 722-4201; $23.93 s, $27.20 d); **Frontier Motel** (75 S. 200 East; tel. 722-2201; $32.70 s, $35.97 d); and **Best Western Inn** (one mile east on US 40; tel. 722-4644 or 1-800-528-1234; $32.70 s, $34.88 d).

## Food

The **Frontier Grill** is a family restaurant open daily for breakfast, lunch, and dinner at 65 S. 200 East, next to the Frontier Motel; tel. 722-3669. **Western Hills Cafe** offers American and Mexican favorites Mon. to Sat. for breakfast, lunch, and dinner; 737 E. 200 North; tel. 722-9225. **Kay's Best Western** is a family-style place open daily for breakfast, lunch, and dinner; located just west of the Best Western Inn (one mile east of downtown); tel. 722-9197. The **Cow Palace** offers steaks in an informal Western setting, open Mon. to Sat. for lunch and dinner; just east of the Best Western Inn (one mile east of downtown); tel. 722-2717. **Pizza Hut** serves pizza daily for lunch and dinner on the east edge of town; tel. 722-4586.

## Events

**Rough Rider Days,** on the 2nd weekend in June, focuses on hunting, fishing, and other outdoor sports. Festivities in the area on July Fourth are the Ute Indian **Pow Wow and Rodeo** at Fort Duchesne and **rodeos** in Neola and Altamont. The **U.B.I.C. (Uintah Basin Industrial Convention)** in early Aug. is Roosevelt's biggest annual event with parades, craft shows, and entertainment.

### Recreation And Services
The **city park** offers picnic tables, playground, and outdoor pool at 90 W. Lagoon; tel. 722-4851. **Roosevelt Golf Course** has 9 holes off W. 200 North; tel. 722-9644. Catch movies at **Roosevelt Twin Theatre** at 21 S. 200 East or **Uinta Theatre** at 41 N. 200 East; tel. 722-2095 for both places. The **post office** is at 81 S. 300 East. **Duchesne County Hospital** is at 250 W. 300 North; tel. 722-4691.

### Information
The **Roosevelt Chamber of Commerce** staff can tell you about points of interest in the area, events, and services; (Box 1417, Roosevelt, UT 84066); tel. 722-4598. Foresters at the **Roosevelt Ranger District** office of the Ashley National Forest know about camping, fishing, hiking, and road conditions on the forest lands north of town, including the High Uintas Wilderness; forest maps, topo maps, and books are sold; open Mon. to Fri. 8 a.m.-noon and 1-5 p.m.; on the west edge of town at 244 W. Hwy. 40 (Box 333-6, Roosevelt, UT 84066); tel. 722-5018. The **public library** is open Mon. to Sat., next to the city park at State and Lagoon; tel. 722-4441.

## VICINITY OF ROOSEVELT

### Ashley National Forest
Moon Lake is in the Uintas about 45 miles due north of Duchesne and 50 miles northwest of Roosevelt. Access roads are paved except for a 7-mile section crossing Indian lands. **Moon Lake Campground** (elev. 8,100 ft.) is open from mid-June to one week after Labor Day with water and a $5 fee. **Moon Lake Resort** offers cabins, boat rentals, store, horseback rides, and guided pack trips from June 1 to Aug. 31; write Mountain Home, UT 84051; tel. 454-3142 (in season). Major access points to the High Uintas Wilderness near Roosevelt are (from west to east): Lake Fork at Moon Lake (3 trails), Center Park at the head of Hells Canyon, Swift Creek on the Yellowstone River (2 trails), Uinta Canyon on the Uinta River, and West Fork of Whiterocks River. In winter,

snowmobilers use trails in the Snake John area north of Whiterocks.

Five campgrounds are located along the Yellowstone River on Forest Routes 119 and 124 northwest of Roosevelt; elevations range from 7,700 feet at **Yellowstone Campground** to 8,100 feet at **Swift Creek Campground;** none of these sites have water or fee.

**Uinta Canyon** and **Wandin** campgrounds and the **U-Bar Ranch** are along the Uinta River at an elevation of about 7,600 feet; take UT 121 and Forest Route 118 north of Roosevelt. The U-Bar Ranch offers cabins, horseback riding, and pack trips from June to Nov.; Box 254, Neola, UT 84053; tel. 722-3560.

The **Pole Creek (Elkhorn) Scenic Loop** on Forest Route 117 winds through canyons and atop ridges east of the Uinta River; some sections may be rough, though the drive is usually passable by cars with good clearance. **Pole Creek Campground** (elev. 10,200 ft.) is at the north end of the loop; no water or fee.

### Big Sand Lake State Park
Fishing attracts most of the visitors at this undeveloped park. The 390-acre reservoir has rainbow trout with some browns and cutthroats and lots of crayfish. People also come to water-ski and swim. Ice fishermen try their luck in winter. A boat ramp is on the southeast shore. No water or other services are available; free admission. The park ranger is based at Starvation State Park near Duchesne; tel. 738-2326. From Roosevelt, go southwest 5 miles on US 40, turn west (then north) 10 miles to Upalco, continue straight (north) 0.7 mile where the main road curves left just past Upalco, then turn left 0.4 mile on a gravel road.

## DUCHESNE

This small community, located at the confluence of the Duchesne and Strawberry rivers, is the seat of thinly settled Duchesne ("doo-SHAYN") County. The name honors a French Catholic nun. Ranching, farming, and the oil industry provide most of the employment. Main attractions for visitors are the High

Uintas Wilderness and other sections of the Ashley National Forest, Starvation Lake, and fishing on the Duchesne and Strawberry rivers.

## Practicalities

Stay at the **Mission Motel** (15 W. Main; tel. 738-2217; $21.80 s, $26.16 d) or **Unique Inn** (220 E. Main; tel. 738-2433; $29.38 s or d). **Frostop Drive-In & Cafe** at 516 W. Main serves breakfast, lunch, and dinner daily except Sunday. **Ann's Cafe** and **Cowan's Cafe** on E. Main serve breakfast, lunch, and dinner daily. For steaks, try the **El Cid Steak House** (339 W. Main; tel. 738-5540) or **Well's Club** (47 E. Main; tel. 738-9693). The **city park** at Main and 200 West has picnic tables, playground, and an outdoor pool (tel. 738-9688). The **Duchesne County Fair** in Aug. features a rodeo, parade, horse show, and other entertainment. People at the **Duchesne Ranger District** office of the Ashley National Forest have information on campgrounds, trailheads, and road conditions of the forest and the High Uintas Wilderness to the north and the Tavaputs Plateau to the south; forest maps, topo maps, and some books are sold; open Mon. to Fri. 8 a.m.-6 p.m. and Sat. 8 a.m.-4:30 p.m. from Memorial Day to Oct. 1, then Mon. to Fri. 8 a.m.-5 p.m.; located at 85 W. Main (Box I, Duchesne, UT 84021); tel. 738-2482.

# VICINITY OF DUCHESNE

## Uinta Mountains

Forest Route 144 turns north from Stockmore off UT 35, then follows the Duchesne River North Fork to **Aspen Grove Campground** (elev. 7,000 ft.), **Hades Campground** (elev. 7,100 ft.), and **Iron Mine Campground** (elev. 7,200 ft.). All 3 campgrounds have water and a $4-6 fee from Memorial Day to one week after Labor Day; Iron Mine Campground also has a group reservation area. **Defa's Ranch**, between Hades and Iron Mine campgrounds, offers cabins ($16 s, $18 d), a cafe (breakfast, lunch, and dinner), RV park, horseback riding, and pack trips; open May to Nov.; Hanna, UT

84031; tel. 848-5590. Forest Route 315 turns east from Defa's Ranch to Grandview Trailhead, an access point for the southwestern part of the High Uintas Wilderness; the grade is steep and rough, though cars with good clearance can make it in dry weather.

The Rock Creek area and the new Upper Stillwater Reservoir are reached by going north from Duchesne on UT 87, turning north to Mountain Home, then west on Forest Route 134. The road is paved to the reservoir. **Miner's Gulch Campground** is at an elevation of 7,500 feet; no water or charge. **Yellow Pine Campground** nearby (elev. 7,600 ft.) has developed sites with water from Memorial Day to one week after Labor Day; $5-8, $15 for group reservation sites. **South Fork Campground** (elev. 7,900 ft.) lies just south of Upper Stillwater Reservoir; sites are open from Memorial Day to one week after Labor Day; no charge. Rock Creek Trailhead near the reservoir leads into the High Uintas Wilderness.

## Starvation State Park

The large Starvation Reservoir sits among rolling hills of high-desert country 4 miles west of Duchesne. Water-skiing is the biggest summer activity, followed by fishing, windsurfing, and sailing. Fishermen catch walleye (a state record was taken here), smallmouth bass, and some largemouth bass and German brown trout. The marina is open mid-April to Labor Day with boat rentals (fishing, jet ski, wave cutters, and ski boats), and store. A developed campground overlooking the water has pull-through and tent sites with showers. This exposed location can be windy. A picnic area near a sand beach is past the campground turnoff. Other facilities are a paved boat ramp, fish-cleaning station, and dump station. The park is open all year. The main season, between Memorial Day and Labor Day weekends, is sometimes extended up to a month earlier and later; $3 day use or $5-8 camping; tel. 738-2326 or (800) 322-3770 (reservations). The campground nearly always has room except on major holiday weekends. Showers and restrooms close during the off-season, though outhouses are available. A paved 4-mile road to the park turns off US 40 just west of Duchesne. Address is Box 584, Duchesne, UT 84021.

### Over The Mountains To Price

From Duchesne, US 191 goes southwest 56 miles over the West Tavaputs Plateau to Price. The route follows the Left Fork of Indian Canyon to a pass at an elevation of 9,100 feet, then descends through Willow Creek Canyon to the Price River. Snow may close the road in winter. **Avintaquin Campground** (elev. 8,800 ft.) is reached by a short gravel road from just south of the pass; sites in a fir and aspen forest have water from Memorial Day to one week after Labor Day; $4; there's also a group reservation area. The Bamberger Monument, between the pass and Price Canyon, commemorates construction of the highway by state prisoners in 1919; Governor Simon Bamberger gave the workers reduced sentences and other benefits for their efforts.

# PRICE

In the beginning, Price was a typical Mormon community. Ranchers and farmers had settled on the fertile land surrounding the Price River in 1879. Four years later, everything changed when the railroad came through. A flood of immigrants from all over the world arrived to work in the coal mines and other rapidly growing enterprises. (An informal census taken in a pool hall at nearby Helper in the 1930s found 32 different nationalities in the room!) Coal mining has had its ups and downs in the last 100 years, but it continues to be the largest industry in the area. Price (pop. 10,000) is a modern city and a good base for exploring the surrounding mountains and desert. The highly recommended Prehistoric Museum and the Price Mural are in town and the Western Mining & Railroad Museum is in Helper to the north. Other places to visit lie tucked into the surrounding backcountry and include Nine Mile Canyon (rock art and historic sites), Cleveland-Lloyd Dinosaur Quarry, San Rafael Swell, and many ghost-town sites. Roads wind up canyons to the cool forests and lakes on the Wasatch Plateau. Information and maps for Carbon and Emery counties can be obtained at the Castle Country Travel Office (see "Information" below). A walking tour leaflet available at the office describes historic buildings in Price.

## SIGHTS

### Prehistoric Museum

Excellent exhibits of the creatures and people that lived in prehistoric Utah fill the rooms.

Dramatic dinosaur displays include a fierce flesh-eating allosaurus, a plant-eating camptosaurus (not to be fooled with either), and a stegosaurus. A complete dinosaur egg is one of the few ever found. Mineralogy exhibits have colorful gemstones. The outstanding Indian collection has artifacts of prehistoric Anasazi and Fremont and the modern Ute, Paiute, and Navajo Indians. The power and mystery of prehistoric rock art is conveyed in a replica of the Barrier Canyon mural. Modern art can be seen too, in rotating exhibits. Kids can explore the hands-on displays in the Children's Room. The College of Eastern Utah operates the museum, open Mon. to Sat. (also Sun. in spring and summer) 10 a.m.-5 p.m.; summer hours may be extended; $1 adult or $2 family. Regional and natural history books, fossils, T-shirts, and postcards are sold. Located at 155 E. Main; tel. 637-5060.

### Price Mural

Artist Lynn Fausett captured the history of Price and Carbon County in a colorful mural 4 feet high and 200 feet long. It extends around all 4 walls in the foyer of the Price Municipal Building (enter from the east side). Ahead, as you walk in, are the first settlers, Abram Powell and Caleb Rhodes. Follow the panels around to the right, past scenes of railroad workers, freight wagons, the first town hall in Price, religious leaders, the 1911 Fourth of July parade, and depictions of coal-mining industries. A brochure available here gives details for each scene and identifies the self-portrait of the artist as a small boy. Fausett, a native of

*a prehistoric petroglyph*

the area, used his own recollections and old photos for the project, on which he worked from 1938 to 1941. He also painted the Barrier Canyon mural replica in the Prehistoric Museum and *The Pioneer Trek* at This Is The Place Monument near Salt Lake City. Open Mon. to Fri. 8 a.m.-5 p.m.; free; located at the corner of Main and 200 East.

### College Of Eastern Utah (CEU)

The 2-year community college began as Carbon Junior College in 1938 and took its present name in 1965. CEU's current enrollment of about 1,400 students meets on a 4-quarter system. Most of the facilities, cultural activities, and sporting events are open to the public. The Division of Continuing Education offers a varied program of evening classes. Gallery East hosts state and national art exhibits during the fall to spring quarters in Room C-109 of Main Building; exhibits change monthly. You'll find the bookstore, snack bar,

cafeteria, and formal dining room in the Student Activities Center. A variety of concerts, plays, choirs, and ballets takes place on campus; call public relations at 637-2120 (ext. 288) for the schedule. The library has a good collection that includes a set of topo maps covering Utah; located in the Learning Resource Center in the middle of campus. River expeditions organized by the college run the Green and Colorado rivers with an educational emphasis; they're open to the public too; contact Wilderness Director Lee Johnson at 637-2120, ext. 236. Sporting events include football, basketball, baseball, and swimming; call 637-1300 for the schedule. The Bunnell-Dimitrich Athletic Center (BDAC) has an exercise room, outdoor track, and facilities for racquetball, handball, basketball, and volleyball; tel. 637-1300. The College of Eastern Utah is at 451 E. 400 North, Price, UT 84501.

## PRACTICALITIES

### Accommodations

In order of increasing costs are **Greenwell Motel** (655 E. Main.; tel. 637-3520; $20.71 s, $25.07 d and up; pool); **Crest Motel** (625 E. Main; tel. 637-1532; $21.70 s, $26.16 d); **El Rancho Siesta Motel and RV Park** (W. Main and 145 N. Carbonville Rd.; tel. 637-2424; $23.98 s, $28.34 d; RVers pay $13.08 w/ hookups; pool); **Carriage House Inn** (590 E. Main; tel. 637-5660 or 800-228-5732 in Utah; $30.47 s, $39.19 d; indoor pool and jacuzzi); **Mr. Sleep** (641 W. Price River Dr.; tel. 637-7000; $32.65 s, $38.10 d); **Days Inn** (838 Westwood Blvd.; tel. 637-8880; $49.05 s, $55.59 d and up; indoor pool, sauna, and jacuzzi).

**Balance Rock Motel** is an older place in a quiet canyon just north of Helper (7 miles north of Price); tel. 472-9942; $21.80 s, $26 d. **Comfort Inn and RV Park** is in the town of Wellington, 7 miles to the southeast; tel. 637-7980 or (800) 228-5150; $35.97 s, $43.60 d; has an indoor pool; RVers stay for $13.72 w/hookups; a restaurant is open daily for breakfast, lunch, and dinner.

## Food

For standard American meals, try **Farlaino's Cafe** (87 W. Main; open Mon. to Sat. for breakfast and lunch); **Mecca Cafe** (71 W. Main; open Mon. to Sat. for breakfast, lunch, and dinner); and **Century Cafe** (57 W. Main; open Mon. to Sat. for breakfast, lunch, and dinner). The **Coffee Shope** is a popular breakfast spot; one block north on Carbonville Road from W. Main; open 24 hours daily; tel. 637-7154. The **Crest Cafe** claims to have the best omelets in town at 601 E. Main; open Mon. to Fri. for breakfast and lunch; tel. 637-0843. **Kay's Restaurant** serves American food at 655 E. Main; open daily for breakfast, lunch, and dinner; tel. 637-1989. **Mandy's Family Restaurant** is an informal place for steak, seafood, chicken, and sandwiches at 1253 E. Main in Castle Rock Square; open daily for lunch and dinner; tel. 637-1111. **Country Kitchen** offers varied fare including steak, prime rib, seafood, and pasta at the Days Inn just west of town; open daily for breakfast, lunch, and dinner; tel. 637-8880. Some people say that the **Matador Steak House** has the best steaks in town; 355 E. Main; open Mon. to Sat. for dinner; tel. 637-9959.

The **Greek Streak** specializes in Greek foods at 30 W. 100 South; open Mon. to Sat. for breakfast, lunch, and dinner; tel. 637-1930. **China City Cafe** features a good selection of Chinese and American items at 350 E. Main; open daily for lunch and dinner; tel. 637-8211. **Julio's** brings south-of-the-border flavor to town at 19 S. Carbon Ave.; open Tues. to Sat. for lunch and dinner; tel. 637-6545. Pick up pizza at **Pizza Hut** on the east edge of town; open daily for lunch and dinner; tel. 637-6410. **Castle Rock Cafe and Pizza Deli,** on the west edge of town in Creekview Shopping Center, is open daily for breakfast, lunch, and dinner; tel. 637-6907).

## Entertainment And Events

Catch movies at the **King Coal Theaters 3** (1171 E. Main); **Price Theatre** (30 E. Main); or **Crown Theatre** (30 W. Main); call 637-1705 for recorded information. The **State Quarter Horse Show** is held in May at the Carbon County Fairgrounds west of town. **Helper Outlaw Day** takes place in June at Helper with games, food, and car show. **Black Diamond Stampede Rodeo** provides plenty of action in June. A **Demolition Derby** is also held in June. The **Greek Festival** in July features music, dancing, food, and tours of the Greek church. Wellington's **Pioneer Day** (July 24) festivities include a parade, rodeo, games, and food. **International Days and Carbon County Fair** in Aug. celebrate the area's ethnic diversity with a parade, rodeo, agricultural exhibits, entertainment, contests, and food.

## Services

For **emergencies** (police, fire, paramedic), call 911. The **post office** is at the corner of Carbon Ave. and 100 South; tel. 637-1638. **Castleview Hospital** is at 300 N. Hospital Dr. on the west edge of town; tel. 637-4800. **Gart Bros. Sporting Goods** has camping and fishing gear in the Creekview Shopping Center on the west edge of town; tel. 637-2077.

## Recreation

**Washington Park** has picnic areas, playground, indoor swimming pool, Desert Wave pool, tennis, volleyball, basketball, and horseshoe courts at 250 E. 500 North; tel. 637-1755. Two historic log cabins dating from the 1880s and a fitness track are across to the north in **Pioneer Park**. **South Price Park** offers a picnic area and tennis courts at 400 South and 100 East. **Carbon Country Club Golf Course** has 9 holes; located 4 miles north of town on US 6/191; tel. 637-9949.

## Information

**Castle Country Travel Office** offers literature and ideas for travel in Price and elsewhere in Carbon and Emery counties; open Mon. to Fri. 9 a.m.-5 p.m. in the Prehistoric Museum at 155 E. Main (Box 1037, Price, UT 84501); tel. 637-3009. **Manti-LaSal National Forest** offices have information about recreation in the beautiful alpine country of the Wasatch Plateau to the west; all the Utah forest maps and some regional books are sold; open Mon. to

Fri. 7:45 a.m.-4:30 p.m. in the Creekview Shopping Center on the west edge of town (599 W. Price River Dr., Price, UT 84501); tel. 637-2817. The **Bureau of Land Management** has the Price River Resource Area and San Rafael Resource Area offices in Price; staff can tell you about exploring the San Rafael Swell, Cleveland-Lloyd Dinosaur Quarry, and Nine Mile Canyon, and about boating the Green River through Desolation, Gray, and Labyrinth canyons; land-use maps are sold; open Mon. to Fri. 7:45 a.m.-4:30 p.m.; both offices have the same address and phone number: corner of 900 North and 700 East (Price, UT 84501); tel. 637-4584. **Price City Library** is next to the Price Municipal Building at 159 E. Main; open Mon. to Fri. in summer and Mon. to Sat. the rest of the year; tel. 637-0744. Bookstores in town include **Serendipity** (95 E. Main; tel. 637-5433); **Walton Books** (1187 E. Main; tel. 637-8640); and the **Eagle's Nest Paperback Exchange** (69 W. Main; tel. 637-5510).

**Transport**
**Greyhound** buses go daily west to Salt Lake City and east to Denver from the stop at Yogurt Express, 590 E. Main; tel. 637-3457. **Amtrak** trains stop in nearby Helper on their runs between Denver and Salt Lake City; tel. (800) 872-7245.

# NORTH OF PRICE

## HELPER

In 1883, the Denver & Rio Grande Western Railroad began a depot, roundhouse, and other facilities here for their new line. Trains heading up the long grade to Soldier Summit needed extra locomotives or "helpers" based at the little railroad community, so the place became known as Helper. Miners later joined the railmen, and the 2 groups still make up most of the current population of 2,800. The fine examples of early 20th C. commercial and residential buildings in downtown Helper have earned its designation as a national historic site. The local economy has suffered downturns by unemployment in the coal industry, reflected by the many vacant structures awaiting new owners. The Western Mining & Railroad Museum offers a look into the past of Helper and surrounding mining towns. Helper is at the entrance to Price Canyon, 7 miles north of Price.

### Practicalities
The old hotels and motels downtown may or may not be open. The **Balance Rock Motel** just north of town has rooms at $21.80 s, $26 d; tel. 472-9942. Places to eat include **Old Time Pies** (202 S. Main) and **Jimbo's Steak House** (330 S. Main). The **city park** has shaded picnic tables, playground, outdoor pool, tennis courts, and a ballpark east across the Price River. **Post office** is at 45 S. Main. The **public library** is open weekday afternoons at 19 S. Main. The **Amtrak train station** is downtown off Main.

### Western Mining And Railroad Museum
A venerable red caboose and examples of coal-mining machinery sit outside next to the museum. Inside, you'll see 2 elaborate model railroad sets and photos of old steam locomotives in action. A mine room has models of coal mines (all are underground in this area) and equipment worn by the miners. Other exhibits illustrate 2 great mine disasters of Utah, the 1900 Scofield tragedy in which 200 men and boys died, and the 1924 Castle Gate explosion that killed 173. Other bits of history include ghost town memorabilia, a Butch Cassidy exhibit, and a dentist's office. Video programs illustrate the area's mine and railroad history. The brick building housing the museum dates from about 1914 when it was the Hotel Helper; from 1942 to 1982 it served as

a YMCA for railroad men. Open Mon. to Sat. 9 a.m.-5 p.m. from mid-May to the end of Sept.; donation; tel. 472-3009. It may also be possible to visit on other days; call the phone number posted on the front door. Located in downtown Helper at 296 S. Main.

## Ghost Towns

Many coal-mining communities have bloomed and died in surrounding canyons and hillsides. Most have fared poorly since they were abandoned, yet their picturesque ruins can be worth seeking out. The mines and decaying buildings are dangerous and shouldn't be entered. One former company town has survived intact. Kenilworth's residents bought their houses at low prices when the mines closed and have continued to live here; the large company store, however, now stands vacant; follow Helper's Main St. a short way south, then turn left (east) 3.8 miles on paved UT 157. See the books *Utah Ghost Towns* by Stephen Carr and *Some Dreams Die* by George Thompson for histories and locations of the towns that have faded away.

## Spring Canyon

Some of the best and most easily visited "ghosts" lie along a paved road up scenic Spring Canyon. The road begins as "Canyon Street" in east Helper (across US 6/191 from downtown Helper). You'll see railroad grades, mines, and ruins along much of the road's 6.7 miles. Sagebrush hides most of the Peerless ghost town site, 2.8 miles in. Only foundations and a few buildings survive of this community, which peaked in the 1920s and '30s with a population of about 300, then died in the '50s. A tramway brought coal down from the mine high on the hillside. Spring Canyon is a total ghost; only a loading platform remains of a community that had up to 1,000 people during the '20s, '30s, and '40s. The site is near a junction 3.8 miles in; keep straight at the junction (the road to the right is still used by mining companies and is gated). A large concrete loading facility on the right greets you on arrival at Standardville, 4.9 miles in. The formerly attractive, well-planned community

had a population of 550 during its best years and was the "standard" for other mining towns. Mines nearby operated from 1912 until 1950. A ghostly 2-story stone building, once the Liberty Fuel Company offices, marks the site of Latuda, 5.9 miles in. Several hundred people lived here from about 1920 to 1950; Latuda died completely in the late 1960s. Extensive ruins of the mine can be seen on the slopes to the left. A wooden change house is on the right in Rains, but only foundations remain from the town of 500; located 6.5 miles from Helper. A large stone ruin, once a store, stands at the site of Mutual, just beyond Rains. Most of the 250 or so residents lived to the north along a fork of Spring Canyon. You may have to park at a gate and walk a short distance on the road to Mutual.

## Price Canyon Recreation Area

This pleasant spot in the woods makes a good stopping place for a picnic or a camp. From the turnoff 8.2 miles north of Helper, follow a narrow paved road 3 miles to the picnic area (free day use), a canyon overlook, and the campground (elev. 8,000 ft.). The camping area has water from Memorial Day to late Oct. and a $4 fee. **Bristlecone Ridge Trail** begins at the far end of the campground loop and winds through a forest of Gambel oak, ponderosa pine, and mountain mahogany to a ridgetop. Grand views from the top take in surrounding mountains and Price and Crandall canyons below. The moderately difficult hike is about 2 miles roundtrip with an elevation gain of 700 feet. Bristlecone pines and lots of chipmunks live on the ridge.

## Scofield State Park

The 3,000-acre reservoir lies in a broad mountain valley at an elevation of 7,600 feet. Fishermen go after rainbow and cutthroat trout and crayfish. Water-skiers and boaters have lots of room to roam. The main campground is on the east shore with a picnic area, showers, dump station, boat ramp, docks, and fish-cleaning station. The North Unit on the northwest side of the lake offers picnic and camping areas near a boat ramp and dock; no water or electricity. A primitive camping area is near the turnoff for the North Unit. The lake is accessible all year, though the park closes down about Thanksgiving; restrooms and showers are open about May to October. In winter, Scofield Reservoir has excellent ice fishing. The State Division of Parks and Recreation grooms snowmobile trails nearby at Pond-Town Canyon (west side of the lake 4 miles north of the town of Scofield) and Left Fork of Whiteriver (near Soldier Summit). Cross-country skiing in the area is good too, though no facilities or trails have been developed. Entrance fees are $3 day use or $5-8 camping; Box 166, Price, UT 84501; tel. 448-9449 during the season, 637-8497 in winter; (800) 322-3770 for reservations. The park nearly always has room except during major summer holidays. **Singleton's Boat Camp,** on the east shore near the main campground, offers a snack bar, small store, and boat rentals on summer weekends. From Price, drive 23 miles north on US 6, then turn left 13 miles on UT 96. Other approaches are from Provo (66 miles) via Soldier Summit or from UT 31 where it crosses the Wasatch Plateau to the south.

### Scofield

Two coal mines operate near this tiny mining town south of Scofield Reservoir. Production began in 1879 and peaked about 1920, when the town had a population of nearly 2,000. Utah's worst mining disaster took place nearby on May 1, 1900, at the Winter Quarters Mine, where about 200 men and boys perished in an explosion of coal dust. Weathered tombstones in the cemetery on the hill east of town still give testimony to the tragedy. A paved road continues south and west from Scofield to UT 31 on the Wasatch Plateau.

### Fish Creek

The forest lands surrounding Scofield have plenty of places for dispersed camping. The

*victims of the mine disaster, Scofield, 1900*

small **Fish Creek Campground** west of the lake has water from about mid-June to mid-Sept.; free. This is also the start of the **Fish Creek National Recreation Trail.** From Scofield, go northwest 3.7 miles on a partly paved road, then turn left 1.5 miles at a fork up Fish Creek Valley. This last section of road is slippery when wet and may be too rough for cars at any time. The easy trail follows the creek through meadows and forests of aspen and evergreens. This is a good area to look for wildlife, including moose, elk, mule deer, black bear, mountain lion, bobcat, and beaver. Fishermen will find many places to cast a line; special fishing regulations (posted) apply in upper Fish Creek. The trail is good for both day and overnight hikes; Skyline Drive is 13 miles upstream.

# EAST OF PRICE

Aside from a few ranches and coal mines, the rugged canyon country of the West Tavaputs Plateau remains largely a wilderness. Two especially good areas to visit here are Nine Mile Canyon (accessible by car) and Desolation and Gray canyons of the Green River (accessible by raft or kayak). Adventurous drivers with high-clearance vehicles can explore other places too; ask the BLM staff in Price about the backcountry roads.

## Nine Mile Canyon

A drive through this scenic canyon takes the visitor back in time to when Fremont Indians lived and farmed here, about 900 years ago. Although their pithouse dwellings can be difficult for a non-archaeologist to spot, the granaries and striking rock art stand out clearly. The canyon is especially noted for its abundant petroglyphs and smaller numbers of pictographs. You'll also see several ranches and the ghost town of Harper. Obtain a brochure for Nine Mile Canyon in Price from the Castle Country Tourist Office, Prehistoric Museum, or the BLM offices. The Roosevelt Chamber of Commerce has a less detailed brochure. Nine Mile Canyon is actually more than 40 miles long; the origin of its misleading name is unclear. The drive is about 120 miles roundtrip from Price and takes most of a day. Another approach is from near Myton in the Uinta Basin via Wells Draw and Gate Canyon. All these roads can be negotiated when dry by cars with good clearance; Gate Canyon is the roughest section and may be impassable after storms. In the late 1800s and early 1900s, these roads through Nine Mile Canyon formed the main highway between Vernal and the rest of Utah. Today the distances and dusty roads may discourage the more casual traveler. This region is also fairly remote with no services; bring water, lunch, and a full tank of gas. From Price, drive 10 miles southeast (3 miles past Wellington) on US 6/191 and turn north on 2200 East (Soldier Creek Road) at a sign for Nine Mile Canyon. The road passes

Soldier Creek Coal Mine after 13 miles (pavement ends), continues climbing to an aspen-forested pass, then drops into Nine Mile Canyon. Turnoff for the northern approach from US 40 is 1.5 miles west of Myton.

## Desolation And Gray Canyons Of The Green River

The Green River leaves the Uinta Basin and slices deeply through the Tavaputs Plateau, emerging 95 miles downstream near the town of Green River. River runners enjoy the canyon scenery, hikes up side canyons, a chance to see wildlife, and visits to Fremont rock art

*Gunnison Butte overlooking lower Gray Canyon*

sites. John Wesley Powell named the canyons in 1869, designating the lower 36 miles as Gray Canyon. Boaters usually start at Sand Wash, site of a ferry from the early 1920s to 1952; a 42-mile road (36 miles are unpaved) south from Myton is the best way in; another road turns east from Gate Canyon near Nine Mile Canyon. Some people save the long 200-mile car shuttle by flying from the town of Green River to an airstrip on a mesa top above Sand Wash. Swasey Rapids, north of the town of Green River is the most common take-out point. The last part of Gray Canyon, between Nefertiti and Swasey rapids, is a good day trip;

see "Vicinity of Green River," p. 347. Although not as difficult as Cataract Canyon, Desolation and Gray canyons do have about 60 rapids and riffles. Some are Class III and require river-running experience. Rafts and kayaks are used. Contact the BLM Price River Resource Area office in Price for information and the required permits; open Mon. to Fri. 7:45 a.m.-4:30 p.m.; corner of 900 North and 700 East (Price, UT 84501); tel. 637-4584. Commercial trips go through the canyons; the BLM can give you names of the companies. The *Desolation River Guide* by Laura Evans and Buzz Belknap has maps and descriptions.

# SOUTH OF PRICE

## CLEVELAND-LLOYD DINOSAUR QUARRY

You can learn more about dinosaurs and see their bones in an excavation here in the desert, 30 miles south of Price. Dinosaurs stalked this land about 147 million years ago, when it had a wetter and warmer climate. Mud in a lake bottom trapped some of the animals and preserved their bones. The mud layer, which later became rock of the Morrison Formation, has yielded more than 12,000 bones of at least 14 different dinosaur species at this site. Local ranchers discovered the bones, then interested the University of Utah in beginning their digs in 1928. Princeton University and Brigham Young University, which currently does excavations, also have participated in the quarry work.

### Visitor Center
The BLM has built the visitor center, quarry exhibits, nature trail, and picnic sites here. Inside the visitor center, you'll see exhibits of the dinosaur family tree, techniques of excavating and assembling dinosaur skeletons, and local flora and fauna. A fierce allosaurus skeleton cast gazes down on you. Related books, postcards, and posters can be pur-

chased. The enclosed dinosaur quarry, about 100 yards behind the visitor center, contains excavation tools and exposed bones of the allosaurus, stegosaurus, camptosaurus, and camarasaurus. **Rock Walk Nature Trail** begins outside; a brochure available at the start explains about geology, dinosaurs, uranium mining, and the ecology at numbered stops; allow 45 minutes. Usually the quarry can be visited from 10 a.m.-5 p.m. on weekends beginning at Easter, then Thurs. to Mon. from Memorial Day to Labor Day weekends; free admission; tel. 637-4584. The drive in is on graded dirt roads, though rains occasionally close them. From Price, drive south 13 miles on UT 10 and turn left 17 miles on UT 155 and unpaved roads. From Huntington, go northeast 2 miles on UT 10 and turn right 20 miles on UT 155 and unpaved roads. Signs at the turnoffs from UT 10 indicate the days and hours the quarry is open. If it's closed, there's nothing to see. Visitors are not allowed to collect dinosaur bones at the quarry or on other public lands; bones are of greater scientific value when researchers can examine them in place.

### Humbug Overlook Driving Tour
A brochure available at the visitor center describes the plants and animals living in this

desert country. The drive begins at the quarry and goes southeast 7 miles to the rim of Humbug Canyon. Cars with good clearance can negotiate the road in dry weather. The **Jump Trail** winds from the viewpoint down to the canyon floor, about ½ mile one way. Curious erosional forms, known as hoodoos, appear on the canyon walls.

### Cedar Mountain Driving Tour

The overlook atop Cedar Mountain has a great panorama to the south across the gently curved dome of the San Rafael Swell and the many canyons cutting into it. Distant ranges include the Wasatch Plateau (west), Thousand Lake Mountains (southwest), Henry Mountains (south), and the Rockies (in Colorado to the east). A picnic area is at the second overlook at the end of the drive. **Fossil Ledge Nature Trail** makes a ¼-mile loop from the picnic area. Distances to the second overlook are 39 miles from Price, 27 miles from Huntington, or 25 miles from Cleveland-Lloyd Dinosaur Quarry. A graded dirt road climbs about 2,000 feet in elevation through woodlands of juniper, pinyon pine, and ponderosa pine. Cars can easily drive the road in dry weather. A brochure describing points of interest along the way is available from the quarry visitor center or the BLM office in Price.

## EXPLORING THE SAN RAFAEL SWELL (NORTHERN HALF)

About 65 million years ago, immense underground forces pushed rock layers into a dome about 80 miles long (north to south) and 30 miles wide. Erosion has exposed the colorful layers and cut deep canyons. I-70 divides the swell into roughly equal north and south halves. In the north, a 29-mile scenic drive, passable by cars in dry weather, branches off the road to Cedar Mountain and goes south past the Wedge Overlook, descends through Buckhorn Wash, crosses the San Rafael River, then winds across desert to I-70. Much of the San Rafael Swell remains wild and remote. Six sections of it are being considered for wilderness designation. The BLM San Rafael Resource Area office in Price has information about travel and wilderness status in this unique land; office is at the corner of 900 North and 700 East (Price, UT 84501); tel. 637-4584. Good books for travel and historical background in this little-known region are *Hiking Utah's San Rafael Swell* by Michael Kelsey and *Utah's Scenic San Rafael* by Owen McClenahan; Kelsey's book emphasizes history and hiking, while McClenahan's

*San Rafael River from Wedge Overlook*

book mostly describes driving tours (about half of which can be done by car).

## Wedge Overlook

An inspiring panorama takes in surrounding mountains and canyons and the 1,000-foot sheer drop into the "Little Grand Canyon." Rain and snowmelt on the Wasatch Plateau feed tributaries of the San Rafael River, which has cut this deep canyon through the San Rafael Swell. Downstream from the Little Grand Canyon, the river plunges through narrow canyons of the Black Boxes and flows across the San Rafael Desert to join the Green River. The signed turnoff for Wedge Overlook is on the way to the San Rafael Bridge and Campground; see the Utah Travel Council's Northeastern Utah map for the different approaches from Price (23 miles), Huntington (15 miles), and Castle Dale (13 miles). Drive in 6.6 miles from the turnoff, keeping left at a fork near the beginning, to the first overlook, then continue to the left 0.9 mile for the best views at the end of the road. This area is fine for picnicking or camping; no water or facilities. Walk along the rim for other views.

## San Rafael Campground

Continue 12 miles past the Wedge Overlook turnoff to the bridge and campground at the San Rafael River. The road descends into the main canyon via pretty Buckhorn Wash and crosses the bridge to the camping area. The cottonwood trees at the campground mysteriously died, giving the area a bleak appearance. Tables and outhouses are provided; water may be available, but it's safer to bring your own. From here the road continues south 20 miles to I-70 at Exit 129.

## Floating The Little Grand Canyon

The 15-mile trip through this canyon provides one of the best ways to enjoy the scenery. The swift waters have a few riffles and small sand waves, but no rapids. Canoes, kayaks, and rafts can do the excursion in 5-6 hours with higher spring flows. An overnight trip will allow

*San Rafael River, just above the campground*

more time to explore side canyons. Best boating conditions occur during the spring runoff in May and June. Some people float through with inner tubes later in the summer. Life jackets should always be worn. No permits are needed for boating; the BLM in Price can advise on river flows and road conditions. Put-in is at Fuller's Bottom; the turnoff is near the Wedge Overlook turnoff, then 5.4 miles to the river. Take-out is at the San Rafael Campground. Extremely dangerous rapids and waterfalls lie downstream of the campground in the Black Boxes; *don't* attempt these sections unless you really know what you're doing! Hikers can explore the canyons above and below the campground on day and overnight trips; autumn has the best temperatures and lowest water levels; wear shoes suitable for wading.

# CASTLE VALLEY TOWNS

High cliffs of the Wasatch Plateau rise fortress-like on the west above the valley. Perennial streams flowing down the canyons enabled farmers to transform the desert into verdant orchards and fields of crops. Mormon pioneers didn't settle this side of the Wasatch Plateau until the 1870s, long after valleys on the other side of the plateau had been colonized. Water and good land began to run short by the time of the second generation of settlers, and many turned to jobs in nearby coal mines. Roads up the canyons lead to lakes and pretty alpine country.

## HUNTINGTON

This small town at the mouth of Huntington Canyon dates from 1878 and has a population of 2,800. **Village Inn Motel** is at 310 S. Main; tel. 687-9888; rooms cost $26.71 s, $32.16 d. The **Lunch Box** has pizza and sandwiches at 165 S. Main. **Canyon Rim Cafe** offers similar fast food on the north edge of town. **The Old Homestead** serves home-style cooking ½ mile north of town; open Mon. to Sat. for breakfast and lunch; tel. 687-2671. The community celebrates **Heritage Days** with a parade and fireworks on July Fourth. Travelers can turn west from town on paved UT 31 and soon be in the cool forests and meadows of the Wasatch Plateau or, by heading east, visit the Cleveland-Lloyd Dinosaur Quarry and the San Rafael Swell.

### Huntington State Park

The 250-acre Huntington Reservoir is a popular destination for picnicking, camping, swimming, fishing, and water-skiing. Lots of grass and shade trees and a swimming beach make the park especially enjoyable in summer. Boaters can use the boat ramp and docks. Fishermen catch mostly largemouth bass and bluegill and some trout; crayfishing is good. The campground is open with showers from March to October. Reservations are a good idea for summer weekends. In winter, the park is open for ice skating and ice fishing. Fees are $3 day use or $8 camping; Box 1343, Huntington, UT 84528; tel. 687-2491 or (800) 322-3770 (reservations). Located one mile north of town on UT 10.

### Huntington Canyon

Highway UT 31 turns west up the canyon from the north edge of town. The giant Huntington power plant looks out of place in the agrarian landscape of the lower canyon. Beyond the power plant, **Bear Creek Campground** offers sites shaded by cottonwoods on the left near Milepost 39 (8.8 miles in from UT 10); it has water and a small charge in summer; elevation is 6,900 feet. The canyon narrows as the road climbs higher and enters groves of spruce, fir, and aspen. **Forks of Huntington Canyon Campground** sits in a side canyon among fir and spruce trees; it has water from early June to mid-Sept.; $4; the turnoff is on the left near Milepost 30 (18 miles in from UT 10); elevation is 7,600 feet. **Left Fork of Huntington Creek National Recreation Trail** begins at the end of the campground road and follows the creek up a pretty canyon. The trail offers easy walking and passes good trout-fishing spots; after 5 miles it comes to an open valley and connects with a jeep road.

Farther up the highway, **Old Folks Flat Campground** has sites in a spruce and aspen forest on the right; it has water and a $6 charge from mid-June to mid-Sept.; also has group sites; located between Mileposts 28 and 27 (20.5 miles in from UT 10); elevation is 7,800 feet. **Electric Lake** offers rainbow and cutthroat trout fishing; a boat ramp is at the upper (north) end; turnoff is on the right near Milepost 14 (34 miles in from UT 10), then 8 miles in. **Skyline Drive** lies near the top of the plateau amidst expansive meadows and groves of fir and aspen. The junction for Skyline Drive to the south is on the left between

Mileposts 14 and 13; turnoff for Skyline Drive to the north is 5 miles farther west along the highway. Roads branch off the northern section of Skyline Drive to Gooseberry Campground (1.5 miles), Flat Campground (4.5 miles), Electric Lake (6 miles), and Scofield (17 miles). **Gooseberry Campground** is near Lower Gooseberry Reservoir; take the (north) Skyline Drive turnoff and follow signs 1.5 miles; sites are open with water and a $5 fee from about mid-June to mid-Sept.; elevation is 8,400 feet. **Flat Canyon Campground** also provides a good base for fishing lakes of the high country; campsites are reached by a 5.5-mile paved road from the (north) Skyline Drive turnoff; open with water and $6 fee from about mid-June to mid-Sept.; elevation is 8,800 feet. From the campground, Boulger Reservoir is ¼ mile away, Electric Lake is 2 miles, and Beaver Dam Reservoir is 2 miles. Other forest roads branch off the highway to more reservoirs and scenic spots; see the Manti-LaSal Forest Map (Manti Division).

Highway UT 31 continues 10 miles down the other side of the plateau to Fairview on US 89. Snowplows keep UT 31 open in winter, though drivers must have snow tires or carry chains from Nov. 1 to March 31. Snowmobilers can use groomed trails on the plateau.

## CASTLE DALE

The story goes that citizens, after founding the community in 1877, applied for a post office for their town of Castle Vale, but the name was recorded wrong. Because they couldn't agree on which side of Cottonwood Creek to settle, 2 towns grew up here—Castle Dale (current pop. 2,300) on the north side and Orangeville (current pop. 1,000) on the south. Castle Dale has a good historical museum and is the seat of Emery County. A memorial in front of the courthouse honors the 27 miners who died nearby in the Wilberg Coal Mine fire on Dec. 19, 1984.

*Castle Valley Pageant*

## Emery County Museum

Period rooms show life in the early days of Castle Valley settlements: a schoolroom, lawyer's office, country store, and kitchen. Pioneer rooms have farm and coal-mining tools and memorabilia of one-time outlaw Matt Warner. Exhibits of the prehistoric Fremont and Anasazi Indians include a rabbit-fur robe, pottery, baskets, tools, and jewelry. Meet a 22-foot allosaurus skeleton cast and see dinosaur bones and other fossils, rocks, and minerals. An art gallery exhibits local works. The museum is a good source of local travel information; literature and books are available. It's usually open Mon. to Fri. 9 a.m.-5 p.m., Sat. 9 a.m.-1 p.m.; donation; in the Castle Dale City Hall, one block north of the courthouse, at the 100 North and 100 East. A new museum building, located diagonally across the street, will eventually house the exhibits.

## Practicalities

**Village Inn Motel** is at 375 E. Main; tel. 381-2309; rooms cost $26.71 s, $32.16 d. **Big Moma's Pizza and Deli** offers pizza, spaghetti, and sandwiches at 340 E. Main; open Mon. to Sat. for lunch and dinner; tel. 381-5080. The **K Bar K Cafe** serves American fare at 41 W. Main; open Mon. to Sat. for breakfast, lunch, and dinner; tel. 381-5474. A supermarket is on E. Main.

**Pioneer Day** (July 24th) is celebrated with a parade, rodeo, and games. **Castle Valley Pageant**, held in early Aug., recounts the faith and trials of the pioneers who settled here; the pageant takes place on a hillside a short drive from town. The **Emery County Fair** is also in Aug.; horse races are run in Ferron to the south, while the horse show, parade, and most exhibits are in Castle Dale.

The indoor **swimming pool** is open May to Sept.; next to the city hall (one block north of the courthouse). The **city park,** between the courthouse and city hall, has covered picnic tables. Castle Dale's **library** is open Mon. to Fri. 11 a.m.-5 p.m.; next door to the city hall.

## The High Country West Of Castle Dale

Head northwest from town toward Joes Valley Reservoir on the paved road along Cottonwood Creek. After about 10 miles you'll reach a fork; an unpaved road turns right (north) along Cottonwood Creek to Upper Joes Valley (10 miles); the main road (UT 29) continues and enters Straight Canyon. Seely Creek below the dam in Straight Canyon has good fishing for German brown trout. Joes Valley Reservoir covers 1,170 acres in a large valley at the upper end of Straight Canyon, 16 miles from Castle Dale. A road turns off the highway at the north end of the lake and goes north to **Upper Joes Valley Campground** (9 miles) and UT 31 (21 miles). Upper Joes Valley Campground is also known as Indian Creek Campground. It's open with water from late June to mid-Sept. and a $5 fee; sites can be reserved with the Ferron Ranger District office; elevation is 9,000 feet.

**Joes Valley Campground** has 2 sections on the west shore of the reservoir; they have water from mid-May to mid-Sept and a $6 fee; one loop stays open all year (no water or charge off-season); elevation is 7,100 feet. A boat ramp and **Joes Valley Marina** are here too; the marina offers boat slips, rentals (fishing boats w/motors, rowboats, and paddle boats), a cafe (breakfast, lunch, and dinner daily), and a small store; tel. 381-2453; open mid-May to early November. Campground and marina are about 20 miles west of Castle Dale. Fishermen catch rainbow and cutthroat trout in the lake. Lowry Fork to the north has good trout fishing in the spring. Water-skiing is popular on the lake, but winds are too erratic for reliable sailing. Pavement ends after the turnoff for Joes Valley Campground. A forest road continues west and climbs 13 miles to Skyline Drive (elev. 10,200 ft.) at the top of the Wasatch Plateau. The clay road surface is usually fine for cars in dry weather but treacherously slippery when wet for *any* vehicle. The road from Castle Dale to the reservoir is kept open in winter for ice fishing and snowmobile access.

North Dragon Road turns south between the 2 sections of Joes Valley Campground and goes about 15 miles to a spectacular overlook above Castle Dale; the San Rafael Swell and distant Henry, La Sal, and Abajo mountains can be seen on a clear day; the road is unpaved but OK when dry for cars with good clearance.

# FERRON

The town's name honors a surveyor who visited the valley in preparation for Mormon settlement. Millsite State Park and Ferron Reservoir are on a scenic road that connects Ferron with Skyline Drive. **Castle Country Motel** is on highway UT 10 with rooms at $25 s or d; tel. 384-2311. The motel has a small cafe open daily for breakfast, lunch, and dinner. The **Wilber & Friends Restaurant** offers a fancier menu and decor around the corner at 35 E. Main; open Mon.-Sat. for breakfast, lunch, and dinner. Ferron (pop. 1,900) celebrates its pioneer heritage in Sept. during **Peach Days** with horse races, a demolition derby, games, craft exhibits, a dance, and fireworks. The **Southeastern Utah Junior Livestock Show** takes place in July. The **Ferron Ranger District** office on the main highway can help you plan a trip to the Wasatch Plateau; open Mon. to Fri. 8 a.m.-noon and 12:30-4:30 p.m.; Box 310, Ferron, UT 84523; tel. 384-2372.

## Canyon Road To Skyline Drive

Turn west on Canyon Road beside the Ferron Ranger District office for a trip to Millsite State Park and the high county of the Wasatch Plateau. **Millsite State Park** is 4 miles from town at an elevation of 5,900 feet. The 450-acre Millsite Reservoir is about twice the size of Huntington Reservoir and has the area's best sailing conditions and the most space for water-skiing. Fishermen come to catch rainbow, cutthroat, and German brown trout. Ice fishing is done in winter. The park has picnic grounds, campground with showers, boat ramp, and dock. Facilities, including drinking water, stay open all year. **Millsite Golf Course**, adjacent to the park, features 9 challenging holes. Off-road vehicle riding is popular in the barren countryside near the reservoir. Day use of the park costs $3, camping $8; tel. 384-2552, 687-2491 (Huntington State Park) or (800) 322-3770 (reservations).

Pavement ends past the state park, but a fairly good gravel road, narrow and winding in places, continues high into the mountains. Stop at Ferron Canyon Overlook (14 miles from town) for a panorama of Millsite Reservoir, surrounding mountains and valleys, and the San Rafael Swell; signs point out features and geology; elevation here is 8,200 feet. The road continues climbing to alpine country with pretty lakes and groves of fir and aspen.

**Ferron Reservoir** (28 miles from town) is the largest of the high-country lakes (57 acres). The forest service campground is open from mid-June to mid-Sept. with water and a $5 fee; elevation is 9,400 feet. **Sky Haven Lodge** on the lake offers cabins, a small cafe (breakfast, lunch, and dinner daily), a small store, and boat rentals (with or without motors). Horseback rides and guided pack trips can be arranged; 242 E. 600 South, Manti, UT 84542; tel. 528-7699. The road to Ferron Reservoir is open for vehicles only from about mid-June to late Sept., but the lodge plans to stay open in winter and organize snowmobile transportation. Skyline Drive is only 2 miles beyond Ferron Reservoir. Turn north on the drive to a fine view of the reservoir and canyon to the east and valleys near Manti to the west. The highest point on Skyline Drive, at 10,897 feet, is just 0.8 mile beyond the viewpoint.

*Pink Cliffs of the Paunsaugunt Plateau*

# SOUTHWESTERN UTAH

## INTRODUCTION

Visitors to Utah's "Dixie" enjoy marvelous scenery and a warm winter sun. The region's climate and varied terrain make it ideal for year-round outdoor recreation. You can hike through serpentine canyons or flower-filled meadows, hit the slopes at the Brian Head ski area, glide on cross-country skis across a high plateau, explore the desert, or play a leisurely round of golf.

### THE LAND

The Mohave Desert, Great Basin, and Colorado Plateau meet here to create a unique combination of climates and ecosystems. Plants and wildlife normally found only in Arizona and southern California live in the arid plains and rocky ranges of the desert. The lofty cliffs of the Colorado Plateau rise east of the desert country with some of the most spectacular scenery on earth—the grandeur and colors have to be seen to be believed. Great faults break the Colorado Plateau into a staircase of lesser plateaus across southern Utah and into northern Arizona. Angular features of cliffs and canyons dominate the plateau landscape. Volcanic cones and lava flows have broken through the surface, some in geologically recent times. Elevations range from 2,350 feet at Beaver Dam Wash to 11,307 feet atop Brian Head Peak.

#### Climate
No matter what the season is, you can nearly always find pleasant temperatures in some part of the region. Ever since Brigham Young

built a winter house at St. George to escape the cold and snow, people have been coming to take advantage of the mild climate. Midwinter temperatures at St. George (elev. 2,880 ft.) may drop below freezing at night, but days are typically in the middle to upper 50s F with bright sunshine. Spring and autumn bring ideal weather. Summer, when the highs often top 100°, is the time to head for the mountains and high plateaus. The alpine meadows and cool forests of the Beaver Dam Mountains, Cedar Breaks National Monument, and Bryce Canyon National Park provide a welcome refuge from summer heat. Precipitation ranges widely from place to place and from year to year, though most falls in winter/early spring and in late summer. Annual precipitation averages 10.4 inches in St. George and more than 20 inches in the high country.

## FLORA AND FAUNA

The land provides habitats for a great variety of plant and animal species. Sparse desert vegetation consists largely of big sagebrush, rabbitbrush, bitterbrush, blackbrush, yucca, cacti, and grasses. The distinctive Joshua tree, a member of the lily family, grows in the extreme southwestern corner of the state. Perennial streams support cottonwood, willow, velvet and single-leaf ash, tamarisk, rushes, and sedges. Creatures of the desert include the chuckwalla, Gila monster (a poisonous lizard), California king snake, and road runner. Above about 4,000 feet, woodlands of pinyon pine and Utah juniper take over from the desert; you'll often find cliffrose, Utah serviceberry, live oak, and Gambel oak here too. At about 7,000-8,000 feet, ponderosa pine, Gambel oak, and Rocky Mountain juniper are common. Thriving in the cool mountain air above 8,000 feet are Douglas fir, subalpine fir, Engelmann spruce, aspen, and wildflowers. Larger wildlife, such as mule deer, elk, mountain lion, and coyote, migrate with the seasons between the high and low country. More than 200 bird species have been spotted in the region. Raptors include bald and golden eagles, red-tailed and Cooper's hawks, peregrine and prairie falcons, and the American kestrel.

## HISTORY

### The Indians
Beginning about 15,000 years ago, groups of Paleo-Indians wandered across the region to hunt and gather wild plants. Only scant evidence remains of their long stay here. The more sophisticated Anasazi and Fremont cultures emerged about A.D. 500 with newly acquired agriculture. Their corn, beans, and squash enabled them to be less reliant on migration and to construct year-round village sites. Although both groups developed crafts such as basketry, pottery, and jewelry, only the Anasazi progressed to construction of masonry buildings in their villages. The Fremont ranged across present-day central Utah, while the Anasazi stayed in what are now southern Utah and adjacent states. The Fremont and Anasazi mysteriously abandoned their Utah villages during the 1200s. Archaeologists have traced the Anasazi to modern pueblo tribes in Arizona and New Mexico but don't know what became of the Fremont.

Nomadic bands of Southern Paiutes, possible descendants of the Paleo-Indians, were inhabiting the region when the first white men came. The Paiutes befriended and guided the early explorers and settlers, but troubles soon began when the Indians saw their lands taken

*Anasazi bowl found near St. George*

over by farmers and ranchers. Unable to maintain their old lifestyle or defeat the newcomers, the Indians settled near the white men's towns. They now have the Shivwits Reservation northwest of St. George and the Kaibab-Paiute Reservation in Arizona southwest of Kanab.

## Explorers And Colonizers

In 1776, Spanish explorers of the Dominguez-Escalante expedition were the first white men to visit and describe the region. They had given up partway through a proposed journey from Santa Fe to California and returned to Santa Fe along a route passing through the sites of present-day Cedar City and Hurricane. In the first half of the 19th C., mountain men like Jedediah Smith and government surveyors such as John C. Fremont explored the land and learned about the Indians. In 1849-50, Mormon leaders in Salt Lake City took the first steps in colonizing the region when they sent an advance party led by Parley P. Pratt. Encouraging reports of rich iron ore west of

Cedar Valley and of fertile land along the Virgin River convinced the Mormons to expand southward. Calls went out for members to establish missions and to mine the iron ore and supply iron products needed for the expanding Mormon empire. Parowan, now a sleepy community along I-15, was the first settlement and Cedar City the second, both established in 1851. In 1855, a successful experiment in growing cotton along Santa Clara Creek, near present-day St. George, aroused considerable interest among the Mormons. New settlements soon arose in the Virgin River Valley. However, poor roads hindered development of the cotton and iron industries, most of which ended when cheaper products began arriving on the transcontinental railroad. Floods, droughts, disease, and hostile Indians discouraged some of Dixie's pioneers, but many of those who stayed prospered by raising food crops and livestock. The past 20 years have brought rapid growth to the region in the form of new industries, tourism, and retirement communities.

*William Carter behind his plow at St. George, Jan. 19, 1893.*
*He also plowed the first furrows at Salt Lake City on July 23, 1847.*

# ST. GEORGE

Southern Utah's largest town lies between lazy bends of the Virgin River on one side and rocky hills of red sandstone on the other. In 1861, more than 300 Mormon families in the Salt Lake City area answered the call to go south to start the Cotton Mission, of which St. George became the center. The settlers overcame great difficulties to farm and to build an attractive city in this remote desert. Brigham Young chose the city's name to honor George A. Smith, who had served as head of the Southern (Iron) Mission during the 1850s. (The title "Saint" means simply that he was a Mormon, a Latter-day Saint.) Visits to some of the historic sites will add to your appreciation of the city's past; ask for the brochure, *St. George Historic Walking Tour,* at the chamber of commerce. The warm climate, dramatic setting, and many year-round recreation opportunities have helped make St. George (pop. 28,000) the fastest-growing city in the state. Local boosters claim that this is where Utah's summer sun spends the winter!

## SIGHTS

### St. George Temple
Visible for miles, the gleaming white temple rises from landscaped grounds in the center of St. George. In 1871, enthusiastic Mormons from all over the territory gathered to erect the temple. Dedication on April 6, 1877, brought great joy to church members because, for the first time, they had a sacred house of worship in the West. The St. George Temple is the oldest Mormon temple in the world that's still in use. It's constructed of stuccoed stone in a castellated Gothic Revival style; a cupola with a weather vane caps the structure. Sacred ceremonies take place inside, so no tours are offered. You're welcome to visit the grounds to admire the architecture. The temple is especially impressive at night when lit up against the black sky. A visitor center on the northeast

corner of the grounds has short films and videos introducing the Mormon religion; it's open daily 9 a.m.-8 p.m. (until 9 p.m. in summer); tel. 673-5181. Visitor center and temple are at the corner of 400 East and 200 South.

### St. George Tabernacle
When Brigham Young visited the Cotton Mission after its first year, he found the community afflicted with difficulties and low morale. Soon after, he ordered construction of a tabernacle to help rally the members. The task, paid for with tithing revenues, took 13 years to complete. Builders used local red sandstone for the walls, and placed a slender white steeple on the roof, reminiscent of a New England church. Tour guides will show you around and explain some of the tabernacle's history and construction details. The 30-minute film, *Windows of Heaven,* shown on request, dramatizes the revelation received here in 1899 by church president Lorenzo Snow. Guides offer free tours daily about 11 a.m.-5 p.m.; occasional concerts (free) and other presentations take place too; tel. 628-4072. The tabernacle is downtown at Main and Tabernacle streets.

### DUP Pioneer Museum
Drop in to see hundreds of pioneer portraits and the tools and clothing used by early settlers. The spinning wheels and looms on display served in the mission's cotton and silk industries. Open Mon. to Sat. 10 a.m.-5 p.m.; donation; tel. 628-7274. The museum, staffed by the Daughters of the Utah Pioneers, is at 145 N. 100 East, behind the old county courthouse.

### Brigham Young Winter Home
Late in life, Brigham Young sought relief from rheumatism and other aches and pains by spending winters in Dixie's mild climate. This also gave him an opportunity to supervise more closely the affairs of the church here,

# ST. GEORGE

1. Bluff Street Park
2. Bureau of Land Management offices
3. Brigham Young Winter Home
4. post office
5. St. George Chamber of Commerce; DUP Pioneer Museum
6. Pioneer Park
7. Greene Gate Village
8. St. George Tabernacle; Washington County Library
9. Pine Valley Ranger District office (USFS)
10. Vernon Worthen Park
11. St. George Temple
12. Dixie Medical Center
13. swimming pool
14. Commercial Center
15. J.C. Snow Park
16. Dixie Center
17. Red Cliffs Mall

TO SNOW CANYON, VEYO, GUNLOCK RESERVOIR, & PINE VALLEY MTNS.

18

DIXIE RED HILLS GOLF COURSE

SUNSET BLVD.

TO JACOB HAMBLIN HOME, SNOW CANYON, & GUNLOCK RESERVOIR

600 NORTH
500 NORTH
400 NORTH
DIAGONAL ST.
400 WEST
300 WEST
200 WEST
200 NORTH
ST. GEORGE BLVD.
SKYLINE DR.
TABERNACLE ST.
100 SOUTH
200 SOUTH
300 SOUTH
400 SOUTH
100 WEST
MAIN ST.
100 EAST
200 EAST
300 EAST
400 EAST
700 EAST
800 EAST
900 EAST
1000 EAST
700 SOUTH
900 SOUTH

TWIN LAKES GOLF COURSE

INDUSTRIAL RD.
HIGHLAND DR.
RED CLIFFS DR.

TO WASHINGTON, ZION N.P., & CEDAR CITY

EXIT 8

DIXIE COLLEGE

0        0.5 mi
0        0.5 km

AIRPORT DR.
AIRPORT
BLUFF ST.

15

EXIT 6

RIVER RD.

INDIAN HILLS DR.
SANTA CLARA RIVER

HILTON DR.

VIRGIN RIVER

TO DINOSAUR TRACKWAYS & OLD FORT PEARCE

ST. GEORGE GOLF COURSE

TONAQUINT DR.
SOUTHGATE GOLF COURSE

TO VIRGIN RIVER GORGE & LAS VEGAS

especially construction of the temple. A telegraph line connected Young's house with Salt Lake City. He moved here late in 1873 and returned each winter until his death in 1877. The carefully restored adobe house contains furnishings of the era, including some that belonged to Young. Fruit and mulberry trees grow in the yard; mulberry leaves once fed silkworms of a short-lived pioneer industry. Free tours begin at Young's office on the east side of the house. Open daily 9 a.m. until about sunset; tel. 673-2517; on 200 North between Main and 100 West.

### Jacob Hamblin Home

No one did more to extend the Mormons' southern settlements and keep peace with the Indians than Jacob Hamblin. He came west in 1850 with 4 children (his first wife refused to come) and settled in the Tooele area with wife number 2. At Brigham Young's request, Hamblin moved to the south in 1856 and helped build the Santa Clara Fort. He built the present sandstone house after floods washed away the fort in 1862. Almost always on the move serving on missions, Hamblin had little time for home life. He moved to Kanab in 1870, then south to Arizona and New Mexico. Even so, he had 4 wives (never more than 2 at a time) and managed to father 24 children. The kitchen, work areas, and living rooms provide a good idea of what pioneer life was like. Free tours show you the house and tell of activities that once took place here. Open daily 9 a.m.-6 p.m. (until 7 p.m. in summer); tel. 673-2161. Located in the village of Santa Clara, 4 miles northwest of St. George.

### Old Cotton Mill

The Mormon Church began construction of this large 3-story stone building in 1865 as part of the Cotton Mission, but it was sold 6 years later to a public cooperative. Mill workers turned out batting, blankets, clothing, and other textiles until the late 1800s, when shortages of raw materials forced cutbacks. Machinery was sold and the mill became a warehouse about 1910. The venerable building, now restored, often hosts community events.

Plans are to make it into a historic park like Pipe Spring National Monument. Tours can be arranged; tel. 673-0375. The mill is in Washington, a small town northeast of St. George; take I-15 Exit 10, go east on Telegraph St. into town, turn right on 200 West, and follow signs.

### Dixie College

A giant "D" on a hillside to the west watches over the "Home of the Rebels" and the surrounding town. The school began in 1911 as the St. George Stake Academy, founded by the Mormon Church. Later the name was changed to Dixie Normal School, then to Dixie Community College, and finally to the present one in 1970. Dixie College is a 2-year community college now run by the state. The approximately 2,500 students and 100 faculty meet on a 4-quarter system. Visitors are welcome to attend cultural and sporting events and to use many of the facilities. The Fine Arts Building (700 East and 100 South) has exhibits inside, but you'll find the biggest work outside on the south wall. A mosaic more than 15 feet high and 127 feet long depicts the region's history from the days of the Fremont Indians to Mormon settlement. To find out what's going on at Dixie College, visit the Administration Building (700 East and 200 South) or call 673-4811, ext. 202 (student productions in the Fine Arts Theater), ext. 276 or 352 (Celebrity Concert Series from Oct. to April), or ext. 383 (sporting events). The library is open during the main terms Mon. to Fri. 8 a.m.-10 p.m., Sat. 10 a.m.-5 p.m., and Sun. 1-8 p.m.; ext. 201. Recreation facilities open to the public include a swimming pool, basketball court, and weight room at Dixie Center, and handball, tennis, and a jogging track at Hansen Stadium; both places are near the corner of 700 East and 400 South. The Student Union in the center of the campus has a cafeteria and snack bar; get your Dixie Rebels clothing and souvenirs at the bookstore. Visitors may park at the southeast corner of 700 East and 100 South (near the Fine Arts Building), along the west side of the gymnasium (700 East and 300 South), or on streets off campus. Mailing address is St. George, UT 84770.

# ST. GEORGE ACCOMMODATIONS

Add 9% tax to all prices

| MOTEL/HOTEL | ADDRESS | RATES | PHONE | FEATURES |
|---|---|---|---|---|
| Bluffs Motel | 1140 S. Bluff St. | $29-65 | 628-6699 | kitchenettes, pool, spa |
| Brower's Desert Edge Inn | 525 E. St. George Blvd. | $27-50 | 673-6137 | kitchenettes, pool |
| Budget 8 Motel | 1230 S. Bluff St. | $25-34 | 628-5234 | pool |
| Chalet Motel | 664 E. St. George Blvd. | $25-60 | 628-6272 | pool |
| Claridge Inn | 1187 S. Bluff St. | $27-42 | 673-7222 | pool, spa |
| Colonial Motel | 299 E. St. George Blvd. | $18-22 | 673-3022 | |
| Comfort Inn | 999 E. Skyline Dr. | $32-52 | 628-4271 or (800) 221-2222 | pool |
| Comfort Suites | 1239 S. Main | $49-59 | 673-7000 or (800) 221-2222 | suites, pool, spa |
| Coral Hills (Best Western) | 125 E. St. George Blvd. | $36-80 | 673-4844 or (800) 542-7733 | pools, spas |
| Coronada Family Inn | 559 E. St. George Blvd. | $25-65 | 628-4436 or (800) 548-6007 | kitchenettes, pool |
| Days Inn & Four Seasons Convention Center | 747 E. St. George Blvd. | $37-125 | 673-6111 or (800) 635-4441 | suites, pool, spa, tennis, Cont. break. |
| Diamond Valley Guest Ranch | 9 miles north on UT 18 | $20-40 | 574-2281 | horseback riding |
| Dixie Palms Motel | 185 E. St. George Blvd. | $20-50 | 673-3531 | |
| Greene Gate Village Bed & Breakfast Inn | 76 W. Tabernacle | $40-75 | 628-6999 | bed and breakfast, pool, spa |
| Heritage Inn | 1165 S. Bluff St. | $29-34 | 628-4481 or (800) 231-4488 | pool, spa, sauna |
| Hilton Inn of St. George | 1450 Hilton Inn Dr. | $61-83 | 628-0463 or (800) 662-2525 | pool, sauna, tennis |
| Holiday Inn | 850 S. Bluff St. | $66-120 | 628-4235 or (800) 457-9800 | rec. area, pool |
| Holiday Resort Realty | 141 Brigham Rd., #A | $44-158 | 673-6172 | golf, tennis, pool, condos |
| Motel 6 | 205 N. 1000 E. (Exit 8) | $25-31 | 628-7979 | pool |
| Oasis Motel | 231 W. St. George Blvd. | $20-35 | 673-3551 | kitchenettes, pool |

# ST. GEORGE ACCOMMODATIONS (CONTINUED)

Add 9% tax to all prices

| MOTEL/HOTEL | ADDRESS | RATES | PHONE | FEATURES |
|---|---|---|---|---|
| Ranch Inn | 1040 S. Main | $27-48 | 628-8000 or (800) 332-0400 | kitchenettes, pool, spa |
| Red Cliffs Inn | I-15 Exit 10 | $27-40 | 673-3537 | pool |
| Red Mesa Motel | 247 E. St. George Blvd. | $19-35 | 673-3163 | kitchenettes, pool |
| Regency Inn | 770 E. St. George Blvd. | $31-48 | 673-6119 | kitchenettes, pool |
| Rodeway Inn | 260 E. St. George Blvd. | $32-55 | 673-6161 | pool, Cont. break. |
| Sands Motel | 581 E. St. George Blvd. | $20-25 | 673-3501 | pool |
| Seven Wives Inn Bed & Breakfast | 217 N. 100 West | $35-70 | 628-3737 | bed and breakfast, pool |
| Shady Corner Bed & Breakfast | 194 S. 600 East | $45-60 | 673-7383 | bed and breakfast |
| South Side Inn | 750 E. St. George Blvd. | $24-39 | 628-9000 | pool, spa |
| Sullivan's Rococo Inn | 511 S. Airport Rd. | $25-45 | 628-3671 | pool, jacuzzi |
| Sun Time Inn | 420 E. St. George Blvd. | $34-60 | 673-6181 | kitchenettes, pool |
| Super 8 Motel | 915 S. Bluff St. | $32-39 | 628-4251 or (800) 844-8888 | pool |
| Thunderbird Lodge (Best Western) | 150 N. 1000 East | $39-56 | 673-6123 or (800) 528-1234 | pool, spa, sauna |
| Travel Inn (Best Western) | 316 E. St. George Blvd. | $34-53 | 673-3541 or (800) 528-1234 | pool, spa |
| TraveLodge East | 175 N. 1000 East | $31-42 | 673-4621 or (800) 255-3050 | pool |
| TraveLodge West | 60 W. St. George Blvd. | $30-40 | 673-4666 or (800) 255-3050 | pool, spa, sauna |
| Western Safari Motel | 310 W. St. George Blvd. | $18-30 | 673-5238 | kitchenettes |
| Weston's Lamplighter Motel | 460 E. St. George Blvd. | $28-44 | 673-4861 | pool, spa |

## PRACTICALITIES

St. George has a large number of places to stay and eat. Most are along the I-15 Business Route of St. George Blvd. (Exit 8) and Bluff St. (Exit 6). You'll find almost every fast-food place known to modern man just off the interstate on St. George Boulevard!

### Campgrounds

**Snow Canyon State Park** has a campground with showers open all year in a pretty canyon setting; go 12 miles north on UT 18, then left 2 miles; tel. 628-2255 or (800) 322-3770 (reservations); $8 or $10 w/hookups. Closer to town are **St. George Campground & RV Park** with pool, laundry, and showers (2100 E. Middleton Dr.; tel. 673-2970; $8.72 tents, $10.90 RV w/hookups); **Temple View RV Resort** with pool, laundry, and showers (975 S. Main; tel. 673-6400; $11.94 tents, $15.21 RV w/hookups); **Redlands RV Park** with pool, store, laundry, and showers (I-15 Washington Exit 10; tel. 673-9700; $13.63 tents, $16.90 RV w/hookups); and **Hillside Palms RV Park** (175 N. 600 East; tel. 673-2102/2809; $10.90 w/hookups; no showers; no tents).

### Food

For American food: **The Shed Restaurant** offers steak, seafood, and other fine dining at the Four Seasons Inn, 747 E. St. George Blvd.; tel. 673-7800; open Mon. to Sat. for dinner. **Jolly King** is a cafe at Weston's Lamplighter, 430 E. St. George Blvd.; tel. 673-2742; open daily for breakfast, lunch, and dinner. The **Sizzler** has an informal atmosphere for steak and seafood at 405 E. St. George Blvd.; tel. 628-1313; open daily for lunch and dinner. **Golden Corral Family Steak House** is at 350 E. St. George Blvd.; tel. 673-4213; open daily for lunch and dinner. **Andelin's Gable House** presents elegant a la carte and 3- and 5-course dinners at 290 E. St. George Blvd.; tel. 673-6796 (reservations advised for multi-course dinners); open Mon. to Sat. for breakfast, lunch, and dinner. **Rene's Restaurant** serves American and some Italian cuisine at Phoenix Plaza, corner of Sunset Blvd. and Valley View Dr.; tel. 628-9300; open Mon. to Sat. for lunch and dinner. **McGuire's** varied menu includes Italian specialties at 531 N. Bluff St.; tel. 628-4066; open Mon. to Sat. for dinner. **The Palms** in the Holiday Inn features steak, prime rib, and seafood dinners and a Sun. brunch at 850 S. Bluff St.; tel. 628-4235; open daily for breakfast, lunch, and dinner. **Sullivan's Rococo Steak House** offers prime rib, steak, seafood, and other specialties with memorable views atop a hill just west of town (take Airport Rd.); tel. 673-3305; open daily for dinner. **Sterling's Hide-a-Way Restaurant** prepares home-style meals at 2 W. St.

mural detail on the
Fine Arts Bldg. at
Dixie College

George Blvd. in Ancestor Square; tel. 628-4622; open Mon. to Sat. for breakfast, lunch, and dinner. **Marie Callender's** menu of American favorites includes their famous pies at 1110 S. Bluff St.; tel. 628-1700; open daily for breakfast, lunch, and dinner. **Dick's Cafe** has been serving customers since 1935 at 114 E. St. George Blvd.; tel. 673-3841; open daily for breakfast, lunch, and dinner. **Trafalga Restaurant** is a cafe at 76 W. St. George Blvd.; tel. 673-2933; open daily for breakfast, lunch, and dinner.

Dine Chinese at the **Rickshaw,** 212 N. 900 East; tel. 628-1511; open Mon. to Sat. for dinner. Authentic Mexican food is prepared at **Los Hermanos** (46 W. St. George Blvd. in Ancestor Square; tel. 628-5989; open Mon. to Sat. for lunch and dinner); **Paula's Cazuela** (745 W. Ridgeview Dr. on the northwest edge of town; tel. 673-6568; open Mon. to Sat. for lunch and dinner); and **Pancho & Lefty's** (1050 S. Bluff St.; tel. 628-4772; open daily for lunch and dinner). Pick up pizza at **Pizza Factory** (1 W. St. George Blvd. in Ancestor Square; tel. 628-1234; open Mon. to Sat. for lunch and dinner); **Pizza Hut** (471 E. St. George Blvd.; tel. 628-2641; and at 932 S. Bluff St.; tel. 628-9290; both are open daily for lunch and dinner); and **Little Caesar's Pizza** (700 E. 700 South; tel. 628-8100; and at 929 W. Sunset Blvd. tel. 628-8595; both are open daily for lunch and dinner).

## Entertainment And Events
Staff at the St. George Chamber of Commerce know about upcoming events; contact them in the old county courthouse at 97 E. St. George Blvd.; tel. 628-1658. They'll know, for example, about concerts at Dixie Center and the Tabernacle and the many small sporting events that take place in St. George. Major annual events include: **January or February:** Sunfest Trade Show of commercial exhibits especially for snow birds. **February:** Dixie Squares Jamboree square dancing. Presidents Day Softball. Spirit of Dixie presents a series of rodeo, entertainment, clogging, crafts, and food events to the community through mid-May. Dixie Invitational Art Show

hosts regional artists; it begins President's Day weekend at the Fine Arts Bldg. on Dixie College campus. **March:** Womens Conference in Dixie, on the first weekend, offers workshops and lectures. Utah Seniors Golf Tournament. St. George 10K Run. Barbershop Show. Spirit of Dixie continues. **April:** Dixie College D-Week (homecoming). St. George Arts Festival (Easter weekend). Horse races at Lions Dixie Downs Race Meet. Spirit of Dixie continues. **May:** Spirit of Dixie concludes mid-month. **June:** Dixie Festival of Performing Arts hosts student and professional concerts. **July:** Fireworks at the Sun Bowl, adjacent to Vernon Worthen Park. Gunlock Rodeo (July 4th; amateur). Enterprise Rodeo (Thurs., Fri., and Sat. of July 24th weekend; amateur). **August:** Washington County Fair at the fairgrounds in Hurricane. Veyo Rodeo. **September:** Lions Dixie Round-Up (PRCA rodeo). **October:** World Senior Games presents a wide variety of olympic-type competitions for seniors; you'll be amazed at the enthusiasm and abilities. St. George Marathon (on first Sat.). **November:** Thanksgiving Day Rodeo (in Santa Clara; amateur). Annual Holiday Festival Parade (Fri. or Sat. after Thanksgiving). **December:** Jubilee of Trees (exhibition of decorated trees and handicrafts on the first Fri. and Sat.). Handel's *Messiah* (early in month).

## Recreation
**Vernon Worthen Park** offers shaded picnic tables, playground, and tennis courts at 400 East and 200 South. **J.C. Snow Park** has picnic tables and playground (but little shade) at 400 East and 900 South. **Pioneer Park** overlooks the city from the north; it's in desert country just off Skyline Drive (see map); the primitive park just has a few picnic tables. The outdoor public **swimming pool** features a hydro slide; open Memorial Day to Labor Day weekends at 250 E. 700 South; tel. 634-5867. **Tennis** players may use the public courts at Dixie College and at Vernon Worthen Park. Green Valley Resort has a tennis college and many courts for their guests (only) at 1515 W. Canyon View Dr.; tel. 628-8060. The city's

**Leisure Services Dept.** offers a wide range of activities for adults and youth, including classes (art, music, sports), field trips, and lectures; tel. 634-5850.

With 7 golf courses, St. George has a reputation as Utah's winter golf capital. **St. George Golf Club** is an 18-hole, par-73 course south of town in Bloomington Hills; tel. 634-5854. **Southgate Golf Course** has 18 holes, par 70, at 1975 S. Tonaquint Dr. on the southwest edge of town; tel. 628-0000. **Bloomington Country Club** is private 18-hole, par-72 course; players need to be members, guests of members, or members of a club with a reciprocal agreement; located southwest of town in Bloomington; tel. 673-2029. **Dixie Red Hills** is a 9-hole, par-34 municipal course at 1000 N. 700 West on the northwest edge of town; tel. 634-5852. **Green Valley Golf Club** has 9 holes, par 27, and a 27-hole miniature golf course at 1200 Dixie Downs Rd. (west of town in Green Valley); tel. 628-3778. **Twin Lakes Golf Course** has 9 holes, par 27, at 660 N. Twin Lakes Dr. on the northeast edge of town (take the I-15 frontage road); tel. 673-4441. **Sunbrook Golf Course** is the area's newest, with 18 holes off Dixie Downs Rd. between Green Valley and Santa Clara; tel. 673-5590.

**Shopping**

Outdoor supplies can be purchased at the **Outdoor Outlet** (1062 E. Tabernacle; tel. 628-3611) and **McKnight's Sporting Goods** (968 E. St. George Blvd.; tel. 673-4919). **Red Cliffs Mall** has the big Z.C.M.I., J.C. Penny, Wal-Mart, and other stores on Red Cliffs Dr., the east frontage road northeast of the I-15 St. George Blvd. junction. The **Commercial Center** is a shopping center with K mart, Albertsons, and other stores at 700 S. Bluff.

**Services**

The **post office** is at 180 N. Main; tel. 673-3312. **Dixie Medical Center** provides hospital care at 544 S. 400 East; tel. 634-4000 (Physician Referral number is 628-6688). **Elder Hostel** education and recreation programs in St. George have been very popular with seniors; tel. 673-3704 or (800) 545-4653. Foreign currency can be exchanged at **First Security Bank,** 410 E. Tabernacle; tel. 628-2831.

**Information**

The **St. George Chamber of Commerce** can tell you about the sights, events, and services of southwestern Utah; they have brochures of accommodations, restaurants, a historic walking tour, and area ghost towns; open Mon. to Fri. 9 a.m.-5 p.m.; tel. 628-1658. The office is in the old county courthouse (built 1866-76) at 97 E. St. George Blvd. (St. George, UT 84770). See the **Pine Valley Ranger District** office for information on fishing, hiking, and camping in the Dixie National Forest north of town; maps of the forest and Pine Valley Wilderness are available; open Mon. to Fri. 8 a.m.-5 p.m.; tel. 673-3431; Room 40 of the Federal Bldg. at 196 E. Tabernacle (St. George, UT 84770). The **Bureau of Land Management** oversees vast lands in Utah's southwest corner and the Arizona Strip; open Mon. to Fri. 7:45 a.m.-4:30 p.m.; the offices for Dixie Resource Area (tel. 673-4654) and the Shivwits and Vermillion resource areas of the Arizona Strip (628-4491) are at 225 N. Bluff St. (St. George, UT 84770); the building is set back from the road behind a row of shops; look for it on the west side of Bluff St. between 200 and 300 North.

**Washington County Library** has a good selection of books; a bulletin board lists community events and classes; open Mon. to Thurs. 9 a.m.-9 p.m., Fri. and Sat. 9 a.m.-6 p.m.; it's just south of the Tabernacle at 50 S. Main; tel. 634-5737. **Dixie College's library** sits in the center of campus; open Mon. to Fri. 8 a.m.-10 p.m., Sat. 10 a.m.-5 p.m., and Sun. 1-8 p.m. during the main terms; tel. 673-4811, ext. 201. **The Book Cellar** offers a good assortment that includes regional and travel books at 380 W. St. George Blvd.; tel. 628-0380. Other sources for Utah books include **R&K's Bookstore** (116 E. City Center; tel. 673-5478) and **Deseret Book Co.** (801 S.

Bluff St.; tel. 628-4495). The **Book Peddler** specializes in used books at 777 E. 700 South; tel. 673-5827.

## Tours And Transport
**Sun Time Aviation** will show you spectacular scenery from the air on a variety of trips, ranging from a half-hour flight over St. George and Snow Canyon ($24/person; minimum of 2) to a 4-hour loop to Zion, Bryce, Grand Canyon, and Lake Powell ($339/person; minimum of 2; a short stop is made at Page); tel. 628-0481. For a cab, call **Pete's Taxi**; tel. 673-5467. See the telephone yellow pages for car rental agencies. **Greyhound Bus** departs from the Trafalga Restaurant at 76 W. St. George Blvd. for Salt Lake City, Denver, Las Vegas, and other destinations; tel. 673-2933. **Skywest Airlines** flies to Salt Lake City (5X daily, $108-127 one way), Page (2X daily, $69 one way), Las Vegas (4X daily, $70 one way), and other destinations; ask about roundtrip and special fares; tel. (800) 453-9417.

*mat penstemon* (Penstemon caespitosus)

# VICINITY OF ST. GEORGE

Some good scenic drives begin at St. George. Whether you're short on time or have all day, a good choice is the 24-mile loop through Snow Canyon State Park via UT 18, the park road (UT 300), and Santa Clara. The old highway to Littlefield (AZ) makes a 67-mile loop with I-15; the route follows former US 91 through the pioneer settlement of Santa Clara, the sparsely settled Shivwits Indian Reservation, and over a 4,600-foot pass in the Beaver Dam Mountains to Littlefield; the I-15 section goes through the spectacular Virgin River Gorge upstream from Littlefield. In summer, the cool forests of the Pine Valley Mountains 37 miles northwest of town are an especially attractive destination: you can make a 130-mile drive with many possible side trips by circling the mountains on UT 18, UT 56, and I-15. Zion National Park, with its grandeur and color, is about 40 miles northeast of St. George. Adventurous motorists may want to try some of the unpaved roads through the desert east and west of St. George; the back way to Hurricane via Fort Pearce can be driven by car in good weather.

## SNOW CANYON STATE PARK

The park is a great place to explore and enjoy the desert scenery. Red-rock canyons, sand dunes, volcanos, and lava flows have formed an incredible landscape. Walls of Navajo Sandstone 500-750 feet high enclose 3-mile-long Snow Canyon. Hiking trails lead into the backcountry for a closer look at the geology, flora, and fauna. Common plants are barrel, cholla, and prickly pear cacti, yucca, Mormon tea, shrub live oak, cliffrose, and cottonwood. Delicate wildflowers bloom mostly in the spring and autumn, following the wet seasons, but cactus and the sacred datura can flower in the heat of summer. Wildlife include the sidewinder and diamondback rattlesnakes, Gila monster, desert tortoise, kangaroo rat, squirrels, cottontail, kit fox, coyote, and mule deer. You may find some Indian rock art, arrowheads, bits of pottery, and ruins. Many of the place names in the park honor Mormon

pioneers. Snow Canyon was named for Lorenzo and Erastus Snow—not for the rare snowfalls. Cooler months have the best weather; summers are too hot for comfortable hiking except in early morning. Highway UT 18 leads past an overlook on the rim of Snow Canyon and to the paved park road (UT 300) that drops into the canyon and follows it to its mouth and the small town of Ivins. Snow Canyon is about 12 miles northwest of St. George. It's reached either by UT 18, the faster way, or via Santa Clara and Ivins. The entrance fee is $3/vehicle for day use, $8 for camping, or $10 for camping w/hookups. Contact Snow Canyon State Park at Box 140, Santa Clara, UT 84765; tel. 628-2255 or (800) 322-3770 (reservations).

### Practicalities

Set within the canyon, **Shivwits Campground** (elev. 2,600 ft.) stays open all year with water, showers, and hookups. Camping reservations are recommended for spring and autumn weekends. Groups can also reserve picnic and overflow areas. **Snow Canyon Riding Stables** offers horseback riding, hay rides, campfire breakfasts, and Western shows year-round; overnight pack trips in the Pine Mountains can be arranged in summer; tel. 628-6677/7665.

### Hiking Trails

The park brochure has an aerial photo of the area on which trails and other features have been drawn in. **Hidden Pinyon Trail,** also signed as "nature trail," begins across the road from the Shivwits Campground entrance, then weaves among sandstone hills and lava flows to Varnish Mountain Overlook above Snow Canyon. At the overlook, desert varnish on sandstone has turned the rock jet black. The easy trail is 1½ miles roundtrip and has a small elevation gain; some sections cross rough rocks and deep sand. It's an easy scramble from the overlook area to the canyon floor below. **West Canyon Trail** is the longest in the park; it begins near the stables (0.7 mile south of the campground) and goes northwest along an old road up Snow Canyon to West Canyon. (You can also take cross-country hikes into other canyons passed on the way.) The trail is 7 miles roundtrip with a small elevation gain. Overnight trips are permitted here, but check in first with a park ranger. **Johnson's Arch Trail** begins near the mouth of Snow Canyon just outside the south boundary of the park (1.9 miles south of the campground). The 1½-mile roundtrip trail crosses Hackleberry Wash and goes up a small canyon to the arch. **Lava Tubes Trail** winds across a lava field to an area of lava caves; 1 mile roundtrip. The caves formed when molten lava broke out of the partly cooled flow and left rooms and tunnels behind. Artifacts indicate that Indians once sheltered in the chambers. Trailhead is 1.5 miles north of the campground. The steep and strenuous **Volcano Trail** ascends a cinder cone northeast of Snow Canyon. The 1,000-year-old volcano is on the east side of UT 18 one mile north of the turnoff for Snow Canyon.

## VEYO AND VICINITY

This little village lies along the Santa Clara River 19 miles northwest of St. George. Nearby in a small canyon, **Veyo Resort** offers a swimming pool fed by warm-water springs. The pretty spot has picnic tables and a snack bar; open from about the last weekend in March to Labor Day; tel. 574-2744; take the Veyo Pool Resort Road from UT 18 southeast of town.

### Gunlock State Park
The 266-acre reservoir is set among red and gray hills 10 miles southwest of Veyo. Parking area, docks, and paved boat ramp lie just off the road near the dam. The red-sand beach across the lake can be reached by boat or by a short walk across the dam. Largemouth bass, channel catfish, bluegill, and the odd trout swim in the waters. At press time, the park lacked a developed picnic area, campground, or water source. Open all year; no charge. A marina and campground are planned; check with Snow Canyon State Park for current info at Box 140, Santa Clara, UT

84765; tel. 628-2255. Gunlock Lake can be reached from St. George via Veyo or by the slightly shorter route through Santa Clara.

### Baker Dam Recreation Site
This 50-acre reservoir on BLM land is on the Santa Clara River upstream from Veyo. Fishermen come for the rainbow and brown trout. An established campground is located just before the dam; drive across the dam to undeveloped camping areas and a boat ramp. Open all year; no water or charge. Go north 4 miles on UT 18 from Veyo, then turn right 0.5 mile on a paved road (between Mileposts 24 and 25).

## PINE VALLEY MOUNTAINS

A massive body of magma, uncovered by erosion, makes up the Pine Valley Mountains. Vegetation ranges from pinyon pine and juniper in woodlands on the lower slopes, to ponderosa pine and aspen at the middle elevations, to Douglas fir, subalpine fir, Engelmann spruce, and limber pine at the heights. Signal Peak (elev. 10,365 ft.) tops the range, much of which has been designated the Pine Valley Mountain Wilderness.

### Pine Valley
In 1856, pioneers arrived at Pine Valley (elev. 6,600 ft.) to harvest the extensive forests and to raise livestock. Lumber from Pine Valley helped build many southern Utah settlements and even went into Salt Lake City's great tabernacle organ. The town's picturesque white chapel was built in 1868 by Ebenezer Bryce, who later homesteaded at what's now Bryce Canyon National Park. Most of today's residents come up just in summer for the cool mountain air. The Branding Iron Steak House serves dinners during the summer. Pine Valley is 32 miles from St. George via Veyo.

### Pine Valley Recreation Area
Continue 3 miles on the paved road past Pine Valley to the picnic areas, campgrounds, and trails in Dixie National Forest. At Pine Valley Reservoir, 2.3 miles up on the right, you can fish for rainbow and some brook trout. There's also fair fishing in the Santa Clara River up-

stream and downstream. **Ponderosa Picnic Area** is 0.4 mile farther on the right; free day use. Turn right just past the picnic area for **Pines Campground** and **Lower Pines Picnic Area** and **Brown's Point Trailhead.** Continue straight for **Blue Springs** and **South and North Juniper campgrounds** and for **Whipple Trailhead.** All the campgrounds have water and a $6 single-unit fee during their May 20 to Oct. 31 season. Elevation is 6,800 feet. Groups can reserve one camping and 3 picnic areas with the Pine Valley Ranger District in St. George.

**Pine Valley Wilderness**

The 50,000-acre wilderness has the best scenery of the Pine Valley Mountains, but it can be seen only on foot or horseback. A network of trails from all directions leads into the wilderness. They're usually open from about mid-June into October. **Summit Trail** is the longest (35 miles one way) and connects with many other trails. Several loops are possible, though most are too long for day hikes. **Whipple National Recreation Trail** is one of the most popular for both day and overnight trips; it ascends 2,100 feet in 6 miles to Summit Trail. **Brown's Point Trail** also climbs to Summit Trail, but in 4 miles. Strong hikers can use the Brown's Point and Summit trails to reach the top of Signal Peak on a day hike; the last part of the climb is a rockscramble. Generally, the trails from Pine Valley are signed and easy to follow; trails in other areas may be unmaintained. Take topo maps and a compass if you're going for more than a short stroll. The Pine Valley Ranger District office in St. George has a recreation map showing trails and trailheads; Room 40 of the Federal Bldg. at 196 E. Tabernacle (St. George, UT 84770); tel. 673-3431. *The Hiker's Guide to Utah* by Dave Hall describes a 15-mile loop in the Pine Valley Mountains.

## WEST OF PINE VALLEY MOUNTAINS

**Mountain Meadows Massacre Historic Site**

A short trip from UT 18 west of the Pine Valley Mountains leads to the site of one of the darkest chapters of Mormon history. The pleasant valley had been a popular rest stop for pioneers about to cross the hot desert country to the west. In 1857, a California-bound wagon train, whose members had already exchanged angry words with Mormons of the region, was attacked by an alliance of local Indians and the Mormons. About 120 people of the wagon train died in the massacre. Only some small children too young to tell the story were spared. The close-knit Mormon community tried to cover up the incident and hindered federal attempts to apprehend the killers. Only John D. Lee, who was in charge of Indian affairs in southern Utah at the time, was ever brought to justice. After nearly 20 years and 2 trials, authorities took him back to this spot to be executed by firing squad. Many details of the massacre remain unknown. The major causes seem to have been the strong anti-Mormon feelings by the travelers, a Mormon fear of invasion, aggressive Indians, and poor communications between the Mormon leadership in Salt Lake City and southern Utah. A simple monument now marks the site of the tragedy; turn west one mile on a gravel road from UT 18 between Mileposts 31 and 32.

**Enterprise Reservoirs**

Rainbow trout lurk in the lower and upper reservoirs. The larger Upper Enterprise Reservoir has a paved boat ramp and easier access. Nearby **Honeycomb Rocks Campground** (elev. 5,700 ft.) has water and a $4 fee from about May 15 to Oct. 31. Its name describes the outcrops of porous volcanic tuff. The open country here supports mostly grass, sage, and some ponderosa pine and Gambel oak. Drive to the town of Enterprise, 41 miles northwest of St. George and 47 miles west of Cedar City, then follow paved roads 11.5 miles west and south.

**Pine Park Campground**

This campground is located farther west from Enterprise in an isolated area of the Dixie National Forest near the Nevada border; open about May 20 to Oct. 31; no water or fee. You may need 4WD, because the last part of the road is steep and rough. Sites are in a canyon eroded from volcanic tuff at an elevation of 6,200 feet.

## NORTH OF PINE VALLEY MOUNTAINS

### Old Irontown

This is one of Utah's best-preserved 19th C. iron smelter sites. The original Iron Mission near Cedar City had poor success during its brief life in the 1850s. In 1870, though, more extensive ore deposits farther west at this site encouraged another attempt at iron making. Daily production rose to nearly 5 tons, and a town of several hundred workers grew up around the smelter. Profits began to decline in the 1880s when cheaper iron from the eastern states flooded in. The town soon died, though mining has since continued on and off in the vicinity. A brick chimney and stone foundations of the smelter and a beehive-shaped charcoal kiln show the layout of the operation. Look around in the sagebrush for remnants of the townsite and for pieces of slag and iron. Drive 16 miles west from Cedar City or 30 miles east from Enterprise to the signed turnoff on UT 56 (just west of Milepost 41), then turn southwest 2.7 miles.

## EAST OF PINE VALLEY MOUNTAINS

### Leeds

This small community has an **RV park** open all year at the gas station; $7.63 w/hookups; tel. 879-2210. Leeds has 2 exits on I-15; southbound traffic on I-15 must use Exit 23 on the north side of town; northbound traffic on I-15 must take Exit 22 south of town.

### Silver Reef

This ghost town is probably Utah's most accessible. In about 1870, prospectors found rich silver deposits in the sandstone here, much to the surprise of mining experts who thought such a combination impossible. The town grew up several years later and boomed from 1878 to 1882. The population peaked at 1,500 and included a sizable Chinese community. Then a combination of lower silver prices, declining yields, and water in the mines forced the operations to close one by one, the last in 1891. Other attempts at mining have since been made from time to time, including some uranium production in the 1950s and '60s, but the town had died.

The **Wells Fargo building**, which once stood in the center of town, is now Silver Reef's main attraction. Built of stone in 1877, it looks as solid as ever. **Jerry Anderson Art Gallery** and the small **Silver Reef Museum** occupy the interior; open Mon. to Sat. 9 a.m.-5 p.m.; tel. 879-2254. Encroaching modern houses detract a bit from the setting, but the ghosts are still here. Stone walls and foundations peek out of the sagebrush. A short walk on the road past the Wells Fargo building takes you to the ruins and tailings of the mills that once shook the town with their racket. Take I-15 Leeds Exit 22 or 23 and follow signs 1.3 miles on a paved road.

### Oak Grove Campground

On the east side of the Pine Valley Mountains, Oak Grove (elev. 6,800 ft.) is in a forest of Gambel and live shrub oak, ponderosa pine, and some spruce. The small campground has water from about May 20 to Oct. 31; no charge. Leeds Creek has trout fishing, but dense shrubbery along the banks can make access difficult. **Oak Grove Trail** winds 3 miles from the campground to Summit Trail in the Pine Valley Mountain Wilderness. Take I-15 Leeds Exit 22 or 23 and go northwest 9 miles. The unpaved road may be rough, especially late in the season; it's usually passable by cars, but isn't recommended for trailers.

### Red Cliffs Recreation Site

Weather-sculptured cliffs of reddish-orange sandstone rise above this pretty spot. The seasonal Quail Creek emerges from a canyon, flows though the middle of the campground, then goes on to Quail Creek Reservoir 2 miles away. The campground/picnic area (elev. 3,240 ft.) is open all year with water; there's a $4 camping fee. **Desert Trail** starts on the left near the beginning of the campground loop and follows the creek ½ mile into the canyon. Idyllic pools and graceful rock formations line the way. You'll need to do some wading to continue upstream past trail's end. A shorter but more rugged trail (¼ mile roundtrip) begins near the end of the campground loop and crosses slickrock to Silver Reef Lookout Point. Here there's a good panorama of the area, though you can't actually see Silver Reef ghost town. Take I-15 Leeds Exit 22 or 23, go south 3 miles on the frontage road, then turn west 1.7 miles on a paved road. Long trailers may drag on dips at stream crossings.

## Quail Creek State Park

Barren rock hills surround the 590-acre reservoir. Most of the water comes from pumps fed by the Virgin River; Quail Creek also contributes its share. Curiously, the reservoir has 2 dams to hold back the waters. The newly developed state park on the west shore offers a campground (water but no showers or hookups), swimming beach, paved boat ramp, and docks. Fishermen come for the largemouth bass, rainbow trout, catfish, and bluegill). Other popular activities include water-skiing, jet-skiing, and windsurfing. The park stays open all year; $3/vehicle day use, $6/vehicle camping; Box 1943, St. George, UT 84770; tel. 879-2378 or (800) 322-3770 (reservations). If coming from the north, take I-15 Leeds Exit 23 and follow the frontage road south 3.4 miles, then turn left 1.5 miles; from the south, take I-15 Hurricane Exit 16, go east 2.6 miles on UT 9, then north 2 miles on a paved road.

# HURRICANE

Legend has it that in the early 1860s a group of pioneers was descending the steep cliffs above the present townsite when a strong wind came up; Erastus Snow compared it with a hurricane and named the place Hurricane Hill. A canal to bring water from the Virgin River to Hurricane Bench took 11 years of hard work to build, beginning in 1893, but it allowed farming in the area for the first time. Settlers founded the town in 1906. Many retirees and winter visitors live here now. Hurricane is also a handy traveler's stop. The **Washington County Fair** is held in August.

## Practicalities

**Weston's Lamplighter Inn (Best Western)** has a pool at 280 W. State; tel. 635-4647; $40.33 s, $50.14 d. **Motel Park Villa** has some kitchenettes at 650 W. State; tel. 635-4010; $25 s, $31.75 d. **Brentwood RV Park** is open year-round with a restaurant, 9-hole golf course, bowling alley, indoor pool, tennis courts, and recreation room; 4.5 miles west of town; tel. 635-2320; $9.81 tent, $13.08 RV w/hookups. **Quail Lake RV Park** is open year-round with pool, jacuzzi, store, and golf driving

Wells Fargo building at Silver Reef ghost town

range; 6 miles west of town; tel. 635-9960; $10.90 w/hookups). **Quail Creek State Park** (see above) is 6.5 miles west, then 2 miles north. The small town of La Verkin, 2.7 miles north of Hurricane, has the **Gateway Trailer Park** (open all year at 513 N. 412 West with showers; $7.63 tent or RV w/hookups; tel. 635-4533) and **Zion RV Park** (open all year at 44 W. 500 North with showers, pool, and store; $13.08 tent, $15.81 RV w/hookups; tel. 635-4272). Cafes include **Grandma's Country Kitchen** and **El Chaparral Restaurant** in Hurricane and the **Brentwood Restaurant** 4.5 miles west.

## Pah Tempe Hot Springs

Hot mineral water gushes from springs along the Virgin River and fills 7 pools (about 106° F) and a swimming pool (high 90s). The Dominguez-Escalante expedition passed by in 1776 and thought these hot springs characteristic of the entire river, which they named the Rio Sulfureo. A small resort at the springs maintains the pools, a bed and breakfast ($40 s, $46 d), a campground ($12 s, $18 d), and a health-food cafe (open daily with vegetarian cooking for breakfast, lunch, and dinner). The resort is open daily about 9 a.m.-10 p.m. (to 11 p.m. on Fri. and Sat.); tel. 635-2879/2353. Admission fees for the pools are $5 adult, $3 children 6-12 and seniors, and $1 children under 6. The resort is on Enchanted Way, just off UT 9 one mile north of Hurricane.

With permission from the resort, you can take the old bridge across the river to see a group of undeveloped hot springs. Hikers can continue farther upstream to explore the canyon. Look for the Hurricane Canal in the cliffs high above the river.

## The Dinosaur Trackways And Old Fort Pearce

Both of these sites illustrate periods of Utah's past. They're easily visited on a scenic backroad drive through the desert between Hurricane and St. George. Most of the road is unpaved and has some rough and sandy spots, but it should be OK for cautiously driven cars in dry weather. From Hurricane, drive south 8 miles on 700 West, then turn west 8.5 miles to the dinosaur trackways turnoff and another 2 miles to the Fort Pearce turnoff. From St. George, head east on 700 South and follow the road as it turns south; turn left (east) 2.1 miles on a paved road immediately after crossing the Virgin River, turn left 3.5 miles on another paved road after a curve, then turn left (east) 5.6 miles on an unpaved road to the Fort Pearce turnoff and another 2 miles to the dinosaur trackways turnoff. Signs for Warner Valley and Fort Pearce point the way at many, but not all, of the intersections.

A group of dinosaur trackways documents the passage of at least 2 different species more than 200 million years ago. The well-preserved tracks, in the Moenave Formation, may have been made by a 20-foot-long herbivore weighing an estimated 8-10 tons and by a carnivore half as long. No remains of the dinosaurs themselves have been found here.

The name of Old Fort Pearce honors Capt. John Pearce, who led Mormon troops of the area during the Black Hawk War with Ute Indians from 1865 to 1869. In 1861, ranchers had arrived in Warner Valley to run cattle on the desert grasslands. Four years later, however, Indian troubles threatened to drive the settlers out. The Black Hawk War and periodic raids by Navajo Indians made life very precarious. Springs in Fort Pearce Wash, the only reliable water for many miles, proved the key to domination of the region. In Dec. 1866, work began on a fort overlooking the springs. The stone walls stood about 8 feet high and were more than 30 feet long. No roof was ever added. Much of the fort and the adjacent corral (built in 1869) have survived to the present. Local cattlemen still use the springs for their herds. Petroglyphs can be seen ¼ mile downstream from the fort along ledges on the north side of the wash.

# ZION NATIONAL PARK

The sheer cliffs and great monoliths of Zion Canyon reach high into the heavens. Energetic streams and other forces of erosion created this land of finely sculptured rock. One can understand why the Mormon pioneers thought the name Zion appropriate here. The large park spreads across 147,000 acres and contains 8 geologic formations and 4 major vegetation zones. Elevations range from 3,666 feet in lower Coalpits Wash to 8,726 feet atop Horse Ranch Mountain.

The highlight for most visitors is Zion Canyon, up to 2,400 feet deep. A scenic drive winds through it along the North Fork of the Virgin River past some of the most spectacular scenery in the park. Hiking trails branch off to lofty viewpoints and narrow side canyons. Adventurous souls can continue on foot past road's end into the eerie depths of the Virgin River Narrows in upper Zion Canyon. The spectacular Zion-Mt. Carmel Highway, with its switchbacks and tunnels, provides access to the canyons and high plateaus east of Zion Canyon. Two other roads enter the rugged Kolob section northwest of Zion Canyon. The Kolob, a Mormon name meaning "The brightest star, next to the seat of God," includes wilderness areas rarely visited by man.

Zion's grandeur extends all through the year. Even rainy days can be memorable as countless waterfalls plunge from every crevice in the cliffs above. Spring and autumn are the choice seasons for the most pleasant temperatures and the best chances of seeing wildlife and wildflowers. From about mid-Oct. to early Nov., cottonwoods and other trees and plants blaze with color. Summer temperatures in the canyons can be uncomfortably hot with highs hovering above 100° F; this is also the busiest season. In winter, nighttime temperatures are near freezing; weather then tends to be unpredictable, with bright sunshine one day and freezing rain the next. Snow-covered slopes contrast with colorful rocks. Snow may block some of the high-country trails and the road to Lava Point, but the rest of the park is open and accessible year-round.

The Zion Canyon Visitor Center, at the mouth of Zion Canyon, is on UT 9 about midway between I-15 and US 89. It's 43 miles northeast of St. George, 60 miles south of Cedar City, 41 miles northwest of Kanab, and 86 miles southwest of Bryce Canyon National Park. Large RVs and bicycles must heed special regulations for the long tunnel on the Zion-Mt. Carmel Highway; see "East of Zion Canyon," p. 270. Visitors short on time usually drop in at the visitor center, travel the Zion Canyon Scenic Drive, and take short walks on Weeping Rock or Gateway to the Narrows trails. A stay of 2 days or longer is better to take in more of the grand scenery and to hike other inviting trails. Kolob Canyons Road, in the extreme northwestern section of the park, begins just off I-15 Exit 40 and climbs to an overlook for great views of the Finger Canyons of the Kolob; the drive is 10 miles roundtrip. Motorists with more time may also want to drive the Kolob Terrace Road to Lava Point for another perspective of the park; this drive is about 44 miles roundtrip from Virgin (on UT 9) and has some unpaved sections. An entry fee of $5 ($2 bus passengers and bicyclists) is charged at the East and South entrance stations year-round; it's good for 7 days. No charge is made for the Kolob Canyons or Lava Point drives.

## Geology

The rock layers at Zion began as sediments of oceans, rivers, lakes, or sand dunes deposited 53-225 million years ago. The Navajo Sandstone, laid down in about the middle of this period, forms most of the cliffs and great temples of the park. Look for the slanting lines of desert sand dunes turned to stone in this formation, which is more than 2,000 feet thick in some places. A gradual uplift of the Colorado Plateau, which continues today, has caused the formerly lazy rivers on its surface to pick up speed and knife through the rock layers. You can really appreciate these erosive powers during flash floods, when the North Fork of the Virgin River or other streams roar through their canyons. Erosion of some of the Virgin River's tributaries couldn't keep up with the main channel and were left as "hanging valleys" on the canyon walls; a good example is Hidden Canyon, reached by trail in Zion Canyon. Faulting has broken the Colorado Plateau into a series of smaller plateaus; those with the greatest uplift had the most layers removed by erosion. At Zion you're on the Kolob Terrace of the Markagunt Plateau, whose rock layers are younger than those of Kaibab Plateau at Grand Canyon National Park and older than those exposed on the Paunsaugunt Plateau at Bryce Canyon National Park.

## Flora And Fauna

Many different plant and animal communities live in the rugged terrain of deep canyons and high plateaus. Because the park lies near the meeting place of the Colorado Plateau, Great Basin, and Mohave Desert, representatives of all 3 regions can be found here. Only desert plants can endure the long dry spells and high temperatures found at lower elevations away from permanent water; they include cacti (prickly pear, cholla, and hedgehog), blackbrush, creosote bush, honey mesquite, and purple sage. Pygmy forests of pinyon pine, Utah juniper, live oak, mountain mahogany, and cliffrose grow between about 3,900 and 5,600 feet. High plateaus and the cooler canyons have ponderosa pine, Douglas fir, white fir, and aspen. Permanent springs and streams support a profusion of greenery such as cottonwood, box elder, willow, red birch, horsetail, and ferns. Watch out for poison ivy in moist, shady areas. Colorful wildflowers pop out of the ground at all elevations from spring through autumn.

You're likely to see mule deer, common throughout the park. Other wildlife includes elk, mountain lion, bobcat, black bear, bighorn sheep (reintroduced), coyote, gray fox, porcupine, ringtail cat, black-tailed jack rabbit, rock squirrel, cliff chipmunk, beaver, and many species of mice and bats. Birders have spotted more than 270 species in and near the park; common birds are red-tailed hawk, turkey vulture, quail, mallard, great horned owl, hairy woodpecker, raven, scrub jay, black-headed grosbeak, blue-gray gnatcatcher, canyon wren, Virginia's warbler, white-throated swift, and broad-tailed hummingbird. Hikers need to watch for western rattlesnakes, though these relatively rare snakes are unlikely to attack unless provoked.

## History

As early as A.D. 500, the Kayenta-Virgin branch of Anasazi Indians built small villages of partly underground pit houses in what's now the park. Their culture gradually developed over the centuries with improved agriculture and crafts until they left the region about 1200. Next came the Kaibab Band of Southern Paiutes, who spent part of the year here on seasonal migrations. The Paiutes relied heavily on wild seeds for food, supplemented by hunting and some agriculture. Anglo settlers and their livestock depleted the range and wildlife so much that the Paiutes had to abandon their old lifestyles.

*Zion Canyon*

Mormon pioneers pushed up the Virgin River Valley in 1859 and founded Grafton, the first of a series of towns south of the present-day park. In 1863, the Isaac Behunin family began farming in Zion Canyon and built a one-room cabin near where Zion Lodge now stands. Other families settled and farmed the canyon until the area's establishment as a national monument. The canyon's naming is credited to Isaac Behunin, who believed this spot to be a refuge from religious persecution. When Brigham Young later visited the canyon, however, he found tobacco and wine in use and declared the place "not Zion," which some dutiful followers then began calling it! A scientific expedition led by John Wesley Powell in 1872 helped make the wonders known to the outside world. Efforts by Stephen T. Mather, first director of the National Park Service, and others led to designation of Mukuntuweap ("Straight Canyon") National Monument in 1909 and establishment of Zion National Park in 1919.

## ZION CANYON

You may want to begin your travels in the park with a stop at the Zion Canyon Visitor Center at the lower end of the canyon. Then drive 0.7 mile north to the turnoff for Zion Canyon Scenic Drive, a 6-mile road following the North Fork of the Virgin River upstream. Monuments along the way include the Three Patriarchs, Mountain of the Sun, Lady Mountain, Great White Throne, Angels Landing, and Weeping Rock. Pullouts and hiking trails allow you to enjoy the many exhilarating views. Grotto Picnic Area offers shaded tables with water and restrooms. The road ends at Temple of Sinawava and the beginning of the Gateway to the Narrows Trail. In the busy summer months, vehicles over 21 feet have special parking restrictions in Zion Canyon; check at the entrance stations or visitor center.

### Zion Canyon Visitor Center
A large exhibit room introduces the rock layers of Zion—how they formed and how they have changed. Photos and dioramas illustrate adaptation of plants and animals to the park's

many habitats. Clay figurines, stone tools, and a clay jar containing 1,000-year-old corn belonged to the Anasazi, the first Indian culture to leave signs of habitation here. The Mormon pioneer exhibit commemorates the determined farmers who settled in the area. Staff will answer your questions about the park; they also have a variety of handouts on hiking, flora and fauna checklists, history, and other aspects of the park. Many nature programs and hikes are offered from late March to Nov.; check the posted schedule. Children's programs are held at Zion Nature Center near South Campground; ask at the visitor center for details. An excellent selection of books in the visitor center covers natural history, human history, and regional travel. Topo and geologic maps, posters, slides, postcards, and film are sold too. The Zion Canyon Visitor Center is open daily all year: 9 a.m.-5 p.m. in winter, extended to 8 a.m.-9 p.m. in summer. For more information, contact the park at Springdale, UT 84767; tel. 772-3256.

### Zion Lodge
The rustic lodge sits in the heart of Zion Canyon, 3 miles up Zion Canyon Scenic Drive. Zion Lodge provides the only accommodations and dining places within the park. It's open year-round, though the restaurant closes in winter; reservations for rooms should be made as far in advance as possible. Costs run $63.77 s or d for the motel, $71.40 s or d for the western cabins, and $103.55 for motel suites. The moderately priced restaurant offers a varied American menu daily for breakfast, lunch, and dinner. Picnic lunches can be ordered in advance; tel. 772-3213, ext. 160. A snack bar serves fast food. Zion Lodge organizes horseback rides along the Virgin River (one hour) and Sand Bench Trail (3 hours) and to Cable Mountain (from the East Entrance Station; all day). Tours in open-air vehicles provide narrated sightseeing trips in Zion Canyon; they run several times daily between Memorial Day and Labor Day weekends. The lodge also has evening programs, a post office counter (open Mon. to Sat.), and a gift shop. Make reservations for Zion Lodge through TW Services, Box 400, Cedar City, UT 84720; tel. 586-7686.

## Zion Canyon Campgrounds

Campgrounds in the park often fill up on Easter and other major holidays and occasionally at other times. **South** and **Watchman campgrounds,** just inside from the South Entrance Station, have sites for $6 with water but no showers or hookups. Only group areas can be reserved. One of the campgrounds stays open in winter. Some of the pioneers' fruit trees in the campgrounds are still producing; you're free to pick what you'll be eating here. Additional campgrounds lie just outside the park in Springdale (see "Vicinity of Zion National Park" below).

# ZION CANYON HIKES

The trails in Zion Canyon provide perspectives of the park not possible from the roads. Much of the hiking requires long ascents, but isn't too difficult at a leisurely pace. Water should be carried on most hikes. Descriptions of the following trails are given in order from the mouth of Zion Canyon to the Virgin River Narrows.

Countless off-trail routes in the canyons and plateaus surrounding Zion Canyon are possible for experienced hikers; rangers can suggest areas. Rappelling and other climbing skills may be needed to negotiate drops in some of the more remote canyons. Overnight hikers must obtain free backcountry permits from either Zion Canyon or Kolob Canyons visitor centers. Normally you won't need advance reservations for backcountry camping. Some areas of the park, mainly those near roads and major trails, are closed to overnight use. Zion Lodge offers shuttle services for hikers.

Rock climbers come to challenge the high cliffs, especially those of Navajo Sandstone. For route descriptions, see the climbing books available for reference at both visitor centers. Check to make sure your climbing area is open; some places are closed to protect wildlife. Climbing alone is discouraged.

## Watchman Trail

From a trailhead north of Watchman Campground, the trail climbs 370 feet to a bench below Watchman Peak, the prominent mountain southeast of the visitor center. You'll enjoy views of lower Zion Canyon and the town of Springdale. The well-graded trail follows a side canyon past some springs, then ascends to the overlook; distance is 2.4 miles roundtrip and takes about 2 hours. A wide variety of trees and plants lines the way. In summer, it's best to get an early start. One trailhead is near the South Campground amphitheater; there's also a trail from Watchman Campground (see the park brochure map). Rangers lead naturalist walks during the main season.

## Court Of The Patriarchs Viewpoint

A short trail from the parking area leads to the viewpoint. The Patriarchs, a trio of peaks to the west, overlook Birch Creek; they are (from left to right) Abraham, Isaac, and Jacob. Mount Moroni, the reddish peak on the far right, partly blocks the view of Jacob. Better views can be obtained by hiking 0.5 mile or so up Sand Bench Trail (see below).

## Sand Bench Trail

This is an easy loop with good views of the Three Patriarchs, the Streaked Wall, and other monuments of lower Zion Canyon. The trail is 1.7 miles long with a 500-foot elevation gain; allow about 3 hours. During the main season, Zion Lodge organizes 3-hour horseback rides on the trail. The horses churn up dust and leave an uneven surface though, so hikers usually prefer to go elsewhere then. You'll soon leave the riparian forest along

*The rock squirrel* (Citellus variegatus) *is a large ground squirrel that lives in rocky areas from high plateaus to the edge of the desert. It's often seen in the park.*

Birch Creek as the trail climbs onto the dry benchland. Pinyon pine, juniper, sand sage, yucca, prickly pear cactus, and other high-desert plants and animals live here. Hikers can park at Court of the Patriarchs Viewpoint, walk across the scenic drive, then follow a service road to the footbridge and trailhead. A 1.2-mile trail along the river connects the trailhead with Zion Lodge. Try to hike in early morning or late afternoon in the warmer months.

### Emerald Pools Trails

Three spring-fed pools, small waterfalls, and views of Zion Canyon make the climb worth-while. You have a choice of 3 trails. Easiest is the paved trail to the Lower Pool; cross the footbridge near Zion Lodge and turn right 0.6 mile. The Middle Pool above can be reached by continuing 0.2 mile on a smaller trail or by taking a different trail from the footbridge at Zion Lodge (after crossing the bridge, turn left, then right up the trail). Together these trails make a 1.8-mile roundtrip loop. The third trail begins from the Grotto Picnic Area, crosses a footbridge and turns left 0.7 mile; the trail forks left to the Lower Pool and right to the Middle Pool. A steep 0.4-mile trail leads from the Middle Pool to Upper Emerald Pool. This magical spot has a white-sand beach and towering cliffs rising above. Allow 1-3 hours to visit the pools. Photographers often get good pictures of rock reflections in the pools.

### West Rim Trail

Some of the best views of Zion Canyon are reached on this strenuous trail. Backpackers can continue on the West Rim Trail to Lava Point and other destinations in the Kolob region. Start from Grotto Picnic Area (elev. 4,300 ft.) and cross the footbridge, then turn right along the river. The trail climbs the slopes and enters the cool and shady depths of Refrigerator Canyon. Walter's Wiggles, a series of 21 closely spaced switchbacks, lead to Scout Lookout and a trail junction, 4 miles roundtrip and a 1,050-foot elevation gain. Scout Lookout has fine views of Zion Canyon. The trail is paved and well graded to this point. Turn right 0.5 mile at the junction to reach the summit of Angels Landing.

Angels Landing is a sheer-walled monolith rising 1,500 feet above the North Fork of the Virgin River. Though the trail to the summit is rough, chains provide security in the more exposed places. The climb is safe with care and good weather. Anyone steady on his feet should be able to make it out, but don't go if the trail is covered with snow or ice or if thunderstorms threaten. Once on top, you'll see why Angels Landing got its name—the panorama makes all the effort worthwhile. Average hiking time for the roundtrip between Grotto Picnic Area and Angels Landing is 4 hours.

Energetic hikers can continue 4.8 miles on the main trail from Scout Lookout to West Rim Viewpoint, which overlooks the Right Fork of North Creek. This strenuous 12.8-mile round-trip from Grotto Picnic Area has a 3,070-foot elevation gain. West Rim Trail continues through Zion's backcountry to Lava Point (elev. 7,890 ft.), where there's a primitive campground. A car shuttle and one or more days are needed for the 13.3 miles (one way) from Grotto Picnic Area. You'll have an easier hike by starting at Lava Point and hiking down to Grotto Picnic Area; even so, be prepared for a *long* dayhike. The trail has little or no water in some years.

### Weeping Rock Trail

A favorite with visitors, this easy trail winds past lush vegetation and wildflowers to a series of cliffside springs above an overhang. Thousands of water droplets glisten in the afternoon sun. The springs emerge where water seeping through more than 2,000 feet of Navajo Sandstone meets a layer of impervious shale. The paved trail is 0.5 mile roundtrip with a 100-foot elevation gain. Signs along the way identify some of the trees and plants.

### East Rim Trail

The strenuous East Rim Trail climbs 2,150 feet in 3.6 highly scenic miles to Observation Point (elev. 6,507 ft.) on the edge of Zion Canyon. Allow about 7 hours for the roundtrip. Trails branch off along the way to Hidden Canyon, upper Echo Canyon, East Entrance, East Mesa, and other destinations. The first of many switchbacks begins a short way up from the trailhead at Weeping Rock parking area. You'll reach the junction for Hidden Canyon Trail (see below) after 0.8 mile. Several switchbacks later, the East Rim Trail enters sinuous Echo Canyon. This incredibly narrow chasm can be explored for short distances upstream and downstream to deep pools and pour-offs. Echo Canyon Trail branches to the right at about the halfway point; this rough trail continues farther up the canyon and connects with trails to Cable Mountain, Deertrap Mountain, and the East Entrance Station (on Zion-Mt. Carmel Highway). The East Rim Trail then climbs slickrock slopes above Echo Canyon with many fine views. Parts of the trail are cut right into the cliffs. You'll reach the rim at last after 3 miles of steady climbing. Then it's an easy 0.6 mile through a forest of pinyon pine, juniper, Gambel oak, manzanita, sage, and some ponderosa pine to Observation Point. Impressive views take in Zion Canyon below and mountains and mesas all around. East Mesa Trail turns right about 0.3 mile before Observation Point and follows the plateau northeast to a dirt road outside the park.

## Hidden Canyon

See if you can spot the entrance of Hidden Canyon from below! Inside the narrow canyon are small sandstone caves, a little natural arch, and diverse plant life. The high walls, rarely more than 65 feet apart, block sunlight except for a short time at midday. Hiking distance on the moderately difficult trail is about 3 miles roundtrip between Weeping Rock parking area and the lower canyon; follow East Rim Trail 0.8 mile, then turn right 0.7 mile on Hidden Canyon Trail to the canyon entrance. Footing can be a bit difficult in places due to loose sand, but chains provide handholds on the more exposed sections. Steps chopped into the rock just inside Hidden Canyon help to bypass some deep pools. Allow 3-4 hours for the roundtrip; elevation change is about 1,000 feet. After heavy rains and spring runoff, the creek forms a small waterfall at the canyon entrance. The canyon is about one mile long and mostly easy walking, though the trail fades away. Look for the arch on the right about 0.5 mile up the canyon.

## Gateway To The Narrows Trail

This is one of the most popular hikes in the park. The nearly level paved trail begins at the end of Zion Canyon Scenic Drive and winds one mile upstream along the river to the Virgin River Narrows. Allow about 2 hours to take in the scenery. Countless springs and seeps on the canyon walls support luxuriant plant growth and swamps. Most of the springs occur at the contact between the Navajo Sandstone and the less permeable Kayenta Formation below. The water and vegetation attract abundant wildlife; keep an eye out for birds and animals and their tracks. At trail's end, the canyon is wide enough for only the river. Hikers continuing upstream must wade and sometimes even swim (see below). Late morning is the best time for photography. In autumn, cottonwoods and maples display bright splashes of color.

## The Narrows

Upper Zion Canyon is probably the most famous backcountry area in the park, yet it's one of the most strenuous. There's no trail and you'll be wading much of the time in the river, which is usually knee- to chest-deep. At places, the high fluted walls of upper North Fork of the Virgin River are only 20 feet apart, and very little sunlight penetrates the depths. Mysterious side canyons beckon exploration. Hikers should be well prepared and in good condition, as river hiking is more tiring than that over dry land. The major hazards are flash floods and hypothermia. Finding the right time to go through can be tricky: spring runoff is too high, summer thunderstorms bring hazardous flash floods, and winter is too cold. That leaves just part of early summer (mid-June to mid-July) and early autumn (mid-Sept. to mid-Oct.) as the best bets. You can get through the entire 16-mile (one way) Narrows in about 12 hours, though 2 days is best to enjoy the beauty of the place. Children under 12 shouldn't attempt hiking the entire canyon. Talk with rangers at Zion Canyon Visitor Center before starting a trip; they also have a handout with useful information on planning a Narrows hike. You'll need a permit for hikes *through* the Narrows even on a day trip. No permit is needed if you're just going part way in and back in one day, though you must first check conditions and the weather forecast with rangers. No camping is permitted below Big Springs. Group size for hiking and camping is limited to 12.

A hike downstream saves not only climbing but the work of fighting the river currents. In fact, the length of the Narrows should only be hiked downstream. The upper trailhead is near Chamberlain's Ranch, reached by an 18-mile dirt road that turns north from UT 9 east of the park. The lower trailhead is at the end of the Zion Canyon Scenic Drive. Elevation change is 1,280 feet. A good half-day trip begins at the end of Gateway to the Narrows Trail and follows the Narrows 1.5 miles upstream to Orderville Canyon, then back the same way.

## EAST OF ZION CANYON

The east section of the park is a land of sandstone slickrock, hoodoos, and narrow canyons. Much of the pretty scenery can be seen along the Zion-Mt. Carmel Highway (UT 9) between the East Entrance Station and Zion Canyon. Most of this region is a place to explore on your own. Try hiking a canyon or heading up a slickrock slope (the pass be- tween Crazy Quilt and Checkerboard mesas is one possibility). Highlights on the plateau include views of the White Cliffs and Checkerboard Mesa (both near the East Entrance Station) and hiking the Canyon Overlook Trail (begins just east of the long tunnel). Checkerboard Mesa's distinctive pattern is due to a combination of vertical fractures and horizontal bedding planes, both accentuated by weathering. The spectacular descent into Zion Canyon goes first through a 530-foot tunnel, then a 5,600-foot tunnel, followed by a series of 6 switchbacks to the canyon floor. Because of the narrowness of the long tunnel (completed in 1930) and the growing numbers of large vehicles visiting Zion, it's necessary for them to travel through in one-way traffic. Any vehicle over 7' 10" wide or 11' 4" high or 40' long (50' w/trailer) must go through in one-way traffic; a $10 fee is charged at the tunnel to do this. Bicycles must be carried through the long tunnel (it's too dangerous to ride). **Zican Indian Store,** just outside of the East Entrance Station, is open all year with a cafe, groceries, gas station, and souvenirs. A primitive campground (no facilities) is across the highway.

### Canyon Overlook Trail
This popular hike features great views from the heights without the stiff climbs found on

*a short hike on Canyon Overlook trail*

most other Zion trails. Allow about an hour for the one-mile roundtrip; elevation gain is 163 feet. A booklet available at the start or at the Zion Canyon Visitor Center describes the geology, plant life, and clues to the presence of wildlife. The trail winds in and out along ledges of Pine Creek Canyon, which opens into a great valley. Panoramas at trail's end take in lower Zion Canyon in the distance. A sign at the viewpoint identifies Bridge Mountain, Streaked Wall, East Temple, and other features. The Great Arch of Zion, termed a "blind arch" because it's open on only one side, lies below; the span is 580 feet high, 720 feet long, and 90 feet deep. Canyon Overlook Trail begins across from the parking area just east of the longer (west) tunnel on the Zion-Mt. Carmel Highway.

## THE KOLOB

North and west of Zion Canyon lies the remote backcountry of the Kolob. This area became a second Zion National Monument in 1937, then was added to Zion National Park in 1956. You'll see all but one of the rock formations present in the park and evidence of past volcanic eruptions. Two roads lead into the Kolob. The paved 5-mile Kolob Canyons Road begins at the Kolob Canyons Visitor Center just off I-15 and ends at an overlook and picnic area; it's open all year. Kolob Terrace Road is paved from the town of Virgin (15 miles west on UT 9 from the South Entrance Station) to near the turnoff for Lava Point; snow usually blocks the way in winter.

### Kolob Canyons Visitor Center
Though small with just a handful of exhibits, the visitor center is a good place to stop for information on exploring the Kolob region. Hikers can learn current trail conditions and obtain the permits required for overnight trips and Zion Narrows day trips. Books, topo and geologic maps, posters, postcards, slides, and film are sold. Open daily 8 a.m.-4:30 p.m., with extended hours between Memorial Day and Labor Day weekends; tel. 586-9548. The visitor center and the start of the Kolob Canyons Road lie just off I-15 Exit 40.

### Campgrounds
The Kolob section of the park doesn't have a campground. The nearest one within the park is Lava Point Campground (see below). **Redledge Campground** in Kanarraville is the closest commercial campground to the Kolob Canyons area; go 2 miles north on I-15, take Exit 42, and continue 4.5 miles into downtown Kanarraville. The campground is open from early April to late Oct. with showers and laundry; $8.72 tents, $13.08 RVs w/hookups; tel. 586-9150. The tiny agricultural community was named after a local Paiute chief. A low ridge south of town marks the southern limit of prehistoric Lake Bonneville.

### Kolob Canyons Road
The 5-mile scenic drive winds past the dramatic Finger Canyons of the Kolob to Kolob Canyons Viewpoint and a picnic area at the end of the road. The road is paved and has many pullouts where you can stop to admire the scenery. The first part of the drive follows the 200-mile-long Hurricane Fault that forms the west edge of the Markagunt Plateau. Look for the tilted rock layers deformed by friction as the plateau rose nearly one mile. Taylor Creek Trail, which begins 2 miles past the visitor center, provides a close look at the canyons (see below). Lee Pass, 4 miles beyond the visitor center, was named after John D. Lee of the infamous Mountain Meadows Massacre; he's believed to have lived nearby for a short time after the massacre. La Verkin Creek Trail begins at Lee Pass Trailhead for trips to Kolob Arch and beyond. Signs at the end of the road identify the points, buttes, mesa, and mountains. The salmon-colored Navajo Sandstone cliffs glow a deep red at sunset. **Timber Creek Overlook Trail** begins from the picnic area at road's end and climbs ½ mile to the overlook (elev. 6,369 ft.); views encompass the Pine Valley Mountains, Zion canyons, and distant Mt. Trumbull.

### Taylor Creek Trail
An excellent dayhike from Kolob Canyons Road. The easy to moderate trail begins on the left 2 miles from Kolob Canyons Visitor Center and heads upstream into the canyon of Middle Fork of Taylor Creek. Double Arch

Alcove is 2.7 miles from the trailhead; a dry fall 0.2 mile farther blocks the way (water flows over it during spring runoff and after rains). A giant rock fall occurred here in June 1990. Other nearby canyons, such as North and South forks of Taylor Creek, can be explored too. South Fork of Taylor Creek Trail leaves the drive at a bend 3.1 miles from the visitor center, then goes in 1.2 miles.

### Hiking To Kolob Arch

Kolob Arch vies with Landscape Arch in Arches National Park as the world's longest natural rock span. Differences in measurement techniques have resulted in a controversy as to which is longer: Kolob Arch's span has been measured variously at 292-310 feet, Landscape Arch's at 291-306 feet. Kolob probably takes the prize because its 310-foot measurement was done with an accurate electronic method. Kolob's height is 330 feet and its vertical thickness is 80 feet. The arch makes a fine destination for a backpack trip. Spring and autumn are the best seasons to go; summer temperature rise into the 90s, and winter snows make the trails hard to follow. You have a choice of 3 moderately difficult trails. **La Verkin Creek Trail** begins at Lee Pass (elev. 6,080 ft.) on Kolob Canyons Scenic Drive, 4 miles beyond the visitor center. The trail drops into Timber Creek (intermittent flow), crosses over hills to La Verkin Creek (flows year-round; some springs too), then turns up side canyons to the arch. The 14-mile roundtrip can be done as a long day trip, but you'll enjoy the best lighting for photos at the arch if you camp in the area and see it the following morning. Carry plenty of water for the return trip; the 800-foot climb to the trailhead can be hot and tiring.

Other ways to reach Kolob Arch are by the **Hop Valley** and **Willis Creek (La Verkin Creek) trails,** both reached from Kolob Terrace Road. Hop Valley Trail is 7 miles one way to Kolob Arch with an elevation drop of 1,050 feet; water is available in Hop Valley and La Verkin Creek. The trail crosses some private land (don't camp there). Willis Creek (La Verkin Creek) Trail is 10 miles one way with an elevation drop of 2,950 feet. It begins near Kolob Reservoir north of the park and also

crosses some private land (permission needed); careful map reading is required to find your way through crisscrossing trails into Willis Creek. Camp on park land only. Willis and La Verkin creeks have water and you may need to do some wading.

### Lava Point

The panorama from Lava Point (elev. 7,890 ft.) takes in the Cedar Breaks area to the north, the Pink Cliffs to the northeast, Zion Canyon Narrows and tributaries to the east, the Sentinel and other monoliths of Zion Canyon to the southeast, and Mt. Trumbull on the Arizona Strip to the south. Signs help identify features. Lava Point, which sits atop a lava flow, is a good place to cool off in summer—temperatures are about 20° cooler than in Zion Canyon. Aspen, ponderosa pine, Gambel oak, and white fir grow here. A small primitive **campground** near the point offers sites during the warmer months; no water or charge.

Two trails begin from West Rim Trailhead; either drive here or walk the one-mile **Barney's Trail** from Site 2 in the campground. **West Rim Trail** goes southeast to Zion Canyon, 13.3 miles one way with an elevation drop of 3,600 feet (3,000 feet in the last 6 miles). Water can normally be found along the way at Sawmill, Potato Hollow (less reliable—was dry in summer 1990), and Cabin springs. **Wildcat Canyon Trail** heads southwest 5 miles to a trailhead on Kolob Terrace Road (16 miles north of Virgin); elevation drop is 450 feet. This trail lacks a reliable water source. You can continue east toward Kolob Arch by taking the 4-mile **Connector Trail** to **Hop Valley Trail.** Snow blocks the road to Lava Point for much of the year; usual season is May or June to early November. Check road conditions with Zion Canyon or Kolob Canyons visitor centers. From the South Entrance Station in Zion Canyon, drive west 15 miles on UT 9 to Virgin, turn north 21 miles on Kolob Terrace Road (signed "Kolob Reservoir"), then right 1.8 miles to Lava Point.

### Kolob Reservoir

This high-country lake north of Lava Point has good fishing for rainbow trout. An unpaved boat ramp is at the south end near the dam.

People sometimes camp along the shore, although there are no facilities. Most of the surrounding land is private. To reach the reservoir, continue north 3.5 miles on Kolob Terrace Road from the Lava Point turnoff. The fair-weather road can also be followed past the reservoir to the Cedar City area. Blue Springs Reservoir, near the turnoff for Lava Point, is closed to the public.

# VICINITY OF ZION NATIONAL PARK

## SPRINGDALE

This small Mormon settlement (pop. 350) dates from 1862. A wife of one of the first settlers chose the name. Springdale lies just outside the park's South Entrance and offers many services for travelers.

### Accommodations And Campgrounds

Places to stay and eat are listed in order of increasing distance from the park entrance. All normally stay open year-round except as noted; rates may drop in winter. Cliffrose Lodge has a motel information service for the area; tel. (800) 342-8824. **Cliffrose Lodge** at 281 Zion Park Blvd. offers luxury rooms, pool, and gardens; tel. 772-3234 or (800) 243-8824; rooms run $66-82.50 s or d; suites are available too. **Flanigan's Inn** at 428 Zion Park Blvd. has a restaurant and pool; tel. 772-3244; rooms start at $39.60 s or d. **Zion Canyon Campground** offers cabins ($27.50 s or d), RV sites ($14.30 w/hookups), and tent sites ($12.10) at 481 Zion Park Blvd.; tel. 772-3237; facilities include store, pizza parlor and movies (both closed in winter), game room, laundry, and showers. **Canyon Ranch Motel** at 668 Zion Park Blvd. has some kitchenettes; tel. 772-3357; rooms are $41.80 s, $46.20 d and up. **Zion House Bed & Breakfast** is at 801 Zion Park Blvd.; tel. 772-3281; rooms (nonsmoking only) are $38.50-51.70 s, $48.40-63.80 d. **Pioneer Lodge Motel** at 838 Zion Park Blvd. has a restaurant and pool; tel. 772-3233; rooms start at $41.80 s or d. **Bumbleberry Inn** at 897 Zion Park Blvd. also has a restaurant; tel. 772-3224; $48.40 s, $53.90 d. **El Rio Lodge** is at 995 Zion Park Blvd.; tel. 772-3205; $37.40 s, $38.50 d and up. **Under the Eaves Guest House** features homey bed and breakfast accommodations at 980 Zion Park Blvd.; tel. 772-3457; $38.50-60.50 s, $49.50-71.50 d. **Terrace Brook Lodge** at 990 Zion Park Blvd. has a pool; tel. 772-3932; $38.50 s, 44 d. **Driftwood Lodge (Best Western)** at 1515 Zion Park Blvd. has a restaurant and pool; tel. 772-3262 or (800) 528-1234; $41.80 s, $44 d.

### Food

**Pizza at the Park** serves pasta, pizza, Italian sandwiches, and American food at Zion Canyon Campground (481 Zion Park Blvd.; tel. 772-3462); open daily for breakfast, lunch, and dinner. **Flanigan's Inn** has varied offerings including trout, New York strip steak, fettuccini, ham steak, and trout at 428 Zion Park Blvd.; tel. 772-3244; open daily for breakfast, lunch, and dinner. The **Pioneer Restaurant** serves American food at 828 Zion Park Blvd.; tel. 772-3467; open daily for breakfast, lunch, and dinner. **Sparky's Cafe** offers gourmet sandwiches, salads, and pasta dinners at 868 Zion Park Blvd.; tel. 772-3901; open daily for lunch and dinner (closed in winter). **Bumbleberry Inn's** menu of American food includes "bumbleberry" pies and pancakes at 897 Zion Park Blvd.; tel. 772-3224; open Mon. to Sat. for breakfast, lunch, and dinner. **Bit & Spur Restaurant** prepares flavorful chicken enchilada, chili relleno, toro Colorado, and other foods of the Southwest at 1212 Zion Park Blvd.; tel. 772-3498; open daily for dinner. **Driftwood Lodge** serves fine American food at 1515 Zion Park Blvd.; tel. 772-3262; open daily for breakfast, lunch, and dinner.

### Other Practicalities

**Springdale Art Center** has an especially busy program during the warmer months with art exhibits, plays, and concerts; located at 868 Zion Park Blvd.; call Sparky's Cafe at

772-3901 for the schedule. You may also want to check out the many art galleries, rock shops, and gift shops along Zion Park Boulevard. The **Grand Circle** multimedia show by Dixie College portrays the splendor and history of Zion and other scenic areas in the Southwest; presented nightly from late May to early Sept. at the O.C. Tanner Amphitheater in town (turnoff is opposite Zion Canyon Campground, then in 0.8 mile); concerts and dance performances occasionally take place too; tel. 1-673-4811, ext. 352. The **Southern Utah Folklife Festival** held in Zion National Park brings back the pioneer days with demonstrations, food, and entertainment; usually held Thurs., Fri., and Sat. following Labor Day. A **Fourth of July Celebration** has a parade and fire works. Roadside stands rent inner tubes in summer for tubing the Virgin River. Bicycles can also be rented in town. **Zion Canyon Medical Clinic** provides emergency services from about May to Oct.; take the turnoff for the O.C. Tanner Amphitheater; tel. 772-3226. The **post office** is in the center of town on Zion Park Blvd.; tel. 772-3950.

## GRAFTON

One of the best-preserved and most picturesque ghost towns in Utah. Photos of Grafton grace the covers of no less than 3 ghost-town books! Mormon families founded Grafton in 1859 near the Virgin River at a spot one mile downstream from the present site, but a big flood 2 years later convinced them to move here. Hostilities with the native Paiutes during the Black Hawk War forced residents to depart again for safer areas from 1866 to 1868. Floods and irrigation difficulties made life hard even in the best of times. Population declined in the early 1900s until only ghosts remained.

Movie makers discovered Grafton and used the site for *Butch Cassidy and the Sundance Kid* and other films. You may notice a few fiberglass chimneys and other "improvements." A schoolhouse, store, houses, cabins, and a variety of outbuildings still stand. One story goes that the Mormon bishop lived in the large 2-story house with wife #1 while wife #2 had to settle for the rough cabin across the

road—probably not an amicable situation! Grafton's cemetery is worth a visit too; it's on the left at a turn 0.3 mile before the townsite. A monument commemorates 3 settlers killed by Indians in 1866. Many of Grafton's families now live in nearby Rockville; they tend the cemetery and look after the old buildings. From Springdale, follow UT 9 southwest 2 miles to Rockville and turn south 4 miles on Bridge Road (200 East). The last 2.5 miles are unpaved but should be OK for cars in dry weather; keep right at a road junction 1.8 miles past Rockville.

## THE VERMILION CLIFFS AND CANAAN MOUNTAIN

The rocky hills south of Springdale and Rockville offer fine scenery for back-road drives or hikes. A 7-mile dirt road from Rockville climbs into the high country and drops down the Vermilion Cliffs to UT 59 between Hurricane and Hilldale on the other side; follow the directions to Grafton but turn left at the road junction 1.8 miles past Rockville. Panoramas take in Zion National Park and the rugged countryside all around. You can also find good places to hike or camp along the way. Cars with good clearance can usually make this trip if the road is dry.

Canaan Mountain (elev. 7,200 ft.), a wilderness study area due south of Springdale, rises more than 2,000 feet above the surrounding land. The summit is a plateau of rolling slickrock, pinnacles, balanced rocks, and deep fractures similar to the plateaus of Zion National Park. High cliffs on 3 sides give you the feeling of being on an island in the sky. Eagle Crags Trailhead (elev. 4,400 ft.) near Rockville provides access from the north past the Eagle Crags, a group of towering sandstone monoliths. Squirrel Canyon Trailhead (elev. 5,100 ft.) near Hilldale is the starting point for hikes from the south via Water or Squirrel canyons. See the USGS 7½-minute topo maps Springdale West, Springdale East, Smithsonian Butte, and Hilldale. Contact the BLM office in St. George (tel. 673-4654) and use *The Hiker's Guide to Utah* by Dave Hall for hiking information.

## VIRGIN

Mormon pioneers settled here in 1857 and named it for the nearby Virgin River. A few small eateries are in town. Kolob Terrace Road turns north to Lava Point in Zion National Park and continues on to Kolob Reservoir, high plateaus, and the Cedar City area. Virgin is on UT 9, 28 miles east of St. George and 15 miles west of the South Entrance to Zion National Park.

# CEDAR CITY

A cultural, tourist, and trade center, Cedar City is a popular stop for travelers. The excellent Utah Shakespearean Festival in summer presents several of the master's plays and a whole array of Elizabethan dances, concerts, sideshows, seminars, and backstage tours. Just east of town rise the high cliffs of the Markagunt Plateau—a land of panoramic views, colorful rock formations, desolate lava flows, extensive forests, and flower-filled meadows. The immense amphitheater of Cedar Breaks National Monument, eroded from the plateau, can be reached by a short but spectacular drive. Other areas to explore in the Cedar City area include Zion National Park to the south, Pine Valley Mountains to the southwest, and the remote desert country to the west and north. Cedar City is just east of I-15, 52 miles northeast of St. George and 253 miles southwest of Salt Lake City; take I-15 Exits 57, 59, or 62.

### History
Cedar City began as a mission in 1851 to supply the Mormon settlements with much-needed iron products. Church leaders, upon hearing of promising iron ore and coal deposits far to the southwest, decided to launch the first major colonizing effort since the settlement of the Salt Lake City area. The first

*the Greenshow, Utah Shakespearean Festival*

wagon loads of families and supplies left Provo in Dec. 1850 for Parowan, 18 miles north of present-day Cedar City. Other settlers arrived at Cedar City late the following year. All had to start from scratch. Farmers planted crops to feed the new communities while miners and engineers laid plans for iron-manufacturing industries. Hard winters, crop failures, floods, and shortages of skilled workmen nearly doomed the whole project. The final blow came when Johnston's Army and others brought cheaper iron from the East. Only a small amount of iron was produced, and operations ceased in 1858. Sizable quantities of iron ore did exist, though; large-scale mining west of Cedar City began in the 1920s, peaked in 1957, and has tapered off in recent years.

Paiute Indians have lived here since before pioneer days. Sponsorship by the Mormon community allowed them to remain when the federal government forced most other Indians in the state to move onto reservations. There's a Paiute village in the northeastern part of Cedar City. The tribe puts on the Paiute Restoration Gathering in mid-June.

## SIGHTS

### Utah Shakespearean Festival
The enthusiasm of the actors and the community make this summer festival come alive. The action centers on one of the most authentic Elizabethan stages in the world. Nearly all the actors and support people are non-equity, receiving only housing and a moderate stipend for their efforts. Yet the festival has such a high reputation and provides such a good learning experience that all participate eagerly. Their enthusiasm is contagious, and visitors soon find themselves caught up in the spirit. The festival presents 3 Shakespearean plays each season, choosing from both the well-known and the rarely performed works. The management's long-term goal is to produce every play from the Shakespeare canon! The new indoor Randall Jones Theatre presents the "Best of the Rest"—works by other great playwrights such as Chekhov, Moliere, and Arthur Miller.

Much work goes on backstage; for every actor, about 7 people are involved with costumes, makeup, sets, electrics, box office, and the many other aspects of staging plays. Production starts months ahead, then becomes frantic in the last weeks before the festival opens. Since it began at Southern Utah State College in 1962, the festival has continued to grow in quality and attendance.

Days at the festival are filled with entertaining and educational activities. Costumed actors put on the popular Greenshow each day before the performances with a variety of Elizabethan comedy skits, Punch and Judy shows, musicians, jugglers, food sellers, and pretty "wenches." Another activity, the Renaissance Feaste, presents dinner and entertainment of Tudor times. Backstage tours of the costume shop, makeup room, and stage show you how the festival works. At literary seminars each morning, actors and Shakespearean scholars discuss the previous night's play. The actors like to meet the audience, and you'll have plenty of opportunities to talk with them. Production seminars, held daily except Sun., take a close look at acting, costumes, stage props, special effects, and other details of play production.

The season begins about early July and lasts to early September. Tickets sales are well managed—you can order exactly what you want ahead of time, purchase tickets at a counter that sells last-minute cancellations, or buy special tickets set aside on the day of the performances. The Greenshow and seminars are free; you'll have to pay for most other events. The main performances cost $8-20, depending on seating and type of ticket. Because the plays often sell out, it's best to purchase tickets well in advance. Both matinee and evening plays are scheduled, so you can plan a visit to see all 6 plays in just 3 days. Detailed brochures listing activities and dates of performances are available at many tourist offices in Utah or by mail from the Utah Shakespearean Festival, Cedar City, UT 84720; tel. 586-7878 (box office), 586-7880 (information *a tense moment during* A Midsummer Night's Dream

desk), 586-7790 (courtesy booth for last-minute ticket sales). The Shakespearean plays are performed at the Adams Memorial Theatre on the Southern Utah University campus near the corner of Center and 300 West. Rain occasionally dampens the performances (Elizabethan theaters lacked a roof over the stage), and the plays move to a conventional theater next door, where the box office is located. The new contemporary Randall Jones Theatre, where the "Best of the Rest" can be seen, is across the street on 300 West.

### Southern Utah University (SUU)

The towns of southern Utah eagerly sought a branch of the state's teacher training school after it had been authorized in 1897 by the Utah Legislature. A committee awarded the school to Cedar City, and classes began the same year in a borrowed church building. Some people say that Cedar City was chosen because it was the only one of the candidate towns without a saloon or pool hall! The school continued as a branch of the University of Utah and Utah State University until 1965, when it became independent as the 4-year Southern Utah State College. In 1991 the college became a university. Major fields of study are education, arts and letters, science,

and business. Graduate programs are offered in education and accounting. The attractively landscaped campus occupies 104 acres just west of downtown. SUU also operates a 1,000-acre farm in a valley west of town and a 3,700-acre ranch in Cedar Canyon to the east. The school year consists of 3 quarters (fall, winter, and spring) and summer sessions.

**Braithwaite Fine Arts Gallery** presents changing exhibits in the Braithwaite Fine Arts Center; open during the Shakespearean Festival Mon. to Fri. 10 a.m.-7:30 p.m., Sat. and Sun. 1-5 p.m.; open the rest of the year Mon. to Thurs. and Sat. 10 a.m.-7:30 p.m., Fri. 10 a.m.-5 p.m.; tel. 586-5432; it's located about one block north of the intersection of 200 South and 400 West. The Utah Shakespearean Festival is the main summer event on campus, but a variety of cultural and sports events takes place all through the year. Noted speakers can be heard at the Convocations Program in the Auditorium, Center and 300 West; programs are usually held Thurs. at 11 a.m. from Oct. to May. The scheduling office can tell you of upcoming convocations and other cultural happenings; tel. 586-7762. Sporting events on campus include football, basketball, baseball, softball, gymnastics, and track; call 586-7872 for the schedule. Sports facilities open to the public are an indoor swimming pool, tennis and racquetball courts, and gym at the Physical Education Building, 600 W. 200 South; tel. 586-7815. The college can be contacted at the Information Services office, Southern Utah University, Cedar City, UT 84720; tel. 586-7752.

### Iron Mission State Park

This large museum is dedicated to the history of the cultures that have lived in and developed Iron County. Exhibits illustrate the Iron Mission's early hardships and the first iron production on Sept. 30, 1852. An old community bell on display was made by members of the Iron Mission. A diverse array of carriages is the museum's main attraction. You'll see everything from a bullet-scarred overland stagecoach to an elegant clarence carriage. All the sleighs, utility wagons, hearses, and many other forms of 19th C. transport have been meticulously restored. Also displayed are artifacts of prehistoric and modern Indian tribes. Pioneer memorabilia include clothing, furniture, saddles, and a bathtub. Out back is a large collection of horse-drawn farm machinery. The museum is open daily 9 a.m.-7 p.m. from June 1 to mid-Sept., then daily 9 a.m.-5 p.m. the rest of the year; closed Thanksgiving, Christmas, and New Year's Day; $1 adult, $.50 age 7-15; tel. 586-9290. Located at 595 N. Main.

### DUP Museum

The Daughters of the Utah Pioneers have put together a good collection of pioneer photos, household items, and farm tools, as well as a kitchen. Open in summer Mon. to Sat. 9 a.m.-5 p.m.; guided tours are often available in the afternoons; free admission. Located in an 1866 pioneer house at the corner of Center and 100 East (across from the Rock Church).

### Rock Church

Depression-era residents needed a new LDS church building but lacked the money to build one. Undaunted, they set to work using local materials and came up with this beautiful structure made of many different types of rocks. Skilled craftsmen made the metal lamps, carpets, western red cedar pews, and most other furnishings. Open for tours in summer; free admission; located at the corner of Center and 100 East.

## PRACTICALITIES

With so much to see in the area and so many things going on in town, Cedar City is popular with visitors. A good selection of places to stay and eat line Main St., the I-15 business route.

### Campgrounds

**Cedar City KOA** at 1121 N. Main is open all year with showers, recreation room, playground, and a pool; tel. 586-9872; $13.08 tent or RV no hookups, $16.90 RV w/hookups. The **RV Park** (Country Aire) at 1700 N. Main is open all year with showers and a pool; tel. 586-2550; $10.90 tent or RV no hookups, $13.08 RV w/hookups.

### Food

The **Black Swan** has an English atmosphere for fine dining at 164 S. 100 West; tel. 586-7673; open in summer Mon. to Sat. for lunch and dinner; also open after evening Festival performances for coffee and desert; call for hours off season. The Western-style **Milt's Stage Stop** lies 5 miles east of town on UT 14 in Cedar Canyon; tel. 586-9344; open daily for dinner. An informal atmosphere for steak and seafood is offered by the **Sizzler** (199 N. Main; tel. 586-0786; open daily for breakfast, lunch, and dinner) and **Golden Corral Family Steak House** (755 S. Main; tel. 586-2396; open daily for lunch and dinner). **Sullivan's Cafe** serves American food at 86 S. Main; tel. 586-6761; open daily for breakfast, lunch, and dinner; its La Tajada Room features steak and seafood dinners. **Sugar Loaf Restaurant** is an American cafe serving some Mexican favorites and Navajo tacos at 281 S. Main; tel. 586-6593; open daily for breakfast, lunch, and dinner.

Three Chinese cafes serve Cantonese-style food: **China Garden Restaurant** (170 N. Main; tel. 586-6042; open daily for lunch and dinner); **Kowloon Restaurant** (50 W. Center;

# CEDAR CITY ACCOMMODATIONS

Add 9% tax to all prices

| MOTEL/HOTEL | ADDRESS | RATES | PHONE | FEATURES |
|---|---|---|---|---|
| American Siesta Motel | 427 S. Main | $18-30 | 586-2700 | kitchenettes |
| Astro Budget Inn | 323 S. Main | $26-45 | 586-6557 | pool |
| Cedar Crest Motel | 583 S. Main | $27-40 | 586-6534 | kitchenettes, pool |
| Comfort Inn | 250 N. 1100 West | $41-58 | 586-2082 or (800) 627-0374 | kitchenettes, pool, spa, hot tub |
| Daystop Motel | 479 S. Main | $40-45 | 586-9471 | Cont. breakfast |
| Economy Motel | 433 S. Main | $19-40 | 586-4461 | |
| El Rey Inn (Best Western) | 80 S. Main | $42-98 | 586-6518 or (800) 528-1234 | suites, pool, sauna, spa |
| Holiday Inn | 1575 W. 200 North | $72-83 | 586-8888 or (800) HOLIDAY | pool, spa, sauna |
| Quality Inn | 18 S. Main | $56-66 | 586-2433 or (800) 221-2222 | pool |
| Raycap Motel | 2555 N. Main | $32-43 | 586-7435 | pool |
| Rodeway Inn | 281 S. Main | $36-52 | 586-9916 or (800) 228-2000 | pool, sauna |
| Super 7 Motel | 190 S. Main | $32-42 | 586-6566 | |
| Thrifty Motel | 344 S. Main | $45-65 | 586-9114 | kitchenettes, pool |
| Town & Country Inn (Best W.) | 200 N. Main | $49-81 | 586-9911 or (800) 528-1234 | pools, spa |
| Village Inn Motel | 840 S. Main | $45-89 | 586-9926 | kitchenettes, pool |
| Woodbury Guest House | 237 S. 300 West | $60-75 | 586-6696 | bed and breakfast |
| Zion Inn | 222 S. Main | $22-40 | 586-9487 | kitchenettes |

tel. 586-3419; open Mon. to Sat. for lunch and daily for dinner); and **Hunan King Restaurant** (501 S. Main; tel. 586-8952; open daily for lunch and dinner). Good places for Mexican and American food are **Pancho and Lefty's** (2107 N. Main; tel. 586-7501; open daily for dinner) and **Miguela's** (231 N. 1100 West, across from Comfort Inn; tel. 586-9772; open Mon. to Sat. for lunch and dinner). For pizza, try the **Pizza Factory** (124 S. Main; tel. 586-

3900; open Mon. to Sat. for lunch and dinner); **Pizza Express** (166 N. Main; tel. 586-7200; open Mon. to Sat. for lunch and dinner); or **Pizza Hut** (579 S. Main; tel. 586-9896; open daily for lunch and dinner).

## Events
**June:** The local Indian community sponsors the Paiute Restoration Gathering with a parade, dances, traditional games, native food, and a beauty pageant, usually the second weekend in June. Utah athletes compete in the Utah Summer Games during late June; events, patterned after the Olympic games, begin with a torch relay and include track and field, 10K and marathon runs, cycling, boxing, wrestling, basketball, tennis, soccer, karate, and swimming. The Leavitt Group Cedar City Amateur Golf Tournament is held in late June or early July. **July:** The Fourth of July is celebrated with a parade, fireworks, and games for the kids. The Highlands Heritage Festival is a gathering of Scottish clans with bagpipe bands, athletic competitions, dancing, drumming, and fiddling. Hey Cedars Square Dance Jubilee features lively dancing. Everyone dresses up in medieval-style clothing for the Utah Midsummer Renaissance Faire of 16th C. entertainment, crafts, and food. Pioneer Day honors Utah's early settlers with Homesteader Days (up Cedar Canyon) and a parade and games (in town) on July 24. **August:** Cowboys and cowgirls show their stuff in the amateur Iron Rangers Rodeo early in the month. Dances by the American Folk Ballet portray America's southern and western folk history. **September:** Iron County Fair presents a parade, rodeos, horse races, exhibits, and entertainment 18 miles north in Parowan during the Labor Day holiday. Golf, softball, and horseshoe tournaments are held during the month.

## Recreation
The main **city park** has picnic tables, playground, and horseshoe courts at Main and 200 North; the Cedar City Chamber of Commerce office is here too. The **municipal swimming pools** at 400 Harding Ave. (400 W. 100 North) have indoor and outdoor areas and a hydrotube; tel. 586-2869. Look for **tennis courts** at Canyon Park (on UT 14, 3 blocks east of Main), the high school (703 W. 600 South), and the middle school (450 W. Center).

## Shopping And Services
The **Renaissance Square** and **South Main Mall** shopping centers are on S. Main at the south edge of town. Camping, skiing, and other outdoor supplies are sold at **Gart Bros. Sporting Goods** (606 S. Main; tel. 586-0687) and **Ron's Sporting Goods** (138 S. Main; tel. 586-9901). **Valley View Medical Center** provides hospital care at 595 S. 75 East; tel. 586-6587. The **post office** is at 10 N. Main; tel. 586-6701.

## Information
**Cedar City Chamber of Commerce** has literature and advice on travel in the area; open Mon. to Fri. (and sometimes Sat.) 8 a.m.-6 p.m. in summer, then 9 a.m.-5 p.m. the rest of the year; located in the main city park at 286 N. Main (Box 220, Cedar City, UT 84720); tel. 586-4022/4484. **Cedar City Ranger District** office of the Dixie National Forest has information on recreation and travel on the Markagunt Plateau; at 82 N. 100 East (Box 627, Cedar City, UT 84721-0627); tel. 865-3200. The **BLM's Cedar City District** office can tell you about the BLM lands in southwestern Utah, including Beaver River, Dixie, Kanab, and Escalante resource areas; open Mon. to Fri. 7:45 a.m.-4:30 p.m.; located just off Main at 176 E. DL Sargeant Dr. on the north edge of town (Cedar City, UT 84720); tel. 586-2401. For more specific info on the southern Wah Wah Mountains and other desert areas northwest of town, visit the **BLM's Beaver River Resource Area** office; open Mon. to Fri. 7:45 a.m.-4:30 p.m.; in the First Interstate Bank Bldg., 444 S. Main, Suite C-3 (Cedar City, UT 84720); tel. 586-2458. **Cedar City Public Library** has good reading at 136 W. Center; open Mon. to Thurs. 9 a.m.-9 p.m., Fri. and Sat. 9 a.m.-6 p.m.; tel. 586-6661. **Mountain West Bookstore** offers a selection of Utah history, travel, general reading, and LDS titles at 99 N. Main; tel. 586-3828.

## Transport

See the telephone yellow pages for car rental agencies. **Greyhound Bus** offers service at least twice daily to Salt Lake City, Denver, St. George, Las Vegas, and other destinations from the 7-11 store at 809 W. 200 North and the C-Mart at 1355 S. Main (near the south I-15 interchange); tel. 586-1204. **Skywest Airlines** flies daily to and from Salt Lake City (5 times daily, $104-119 one way), St. George (4 times, $28 one way), Las Vegas (3 times, $81 one way), and other regional cities; call for roundtrip and special fares; tel. (800) 453-9417.

## PAROWAN

Although just a small town, Parowan (pop. 1,800) is southern Utah's oldest community and the seat of Iron County. Highway UT 143 turns south from downtown to the Brian Head Ski Area, Cedar Breaks National Monument, and other scenic areas on the Markagunt Plateau. To the west lies Utah's desert country. Accommodations in town offer a less expensive alternative to those in Brian Head. **Iron County Fair** presents a parade, rodeos, horse races, exhibits, and entertainment during the Labor Day holiday. The **Parowan City Office** will answer your questions about the area; open Mon. to Fri. 9 a.m.-4 p.m. at 5 S. Main (Box 576, Parowan, UT 84761); tel. 477-3331. Parowan is 18 miles northeast of Cedar City and 14 miles north of Brian Head; take I-15 Exits 75 or 78.

### Parowan Gap Petroglyphs

Indians have pecked many designs into the rocks at this pass 10.5 miles northwest of Parowan. The gap was on the route of Indians and wildlife crossing the Red Hills, and it may have been an important site for hunting rituals.

The meanings of this rock art haven't been deciphered, but it probably represents the thoughts of many different Indian tribes over the past 1,000 or more years. Geometric designs, snakes, lizards, mountain sheep, bear claws, and human figures can be recognized. You can get here on a good gravel road from Parowan by going north on Main and turning left 10.5 miles on the last street (400 North). Or, from Cedar City, go north on Main (or take I-15 Exit 62), follow signs for UT 130 north 13.5 miles, then turn right 2.5 miles on a good gravel road (near Milepost 19).

### Practicalities

**Jedediah's Inn and Restaurant** has rooms ($50.14 s, $53.41 d), restaurant (open daily for breakfast, lunch, and dinner), and horse-drawn carriage rides at 625 W. 200 South; tel. 477-3326. **Swiss Village Motel (Best Western)** offers rooms ($35.97 s, $42.51 d), a pool, jacuzzi, and restaurant (open daily for breakfast and dinner) at 580 N. Main; tel. 477-3391 or (800) 528-1234. **Ace Motel** costs $21.54 s, $26.94 d; 72 N. Main; tel. 477-3384. **Old Mill Lodge Bed & Breakfast** lies one mile up Parowan Canyon (UT 143); $26.16-34.88 d; tel. 477-9994. The **Pit Stop Restaurant** (fast food) has a campground with coin-operated showers at 492 N. Main; $3.27 tents, $5.45 RV no hookups, $10.36 RV w/hookups; tel. 477-9990. **Parowan Cafe** is open daily for breakfast, lunch, and dinner at 33 N. Main.

**Vermillion Castle Campground** is in the Dixie National Forest at an elevation of 7,000 feet; open with water and a $4 fee from early May to mid-Nov.; it may be open without water or fee the rest of the year; sites are among juniper and cottonwood trees along Bowery Creek; go south 4 miles on UT 143, then left 1.4 miles on the road to Yankee Meadows Reservoir.

# THE MARKAGUNT PLATEAU

Markagunt is an Indian name for "Highland of Trees." The large, high plateau is mostly gently rolling country of forests and lakes. Black tongues of barren lava extend across some parts of the landscape. Cliffs at Cedar Breaks National Monument are the best-known feature of the plateau, but the land also drops away in the colorful Pink Cliffs farther southeast. Popular activities on the Markagunt include fishing, hiking, mountain bicycling, downhill and cross-country skiing, snowmobiling, and scenic drives. Highways UT 143 (across the northern part) and UT 14 (across the southern part) provide year-round access to the plateau. Contact the Cedar City Ranger District of the Dixie National Forest for a forest map and information on exploring the area at 82 N. 100 East (Box 627, Cedar City, UT 84721-0627); tel. 865-3200. In summer, you can sometimes find foresters at the office on UT 14 opposite the Duck Creek Campground turnoff. Picnickers may stop at Duck Creek, Panguitch Lake, and Vermillion Castle campgrounds free of charge for up to 2 hours.

## BRIAN HEAD

At an elevation of 9,850 feet, Brian Head is the highest municipality in Utah. Skiers like Brian Head for its abundant snow, challenging ski terrain, and good accommodations. Summer visitors come to enjoy the high country. The beautiful colors of Cedar Breaks National Monument lie just a few miles south. Panguitch Lake, to the east, receives high ratings for its excellent trout fishing. A winding paved highway provides year-round access to Brian Head's resort facilities; turn south 14 miles on UT 143 from Parowan (I-15 Exits 75 and 78). Other ways in are from Cedar City or Long Valley Junction via Cedar Breaks National Monument (road closed in winter) or from the town of Panguitch via Panguitch Lake (road usually open all year).

### Brian Head Peak
The town takes its name from the flat-topped peak towering above to the east. Originally called Monument Peak, it got its present (misspelled) name in 1890 to honor the famed orator and politician, William Jennings Bryan. You can drive all the way to the 11,307-foot summit by car when the road is dry, usually from July to October. Panoramas from the top take in much of southwestern Utah and beyond into Nevada and Arizona. Sheep graze the grassy slopes below. From Brian Head, follow the highway about 2 miles south, then turn left (northeast) 3 miles on a gravel road to the summit. The stone shelter here was built by the Civilian Conservation Corps in the 1930s.

### Downhill Skiing
The town comes alive during the skiing season, from about mid-Nov. to early May. Five triple and 2 double chairlifts carry skiers up both sides of the narrow valley to 40 runs. Twenty percent of the terrain is rated beginner

*bobcat* (Lynx rufus)

(11 runs), 40% is intermediate (21 runs), and 40% is advanced (8 runs). The highest lift reaches an elevation of 10,920 feet on Brian Head Peak for a vertical drop of 1,150 feet. Lift tickets cost $26 adult full day, $18 adult half day. Rentals, lessons, shops, and children's day care are available. Contact the resort at Box F, Cedar City, UT 84720; tel. 677-2035 or (800) 272-7426 (snow report).

**Cross-country Skiing**
**Brian Head Cross-Country Center** (in the Brian Head Hotel) grooms about 22 km of trails in the area; ask for its map; tel. 677-2012. The short **North Rim Trail** goes to overlooks in Cedar Breaks National Monument. Experienced skiers with map and compass can head out on backcountry routes to the summit of Brian Head Peak and many other areas.

**Accommodations**
**Brian Head Hotel** is on the north (lower) side of town; rooms go for $55-77 d in summer, $88 d winter weekdays, and $104.50 d winter weekends; suites are available too; tel. 677-3000 or (800) 468-4898. **Brian Head Royale Hotel** across the street has rooms at $44-48.40 d in summer, $90.75 d in winter; tel. 677-2800 or (800) 288-8824. The centrally located **Cosmos Motel** costs $33-66 d (may go up in winter); tel. 677-3663. **Bristlecone Hostel,** near cross-country ski trails on the south side of town, has dorm spaces (ski season rates: $17.60 weekdays, $19.80 weekends, $22 holidays; prices drop 50% off season); the 18-bed hostel can also be reserved by groups at a savings; tel. 677-2059 or 586-7465. Nearly 20 **condominium** projects in town offer luxury accommodations with prices starting at about $50 d in summer; during the ski season expect to pay at least $61 d weekdays, $67 d weekends, $105 d holidays. You can either write the chamber of commerce for a list of condominiums or contact one of the reservation offices: the **Accommodation Station** (Box 44, Brian Head, UT 84719; tel. 677-3333 or 800-572-9705 out of state); **Brian Head Condo Reservations** (Box 217, Brian Head, UT 84719; tel. 677-2045 or 800-722-4742 out of state); or **Brian**

**Head Reservation Center** (Box 55, Brian Head, UT 84719; tel. 677-2042). Many condominiums in town also offer ski packages.

**Food**
**Cosmos** has a varied menu of pasta, veal, and Italian sandwiches; open daily for lunch and dinner (may close Mon. in summer); tel. 677-FOOD. **The Edge** prepares steak and seafood daily for dinner; closed part of spring and autumn; tel. 677-3343. **Brian Head Hotel's** restaurant offers American cuisine daily for breakfast, lunch, and dinner; there's a deli, too; tel. 677-3000. The **Brian Head Royale Hotel** has an American restaurant open daily in winter for breakfast, lunch, and dinner; call for summer hours; tel. 677-2800. The **Tele Deli** serves breakfasts and sandwiches in the Brian Head Mall; open daily for breakfast, lunch, and dinner (breakfast and lunch in summer); tel. 677-2258. **Big O Pizza** dishes up pizza, spaghetti, and Italian sandwiches daily for lunch and dinner; tel. 677-2300. **Sunburst Restaurant** serves breakfast and lunch daily during the ski season next to Chair 2; tel. 677-2400. **Brian Head Station** serves breakfast and lunch daily during the ski season next to Chairs 4 and 6; tel. 677-2035.

**Services**
**Post office** is in Brian Head Mall, near the center of town. Several shops have downhill ski rentals and supplies near the bases of the ski lifts. **Brian Head Cross-Country Center** specializes in cross-country skiing with rentals, instruction, guided tours, and sales; in summer the shop offers mountain bicycles (rentals, tours, and sales), and hiking supplies; located in the Brian Head Hotel (Box 65, Brian Head, UT 84719); tel. 677-2012. **Crystal Mountain Recreation** offers guided snowmobile tours in winter and guided ATV tours in summer; at the north edge of town; tel. 677-2386.

**Information**
**Brian Head Chamber of Commerce** can be reached at Box 325, Brian Head, UT 84719; tel. 677-2810.

# CEDAR BREAKS NATIONAL MONUMENT

Erosion on the west edge of the Markagunt Plateau has carved a giant amphitheater 2,500 feet deep and more than 3 miles across. A fairyland of forms and colors appears below the rim. Ridges and pinnacles extend like buttresses from the steep cliffs. Cottony patches of clouds often drift through the craggy landscape. Traces of iron, manganese, and other minerals have tinted the normally white limestone a rainbow of warm hues. The intense colors blaze during sunsets and glow even on a cloudy day. Rock layers look much like those at Bryce Canyon National Park and, in fact, are the same Claron Formation, but here they're 2,000 feet higher. Elevations range from 10,662 feet at the highest point on the rim to 8,100 feet at Ashdown Creek below. Cedar City and the valleys and ranges of the desert can be seen in the distance beyond the amphitheater. Dense forests broken by large alpine meadows cover the rolling plateau country away from the rim. More than 150 species of wildflowers brighten the meadows during summer; the colorful display peaks during the last 2 weeks in July.

A 5-mile scenic drive leads past 4 spectacular overlooks, each with a different perspective. Avoid overlooks and other exposed areas during thunderstorms, which are common in summer afternoons. Heavy snows close the road most of the year. You can drive in only from about late May until the first big snowstorm of autumn, usually sometime in October. Winter visitors can come in on snowmobiles (unplowed roads only), skis, or snowshoes from Brian Head (2 miles north of the monument) or from UT 14 (2.5 miles south). Cedar Breaks National Monument is 24 miles east of Cedar City, 17 miles south of Parowan, 30 miles southwest of Panguitch, and 27 miles northwest of Long Valley Junction. Nearest accommodations and restaurants are 2 miles north in Brian Head.

## Visitor Center And Campground

A log cabin contains exhibits and an information desk. The exhibits provide a good introduction to the Markagunt Plateau and identify local rocks, wildflowers, trees, animals, and birds. Related books, topo and forest maps, posters, slides, and film are sold. Staff offer nature walks, geology talks, and campfire programs; see the schedule posted in the visitor center and at the campground. Open 8 a.m.-6 p.m. weekdays and 8 a.m.-7 p.m. weekends from about June 1 to mid-October. A $3/vehicle entrance fee is collected near the visitor center; there's no charge if you're just driving through the monument without stopping. The small campground to the east has water and a $5 fee; camping is first come, first served. The campground is open from about June 1 to mid-September. There's a picnic area near the campground. Contact the monument at Box 749, Cedar City, UT 84720; tel. 586-9451.

## Hiking Trails

Two easy trails near the rim give an added appreciation of the geology and forests here. Allow extra time while on foot—it's easy to get out of breath at these high elevations! Regulations prohibit pets on the trails. **Spectra Point/Wasatch Rampart Trail** begins at the visitor center, then follows the rim along the south edge of the amphitheater to an overlook. The hike is 4 miles roundtrip with some ups and downs. Weather-beaten bristlecone pines grow at Spectra Point, about halfway on the trail.

**Alpine Pond Trail** forms a 2-mile loop that drops below the rim into one of the few densely wooded areas of the amphitheater. The trail winds through enchanting forests of aspen, subalpine fir, and Engelmann spruce. Hiking distance can be cut in half with a car shuttle between the 2 trailheads or by taking a connector trail that joins the upper and lower parts of the loop near Alpine Pond. Begin from either Chessmen Ridge Overlook or the trailhead pullout 1.1 miles farther north. A trail guide is available at the start or at the visitor center.

*Cedar Breaks Amphitheater from Chessmen Ridge Overlook*

Experienced hikers can enter the monument's lower valleys from the **Ashdown Gorge Wilderness** on the west. Although no trails within the monument itself wind from the rim down to the bottom, you can take **Rattlesnake Creek Trail** from a trailhead on the rim just outside the monument's north boundary. The rugged trail drops 3,400 feet in 9 miles, following Rattlesnake and Ashdown creeks to the lower trailhead on UT 14 about 7 miles east of Cedar City. Upon reaching Ashdown Creek, you have a choice of heading several miles upstream into the monument or of entering the depths of Ashdown Gorge downstream. Check the weather forecast beforehand to avoid getting caught in a flash flood within the gorge. Hikers must be good at map reading and keeping an eye out for the next cairn or tree blaze. Rattlesnake and Ashdown creeks usually have water, though it can be silty or polluted by livestock. Some wading may have to be done in the gorge. Topo maps are the 7½-minute Flanigan Arch or 15-minute Cedar Breaks. Check with staff at Cedar Breaks National Monument or Cedar City Ranger District for current trail conditions.

## PANGUITCH LAKE AND VICINITY

This 1,250-acre reservoir sits in a volcanic basin surrounded by forests and barren lava flows. The cool waters have a reputation for outstanding trout fishing, most of which is for rainbow. Some German browns can also be caught in the lake and downstream in Panguitch Creek. The U.S. Forest Service has 3 campgrounds nearby; all are open with water from early June to mid-September. **Panguitch Lake North Campground,** on the southwest side of the lake, has developed sites in a ponderosa pine forest at an elevation of 8,400 feet; $6-12 fee. **Panguitch Lake South Campground,** across the highway, is more suited for small rigs; $4 fee. **White Bridge Campground** (elev. 7,900 ft.) lies among cottonwoods and junipers along Panguitch Creek 4 miles northeast of the lake; $6 fee. A **visitor center** staffed by the Dixie Interpretive Association is open Fri., Sat., and Sun. about 10 a.m.-5 p.m., on W. Lakeshore Dr., just off UT 143. Panguitch Lake lies along UT

143 about 16 miles southwest of Panguitch and 14 miles northeast of Cedar Breaks National Monument.

## Panguitch Lake Resorts

Several fishing resorts encircle the lake. **Rustic Lodge** on the west shore offers cabins ($54.50 up to 4), RV park with showers and laundry ($7.63 tent, $15.26 RV w/hookups), restaurant (open daily for breakfast, lunch, and dinner), small store, boat rentals, mountain bicycle rentals, and horseback riding; open year-round; tel. 676-2639; turn in 2 miles on W. Lakeshore Rd. from UT 143. **Beaver Dam Lodge** on the north shore has motel rooms ($54.50-70.85), restaurant (open daily for breakfast, lunch, and dinner), small store, and boat rentals; open year-round; tel. 676-8339; turn in 3 miles on W. Lakeshore Rd. from UT 143. **Panguitch Lake General Store,** near the turnoff for W. Lakeshore Rd., has groceries and fishing supplies. **Panguitch Lake Resort** on the south shore has cabins ($54.50 up to 4), RV park with showers ($13.63 w/hookups; no tents), restaurant (open daily for breakfast, lunch, and dinner), small store, and boat rentals; open between about Memorial Day and Labor Day weekends; tel. 676-2657 (in season) or 676-2349 (winter). **Lake View Resort** is on the east shore with cabins ($43.60-59.95), RV park ($13.08 w/hookups), small store, and boat rentals; open between about Memorial Day and Labor Day weekends; tel. 676-2650 (in season) or 628-2719 (winter).

## Mammoth Springs

Moss and luxuriant streamside vegetation surround the crystal-clear spring waters at this beautiful spot. Mammoth Springs is about 5½ miles south of Panguitch Lake; the last 2 miles are on gravel Forest Route 068. See the Dixie National Forest map (Pine Valley and Cedar City ranger districts). A foot bridge leads across the stream to the springs.

## Mammoth Cave

Step a few feet underground to explore the inside of a lava flow. When this mass of lava began to cool, the molten interior burst through the surface and drained out through a network of tunnels. A cave-in revealed this section of tunnel, which has 2 levels. One of the upper levels can be followed through to another opening. The lower tunnel with the large entrance goes back about ¼ mile. To explore beyond that or to check out other sections, you'll have to stoop or crawl. Bring at least 2 reliable flashlights—the caves are *very* dark! Mammoth Cave is about 14 miles south of Panguitch Lake; roads also lead in from Duck Creek on UT 14 and Hatch on US 89. You'll need the forest map to navigate the back roads, though there are some signs for Mammoth Cave.

# RECREATION AREAS ALONG UT 14 (WEST TO EAST)

## Cedar Canyon Campground

Sites lie along Crow Creek among aspen, fir, and spruce in a pretty canyon setting; elevation is 8,100 feet. Open with water from early June to mid-Sept.; $4. Located 12 miles east of Cedar City on UT 14.

## Zion Overlook

A sweeping panorama takes in the deep canyons and monuments of Zion National Park to the south. Located 16.5 miles east of Cedar City on the south side of the road. (The parking area is accessible only to eastbound traffic.)

## Bristlecone Pine Trail

This easy ½-mile loop, graded for wheelchair access, leads to the rim of the Markagunt Plateau and excellent views. A dense spruce-fir forest opens up near the rim, where storm-battered limber and bristlecone pines cling precariously near the edge. The bristlecone pines can be identified by their short-needled, "bottle-brush" branches. The trailhead is 17 miles east of Cedar City on the south side of UT 14.

## Navajo Lake

Lava flows dammed this unusual 3½-mile-long lake, which has no surface outlet. Instead, water drains through sinkholes in the limestone underneath and emerges as Cascade Falls (in the Pacific Ocean drainage) and

Duck Creek (Great Basin drainage). From a pullout along the highway, 24 miles east of Cedar City, you can sometimes see 3 of the sinkholes at the east end; a dam prevents the lake from draining into them. Take the Navajo Lake turnoff, 25.5 miles east of Cedar City, for the campgrounds, marina, and lodge along the south shore. The U.S. Forest Service maintains **Spruces** and **Navajo campgrounds** along the lake and **Te-Ah Campground** 1.5 miles west of the lake; all have water and a $6 fee from mid-June to mid-Sept.; expect cool nights at the 9,200-foot elevation. Aspen, spruce, and fir grow along the lake. Boats can be rented at **Behmer Lodge and Landing,** between Spruces and Navajo campgrounds. **Navajo Lake Lodge,** at the west end of the lake, has cabins, a small cafe, store, and boat rentals; open Memorial Day weekend to late September. Fishermen catch rainbow trout and occasionally some eastern brook and brown trout; ice fishing is done in winter. Small boats can be hand launched at Spruces and Navajo campgrounds or from boat ramps at Navajo Lake Lodge and Behmer Lodge & Landing.

## Cascade Falls National Recreation Trail

Splendid views and a waterfall make this an exciting trip. The easy trail is 1.1 miles round-trip with some ups and downs. It begins at the south rim of the Markagunt Plateau, drops a short way down the Pink Cliffs, then winds along the cliffs to the falls. The falls gush from a cave and bounce their way down to the North Fork of the Virgin River and Zion Canyon. The flow peaks during spring runoff. Take the Navajo Lake turnoff from UT 14, go 0.3 mile, then turn left 3 miles on a gravel road to its end.

## Duck Creek Campground

Turn north from UT 14 at Duck Lake, about 28 miles east of Cedar City. Sites (elev. 8,600 ft.) are open early June to mid-Sept. with water and a $6 fee. The adjacent creek and lake have trout fishing. You'll see why Duck Lake got its name. A **visitor center,** staffed by the Dixie Interpretive Association, is open daily 10 a.m.-5 p.m. in summer; it's across the highway from the campground turnoff.

## Duck Creek Village

Hollywood has used this area since the 1940s to film such productions as *How the West Was Won, My Friend Flicka,* and the Daniel Boone TV series. The village lies at the edge of a large meadow (elev. 8,400 ft.) about 30 miles east of Cedar City. The surrounding countryside is excellent for snowmobiling, a popular winter sport here. A big snowmobile race takes place on the weekend closest to Valentine's Day. Cross-country skiing is good too, on a variety of meadow, forest, and bowl terrain. The snow season lasts from about late Nov. to late March. **Meadeau View Lodge** operates a bed and breakfast all year; tel. 682-2495; rates are $36.30-47.30 s, $55-66 d. **Falcon's Nest** offers cabins in the village; tel. 682-2556; $41.42-52.32 in summer and $52.32-54.50 in winter. **Thunder Inn Cafe** is open daily except Tues. all year for breakfast, lunch, and dinner. **Loose Wheels** runs snowmobile tours, repairs snowmobiles, and rents cross-country skis; off-road vehicle tours are offered in summer; tel. 682-2526.

To reach the rest of Duck Creek Village, including the post office, drive one mile east, then 0.5 mile south. **Pinewoods Inn** rents condominiums in the forest May to Oct.; tel. 682-2512; $76.30 d. The **Pinewoods Restaurant** prepares prime rib, steak, seafood, and other fare during its late May to late Sept. season; tel. 682-2512; open daily except Mon. for breakfast, lunch, and dinner (closes 2-5 p.m.). **Whispering Pines Lodge** has condominiums available all year; tel. 682-2378; $65 up to 4.

## Strawberry Point

A magnificent panorama takes in countless ridges, canyons, and mountains south of the Markagunt Plateau. Zion National Park and even the Arizona Strip can be spotted from this lofty perch (elev. 9,016 ft.). Erosion has cut delicate pinnacles and narrow canyons into the Pink Cliffs on either side below the viewpoint. Turn south from UT 14 between Mileposts 32 and 33 (32.5 miles east of Cedar City) onto a gravel road and go 9 miles to its end. A 500-foot path continues to Strawberry Point. Take care near the edge—the rock is crumbly and there are no guard rails.

# BRYCE CANYON NATIONAL PARK

A geologic fairyland of rock spires rises beneath the high cliffs of the Paunsaugunt Plateau. This intricate maze, eroded from a soft limestone, now glows with warm shades of reds, oranges, pinks, yellows, and creams. The rocks provide a continuous show of changing color through the day as the sun's rays and cloud shadows move across the landscape. Visitors perceive a multitude of wondrous forms. The natural rock sculptures can be Gothic castles, Egyptian temples, a subterranean world inhabited by dragons, or vast armies of a lost empire. Paiute Indians related a tale of the Legend People, various animals and birds living in a beautiful city built for them by Coyote. The Legend People then began behaving badly toward Coyote, who transformed them all into stone. Bryce Canyon National Park contains some of the best scenery, though what's popularly called Bryce Canyon isn't a canyon at all, but the largest of a series of massive amphitheaters cut into the Pink Cliffs. You can gaze into the depths from viewpoints and trails on the plateau rim or descend moderate grades winding among the spires. More of the park can be seen along a 17-mile scenic drive going past Bryce Canyon to other overlooks and trailheads. The nearly 36,000 acres of Bryce Canyon National Park offers many opportunities to explore spectacular rock features, dense forests, and expansive meadows. A variety of wildlife and plant communities make their homes in the park.

Cool temperatures prevail most of the year at the park's 6,600- to 9,100-foot elevations. Expect pleasantly warm days in summer, frosty nights in spring and autumn, and snow in winter. The visitor center, scenic drive, and a campground stay open through the year. Allow a full day to see the visitor center exhibits, enjoy the viewpoints along the scenic drive, and to take a few short walks. Photographers usually obtain best results early and late in the day when shadows set off the brightly colored rocks. Memorable sunsets and sunrises reward visitors who stay overnight. Moonlit nights reveal yet another spectacle.

From Bryce Junction to the west (on US 89, 7 miles south of Panguitch), turn east 14 miles on UT 12, then south 3 miles on UT 63. Or, from Torrey to the east (near Capitol Reef National Park), head west 103 miles on UT 12, then turn south 3 miles; winter snows occasionally close this section of UT 12. Both approaches have spectacular scenery. The park entrance fee of $5/vehicle ($2 bicyclists and bus passengers) is good for 7 days. A brochure available at the entrance station and visitor center has a map of major scenic features, drives, and trails.

## The Hoodoos

The park's landscape originated about 60 million years ago as sediments in a large body of water, named Lake Flagstaff by geologists. Silt and calcium carbonate and other minerals settled on the lake bottom. These sediments consolidated and became the Claron Formation, a soft silty limestone with some shale and sandstone. Lake Flagstaff had long since disappeared when the land began to rise as part of the Colorado Plateau uplift about 16 million years ago. Uneven pressures beneath the plateau caused it to break along fault lines into a series of smaller plateaus at different levels known as the "Grand Staircase." Bryce Canyon National Park occupies part of one of these plateaus—the Paunsaugunt. The spectacular Pink Cliffs on the east edge contain the famous erosional features known as the "hoodoos," carved in the Claron Formation. Variations in hardness of the rock layers result in these strange features which seem almost alive. Traces of iron and manganese provide the distinctive coloring. The hoodoos continue to change—new ones forming and old ones fading away. Despite appearances, wind plays little role in creation of the landscape; it's the freezing and thawing, snowmelt, and rainwater that dissolve weak layers, pry open

*hoodoo at Agua Canyon Overlook*

Larger wildlife visit the higher elevations in summer, then move down out of the park as winter snows arrive. You can often spot mule deer grazing in meadows, especially in morning and evening. Other residents include mountain lion, black bear, coyote, bobcat, gray fox, striped skunk, badger, porcupine, Utah prairie dog, yellow-bellied marmot, Uinta chipmunk, and golden-mantled ground squirrel. Beaver live near the park on the East Fork of Sevier River. (Paunsaugunt is Paiute for "Home of the Beaver.") A few reptiles can be found despite the cool climate; look for the short horned lizard, skink, and Great Basin rattlesnake. Birds appear in greatest numbers from May to October. Violet-green swallows and white-throated swifts dive and careen among the hoodoos in hot pursuit of flying insects. Other summer visitors are the golden eagle, red-tailed hawk, western tanager, and mountain bluebird. Year-round residents include woodpeckers, owls, raven, Steller's jay, Clark's nutcracker, and blue grouse. Although some wild creatures may seem quite tame, they must not be fed or handled—rodents may have diseases, and young deer contaminated with human scent might be abandoned by their mothers.

cracks, and carve out the forms. The plateau cliffs, meanwhile, recede at a rate of about one foot every 50-65 years; look for trees on the rim that now overhang the abyss. Listen, and you might hear the sounds of pebbles falling away and rolling down the steep slopes.

### Flora And Fauna
Vegetation in the park changes considerably with elevation. Pinyon pine, Utah juniper, and Gambel oak dominate the warmer and drier slopes below about 7,000 feet. Ponderosa pines rise majestically over greenleaf manzanita and other shrubs between elevations of 7,000 and 8,500 feet. Blue spruce, white fir, Douglas fir, limber pine, bristlecone pine, and aspen thrive in the cool moist conditions above 8,500 feet. Wildflowers put on a showy display from spring to early autumn. Springs and seeps below the rim support pockets of water birch, bigtooth maple, willows, and narrow-leaf cottonwood.

### History
Prehistoric Anasazi lived in the lower country surrounding Bryce and probably made frequent trips into the park area to hunt game and gather pinyon nuts and other wild foods. Nomadic groups of Paiute Indians later wandered into the area on seasonal migrations. Mormon pioneer Ebenezer Bryce homesteaded near the townsite of Tropic in 1875, but the work of scratching a living from the rugged land became too hard. He left 5 years later for more promising areas in Arizona. The name of the park and his remark, "Well, it's a hell of a place to lose a cow," commemorate his efforts. A later settler, Ruben "Ruby" Syrett, recognized the tourist potential and opened the first small lodge near Sunset Point in 1919, then Ruby's Inn in 1924. Enthusiasm for the scenic beauty led to creation of Bryce Canyon National Monument in 1923. The name changed to Utah National Park in the following

year, then took its current name in 1928. Tours organized by the Union Pacific Railroad, beginning in the late 1920s, made Bryce well known and easily visited.

## Visitor Center

From the turnoff on UT 12, follow signs past Ruby's Inn to the park entrance; the visitor center is a short distance farther on the right. A brief slide show, given on request, introduces the park. Geologic exhibits illustrate how the land was formed and how it's changed. There are historic displays of the Paiute Indians, early explorers, and the first settlers. Trees, flowers, and wildlife are identified. Rangers present a variety of naturalist programs, including short hikes, from mid-May to early Sept.; the schedule is posted. Staff sell natural history and travel books, maps of the park and adjacent Dixie National Forest, posters, postcards, slides, and film. Open daily all year (except Christmas) 8 a.m.-4:30 p.m., with extended hours during the warmer months. Contact the park at Bryce Canyon, UT 84717; tel. 834-5322.

Special hazards you should be aware of include crumbly ledges and lightning strikes. People who have wandered off trails or gotten too close to the drop-offs have had to be pulled out by rope. Avoid cliffs and other exposed areas during electrical storms (most common in late summer).

## Winter Visits

Try a visit during the winter too. Snow on the rocks appears like frosting on a cake. The deep blue sky and crystal-clear air between storms make panoramas particularly inspiring. Roads and most viewpoints are plowed. Snowshoes (loaned free at the visitor center) or cross-country skis (rented at Ruby's Inn) allow excursions into the backcountry. **Paria Ski Trail** (5-mile loop) and **Fairyland Ski Trail** (2.5-mile loop) are marked for snowshoers and cross-country skiers. A free backcountry permit is needed for overnight excursions.

## SCENIC DRIVE

From elevations of about 8,000 feet near the visitor center, the scenic drive gradually winds 1,100 feet higher to Rainbow Point. About midway you'll notice a change in the trees from largely ponderosa pine to spruce, fir, and aspen. On a clear day, you can enjoy vistas of more than 100 miles from many of the viewpoints. Because of parking shortages on the drive, trailers must be left at the visitor center or campsite.

### Fairyland Point

To reach the turnoff (just inside the park boundary), go north 0.8 mile from the visitor center, then east one mile. Whimsical forms line Fairyland Canyon a short distance below. You can descend into the "fairyland" on the **Fairyland Loop Trail** or follow the **Rim Trail** for other panoramas.

### Sunrise And Sunset Points

These overlooks are off to the left about one mile past the visitor center; they're connected by a ½-mile paved section of the **Rim Trail**.

*a misty morning at Sunrise Point*

Panoramas from each point take in large areas of Bryce Amphitheater and beyond. The lofty Aquarius and Table Cliff plateaus rise along the skyline to the northeast; you can recognize the same colorful Claron Formation in cliffs that faulting has raised about 2,000 feet higher. **Queen's Garden Trail** from Sunrise Point and **Navajo Trail** from Sunset Point provide different experiences within the amphitheater. **Sunrise Nature Center,** near the parking area for Sunrise Point, has book sales, a few exhibits, and ranger information.

### Inspiration Point

Walk south ¾ mile along the **Rim Trail** from Sunset Point or drive a bit more than a mile to see a fantastic maze of hoodoos in the "Silent City." Weathering along vertical joints has cut many rows of narrow gullies, some more than 200 feet deep.

### Bryce Point

This overlook at the south end of Bryce Amphitheater has memorable views to the north and east. It's also the start for the **Rim, Peekaboo Loop,** and **Under-the-Rim trails.** From the turnoff 2 miles south of the visitor center, follow signs 2.1 miles in.

### Paria View

Cliffs drop precipitously into the headwaters of Yellow Creek, a tributary of the Paria River. You can see a section of Under-the-Rim Trail winding up a hillside near the mouth of the amphitheater below. Distant views take in the Paria River Canyon, White Cliffs (of Navajo Sandstone), and Navajo Mountain. The plateau rim in the park forms a drainage divide. Precipitation falling west of the rim flows gently into the East Fork of Sevier River and the Great Basin; that landing east of the rim rushes through deep canyons in the Pink Cliffs to the Paria River and on to the Colorado River and finally the Pacific Ocean. Take the turnoff for Bryce Point, then keep right at the fork.

### Farview Point

The sweeping panorama takes in a lot of geology. You can see levels of the Grand Staircase that include the Aquarius and Table Cliff plateaus to the northeast, Kaiparowits Plateau to the east, and White Cliffs to the southeast. Look beyond the White Cliffs to see a section of the Kaibab Plateau that forms the north rim of the Grand Canyon in Arizona. The overlook is on the left 9 miles south of the visitor center.

### Natural Bridge

This large feature lies just off the road on the left, 1.7 miles past Farview Point. The span is 54 feet wide and 95 feet high. Most likely it formed due to weathering from rain and freezing, rather than by stream erosion as with a true natural bridge. Once the opening reached ground level, runoff began to enlarge the hole and to dig a gully through it.

### Agua And Ponderosa Canyons

Sheer cliffs and hoodoos can be admired from Agua Canyon overlook on the left, 1.4 miles past Natural Bridge. With a little imagination, you might be able to pick out the Hunter and the Rabbit below. Ponderosa Canyon overlook, on the left 1.8 miles farther, offers a panorama similar to that at Farview Point.

### Yovimpa Point And Rainbow Point

The land drops away in rugged canyons and fine views at the end of the scenic drive, 17 miles south of the visitor center. At an elevation of 9,105 feet, this is the highest area of the park. Yovimpa and Rainbow points lie only a short walk apart, yet they offer different vistas. **Bristlecone Loop Trail** is an easy one-mile loop from Rainbow Point to ancient bristlecone pines along the rim. **Riggs Spring Loop Trail** makes a good day hike; you can begin from either Yovimpa Point or Rainbow Point and descend into canyons in the southern area of the park. **Under-the-Rim Trail** starts from Rainbow Point and winds 22½ miles to Bryce Point; day hikers could make a 7¾-mile trip by using the Agua Canyon Connecting Trail and a car shuttle.

## HIKING

Hikers enjoy close-up views of the wondrous erosional features. The approximately 61 miles of trails also add to an appreciation of the geology at Bryce. Most of the hiking is moderately difficult, with many ups and downs, but the paths are well graded and signed. Hikers not accustomed to the 7,000- to 9,000-foot elevations will find the going relatively strenuous and should allow extra time. A hat and sunscreen protect against sunburn, more likely at these elevations. Don't forget rain gear because storms can come up suddenly. Usually you'll need to carry water for day trips as only a few natural sources exist. Ask at the visitor center for hiking maps, current trail conditions, and water sources. Snow may block some trail sections in winter and early spring. Overnight hikers can obtain the required backcountry permits at the visitor center (camping is allowed only on the Under-the-Rim and Riggs Spring Loop trails). Backpack stoves must be used for cooking, because open fires and wood gathering damage the natural environment. Horses are permitted only on Peekaboo Loop. Pets must stay above the rim; they're allowed on the Rim Trail only between Sunset and Sunrise points. Don't expect much solitude during the summer on the popular Rim, Queen's Garden, Navajo, and Peekaboo Loop trails. Fairyland Loop Trail is less used and the backcountry trails are almost never crowded. September and Oct. are the choice hiking months—the weather is best and the crowds smallest, though nighttime temperatures in late Oct. can dip well below freezing.

### Rim Trail

This easy trail follows the edge of Bryce Amphitheater for 5½ miles between Fairyland Point and Bryce Point; elevation change is 540 feet. Most people walk just sections in leisurely strolls or use the trail to connect with 5 others. The ½-mile section near the lodge between Sunrise and Sunset points is paved and nearly level; other parts are gently rolling.

### Fairyland Loop Trail

The trail winds in and out of colorful rock spires in the northern part of Bryce Amphitheater. Though it's well graded, remember the 900-foot climb to come out. You can make a loop hike of 8 miles from either Fairyland Point or Sunrise Point by using a section of the **Rim Trail;** a car shuttle saves 3 hiking miles. The whole loop is too long for many visitors, who enjoy short trips down and back to see this "fairyland."

### Queen's Garden Trail

This trail is many people's favorite. From Sunrise Point, it drops through impressive features in the middle of Bryce Amphitheater to a hoodoo resembling a portly Queen Victoria. The hike is 1½ miles roundtrip and has an elevation change of 320 feet, which you'll have to climb on the way back. This is the easiest excursion below the rim and takes about 1½ hours. Queen's Garden Trail also makes a good loop hike with **Navajo** and **Rim trails;** most people who do the loop prefer to descend the steeper Navajo and climb out on Queen's Garden Trail for a 3½-mile hike. Trails also connect with the **Peekaboo Loop Trail** and go to the town of Tropic.

### Navajo Loop Trail

From Sunset Point, you'll drop 520 feet in ¾ mile through a narrow canyon. At the bottom, the loop leads into the deep, dark **Wall Street**—an even narrower canyon ½ mile long, then returns to the rim; total distance is about 1½ miles. Other destinations from the bottom of Navajo Trail are **Twin Bridges, Queen's Garden Trail, Peekaboo Loop Trail,** and the town of Tropic. The 1½-mile trail to Tropic isn't as scenic as the other trails, but it does provide another way to enter or leave the park; ask at the visitor center or in Tropic for directions to the trailhead.

### Peekaboo Loop Trail

An enchanting walk full of surprises at every turn—and there are lots of turns! The trail is in the southern part of Bryce Amphitheater, which has some of the most striking rock features. You can start from Bryce Point (6½ miles roundtrip), from Sunset Point (5½ miles roundtrip via Navajo Trail), or from Sunrise Point (7 miles roundtrip via Queen's Garden Trail). The loop itself is 3½ miles long with many ups and downs and a few tunnels. Elevation change is 500-800 feet, depending on the trailhead you choose.

## Under-the-Rim Trail
The longest trail in the park winds 22½ miles below the Pink Cliffs between Bryce Point in the north to Rainbow Point in the south. Allow at least 2 days to hike the entire trail; elevation change is about 1,500 feet with many ups and downs. Four connecting trails from the scenic drive allow you to travel Under-the-Rim Trail as a series of day hikes too. Another option is to combine Under-the-Rim and **Riggs Spring Loop** trails for a total of 31½ miles.

The **Hat Shop** of delicate spires capped by erosion-resistant rock makes a good day-hiking destination; begin at Bryce Point and follow **Under-the-Rim Trail** for about 2 miles. Most of this section is downhill (elevation change of 900 feet), which you'll have to climb on the way out.

## Bristlecone Loop Trail
The easy one-mile loop begins from either Rainbow or Yovimpa points and goes to view-points and ancient bristlecone pines along the rim. These hardy trees survive fierce storms and extremes of hot and cold where no other tree can. Some of the bristlecone pines here are 1,700 years old.

## Riggs Spring Loop
One of the park's more challenging day hikes or a leisurely overnighter, this trail begins from either Yovimpa Point or Rainbow Point and descends into canyons in the southern area of the park. The loop is about 9 miles with an elevation change of 1,625 feet. A shortcut bypassing Riggs Spring saves ¾ mile.

## Mossy Cave Trail
This easy trail near the east edge of the park goes up Water Canyon to a cool alcove of dripping water and moss. Sheets of ice and icicles add beauty to the scene in winter. The hike is only one mile roundtrip with a small elevation gain. A side trail, just before the cave, branches right a short distance to a little waterfall; look for several small arches in the colorful canyon walls above. Although the park lacks perennial natural streams, the stream in Water Canyon flows even during dry spells. Mormon pioneers labored 3 years to channel water from the East Fork of the Sevier River through a canal and down this formerly intermittent wash to the town of Tropic. Without this irrigation water, the town might not even exist. From the visitor center, return to UT 12 and turn east 3.7 miles toward Escalante; the parking area is on the right just after a bridge (between Mileposts 17 and 18). Rangers schedule guided walks to the cave and waterfall during the main season.

# PRACTICALITIES IN THE PARK

Accommodations and campsites can be hard to find from April to Oct. in both the park and nearby areas. Advance reservations at lodges and motels are a good idea then; otherwise, plan to arrive by late morning. An area reservation service can be reached at tel. (800) 444-6689. Park campgrounds operate on a first-come, first served basis; arrive by noon in the main season to be assured of a spot.

## Bryce Canyon Lodge
Set among ponderosa pines a short walk from the rim, Bryce Canyon Lodge has by far the best location. It's open from about early May to mid-October. You have a choice of motel rooms ($64.47 s or d) or western cabins ($76.19 s or d). The lodge dining room offers a varied menu with moderate prices; open daily in season for breakfast, lunch, and dinner (reservations advised for dinner). Box lunches can be ordered 8 hours before. The lodge organizes horseback rides, park tours, evening entertainment, and ranger talks; a gift shop sells souvenirs. Try to make reservations for accommodations as far in advance as possible with TW Services, Box 400, Cedar City, UT 84720; tel. 586-7686 (reservations service) or 834-5361 (Bryce Canyon Lodge).

## North And Sunset Campgrounds
The 2 campgrounds have water, some pull-through spaces, and a $6 fee. North Campground is on the left just past the visitor center; Loop A has heated restrooms and stays open all winter. Sunset Campground is about 2.5

miles farther on the right, across the road from Sunset Point; both campgrounds have a loop for tenters. Groceries, camping supplies, and coin-operated showers and laundry are available from mid-May to late Sept. at **General Store**, between North Campground and Sunrise Point; during the rest of the year, you can go outside the park to Ruby's Inn for these services. Try to arrive early for a space during the busy summer season; both campgrounds usually fill by 1 or 2 p.m. then. Only group areas may be reserved.

## PRACTICALITIES OUTSIDE THE PARK

### Ruby's Inn
The large motel, part of the Best Western chain, offers many year-round services just north of the park boundary on UT 63. Rooms start at $70.85 s or d in summer and $38.15 s or d in winter; kitchenettes and family rooms cost extra. An indoor heated pool is open except in winter. The restaurant serves breakfast, lunch, and dinner daily; no reservations needed. A snack bar is open for lunch and dinner from April to October. The **campground** is open from early April to late Oct. with spaces for tents ($10.90) and RVs ($16.90 w/hookups); showers and laundry are open all year. The **general store** has a large stock of groceries, camping and fishing supplies, film and processing, Indian crafts, books, and other souvenirs. The **Bryce post office** is at the store too. Horseback rides, helicopter tours, and airplane rides are arranged in the lobby. In winter, cross-country skiers can rent gear and use trails located near the inn as well as in the park. Snowmobile rentals and trails are available too, but snowmobiles may not be used within the park. Western-fronted shops across from Ruby's Inn offer trail rides, chuckwagon dinners, mountain bicycle rentals, souvenirs, and a petting farm. **Rodeos** take place in the nearby arena nightly Mon. to Sat. in season. Rooms should be reserved as far in advance as possible for the April to Oct. season; Bryce, UT 84764; tel. 834-5341 or (800) 528-1234.

### Pink Cliffs-Bryce Village Motel
This motel is on UT 12 at the turnoff for the park. Rooms cost $21.80-47.96 s, $27.25-52.32 d from April 1 to Oct. 31 and $21.80 s or d the rest of the year; tel. 834-5303. Its cafe is open daily for breakfast, lunch, and dinner; closed in winter. A barbecue restaurant serves dinner daily in season. The adjacent **RV park** has sites for tents ($4.36) and RVs ($8.72 w/hookups), showers, and laundry; closed in winter; (same phone number). **Foster's Family Steak House**, about 2 miles west on UT 12, serves breakfast, lunch, and dinner daily (dinner only in winter) and has a **motel** ($53.41 s or d in season; $38.15 s or d in winter), supermarket, and bakery; tel. 834-5227.

### Bryce Canyon Pines
The motel is 6 miles west on UT 12 from the park turnoff. Rooms cost $54.50 s, $59.95 d from May 1 to Oct. 31; rates drop off-season; a covered pool is open during the warmer months; tel. 834-5336. The restaurant is open daily for breakfast, lunch, and dinner from early April to late October. The **Country Store** 1/4 mile west of the motel has a campground for tents ($7.63 and RVs ($12 w/hookups) with showers, laundry, store, and pool; open about March 1 to Oct. 31; tel. 834-5218.

### Dixie National Forest Campgrounds
All 3 campgrounds have a scenic setting in the woods. Often they'll have room when campgrounds in the park have filled. Group sites can be reserved but the rest are available on a first-come, first-served basis. The campgrounds may also be open before and after the main season without water or charge. **Kings Creek Campground** is in a ponderosa pine forest at 8,000 feet on the west shore of Tropic Reservoir; open with water and a $5 fee from late May to late Sept.; drive west 2.8 miles on UT 12 from the park turnoff, then turn south 7 miles on the gravel East Fork Sevier River Road. Tropic Reservoir has a boat ramp and fair trout fishing. **Red Canyon Campground** lies in a ponderosa pine forest at 7,400 feet below brilliantly colored cliffs; open with water and a $6 fee from late May to late

Sept.; drive west 10 miles on UT 12 from the park turnoff (or 4 miles east on UT 12 from US 89). **Red Canyon Campground Trail** begins at Site #23 in the campground and climbs 450 feet in 0.8 mile for fine views of erosional forms and Red Canyon. **Pine Lake Campground** is just east of Pine Lake in a forest of ponderosa pine, spruce, and juniper at 7,700 feet; open with water and a $5 fee from mid-June to mid-Sept.; from the highway junction north of the park, head northeast 11 miles on UT 63 (gravel), then turn southeast 6 miles. Contact the Powell Ranger District office in Panguitch (tel. 676-8815) for more information on Kings and Red Canyon campgrounds, and the Escalante Ranger District office in Escalante (tel. 826-4221) for Pine Lake.

### Red Canyon Indian Store And RV Park

The campground has showers and sites for tents ($8.72) and RVs ($12 w/hookups) from late March to late Oct.; cabins cost $18.53 s, $23.98 d; tel. 676-2690. The adjacent Indian Store has Indian crafts, souvenirs, and a rock shop; closed in winter. Harold's Place Cafe is nearby across the highway. Located 0.9 mile east of US 89 on UT 12.

*black bear* (Ursus americanus)

# VICINITY OF BRYCE CANYON NATIONAL PARK

## Red Canyon

The drive on UT 12 between US 89 and the turnoff for Bryce Canyon National Park passes through this well-named canyon. You may think that it should have been included in the national park, as the brightly colored rocks belong to the same Claron Formation that's exposed at Bryce. Staff at **Red Canyon Visitor Center** can tell you of scenic backcountry roads, horseback trails, and hiking routes that wind through the area; books and maps are sold; open daily about 8 a.m.-6 p.m. during the warmer months; located between Mileposts 3 and 4 on UT 12, ¼ mile west of Red Canyon Campground. You can contact the Powell Ranger District office in Panguitch for information year-round; tel. 676-8815. For details about **Red Canyon Campground,** see "Practicalities Outside the Park" above.

The U.S. Forest Service has 4 hiking trails winding back from the highway to give you a closer look at the geology. **Pink Ledges Trail,** the easiest and most popular, loops 0.6 mile past intriguing erosional features from Red Canyon Visitor Center. Signs identify some of the trees and plants; elevation gain is 70 feet. **Birdseye Trail** winds up through formations and connects the visitor center with a parking area on UT 12 just inside the forest boundary, about ¾ mile away. **Red Canyon Campground Trail** begins from Site #23 in the campground and climbs 450 feet in ¾ mile for views of erosional forms and Red Canyon; the campground is on the south side of UT 12 between Mileposts 3 and 4. **Tunnels Trail** ascends 300 feet in ½ mile for fine views of the canyon. The trail begins from a pullout on the south side of UT 12 just west of a pair of tunnels, crosses the stream bed, then climbs a ridge to viewpoints on the top.

## Powell Point

Even in a state with many superb viewpoints, Powell Point (elev. 10,188 ft.) is outstanding. Yet surprisingly few people know about this lofty perch at the southern tip of the Table Cliff Plateau, a southwestern extension of the Aquarius Plateau. Its light-colored cliffs stand about 15 air miles northeast of Sunset Point in Bryce Canyon National Park. Getting to Powell Point involves a bit of adventure. Cars with good clearance can be driven within 4.3 miles of the point; high-clearance vehicles can go to within 0.6 mile of the point. From the highway junction north of the national park, drive northeast 11 miles on UT 63 (gravel), turn southeast 6 miles to Pine Lake, continue east 6 miles on Forest Route 132 up onto the plateau, then look for the one-lane dirt road on the right to Powell Point; high-clearance vehicles can turn in 3.7 miles to the Powell Point trailhead. If you're not equipped for driving this rough road, you'll still find it good for hiking or mountain bicycling. The road ends where the ridge becomes too narrow for it; a clearing here is fine for camping (no facilities). A foot trail continues 0.6 mile to the very end of Powell Point. On the way you'll pass through an extremely weather-beaten and picturesque forest of bristlecone and limber pine. Panoramic views begin well before trail's end and at the point itself you'll feel as though you're at the end of the world. Much of southern Utah and northern Arizona stretches out below to the far horizons. The colorful cliffs of the Claron Formation lie directly underfoot; take care near the crumbly cliff edges. Avoid Powell Point if thunderstorms threaten. (Note the many lightning scars on trees here!) The Escalante Ranger District office may be able to give current road conditions to Powell Point; tel. 826-4221.

## Tropic

Mormon pioneers settled 6 villages near the upper Paria River between 1876 and 1891. The towns of Tropic, Cannonville, and Henrieville still survive. Tropic lies just east of Bryce Canyon National Park and can be seen from many of the park's viewpoints. A log cabin built by Ebenezer Bryce has been moved to a site beside the Bryce Pioneer

Village Motel; ask to go inside the cabin to see a small collection of pioneer and Indian artifacts. **Bryce Pioneer Village Motel** has rooms at $38.15-54.50 s or d regular, $54.50 d kitchenette and family; the RV park has showers and costs $5.30 no hookups, $11.13 w/hookups; motel and RV park close in winter; tel. 679-8546. **Bryce Village Inn** has rooms ($43.60-56.68 s, $49.05-58.86 d), restaurant (breakfast, lunch, and dinner daily), and a gift shop; tel. 679-8811 or (800) 453-4511. **Doug's Place** serves breakfast, lunch, and dinner daily except Sun. on the north edge of town; has a store; open all year; tel. 679-8633. A **tourist booth** in the center of town is open daily about 9 a.m.-7 p.m. from early May to late October.

## KODACHROME BASIN STATE PARK

Visitors come to this basin southeast of Bryce Canyon National Park to see not only colorful cliffs but also strange-looking rock pillars that occur nowhere else in the world. Sixty-seven rock pillars (here called "sand pipes") found in and near the park range in height from 6 to nearly 170 feet. One theory of their origin is that earthquakes caused sediments deep underground to be churned up by water under high pressure. The particles of calcite, quartz, feldspar, and clay in the sand pipes came from underlying rock formations, and the pipes appeared when the surrounding rock eroded away. Most of the other rocks visible in the park are Entrada Sandstone: the lower orange layer is the Gunsight Butte Member and the white layer with orange bands is the Cannonville Member. Signs name some of the rock features. "Big Stoney," the XXX-rated sand pipe overlooking the campground, is so explicit that it doesn't need a sign! An article, "Motoring into Escalante Land," by Jack Breed in the Sept. 1949 *National Geographic* brought attention to the scenery and renamed the area "Kodachrome Flat." The state park makes a worthwhile stop, both as a day trip to see the geology and as a pleasant spot to camp. Entrance costs $3/vehicle day use or $8/vehicle camping; Box 238, Cannonville,

UT 84718; tel. 679-8562/8575 or (800) 322-3770 (reservations).

To reach the park, drive to Cannonville (on UT 12, 12 miles southeast of the Bryce Canyon National Park turnoff and 36 miles southwest of Escalante) and follow signs south and east for 9 miles on paved roads. Adventurous drivers can also approach the park from US 89 to the south via the Cottonwood Canyon road (39 miles) or the Skutumpah road through Bull Valley Gorge and Johnson Canyon (48 miles). These routes may be impassable in wet weather but are usually OK for cars with good clearance in dry weather; ask about current conditions at Kanab, Paria Ranger Station (on US 89 near Milepost 21), or the visitor center at Glen Canyon Dam.

### Campground

The state park's campground sits in a natural amphitheater at an elevation of 5,800 feet. It's open all year and has restrooms and showers

*a sand pipe*

(showers may close in winter). The campground nearly always has room, though reservations can be made.

## Hiking Trails

The short **Nature Trail** introduces the park's ecology. **Panorama Trail** loops through a highly scenic valley with sand pipes and colorful rocks; the easy trail is 3 miles roundtrip and takes about 2 hours. **Angel's Palace Trail** begins just east of the group campground and makes a ¾-mile loop with fine views; elevation gain is about 300 feet. **Eagles View Trail,** a historic cattle trail, climbs nearly 1,000 feet up steep cliffs above the campground, then drops into Henrieville, 2 miles away; the highest overlook is a steep ½-mile ascent from the campground. **Arch Trail** is a ½-mile roundtrip hike to a natural arch; the trail can be reached by a signed dirt road or on a 2-mile (roundtrip) trail; a brochure and numbered stops identify local plants.

## Horseback Riding

**Scenic Safaris** operates guided horseback and horse-drawn coach rides in the park. You can arrange rides at **Trailhead Station,** a small store in the park that sells groceries and camping supplies from April to Sept., or contact Box 278, Cannonville, UT 84718; tel. 679-8536/8787.

# SOUTH OF KODACHROME BASIN STATE PARK

Several highly scenic canyon systems cut deep into the plateaus south of Kodachrome Basin. The book *Hiking and Exploring the Paria River* by Michael Kelsey outlines some of the hiking possibilities in the region. The BLM staff at the Paria Ranger Station (on US 89 near Milepost 21) or at their office in Kanab (tel. 644-2672) know about current road and hiking conditions. Hikers may encounter cattle and off-road vehicles in some areas, but most of the land remains a wilderness. Spring and autumn are the best hiking seasons, when you'll avoid the desert extremes found in winter and summer. Gnats and biting flies can be troublesome from late May into July; bring repellent and long pants then.

## Cottonwood Canyon And Grosvenor Arch

The road from Cannonville continues past the turnoff to Kodachrome Basin State Park and drops into the upper reaches of Cottonwood Creek (a tributary of the Paria River) and follows it for about 15 miles. Total distance on this scenic drive between Cannonville and US 89 is 46 miles one way, nearly all of which is dirt. If coming from the south, look for the turnoff on US 89 between Mileposts 17 and 18. Cars with good clearance can do the trip any time of year if the road is dry. Be especially cautious if any of the washes have water—cars sometimes get stuck in them. When wet, the road is slippery and hazardous even with 4WD vehicles. Check current conditions at Kodachrome Basin State Park, Paria Ranger Station (on US 89 near Milepost 21), Kanab, or the visitor center at Glen Canyon Dam. A one-mile side road leads to the magnificent Grosvenor Arch; the largest of the 2 openings is 99 feet across. The 1949 National Geographic Society expedition named the double arch in honor of the society's president. Turnoff is 10 miles from the state park turnoff and 29 miles from US 89.

## Hackberry Canyon

Hikers can travel the 18-mile length of this scenic canyon in 2-3 days. The headwaters lie just south of the Cottonwood Canyon road between Kodachrome Basin State Park and Grosvenor Arch at an elevation of about 6,000 feet. The lower canyon meets Cottonwood Canyon at an elevation of 4,700 feet. Cottonwood Canyon road provides access to both ends. A small spring-fed stream flows down the lower half of Hackberry. Many side canyons invite exploration. One of them, Sam Pollock Canyon, is on the west about 4½ miles upstream from the junction of Hackberry and Cottonwood canyons; follow it 1¾ miles up to **Sam Pollock Arch** (60 ft. high and 70 ft. wide). Topo maps are the metric 1:100,000 Smoky Mountain or the 7½-minute Slickrock Bench and Calico Peak. Kelsey's book contains trail and trailhead information and a history of the Watson homestead, located a short way below Sam Pollock Canyon.

### Upper Paria River Canyon

Although not as well known as the lower canyon, the upper section has some beautiful scenery and offers many side canyons to explore too. The Paria lies west of both Hackberry and Cottonwood canyons. Access to the upper end is from the Skutumpah or Cottonwood Canyon roads near Kodachrome Basin State Park (elev. about 5,900 ft.). The usual lower entry is from near Pahreah ghost town (elev. 4,720 ft.); turn north 6 miles from US 89 between Mileposts 30 and 31 and continue past the Pahreah movie set to road's end. (The clay road surface is very slippery when wet but is OK for cars when dry.) The upper canyon is about 25 miles long, and the hike takes 3-4 days (allowing some time to explore side canyons). Water can be found at springs along the main canyon and in many side canyons (purify first); try not to use water from the river itself as it may contain chemical pollution. Topo maps are the metric 1:100,000 Kanab and Smoky Mountain or the 7½-minute Cannonville, Bull Valley Gorge, Deer Range Point, and Calico Peak. Again, Kelsey's book is a good source of history and hiking information for this area.

# ALONG US 89: PANGUITCH TO KANAB

## PANGUITCH

Pioneers arrived in 1864, but hostile Ute Indians forced evacuation just 2 years later. A second attempt by settlers in 1871 succeeded, and Panguitch (Indian for "Big Fish") is now the largest town in the area. The early 20th C. commercial buildings downtown have some of their original facades. On side streets you can see sturdy brick houses built by the early settlers. Stop by the **DUP Museum** in the old bishop's storehouse at 100 East and Center to see historic exhibits of Panguitch; open Mon. to Sat. about 4-8 p.m. in summer and by appointment the rest of the year; phone numbers are on the door.

### Practicalities

About 11 motels and 6 cafes line US 89 (Main and Center) in town. **Hitch-N-Post Campground** at 420 N. Main offers year-round spaces for tents ($8.72) and RVs ($13.08 w/hookups); has showers and laundry; tel. 676-2436. **Big Fish KOA Campground** is at 555 S. Main on the road to Panguitch Lake; open April 1 to Oct. 31 with a pool, recreation room, laundry, and showers; $13.08 tent or RV no hookups, $17.44 RV w/hookups; tel. 676-2225. **Sportsman's Paradise RV Park** is 2 miles north on US 89; open May to Oct. for tents ($8.72) and RVs ($10.90 w/hookups); has a store, showers, and laundry; tel. 676-8348. Major annual **events** include July Fourth celebrations (parade, fireworks, and FFA junior rodeo in town; also fireworks at Panguitch Lake), Pioneer Day on July 24 (parade and rodeo), and Garfield County Livestock Show and Fair in August. The **city park** on the north edge of town has picnic tables, a playground, tennis courts, and a tourist information cabin.

The **post office** is at 65 N. 100 West; tel. 676-8853. **Garfield Memorial Hospital** provides medical services at 200 N. 400 East; tel. 676-8811 (hospital), 676-8842 (clinic). The **Information Center** in the city park offers brochures and suggestions for services in Panguitch and travel to Bryce Canyon National Park and other scenic destinations nearby; open daily 9 a.m.-7 p.m. from early May to late Oct.; closed in winter; tel. 676-8131 or (800) 444-6689. Garfield County Travel Council can be contacted year-round at Box 200, Panguitch, UT 84759; tel. 676-2311. The **Powell Ranger District** of the U.S. Forest Service has information for campgrounds, hiking trails, fishing, and scenic *wooden Indian in front of a Panguitch store*

drives in the forest and canyons surrounding Bryce Canyon National Park; open Mon. to Fri. 8 a.m.-4:30 p.m. at 225 E. Center (US 89) or write Box 80, Panguitch, UT 84759; tel. 676-8815. The **public library** is at 75 E. Center; tel. 676-2431.

## HATCH

The Hatch family started a ranch in the upper Sevier River Valley during the early 1870s. Colorful cliffs of the Paunsaugunt Plateau contrast with the blue sky to the east. Stop in at the **DUP Museum** to learn about the pioneers and see their artifacts; it's usually open summer afternoons (except Sun.), or you can call the telephone numbers posted on the front; turn west one block at the sign in the center of town. **Mountain Ridge Motel** is open about April to Oct.; tel. 735-4258; rooms cost $36 s or d; an RV park with showers has

spaces for tents ($10) and RVs ($12 w/hookups). **New Bryce Motel** has a cafe (open daily for breakfast, lunch, and dinner) and rooms ($39.24 s, $44.69 d); open about mid-March to late Oct.; tel. 735-4265. **Galaxy Motel** also has a cafe (open daily for breakfast, lunch, and dinner) and rooms ($29.34 s, $34.88 d); tel. 735-4327. **Riverside Campground** is just north of town with sites for tents ($10.90) and RVs ($14.17) from about early May to late Sept.; has trout fishing in the Sevier River, laundry, and showers; tel. 735-4223. **Garfield Information Center,** just south of town, is open daily 9 a.m.-7 p.m. from early May to late Oct. with literature and advice for travel in Garfield County. (The county is named for former U.S. President Garfield, not the cat!)

### Mammoth Creek Hatchery
This is one of about 11 state hatcheries producing trout and other game fish. You're welcome to visit during daylight hours. Indoor areas house the eggs and fry; larger fish swim in the outdoor raceways. Go one mile south of Hatch on US 89 and turn west 2 miles on a paved road at the sign. An unpaved road continues to Mammoth Cave and other attractions on the Markagunt Plateau.

## LONG VALLEY

Highway US 89 follows the East Fork of the Virgin River past a series of small Mormon towns north of Kanab. Nearly all travelers visiting the national parks of the region will pass through this forested valley. Most of the towns in Long Valley offer a handful of motels, campgrounds, and restaurants.

### Long Valley Junction
The junction (elev. 7,200 ft.) marks the divide between the East Fork of the Virgin River to the south and the Sevier River to the north. Turn west on UT 14 to visit Cedar Breaks National Monument and the alpine country of the Markagunt Plateau. Continue south 13 miles for Glendale or north 13 miles on US 89 for Hatch.

## Glendale

The original settlers named their community Berryville in 1864. A small fort helped protect against Navajo raids, but continued Indian troubles forced all the valley's inhabitants to leave by 1866. A new group arrived in 1871 and renamed the site Glendale after the town in Scotland. **Bryce-Zion KOA Campground,** 5 miles north of Glendale, has a pool, store, horseback rides, laundry, and showers; open May 1 to Oct. 15; tel. 648-2490; $14.72 tent or RV no hookups, $18.53 w/hookups.

## Orderville

Residents began a communal life in 1875 as part of the Mormon United Order. Everyone worked on cooperative farms and industries, divided income according to need, shared meals at a common table, and met twice daily for worship. The experiment succeeded admirably for about 10 years, longer than in any other Mormon town. A combination of internal disagreements and external pressures eventually convinced community leaders to end the United Order and to return its property to private ownership. The **Orderville DUP Museum** contains pioneer artifacts; open on request (call telephone numbers posted on door). Inexpensive accommodations are offered by the **Orderville Motel** (tel. 648-2271), **Parkway Motel** (tel. 648-2380), and **Baca's Starlight Motel** (tel. 648-2562). Orderville also has 2 or 3 cafes. **Tortoise and the Hare Campground** just north of town has sites for tents and RVs (both $7.65 w/hookups) with showers and laundry; open early April to late Oct.; tel. 648-2312.

## Mt. Carmel

This agricultural community, a few miles north of Mt. Carmel Junction, was first settled in 1865 as Winsor. Threats by Navajo and Paiute Indians forced its abandonment a year later and it wasn't reestablished until 1871, when it was named Mt. Carmel for a mountain in Palestine. The Elkhart Cliffs of white Navajo Sandstone rise to the east. **Mt. Carmel Motel and RV Park** is a small place on the south edge of town; closed in winter; tel. 648-2323; rooms are $21.80-26.16 s or d; the RV park is $5.45 for tents, $8.15 RVs w/hookups.

## Mt. Carmel Junction

Highway UT 9 turns west here from US 89 to Zion National Park. **Thunderbird Motel (Best Western)** features a restaurant, 9-hole golf course, and a pool; tel. 648-2203 or (800) 528-1234; $57.77-64.31 s or d in summer. **Thunderbird Restaurant** serves breakfast, lunch, and dinner daily. **Golden Hills Motel** (tel. 648-2268) costs $30.52 s, $37.06 d in summer; **Golden Hills Restaurant** serves breakfast, lunch, and dinner daily. **East Zion Trailer Park** has RV sites (closed in winter) for $11 w/hookups (no tents) next to the Shell station; tel. 648-2326. **Riverside RV Park** offers sites year-round for self-contained units at $7.63 w/hookups (no restrooms or showers); tel. 648-2262; check in at the Thunderbird Motel across the street.

*whiptail lizard*

Kanab, beneath the Vermilion Cliffs, late 1800s

# KANAB AND VICINITY

Striking scenery surrounds this small town in Utah's far south. The Vermilion Cliffs to the west and east glow with a fiery intensity at sunrise and sunset. Streams have cut splendid canyons into surrounding plateaus. The Paiute Indians knew the spot as Kanab, meaning "Place of the Willows," which still grow along Kanab Creek. Mormon pioneers arrived in the mid-1860s and tried to farm along the unpredictable creek. Irrigation difficulties culminated in the massive floods of 1883, which in just 2 days gouged a section of creekbed 40 feet below its previous level. Ranching proved better suited to this rugged and arid land. Hollywood discovered the dramatic scenery in the 1920s and has filmed more than 150 movies and TV series here since. Several western sets near Kanab have been constructed by film crews, but most lie on private land and are difficult to visit. The Pahreah set east of town, however, is on BLM land and open to the public.

Travelers find Kanab (pop. 3,500) a handy stopover on trips to Bryce, Zion, and Grand Canyon national parks and to the Glen Canyon National Recreation Area. A good selection of motels and restaurants lines US 89, which zigzags through town. Short detours on many of the side streets reveal 19th C. houses of Kanab's pioneer days.

## SIGHTS

### Kanab Heritage House

This 1895 Queen Anne-style Victorian house reflects the prosperity of 2 of Kanab's early Mormon residents. Henry Bowman built it, but he lived here only 2 years before going on a mission. He sold the property to Thomas Chamberlain, who led a busy life serving as a leader in the Mormon's United Order and caring for his 6 wives and 55 children. (There's a family photo in the sitting room.) A guide will show you around the house and explain its architectural details. Photos, furnishings, and artifacts give an idea of what life was like in early Kanab. The town had no stores when the house was built, so each family grew its own vegetables and fruit. The grape arbor, berry bushes, and trees here represent those grown during pioneer times; fruit is free for the picking to visitors. The house is usually open for tours in summer Mon. to Fri. 9:30 a.m.-noon and 1:30-5 p.m.; free admission. You might be able to visit at other times by appointment; call the city clerk (tel. 644-2534) or the number posted on the front of the house. Located one block off US 89 at the corner of Main and 100 South.

## Lopeman's Frontier Movie Town

The owners assembled this movie-set replica in Kanab to show tourists a bit of the "Old West." Some of the buildings have seen actual use in past movies and TV shows; you can take a close look and learn in what they appeared. Many small exhibits display western and movie memorabilia. Shops sell handicrafts and snacks. Local tour information is available too. Groups can arrange cowboy cookouts and western shows. Movie Town entry costs $2 age 12 and up; it's open April 1 to Oct. 31 about 10 a.m.-9 p.m.; tel. 644-5337. Turn in off W. Center between Brandon Motel and Gift City.

## Squaw Trail

This well-graded trail provides a close look at the geology, plant life, and animals of the Vermilion Cliffs just north of town. Allow about an hour on the moderately difficult trail to reach the first overlook (2 miles roundtrip with a 400-foot elevation gain) or 1½ hours to go all the way up (3 miles roundtrip with an 800-foot elevation gain). Views to the south take in Kanab, Fredonia, Kanab Canyon, and the vast Kaibab Plateau. At the top, look north to see the White, Gray, and Pink cliffs of the Grand Staircase. Some maps show the trail continuing across the mesa to Hog Canyon, but this section hadn't been completed at press time. Trailhead is at the north end of 100 East near the city park. Pick up a trail guide at the Information Center (brochures may also be available at the trailhead or BLM office). Bring water. Try to get a very early start in summer.

## Moqui Cave

A tourist attraction with a large collection of Indian artifacts. Most of the arrowheads, pottery, sandals, and burials have been excavated locally. A diorama recreates an Anasazi ruin (not open to the public) located 5 miles away in Cottonwood Wash. Fossils, rocks, and minerals are exhibited too, including what's claimed to be the largest fluorescent mineral display in the country. The collections and a gift shop lie within a spacious cave that stays pleasantly cool even in the hottest weather. Open daily except Sun. from early March to mid-Nov.; summer hours are 8:30 a.m.-7:30 p.m., with shorter hours in spring and autumn; $3 adult, $1.50 children 13-17, and $.50 age 6-12. The cave is 5.5 miles north of Kanab on US 89.

# PRACTICALITIES

## Canyonlands International Youth Hostel

A great place to meet other travelers, many from foreign countries. Guests stay in simple dorm-style accommodations. Facilities include kitchen, laundry, TV room, patio, lawn, locked storage, and a reference library of regional maps and books. Open year-round; the hostel closes during the day, so you need to check in 7-10 a.m. or 6-11 p.m.; $8 with hostel card, $10 nonmembers; tel. 644-5554. Centrally located ½ block off US 89 at 143 E. 100 South.

## Motels

Reservations are a good idea during the busy summer months. Motels are listed in order of increasing price. (Summer rates shown; they may drop several dollars in winter.) All of the motels and campgrounds lie along US 89, which follows 300 West, Center, 100 East, and 300 South through town.

**Premium Motel** has basic accommodations at the corner of US 89 and 100 South (99 S. 100 East); tel. 644-2449; $18.53 s, $21.80 d. **Coral Sands Motel** is at 60 S. 100 East; tel. 644-2616; $31.20 s, $33.30 d and up. **Treasure Trail Motel** is at 150 W. Center with a pool; tel. 644-2687; $32.70 s or d. **Aiken's Lodge** is at 79 W. Center with a pool; tel. 644-2625; $32.70 s or d and up. **Brandon Motel** is at 223 W. Center with a pool; tel. 644-2631; $32.70-43.60 s or d. **Sun-N-Sand Motel** at 347 S. 100 East has a pool, jacuzzi, and kitchenettes; tel. 644-5050; $32.70 s, $37.06 d and up. **K-Motel** is at 330 S. 100 East; tel. 644-2611; $32.90 s, $39.50 d. **Twin Pines Motel** is at 249 S. 100 East; tel. 644-2982; $38.15 s or d. **Quail Park Lodge** at 125

N. 300 West has a pool; tel. 644-2639; $43.60 s, $45.78 d. **Four Seasons Motel** at 22 N. 300 West has a pool; tel. 644-2635; $53.41 s, $59.95 d, $75.21 family. **Parry Lodge** is a large white colonial building at 89 E. Center with a pool; tel. 644-2601; $53.41 s, $58.86 d. (Parry Lodge has hosted many famous movie stars; ask for the room where your favorite star has stayed. Ronald Reagan once had #125!) **Red Hills Motel (Best Western)** at 124 W. Center has a pool; tel. 644-2675 or (800) 528-1234; $54.50 s, $59.95 d. **Shilo Inn** features a pool, spa, free continental breakfast, and mini suites at 296 W. 100 North; tel. 644-2562 or (800) 222-2244; $70.85 s or d.

### Campgrounds

**Hitch'n Post RV Park** has sites with showers for tents and RVs; open all year at 196 E. 300 South; tel. 644-2681; $6.89 no hookups, $11.66 w/hookups. **Coleman's Exxon RV Park** offers sites with showers for RVs; open all year at 355 E. 300 South; tel. 644-2922; $6.50 w/hookups. **Crazy Horse Campark** has sites with pool, store, game room, and showers; open mid-April to late Oct. at 525 E. 300 South; tel. 644-2782; $9.27 tent, $11.45 RV w/hookups.

### Food

**Parry's Lodge** features steak and seafood at 89 E. Center; tel. 644-2601; open daily for breakfast, lunch, and dinner (closed 2-5 p.m.); photos of former movie-star guests decorate the walls. The **Territorial Inn** has steak and seafood in a Western atmosphere at 625 E. 300 South; tel. 644-5744; open daily for dinner. Other good places for American food are **Richard's Family Restaurant** (22 N. 300 West; tel. 644-2635; open daily for breakfast, lunch, and dinner); **Chef's Palace Restaurant** (176 W. Center; tel. 644-5052; open daily for breakfast, lunch, and dinner; offers steak, prime rib, and seafood); **Quackers** (310 S. 100 East in Heritage Center; tel. 644-2500; open daily for breakfast, lunch, and dinner with a homey atmosphere); and **Paula's Gold Dust Cafe** (176 S. 100 East; tel. 644-5938;

open Mon. to Sat. for breakfast and lunch). **Downstream Deli** has a long list of sandwiches and pizza at the north edge of town on US 89; tel. 644-5987; open daily for lunch and dinner (closed Mon. and Tues. in winter). For a choice of Mexican and American cuisine, try **Houston's Trail's End Restaurant** (32 E. Center; tel. 644-2488; open daily for breakfast, lunch, and dinner) or **Rosa's Cafe** (323 S. 100 East; tel. 644-5045; open daily for dinner). **Pizza Hut** serves up pizza daily for lunch and dinner at 421 S. 100 East; tel. 644-2513. **J.J. Hunan Chinese Restaurant** has oriental cuisine at 86 S. 200 West; open Mon. to Sat. for lunch and dinner; closed in winter.

### Entertainment And Events

**Kanab Theatre** has movies at 38 W. Center; tel. 644-2334. **Zane Grey Horse Show** takes place the fourth weekend in June. **July Fourth** is celebrated with a parade, cookout, and fireworks. Another parade and a cookout commemorate **Pioneer Day** on July 24. **Kane County Fair**, on the third weekend in Aug., presents rodeo action, livestock shows, and arts and crafts at Orderville (22 miles north). **Kanab West Fest** features a rodeo, western art, and festivities in October.

### Services And Shopping

The **city park** has picnic tables, playground, tennis courts, and a ball field at the north end of 100 West; the trailhead for Squaw Trail starts here (see "Squaw Trail" above). An outdoor **swimming pool** is open in summer at 44 N. 100 West (behind the State Bank); tel. 644-5870. **Coral Cliffs Golf Course** has 9 holes and a driving range on the east edge of town; tel. 644-5005. **Post office** is at 34 S. Main; tel. 644-2760. **Kane County Hospital** provides emergency care at 221 W. 300 North tel. 644-5811.

**Gift City,** at 288 W. Center across from Four Seasons Motel, specializes in "Kanab Wonderstone" slabs; this natural sandstone, found nearby, has curious patterns (possibly caused by mineral springs) that resemble scenic landscapes; prices range from a few dollars for a pocket-sized piece to $1,000 for a 5-foot by 2½-foot work. Several other shops sell Indian crafts and assorted souvenirs.

### Information

Staff at the **Information Center** offer literature and advice for services in Kanab and travel in Kane County, they're in the center of town at 41 S. 100 East (Kanab, UT 84741); open Mon. to Sat. 8 a.m.-6 p.m. from mid-March to late Oct. and Mon. to Fri. 9 a.m.-5 p.m. the rest of the year; tel. 644-5033. Visit the **BLM** office to learn about hiking and back roads in the Kanab area at 318 N. 100 East (Kanab, UT 84741); open Mon. to Fri. 7:45 a.m.-4:30 p.m.; tel. 644-2672. The **public library** is at 13 S. 100 East; tel. 644-2394.

### Tours

**Kanab Air Service** flies 2 scenic loops: their 35-minute flight takes you over the western Grand Canyon ($45/person with a minimum of 3); the 125-minute trip includes Havasupai and some of the eastern Grand Canyon as well ($95/person with a minimum of 3); tel. 644-2904. The airport is 3 miles south of town on US 89A, toward Fredonia. You can travel like pioneers in covered wagons, ride horseback, or participate in cattle drives across southern Utah and northern Arizona with the **Honeymoon Trail Company,** Moccasin, AZ 86022; tel. (602) 643-7292.

### CORAL PINK SAND DUNES STATE PARK

Churning air currents, funneled by surrounding mountains, have deposited huge sand dunes in this valley west of Kanab. The ever-changing dunes reach heights of several hundred feet and cover about 2,000 of the park's 3,700 acres. Movie makers have used the location for filming. Tiny particles of quartz make up the sand; the "coral pink" refers only to the color. Average summer temperatures at the 6,000-foot elevation range from about 55° F at night to 95° during the day; winter days have highs of about 55°, falling to below freez-

ing at night. Most wildlife is difficult to spot, though you may see their tracks in the sand. Coyotes are often heard at night. Wildflowers put on a fine show in June and July. Different areas in the park have been set aside for hiking, off-road vehicles, and a campground. If you see what looks like a family reunion, it might be just a man with 3 or 4 wives from the nearby polygamist settlements of Colorado City or Hilldale!

From Kanab, go 13.5 miles north on US 89, then turn south 11 miles on a paved road; the turnoff is 3.5 miles south of Mt. Carmel Junction. A shortcut from Kanab on a gravel road via Ponderosa Grove Campground saves several miles, but it can be hard to find; see "Other Areas" below. The back road from Cane Beds in Arizona has about 16 miles of gravel and dirt with some sandy spots; ask a park ranger for current conditions. Entrance fees are $3/vehicle for day use or $8/vehicle for camping. The park can be contacted at Box 95, Kanab, UT 84741; tel. 874-2408 or (800) 322-3770 (reservations).

### Day-use Area
Located on the left just past the contact station. A short boardwalk leads into a protected section of the dunes; signs explain the geology and illustrate some animals and plants that live in this semiarid desert. Photographers and families can explore on foot and use the sheltered picnic area.

### Riding The Dunes
Drivers of off-road vehicles can head for the sands from a trailhead between the day-use area and campground. The thrills of traveling across the Sahara-like landscape attract motorcyclists, ATVers, and dune buggy enthusiasts. Paddle-type tires work best on the soft sand. Park regulations ask drivers to attach an 8-foot whip with a flag to their vehicle, to observe quiet hours from 10 p.m. to 9 a.m., and to avoid riding across vegetation. All vehicles must be registered for off-highway use. It's a good idea to ride where you can be seen by other drivers. Rangers have a complete list of regulations.

### Campground
The pleasant campground sits in a pinyon pine, juniper, and oak woodland. Facilities include restrooms with showers, paved pull-through sites, and a dump station. Ice, fire wood, and off-road vehicle whips may be sold by park staff. Open all year, but the water is shut off from late Oct. until Easter; winter campers need to bring their own. Reservations are recommended for the busy Memorial Day to Labor Day season.

### Other Areas
The canyon country surrounding the park has good opportunities for hiking and off-road vehicle travel; the BLM office in Kanab can supply maps and information. The BLM maintains **Ponderosa Grove Campground** on the north edge of the dunes; no water or fee; it's on a gravel road that turns off one mile north of the park or 8 miles north of Kanab from US 89 (between Mileposts 72 and 73). Turnoffs may not be signed. The campground is 2 miles in from the road to the park and 7.3 miles in from US 89. Drivers with 4WD vehicles can turn south on Sand Springs Road (1.5 miles east of Ponderosa Grove Campground) and go one mile to Sand Springs and another 4 miles to South Fork Indian Canyon Pictograph Site in a pretty canyon. Visitors may not enter the Kaibab-Paiute Indian Reservation, which is south across the Arizona state line, from this side.

*horned lark*
(Eremophila alpestris)

# THE ARIZONA STRIP

Lonely and vast, the "Strip" lies north and west of the Colorado River and south of Utah. Phoenix and the rest of Arizona seem a world away. The Arizona Strip's history and geography actually tie it more closely to Utah. Some beautiful desert and mountain country await the adventurous traveler. In addition to Grand Canyon National Park, 9 designated wilderness areas totaling nearly 400,000 acres protect the most scenic and unique sections. Several tiny communities in the Arizona Strip offer food and accommodations for travelers. More extensive facilities lie just outside the region: Kanab and St. George across the Utah border to the north and Page across the river to the east.

## PIPE SPRING NATIONAL MONUMENT

Step back to the days when cowboys and pioneers first settled this land. Excellent exhibits in Winsor Castle, an early Mormon ranch southwest of Kanab, provide a look into frontier life. Abundant spring water attracted prehistoric Indians, who settled nearby more than 1,000 years ago, then departed. Nomadic Paiute Indians came more recently and now live on the surrounding Kaibab-Paiute Indian Reservation. Mormons discovered the springs in 1858 and began ranching 5 years later, but swift Navajo raiding parties stole some stock and killed 2 men who pursued the Indians. A treaty signed in 1870 between the Mormons and Navajo ended the raids and opened the land to development.

Brigham Young, the Mormon president, then decided to locate the church's southern Utah tithing herd at Pipe Spring. A pair of 2-story stone houses went up, with walls connecting the ends to form a protected courtyard. Workmen added gun ports "just in case," but the settlement was never attacked. The structure became known as Winsor Castle because the ranch's superintendent, Anson P.

Winsor, possessed a regal bearing and was thought to be related to the English royal family. Winsor built up a sizable herd of cattle and horses and oversaw dairying and farming at the ranch. A telegraph office (Arizona's first) which opened in 1871 brought Utah and the rest of the world closer. Travelers frequently stopped by. In fact, so many newlyweds passed through, after having been married in the St. George Temple, that their route became known as the Honeymoon Trail. In the 1880s, the Mormon Church entered a period of turmoil and feared that the federal government would seize church property in the dispute over polygamous marriages. Winsor Castle, whose importance to the church had been declining, was sold to a non-Mormon.

President Harding proclaimed Pipe Spring a national monument in 1923 "as a memorial of Western pioneer life." National Park Service staff keep the frontier spirit alive by maintaining the ranch as it was in the 1870s. Activities such as cattle branding, gardening, weaving, spinning, quilt-making, and baking still take place on a small scale. You can take a short tour of Winsor Castle or explore the restored rooms and outbuildings on your own. A half-mile loop trail climbs the small ridge behind the ranch to a viewpoint; signs tell of local history and geology.

### Visitor Center
Historic exhibits are open daily 8 a.m.-4 p.m. year-round; $1/person admission; tel. 643-7105. A short video introduces the monument. Demonstrations of blacksmithing, branding, and other cowboy skills sometimes take place in the summer months. Produce from the garden and goodies from the kitchen may be sold or given away. A shop offers regional books and Southwestern Indian arts and crafts. The snack bar's menu includes such items as cowboy beans and beef similar to those eaten here 100 years ago. The Paiute tribe operates **Heart Canyon Campground** 1/2 mile north-

east of the monument; sites have showers and stay open all year: $5 or $10 w/hookups. Nearest grocery stores, restaurants, and motels are in Fredonia. Pipe Spring National Monument is just off AZ 389, 21 miles southwest of Kanab.

## PARIA CANYON

The wild and twisting canyons of the Paria River and its tributaries offer a memorable experience for experienced hikers. Silt-laden waters have sculptured the colorful canyon walls, revealing 200 million years of geologic history. Paria means "Muddy Water" in the Paiute language. You enter the 2,000-foot-deep gorge of the Paria in southern Utah, then hike 37 miles downstream to Lees Ferry in Arizona, where the Paria empties into the Colorado River.

Ancient petroglyphs and campsites show that pueblo Indians traveled the Paria more than 700 years ago. They hunted mule deer and bighorn sheep while using the broad, lower end of the canyon to grow corn, beans, and squash. The Dominguez-Escalante Expedition stopped at the mouth of the Paria in 1776 and were the first white men to see the river. John D. Lee and 3 companions traveled through the canyon in 1871 to bring a herd of cattle from the Pahreah settlement to Lees Ferry. After Lee began the Colorado River ferry service in 1872, he and others farmed the lower Paria Canyon. Prospectors came here to search for gold, uranium, and other minerals, but much of the canyon remained unexplored. In the late 1960s, the Bureau of Land Management organized a small expedition whose research led to protection of the canyon as a primitive area. The Arizona Wilderness Act in 1984 designated Paria Canyon a wilderness, along with parts of the Paria Plateau and Vermilion Cliffs.

Allow 4-6 days to hike Paria Canyon on account of the many river crossings and because you'll want to make side trips up some of the tributary canyons. The hike is considered moderately difficult. Hikers should have enough backpacking experience to be self-sufficient, as help may be days away. Flash floods can race through the canyon,

especially from July to September. Rangers close the Paria if they think a danger exists. Because the upper end has the narrowest passages (between Miles 4.2 and 9.0), rangers require that all hikers start here in order to have up-to-date weather information. You must have a permit, which is issued free (no more than 24 hours in advance) by the BLM rangers at either the Paria Canyon Ranger Station near the trailhead (open Thurs. to Mon. 8-11 a.m. from mid-March to mid-Nov.) or at the Kanab Area Office at 318 N. 100 East in Kanab, Utah, 84741 (open Mon. to Fri. 7:45 a.m.-4:30 p.m. year-round); tel. 644-2672. Both offices provide weather forecasts and brochures with map and hiking information.

All visitors need to take special care to minimize impact on this beautiful canyon. Check the BLM "Visitor Use Regulations" for the Paria before you go. They include no campfires in the Paria and its tributaries, a pack-in/pack-out policy, and that latrines be made at least 100 feet away from river and

*the Paria Narrows*

campsite locations. Also, remember to take some plastic bags to carry out toilet paper; the stuff lasts years and years in this desert climate. You don't want to haunt future hikers with TP flowers!

Best times to travel along the Paria are from about mid-March to June and Oct. and November. Winter hikers often complain of painfully cold feet. Wear shoes suitable for frequent wading; canvas shoes are better than heavy leather hiking boots. You can get good drinking water from springs along the way (see the BLM hiking brochure for locations); it's best not to use the river water because of possible chemical pollution from farms and ranches upstream. Normally the river is only ankle deep, but it can be waist deep in a few spots in the spring or after rainy spells. During thunderstorms, it can be over 20 feet deep in the Paria Narrows, so heed weather warnings! Quicksand, most prevalent after flooding, is more of a nuisance than a danger—usually it's just knee deep. Many hikers carry a walking stick to probe the opaque waters for good crossing places.

### Wrather Canyon Arch
One of Arizona's largest natural arches lies about one mile up this side canyon. The massive structure has a 200-foot span. Turn right (southwest) at Mile 20.6 on the Paria hike. (The mouth of Wrather Canyon and other points along the Paria are unsigned; you need to follow your map.)

### Trailheads
The BLM Paria Canyon Ranger Station is in Utah, 43 miles east of Kanab on US 89 near Milepost 21. It's on the south side of the highway, just east of the Paria River. The actual trailhead is 2 miles south on a dirt road near an old homestead site called White House Ruins. Exit trailhead is in Arizona at Lonely Dell Ranch of Lees Ferry, 44 miles southwest of Page via US 89 and 89A (or 98 miles southeast of Kanab on US 89A).

### Shuttle Services
You'll need to do a 150-mile-roundtrip car shuttle for this hike or make arrangements for someone else to do it for you, using either your

car (about $55) or theirs ($125-150). Contact: Marble Canyon Lodge (tel. 602-355-2225), Ken Berlin (602-355-2286), Richard Clark (602-355-2281), or Steve Knisely (602-355-2295); all can be reached at Marble Canyon, AZ 86036. In Fredonia, there's Dick Walker (602-643-7494/7333). In Page, try Harley Stomberg (602-645-9471).

### Buckskin Gulch
This amazing tributary of the Paria has convoluted walls hundreds of feet high, yet it narrows to as little as 4 feet in width. In places the walls block out so much light that it's like walking in a cave. Be *very* careful to avoid times of flash-flood danger. Hiking can be strenuous with rough terrain, deep pools of water, and log and rock jams that may require the use of ropes. Conditions vary considerably from one year to the next. You can descend into Buckskin from 2 trailheads, Buckskin and Wire Pass, both reached by a dirt road. The hike from Buckskin Trailhead to the Paria River is 16.3 miles long (one way) and takes 12 or more hours. From Wire Pass Trailhead it's 1.7 miles to Buckskin Gulch, then 11.8 miles to the Paria. You can climb out on a trail to a safe camping place about halfway down Buckskin Gulch. Carry water to last until the mouth of Buckskin Gulch.

### Lees Ferry
The deeply entrenched Colorado River cuts one gorge after another as it crosses the high plateaus of southern Utah and northern Arizona. Settlers and travelers found the river a dangerous and difficult barrier until well into this century. A break in the cliffs above Marble Canyon provided one of the few places to build a road to the water's edge. Until 1929, when Navajo Bridge spanned the canyon, vehicles and passengers had to cross by ferry. Zane Grey expressed his thoughts about Lees Ferry, in *The Last of the Plainsmen* (1908): "I saw the constricted rapids, where the Colorado took its plunge into the box-like head of the Grand Canyon of Arizona; and the deep, reverberating boom of the river, at flood height, was a fearful thing to hear. I could not repress a shudder at the thought of crossing above that rapid."

The Dominguez-Escalante Expedition tried to cross at what's now known as Lees Ferry in 1776, but without success. The river proved too cold and wide to swim safely, and winds frustrated the attempts to raft across. The Spaniards had to go 40 miles upstream into present-day Utah before finding a safe ford. About 100 years later, Mormon leaders began eyeing the Lees Ferry crossing as the most convenient route for expanding Mormon settlements from Utah into Arizona. After Jacob Hamblin led a failed attempt at rafting the river in 1860, he returned 4 years later and made it across safely. Mormons built a guard post in 1869 to prevent others from taking over the strategic spot. Although Hamblin was the first to recognize the value of this crossing, it now bears the name of John D. Lee. This colorful character gained notoriety in the 1857 Mountain Meadows Massacre (see p. 260). To get Lee out of sight, the Mormon Church leaders asked him to start a regular ferry service on the Colorado River, which he began in 1872.

One of Lee's wives remarked on seeing the isolated spot, "Oh, what a lonely dell!" which became the name of their place. Lee managed to establish the ferry service despite boat accidents and sometimes hostile Navajo, but his past caught up with him. In 1877, authorities took Lee back to Mountain Meadows where a firing squad and casket awaited.

Miners and farmers came to try their luck along the Colorado River and its tributaries. The ferry service continued too, though it suffered fatal accidents from time to time. The last run took place in June 1928 while the bridge was being constructed 6 miles downstream. The ferry operator on that trip lost control in strong currents and the boat capsized; all 3 persons aboard and a Model-T Ford were lost. Fifty-five years of ferryboating had come to an end. Navajo Bridge opened in Jan. 1929, an event hailed by the Flagstaff *Coconino Sun* as the "Biggest News in Southwest History."

Jacob Hamblin

John Doyle Lee

# SOUTHEASTERN UTAH

## INTRODUCTION

The Colorado River and its tributaries have carved extraordinary landscapes in southeastern Utah. The intricate mazes of canyons, delicate arches, and massive rock monoliths make this a region like no other. First-time visitors often need a while to appreciate this strange land, until they're won over by the infinite colors and beauties of the sculptured rock. The thousands of canyons invite exploration—they offer solitude, ruins of prehistoric villages, wildlife, and dramatic records of geologic history.

### THE LAND

Beginning about 300 million years ago, the land was at times a great Sahara-like desert and at other times covered by water. Thick layers of sediments built up one on top of the other. Then, during the last 50 million years, powerful forces within the earth slowly pushed the entire region a mile upward. The ancestral Colorado River and other streams appeared and began to carve the deep gorges seen today. Some of the younger rock layers of the uplifted Colorado Plateau have been eroded away, yet the deposits that remain represent more than 150 million years. Ancient dunes-turned-to-stone make up many of the sheer canyon cliffs, arches, and spires of the region. Delicate crossbedded lines of the former dunes add grace to these features. Forces within the restless plateau have also buckled and folded rock layers into great reefs as long as 100 miles. Weathering then carved them into rainbow-hued rock monuments. Volcanic

pressures deep in the earth also shaped the land. Thick sediments above, however, prevented most of the molten rock from reaching the surface. Massive intrusions of magma bowed up overlying rock layers before cooling and solidifying. Erosion has since uncovered 4 of these dome-shaped complexes in southeastern Utah—the Henrys, La Sals, Abajos, and Navajo Mountain. Rain and snowmelt captured by these high peaks nourish the plants and wildlife of the region.

## Climate

The high-desert country of southeastern Utah lies mostly between 3,500 and 6,500 feet. Annual precipitation ranges from an extremely dry 3 inches, at places, to about 10 inches over much of the land. Mountains rising between 10,000 and nearly 13,000 feet receive abundant rainfall in summer and heavy snows in winter. The rugged character of the canyon country causes many localized variations in climate. A canyon seep surrounded by hanging gardens or a mountain meadow filled with wildflowers provides a refreshing contrast to the parched desert. Sunny skies prevail through all 4 seasons. Spring comes early to the canyon country with weather that's often windy and rapidly changing. Summer can make its presence known in April, though the real desert heat doesn't set in until late May or early June. Temperatures then soar into the 90s and 100s F at midday, though the dry air makes the heat more bearable. Early morning is the choice time for travel in summer. Other ways to beat the heat include hiking in the mountains and river rafting. Huge billowing thunderstorm clouds in late summer bring refreshing rains and coolness. Autumn begins after the rains and lasts into Nov. or even Dec.; days are bright and sunny with ideal temperatures, but nights become cold. Winter lasts only about 2 months at the lower elevations. Light snows on the canyon walls add new beauty to the rock layers. Nighttime temperatures commonly dip into the teens—too cold for most campers. Otherwise winter can be a fine time for travel. Heavy snows rarely occur below 8,000 feet.

## Flash Floods

The bare rock and loose soils so common in the canyon country do little to hold back the flow of water. A summer thunderstorm or a rapid late-winter snowmelt can send torrents of mud and boulders rumbling down dry washes and canyons. Backcountry drivers, horseback riders, and hikers need to avoid hazardous locations when storms threaten or unseasonably warm winds blow on the winter snowpack. Logs and other debris wedged high on canyon walls give proof enough of past floods.

## FLORA AND FAUNA

The region's elevation range—from 3,700 feet at Lake Powell to 12,721 feet atop the La Sal Mountains—provides a wide variety of habitats. Yet the dry conditions and thin or nonexistent soils limit both plant and animal life. Annuals simply wait for a wet year before quickly flowering and spreading their seeds. Pinyon pines, junipers, and other plants often adapt by growing in rock cracks that concentrate moisture and nutrients. Small mammals such as mice, wood rats, rock squirrels, and chipmunks find food and shelter in these outposts of vegetation. Even meager soils permit growth of hardy shrubs like blackbrush, greasewood, sagebrush, rabbitbrush, and Mormon tea. Prickly pear and other types of cacti do well in the desert too. Perhaps the most unusual plant communities are the cryptogamic crusts found on sandy soils. Mosses, lichens, fungi, algae, and diatoms live together in a gray-green to black layer up to several inches thick. Microclimates surrounding canyon seeps and springs provide a haven for hanging gardens of grasses, ferns, orchids, columbines, mosses, and other water-loving plants. River and stream banks have their own vegetation including river willows, cattails, tamarisk, and cottonwoods. Wildlife you might see in the semi-arid desert are mule deer, desert bighorn sheep, pronghorns, coyotes, bobcats, foxes, skunks, porcupines, and many species of rodents. Ravens, eagles, *desert bighorn sheep* (Ovis canadensis)

hawks, owls, falcons, magpies, and smaller birds fly overhead. Watch out for the poisonous rattlesnakes and scorpions, though these shy creatures won't attack unless provoked.

At elevations between 7,000 and 8,500 feet, the desert gives way to forests of aspen, Gambel oak, ponderosa pine, and mountain mahogany. Conifers dominate higher up as far as tree line, at about 12,000 feet. Alpine flowering plants, grasses, sedges, and mosses cling to the windy summits of the La Sal Mountains. Wildlife of the forests includes many of the desert dwellers, as well as elk, bear, mountain lion, marmot, and pika. A herd of introduced bison roam freely in the Henry Mountains; the surrounding desert keeps them from going elsewhere.

# HISTORY

## Prehistoric Indians

Nomadic bands of hunter-gatherers roamed the canyon country for at least 5,000 years. The climate was probably cooler and wetter when the first Indians arrived; food plants and game animals would have been more abundant than today. Agriculture introduced from the south about 2,000 years ago brought about a slow transition to a settled village life.

The Fremont culture emerged in the northern part of the region and the Anasazi in the southern part. Thousands of stone dwellings, ceremonial kivas, and towers built by the Anasazi still stand. Both groups also left behind intriguing rock art, either pecked in (petroglyphs) or painted (pictographs). The Anasazi and Fremont departed from this region about 800 years ago, perhaps because of drought, warfare, or disease. Some of the Anasazi moved south and joined the pueblo tribes of present-day Arizona and New Mexico. The fate of the Fremont Indians remains a mystery.

After the mid-1200s and until white men arrived to settle in the late 1800s, small bands of nomadic Ute and Paiute moved through southeastern Utah. The Navajo began to enter Utah in the early 1800s. None of the 3 Indian groups established firm control of the region north of the San Juan River. A remnant of the Ute and Paiute Indian tribes now lives on the small White Mesa Reservation south of Blanding.

## The Navajo

Relatives of the Athapascans of western Canada, the seminomadic Navajo wandered into New Mexico and Arizona between A.D. 1300 and 1500. This adaptable tribe learned agriculture, weaving, pottery, and other skills from their pueblo neighbors, and they became expert horsemen and sheepherders with livestock obtained from the Spanish. Later, though, the old Navajo habits of raiding neighboring tribes and white men almost caused their downfall. In 1863-64 the U.S. Army rounded up all the Navajo they could find and forced the survivors on "The Long Walk" from Fort Defiance in northeastern Arizona to a bleak camp in eastern New Mexico. This attempt at domestication failed dismally, and the Navajo were released 4 years later.

In 1868 the federal government "awarded" land to the Navajo that has since grown to become a giant reservation spreading from northeastern Arizona into adjacent Utah and New Mexico. The Navajo Nation, with 172,000 members, now ranks as the largest Indian tribe in the country. Their Utah land lies mostly

*Navajo medicine man with his ceremonial sand painting*

south of Lake Powell and the San Juan River in the extreme southeastern corner of the state but includes some acreage north of the San Juan near Montezuma Creek. Oil, gas, and ranching are important sources of income. The Navajo own the spectacular Monument Valley Tribal Park on the Utah-Arizona border.

Religion forms a vital part of Navajo culture. Most ceremonies involve healing and often take place late at night. If someone is sick, his family calls in a medicine man who uses sand paintings, chants, and dancing to effect a cure. The Navajo have become highly skilled at crafts, especially silver jewelry and woven rugs. You'll see these in trading posts on and off the reservation. Colorful velveteen blouses and long flowing skirts like those worn by Navajo women can sometimes be purchased at trading posts too. The style was adopted during the tribe's New Mexico internment in the 1860s. It was what the U.S. Army wives were then wearing!

## Exploration And Settlement
The Spanish Dominguez-Escalante expedition skirted the east edge of the region in 1776 in an unsuccessful attempt to find a route west to California. Retreating back to New Mexico,

they encountered great difficulties in the canyons of southern Utah before finding a safe ford across the Colorado River. This spot, known as the "Crossing of the Fathers," now lies under Lake Powell. Later explorers established the Old Spanish Trail through Utah to connect New Mexico with California. The route crossed the Colorado River near present-day Moab and was used from 1829 to 1848, when the United States acquired the western territories. Fur trappers also traveled the canyons in search of beaver and other animals during the early 1800s; some inscriptions carved into the sandstone record their passage. The U.S. Army's Macomb Expedition visited southeastern Utah in 1859 and made the first documented description of what's now Canyonlands National Park. Major John Wesley Powell's pioneering river expeditions down the Green and Colorado in 1869 and 1871-72 filled in many blank areas on the maps.

Hostile Indians discouraged early attempts by the Mormons to start settlements in southeastern Utah. The Elk Ridge Mission, founded in 1855 near present-day Moab, lasted only a few months before Ute Indians killed 3 Mormons and sent the rest fleeing for their lives. Church members had better success during the 1870s in the Escalante area (1876) and Moab (1877). But for sheer effort and endurance, no group of pioneers is remembered as much as the Hole-in-the-Rock Expedition of 1879-80. Sixty families with 83 wagons and more than 1,000 head of livestock crossed some of the West's most rugged canyon country in an attempt to settle at Montezuma Creek on the San Juan River. They almost didn't make it. A journey expected to take 6 weeks turned into a 6-*month* ordeal. The exhausted company arrived on the banks of the San Juan River on April 5, 1880. Too tired to continue just 20 easy miles to Montezuma Creek, they stayed and founded the town of Bluff. The Mormons established other towns in southeastern Utah too, relying for their livelihoods on ranching, farming, and mining. None of the communities in the region ever reached a large size; Moab is the biggest with a population of 4,600. More and more people have come to realize that the scenery and wilderness qualities of this unique land are its most valuable resources.

# ESCALANTE

The outstanding scenery of the countryside surrounding the town of Escalante has just begun to be discovered. Highlights of a visit include seeing the Escalante River system's magnificent canyons, driving the historic Hole-in-the-Rock Road across a landscape little changed from pioneer days, fishing the trout lakes on the high Aquarius Plateau, and enjoying splendid panoramas. Motorists traveling between Capitol Reef and Bryce Canyon national parks can take a shortcut through the town of Escalante, thanks to recent completion of paved UT 12. The drive provides a good introduction to the region's wonders.

## History

Anasazi and Fremont Indians lived here from about A.D. 1050 to 1200. You can spot their petroglyphs, pictographs, artifacts, storage rooms, and village sites while you're hiking in canyons of the Escalante River and its tributaries. Check the floors of sandstone caves for things left behind—pieces of pottery, arrowheads, mats, sandals, and corncobs. (Federal laws prohibit removal of artifacts; please leave *everything* for the next person to enjoy seeing.) High alcoves in canyon walls protect small stone granaries. You can visit an excavated Anasazi village along with a replica village 27 miles east in Boulder.

Southern Paiute arrived by the 1500s and stayed until white settlers took over. The nomadic Paiute had few possessions and left little behind despite their long stay. Mormon colonists didn't learn about the Escalante region until 1866, when Captain James Andrus led his cavalry east from Kanab in pursuit of troublesome Paiute. Reports of the expedition described the upper Escalante, which was named Potato Valley after the wild tubers growing there. Major John Wesley Powell's expedition down the Green and Colorado rivers in 1869 had failed to recognize the mouth of the Escalante River; it seemed too shallow and narrow for a major tributary. In 1872, a detachment of Powell's second expedition led by Almon H. Thompson and Frederick S. Dellenbaugh stumbled across the Escalante on an overland journey. After some confusion they realized that an entire new river had been found, and they named it for Spanish explorer and priest Silvestre Valez de Escalante. The elusive river was the last to be discovered in the contiguous United States. Mormon ranchers and farmers arrived in the upper valleys of the Escalante in 1876 from Panguitch and other towns to the west, coming not as part of a church-directed mission but simply for new and better lands.

At first glance Escalante looks like a town that time passed by. Only 650 people live here, in addition to the resident cows, horses, and chickens that you'll meet just a block off Main Street. Yet this little community is the biggest place for more than 60 miles around and a center for ranchers and travelers. Escalante (elev. 5,813 ft.) has the neatly laid-out streets and trim little houses typical of Mormon settlements. The former LDS Tithing Office (behind the Griffin grocery store) dates from 1884. Pioneers here had little cash then and paid their tithes in potatoes, fruit, and other produce.

## PRACTICALITIES

### Accommodations

**Moqui Motel** has rooms ($27.25 s, $32.70-38.15 d) and an RV park ($10.60 w/hookups; no tents) at 480 W. Main; tel. 826-4210. **Circle D Motel** has rooms ($32.70 s, $38.15-43.60 d) at 475 W. Main; tel. 826-4297. **Quiet Falls Motel** has rooms ($24.07 s, $30.52-34.88 d) at the corner of W. Main and 100 West; tel. 826-4250. The **Padre Motel** offers rooms ($31.61-37.06 s or d) at 20 E. Main; tel. 826-4276.

### Campgrounds

**Triple-S RV Park** has cabins ($21.20), sites for tents and RVs ($8.48 no hookups, $10.60 w/hookups), and showers; located at 495 W. Main; tel. 826-4959. **Escalante Petrified Forest State Park,** just northwest of town, is a pleasant place to camp or picnic. The campground stays open all year with drinking water and showers but no hookups. The adjacent 30-acre Wide Hollow Reservoir offers fishing, boating, and bird-watching. For a look at some colorful petrified wood, follow the **Wide Hollow Trail** from the campground up a hillside wooded with pinyon pine and juniper. After reaching the top of the 240-foot-high ridge, continue on a loop trail to the petrified wood; allow 45-60 minutes for the one-mile round trip. **Rainbow Loop Trail** (¾ mile) branches off the Wide Hollow Trail to more areas of petrified wood. (The origin of the petrified wood is described below in "Vicinity of Escalante.") The park is 1.5 miles west of town on UT 12, then 0.5 mile north on a gravel road; $3 vehicle day use, $8 vehicle to camp; Box 350, Escalante, UT 84726; tel. 826-4466 or (800) 322-3770 (reservations).

**Calf Creek Recreation Area** lies in a pretty canyon 15.5 miles east of Escalante on UT 12; sites are open with drinking water year-round;

$4; group sites can be reserved through the BLM office. **Calf Creek Falls Trail** (5½ miles roundtrip) begins at the campground and follows the creek upstream to the 126-foot-high falls.

Campgrounds at **Posey Lake** (16 miles north) and **Blue Spruce** (19 miles north) sit atop the Aquarius Plateau in Dixie National Forest. Sites are open with water from about Memorial Day weekend to mid-September. Camping at Posey Lake costs $5, Blue Spruce, $4. Take the dirt Hell's Backbone Road from the east edge of town.

### Food

The **Circle D Restaurant** serves American and Mexican food at 475 W. Main; tel. 826-4297. **Golden Loop Cafe** has standard American fare at 39 W. Main; tel. 826-4433. Both are open daily for breakfast, lunch, and dinner. The **Frosty Shop,** open daily, serves carryout fast food across from the Padre Motel. Buy groceries at either of the 2 general stores on Main Street.

### Services And Information

**Kazan-Ivan Memorial Clinic** (on Center St. behind Escalante General Merc.) offers medical care Mon., Wed., and Fri.; tel. 826-4374. The **Municipal Park** on the west edge of town has covered picnic tables, restrooms with water (except in winter), grills, and a small playground. Obtain travel advice and literature from the **information booth,** open daily 10 a.m.-6 p.m. from mid-May to mid-Sept., across from Padre Motel. The **Dixie National Forest** office at 370 W. Main sells maps and can tell you about road conditions, camping, hiking, and fishing in the high country north of Escalante; Box 246, Escalante, UT 84726; tel. 826-4221. Travelers and hikers headed for the remote canyons of the Escalante River should visit the **Bureau of Land Management (BLM)** or **National Park Service (NPS)** offices one mile west of town (near Milepost 59 on UT 12). Either office can advise on road and hiking conditions as well as issue the free permits required for overnight trips. The BLM office is open Mon. to Fri. 7:45 a.m.-4:30 p.m. and sometimes on Sat. from May to Sept.; staff sell BLM maps of the Escalante Recreation Area and other literature; Box 225, Escalante, UT 84726; tel. 826-4291. The National Park Service office next door is open intermittently Mon. to Fri. 8 a.m.-4:30 p.m. (usually daily from March to June and Sept. to Nov.); they have literature and sell topo maps of the area; Box

511, Escalante, UT 84726; tel. 826-4315. Technically the BLM administers the upper Escalante River while the NPS takes care of the lower section within Glen Canyon N.R.A., but only a single permit is needed for an overnight hiking trip. If nobody's home at either office, obtain the permit from a registration box outside or at trailheads.

# VICINITY OF ESCALANTE

### Petrified Wood Areas
Rivers of 140 million years ago carried trees to the site of present-day Escalante and buried them in sand and gravel. Burial prevented decay as crystals of silicon dioxide gradually replaced the wood cells. Mineral impurities added a rainbow of colors to the trees-turned-to-stone. Weathering has exposed this petrified wood, water-worn pebbles, and sand of the Morrison Formation in 2 places near town. **Wide Hollow** and **Rainbow Loop** trails in Escalante Petrified Forest State Park lead to small outcrops. More abundant petrified wood can be reached by trail from **Baily Wash,** also in the state park. From Escalante, turn north on 300 West beside the forest service office, go 0.8 mile across the Escalante River ford to a junction flanked by large cottonwood trees, turn left 0.5 mile to a hilltop, then right 100 yards to the parking area (go slowly or you'll miss this last turn). A ¾-mile-roundtrip nature trail crosses the dry wash, climbs a small hill, and loops through the colorful petrified wood.

### Hell's Backbone Road
This scenic 38-mile drive climbs high into the forests north of Escalante with excellent views of Death Hollow and Sand Creek canyons and the distant Navajo, Fiftymile, and Henry mountains. **Posey Lake Campground** (elev. 8,700 ft.) offers sites amid aspen and ponderosa pines; open with drinking water from Memorial Day weekend to mid-Sept.; $5. Rainbow and brook trout swim in the adjacent lake. A hiking trail (2 miles roundtrip) begins near Space #14 and climbs 400 feet to an old fire lookout tower with good views of the lake

and surrounding country. Posey Lake is 14 miles north of Escalante, then 2 miles west on a side road. **Blue Spruce Campground** (elev. 7,860 ft.) is another pretty spot but has only 6 sites. Fishermen can try for pan-size trout in a stream. The campground, surrounded by blue spruce, aspen, and ponderosa pine, has drinking water from Memorial Day weekend to mid-Sept.; $4; go north 19 miles from town, then turn left 0.5 mile. Hell's Backbone Road reaches an elevation of 9,200 feet on the slopes of Roger Peak before descending to Hell's Backbone, 25 miles from town. This narrow ridge, with precipitous canyons on each side, was used by mule teams to reach Boulder until the 1930s. At that time a bridge built by the Civilian Conservation Corps allowed the first vehicles to make the trip. You can still see the old mule path below the bridge. After 38 miles the road ends at UT 12; turn right 24 miles to return to Escalante or turn left 3 miles for Boulder. Cars can usually manage the gravel and dirt Hell's Backbone Road when it's dry. Snows and snowmelt, however, block the way until about late May. Check with the U.S. Forest Service office in Escalante for current conditions. Trails and rough dirt roads lead deeper into the backcountry to more vistas and fishing lakes.

## HOLE-IN-THE-ROCK ROAD

The building of this road by determined Mormons was one of the great epics in the colonization of the West. Church leaders organized the Hole-in-the-Rock Expedition to settle the wild lands around the San Juan River of southeastern Utah. A Mormon presence would aid

# ESCALANTE AREA AND CAPITOL REEF NATIONAL PARK

in ministering to the Indians there and prevent non-Mormons from moving in. In 1878, the Parowan Stake issued the first call for a colonizing mission to the San Juan, even before a site had been selected. Preparations and surveys took place the following year as the 236 men, women, and children received their calls. Food, seed, farming and building tools, 200 horses, and more than 1,000 head of cattle would be taken along. Planners discarded lengthy routes through northern Arizona or eastern Utah in favor of a straight shot via Escalante that would cut the distance in half. The expedition set off in the autumn of 1879, convinced that they were part of a divine mission. Yet hints of trouble to come filtered back from the advance group as they discovered the Colorado River crossing to be far more difficult than first believed. Lack of springs along the way added to their worries. From their start at Escalante, road builders progressed rapidly for the first 50 miles, then slowly over rugged slickrock for the final 6 miles to Hole-in-the-Rock. A 45-foot sheer drop below this narrow notch was followed by ¾ mile of extremely steep slickrock to the Colorado River. The route looked impossible, but 3 crews of workers armed with picks and blasting powder worked simultaneously to widen the notch and to construct a precarious wagon road down to the river and up cliffs on the other side. The job took 6 weeks. Miraculously, all the people, animals, and wagons made it down and were ferried across the Colorado River without a serious accident. Canyons and other obstacles continued to block their way as the weary group pressed on. Only after 6 months of exhausting travel did they stop at the present-day site of Bluff on the San Juan River.

Today, on a journey from Escalante, you can experience a bit of the same adventure the pioneers knew. Except for scattered signs of ranching, the land remains unchanged. If the road's dry, vehicles with good clearance can drive to within a short distance of Hole-in-the-Rock. Though people do make the trip in cars, trucks are more suited for the rough conditions encountered past Dance Hall Rock. Bring sufficient gas, food, and water for

the entire 126-mile roundtrip from Escalante. Turnoff from UT 12 is 5 miles east of town. In addition to rewarding you with scenic views, Hole-in-the-Rock Road passes many side drainages of the Escalante River to the east and some very remote country of the Kaiparowits Plateau high above to the west. Either the NPS or BLM offices just west of Escalante can give current road conditions and suggest hikes.

Metate Arch and other rock sculptures decorate **Devil's Garden,** 12.5 miles down Hole-in-the-Rock Road. Turn west 0.3 mile at the sign to the parking area, as you can't really see the "garden" from the road. Red- and cream-colored sandstone formations sit atop pedestals or tilt at crazy angles. Delicate bedding lines run through the rocks. There are no trails or markers—just wander about at your whim. The BLM has provided picnic tables, grills, and outhouses.

**Dance Hall Rock** (38 miles down Hole-in-the-Rock Road) jumped to fiddle music and lively steps of the expedition members in 1879. Its natural amphitheater has a relatively smooth floor and made a perfect gathering spot. The Hole-in-the-Rock group had to wait 3 weeks at nearby Fortymile Spring for road work ahead to be completed. Dance Hall Rock is an enjoyable place to explore and only a short walk from the parking area. Solution holes pockmark the Entrada Sandstone structure.

At road's end (57 miles from UT 12) continue on foot across slickrock to the notch and views of the blue waters of Lake Powell below. Rockslides have made the descent impossible for vehicles, but hikers can scramble down to the lake and back in about an hour. Elevation change is 600 feet. The ½-mile roundtrip is strenuous. After a steep descent over boulders, look for steps of Uncle Ben's Dugway at the base of the notch. Below here the grade is gentler. Drill holes in the rock once held oak stakes against which logs, brush, and earth supported the outer wagon wheels. The inner wheels followed a narrow rut 4-6 inches deep. About two-thirds of the route down is now under water, though the most impressive road work is still to be seen.

Elizabeth Morris Decker described the descent in a letter to her parents on Feb. 22, 1880: "If you ever come this way it will scare you to death to look down it. It is about a mile from the top down to the river and it is almost strait down, the cliffs on each side are five hundred feet high and there is just room enough for a wagon to go down. It nearly scared me to death. The first wagon I saw go down they put the brake on and rough locked the hind wheels and had a big rope fastened to the wagon and about ten men holding back on it and then they went down like they would smash everything. I'll never forget that day. When we was walking down Willie looked back and cried and asked me how we would get back home."

## Calf Creek Falls Trail

This trip offers a good introduction to the pleasures of hiking in the Escalante River system. Walking between high cliffs of Navajo Sandstone streaked with desert varnish, you'll see beaver ponds, Indian ruins and pictographs, and the misty 126-foot-high Lower Calf Creek Falls. A brochure available at the trailhead identifies many of the desert and riparian plant species along the way. Round-trip distance is 5½ miles with only a slight gain in elevation; bring water and perhaps a lunch. Summer temperatures can soar but the falls and the crystal-clear pool beneath stay cool. Sheer cliffs block travel farther upstream. Trailhead is at the campground in Calf Creek Recreation Area, 15.5 miles east of Escalante on UT 12.

Adventurous hikers can also visit **Upper Calf Creek Falls** by taking a different approach. Trailhead for the upper falls is near Milepost 81 on UT 12 (between the Escalante River bridge and Boulder), but it may not be signed. Follow a rocky dirt road west to a clearing, where cairns mark the steep slickrock descent. At a trail fork the main path turns left to below the falls, and the right fork continues to their top. Roundtrip distance for this strenuous hike is 3 miles. The creek offers pretty scenery and swimming holes both above and below the falls. A walk downstream winds past side canyons, hanging gardens,

and through a narrows to the lip of Lower Calf Creek Falls, 3 miles from the upper falls. You'll have to swim across a deep pool just before this point. The Calf Creek 7½-minute topo map covers the entire creek.

## HIKING THE ESCALANTE RIVER AND ITS TRIBUTARIES

The maze of canyons presents exceptional hiking opportunities. You'll find everything from easy day hikes to challenging backpacking treks. The Escalante's canyon begins just downstream from the town of Escalante and ends at Lake Powell about 85 miles beyond. In all this distance only one road (UT 12) bridges the river. Many side canyons provide additional access to the Escalante and most

*Tony Rose on the Escalante River
(near Silver Falls Creek)*

are as beautiful as the main gorge. The river system covers such a large area that you can find solitude even in spring, the busiest hiking season. The many eastern canyons remain virtually untouched. The Escalante canyons preserve some of the quiet beauty once found in Glen Canyon, now lost under the waters of Lake Powell. Prehistoric Anasazi and Fremont Indians have left ruins, petroglyphs, pictographs, and artifacts in many locations. These archaeological resources are protected by federal law. Please don't collect or disturb them.

## Practicalities
Visit the NPS or BLM people in Escalante for the required permit and the latest trail and road conditions before setting out (see Escalante "Services and Information" above). You can also obtain topo maps and literature that show trailheads, mileages, and other info useful in planning trips. A useful book, *Hiking the Escalante* by Rudi Lambrechtse, introduces the region and describes 43 trips with comments on the geology, flora and fauna, and history. Best times for a visit are early March to early June and mid-Sept. to early November. Summertime is possible too—just be prepared for higher temperatures and greater flash-flood danger in narrow canyons. Travel along the Escalante River involves frequent crossings. There's always water in the main canyon, usually ankle to knee deep. Pools in the "Narrows" section between Scorpion Gulch and Stevens Canyon can be up to chest deep in spots (which you can bypass), but that's the exception. All this wading can destroy leather boots, so it's best to wear canvas shoes or boots. High-topped "Vietnam boots," available at surplus stores, work well and prevent gravel getting inside. Occasional springs, some tributaries, and the river itself provide drinking water. Always purify it first; the NPS and BLM warn of the unpleasant disease giardiasis, caused by an invisible protozoan. Don't forget insect repellent—mosquitos and deer flies seek out hikers in late spring and summer. Long-sleeved shirts and long pants also discourage biting insects and protect against the brush.

## Walking Softly
Only great care and awareness can preserve the pristine canyons. You can help if you pack out all nonburnable trash, avoid trampling on the fragile cryptogamic soils (dark areas of symbiotic algae and fungus on the sand), travel in groups of 12 or less to better appreciate the wilderness, don't disturb Indian artifacts, and leave your dogs at home to protect wildlife. (Dogs must be leashed within Glen Canyon N.R.A.) Most important—bury human waste well away from water sources, trails, and camping areas; unless there's a fire hazard, burn toilet paper to aid decomposition. Some parts of the canyons have abundant firewood; try to use only existing fire rings or build your fire without rings below the floodline. The NPS is considering a ban on campfires in their Escalante subdistrict to better preserve the land. The use of backpacker stoves is recommended.

## Floating The Escalante
For most of the year, shallow water and rocks make boat travel impossible, but river levels may rise high enough for 2-3 weeks during spring runoff, which peaks between early April and late May. (In some years there may not be enough water at any time.) Keep in touch with the NPS or BLM in Escalante to hit the river at its highest. Shallow draft and maneuverability are essential, so inflatable canoes or kayaks work best. Also, they are easier to carry out at trip's end or if water levels drop too low for floating. Not recommended are rafts (they're too wide and bulky) and hard-shelled kayaks and canoes (they get banged up on the many rocks). Usual put-in is the UT 12 bridge. Take-out could be Coyote Gulch (13-mile hike), Crack in Wall route (1½-mile hike on steep sand from junction of Coyote and Escalante canyons to Forty-Mile Ridge Trailhead, 4WD needed; a rope is required to negotiate vessel over the canyon rim), or Hole-in-the-Rock (a 600-foot ascent over boulders, rope suggested). You could also be picked up by boat from the Halls Crossing or Bullfrog marinas. Boaters need a backcountry permit from either the BLM or NPS.

## Trailheads

The many approaches allow all sorts of trips. Besides the road access at Escalante and the UT 12 bridge, hikers can reach the Escalante River through western side canyons from Hole-in-the-Rock Road or eastern side canyons from Burr Trail Road. The western-canyon trailheads on Hole-in-the-Rock Road can be more easily reached by car, thus facilitating vehicle shuttles. To reach eastern-canyon trailheads, with the exceptions of Deer Creek and The Gulch on Burr Trail Road, you'll need lots of time and, if the road is wet, 4WD vehicles. You'll also need to carry water for these more remote canyons. With the exception of Deer Creek, they're usually dry.

## Town Of Escalante To UT 12 Bridge
(15 miles)

This first section of canyon offers easy walking and stunning canyon scenery. Tributaries and sandstone caves invite exploration. You'll find good camping areas all along. Usually the river here is only ankle deep. Either enter Escalante River at the bridge next to the sawmill, or go one mile east of town on UT 12 and turn north past the cemetery (visible from highway) and town dump. Almost immediately the river knifes its way through the massive cliffs of the Escalante Monocline, leaving the broad valley of the upper river behind.

**Death Hollow,** far prettier than the name suggests, comes in from the north after 7½ miles. Several good swimming holes carved in rock lie a short hike upstream from the Escalante; watch for poison ivy among the greenery. Continue farther up Death Hollow to see more pools, little waterfalls, and outstanding canyon scenery. Some pools can be bypassed, others have to be swum (bring a little inflatable boat, air mattress, or waterproof bag to ferry packs). Hikers looking for a real challenge can start from a trailhead 24 miles north of town on Hell's Backbone Road, then rockscramble and swim their way to the Escalante River (22½ extremely strenuous miles one way), then walk the Escalante 7½ miles to town or the UT 12 bridge. The first 11 miles of this route are dry, then you're swimming! Allow 4 or 5 days. The average hiker would

most enjoy exploring Death Hollow up from its confluence with the Escalante River.

**Sand Creek,** on the Escalante's north side 4½ miles downstream from Death Hollow, is also worth exploring; deep pools begin a short way up from the mouth. After another ½ mile down the Escalante, a natural arch appears high on the canyon wall. Then the Escalante Natural Bridge comes into view just ½ mile farther. Here you're just 2 miles from the UT 12 bridge. In fact, Escalante Natural Bridge makes a good dayhike destination from the highway.

## UT 12 Bridge To Harris Wash
(26½ miles)

The Escalante Canyon puts on a varied show for this section. At places the walls close in to make constricted narrows, at other places they step back to form great valleys. Side canyons filled with lush greenery and sparkling streams contrast with dry washes of the desert, yet all can be fun to explore. A good hike of 4-6 days begins at the highway bridge, goes down the Escalante to Harris Wash, then up Harris to a trailhead off Hole-in-the-Rock Road (37 miles total).

From the UT 12 parking area, a trail leads to the river. Canyon access goes through private property; cross the river where signs indicate to avoid barking dogs at the ranch just downstream. **Phipps Wash** comes in from the south (right side) after 1½ miles and several more river crossings. Turn up its wide mouth ½ mile to see Maverick Bridge in a drainage to the right. To reach Phipps Arch, continue another ¾ mile up the main wash, turn left into a box canyon, and scramble up the left side (see 7½-minute Calf Creek topo map).

**Bowington (Boynton) Arch** is an attraction of a north-side canyon known locally as Deer Creek. Look for this small canyon on the left one mile beyond Phipps Wash; turn up it one mile past 3 deep pools and turn left a short way into a tributary canyon. In 1878, gunfire resolved a quarrel between local ranchers John Boynton and Washington Phipps. Phipps was killed, but both their names live on.

Waters of **Boulder Creek** come rushing into the Escalante from the north in the next major side canyon, 5¾ miles below the UT 12 bridge. The creek, along with its Dry Hollow and Deer Creek tributaries, provides good canyon walking; deep areas may require swimming or climbing up on the plateau. (You could also start down Deer Creek from the Burr Trail Road where they meet, 6.5 miles southeast of Boulder at a primitive BLM campground; starting at the campground, follow Deer Creek 7½ miles to Boulder Creek, then 3½ miles down Boulder to the Escalante.) Deer and Boulder creeks have water year-round.

High sheer walls of Navajo Sandstone constrict the Escalante River in a narrow channel below Boulder Creek, but the canyon widens again above **The Gulch** tributary, 14 miles below the highway bridge. Hikers can head up The Gulch on a day hike or start from the Burr Trail Road (trailhead is 10.8 miles southeast of Boulder). The hike from the road down to the Escalante is 12½ miles, but there's one difficult spot. A 12-foot waterfall in a section of narrows about halfway down has to be bypassed. When Rudi Lambrechtse, author of *Hiking the Escalante,* tried friction climbing around the falls and the pool at their base, he fell 12 feet and broke his foot. That meant a painful 3-day hobble out. Instead of taking the risk, Rudi recommends backtracking about 300 feet from the falls and friction climbing out from a small alcove in the west wall (look for a cairn on the ledge above). Climb up Brigham Tea Bench, walk south, then look for cairns leading back east to the narrows, and descend to the streambed (a rope helps to lower packs in a small chimney section).

Most springs along the Escalante are difficult to spot. One that's easy to find is in the first south bend after The Gulch; water comes straight out of the rock a few feet above the river. The Escalante Canyon becomes wider as the river lazily meanders along. Hikers can cut off some of the bends by walking in the open desert between canyon walls and riverside willow thickets. A bend cut off by the river itself loops to the north just before Horse Canyon, 3 miles below The Gulch. Along with its tributaries **Death Hollow** and **Wolverine Creek, Horse Canyon** drains the Circle Cliffs

to the northeast. Floods in these mostly dry streambeds wash down pieces of black petrified wood. (Vehicles with good clearance can reach the upper sections of all 3 canyons from a loop road off the Burr Trail Road.) Horse and Wolverine Creek canyons offer good easy-to-moderate hiking, but if you really want a challenge, try Death Hollow (sometimes called "Little Death Hollow" to distinguish it from the larger one near Hell's Backbone Road). Starting from the Escalante River, go about 2 miles up Horse Canyon and turn right into Death Hollow; rugged scrambling over boulders takes you back into a long section of twisting narrows. Carry water for upper Horse Canyon and its tributaries; Lower Horse Canyon usually has water.

About 3½ miles down the Escalante from Horse Canyon, you'll enter Glen Canyon N.R.A. and come to Sheffield Bend, a large grassy field on the right. Only a chimney remains from Sam Sheffield's old homestead. Two grand amphitheaters lie beyond the clearing and up a stiff climb in loose sand. Over the next 5½ river miles to Silver Falls Creek you'll pass long bends, dry side canyons, and a huge slope of sand on the right canyon wall. Don't look for any silver waterfalls in **Silver Falls Creek**—the name comes from streaks of shiny desert varnish on the cliffs. Upper Silver Falls Creek can be approached by a rough road from the Burr Trail Road, but a car shuttle between here and any of the trailheads on the west side of the Escalante River would take all day! Most hikers visit this drainage on a day hike from the river. Carry water.

When the Hole-in-the-Rock route proved so difficult, pioneers figured there had to be a better way to the San Juan Mission. Their new wagon road descended Harris Wash to the Escalante River, climbed part of Silver Falls Creek, crossed the Circle Cliffs, descended Muley Twist Canyon in the Waterpocket Fold, then followed Hall's Creek to Hall's Crossing on the Colorado River. Charles Hall operated a ferry there from 1881 to 1884. Old maps show a jeep road through Harris Wash and Silver Falls Creek canyons, used before the National Park Service closed off the Glen

Canyon N.R.A. section. Harris Wash lies just ½ mile downstream and across the Escalante from Silver Falls Creek.

## Harris Wash
(10¼ miles one way from trailhead to river)
Clear shallow water glides down this gem of a canyon. High cliffs streaked with desert varnish are deeply undercut and support lush hanging gardens. Harris Wash provides a beautiful route to the Escalante River, but it can also be a destination in itself; tributaries and caves can be explored along the way. The sand and gravel streambed makes for easy walking. Reach the trailhead from UT 12 by turning south 10.8 miles on Hole-in-the-Rock Road, then left 6.3 miles on a dirt road (keep left at the fork near the end). Don't be dismayed by the drab appearance of upper Harris Wash. The canyon and creek appear a few miles downstream.

## Harris Wash To Lake Powell
(42¾ miles)
The Escalante continues its spectacular show of wide and narrow reaches, side canyons to explore, and intriguing rock formations. A trip all the way from Harris Wash Trailhead to the Escalante, down the Escalante to near Lake Powell, then out to the Hurricane Wash Trailhead is 66¼ miles, taking 8-10 days. Many shorter hikes using other side canyons are possible too.

Still in a broad canyon, the Escalante flows past **Fence Canyon** (on the west) at 5½ miles from Harris Wash. Fence Canyon has water and is a strenuous 3½-mile cross-country route out to the end of Egypt Road. Get trail directions from a ranger and bring a topo map. (Adventurous hikers could do a 3-day, 20-mile loop via Fence Canyon, the Escalante River, and the northern arm of Twentyfive Mile Wash.) To reach the trailheads, take Hole-in-the-Rock Road 17.2 miles south of UT 12, then turn left (east) 3.7 miles on the Egypt Road for Twentyfive Mile Wash Trailhead or 9.1 miles for Egypt Trailhead.

**Twentyfive Mile Wash,** on the west side 11¼ miles below Harris Wash, is a good route for entering or leaving the Escalante River. The moderately difficult hike is 13 miles one way from trailhead to river. Scenery transforms from that of an uninteresting dry wash in the upper part to a beautiful canyon with water and greenery in the lower reaches. To get to the trailhead, take Hole-in-the-Rock Road 17.2 miles south of UT 12, then turn left 3.7 miles on Egypt Road.

**Moody Creek** enters the Escalante 6 meandering river miles below Twentyfive Mile Wash (or just 2¼ miles as the crow flies). A rough road off the Burr Trail Road gives access to Moody Creek, purple hills, and other eroded features. Distance from trailhead to river is 7 miles one way (moderately strenuous), though most hikers find it more con-

*Colleen Huston in the Escalante River Canyon (below Sheffield Bend)*

venient to hike up from the Escalante. **Middle Moody Creek** enters Moody Creek 3 miles above the Escalante. Moody and Middle Moody canyons feature colorful rock layers, petrified wood, a narrows, and solitude. Carry water, as springs and waterpockets cannot be counted on. Canyons on the east side of the Escalante tend to be much drier than those on the west side.

**East Moody Canyon** enters the Escalante 1½ miles downstream from Moody Canyon, and it too makes a good side trip. There's often water about ½ mile upstream. Continuing down the Escalante, look on the left for a rincon, a meander cut off by the river. **Scorpion Gulch** enters through a narrow opening on the right, 6½ miles below Moody Canyon. A strenuous 8-mile climb up Scorpion Gulch over rockfalls and around deep pools brings you to a trailhead on Early Weed Bench Road. Experience, directions from a ranger, and a topo map are needed. A challenging 4-day, 30-mile loop hike uses Fox Canyon, Twenty-five Mile Wash, the Escalante River, and Scorpion Gulch. Water is found only in lower Twentyfive Mile Wash, the river, and lower Scorpion Gulch. Early Weed Bench turnoff is 24.2 miles south on Hole-in-the-Rock Road from UT 12; head in 5.8 miles to Scorpion Gulch Trailhead.

In the next 12 miles below Scorpion Gulch, Escalante Canyon is alternately wide and narrow. Then the river plunges into the **Narrows,** a 5-mile-long section choked with boulders; plan on spending a day picking a route through. Watch out for chest-deep water here! Remote and little visited, **Stevens Canyon** enters from the east near the end of the Narrows. Stevens Arch stands guard 580 feet above the confluence; the opening measures 225 feet wide and 160 feet high. The upper and lower parts of Stevens Canyon usually have some water.

**Coyote Gulch,** on the right 1½ miles below Stevens Canyon, marks the end of the Escalante for most hikers. Lake Powell often comes within one mile of Coyote Gulch and occasionally floods the canyon mouth. Coyote can stay flooded for several weeks, depending on release flow of Glen Canyon Dam and

water volume coming in. The river and lake don't have a pretty meeting place—quicksand and dead trees are found here. Log jams make it difficult to travel in from the lake by boat.

Coyote Gulch has received more publicity than other areas of the Escalante, and you're more likely to meet other hikers here. Two arches, a natural bridge, graceful sculpturing of the streambed and canyon walls, deep undercuts, and a cascading creek make a visit well worthwhile. The best route in starts where Hole-in-the-Rock Road crosses Hurricane Wash, 34.7 miles south of UT 12. It's 13¼ miles one way from the trailhead to the river and the hike is moderately strenuous. For the first mile you follow the dry sandy wash without even a hint of being in a canyon. Water doesn't appear for 3 more miles. You'll reach Coyote Gulch, which has water, at 5¼ miles from the trailhead. Another way into Coyote Gulch begins at the Red Well Trailhead; it's 31.5 miles south on Hole-in-the-Rock Road, then 1.5 miles east (keep left at the fork). A start from Red Well adds ¾ mile more to the hike than the Hurricane Wash route but is less crowded.

**Other Adventures**

Dry Fork of Coyote Gulch contains 3 enchanting canyons named Peek-a-boo, Spooky, and Brimstone. Enjoy the narrows, natural bridges, and deep pools. See *Hiking the Escalante* for directions.

Three canyons near the end of Hole-in-the-Rock Road lead down to Lake Powell: Fortymile Gulch (strenuous, 12 miles roundtrip), Willow Gulch (moderately difficult, 6 miles roundtrip), and Fiftymile Creek (easy to moderately difficult, 8 miles roundtrip). As none are signed, you'll need a topo map or directions from a ranger or *Hiking the Escalante* to find them.

# BOULDER

About 125 people live in this farming community at the base of Boulder Mountain. Ranchers began drifting in during the late 1870s, though not with the idea of forming a town. By the mid-1890s Boulder had established itself as a ranching and dairy center. Remote and hemmed in by canyons and mountains, Boulder remained one of the last communities in the country to rely on pack trains for transport. Motor vehicles couldn't drive in until the 1930s. Today Boulder is worth a visit to see an excavated Anasazi village and the spectacular scenery along the way. Take paved UT 12 either through the canyon and slickrock country from Escalante or over the Aquarius Plateau from Torrey (near Capitol Reef National Park). The fair-weather Burr Trail Road connects Boulder with Capitol Reef National Park's southern district via Waterpocket Fold and Circle Cliffs. A fourth way in is from Escalante on the dirt Hell's Backbone Road, which comes out 3 miles west of Boulder at UT 12.

### Anasazi State Park
Museum exhibits, an excavated village site, and a pueblo replica provide a look into the life of these ancient people. The Anasazi stayed here for 50-75 years sometime between 1050 and 1200. They grew corn, beans, and squash in fields nearby. Village population peaked at about 200, with an estimated 40-50 dwellings. Why the Anasazi left or where they went aren't known for sure, but a fire swept through much of the village before it was abandoned. Perhaps they burned the village on purpose, knowing they would move on. University of Utah students and faculty excavated the village, known as the Coombs Site, in 1958 and 1959. Pottery, ax heads, arrow points, and other tools found at the site can be seen in the museum, as can more perishable items like sandals and basketry that came from more protected sites elsewhere. A diorama shows how the village might have appeared in its heyday. Video programs on the Anasazi and modern tribes can be seen on request.

Borrow a pamphlet for the self-guided tour of the ruins behind the museum. You'll see a whole range of Anasazi building styles—a pithouse, masonry walls, jacal walls (mud reinforced by sticks), and combinations of masonry and jacal. Replicas of habitation and storage rooms behind the museum show complete construction details. The monument is open daily 8 a.m.-6 p.m. from mid-May to mid-Sept., then 9 a.m.-5 p.m. the rest of the year; admission is $1 adult, $.50 children 6-15, or $3/vehicle (whichever is less); tel. 335-7308. Books, videos, T-shirts, and postcards are sold. Located on UT 12, 28 miles northeast of Escalante and 38 miles south of Torrey.

### Practicalities
**Circle Cliffs Motel** has just 3 units ($21.80 s or d) on UT 12; tel. 355-7329. **Hall's Store** runs a small RV park ($6.54) next to Anasazi State Park. **Flying F Ranch RV Park** offers sites for self-contained RVs; $4 w/hookups; located 4 miles north on UT 12. **Griffin's Drive-in** (closed in winter) sits across from the state park. **Burr Trail Cafe** (open Memorial Day weekend until autumn) is at the intersection of UT 12 and Burr Trail Road. Look for a **visitor information** booth in town during the summer; usually it's in front of Burr Trail Cafe. The 2 gas stations in Boulder sell groceries and snack food.

# BOULDER MOUNTAIN SCENIC DRIVE

Utah 12 climbs high into forests of ponderosa pine, aspen, and fir on Boulder Mountain between the towns of Boulder and Torrey. The modern highway replaces what used to be a rough dirt road. Travel in winter is usually possible now, though heavy snows could close the road. Viewpoints along the drive have sweeping panoramas of the Escalante canyon country, Circle Cliffs, Waterpocket Fold, and the Henry Mountains. Hikers and fishermen can explore the alpine country of Boulder Mountain and seek out the 90 or so lakes swimming with trout. The Dixie National Forest map (Escalante and Teasdale ranger districts) shows the back roads, trails, and lakes. The U.S. Forest Service has 3 developed campgrounds about midway on this scenic drive: **Oak Creek** (18 miles from Boulder; elev. 8,800 ft.), **Pleasant Creek** (19 miles from Boulder; elev. 8,700 ft.), and **Singletree** (24 miles from Boulder; elev. 8,600 ft.). Season with water lasts from about late May to mid-Sept.; sites cost $5; campgrounds may also be open in spring and autumn without water or charge. **Lower Bowns Reservoir** (elev. 7,400 ft.) has primitive camping (no water or fee) and fishing for rainbow and some cutthroat trout; turn east 5 miles on a rough dirt road (not recommended for cars) just south of Pleasant Creek Campground. Contact the Teasdale Ranger District office (near Torrey; tel. 425-3702) for recreation information in the northern and eastern parts of Boulder Mountain; contact the Escalante Ranger District office (Escalante; tel. 826-4221) for the southern and western parts.

## TORREY AND VICINITY

This little town is only 11 miles west of the Capitol Reef National Park visitor center. **Wonderland Inn** recently opened just east of town near the UT 12 turnoff for Boulder; $34.88 s, $41.42 d; tel. 425-3775. **Chuck Wagon Motel** offers motel rooms ($30.52 s, $34.88 d), campground with showers ($5 tent or RV no hookups, $10 RV w/hookups), and a grocery store; open mid-April to mid-Nov.; tel. 425-3288. **Capitol Reef Motel** (closed in winter) has rooms ($34.88 s, $39.24 d), a small cafe serving lunch and dinner, and a gift shop; tel. 425-3271. **Thousand Lakes RV Park,** one mile west of town on UT 24, has

sites with showers, laundry, and store from April 1 to Oct. 31; $5.30 tent, $7.45 RV no hookups, $10.65 RV w/hookups; tel. 425-3500. **La Buena Vida Mexican Food** prepares excellent south-of-the-border meals for lunch and dinner; open daily in summer, then Wed. to Sun. the rest of the year; located on the west edge of town in a little white house with red trim; tel. 425-3759. **Teasdale Ranger Station** of the Dixie National Forest has info about hiking, horseback riding, and road conditions in the northern and eastern parts of Boulder Mountain and the Aquarius Plateau; books and forest maps are sold; office is 2 miles west of Torrey on UT 24, then 1.5 miles south to Main and 100 East (Box 99, Teasdale, UT 84773); open Mon. to Fri. 8 a.m.-4:30 p.m.; tel. 425-3702. **Hondoo Rivers & Trails** leads hiking, horseback, rafting, and driving tours of one to 8 days in the scenic backcountry of southern Utah; Box 98, Torrey, UT 84775; tel. 425-3519.

### Rim Rock Ranch

This motel complex, 3 miles east of Torrey on UT 24, sits on a hill all by itself with fine views of Capitol Reef. Rooms cost $32.70 s, $38.15 d; has a pool; the campground (closed in winter) has showers, $8.72 tent or RV no hookups, $10.90 RV w/hookups; Torrey, UT 84775; tel. 425-3843. The Stagecoach Inn Restaurant features trout, chicken, steaks,

*Chriss Lake, one of many pretty spots on Boulder Mountain.*

and sandwiches; open daily for breakfast, lunch, and dinner. A general store is open during the summer season. Color Country Outfitters at the ranch leads horseback rides in the Capitol Reef area.

### Bicknell
This small town is 8 miles west of Torrey on UT 24. The **Sunglow Motel** has rooms ($23.95 s, $30.50 d) and a cafe (open daily for breakfast, lunch, and dinner); tel. 425-3821. The **Aquarius Motel** offers rooms ($27.25 s, $30.50 d), kitchenettes ($35.94 s or d), and a restaurant (open daily for breakfast, lunch, and dinner); tel. 425-3835. The Aquarius Motel also has sites 4 blocks away for self-contained RVs; $7 w/hookups. **Sunglow Campground** (U.S. Forest Service) is just east of Bicknell; sites are open mid-May to late Oct. with water and a $5 charge; elevation is 7,200 feet; the surrounding red cliffs really light up at sunset.

The **J. Perry Egan Fish Hatchery** produces 25-30 million trout eggs a year. It's the largest in Utah and supplies eggs for most of the state's other hatcheries. Visitors are welcome to see the operation, open during daylight hours. The raceways have fish divided according to species, strain, and age. Trout spawn when 3 years old and are kept to produce here for another 3 years, after which they're released into high-pressure fishing areas. You'll see cutthroat, German brown, brook, and 4-6 strains of rainbow trout (including albinos). Turn south off UT 24 between Mileposts 63 and 64 (southeast of Bicknell), then go 2.5 miles on a paved road.

# CAPITOL REEF NATIONAL PARK

Wonderfully sculptured rock layers in a rainbow of colors put on a fine show here. Though you'll find these same rocks through much of the Four Corners region, their artistic variety has no equal outside Capitol Reef National Park. About 70 million years ago, gigantic forces within the earth began to uplift, squeeze, and fold more than a dozen rock formations into the central feature of the park today—Waterpocket Fold, so named for the many small pools of water trapped by the tilted strata. Erosion has since carved the spires, graceful curves, canyons, and arches. Waterpocket Fold extends 100 miles between Thousand Lake Mountain in the north and Lake Powell in the south. The most spectacular cliffs and rock formations of Waterpocket Fold form Capitol Reef, located north of Pleasant Creek and curving northwest across the Fremont River toward Thousand Lake Mountain. The reef was named by explorers who found Waterpocket Fold a barrier to travel and likened it to a reef blocking passage on the ocean. The rounded sandstone hills reminded them of the Capitol dome in Washington, D.C.—hence the name Capitol Reef.

Roads and hiking trails in the park provide access to the colorful rock layers and to the plants and wildlife that live here. You'll see remnants of the area's long human history too—petroglyphs and storage bins of the prehistoric Fremont Indians, a schoolhouse and other structures built by Mormon pioneers, and several small uranium mines of the 20th century. Legends tell of Butch Cassidy and other outlaw members of the "Wild Bunch" who hid out in these remote canyons in the 1890s.

## NATURAL HISTORY

### The Geologic Story
Exposed rocks reveal windswept deserts, rivers, mud flats, and inland seas of long ago. Nearly all the layers date from the Mesozoic Era (65-230 million years ago), when dinosaurs ruled the earth. Later uplift and twisting of the land—which continue to this day—built up the Colorado Plateau of southern Utah and also the Rocky Mountains to the east. Immense forces squeezed the rocks until they bent up and over from east to west in the massive crease of Waterpocket Fold.

## Climate

Expect hot summer days (highs in upper 80s and low 90s) and cool nights. Winter brings cool days (highs in 40s) and night temperatures dropping into the low 20s and teens. Snows accent the colored rocks while rarely hindering traffic on the main highway. Winter travel on the back roads and trails may be halted by snow, but it soon melts when the sun comes out. Annual precipitation averages only 7 inches, peaking in the July-Aug. thunderstorm season.

## Flora And Fauna

Ponderosa pine and other cool-climate vegetation grow on the flanks of Thousand Lake Mountain (7,000-9,000 ft. high) in the northwest corner of the park. Most of Waterpocket Fold, however, is at 5,000-7,000 feet, covered with sparse juniper and pinyon pine that cling precariously in cracks and thin soils of the slickrock. The soil from each rock type generally determines what will grow. Mancos Shale forms a poor clay soil supporting only saltbush, shadscale, and galleta grass. On Dakota Sandstone you'll see mostly sage and rabbitbrush. Clays of the Morrison Formation repel nearly all plants, while its sandstones nurture mostly juniper, pinyon pine, and cliffrose; uranium prospectors discovered that *astragalus* and prince's plume commonly grow near ore deposits. Sands of the Summerville Formation nourish grasses and fourwing saltbush. The Fremont River and several smaller creeks provide a lush habitat of cottonwood, tamarisk, willow, and other water-loving plants.

Streamside residents include beaver, muskrat, mink, tree lizard, Great Basin spadefoot toad, Rocky Mountain toad, and leopard frog. Spadefoot toads, fairy shrimp, and insects have adapted to the temporary water pockets by completing the aquatic phase of their short life cycles in a hurry. Near water or out in the drier country, you might see mule deer, coyote, gray fox, porcupine, spotted and striped skunks, badger, black-tailed jack rabbit, desert cottontail, yellowbelly marmot, rock squirrel, Colorado chipmunk, Ord's kangaroo rat, canyon mouse, and 5 known species of bats. With luck, you may sight a relatively rare mountain lion or black bear. While you can't miss seeing the many small lizards along the trails, snakes tend to be more secretive; those in the park include the striped whipsnake, Great Basin gopher snake, wandering garter snake, and the rarely seen desert faded pygmy rattlesnake. Some common birds are the sharp-shinned hawk, American kestrel, chukar, mourning dove, white-throated swift, black-chinned and broad-tailed hummingbirds, violet-green swallow, common raven, pinyon and scrub jays, canyon and rock wrens, and rufous-sided towhee. Most wildlife, except birds, wait until evening to come out, and they disappear again the following morning.

## HUMAN HISTORY

### Prehistoric Man

By A.D. 700, Fremont Indians had found good farming land in some of the valleys. They grew corn, beans, and other crops to supplement

*plain titmouse (Parus inornatus), a common year-round resident in the park* hunting and the gathering of wild plants. They protected food from rodents and insects by carefully constructing stone or wooden storage rooms. Many of these have survived in sheltered cliff overhangs, but the pithouse dwellings have nearly vanished. Intriguing pictographs and petroglyphs portray the Fremont adorned with headdresses, shields, sashes, and jewelry. Figures of desert bighorn sheep are seen too. Was this artwork casual doodlings? Or did it have religious importance? Its meaning hasn't been deciphered. Archaeologists first described and named the Fremont Culture from sites along the Fremont River at Capitol Reef in 1929. Droughts and possible conflict with other tribes may have been factors in the disappearance of the Fremont from the area about 1250. Until the white man came, small groups of Ute and Paiute spent winters hunting here, then moved to the high country in summer.

## Mormon Settlement

We can see why early explorers detoured around this natural barrier, though some trappers may have entered its canyons. Capitol Reef remained one of the last places in the West to be discovered. First reports came in 1866 from a detachment of Mormon militia pursuing renegade Indians. In 1872, Professor Almon H. Thompson of the Powell expedition led the first scientific exploration in the fold country and named several park features along the group's Pleasant Creek route. Mormons, expanding their network of settlements, arrived in the upper Fremont Valley in the late 1870s and spread downriver to Hanksville. Junction (renamed Fruita in 1902) and nearby Pleasant Creek (Sleeping Rainbow/Floral Ranch) were settled about 1880. Floods, isolation, and transport difficulties forced many families to give up, especially downstream from Capitol Reef. Irrigation and hard work paid off in Fruita with prosperous fruit orchards and the sobriquet "the Eden of Wayne County." Fruita averaged about 10 families who grew alfalfa, sorghum (for syrup), vegetables, and a wide variety of fruit. Getting the produce to market required long and difficult journeys

by wagon. The region remained one of the most isolated in Utah until after WW II.

## Creation Of The Park

In the 1920s local residents began to extol the wonders of Capitol Reef to the outside world. Impressed visitors lobbied for a national monument, which President Franklin D. Roosevelt proclaimed in 1937. The original 37,060-acre Capitol Reef National Monument included the highly scenic areas around the Fremont River canyon and Capitol Gorge. Expansions to the north and south in 1969, followed by more additions and national park status in 1971, brought the park to its current 241,904 acres. Fruita residents moved out in the 1960s as the National Park Service purchased the old homesteads. The schoolhouse, Behunin cabin, Merin Smith's blacksmith shop, and other buildings survive to commemorate Fruita's pioneer settlers. And the orchards still produce fruit that visitors may pick.

# VISITING THE PARK

The visitor center and main highway (UT 24) through Capitol Reef stay open all year. Even travelers short on time will enjoy a quick look at visitor center exhibits and a drive on UT 24 through an impressive cross section of Capitol Reef cut by the Fremont River. More of the park can be seen on the Scenic Drive, a good paved road that heads south from the visitor center. The drive passes beneath spectacular cliffs of the reef and enters scenic Grand Wash and Capitol Gorge canyons; allow at least 1½ hours for the 25-mile round trip. The fairweather Notom Road (dirt) heads south along the other side of the reef for almost 80 miles with fine views of Waterpocket Fold. Burr Trail Road (dirt) in the south actually climbs over the fold in a steep set of switchbacks, connecting Notom Road with Boulder. Only high-clearance vehicles can explore the park's northern district. All these roads provide access to viewpoints and hiking trails. A $3/vehicle park entrance fee is collected on the Scenic Drive from April to October.

## Visitor Center

Start with a 10-minute slide show, shown on request, introducing Capitol Reef's natural wonders and history. A giant relief map gives you a bird's-eye view of the entire park. Rock samples and diagrams illustrate 7 of the geologic formations you'll be seeing. Photos identify plants and birds found here. Prehistoric Fremont Indian artifacts on display include petroglyph replicas, sheepskin moccasins, pottery, basketry, stone knives, spear and arrow points, and bone jewelry. Other historic exhibits outline exploration and early Mormon settlement. Visitors headed for the back roads should ask at the desk about conditions and the weather forecast. Hikers planning overnight trips can get the required free backcountry permit. Besides answering questions, rangers will give out info sheets for special interests—hikers can pick up a map of trails that are near the visitor center and of longer routes in the southern park areas; naturalists will want the checklists of plants, birds, mammals, and other wildlife; and history buffs can learn more about the area's settlement and founding of the park. You can also choose from a good selection of pamphlets and books about the park, natural history, archaeology, pioneer history, and regional travel. Topo maps, posters, postcards, film, petroglyph replicas, and other souvenirs can be purchased too. Rangers offer nature walks, campfire programs, and other special events from May to Sept.; the bulletin board outside the visitor center lists what's on. Hours at the visitor center are daily 8 a.m.-7 p.m. from June to Sept., and daily 8 a.m.-4:30 p.m. the rest of the year. The visitor center is on UT 24 at the turnoff for Fruita Campground and the Scenic Drive. For more information, contact Capitol Reef National Park, Torrey, UT 84775; tel. 425-3791.

## Hiking And Rock Climbing

Fourteen day-hiking trails begin within a short drive of the visitor center. Of these, only Grand Wash, Capitol Gorge, Sunset Point, and Goosenecks are easy. The others involve moderately strenuous climbs and travel over irregular slickrock. Signs and rock cairns mark the way, but it's all too simple to wander off if you don't pay attention to the route. Rewards of hiking in the park include superb views, a chance to see wildlife and flora, and a deeper appreciation of the geologic history. Innumerable canyon and cross-country possibilities exist all over the park; talk to the rangers for ideas. To avoid intimidating the wildlife, pets may not be taken on trails or into the backcountry. Be cautious on slickrock; although it's not really slippery unless wet, hikers have gotten into trouble by attempting too steep a slope. You'll need a canteen on most hikes because few of the canyons and natural waterpockets are reliable water sources. Spring and autumn offer the most comfortable temperatures and less chance of bothersome insects (worst from mid-May to late June). Though most trails can easily be done in a day, backpackers might want to try longer trips in Chimney Rock Canyon in the north or Muley Twist Canyon and Halls Creek in the south. Obtain the required backcountry permit (free) from a ranger and camp at least ½ mile from the nearest maintained road or trail. (Cairned routes like Chimney Rock Canyon, Muley Twist Canyon, and Halls Creek don't count as trails.) Bring a stove for cooking, as backcountry users may not build fires. Avoid camping or parking in washes at any time—torrents of mud and boulders can carry away everything! Technical rock climbers should check with rangers to learn about restricted areas; registration is voluntary. Climbers must use "clean" techniques (no pitons or bolts) and keep at least 25 feet from rock art panels.

## Fruit Picking

Though Fruita's citizens have departed, the National Park Service still maintains the old orchards. Visitors are welcome to pick and carry away the cherries, apricots, peaches, pears, and apples during the harvest seasons. Harvest times begin in late June or early July and end in October. You'll be charged about the same as in commercial pick-your-own orchards. You may also wander through any orchard and eat all you want on the spot before and during the designated picking season (no charge).

## PRACTICALITIES

### In The Park

**Fruita Campground** stays open all year and has drinking water but no showers or hook-ups; $5; from Nov. to April there's no fee and you have to get water from the visitor center. Surrounding orchards and lush grass make this an attractive spot, one mile from the visitor center on the Scenic Drive. Sites often fill by early afternoon in the busy May to Oct. season. Two group campgrounds (by reservation only) and a picnic area are nearby. If you're just looking for a place to park for the night, check out the public land east of the park boundary off UT 24; areas on both sides of the highway (about 9 miles east of the visitor center) may be used for primitive camping; no facilities or charge. The 5-site **Cedar Mesa Campground** is in the park's southern district just off Notom-Bullfrog Road (dirt); campers here enjoy fine views of Waterpocket Fold and the Henry Mountains. Open all year, no water or charge; from the visitor center, go east 9.2 miles on UT 24, then turn right 22 miles on Notom-Bullfrog Road (avoid if wet). The **Cathedral Valley Campground** serves the park's northern district; it has 5 sites (no water or charge) near the Hartnet Junction, about 30 miles north of UT 24; take either the Caineville Wash or Hartnet (has a river ford) roads; both are dirt and should be avoided if wet.

### Other Areas

Accommodations, campgrounds, and restaurants are at Rim Rock Ranch (8 miles west of the visitor center), Torrey (11 miles west of the visitor center) and Bicknell (19 miles west of the visitor center); see "Torrey and Vicinity" earlier in this chapter. The U.S. Forest Service has 3 developed campgrounds (open with water from late May to mid-Sept.) on UT 12 between Torrey and Boulder. With distances from the park and elevations, they are: **Singletree** (22 miles, 8,200 ft.); **Pleasant Creek** (27 miles, 8,600 ft.); and **Oak Creek** (28 miles, 8,800 ft.). **Lower Bowns Reservoir** has primitive camping (no water or fee) and fishing for rainbow trout and some cutthroat (elev.

7,400 ft.); turn east 5 miles on a dirt road just south of Pleasant Creek Campground. **Hondoo Rivers & Trails** offers 4WD, horseback, and hiking tours of the park and nearby areas; Box 98, Torrey, UT 84775; tel. 425-3591. Horseback trips are also offered by **Color Country Outfitters,** Rim Rock Ranch, Torrey, UT 84775; tel. 425-3598.

## SIGHTS AND DAY HIKES ALONG UTAH 24 (LISTED WEST TO EAST)

### Chimney Rock Trail

Trailhead is 3 miles west of the visitor center on the north side of the highway. Towering above the highway, Chimney Rock is a fluted spire of dark-red rock (Moenkopi Formation) capped by a block of hard sandstone (Shinarump Member of the Chinle Formation). A 3½-mile loop trail ascends 540 feet from the parking lot (elev. 6,100 ft.) to a ridge overlooking Chimney Rock; allow 2½ hours. Panoramic views take in the face of Capitol Reef. Petrified wood along the trail has been eroded from the Chinle Formation (the same rock layer found in Petrified Forest National Park in Arizona).

### Chimney Rock Canyon Route

This moderately difficult hike begins at the top of the Chimney Rock trail. The wonderfully eroded forms of Navajo Sandstone present a continually changing exhibition. The riverbed

*leopard frog* (Rana pipiens)

is normally dry; allow about 6 hours for the 10-mile (one way) trip from Chimney Rock parking area to the Fremont River and UT 24. Check with rangers for the weather forecast before setting off—flash floods can be dangerous, and the Fremont River (which you must wade across) can be high. Normally the river is easily crossed (less than knee deep) to UT 24 (3.7 miles east of the visitor center). With luck you'll have a car waiting for you. Summer hikers can beat the heat with a crack-of-dawn departure. Carry water, as this section of canyon lacks a reliable source. From the Chimney Rock parking area, hike Chimney Rock Trail to the top of the ridge and follow signs for Chimney Rock Canyon. Enter the unnamed lead-in canyon and follow it downstream. A sign marks Chimney Rock Canyon, which is 2½ miles from the start. Turn right 6½ miles (downstream) to reach the Fremont River. A section of narrows requires some rockscrambling (bring a cord to lower backpacks), or the area can be bypassed on a narrow trail to the left above the narrows. Farther down, a natural arch high on the left marks the halfway point.

Upper Chimney Rock Canyon could be explored on an overnight trip. A spring (purify before drinking) is located in an alcove on the right side about one mile up Chimney Rock Canyon from the lead-in canyon. Wildlife use this water source, so camp at least ¼ mile away. Chimney Rock Canyon, the longest in the park, begins high on the slopes of Thousand Lake Mountain and descends nearly 15 miles southeast to join the Fremont River.

## Sulphur Creek Route

This moderately difficult hike begins by following a wash across the highway from the Chimney Rock parking area, descending to Sulphur Creek, then heading down the narrow canyon to the visitor center. The trip is about 5 miles long (one way) and takes 3-5 hours. Park rangers sometimes schedule guided hikes on this route. Warm weather is the best time because you'll be wading in the normally shallow creek. Three small waterfalls can be bypassed fairly easily; two falls are just below the

goosenecks and the third is about ½ mile before coming out at the visitor center. Carry water. The creek's name may be a mistake as there's no sulphur along it; perhaps outcrops of yellow limonite caused the confusion. You can make an all-day 8-mile hike in Sulphur Creek by starting where it crosses the highway between Mileposts 72 and 73, 5 miles west of the visitor center.

## Panorama Point, The Goosenecks, And Sunset Point

Turnoff is 2.5 miles west of the visitor center on the south side of the highway. Follow signs south for 0.15 mile to Panorama Point and views of Capitol Reef to the east and Boulder Mountain to the west. A sign explains how glacial meltwaters carried basalt boulders from Boulder Mountain to the reef 8,000-200,000 years ago. Goosenecks of Sulphur Creek are 0.9 mile farther on a gravel road. A short trail leads to the Goosenecks Overlook on the rim (elev. 6,400 ft.) for dizzying views to the creek below. Canyon walls display shades of yellow, green, brown, and red. Another easy trail leads ⅓ mile to Sunset Point and panoramic views of the Capitol Reef cliffs and the distant Henry Mountains.

## Fruita Schoolhouse

Located 0.8 mile east of the visitor center on the north side of the highway. Early settlers completed the one-room log structure in 1896. Teachers struggled at times with rowdy students, but the kids learned their 3 R's in grades 1 through 8. Mormon church meetings, dances, town meetings, elections, and other community gatherings took place here. Lack of students caused the school's closing in 1941. Rangers are on duty some days in summer (ask at the visitor center). At other times you can peer inside the windows and listen to a recording of a former teacher recalling what school life was like.

## Petroglyphs

Located 1.2 miles east of the visitor center on the north side of the highway. Fremont petroglyphs of several human figures with head-

*Indian artifacts illustrate a talk at the petroglyphs.*

dresses and mountain sheep decorate the cliff. More petroglyphs can be seen by walking to the left and right along the cliff face.

### Hickman Natural Bridge, Rim Overlook, And Navajo Knobs Trails

Trailhead is 2 miles east of the visitor center on the north side of the highway. The graceful Hickman Natural Bridge spans 133 feet across a small streambed. Numbered stops along the self-guiding trail correspond to descriptions in a pamphlet available at the trailhead or visitor center. Starting from the parking area (elev. 5,320 ft.), the trail follows the Fremont River's green banks a short distance before gaining 380 feet in the climb to the bridge. The last section of trail follows a dry wash shaded by cottonwood, juniper, and pinyon pine trees. You'll pass under the bridge (eroded from the Kayenta Formation) at trail's end. Capitol Dome and other sculptured features of the Navajo Sandstone surround the site. The 2-mile (roundtrip) hike takes about 1½ hours. Joseph Hickman served as principal of Wayne County High School and later in the state legislature during the 1920s; he and another local man, Ephraim Pectol, led efforts to promote Capitol Reef.

A splendid overlook 1,000 feet above Fruita beckons hikers up the Rim Overlook Trail.

Take the Hickman Natural Bridge Trail ¼ mile from the parking area, then turn right 2 miles at the signed fork. Allow 3½ hours from the fork for this hike. Panoramic views take in the Fremont River valley below, the great cliffs of Capitol Reef above, the Henry Mountains to the southeast, and Boulder Mountain to the southwest.

Continue another 2.2 miles and more than 500 feet higher from the Rim Overlook to reach Navajo Knobs. Rock cairns lead the way over slickrock along the rim of Waterpocket Fold. A magnificent panorama at trail's end takes in much of southeastern Utah.

### Cohab Canyon And Frying Pan Trails

Park at Hickman Natural Bridge trailhead, then walk across the highway bridge. This trail climbs Capitol Reef for fine views in all directions and a close look at the swirling lines in the Navajo Sandstone. After ¾ mile and a 400-foot climb, you'll reach a trail fork: keep right one mile to stay on Cohab Canyon Trail and descend to Fruita Campground or turn left onto Frying Pan Trail to Cassidy Arch (3½ miles away) and Grand Wash (4 miles away). All these interconnecting trails give you many hiking possibilities, especially if a car shuttle can be arranged. For example, you could start up Cohab Canyon Trail from UT 24, cross over the reef on Frying Pan Trail, make a side trip to Cassidy Arch, descend Cassidy Arch Trail to Grand Wash, walk down Grand Wash to UT 24, then walk (or car shuttle) 2.7 miles along the highway back to the start (10½ miles total). Cohab is a pretty little canyon in the Wingate Sandstone overlooking the campground. Mormon polygamists supposedly used the canyon to escape federal marshals during the 1880s. Hiking the Frying Pan Trail involves an additional 600 feet of climbing from either Cohab Canyon or Cassidy Arch trails. Once atop Capitol Reef, the trail follows the gently rolling slickrock terrain.

### Grand Wash

Trailhead is 4.7 miles east of the visitor center on the south side of the highway. One of only 5 canyons cutting completely through the reef, Grand Wash offers easy hiking and great scenery. There's no trail—just follow the dry gravel riverbed. Flash floods can occur during storms. Canyon walls of Navajo Sandstone rise 800 feet above the floor and close in to as little as 20 feet in width. Cassidy Arch trailhead (see below) is 2 miles away, and parking for Grand Wash from the Scenic Drive is ¼ mile farther.

### Behunin Cabin
Located 6.2 miles east of the visitor center on the south side of the highway. Elijah Cutlar Behunin used blocks of sandstone to build this cabin about 1882. He moved on, though, when flooding made life too difficult. Small openings allow a look inside the dirt-floored structure, but no furnishings remain.

### Small Waterfall In The Fremont River
Parking is 6.9 miles east of the visitor center on the north side of the highway. The river twists through a narrow crack in the rock before making its final plunge into a pool below. A sign warns of hazardous footing above the falls, which is dangerous for children. Instead, take the sandy path from the parking area to below the falls where they can be safely viewed. Use extreme caution if you intend to cool off in the pool at the base of the waterfall, as there is a very strong and dangerous undertow.

## SIGHTS AND DAY HIKES ALONG THE SCENIC DRIVE

Turn south from UT 24 at the visitor center to experience some of the reef's best scenery and to learn more about its geology. An illustrated pamphlet, available on the drive or in the visitor center, has keyed references to numbered stops along the 25-mile (roundtrip) drive. Descriptions identify rock layers and explain how they were formed. Just a quick tour takes 1½ hours, but several hiking trails may tempt you to make a longer stay. The Scenic Drive is paved, though side roads have gravel surfaces. You'll first pass orchards and several of Fruita's buildings. A **blacksmith** shop (0.7 miles from the visitor center on the right) displays tools, harnesses, farm machinery, and Fruita's first tractor. The tractor didn't arrive until 1940—long after the rest of the country had modernized. In a recording, a rancher tells about living and working in Fruita.

### Picnic Area
Located 0.8 mile from the visitor center on the left, fruit trees and grass make this a pretty spot for lunch. A short trail crosses orchards and the Fremont River to the Fruita Schoolhouse.

### Cohab Canyon Trail
Trailhead is across the road from Fruita Campground, 1.3 miles from the visitor center. The trail follows steep switchbacks during the first ¼ mile, then more gentle grades to the top, 400 feet higher and one mile from the campground. You can take a short trail to viewpoints or continue ¾ mile down the other side of the ridge to UT 24. See description under "Sights and Day Hikes Along Utah 24" above. Another option is to turn right at the top on Frying Pan Trail to Cassidy Arch (3½ miles one way) and Grand Wash (4 miles one way).

### Fremont Overlook Trail
Trailhead is behind Fruita Campground, 1.3 miles from the visitor center. After a leisurely ½-mile walk through orchards along the Fremont River (elev. 5,350 ft.), take a steep winding trail to a viewpoint on Miner's Mountain. Sweeping views take in Fruita, Boulder Mountain, and the reef. The roundtrip distance of 2½ miles takes about 1½ hours; elevation gain is 770 feet.

### Grand Wash Road
Turn left off the Scenic Drive 3.6 miles from the visitor center. This side trip follows the twisting Grand Wash for one mile. At road's end you can continue on foot 2¼ miles (one way) through the canyon to its end at the Fremont River (see Grand Wash under "Sights and Day Hikes Along Utah 24" above). Another good hike is the climb to Cassidy Arch.

**Cassidy Arch Trail** begins near the end of Grand Wash Road. Energetic hikers will enjoy good views of Grand Wash, the great domes of Navajo Sandstone, and the arch itself. The 3½-mile roundtrip trail ascends the north wall of Grand Wash (Wingate and Kayenta formations), then winds across the slickrock of Kayenta Formation to a vantage point close to the arch, also of Kayenta. Allow about 3 hours, as the elevation gain is nearly 1,000 feet. The notorious outlaw Butch Cassidy may have traveled through Capitol Reef and seen this arch. Frying Pan Trail branches off Cassidy Arch Trail at the one-mile mark, then wends its way across 3 miles of slickrock to Cohab Canyon; see "Sights and Day Hikes Along Utah 24" above.

## Old Wagon Trail

Wagon drivers once used this route as a shortcut between Grover and Capitol Gorge. Look for the trailhead 0.7 mile south of Slickrock Divide, between Grand Wash and Capitol Gorge. The old trail crosses a wash to the west, then ascends steadily through pinyon and juniper woodland on Miners Mountain. After 1.5 miles, the trail leaves the wagon road and goes north 0.5 mile to a high knoll for the best views of the Capitol Reef area. The 4-mile, roundtrip hike climbs 1,000 feet.

## Pleasant Creek Road

Turn right 8.3 miles from the visitor center where the Scenic Drive curves east toward Capitol Gorge. Pleasant Creek Road turns south and continues below the face of the reef. After 3 miles the sometimes rough, dirt road passes **Sleeping Rainbow/Floral Ranch** (closed to public) and ends at Pleasant Creek. A rugged 4WD road continues on the other side but is much too rough for cars. Floral Ranch dates back to Capitol Reef's early years of settlement. In 1939 it became the Sleeping Rainbow Guest Ranch, from the Indian name for Waterpocket Fold. Now the ranch belongs to the park, but the former owners still live here. Pleasant Creek's perennial waters begin high on Boulder Mountain to the west and cut a scenic canyon completely through Capitol Reef. Hikers can head downstream through the 3-mile-long canyon and return, or continue another 3 miles cross-country to Notom Road.

## Capitol Gorge

This is the end of the Scenic Drive, 10.7 miles from the visitor center. Capitol Gorge is a dry canyon through Capitol Reef much like Grand Wash, though with a somewhat different character. Believe it or not, the narrow, twisting Capitol Gorge was the route of the main state

*The "Castle" stands near the visitor center.*

highway through southcentral Utah for 80 years! Mormon pioneers laboriously cleared a path so wagons could go through, a task repeated every time flash floods rolled in a new set of boulders. Cars bounced their way down the canyon until 1962, when the present UT 24 opened, but few traces of old road remain today. Walking is easy along the gravel riverbed, but don't enter if storms threaten. The first mile downstream is the most scenic: Fremont Indian petroglyphs (in poor condition) appear on the left after 0.1 mile; narrows of Capitol Gorge close in at 0.3 mile; a "pioneer register" on the left at ½ mile consists of names and dates of early travelers and ranchers scratched in the canyon wall; natural water tanks on the left at ¾ mile are typical of those in Waterpocket Fold. Hikers can continue another 3 miles downstream to the Notom Road.

**Golden Throne Trail** also begins at the end of the Scenic Drive. Instead of heading down Capitol Gorge from the parking area, turn left up this trail for dramatic views of the reef and surrounding area. Golden Throne is a massive monolith of yellow-hued Navajo Sandstone capped by a thin layer of red Carmel Formation. The 4-mile roundtrip trail climbs 1,100 feet in a steady grade to a viewpoint near the base of Golden Throne; allow 4 hours.

## THE NORTH DISTRICT

Only the most adventurous travelers get into the remote canyons and desert country of the north. The few roads *cannot* be negotiated by ordinary cars. In good weather, high-clearance vehicles can enter the region from the east, north, and west. The roads lead through stately sandstone monoliths of Cathedral Valley, volcanic remnants, badlands country, many low mesas, and vast sand flats. Foot travel allows closer inspection of these features or lengthy excursions into the canyons of Polk, Deep, and Spring creeks, which cut deeply into the flanks of Thousand Lake Mountain. Much of the north district is good

for horseback riding too. **Cathedral Valley Campground's** 5 sites provide a place to stop for the night; rangers won't permit car camping elsewhere in the district. Hikers with a backcountry permit must camp at least ½ mile from the nearest road. A small guide to this area can be purchased at the visitor center.

## THE SOUTH DISTRICT

### Notom-Bullfrog Road

Capitol Reef is only a small part of Waterpocket Fold. By taking the fair-weather Notom-Bullfrog Road, you'll see nearly 80 miles of the fold's eastern side. This route crosses some of the younger geologic layers, such as those of the Morrison Formation that form colorful hills. In other places, eroded layers of the Waterpocket Fold jut up at 70-degree angles. The Henry Mountains to the east and the many canyons on both sides of the road add to the memorable panoramas. Keep an eye on the weather before setting off—usually the dirt and gravel surface is OK for cars when dry but can be too slippery and gooey for *any* vehicle when wet. Sandy spots and washouts may present a problem for low-clearance vehicles; contact the visitor center to check current conditions. Have a full gas tank and carry extra water and food because no services are available between UT 24 and Bullfrog Marina. A small guide to this area can be purchased at the visitor center. Features and mileage along the drive from north to south include:

**Mile 0.0:** The turnoff from UT 24 is 9.2 miles east of the visitor center and 30.2 miles west of Hanksville (another turnoff from UT 24 is 3 miles east).
**Mile 2.2:** Pleasant Creek; the mouth of the canyon is 5-6 miles upstream, though it's only about 3 miles by heading cross-country from south of Notom. The canyon cuts 3 miles through Capitol Reef to Pleasant Creek Road (off the Scenic Drive).
**Mile 4.1:** Notom Ranch is to the west; once a small town, Notom is now a private ranch.

**Mile 8.1:** Burrow Wash; hikers can explore the narrow canyon upstream.

**Mile 9.3:** Cottonwood Wash; another canyon hike just upstream.

**Mile 10.4:** Five Mile Wash; yet another canyon hike.

**Mile 13.3:** Sheets Gulch; a scenic canyon lies upstream here too.

**Mile 14.1:** Sandy Ranch junction; high-clearance vehicles can turn east 16 miles to the Henry Mountains.

**Mile 14.2:** Oak Creek Access Road to the west; turn here for Oak Creek. The creek cuts a 2-mile-long canyon through Capitol Reef that's a good dayhike. Backpackers sometimes start upstream at Lower Bowns Reservoir (off UT 12) and hike the 15 miles to Oak Creek Access Road. The clear waters of Oak Creek flow all year but must be treated for drinking.

**Mile 14.4:** Oak Creek crossing.

**Mile 20.0:** Entering Capitol Reef National Park; a small box has info sheets.

**Mile 22.3: Cedar Mesa Campground** to the west; the small 5-site campground is surrounded by junipers and has fine views of Waterpocket Fold and the Henry Mountains. Sites have tables and grills; there's an outhouse but no drinking water; free. **Red Canyon Trail** begins here and heads west into a huge box canyon in Waterpocket Fold; 4 miles roundtrip.

**Mile 26.0:** Bitter Creek Divide; streams to the north flow to the Fremont River; Halls Creek on the south side runs through Strike Valley to Lake Powell, 40 miles away.

**Mile 34.1:** Burr Trail Road junction; turn west up the steep switchbacks to ascend Waterpocket Fold and continue to Boulder and UT 12 (36 miles). Burr Trail is the only road that actually crosses the top of the fold and it's one of the most scenic in the park. Driving conditions are similar to the Notom-Bullfrog Road—OK for cars when dry. No services until Boulder.

**Mile 36.0:** Surprise Canyon trailhead; a hike into this narrow, usually shaded canyon takes 1-2 hours.

**Mile 36.6:** The Post; a small trading post here

once served sheep herders and some cattle men, but today this spot is just a reference point. Park here to hike to Headquarters Canyon. A trailhead for Lower Muley Twist Canyon via Halls Creek lies at the end of a ½-mile-long road to the south.

**Mile 37.5:** Leaving Capitol Reef National Park; a small box has info sheets.

**Mile 45.5:** Road junction; turn right (south) to continue to Bullfrog Marina (25 miles) or go straight (east) for Starr Springs Campground (23 miles) and the Henry Mountains.

**Mile 46.4:** The road to the right (west) goes to Halls Creek Overlook. This turnoff is poorly signed and easy to miss; look for it 0.9 mile south of the previous junction. Turn in and follow the road 3 miles, then turn right at a fork 0.4 mile to the viewpoint. The last 0.3 mile may be too rough for low-clearance cars. A picnic table is the only "facility" here. Far below in Grand Gulch, Halls Creek flows south to Lake Powell. Look across the valley for the double Brimhall Bridge in the red sandstone of Waterpocket Fold. A steep trail descends to Halls Creek (1.2 miles one way) and it's possible to continue another 1.1 miles up Brimhall Canyon to the bridge. A register box at the overlook has info sheets on this route. Note, however, that the last part of the hike to the bridge requires difficult rockscrambling and wading or swimming through pools! Hikers looking for another adventure might want to follow Halls Creek 10 miles downstream to the narrows. Convoluted walls rise nearly 700 feet, yet narrow to little more than arms' length apart. This beautiful area of water-sculpted rock sometimes has deep pools that require swimming.

**Mile 49.0:** Colorful clay hills of deep reds, creams, and grays rise beside the road. This clay turns to goo when wet, providing all the traction of axle grease.

**Mile 54.0:** Beautiful panorama of countless mesas, mountains, and canyons. Lake Powell and Navajo Mountain can be seen to the south.

**Mile 65.3:** Junction with paved UT 276; turn left (north) for Hanksville (59 miles) or right (south) to Bullfrog Marina (5.2 miles).

**Mile 70.5:** Bullfrog Marina (see pp. 420-421 in the "Glen Canyon National Recreation Area" section).

## Lower Muley Twist Canyon

"So winding that it would twist a mule pulling a wagon," said an early visitor. This canyon has some of the best hiking in the southern district of the park. In the 1880s, Mormon pioneers used the canyon as part of a wagon route between Escalante in the west and new settlements in southeastern Utah, replacing the even more difficult Hole-in-the-Rock route. Unlike most canyons of Waterpocket Fold, Muley Twist runs lengthwise along the crest for about 18 miles before finally turning east and leaving the fold. Hikers starting from Burr Trail Road can easily follow the twisting bends down to Halls Creek, 12 miles away. Two trailheads and the Halls Creek route allow a variety of trips. You could start from Burr Trail Road near the top of the switchbacks (2.2 miles west of Notom-Bullfrog Road) and hike down the dry gravel streambed. After 4 miles you have the options of returning the same way, taking the Cut Off route east 2½ miles to the Post trailhead (on Notom-Bullfrog Road), or continuing 8 miles down Lower Muley Twist Canyon to its end at Halls Creek. Upon reaching Halls Creek, turn left (north) 5 miles up the creekbed or the old jeep road beside it to the Post. This section of creek lies in a open dry valley. With a car shuttle, the Post would be the end of a good 2-day, 17-mile hike, or you could loop back to Lower Muley Twist Canyon via the Cut Off route and hike back to Burr Trail Road for a 23½-mile trip. It's a good idea to check the weather beforehand and avoid the canyon if storms threaten.

Cream-colored cliffs of Navajo Sandstone lie atop the red Kayenta and Wingate formations. Impressively deep undercuts have been carved in the lower canyon. Spring and autumn offer the best conditions (summer temperatures can exceed 100° F). Elevations range from 5,640 feet at Burr Trail Road to 4,540 feet at the confluence with Halls Creek to 4,894 feet at the Post. An info sheet available at the visitor center and trailheads has a small map and route details. Topo maps are Wagon Box Mesa, Mt. Pennell, and Hall Mesa or the 1:100,000-scale Escalante and Hite Crossing; they are sold at the visitor center. You'll also find this hike described in Dave Hall's *Hiker's Guide to Utah* and in Michael Kelsey's *Canyon Hiking Guide to the Colorado Plateau* and *Utah Mountaineering Guide*. Carry all water for the trip, as natural sources are often dry or polluted.

## Upper Muley Twist Canyon

This part of the canyon has plenty of scenery too. Large and small natural arches along the way add to its beauty. Upper Muley Twist Road turns north off Burr Trail Road about one mile west from the top of the switch backs. Cars can go in 0.5 mile to a trailhead parking, while high-clearance 4WD vehicles can head another 2.5 miles to the end of the primitive road. Look for natural arches on the left along this last section. From the end of the road, you can hike as far as 6½ miles (one way) to the head of Upper Muley Twist Canyon. **Strike Valley Overlook Trail** (¾ mile roundtrip) also begins at the end of the road and leads to a magnificent panorama of Waterpocket Fold and beyond. Return to the canyon and continue on foot upstream to see 2 large arches. Saddle Arch, the second one on the left, is 1¾ miles away. Proceed upcanyon to see several more arches. A very narrow section of canyon beginning about 4 miles from the end of the road must be bypassed to continue; look for rock cairns showing the way around. At 4¾ miles from the end of the road, look for a sign to the Rim route. This route climbs the canyon wall, follows the rim (good views of Strike Valley and the Henry Mountains) back to a point opposite Saddle Arch, and descends to the canyon bottom. Continuing up the canyon past the Rim route sign will take you to several small drainages marking the upper end of Muley Twist Canyon. Climb a high tree-covered point on the west rim for great views; experienced hikers with a map can follow the rim back to Upper Muley Road (no trail or markers on this route). Bring all the water you'll need, as there are no reliable sources in Upper Muley Twist Canyon.

# EAST OF CAPITOL REEF NATIONAL PARK

## HANKSVILLE

Ebenezer Hanks and other Mormon settlers founded this out-of-the-way community in 1882 along the Fremont River, then known as the Dirty Devil River. The isolation attracted polygamists like Hanks, who had 2 wives, and other fugitives from the law. Butch Cassidy and his gang found refuge in the rugged canyon country of "Robbers' Roost" east of town. Hanksville hasn't grown much. The population is only about 400, but it has outlasted several other farm communities upstream. Today most people work at ranching, farming (hay, corn feed, and watermelons), mining, or tourism. The old stone church (on Center one block south of the highway) and several houses survive from the 19th century. Travelers exploring this scenic region find Hanksville a handy stopover; Capitol Reef National Park lies to the west, Lake Powell and the Henry Mountains to the south, the remote Maze District of Canyonlands National Park to the east, and Goblin Valley State Park to the north. The book *Hiking and Exploring Utah's Henry Mountains and Robbers Roost* by Michael Kelsey has a wealth of history and travel information about the Hanksville area.

### Wolverton Mill

E.T. Wolverton built this ingenious mill during the 1920s at his gold-mining claims in the Henry Mountains. A 20-foot waterwheel, still perfectly balanced, powered ore-crushing machinery and a sawmill. Owners of claims at the mill's original site didn't like a steady stream of tourists coming through to see the mill, so it was moved to the BLM office at Hanksville. Drive south ½ mile on 100 West to see the mill and some of its original interior mechanism.

### Practicalities

**Poor Boy Motel** has rooms for $34.88 s, $41.42 d; on UT 24 in the center of town; tel. 542-3471. **Fern's Place** has several kitchenettes at $27.25-38.15 s or d; one-quarter mile west on UT 24; tel. 542-3251. **Redrock Campground,** also in the center of town, offers sites for tents and RVs, $8.48 tent, $9.54 RV no hookups, $11.66 RV w/hookups; has showers and laundry; open March 15 to Oct. 31; tel. 542-3235. The **Redrock Restaurant** (adjacent to the campground) serves American food daily for breakfast, lunch, and dinner; closed in winter. **Tropical Jeem's** cafe one mile north on UT 24 offers Mexican and American meals daily for breakfast, lunch, and dinner; may close in winter. **Stan's Burger Shack** on the south edge of town is open daily with fast food. **Luna Mesa Cantina** serves Mexican/American lunches and dinners daily in Caineville, between Hanksville and Capitol Reef; closed winter. **Hanksville Information Center** has regional travel brochures and info at the junction of UT 24 and UT 95; open Mon. to Sat. 9 a.m.-4 p.m. from about May to September. The **Bureau of Land Management** staff can tell you about road conditions, hiking, camping, and the buffalo herd in the Henry Mountains. A recreation map and USGS topo maps are available; open Mon. to Fri. 8 a.m.-5 p.m.; turn south ½ mile on 100 West from UT 24 or write Box 99, Hanksville, UT 84734; tel. 542-3461.

## HENRY MOUNTAINS AND VICINITY

Great domes of intrusive igneous rock pushed into and deformed surrounding sedimentary layers about 70 million years ago. Erosion later uncovered the domes, revealing mountains towering 5,000 feet above the surrounding plateau. Mount Ellen's North Summit Ridge (elev. 11,522 ft.) and Mt. Pennell (elev. 11,320 ft.) top the range. Scenic views and striking geologic features abound in and around the Henrys. Rock layers tilt dramatically in Waterpocket Fold to the west and in

Mt. Ellen in the
Henry Mountains,
from Burr Trail Road

the Pink Cliffs on the south side of Mt. Hillers. Sheer cliffs of The Horn, between Mt. Ellen and Mt. Pennell, attract rock climbers.

The arid land and rugged canyons surrounding the Henry Mountains so discouraged early explorers and potential settlers that the range wasn't even named or described until 1869, when members of the Powell river expedition sighted it. Powell later named the range in honor of one of his supporters, Professor Joseph Henry of the Smithsonian Institution. Tales by Indians of a lost Spanish gold mine have long enticed prospectors, yet only modest amounts of the yellow metal were found. Bromide Basin has been the major site for gold and silver mines of the past and present. A brief gold boom here in the early 1890s gave rise to Eagle City mining camp along Crescent Creek. The rich vein soon worked out and the town faded away. Other minerals occur in the area too; a uranium mine is just south of the Henrys in Shootaring Canyon, near Ticaboo.

Vegetation ranges from sparse desert plants such as galleta grass and blackbrush on the lower slopes to pinyon pine and juniper woodlands higher up, then to forests of ponderosa pine, aspen, Douglas fir, spruce, and bristlecone pine. Alpine plants and grasslands cover the highest summits. Buffalo, brought to the Henrys from Yellowstone National Park in 1941, form one of the few free-roaming herds in the United States. They winter in the southwestern part of the mountains, then move higher as the snow melts. Mule deer keep mostly to the higher elevations, while pronghorn stay in the desert country to the east. Most of the bighorn sheep are found in the Little Rockies, a southeastern extension of the Henry Mountains. Mountain lions live near the Henrys too, but they're more likely to see you than you are to see them!

**Exploring The Henry Mountains**
Roads with panoramic views cross the range between the high peaks at Bull Creek, Pennellen, and Stanton passes. Most driving routes are best suited for high-clearance vehicles. The road through Bull Creek Pass (elev. 10,485 ft.) is snow-free only from about early July to late October. Rains, which peak in Aug., occasionally make travel difficult in late summer. Roads tend to be at their best after grading in autumn, just before the deer-hunting season. Travel at the lower elevations is possible all year, though spring and autumn have the most pleasant temperatures. Check in first with the BLM office in Hanksville before exploring the backcountry. They can advise on road and trail conditions and, in case of trouble, they will have an idea of where to look for you. Take precautions for desert travel, and

have water, food, and extra clothing with you. The Henry Mountains remain a remote and little-traveled region.

## Campgrounds
**Starr Springs Campground** sits in an oak forest at the base of Mt. Hillers. Sites (elev. 6,300 ft.) stay open all year and have water (and a small charge) from early May to early October. **Panorama Knoll Trail** begins from the campground and makes a ½-mile loop to an overlook. A good gravel road to Starr Springs Campground turns off UT 276 near Milepost 17 (23 miles north of Bullfrog and 43 miles south of Hanksville) and goes in 4 miles. **Lonesome Beaver Campground** lies in a very pretty spot surrounded by ponderosa pine and Douglas fir; season runs May to Oct. (elev. 8,000 ft.); its 5 sites may not be maintained or have water. To get here from Hanksville, turn south 27 miles on 100 East (next to the post office) or follow the road along Crescent Creek from UT 95 to the east; both unpaved roads are marginal for cars (check first with the Hanksville BLM office). **McMillan Springs Campground** is in a ponderosa pine forest at an elevation of 8,400 feet with a great view of Waterpocket Fold, especially at sunrise; open April to Nov.; no water; located on a rough road (not recommended for cars) between Notom Road and Bull Creek Pass.

## Hiking
Countless mountain and canyon hiking possibilities exist in the range; Kelsey's book on the Henry Mountains has trip suggestions and practical advice. Most routes go cross-country or follow old mining roads. The summit of Mt. Ellen is a good day-hike destination and probably attracts the greatest number of hikers. Easiest way is to follow the ridge north from Bull Creek Pass; elevation gain is 1,030 feet. Another popular approach is from Lonesome Beaver Campground; there's no real trail but you can follow an old road that climbs the slopes part of the way; elevation gain is 3,400 feet. Either route is about 8 miles roundtrip and takes most of a day. Interestingly, Mt. Ellen Peak shown on the maps isn't the true high point: the North Summit Ridge of Mt. Ellen, 1½ miles to the north, is 16 feet higher at 11,522 feet. See the 7½-minute Mount Ellen and Dry Lakes Peak or the 15-minute Mt. Ellen topo maps.

## Little Egypt
Eerie rock formations similar to those in Goblin Valley, but covering a smaller area, lie east of the Henrys. Kids will enjoy exploring the area and it's a fine place for a picnic. Turn southwest 1.5 miles from UT 95 between Mileposts 20 and 21; the gravel road is usually OK for cars when dry. No facilities or even a sign mark the site, so note mileage from UT 95.

## Dirty Devil Canyon Overlook
The muddy waters of the Dirty Devil River have carved an impressive canyon southeast of Hanksville. Views from the overlook at Burr Point take in some impressive scenery. Desperadoes around the turn of the century hid

*Dirty Devil River*

out in the rugged canyonlands of "Robbers' Roost" across the river. In 1869, when one of Powell's expedition members was asked if the waters had trout, he replied with disgust that the smelly and muddy river was "a dirty devil." An unpaved road winds east for 11 miles from UT 95 (between Mileposts 15 and 16). Cars with good clearance should be OK in dry weather. Park near where the road makes a sharp right just before the edge, or follow the road south for other views. Walking along the rim also affords different perspectives.

## GOBLIN VALLEY STATE PARK

Thousands of spooky rock formations inhabit this valley. Little eyelike holes in the "goblins" make you wonder who's watching whom. All of the goblins have weathered out of the Entrada Formation, here a soft red sandstone and even softer siltstone. **Carmel Canyon Trail** begins from the northeast side of the parking lot at road's end, then leads into the strange landscape of goblins, spires, and balanced rocks. Just wander about at your whim; this is a great place for the imagination! **Curtis Canyon Trail** begins from the southwest side of the parking lot, goes west to a viewpoint of the Henry Mountains, then turns north to Curtis Bench Trailhead (on the road between the parking lot and the campground); cairns mark the 1½-mile (one way) route. The state park provides a campground with showers on the drive in and a covered picnic area and an overlook at the end of the road. The park stays open all year; $3/vehicle day use or $8/vehicle camping; Box 93, Green River, UT 84525; tel. 564-8110 or (800) 322-3770 (reservations). The turnoff from UT 24 is 21 miles north of Hanksville and 24 miles south of I-70; follow signs west 5.3 miles on a paved road, then south 7 miles on a gravel road.

The park is also a good base for exploring the **San Rafael Swell** area to the northwest. Deep canyons, otherworldly landscapes of rock and sand, old uranium mines, and Hondoo Arch await discovery here. **Temple Mountain Bike Trail,** marked for use by trail motorcycles, traverses old mining roads, ridges, and wash bottoms about 12 miles north of the state park. Rangers at the park can tell you about the San Rafael Swell area; for more detailed info contact the BLM San Rafael Resource Area, 900 North and 700 East, Price, UT 84501; tel. 637-4584.

## GREEN RIVER

The small town began in 1878 as a mail station on the long run between Salina in central Utah and the Colorado border. Today Green River is still the only sizable settlement on this route, now I-70. Travelers can stop for a rest or meal here, or use it as a base for exploring the scenic San Rafael Swell country nearby.

**River Running**

Boaters enjoy trips on the Green River. Desolation and Gray canyons lie upstream of the town of Green River, while Labyrinth and Stillwater canyons are downstream. River companies organize trips through these areas; ask at the Green River Information Center for names and details. **Holiday River Expeditions** offers day trips through Gray Canyon from Memorial Day to Labor Day weekends; costs are $40 adult, $35 age 12-18, and $30 under 12; tel. 564-3273. The office is on the north side of the I-70 business route, ¼ mile east of the Green River bridge. You can also drive or do your own boat trip through this section of canyon; see "Green River Scenic Drive" below. Most river running on the Green is done with rafts, though regular power boats can also follow the river below town to the confluence with the Colorado River and head up the Colorado to Moab, 2-3 days and 186 river miles away. The town of Green River sponsors an annual **Friendship Cruise** on this route on Memorial Day weekend. A popular 4-day canoe or raft trip goes to Mineral Bottom, 70 miles south near Canyonlands National Park; **Tex's Riverways** provides canoes and shuttle services: Box 67, Moab, UT

84532; tel. 259-5101. Most boaters use the launch area at Green River State Park, 150 S. Green River Boulevard.

### John Wesley Powell Museum

Stop by this new museum to learn about Powell's daring expeditions down the Green and Colorado rivers in 1869 and 1871-72. Historic river boats on display include a replica of Powell's *Emma Dean*. Other exhibits show places to visit in the area. The Green River Information Center in the museum has local travel information. A gift shop sells books, maps, Indian crafts, T-shirts, and other souvenirs. The Powell Museum, on the east bank of the Green River, is at 885 E. Main (the I-70 business route through town); tel. 564-3427/3428. Open daily 9 a.m.-9 p.m. in summer and reduced hours the rest of the year.

### Practicalities

Travelers have a selection of 10 motels and a similar number of restaurants and fast-food places. You'll find these along the business route (Main St.) between I-70 Exits 158 and 162. To really get away, **Tavaputs Plateau Ranch** offers guest accommodations and activities in the high country north of Green River, reached by a long drive or short charter flight; Box 139, Green River, UT 84525; tel. 564-3463 or 637-1236.

Four campgrounds, all with showers, have sites for tents and RVs: **Shady Acres RV Park** at 360 E. Main costs $8.76 no hookups, $11.50 w/hookups; open all year with store, showers, and laundry; tel. 564-8290. **United Campground** at 910 E. Main is $9.86 no hookups, $14.24 w/hookups; open April 1 to Oct. 15 with a pool, store, showers, and laundry; tel. 564-8195. **Green River State Park** at 150 S. Green River Blvd. offers pleasant sites shaded by large cottonwoods and a boat ramp for $3 day use, $8 camping; open all year; tel. 564-3633 or (800) 322-3770 (reservations). **Green River KOA** at 550 S. Green River Blvd. runs $10.90 tent, $13.08 RV no hookups, $16.90 w/hookups; open April 1 to Oct. 15 with a pool, store, and laundry; tel. 564-3651.

The community is famed for its excellent melons, available in season at fruit stands along Main Street. **Melon Days** celebrates the harvest on the third weekend of Sept. with a parade, city fair, music, canoe race, games, and free melons.

A pleasant **city park** offers shaded tables, playground, and tennis courts at the corner of Main and 100 East. **Green River Information Center** has information about services in town

*The Green River flows placidly below Gray Canyon.*

and places to see in the area; open daily 9 a.m.-9 p.m. in summer, then reduced hours the rest of the year; located at 885 E. Main in the John Wesley Powell Museum (Box 335, Green River, UT 84525); tel. 564-3526. The **post office** is on E. Main. **Green River Medical Clinic** offers services Mon. to Fri. 9 a.m.-5 p.m.; turn south at 250 E. Main; tel. 564-3434 or 564-8111 (after-hours emergencies). See some of southeastern Utah's incredible landscape with **Redtail Aviation**; flights normally leave from the airport 18 miles north of Moab, but the pilot will pick you up at Green River for $10 extra per person. You can fly over Canyonlands National Park (Needles, Island in the Sky, and the Maze), Dead Horse Point, and other spectacular landscapes. Flights operate all year; Box 515, Moab, UT 84532; tel. 259-7421 (Moab) or 564-3412 (Green River). Green River's airport is south of town.

## VICINITY OF GREEN RIVER

### Green River Scenic Drive

Splendid cliffs of Gray Canyon enclose the Green River 10 miles north of town. An unpaved road winding 8.5 miles into the canyon allows drivers easy access to the scenery. Cars with good clearance can travel through the canyon in dry weather. (When wet, the clay road surface shouldn't be attempted by any vehicle.) From downtown Green River, head east on Main Street and turn north on Hastings Road (1200 East); it's the first paved road to the north past the bridge. After 2 miles the road follows the banks of Green River a short way with views north to the castle-like cliffs of the Beckwith Plateau, through which the Green River has carved Gray Canyon. At 6.3 miles after turning off Main, make a right turn on an unpaved road just before the paved road enters a ranch. The turn may have a small sign for "Nefertiti." Follow the unpaved road 3.8 miles across a wash, then along the river to Swasey Beach and Rapids near the mouth of Gray Canyon. A primitive camping area under the cottonwoods is an inviting place to spend the night. The campground has an outhouse;

no drinking water or charge. A large sandy beach stretches along the shore just below the rapids. The road becomes a bit rougher and single lane in spots past Swasey Beach for the 8.5 spectacular miles to road's end at Nefertiti. You'll see Price River Canyon entering Gray Canyon on the other side of the river 2 miles before Nefertiti. Look for petroglyphs near the end of the road. Hikers can explore many rugged side canyons or follow cattle trails a long distance upstream. Cowboys on horseback still work the range on the plateaus to the north much as they've always done. Cattle are driven on these trails to the high country in spring and brought back down in autumn. Kelsey's book *Canyon Hiking Guide to the Colorado Plateau* details hiking possibilities through Gray and Desolation canyons and their side canyons. Commercial raft trips provide a more relaxed way of enjoying this extremely remote part of Utah; see "Desolation and Gray Canyons of the Green River," pp. 237-238.

River runners enjoy half a dozen lively rapids on the section of river from the boat launch just above Nefertiti Rapid to the takeout at Swasey Beach. This makes a good day trip with rafts or kayaks; canoeists will find the whitewater very challenging. All boaters must wear life jackets and carry proper equipment (spare oar or paddle, extra life jacket, and bail bucket or pump). You won't need a permit, though the BLM has a register at the put-in.

### San Rafael Swell

This massive fold and uplift of the earth's crust is crossed by I-70 about 19 miles west of Green River. The east face and "flat irons" of the Swell, known as the San Rafael Reef, rise dramatically 2,100 feet above the desert. View areas allow stopping for a look at the colorful rock layers. San Rafael Swell is 80 miles long (north to south) and 30 miles wide. The geology, sheer cliffs, and narrow canyons attract adventurous travelers to the backroads and hiking routes. This little-known region also has a rich history of outlaws, ranchers, and miners. Boaters with canoes or rafts can float a section of the San Rafael River beneath

1,000-foot-high canyon walls *upstream* of the San Rafael Campground; see "Floating the Little Grand Canyon," p. 240. Good books for background and travel are *Hiking Utah's San Rafael Swell* by Michael Kelsey and *Utah's Scenic San Rafael* by Owen McClenahan; Kelsey's book emphasizes history and hiking, while McClenahan's book mostly describes driving tours (about half of which can be done by car). The BLM is studying 6 areas within the San Rafael for wilderness designation. Their San Rafael Resource Area office administers this region: 900 North and 700 East, Price, UT 84501; tel. 637-4584.

## Black Dragon Canyon

Don't worry about the dragon; he doesn't bite. This narrow canyon in the San Rafael Swell is just off I-70, 15 miles east of Green River. A ¼-mile walk up the streambed leads to a pair of pictograph panels of the dragon (he's actually red), human figures, a dog, and geometric designs. Continue farther upcanyon for more good scenery. To reach the trailhead, turn north on a dirt road from the I-70 westbound lane just past Milepost 145; this isn't a regular exit and may not be signed. If coming from the west, you'll have to turn around at the Hanksville Exit 147 and backtrack 2 miles. The dirt road crosses a wash (best to walk from here if it's filled with water), goes through a second gate, and crosses the streambed from Black Dragon Wash, 1.1 miles from I-70. Turn left 0.4 mile up the streambed (normally dry) to the canyon entrance. High-clearance vehicles can drive a short way up the canyon.

## Crystal Geyser

With some luck, you'll catch the spectacle of this cold-water geyser on the bank of the Green River. The gusher shoots as high as 60 feet but only 3-4 times daily, so you may have to spend a half day here in order to see it. Camping is possible nearby (no facilities), so you might be able to see the geyser by moonlight. Staff at the Green River Information Center often know the latest eruption schedule. An eruption typically lasts 7 minutes and discharges 4,350 cubic feet of salt water. Carbon dioxide and other gases power the gushing water. A 2,267-foot-deep petroleum test well dug in 1935-36 concentrated the geyser flow, but thick layers of old travertine deposits attest that mineral-laden springs have long been active at this site. Colorful newer travertine forms delicate terraces around the opening and down to the river. The orange and dark red of the minerals and algae make this a pretty spot, even if the geyser is only quietly gurgling.

Crystal Geyser is 10 miles south of town by road (boaters should look for the geyser deposits on the left about 4½ river miles downstream from Green River). From downtown, drive east one mile on Main, turn left 3 miles on signed Frontage Road (near Milepost 4), then turn right 6 miles on a narrow paved road just after going under a railroad overpass. The road goes under I-70, then is unpaved for the last 4.5 miles; keep right at a fork near some power lines. Some washes have to be crossed, so the drive isn't recommended after rains. Other times it's OK for cars. Buildings and antennas passed on the way belong to the Utah Launch Complex of White Sands Missile Range. From 1963 to 1979 several hundred Pershing and Athena rockets blasted off for targets at White Sands, New Mexico, 400 miles away.

## Woodside Geyser

This geyser is a smaller version of Crystal. Woodside goes up more often than Crystal and sometimes puts on a good show. Colorful travertine terraces surround the opening. When railroad workers drilled for water here in 1910 they got a 75-foot spout of useless mineral water! The geyser sits just west of US 191/6, 23 miles northwest of Green River and 37 miles southeast of Price. Look for an abandoned gas station on the west side of the road and turn in about 1,000 feet to a group of large trees surrounding the geyser. The site was once a developed tourist attraction.

# SEGO CANYON AND GHOST TOWN

Prehistoric rock art and ruins of a coal-mining town lie within scenic canyons of the Book

Cliffs just a short drive north from Thompson and I-70. In the early 1900s, a local rancher discovered thick seams of high-quality coal here. A mining camp, served by the Ballard and Thompson Railroad, sprang to life at the site. Residents named their little town after Utah's state flower, the sego lily, which grew profusely in the canyons. Population peaked at about 500; families lived in fine houses or in rustic dugouts, while the bachelors stayed in a 2-story boarding house. Production continued through water shortages, fires, and management troubles until the early 1950s, when the railroads switched to diesel locomotives and no longer needed Sego's coal. The town folded and was sold for salvage. Plenty of good coal remains; if steam locomotives ever come back into style, perhaps Sego will too!

Stone walls of the company store, the frame boarding house, dugout houses, railroad grades, and foundations of coal-handling structures can still be seen. The road in can be traveled by cars with good clearance if the weather is dry; don't enter the canyons after recent rains or if storms threaten. Take I-70 Thompson Exit 185 (25 miles east of Green River or 5 miles east of the US 191 turnoff to Moab) and drive one mile north to Thompson. The small railroad community has a cafe and convenience store near I-70. Continue north across the tracks on a paved road, which becomes dirt after 0.5 mile, into Thompson Canyon. At the first creek ford, 3.5 miles from town, look for petroglyphs and pictographs on cliffs to the left. More rock art, though in poorer condition, can be seen to the right at the second ford, just past the first. Look for a road fork on the right leading through a notch into Sego Canyon 0.3 mile after the second ford. This turnoff is easily missed. The ghost town lies one mile up Sego Canyon. Both the Sego and Thompson canyon roads lead deeper into the rugged Book Cliffs. Drivers with 4WD and hikers can explore more of this land, seldom visited except in deer season.

*long-tailed weasel* (Mustela frenata)

# MOAB

By far the largest town in southeastern Utah, Moab (pop. 4,600) makes an excellent base for exploring the surrounding canyon country. The area offers Arches and Canyonlands national parks, scenic drives, jeep touring, river running, mountain bicycling, and hiking. Moab lies near the Colorado River in a green valley enclosed by high sandstone cliffs. The original Moab was a biblical kingdom at the edge of Zion. Early settlers must have felt themselves at the edge of their world too, being so isolated from Salt Lake City, the Mormon city of Zion. Moab's existence on the fringe of Mormon culture and the sizable gentile population have given the town a unique character. Yet the incredible canyons, mesas, and mountains all around Moab remain the biggest draw. Movie and advertising photographers come from all over the world to work in these dramatic settings.

The landscape invites exploration. Adventurous drivers with 4WD vehicles have many places to go; a set of booklets and maps of off-road vehicle and mountain bicycle trails by F.A. Barnes (see "Booklist") will get you started. Mountain bicyclists enjoy the challenges of the back roads too and delight in riding the Moab Slickrock Bike Trail. The Trails Illustrated "Bike Map" #501 of the Moab area has mountain bicycle routes color coded according to difficulty. Hikers can visit even more places; talk to the National Park Service, BLM, and U.S. Forest Service people. The books *Canyon Country Hiking* by Barnes and *Canyon Hiking Guide to the Colorado Plateau* by Kelsey describe hiking areas near Moab. High daytime temperatures prevail at the low 4,000-foot elevation here in summer, when it's worth getting an extra early start in the cool of the morning.

## History

Prehistoric Fremont and Anasazi Indians once lived and farmed in the canyon bottoms. Their rock art, granaries, and dwellings can still be seen. Nomadic Ute Indians had replaced the earlier groups by the time the first white men arrived. The Old Spanish Trail, opened in 1829 between New Mexico and California, passed through Spanish Valley and crossed the Colorado near present-day Moab. Mormon missionaries tried to establish the Elk Mountain Mission here in 1855. They managed to plant some fields, build a stone fort, and convert some of the Utes before a series of attacks killed 3 missionaries and sent the others fleeing back to civilization. The valley reverted to the Indians and small numbers of

## MOAB

1. Slickrock Country Campground, Sundowner Restaurant, and Western River Expeditions
2. Grand Old Ranch House
3. Mi Vida Restaurant (Steen Mansion)
4. Moab Visitor Center
5. Allen Memorial Hospital
6. Holiday Haven RV Park
7. City Park and swimming pool
8. Moab Rock Shop (Lin Ottinger's Tours)
9. North American River Expeditions & Canyonlands Tours
10. Tag-A-Long Tours
11. Rim Cyclery & Rim Tours
12. Honest Ozzie's Cafe
13. Grand Emporium
14. post office
15. Hollywood Stuntmen's Hall of Fame
16. Moab (Dan O'Laurie) Museum and Grand County Public Library
17. National Park Service and U.S. Forest Service
18. Canyonlands Campark
19. Miller's Shopping Center
20. BLM District Office
21. Bar M Chuckwagon Supper
22. Moab Rotary Park
23. BLM Grand Resource Area Office
24. Moab Lanes
25. Lazy Lizard Hostel
26. Grand Cinema

explorers, outlaws, ranchers, and trappers for the next 20 years. Settlers with better success founded Moab in the 1870s. Indian troubles ceased after 1881 and the community became a quiet farming and ranching center. Oil exploration in the 1920s caused some excitement, but nothing like that of the uranium boom that began in 1952. Moab's population tripled in just 3 years as eager prospectors swarmed into the canyons. One of these hopefuls, Charlie Steen, did hit it big. Experts had laughed at Charlie's efforts until he discovered the Mi Vida uranium bonanza about 30 miles south of town. An instant multimillionaire, he built a large mansion overlooking Moab and hosted lavish parties attended by Hollywood celebrities. Charlie Steen and most of the prospectors have moved on, but Moab has never been the same since.

## Moab (Dan O'Laurie) Museum

Step inside to learn about Moab's and Grand County's past. Prehistoric Indian artifacts include pottery, baskets, sandals, and tools. More recent crafts represent the Ute Indians, who no longer live near Moab. An exhibit of early explorers commemorates work of daring Spanish and American expeditions. Photos and tools show pioneer Moab life, much of which centered around ranching or mining. See colorful rocks and minerals, as well as bones of huge dinosaurs that once tracked across this land. Visiting shows can be seen too. Step upstairs to see rotating art exhibits. Ask for a *Moab Area Historic Walking Tour* leaflet to learn about historic buildings in town. Open in summer Mon.-Sat. 1-5 p.m. and 7-9 p.m., then the rest of the year Mon.-Thurs. 3-5 p.m. and 7-9 p.m., Fri. and Sat. 1-5 p.m. and 7-9 p.m.; free admission; tel. 259-7985. Located at 118 E. Center.

## Hollywood Stuntmen's Hall Of Fame And Museum

Action photos show the amazing stunts done in movies and television, from the early days to the present. You'll also see many costumes, weapons, and stunt equipment used. This Hall of Fame/Museum—said to be the only one of its kind—is dedicated to preserving the history of the stunt profession in movies and TV. The Dave Sharpe Action Theatre presents a variety of old and new films. A gift shop sells stunt and movie memorabilia. Open in spring and summer daily Mon.-Fri. noon-9 p.m., Sat. and Sun. noon-6 p.m.; call for hours off-season; tel. 259-6100. Entry costs $3 adult, $2 age 12-18 and seniors, and $1 age 3-11. Located one block north of the Dan O'Laurie Museum at 111 E. 100 North.

## Hole 'N The Rock

In the mood for something touristy? Albert Christensen worked 12 years to excavate his dream home within a sandstone monolith south of town. When he died in 1957, his wife Gladys worked another 8 years to complete the project. The interior has notable touches like a 65-foot chimney drilled through the rock ceiling, paintings, taxidermy exhibits, and a lapidary room. The 14-room home is open for tours daily 8 a.m.-8 p.m. in summer and daily 9 a.m.-5 p.m. the rest of the year; $1.50 adult, $.50 age 5-12; it also has a gift shop; tel. 686-2250. A picnic area and snack bar are outside. Located 15 miles south of Moab on US 191.

# PRACTICALITIES

## Youth Hostel

The **Lazy Lizard** hostel costs just $6.54 a night for simple dorm-style accommodations, no hostel card needed; includes hot tub, kitchen, and coin-op laundry. Camping ($4/person), single rooms ($10.90), and doubles ($16.35) are offered too; tel. 259-6057. Located one mile south of town in the red and white house behind A-1 Storage; turnoff is about 200 yards south of Moab Lanes.

## Campgrounds

**Canyonlands Campark** is open all year at 555 S. Main; has showers, laundry, store, and pool; sites cost $11.55 tent or RV (no hookups) and $17.05 w/hookups; tel. 259-6848. **Slickrock Country Campground** is open all year, one mile north on US 191; has showers, store, outdoor cafe, and pool; sites go for $10.90 tent or RV (no hookups), $16.35

# MOAB ACCOMMODATIONS

(summer rates shown; those in winter typically drop $5)
Add 10% tax to all prices

| LODGING | ADDRESS | RATES | PHONE | FEATURES |
|---|---|---|---|---|
| Apache Motel | 166 S. 400 East | $42-44 | 259-5727 | kitchenettes, pool |
| Bowen Motel | 169 N. Main | $32-56 | 259-7132 | kitchenettes, pool |
| Canyon Country Bed & Breakfast | 590 N. 500 West | $35-55 | 259-7882 or (800) 635-1792 | mtn. bike rentals |
| Canyonlands Motel | 16 S. Main | $25-34 | 259-5167 | kitchenettes |
| Castle Valley Inn Bed & Breakfast | in Castle Valley 2.3 mi. in from UT 128 | $40-70 | 259-6012 | dinners, hot tub, wilderness setting |
| Cedar Breaks Condos | Center and 400 East | $50-55 | 259-7830 | kitchenettes |
| Colorado River Lodge | 512 N. Main | $33-39 | 259-6122 | |
| Cottonwood Condos | 338 E. 100 South | $35-45 | 259-8897 | kitchenettes |
| Greenwell Motel | 105 S. Main | $69 | 259-6151 | pool |
| Inca Inn Motel | 570 N. Main | $28-34 | 259-7261 | pool |
| Kokopelli Lodge | 72 S. 100 East | $35-47.50 | 259-7615 | |
| Landmark Motel | 168 N. Main | $56-76 | 259-6147 | pool |
| Moab TraveLodge | 550 S. Main | $48-64 | 259-6171 | pool |
| Nichols Lane Accommodations | 543 Nichols Lane | $40-45 | 259-8184 | kitchens |
| Pack Creek Ranch | La Sal Mtns. foothills | $40-200 | 259-5505 | kitchenettes, riding |
| Prospector Lodge | 186 N. 100 West | $20-30 | 259-5145 | |
| Ramada Inn | 182 S. Main | $64-68 | 259-7141 | pool |
| Red Rock Lodge | 51 N. 100 West | $29-48 | 259-5431 | hot tub |
| Ron Tez | 450 E. 200 South | $50 | 259-7273 | kitchens |
| Rustic Inn Motel | 120 E. 100 South | $45-65 | 259-6177 | kitchenettes, pool |
| Sandi's Bed & Breakfast | 450 Walker St. | $35-50 | 259-6359 | |
| Sunflower Hill Bed & Breakfast | 185 N. 300 East | $35-45 | 259-2974 | |
| Sunset Motel | 41 W. 100 North | $27-65 | 259-5191 | kitchenettes, pool |
| Super 8 Motel | 889 N. Main | $52.88 | 259-8868 | pool, hot tub |
| The Virginian Motel | 70 E. 200 South | $26-33 | 259-5951 | kitchenettes |
| Westwood Guest House | 81 E. 100 South | $35-45 | 259-7283 | kitchenettes |

w/hookups, or $19.62 for cabins; tel. 259-7660. **Big Sky RV Park** is open all year, 11 miles north on US 191 near the turnoff for Dead Horse Point; has a store but no showers; sites run $7.09 tent or RV (no hookups) and $9.27 w/hookups; tel. 259-7854. **Holiday Haven RV Park** is open all year at 400 North and 500 West (register at K&R Foods across the street); has laundry and pool; RV sites cost $14 w/hookups; tel. 259-8526. **Moab KOA** is open Feb. 15 to Nov. 15, 4 miles south on US 191; has showers, laundry, store, mini golf, and pool; sites cost $12.26 tent or RV (no hookups) and $16.62 w/hookups; tel. 259-6682. You'll also find campgrounds farther out at Arches (see p. 369) and Canyonlands (pp. 381, 383, and 385) national parks, Dead Horse Point State Park (p. 374), La Sal Mountains (p. 367), and Canyon Rims Recreation Area (p. 390).

## Food

The **Grand Old Ranch House** serves elegant meals in an 1896 pioneer house; specialties include German cuisine, steak, prime rib, veal, seafood, and trout; open daily for dinner on the north edge of town; tel. 259-5753 (reservations recommended). **Mi Vida Restaurant** in Charlie Steen's mansion has a sweeping view of the valley; chefs offer steak, seafood, and other fare; open Sat. and Sun. for brunch, Mon.-Fri. for lunch, and daily for dinner; take the signed drive on the north edge of town; tel. 259-7146. **Sundowner Restaurant** prepares German and Southwestern cuisines; open daily for dinner on the north edge of town (next to Slickrock Country Campground); tel. 259-5201. **Honest Ozzie's Cafe** features tasty breakfasts and dinners made with natural ingredients; also the best selection of vegetarian food in town; open daily at 60 N. 100 West; tel. 259-8442. The **Rio Colorado Restaurant** can fill the bill for 'most any appetite—sandwiches, Mexican food, steak, seafood, chicken, pasta, and salads; open daily for lunch and dinner, turn west one block on Center from Main; tel. 259-6666. **Bar M Chuckwagon Supper** serves up tasty cowboy food, followed by a variety of live western entertain-

ment; open for dinner (call to check on time) Mon. to Sat. from June to Sept.; located on the banks of Mill Creek at 541 S. 400 E. Mulberry Lane (see Moab map); tel. 259-2276. **Cattleman's Inn** rustles up American food including steak and seafood; open 24 hours daily for breakfast (served anytime), lunch, and dinner; the adjacent lounge has dancing with live country/Western or rock bands on Fri. and Sat. nights; located 2 miles south of town on US 191; tel. 259-6585. **Westerner Grill** is a favorite with locals; open 24 hours daily for breakfast (anytime), lunch, and dinner at 331 N. Main; tel. 259-9918. The **Ramada Inn** offers varied American fare in the Arches and Pancake Haus dining rooms, including sirloin, prime rib, and trout; open daily for breakfast, lunch, and dinner at 182 S. Main; tel. 259-7141. **Golden Stake Restaurant** has the American favorites including steak and seafood; open daily for breakfast, lunch, and dinner at 550 S. Main; tel. 259-7000. **Canyonlands Cafe** serves American meals; open daily for breakfast (anytime), lunch, and dinner at 16 S. Main; tel. 259-6872. **JR's Cafe** features Western-style breakfasts; open daily for breakfast and lunch at 1075 S. US 191 (south edge of town); tel. 259-8352. **Pack Creek Ranch** offers fine dining in a remote mountain setting; open daily for dinner 16 miles southeast of Moab off the LaSal Mountain Loop Road; tel. 259-5505 (reservations recommended).

**La Hacienda** offers Mexican and gringo food; open daily for breakfast, lunch, and dinner at 574 N. Main; tel. 259-6319. **Creekside Restaurant** also has a menu with a choice of Mexican and American items; open daily for breakfast, lunch, dinner, and takeout at 105 S. Main; tel. 259-5371. **Dos Amigos** presents a long list of Mexican specialties; you can dine indoors on out on the patio; open daily for breakfast, lunch, and dinner at 56 E. 300 South; tel. 259-7903. **Catarina's** serves Italian cuisine with choices of vegetarian, meat, and seafood entrees (pizza too) in both indoor and outdoor settings; open daily except Mon. for lunch and dinner at 51 N. Main; closed in winter; tel. 259-6070. **Pizza Hut** specializes in pizza; open daily for lunch and dinner at 265 S. Main; tel. 259-6345. **Grand Ice Cream Parlor** is a popular spot for fast food and ice cream; open daily for breakfast, lunch, and dinner at the corner of Main and 200 South; tel. 259-5853. You'll find an old-fashioned **soda fountain** in the T-Shirt Shop, 61 N. Main. **Moab Natural Foods** is a grocery store offering health food and a variety of books, 111 N. 100 West; tel. 259-5712.

## Entertainment And Events
The **Grand Cinema** shows movies at 1382 Mill Creek Dr.; tel. 259-6053. *The Canyon's Edge,* a multimedia presentation on the wonders of the Colorado Plateau, is given at Western Plaza (Main and Center) from April to Oct.; $2.50 admission; tel. 259-7750. Tag-A-Long Expeditions presents **Canyon Classics,** performances of classical music, ballet, and opera in a wilderness setting, accessible by jetboat or raft tours on the Colorado River; tel. 259-8946 or (800) 453-3292.

To find out about local happenings, contact the Moab Visitor Center (tel. 259-8825). Softball, golf, and other sport competitions take place through the warmer months. Major annual events include: **March:** Moab Half Marathon (third Sat.) and Jeep Safari (Easter weekend). **April:** Moab Bicycle Stage Race. **May:** Green River to Moab Friendship Cruise (Memorial Day weekend). **June:** Canyonlands Rodeo (with rodeo parade, dance, horse racing, and 4-H gymkhana; third or fourth weekend). **July-August:** Celebration on July Fourth, Little Buckaroo Rodeo, Grand County Fair (agricultural, crafts, and arts judging in August). **September:** Moab Movie Jubilee (Moab Film Commission shows films made in the area; early Sept.), Desert Duster Ladies Golf Tournament (mid-Sept.), Jeep Safari (overnight; on Labor Day weekend). **October:** Arts Festival of the Canyonlands (art sales, music, Greek theater; early Oct.), Gem and Mineral Show (second weekend), Fat Tire Festival (mountain bicycle guided tours, hill climb, workshops, and entertainment; late Oct.), and Moab Music Festival (jazz, bluegrass, and other groups; same weekend as

Fat Tire Festival. **November-December:** Christmas Parade and Crafts Fair (late Nov. or early Dec.) and Winter Sun Run (first or second weekend in Dec).

## Shopping And Services
Rockhounds and anyone wanting to learn more about geology will enjoy a stop at **Lin Ottinger's Moab Rock Shop,** 600 N. Main; tel. 259-7312. From May to Sept. Lin Ottinger leads tours of the area during the day and presents free slide shows of the backcountry in the evening. The **Grand Emporium** at Main and W. Center has art galleries and Indian art and craft shops; other shops lie scattered around town. Artists find the canyon country an inspiring place to work; the **Moab Arts Center** offers classes and excursions of 1-7 days; contact the Helen M. Knight Studio, 168 W. 400 North, Moab, UT 84532; tel. 259-7350. **Rim Cyclery** sells outdoor gear for bicycling, backpacking, climbing, river running, and skiing; rentals include mountain bicycles, and cross-country skis; day and overnight mountain bicycle tours are offered in spring and autumn; 94 W. 100 North; tel. 259-5333. **Canyon Climber ATVs** rents all-terrain vehicles (4-wheelers) and has a recreational track and guided tours; located 1.5 miles south of town on US 191; tel. 259-6274/5301.

The **post office** is downtown at 50 E. 100 North; tel. 259-7427. **Allen Memorial Hospital** provides medical care at 719 W. 400 North; tel. 259-7191. For **emergencies** (ambulance, sheriff, police, or fire), dial 911.

## Recreation
The **City Park** has shaded picnic tables, a playground, and an outdoor swimming pool (tel. 259-8226) at 181 W. 400 North. The **Lions Park** offers picnicking along the Colorado River 2 miles north of town. **Tennis courts** are beside the Grand County Middle School, 217 E. Center. **Moab Lanes** has bowling action on US 191 at the south edge of town; tel. 259-5188. **Moab Golf Club** features an 18-hole course, driving range, and pro shop; at 2705 SE Bench Road (go south 3 miles on US 191, turn left 3 miles on Spanish

Trails Road, then right ¼ mile on Murphy Lane); tel. 259-6488. **Pack Creek Ranch** offers 2-hour horseback rides in Arches National Park and the La Sal Mountains; pack trips tour the La Sals and canyon country; tel. 259-5505.

## Information

**Moab Visitor Center** staff know about services in town and can suggest many places to go in the area; lots of free literature is available and some good books and maps are sold. Free brochures include hiking trails, mountain bike trails, jeep trails, and auto tours. Hours from April to Oct. are Mon.-Fri. 8 a.m.-6 p.m., Sat. and Sun. 8 a.m.-6 p.m. (extended daily to 7 p.m. Memorial Day to Labor Day weekends); hours from Nov. to March are Mon. to Sat. 8 a.m.-6 p.m. Located on the north edge of town at 805 N. Main (Box 550, Moab, UT 84532); tel. 259-8825 or (800) 635-6622. The **National Park Service** office in Moab is headquarters for Canyonlands and Arches national parks and Natural Bridges National Monument; staff will answer your questions about their areas and sell related books and topo maps; open Mon.-Fri. 8 a.m.-4:30 p.m.; 125 W. 200 South (Moab, UT 84532); tel. 259-7164. **Manti-La Sal National Forest** people can tell you about the roads, camping, hiking, fishing, and cross-country skiing in the cool La Sal Mountains southeast of Moab; open Mon.-Fri. 8 a.m.-noon and 12:30-4:30 p.m.; 125 W. 200 South (Moab, UT 84532); tel. 259-7155. The **Bureau of Land Management** has 2 offices in Moab, the BLM District office (82 E. Dogwood on the south side of town next to Miller's Shopping Center; Box 970, Moab, UT 84532; tel. 259-6111) and Grand Resource Area office (Sand Flats Rd. off Mill Creek Dr. on the east side of town; Box M, Moab, UT 84532; tel. 259-8193). Both places sell regional books and land-use maps and can advise on backcountry travel. River runners need to visit the Grand Resource Area office for Colorado River info and Westwater Canyon permits. Most river runners obtain their permit by making an application in Jan. and Feb. for a March drawing; the office can ad-

vise on this process and on cancellations available. Both offices are open Mon.-Fri. 7:45 a.m.-4:30 p.m.

The **Grand County Public Library** is a good place for local history and general reading; open Mon. to Thurs. 1-9 p.m., Fri. 1-5 p.m., and Sat. 10 a.m.-2 p.m.; 25 S. 100 East (next to the Dan O'Laurie Museum); tel. 259-5421.

## River Tours

Rafts and other watercraft can take you through beautiful canyons near Moab. Western River Expeditions and Tag-A-Long rent rafts and inflatable kayaks for those who would rather organize their own boat trips. The most popular run near Moab starts upstream on the Colorado River near Fisher Towers and bounces through several moderate rapids on the way back toward town. The Green and Colorado rivers also offer relatively gentle travel above their confluence; see "Canyonlands River District," pp. 379-380. The longer river trips provide more of a wilderness experience (thrilling rapids too in Westwater, Cataract, and Desolation canyons). Most one-day raft excursions cost about $35 per person. Expect to pay $100-150 per person per day for overnight trips. The rafting season runs April to Sept.; jet boat tours are Feb. to November. Contact the Moab Information Center and the National Park Service office for lists or brochures of tour operators.

**Canyonlands by Night** tours leave at sunset in an open boat and go several miles upstream on the Colorado River; a guide points out canyon features then. The sound and light show begins on the way back; music and historic narration accompany the play of lights on canyon walls; $16 adult, $8 age 6-17; boats run May to mid-October. **Canyonlands by Day** trips go downriver into the Colorado River canyon near Dead Horse Point; $45 adult, $30 age 6-17, $5 under 6; tour operates March to October. Trips depart from the office and dock just across the Colorado River and on the left from Moab; tel. 259-5261. **Canyonlands River Expeditions** runs one-day raft trips (oar) on the river above

Moab ($35 adult, $30 seniors, $24 children 12-17, $20 children 5-11); half-day, sunset cookout, and overnight trips can be taken too; 401 N. Main (Box 336, Moab, UT 84532); tel. 259-5126.

**Adrift Adventures** leads one-day raft trips (oar) on the Colorado River upstream from Moab ($35 adult, $24 children 7-17); half-day and sunset trips are available too; half-day jet boat trips cost $42-45, or you can take the full-day combination jeep tour/jet boat trip for $69; 378 N. Main (Box 577, Moab, UT 84532); tel. 259-8594 or (800) 874-4483.

**Sheri Griffith Expeditions** leads trips upstream on the Colorado River (one day by oar: $38 adult, $29 children 5-16), through Westwater Canyon (2-3 days by oar), Cataract Canyon (5 days by oar, 3-4 days by motorized), Dolores River (3-5 days by oar), and Green River canyons (4-6 days by oar); Box 1324, Moab, UT 84532 (office is 3 miles south of downtown on US 191); tel. 259-8229 or (800) 332-2439.

**Western River Expeditions** guides one-day trips (oar) upstream on the Colorado ($35 adult, $25 children 17 and under); 1371 N. Main, Moab, UT 84532; tel. 259-7019. Western River Expeditions also runs longer raft trips through Westwater Canyon (3 days by oar), Cataract Canyon (4 days by motorized),

Grand Canyon (3-6 days by motorized, 10 days by oar), and canyons of the Green River (4-5 days oar or paddle); 7258 Racquet Club Dr., Salt Lake City, UT 84121; tel. 942-6669 or (800) 453-7450 out of state.

**Tag-A-Long Tours** offers raft trips (oar) on the Colorado River above Moab (half day: $28 adult, $24 children under 17; full day: $35 adult, $28 children under 17) and half-day jet boat excursions ($55 adult, $45 children under 17); longer raft trips go through Westwater Canyon (2 days by oar), Cataract Canyon (3-4 days by motorized), and Green River canyons (4-5 days by oar in rafts or inflatable kayaks, 4 days in canoes); a shuttle service from the Green-Colorado confluence is provided too; 452 N. Main; Moab, UT 84532; tel. 259-8946 or (800) 453-3292.

**North American River Expeditions & Canyonlands Tours** operates raft trips (oar) on the Colorado above Moab (full day: $35 adult, $26 children under 17; half day: $26 adult, $17 children under 17), half-day jet boat trips ($45 adult, $29 children under 100 lbs.), full-day jet boat and jeep tour combinations ($71 adult, $55 children under 17), and 2-5 day raft trips (motorized) through Cataract Canyon; 543 N. Main, Moab, UT 84532; tel. 259-5865 or (800) 342-5938 out of state.

**Descent River Expeditions** runs one-day

a peaceful morning on
the Colorado River,
below Moab

trips on the Colorado upstream of Moab ($35 adult, $22 children under 17), Westwater Canyon (1-2 days by oar), Cataract Canyon (3 days by motorized sportboat, 4 days by motorized raft, or 5 days by oar); 321 N. Main St., Moab, UT 84532; tel. 259-7252.

**Navtec Expeditions** organizes one-day Colorado River trips above Moab by oar-powered raft or motorized sportboats ($35-64 adult, $26-49 children) and one-day trips downriver to Dead Horse Point by motorized sportboats ($45 adult, $29 children 12 and under); longer excursions travel through Cataract Canyon in 2 or 3 days by motorized sportboats; Box 1221 (40 W. 100 North and 600 N. Main), Moab, UT 84532; tel. 259-7983.

**Tex's Riverways** takes visitors on jet boat trips down the Colorado into Canyonlands National Park (call for schedule and rates) and provides canoe packages, including canoes and shuttle services from the Green-Colorado confluence, for trips down the Green River (4-10 days); Box 67, Moab, UT 84532; tel. 259-5101.

### Road Tours

**Lin Ottinger's Tours** offers backcountry driving trips from May to Sept.; Lin has been poking around the canyons of this area since the uranium boom of the 1950s, and he knows the best places; frequent stops allow plenty of time to walk around for a look at Indian art and scenic and geologic features; $30-35 all day; 600 N. Main, Moab, UT 84532; tel. 259-7312.

**Tag-A-Long Tours** has a variety of one-day ($55-85) and multi-day ($385; 3 days) jeep tours from April to Oct.; 452 N. Main, Moab, UT 84532; tel. 259-8946 or (800) 453-3292.

**North American River Expeditions & Canyonlands Tours** explore the backcountry of the Island in the Sky and Needles districts of Canyonlands National Park year-round; $49-78 all day; 543 N. Main, Moab, UT 84532; tel. 259-5865 or (800) 342-5938 out of state.

**Adrift Adventures** has a half-day jeep tour to Dead Horse Point and Island in the Sky at $37 or you can take a full-day combination jeep tour/jet boat trip for $69; 378 N. Main (Box

577, Moab, UT 84532); tel. 259-8594 or (800) 874-4483.

**Canyonlands Field Institute** offers many educational programs—hiking, driving, rafting, and canoeing tours, naturalist walks, photography workshops, seminars, and youth programs; 38 S. 100 West (Box 68, Moab, UT 84532); tel. 259-7750.

### Mountain Bicycle Tours

**Rim Tours** leads day ($26-35) and multi-day ($90-200) trips on mountain bicycles through the canyon country; some tours combine a river excursion too; bicycles can be rented or you can bring your own; 94 W. 100 North, Moab, UT 84532; tel. 259-5223.

**Kaibab Desert and Mountain Bike Tours** explore Canyonlands National Park and other scenic areas; in summer, daily trips drop you off high in the La Sals, meet you for lunch, then again at the bottom of the descent ($50); spring and autumn dailies visit Island in the Sky of Canyonlands ($50); multi-day trips operate mostly in spring and autumn to Maze District of Canyonlands (2 days bicycling, one day hiking, and 2 days rafting through Cataract Canyon; $695), White Rim of Canyonlands (4 days; $320), and Behind the Rocks (2 days; $150); rentals, supplies, and shuttle services are offered too; 37 S. 100 West, Moab, UT 84532; tel. 259-7423.

**Western Spirit Cycling** specializes in multi-day tours of the Moab area during spring and autumn and the high country of Colorado, Idaho, and Montana in summer; Utah trips include the White Rim (4-5 days; $375-460), La Sals (3-4 days; $275-350), Abajos (4-5 days; $400-485), Lockhart Basin Trail (2 days; $180), and Kokopelli's Trail (5 days; $485); day trips (on request with a 4-person minimum), rentals, and instructional clinics are offered too; 545 Locust Lane, Moab, UT 84532; tel. 259-8732.

**Adrift Adventures** leads a variety of trips from mid-Sept. to late Nov. and early March to late April; destinations include a half-day tour to Arches ($26), full-day to Gemini Bridges ($40), full-day to Porcupine Rim ($40), and

4-day to White Rim ($395); 378 N. Main (Box 577, Moab, UT 84532); tel. 259-8594 or (800) 874-4483.

## Air Tours

You'll have a bird's-eye view of southeastern Utah's incredible landscape with **Redtail Aviation** from Moab or Green River airports. Flights feature Canyonlands National Park (Needles, Island in the Sky, and the Maze districts; one hour; $40); longer tours available too. Rates are based on 3 or more persons; add $10 per person for tours out of Green River. Flights operate all year; Box 515, Moab, UT 84532; tel. 259-7421 (Moab) or 564-3412 (Green River). The airport is 18 miles north of Moab on US 191.

## Transport

**Tag-A-Long Adventure Rentals** will put you in the seat of a jeep, auto, mountain bicycle, canoe, or inflatable kayak!; 452 N. Main; tel. 259-8946 or (800) 453-3292. Rent jeeps and other 4WD vehicles at **Farabee 4X4 Rentals** (550 N. Main; tel. 259-7494), **North Main Service** (284 N. Main; tel. 259-5242), **Slick Rock 4X4 Rental** (83 S. Main; tel. 259-5304), and **Certified Ford** (500 S. Main; tel. 259-6107). **KJ Cab** taxi service includes shuttles for bicyclists and river runners; tel. 259-TAXI. **Alpine Air** flies most days from Salt Lake City to Moab with connections on to Monticello and Blanding, then back to Salt Lake City; tel. 373-1508 (Provo) for reservations.

*rafting the Colorado River above Moab;*
*Ed Crosby at the oars*

# EXPLORING THE CANYON COUNTRY NEAR MOAB

Except for the La Sals and national parks, most of the canyon country surrounding Moab is administered by the Bureau of Land Management (BLM). Staff can offer advice for exploring their lands at the 2 BLM offices in Moab (see Moab "Information,") p. 356. The offices also have literature, books, and maps.

## MOAB SLICKROCK BIKE TRAIL

Undulating slickrock just east of Moab challenges even the best mountain bicycle riders. Originally motorcyclists laid out this route, though now about 90% of riders rely on leg and lung power. The practice loop near the beginning allows first-time visitors a chance to get a feel for the slickrock. The "trail" consists only of painted white lines. Riders following it have less chance of getting lost or finding themselves in hazardous areas. Plan on about 5 hours to do the 10.3-mile main loop and expect to do some walking. Side trails

lead to viewpoints overlooking Moab, the Colorado River, and arms of Negro Bill Canyon. Panoramas of surrounding canyon country and the La Sals add to the pleasure of biking. Take care if venturing off the trail—it's a long way down some of the sheer cliff faces! The trail's steep slopes and sharp turns can be tricky—a helmet is a must. Knee pads and riding gloves also protect from scrapes and bruises. Fat bald tires work best on the rock; partially deflated knobby tires do almost as well. Carry plenty of water—one gallon in summer, ½ gallon in cooler months. Tiny microbiotic plant associations, which live in fragile cryptogamic soil, don't want you tearing through their homes; please stay on the rock and avoid sand areas. Rim Cyclery and Kaibab Desert & Mountain Bike Tours in Moab offer rentals, supplies, books, and tours. Obtain a trail map there or from the Moab Visitor Center or either BLM office. To reach the trailhead from Main St. in Moab, turn east 0.4 mile on 300 South, turn right 0.1 mile on 400 East, turn left (east) 0.5 mile on Mill Creek Dr.,

*on the Moab Slickrock Bike Trail; La Sals stand in distance* then left 2.5 miles on Sand Flats Road. The Grand Resource Area BLM office is at the Sand Flats Road turnoff.

The practice loop also makes an enjoyable 2½-mile hike. Precipitous drop-offs into tributaries of Negro Bill Canyon have breathtaking views. It's best to walk off to the side of the white lines marking the route. You'll reach the practice loop ¼ mile from the trailhead.

### Kokopelli's Trail

Mountain bicyclists have linked together a series of back roads through the magical canyons of eastern Utah and western Colorado. You can start on Sand Flats Road in Moab and ride east to Castle Valley (21.1 miles), Fisher Valley (44.9 miles), Dewey Bridge (62.9 miles), Cisco Boat Landing (83.5 miles), Rabbit Valley (108 miles), and Loma (127.5 miles). Lots of optional routes and access points allow for many possibilities. See the small book *The Utah-Colorado Mountain Bike Trail System, Route 1—Moab to Loma* by Peggy Utesch for detailed descriptions.

# KANE CREEK SCENIC DRIVE AND TRAILS

This road heads downstream along the Colorado River on the same side as Moab. The 4 miles through the Colorado River's canyon are paved, followed by 6 miles of good dirt road through Kane Springs Canyon. People with high-clearance vehicles or mountain bicycles can continue across a ford of Kane Springs Creek to Hurrah Pass and an extensive network of 4WD trails. The book and separate map *Canyon Country Off-Road Vehicle Trails: Canyon Rims & Needles Areas* by F.A. Barnes has detailed back-road information.

### Moab Rim Trail

The high cliffs just southwest of town provide fine views of the Moab Valley, highlands of Arches National Park, and the La Sal Mountains. The trail turns off Kane Creek Blvd. 1.5 miles downriver from Moab. (Total driving distance from the junction of Main St. and

Kane Creek Blvd. is 2.6 miles; look for the trailhead on the left 0.1 mile after a cattle guard.) The sky can be seen through Little Arch across the river from the trailhead. Jeep-type vehicles can also ascend the Moab Rim Trail, though the rough terrain is considered difficult for them; the first 200 yards will give drivers a feel for the difficulty. The trail climbs northeast 1½ miles along tilted rock strata of the Kayenta Formation to the top of the plateau. This is a moderately difficult hike with good views nearly all the way. Elevation gain is 940 feet. Once on top, hikers can follow jeep roads southeast to Hidden Valley Trail and descend to US 191 south of Moab, a 5½-mile trip (total one way). Experienced hikers can also head south from the rim to Behind the Rocks, a fantastic maze of sandstone fins.

To reach the Hidden Valley Trail, continue on the jeep road, which turns south and drops into a slickrock area flanked by 2 large domes of Navajo Sandstone. The road follows a wash at the bottom, then climbs a large sand hill (several ways up). About ½ mile farther, 2 side roads turn left to viewpoints; the main road continues south into a wash, curves to the east up a slope, and ends near the upper end of Hidden Valley Trail. From here it's a ⅓-mile hike to a low divide and another 2 miles to the lower trailhead near US 191. You'll need a car shuttle for a one-way hike.

### Hidden Valley Trail

You'll see not only a "hidden valley" but also panoramas of the Moab area and Behind the Rocks. The moderately difficult trail ascends 500 feet in a series of switchbacks to a broad shelf below the Moab Rim, then follows the shelf ("hidden valley") to the northwest. It then crosses a low pass and follows a second shelf in the same direction. Near the end of the second shelf, the trail turns left to a divide, from which you can see a portion of the remarkable fins of Behind the Rocks. This divide is 2 miles from the start (one way) and 680 feet higher in elevation. The trail continues ⅓ mile from the divide down to the end of the Moab Rim Trail, a jeep road and hiking trail. Or, instead of turning left to the divide, you can make a short side trip (no trail) to the right for views of Moab. To reach the Hidden Valley Trailhead, drive south 3 miles on US 191 from Moab, turn right 0.4 mile on Angel Rock Road to its end (turnoff is just south of Milepost 122), then right 0.3 mile on Rimrock Lane.

## Behind The Rocks

A look at the topo map will show that something strange is going on here. Massive fins of Navajo Sandstone 100-500 feet high, 50-200 feet thick, and up to ½ mile long cover a large area. Narrow vertical cracks, sometimes only a few feet wide, separate the fins. Archaeological sites and several arches are in the area. No maintained trails exist here, and some routes require technical climbing skills. The maze offers endless exploration routes. If you get lost (very easy to do), remember that the fins are oriented east-west; the rim of the Colorado River canyon is reached by going west and Spanish Valley by going east. Bring plenty of water, a topo map (Moab 15-minute), and a compass. Access routes are Moab Rim and Hidden Valley trails (from the north and east) and Pritchett Canyon (from the west and south). Though only a couple of miles from Moab, Behind the Rocks seems a world away. The BLM is studying a possible wilderness designation to protect the solitude and character of this strange country.

## Pritchett Canyon

A very difficult jeep road, also popular with mountain bicyclists, winds up this canyon to Pritchett Arch (4½ miles one way) and several other arches. Canyon scenery and good views of Behind the Rocks are other attractions. Turnoff is on the left 4.8 miles down Kane Creek Blvd., just before the road turns up Kane Creek Canyon; look for a small canyon with tamarisk growing in it.

## Hunters Canyon

Hikers enjoy seeing the arch and other rock formations in the canyon walls and the lush vegetation along the creek. Off-road vehicles have made tracks a short way up, then you'll be walking mostly along the creekbed. Short sections of trail lead around thickets of tamarisk and other water-loving plants. Look for

Hunters Arch on the right about ½ mile up. Most of the water in Hunters Canyon comes from a deep pool surrounded by hanging gardens of maidenhair fern. This pretty spot is 3 miles (one way) and 240 feet higher than the start. A dry fall and a small natural bridge lie above the pool. To reach the trailhead from Moab, drive 8 miles on Kane Creek Blvd. along the Colorado River and up Kane Creek Canyon. The road is asphalted where it fords Hunter Creek.

A longer hike can be made by going up Hunters Canyon and descending on Pritchett Canyon Road. The road crosses the normally dry creekbed just upstream of the deep pool. To bypass the dry fall above the pool, backtrack 300 feet down the canyon and rock-scramble up a short, steep slope (on the right heading upstream). At a junction just east of here, a jeep road along the north rim of Hunters Canyon meets Pritchett Canyon Road. Walk northeast ½ mile on Pritchett Canyon Road to a spur trail on the left leading to Pritchett Arch. Then continue 4½ miles on Pritchett Canyon Road to Kane Creek Boulevard. This country is more open and desertlike than Hunters Canyon. A 3.2-mile car shuttle or hike is needed to return to Hunters Canyon Trailhead.

# UTAH SCENIC BYWAY 279 AND TRAILS

Utah Highway 279 goes downstream through the Colorado River canyon on the other side of the river from Moab. Pavement extends 16 miles past fine views, prehistoric rock art, arches, and hiking trails. A potash plant marks the end of the highway, where a rough dirt road continues to Canyonlands National Park. From Moab, head north 3.5 miles on US 191, then turn left on UT 279. Soon you'll see Moab's radioactive lake on the left atop a huge pile of uranium tailings next to a plant owned by Atlas Minerals. Charlie Steen built the mill in the mid-1950s to process ore from his Mi Vida Mine. The water helps keep the hazardous dust down. Needless to say, no swimming or trespassing is allowed! The highway enters the canyon at the "Portal," 2.7 miles from the turnoff. Towering cliffs of sandstone rise on the right and the Colorado River is just below on the left.

### Indian Ruins Viewpoint
Stop at a signed pullout on the left to see a small prehistoric Indian ruin tucked under a ledge across the river. The stone structure was probably used for food storage. Viewpoint is 0.6 mile past the canyon entrance.

### Portal Overlook Trail
A trail switchbacks up a slope, then follows a sloping sandstone ledge of the Kayenta Formation to an overlook. A panorama takes in the Colorado River, Moab Valley, Arches National Park, and the La Sals. The hike is 1½ miles (one way) with an elevation gain of 980 feet. This trail is a twin of the Moab Rim Trail across the river. Signed parking is on the left, 3.7 miles from the turnoff at US 191. You can also begin the hike from an attractive picnic area shaded by mulberry trees, next to the highway a short distance beyond the main trailhead.

### Petroglyphs
Groups of petroglyphs cover cliffs along the highway 5.2 miles from US 191. These may not be signed, but they are 0.7 mile beyond Milepost 11. Look across the river to see The Fickle Finger of Fate among sandstone fins of Behind the Rocks. A petroglyph of a bear is 0.2 mile farther down the highway. Archaeologists think that Fremont and the later Ute Indians did most of the artwork in this area.

*bear petroglyph*

### Dinosaur Tracks
Tracks and petroglyphs are visible on rocks above to the right. Sighting tubes help locate the features. It's possible to hike up the steep hillside for a closer look. The signed pullout is on the right, 6.2 miles from US 191.

### Corona Arch And Bowtie Arch
A 1½-mile (one way) hike across slickrock country leads to these impressive arches. You can't see them from the road, though a third arch—Pinto—is visible. Signed trailhead is on the right 10.0 miles from US 191 (midway between Mileposts 5 and 6); you'll see railroad tracks just beyond when you reach the trailhead. The trail climbs up from the parking area, crosses the tracks, and follows a bit of a jeep road and a small wash to an ancient gravel bar. Pinto (or Gold Bar) Arch can be seen to the left, though there's no trail to it. Follow cairns to Corona and Bowtie. Handrails and a ladder help in the few steep spots. Despite being only a few hundred yards apart, each arch has a completely different character and history. Bowtie formed when a pothole in the cliffs above met a cave underneath. It used to be called "Paul Bunyan's Potty" before the name was appropriated for an arch in Canyonlands National Park. The hole is about 30 feet in diameter. Corona Arch, reminiscent of the larger Rainbow Bridge, eroded out of a sandstone fin. The graceful span is 140 feet long and 105 feet high. Both arches are composed of Navajo Sandstone. If you have time for only one hike in the Moab area, this one is especially recommended.

### Jug Handle Arch
This aptly named formation is close to the road on the right, 13.6 miles from US 191. The opening is 46 feet high and 3 feet wide. Ahead the canyon opens up. Underground pressures of salt and potash have folded the rock layers into an anticline.

### Moab Salt Plant
The mine injects water underground to dissolve the potash and other chemicals, then pumps the solution to evaporation ponds. The

ponds are dyed blue to hasten evaporation, which takes about a year. These colorful solutions can be seen from Dead Horse Point and Anticline Overlook on the canyon rims. High-clearance vehicles can continue on the unpaved road beyond the plant. The road passes through varied canyon country with views overlooking the Colorado River. At a road junction in Canyonlands National Park (Island in the Sky District), you have a choice of turning left for the 100-mile White Rim Trail (4WD only past Musselman Arch) or continuing up the steep switchbacks of the Shafer Trail Road (4WD recommended) to the paved park road or returning the way you came.

## UTAH SCENIC BYWAY 128 AND TRAILS

Utah Highway 128 turns northeast from US 191 just south of the Colorado River bridge, 2 miles north of Moab. This exceptionally scenic canyon route follows the Colorado for 30 miles upstream before crossing at Dewey Bridge and turning north to I-70. The entire highway is paved. In 1986, a new bridge replaced the narrow Dewey suspension bridge that once caused white knuckles on drivers of large vehicles. Lions Park picnic area at the turnoff from US 191 is a pleasant stopping place. Big Bend picnic area is another good spot 7.5 miles up UT 128. A popular one-day raft trip with mild rapids begins from the Hittle Bottom boat launch, 23.5 miles up UT 128 near Fisher Towers, and ends 14 river miles downstream at Sandy Beach, 10.3 miles up UT 128 from US 191. Rafts and life jackets (required) can be rented in Moab. No permit is needed on this section of river. A network of highly scenic jeep roads branches off Castle Valley and Onion Creek roads into side canyons and the La Sal Mountains. These are described in the book and separate map *Canyon Country Off-Road Vehicle Trails: Arches & La Sals Areas* by F.A. Barnes.

### Negro Bill Canyon

The route follows a lively stream surrounded by abundant greenery and sheer canyon cliffs.

Beaver and other wildlife live here. Morning Glory Natural Bridge, in a side canyon, is the sixth longest natural rock span in the country at 243 feet. The trailhead is on the right just after crossing a concrete bridge 3 miles from US 191. A trail leads upcanyon, at some places along the creek, at others high on the banks. Small beaver ponds provide a place to cool off on a hot day. To see Morning Glory Natural Bridge, head 2 miles up the main canyon to the second side canyon on the right, then follow a good side trail ½ mile up it to the long slender bridge. The spring and small pool underneath keep the air cool even in summer; ferns, columbines, and poison ivy grow here. Elevation gain is 330 feet. William ("Nigger Bill") Granstaff was a mulatto who lived in the area from about 1877 to 1881. Modern sensibilities have changed his old nickname to "Negro Bill."

Experienced hikers can continue up the main canyon about 8 miles and rockscramble (no trail) up the right side, then drop into Rill Creek that leads to the North Fork of Mill Creek and into Moab. Total distance is about 16 miles one way; you'll have to find your own way between canyons. The upper Negro Bill and Rill canyons can also be reached from Sand Flats Road. The Moab and Castle Valley 15-minute and Moab 1:100,000 topo maps cover the route. This would be a good overnight trip, though fast hikers have done it in a day. Expect to do some wading and rockscrambling. Water from the creeks and springs is available in both canyon systems; purify first. A car shuttle is necessary between the Negro Bill and Mill Creek trailheads. Mill Creek is reached from the end of Powerhouse Lane on the east edge of Moab (see the Moab map), but DON'T PARK HERE. Vehicle break-ins are a serious problem. Either have someone meet or drop you off here or park closer to town near houses. Although the end of Powerhouse Lane is badly trashed, a hike up the North Fork is very pretty. A deep pool and waterfall lie ¾ mile upstream; follow Mill Creek upstream and take the left (north) fork. Negro Bill and Mill Creek canyons may be better protected in the future; both are BLM wilderness study areas.

## La Sal Mountain Loop Road

This paved scenic road goes through Castle Valley, climbs high into the La Sals, then loops back to Moab. Allow at least 3 hours to drive the 62-mile loop. Turnoff from UT 128 is 15.5 miles up from US 191. See "La Sal Mountains" below.

## Onion Creek Road

A graded county road turns southeast off the highway 20 miles from US 191 and heads up Onion Creek, crossing it many times. Avoid this route if storms threaten. The unpleasant-smelling creek contains poisonous arsenic and selenium. Colorful rock formations of dark-red sandstone line the creek, and you'll cross an upthrusted block of crystalline gypsum. After about 8 miles the road climbs steeply out of Onion Creek to upper Fisher Valley and a junction with Kokopelli's Trail, which follows a jeep road over this part of its route.

## Fisher Towers

Gothic spires of dark-red sandstone soar as high as 900 feet above Professor Valley. The BLM has a picnic area nearby and a hiking trail skirting the base of the 3 main towers; Titan, the highest, is the third one. Titan is one mile from the picnic area, and a viewpoint overlooking Onion Creek is 1.1 miles farther. Carry water for this moderately difficult hike. In 1962, 3 climbers from Colorado made the first ascent of Titan Tower. The almost vertical rock faces, overhanging bulges, and sections of rotten rock made for an exhausting 3½ days of climbing (the party descended to the base for 2 of the nights). Their final descent from the summit took only 6 hours. See the Nov. 1962 *National Geographic* magazine for the story and photos. Supposedly, the name "Fisher" is not that of a pioneer, but a corruption of the geologic term "fissure" (a narrow crack). An unpaved road turns southeast off UT 128 near Milepost 21 (21 miles from US 191) and goes in 2 miles to the picnic area.

## Dewey Bridge

A modern 2-lane concrete bridge has replaced the picturesque wood and steel suspension bridge built in 1916. The drive through the Colorado River's canyon ends a short way past the bridge. Bicyclists and hikers can still use the old bridge; an interpretive sign has its history. Drivers can continue on the highway to I-70 through rolling hills nearly devoid of vegetation.

## Westwater Canyon

Wild rapids lie upstream of Dewey Bridge. The Colorado River cut this narrow gorge into dark metamorphic rock. A river trip by raft or kayak can be done in one day or in a more leisurely 2-3 days. Unlike most desert rivers, this section of the Colorado also offers good river running at low water levels in late summer and autumn. Westwater Canyon's inner gorge, where boaters face their greatest challenge, is only about 3½ miles long. Scenic sandstone canyons, however, are enjoyed upstream and downstream. Boaters can put in at the BLM's Westwater Ranger Station in Utah or at Loma boat launch in Colorado. A start at Loma adds a day or two to the trip and the sights of Horsethief and Ruby canyons. Normal take out is at Cisco, though it's possible to continue 16 miles on slow-moving water through open country to Dewey Bridge. The **Dolores River**, also enjoyed by river runners, joins the Colorado about 2 miles upstream from Dewey Bridge. The season lasts mid-May to mid-June—none at all in dry years. Boaters need a permit and experience for both rivers; kayakers should have their rolls down well. The BLM Grand Resource Area office in Moab handles permits and provides information for these rivers.

## Top-Of-The-World Road

This easy 4WD road climbs to an overlook with outstanding views of Fisher Towers, Fisher Valley, Onion Creek, and beyond. Turn right (east) on the Entrada Bluffs Road (just before crossing Dewey Bridge). After 5.5 miles, keep straight on a dirt road when the main road curves left, then immediately turn right (south) and go uphill 100 yards through a gate (gateposts are railroad ties) and continue about 4.5 miles on the Top-of-the-World Road to the rim. Elevation here is 6,800 feet, nearly 3,000 feet higher than the Colorado River.

# LA SAL MOUNTAINS

The forests and lakes in Utah's second-highest mountain range provide a dramatic contrast to the barren slickrock and sands of the surrounding desert. Mount Peale (elev. 12,721 ft.) crowns the range at a height nearly 9,000 feet above the Colorado River. Volcanic intrusions formed the La Sals about 30 million years ago, twisting and upturning surrounding rock layers at the same time. Streams and glaciers later carved knife-like ridges in the peaks and deep canyons in the foothills. The range comprises 3 distinct mountain groups in an area about 15 miles long from north to south and 6 miles wide. Major peaks in the northern part are Mt. Waas (12,331 ft.), Manns Peak (12,273 ft.), and Mt. Tomasaki (12,230 ft.). The middle group contains Mt. Mellenthin (12,646 ft.), Mt. Peale (12,721 ft.), and Mt. Tukuhnikivatz (12,483 ft.). The Indian name of this last mountain is reputed to mean "Land Where the Sun Shines Longest." South Mountain (11,798 ft.) dominates the southern group.

Wildlife you might see includes black bear (one of the state's largest populations lives here), Rocky Mountain elk, mule deer, mountain lion, badger, ringtail cat, porcupine, pika, Merriam's turkey, and golden eagle. Native cutthroat and some brook and brown trout swim in streams at the middle to higher elevations. Reservoirs and Mill Creek contain rainbow trout. Early Spanish explorers, seeing the range when it was covered with snow, named it La Sal ("Salt"). Other names include "Salt Mountains" and "Elk Mountains." Gold fever peaked here at the turn of the century with activity concentrated in Miners and Gold basins. Old mines and ruins of former mining camps can still be found in these areas.

## Hiking In The La Sals

Miners traveling through the mountains during the boom years built many of the trails in use today. The current network of about 18 trails totals about 65 miles. Trails cross the range from north to south and branch off to scenic lakes, basins, and canyons. Hiking conditions range from easy to difficult. Horseback riders can use the trails too. Signs mark most trailheads and junctions, but backcountry users should still have topo maps and a compass. Nearly all the canyons and valleys have springs or streams (purify first). Climbers can choose from half a dozen peaks exceeding 12,000 feet. All summit routes require rock-scrambling and route-finding skills. Hazards include loose rock, lightning, and altitude sickness. Mount Peale can be climbed from the south off La Sal Pass Road (from about one mile east of La Sal Pass) or from the pass itself via Mt. Tukuhnikivatz. See the 15-minute La Sal and La Sal Junction or the 1:100,000 La Sal topo maps. The U.S. Forest Service office in Moab is the best source for trail and climbing information (125 W. 200 South; tel. 259-7155).

## Winter Sports

No developed facilities exist yet. Cross-country skiers often head to Miners Basin, Beaver Basin, Geyser Pass, Gold Basin, La Sal Pass, and Dark Canyon. Snowmobilers may use any of the roads in the mountains. Travelers here need proper experience, equipment, and knowledge of avalanche hazards and means of rescue. Always go with a companion.

# LA SAL MOUNTAINS LOOP ROAD

This paved road on the west side of the range provides a good introduction to the high country. Side roads and trails lead to lakes, alpine meadows, and old mining areas. Viewpoints overlook Castle Valley, Arches and Canyonlands national parks, Moab Rim, and other scenic features. Vegetation along the drive runs the whole range from cottonwoods, sage, and rabbitbrush of the desert to forests of aspen, fir, and spruce. The 62-mile loop road can easily take a full day with stops for scenic overlooks, a picnic, and a bit of hiking or fishing. Because of the high elevations, the loop's season usually lasts May through October. The following road log lists the major points of interest along the way (the loop is equally good driven in the other direction too). Stock up on supplies in Moab, as there aren't any stores or gas stations after leaving town. It's a good idea to check current back-road conditions with the U.S. Forest Service office in Moab before venturing off the Loop Road.

**Mile 0.0:** Downtown Moab; head south on US 191 (Main St.).

**Mile 8.0:** Turn left (east) on the La Sal Mountains Loop Road near Milepost 118.

**Mile 10.1:** Ken's Lake, an undeveloped fishing and swimming area, is reached by a gravel road to the left. Fishermen angle for rainbow trout and bass. A 645-foot tunnel brings water from Mill Creek.

**Mile 13.4:** Pack Creek Picnic Area is 3 miles to the right on a paved road; elevation is 6,800 feet. The nearby Pack Creek Ranch offers accommodations, meals, and guided pack trips (tel. 259-5505). The La Sal Pass Road (high-clearance vehicles recommended) continues past the picnic area to the 10,100-foot pass south of Mt. Tukuhnikivatz and Mt. Peale. The pass usually doesn't open until late June.

**Mile 20.1:** Geyser Pass Road (dirt) on the right climbs to Gold Basin (7.5 miles), 10,600-foot Geyser Pass (8 miles), and other areas in the La Sals. Cars can usually be driven to the lower edge of Gold Basin; elsewhere high-clearance vehicles may be needed. Geyser Pass doesn't open until late June in most years.

**Mile 21.5:** Mill Creek bridge; Oowah Lake is 3 miles to the right on an unpaved road (usually OK for cars when dry). Steep forested slopes enclose this pretty reservoir at an elevation of 8,800 feet. A small **campground** near the lake is free; no drinking water. Trails go to Warner Lake (1¾ miles), Clark Lake (1½ miles), Boren Mesa (½ mile), Geyser Pass Road (3 miles), and other destinations.

**Mile 22.8:** Warner Lake is 5.5 miles to the right on a gravel road, which follows a ridge with good views of the peaks to the east and canyon country to the west. **Warner Campground** at the end of the road has drinking water from early June to early Oct. ($4); elevation is 9,200 feet. A short walk across a meadow leads to Warner Lake. Trail destinations from the road's end include Oowah Lake (1¾ miles), Burro Pass (3½ miles), and Dry Fork (1½ miles).

**Mile 25.3:** Sand Flats Road to Moab (20 miles) turns left; a high-clearance vehicle is recommended.

**Mile 27.7:** Overlook on the left side of the road with a great panorama of Castle Valley and Arches National Park.

**Mile 29.2:** Miners Basin is 3 miles right and Pinhook Battleground Monument is 2 miles left; a high-clearance vehicle may be needed for either road. The lure of gold still brings prospectors to Miners Basin; some claims may be closed to visitors. The last Indian conflict in the region took place in 1881 in Pinhook Valley. A headstone marks the grave of 8 whites killed in the engagement.

**Mile 33.8:** Gateway Road to right. This road crosses the northern slopes of the La Sals to the old mining town of Gateway, Colorado. Backroads branch south into the La Sals and north into canyon country. Castleton townsite is near the Gateway Road turnoff. Castleton was founded in about 1890 as a supply center for miners and ranchers. Its population quickly exceeded that of Moab, but it faded away in the early 1900s and little remains today.

**Mile 37.5:** Round Mountain, an old volcanic neck, rises from the center of Castle Valley.

**Mile 39.5:** The prominent rock spires of Castle Rock and of the Priest and Nuns tower above the north side of the valley.

**Mile 44.5:** Junction with UT 128 along the Colorado River. Turn left 17.5 miles for Moab to complete the loop or right for Fisher Towers and Dewey Bridge. See "Dewey Bridge Road" above.

# ARCHES NATIONAL PARK

A concentration of arches of marvelous variety has formed within the maze of sandstone fins at the park. Balanced rocks and tall spires add to the splendor. Early explorers likened the giant arches and other rock formations in the Windows Section to remains of a lost civilization. Paved roads and short hiking trails provide easy access to some of the more than 1500 arches in the park. If you're short on time, a drive to the Windows Section (23.5 miles roundtrip) allows a look at many of the major arches. To visit all the stops and to hike a few short trails would take all day. The entrance fee of $3 per vehicle ($1 bicyclists and bus passengers) is good for 7 days at Arches only. The park brochure available at the entrance station and visitor center has a map of major scenic features, drives, trails, and back roads.

## How The Arches Got Here

An unusual combination of geologic forces created the arches. About 300 million years ago, evaporation of inland seas left behind a salt layer more than 3,000 feet thick in the Paradox Basin of this region. Sediments, including those that later became the arches, then covered the salt. Unequal pressures caused the salt to gradually flow upward in places, bending the overlying sediments as well. These upfolds, or anticlines, later collapsed when ground water dissolved the underlying salt. The faults and joints caused by the uplift and collapse opened the way for erosion to carve hundreds of free-standing fins. Alternate freezing and thawing action and exfoliation (flaking caused by expansion when water or frost penetrates the rock) continued to peel away more rock until holes formed in some of the fins. Rockfalls within the holes helped to enlarge the arches. Nearly all arches in the park eroded out of Entrada Sandstone.

Eventually all the present arches will collapse, but we should have plenty of new ones by the time that happens! The fins' uniform strength and hard upper surfaces have proved ideal for arch formation. Not every hole in the rock is an arch. The opening must be at least 3 feet across in one direction and light must be able to pass through. Although the term "windows" often refers to openings in large walls of rock, windows and arches are really the same. Water seeping through the sandstone from above has created a second type of arch—the pothole arch. You may also come across a few natural bridges, cut from the rock by perennial water run-off.

## Desert Life

Elevations at the park range from 3,960 feet along the Colorado River to 5,653 feet in the Windows area. Annual precipitation averages only 10-11 inches. Even so, plants and wildlife have found niches in this rugged high desert country. Shrubs and grasslands cover most of the land not occupied by barren rock. Cottonwood trees grow along some of the washes while pinyon pine and juniper form pygmy forests at the higher elevations. Specially adapted plant communities can be found in the dark microbiotic crusts on the soil. Hanging gardens surround springs and seeps.

ringtail cat
(Bassariscus astutus)

Tracks across the sands show the presence of shy or nocturnal wildlife. Animals include mule deer, coyote, gray fox, porcupine, bobcat, ringtail cat, kangaroo rat, antelope ground squirrel, collared lizard, and midget faded rattlesnake.

## History

Prehistoric Anasazi and Fremont Indians hunted in the area and may have planted crops in the few places having sufficient soil and moisture. The modern Utes hunted here too. Rock art and artifacts mark the former presence of these tribes. Most of the early settlers and cowboys of the region paid little attention to the scenery. However, in 1923 a prospector by the name of Alexander Ringhoffer interested officials of the Rio Grande Railroad in the scenic attractions at what he called "Devils Garden" (now known as Klondike Bluffs). The railroad men liked the area and contacted Stephen Mather, first director of the National Park Service. Mather started the political process that led to designation of 2 small areas as a national monument in 1929, but Ringhoffer's Devils Garden wasn't included until later. Early visitors had to endure travel over nonexistent or barely passable roads; see the Aug. 1947 issue of *National Geographic* magazine for a well-written account of the monument as it once was. It grew in size over the years and became Arches National Park in 1971. The park now has 73,379 acres—small enough to be appreciated in one day, yet large enough to warrant extensive exploration.

## Visitor Center

Located just past the entrance booth, the visitor center provides a good introduction of what to expect ahead. Exhibits identify the rock layers, describe the geologic and human history, and illustrate some of the wildlife and plants of the park. Staff present a short slide program upon request and answer your questions. Details of special activities are posted. Rangers host campfire programs and lead a wide variety of guided walks during the main season (April to Labor Day). Checklists, pamphlets, books, maps, posters, postcards, and film can be purchased. Backpackers may obtain advice and the required free backcountry permit from a ranger. The easy 0.2-mile **Desert Nature Trail** begins in front of the visitor center and identifies some of the native plants. Picnic areas are located outside the visitor center and at Balanced Rock and Devils Garden. The park is open all year; visitor center hours are daily 8 a.m.-4:30 p.m. (may be extended in summer); tel. 259-8161. Arches National Park is 5 miles north of downtown Moab on US 191.

## Devils Garden Campground

The park's campground is located near the end of the 18-mile scenic drive. It's open all year with water; $5. Try to arrive early during the busy Easter to Oct. season; only groups can reserve spaces. Elevation here is 5,355 feet. During summer evenings, rangers at the Campfire Circle tell about the park's geology, history, wildlife, flora, and environment.

## Hiking And Climbing

Established trails lead to many fine arches and overlooks that can't be seen from the road. You're free to wander cross-country too. Wear good walking shoes with rubber soles for travel across slickrock. The summer sun can be especially harsh on the unprepared hiker—don't forget water, hat, and sunscreen. The desert rule is to carry at least one gallon of water per person for an all-day hike. Take a map and compass for off-trail hiking. Be cautious on the slickrock; the soft rock can crumble easily. Also, remember that it's easier to go up a steep slickrock slope than to come back down! Almost any spot in the park can be reached on a day hike, though there are some good overnight possibilities. Areas for longer trips include Courthouse Wash in the southern part of the park and Salt Wash in the eastern part. All backpacking is done off trail. A backcountry permit must be obtained from a ranger before camping in the backcountry. Hiking regulations include no fires, no pets, camping out of sight of any road (at least one mile away) or trail (at least ½ mile away), and camping at least 300 feet from a recognizable archaeological site or nonflowing water source. Rock climbers don't need a permit, though they should first discuss their plans with a ranger; most features named on USGS maps are *closed* to climbing.

# SIGHTS AND HIKES ALONG THE PARK ROAD

A road guide to Arches National Park, available at the visitor center, has detailed descriptions that correspond to place names along the main road. Be sure to stop only in parking lots and designated pullouts. Watch out for others who are sightseeing in this popular park. The following are major points of interest.

## Moab Fault

The park road begins a long but well-graded climb from the visitor center up the cliffs to the northeast. A pullout on the right after 1.1 miles gives a good view of Moab Canyon and its geology. The rock layers on this side of the canyon have slipped down more than 2,600 feet in relation to the other side. Movement took place about 6 million years ago along the Moab Fault, which follows the canyon floor. Rock layers at the top of the far cliffs are nearly the same age as those at the *bottom* on this side! If you could stack the rocks of this side on top of rocks on the other side, you'd have a complete stratigraphic column of the Moab area—more than 150 million years' worth.

## Park Avenue

South Park Avenue Overlook and Trailhead are on the left 2.1 miles from the visitor center. Great sandstone slabs form a "skyline" on each side of this dry wash. A trail goes north one mile down the wash to North Park Avenue Trailhead (1.3 miles ahead by road). Arrange to be picked up there or backtrack to your start. The large rock monoliths of Courthouse Towers rise north of Park Avenue. Only a few small arches exist now, though major arches may have formed in the past.

## Balanced Rock

This gravity-defying formation is on the right 8.5 miles from the visitor center. A boulder more than 55 feet high rests precariously atop a 73-foot pedestal. Chip Off the Old Block, a much smaller version of Balanced Rock, stood nearby until it collapsed in the winter of 1975-76. For a closer look at Balanced Rock, take the 0.3-mile trail that encircles it. There's a picnic area across the road. Author Edward Abbey lived in a trailer near Balanced Rock during a season as a park ranger in the 1950s; his journal became the basis for the classic *Desert Solitaire.*

## Windows Section

Turn right 2.5 miles on a paved road past Balanced Rock. Short trails about ¼ mile long (one way) lead from the road's end to some massive arches. Windows Trailhead is the start for North Window (an opening 51 feet high and 93 feet wide), South Window (66 feet high and 105 feet wide), and Turret Arch (64 feet high and 39 feet wide). Double Arch, a short walk from a second trailhead, is an unusual pair of arches; the larger opening measures 105 feet high and 163 feet wide—best appreciated by walking inside. The smaller opening is 61 feet high and 60 feet wide. Together, the 2 arches frame a large opening overhead, but this isn't considered a true arch.

Garden of Eden Viewpoint, on the way back to the main road, has a good panorama of Salt Valley to the north. Under the valley, the massive body of salt and gypsum that's responsible for the arches comes close to the surface. Tiny Delicate Arch (described below) can be picked out on a sandstone ridge with the aid of a sighting tube. Early visitors to the Garden of Eden saw rock formations resembling Adam (with an apple) and Eve. Two other viewpoints of the Salt Valley area lie farther north on the main road.

## Wolfe Ranch And Delicate Arch

Drive north 2.5 miles on the main road from the Windows junction and turn right 1.8 miles to the Wolfe Ranch, where a bit of pioneer history survives. John Wesley Wolfe came to this spot in 1888, hoping the desert climate would provide relief for health problems related to a Civil War injury. He found a good spring high in the rocks, grass for cattle, and water in Salt Wash to irrigate a garden. The ranch that he built provided a home for him and some of his family for more than 20 years, and cattlemen later used it as a line ranch. Then sheepherders brought in their animals, which so overgrazed the range that the grass has yet to recover. A trail guide available at the entrance tells about the Wolfe family and features of their ranch. The weather-beaten cabin built in 1906 still survives. You can see petroglyphs above Wolfe Ranch by walking across the swinging bridge and turning left off the trail a short distance. Figures of horses indicate that Ute Indians did the artwork.

Delicate Arch stands in a magnificent setting atop gracefully curving slickrock. Distant canyons and the La Sal Mountains lie beyond. The span is 45 feet high and 33 feet wide. A moderately strenuous hike to the arch begins at Wolfe Ranch and crosses the swinging bridge, climbs a slickrock slope, follows a gully, then contours across steep slickrock to the main overlook. Roundtrip distance is 3 miles with an elevation gain of 500 feet; carry water. This is one of the most scenic hikes in the park. Just before the end of the trail, walk up to a small arch for a framed view of the final destination. The classic photo of Delicate Arch is taken late in the afternoon when the sandstone glows with golden hues.

Another perspective of Delicate Arch can be obtained by driving 1.2 miles beyond Wolfe Ranch. Look for the small arch high above. A steep trail (½ mile roundtrip) climbs a hill for the best panorama.

### Fiery Furnace

Return to the main road and continue 3 miles to the Fiery Furnace Viewpoint and Trailhead on the right. Closely packed sandstone fins form a maze of deep slots, with many arches and at least one natural bridge inside. The Fiery Furnace can be fun to explore, though route-finding is tricky. Drop-offs and ridges make straight-line travel impossible. It's easy to get lost! Ranger-led hikes of about 2 hours during the summer season provide the best way to see the wonders within. You'll need a reservation for this trip, obtainable in person only from the visitor center up to 48 hours in

*Delicate Arch*

*deep within the Fiery Furnace
on a ranger-led hike*

advance. The Fiery Furnace gets its name from sandstone fins that turn flaming red on occasions when thin cloud cover at the horizon reflects the warm light of sunrise or sunset. Actually, the shady recesses provide a cool respite from the hot summer sun.

### Sand Dune And Broken Arches

Trailhead is on the right 2.4 miles past the Fiery Furnace turnoff. A short trail leads to small Sand Dune Arch (opening is 8 feet high and 30 feet wide) tucked within fins. A longer trail (one mile roundtrip) crosses a field to Broken Arch, which you can also see from the road. Opening is 43 feet high and 59 feet wide. When you get close, you'll see that the arch isn't really broken. These arches can also be reached by trail from near comfort station #3 of Devils Garden Campground.

### Skyline Arch

Located on the right one mile past Sand Dune/

Broken Arch Trailhead. In desert climates, erosion may proceed imperceptibly for centuries until a cataclysmic event happens. In 1940, a giant boulder fell from the opening of Skyline Arch, doubling the size of the arch in just seconds. The hole is now 45 feet high and 69 feet wide. A short trail leads to the base of the arch.

### Devils Garden Trail

The trailhead, Devils Garden Picnic Area, and the campground all lie near the end of the main park road. A trail brochure is available at the start and at the visitor center. Devils Garden offers fine scenery and more arches than any other section of the park. The trail leads past large sandstone fins to Landscape and 6 other named arches. Carry water if the weather is hot or if you want to continue past the one-mile point at Landscape Arch. Adventurous hikers could spend days exploring the maze of canyons among the fins.

The first 2 arches lie off a short side trail to the right. Tunnel Arch has a relatively symmetrical opening 22 feet high and 27 feet wide. The nearby Pine Tree Arch is named for a pinyon pine that once grew inside; the arch has an opening 48 feet high and 46 feet wide. Continue on the main trail to Landscape Arch, which has an incredible 306-foot span (6 feet longer than a football field!). This is one of the longest unsupported rock spans in the world. The thin arch looks ready to collapse at any moment, but it may well have been like this for centuries. Height is 106 feet. Distance from the trailhead is 2 miles roundtrip, an easy one-hour walk.

The trail narrows past Landscape Arch and continues ¼ mile to Wall Arch, in a long wall-like fin. The opening is 41 feet high and 68 feet wide. A short side trail branches off to the left beyond Wall to Partition Arch (26 feet high and 28 feet wide) and Navajo Arch (13 feet high and 41 feet wide). Partition was so named because a piece of rock divides the main opening from a smaller hole 8 feet high and 8½ feet wide. Navajo Arch is a rock-shelter type; perhaps prehistoric Indians camped here. The main trail continues northwest and ends at Double O Arch (4 miles roundtrip from the trailhead). Double O has a large oval-shaped opening (45 feet high and 71 feet wide) and a smaller hole (9 feet high and 21 feet wide) underneath. Dark Angel is a distinctive rock pinnacle ¼ mile northwest; cairns mark the way. Another primitive trail loops back to Landscape Arch via Fin Canyon. This route goes through a different area of Devils Garden but adds about one mile to your trip (3 miles back to the trailhead instead of 2). Pay careful attention to the trail markers to keep on the correct route.

### Klondike Bluffs And Tower Arch
Relatively few visitors come to the spires, high bluffs, and fine arch in this northwestern section of the park. A fair-weather dirt road turns off the main drive 1.3 miles before Devils Garden Trailhead, winds down into Salt Valley, and heads northwest. After 7.5 miles, turn left one mile on the road signed "Klondike Bluffs" to the Tower Arch Trailhead. These roads may be washboarded but are usually OK in dry weather for cars; don't drive on them if storms threaten. The trail to Tower Arch winds past

the Marching Men and other rock formations; distance is 3 miles roundtrip. Alexander Ringhoffer, who discovered the arch in 1922, carved an inscription on the south column. The area can also be fun to explore off trail (map and compass needed). Those with 4WD vehicles can drive close to the arch on a separate jeep road. Tower Arch is 34 feet high by 92 feet wide. A tall monolith nearby gave the arch its name.

### Four-Wheel-Drive Road
A rough road near Tower Arch in the Klondike Bluffs turns southeast past **Eye of the Whale Arch** in Herdina Park to Balanced Rock on the main park road, 10.8 miles away. The road isn't particularly difficult for 4WD enthusiasts, though normal backcountry precautions should be taken. A steep sand hill north of Eye of the Whale Arch is very difficult to climb for vehicles coming from Balanced Rock; it's recommended to drive from the Tower Arch area instead.

# DEAD HORSE POINT STATE PARK

The land drops away in sheer cliffs from this lofty perch west of Moab. Nearly 5,000 square miles of rugged canyon country lies in the distance. Two thousand feet below, the Colorado River twists through a gooseneck on its long journey to the sea. The river and its tributaries have carved canyons that reveal a geologic layer cake of colorful rock formations. Even in a region of impressive views around nearly every corner, Dead Horse Point stands out for its exceptional panorama. You'll also see below you, along the Colorado River, the result of powerful underground forces: salt, under pressure, has pushed up overlying rock layers into an anticline. This formation, the Shafer Dome, contains potash that is being processed by the Moab Salt plant. You can see the mine buildings, processing plant, and evaporation ponds (tinted blue to hasten evaporation).

A narrow neck of land only 30 yards wide connects the point with the rest of the plateau. Cowboys once herded wild horses onto the

point, then placed a fence across the neck to make a 40-acre corral. They chose the desirable animals from the herd and let the rest go. According to one tale, a group of horses was left behind after such a roundup. Confused by the unusual geography of the point, they couldn't find their way off and circled repeatedly around it. Finally they perished from thirst while within sight of the river below. You may hear other stories, too, about how the park got its name. Besides the awe-inspiring views, the state park offers a visitor center, campground, picnic area, group area, nature trail, and hiking trails. Dead Horse Point is easily reached by paved road, either as a destination in itself, or as a side trip on the way to Island in the Sky District of Canyonlands National Park. From Moab, head northwest 10 miles on US 191, then turn left 25 miles on UT 313. The drive along UT 313 climbs through a scenic canyon and tops out on a ridge with a panorama of distant mesas, buttes, mountains, and canyons.

*Colorado Gooseneck and canyon country from Dead Horse Point*

## Visitor Center And Campground
Stop here for registration ($3/vehicle day use or $6/vehicle camping) and exhibits about the park. Staff will answer questions and provide checklists of local flora and fauna. A short slide presentation is shown on request. In summer, rangers give talks at the amphitheater behind the visitor center. Books, maps, posters, postcards, film, T-shirts, charcoal, ice, and soft drinks can be purchased. Open daily 8 a.m.-6 p.m. in summer (May 16 to Sept. 15) and 9 a.m.-5 p.m. the rest of the year. Contact the park at Box 609, Moab, UT 84532; tel. 259-6511 or (800) 322-3770 (reservations). A short nature trail that begins outside introduces the high-desert country and its plants. Continue 1.5 miles on the main road to viewpoints and picnic areas on the point itself. Primitive trails connect the point with several other overlooks, the visitor center, and the campground. Ask for a map at the visitor center.

**Kayenta Campground,** just past the visitor center, offers sites with water and electric hookups but no showers; open early April to late October. The campground nearly always fills up during the main season. Either make reservations or try to arrive by early afternoon to be assured of a space. Winter visitors may camp on the point; no hookups are available but the restrooms have water.

# CANYONLANDS NATIONAL PARK

The canyon country of southeastern Utah puts on its supreme performance in this vast park, which spreads across 527 square miles. The deeply entrenched Colorado and Green rivers meet in its heart, then continue south as the mighty Colorado through tumultuous Cataract Canyon Rapids. These 2 rivers form the **River District** and divide Canyonlands National Park into 3 other districts. **Island in the Sky** lies north between the rivers, the **Maze** is to the west, and the **Needles** is to the east. Each has its own distinct character. No bridges connect the 3 land districts, so most visitors have to leave the park to go from one region to another. The huge park can be seen in many ways and on many levels. Paved roads reach a few areas, 4WD roads go to more places, and hiking trails reach still more, yet much of the land shows no trace of man's passage. To get the big picture, fly over this incredible complex of canyons (see "Air Tours" in the Moab section). However, only a river trip or a hike lets you experience the solitude and small details of the land. The park can be visited in any season of the year, but spring and autumn are the best choices. Summer temperatures can get into the 100s F; carrying (and drinking) water becomes critical then; carry at least one gallon/person per day. Arm yourself with insect repellent from late spring to midsummer. Winter days tend to be bright and sunny, though nighttime temperatures can dip into the teens or subzeros. Visitors coming in winter should inquire about travel conditions, as snow and ice occasionally close roads and trails at the higher elevations.

## Visiting The Park

Come to any of the districts for great views, spectacular geology, a chance to see wildlife, and endless opportunities to explore. You won't find crowds or elaborate park facilities—most of Canyonlands remains a primitive backcountry park.

**Island in the Sky District** has paved roads on its top to impressive overlooks and to Upheaval Dome, a strange geologic feature. If you're short on time or don't want to make a rigorous backcountry trip, you'll find this district the best choice. The "Island," actually a large mesa, is much like Dead Horse Point on a giant scale. A narrow neck of land connects the north side of the Island with the "mainland." Hikers and those with suitable vehicles can drop off the Island in the Sky and descend about 1,300 feet to the White Rim 4WD Trail, which follows cliffs of the White Rim around most of the Island.

Few visitors make it over to the **Maze District,** some of the wildest country in the United States. Access is provided by only the rivers and a handful of 4WD roads and hiking trails. Experienced hikers can explore the "maze" of canyons on unmarked routes. **Horseshoe Canyon Unit,** a detached section of Canyonlands National Park west of the Maze District, protects the Great Gallery, a group of pictographs left by prehistoric Indians.

Colorful rock spires prompted the name of the **Needles District.** Splendid canyons contain many arches, strange rock formations, and archaeological sites. Hikers enjoy day hikes and backpack treks on the network of well-marked trails and routes within the district. Drivers with 4WD vehicles have their own challenging roads through canyons and other highly scenic areas. Overlooks and short nature trails can be enjoyed from the paved scenic drive in the park. A highway branching off US 191 south of Moab provides easy access to the Needles District.

The **River District** includes long stretches of the Green and Colorado. River running provides one of the best ways to experience the inner depths of the park. Boaters can obtain helpful literature and advice from park rangers. Groups planning their own trip through Cataract Canyon need a river-running permit.

## Geology

Deep canyons of the Green and Colorado have sliced through rocks representing 150 million years of deposition. The Paradox Formation, exposed in Cataract Canyon, contains salt and other minerals responsible for some of the folded and faulted rock layers in the region. Under immense pressure of overlying rocks, the Paradox flows like plastic, forming domes where the rock layers are thinnest and causing cracks or faults as pressures rise and fall. Each of the overlying formations has a different color and texture; they're the products of ancient deserts, rivers, and seas that once covered this land. Views from any of the overlooks reveal that an immense quantity of rock has already been washed downriver toward California. Not so evident, however, is the 10,000 vertical feet of rock that geologists say once lay across the high mesas. The dry climate and sparse vegetation allow clear views of the remaining rock layers and the effects of erosion and deformation. You can read the geologic story at Canyonlands National Park in the 3,500 feet of strata that remain, from the bottom of Cataract Canyon to the upper reaches of Salt Creek in the Needles District.

## Desert Life

Extremes of flash flood and drought, hot summers and cold winters, discourage all but the most hardy and adaptable life. Desert grasses, small flowering plants, cacti, and shrubs like blackbrush and saltbush survive on the mostly thin soils and meager 10-11 inches of annual precipitation. Trees either grow in cracks that concentrate rainfall and nutrients or rely on springs or canyon streams for moisture. Pinyon pine and juniper prefer the higher elevations of the park, while cottonwoods live in the canyon bottoms having permanent subsurface water. Tamarisk, an exotic streamside plant, and willows often form dense thickets on sandbars along the Green and Colorado rivers. The hanging gardens of lush vegetation that surround cliffside springs or seeps seem oblivious to the surrounding desert. Fragile desert ecology can easily be upset. Cattle, especially in the Needles District, once overgrazed the grasslands and trampled microbiotic crusts and other vegetation. Increased erosion and growth of undesirable exotic plants like cheatgrass have been the result. Scars left by roads and mines during the uranium frenzy of the 1950s can still be seen, most commonly in the Island in the Sky District.

Less than 10 species of fish evolved in the canyons of the Colorado and the Green. These fish developed streamlined bodies and strange features, such as humped backs, to cope with the muddy and highly changeable river waters. Species include the Colorado squawfish, humpback chub, bonytail chub, and humpback sucker; most of these live nowhere else. All have suffered greatly reduced populations and restricted ranges due to recent dam building. Of the approximately 65 mammal species living in the park, about one-third are rodents and another third are bats. You're most likely to see chipmunk, antelope ground squirrel, and rock squirrel, which are often active during the day. Most other animals wait until evening to come out and feed; in the morning look for tracks of mule deer, bighorn sheep, coyote, gray fox, badger, porcupine, spotted skunk, beaver, black-tailed jack rabbit, wood rat, kangaroo rat, and many species of mice.

## History

Prehistoric Anasazi Indians ranged through the entire area, while the Fremont lived mostly west of the Green and Colorado rivers. Both groups departed from the region in the middle to late 1200s. They left behind hundreds of archaeological sites with rock art, granaries, dwellings, and stone tools. Nomadic Ute Indians later roamed through the canyons and drew rock art of their own. The Navajo may have made trips into the park area from the south during the 1800s.

At least one mountain man, Denis Julien, visited the Colorado and Green canyons in

# ENDANGERED FISH OF THE COLORADO RIVER BASIN

*Colorado squawfish (Ptychocheilus lucius)*
*Native only to the Colorado and its major tributaries, this species is the largest minnow in North America. It has been reported as weighing up to 100 pounds and measuring 6 feet long. Loss of habitat due to dam construction has* *greatly curtailed its size and range. Fishermen often confuse the smaller and more common roundtail chub (Gila robusta) with the Colorado squawfish; the chub is distinguished by a smaller mouth extending back only to the front of the eye.*

*humpback chub (Gila cypha)*
*Scientists first described this fish only in 1946 and know little about its life. The small fish usually weighs in under 2 pounds and under 13 inches. Today the humpback chub hangs on the verge of extinction; it has retreated to a few small* *areas of the Colorado River where the water still runs warm, muddy, and swift. The bonytail chub (Gila robusta elegans) has a similar size and shape, but without a hump; its numbers are also rapidly declining.*

*humpback or razorback sucker (Xyrauchen texanus)*
*This large sucker grows to weights of 10-16 pounds and lengths of about 3 feet. Its numbers have been slowly decreasing, especially above the Grand Canyon. They require warm, fast-flowing water to reproduce. Mating is done as a* *bizarre ritual in the spring. When the female has selected a suitable spawning site, 2 male fish press against the sides of her body. The female begins to vibrate her body until the eggs and spermatazoa are expelled simultaneously. One female can spawn 3 times, but she uses a different pair of males each time.*

1836, leaving his signatures but little else to tell of his travels. Julien may have been the first person to raft the rivers here. In 1859, Captain John Macomb and his party noted the beautiful rock sculptures in Needles on an overland trip, but they judged the country worthless. Major John Wesley Powell led the first scientific expedition by boat through the Green and lower Colorado river canyons in 1869, then repeated the journey in 1871-72. Cowboys brought in cattle during the 1870s. Some of their camps, corrals, and inscriptions still survive, though grazing no longer takes place in the park. The Powell expedition and the later cowboys named many of the park's features. Uranium prospectors swarmed through the area with Geiger counters during the 1950s, staking thousands of claims and opening some mines. Most of the jeep roads in use today date from that time.

Serious interest in establishing a park didn't begin until the early 1960s. Stewart Udall, secretary of the interior under President Kennedy, realized the area's potential as a national park while flying over the Colorado River to examine a possible dam site. The superintendent of Arches National Monument, Bates Wilson, also worked hard for creation of a new park here. Canyonlands National Park became a reality in 1964 and was enlarged to its present size in 1971.

### Visitor Centers And Information
Each of the 3 land districts has a small ranger office/visitor center near the park entrance, but you may find it convenient to stop at the National Park Service offices in Moab or Monticello. The headquarters address for Canyonlands National Park is 125 W. 200 South, Moab, UT 84532; tel. 259-7164 (weekdays) or 259-8161 (weekends). Any of the 5 offices has brochures, maps, and books, as well as someone to answer your questions. Vehicular camping is allowed only in established campgrounds and designated backcountry campsites. Except for the main campgrounds at Willow Flat (Island in the Sky) and Squaw Flat (Needles), you'll need a backcountry permit

for overnight stays. Backcountry permits will also be needed for any technical climbing and trips with stock; check with a ranger for details. Pets aren't allowed on trails and must always be leashed. No firewood collecting is permitted in the park; backpackers need stoves for cooking. Vehicle campers can bring in firewood but must use grills or fire pans. The best maps for the park are a series of 3 topos (one for each district) printed on waterproof paper by Trails Illustrated; these cost $6 each and have the latest trail and road information. A giant topo map, Canyonlands National Park and Vicinity, by the USGS has the same 1:62,500 scale for only $4, but without the updated information and fancy paper. Handouts from the ranger offices describe natural history, travel, and other aspects of the park.

### Back-road Travel
Canyonlands National Park offers hundreds of miles of exceptionally scenic jeep roads. Normally you must have a vehicle with both 4WD *and* high clearance. Park regulations require ALL motorized vehicles to have proper registration and licensing for highway use; drivers must be licensed as well. (ATV's are prohibited.) It's essential for both motor vehicles and bicycles to stay on existing roads to prevent damage to the delicate desert vegetation. Carry tools, extra fuel, water, and food in case of breakdown in a remote area. Mountain bicyclists enjoy travel on the backcountry roads too. Before making a trip, drivers and cyclists should talk with a ranger to register and to learn of current road conditions, which can change drastically from one day to the next. Also, the rangers will be more knowledgeable about where to look in case you become stuck. Primitive campgrounds are provided on most of the roads; no charge, but you'll need a backcountry permit from a ranger. Local author F.A. Barnes has written 2 sets of guidebooks and maps covering parts of Canyonlands National Park: *Canyon Country Off-Road Vehicle Trails: Island Area* and *Canyon Country Off-Road Vehicle Trails: Canyon Rims & Needles Areas*.

# RIVER DISTRICT

## River Running
## Above The Confluence

Both the Green and Colorado rivers flow smoothly through their canyons above the confluence. Almost any shallow-draft boat can navigate these waters. Canoes, kayaks, rafts, and power boats are commonly used. Any travel requires advance planning because of the remoteness of the canyons and the few points of access to the rivers. No campgrounds, supplies, or other facilities exist past Moab on the Colorado River or the town of Green River on the Green. All river runners must follow park regulations, which include the carrying of life jackets, use of a fire pan for fires, and packing out all garbage and solid human waste. The river flow on both the Colorado and the Green averages a gentle 2-4 mph (7-10 mph at high water). Boaters typically do 20 miles per day in canoes and 15 miles per day in rafts.

The Colorado has one modest rapid called the Slide, 1½ miles above the confluence, where rocks constrict the river to one-third of its normal width; the rapid is roughest during high water levels in May and June. This is the only difficulty on the 64 river miles from Moab. Inexperienced canoeists and rafters may wish to portage around it. The most popular launch points on the Colorado are the Moab Dock (just upstream from the US 191 bridge near town) and the Potash Dock (17 miles downriver at the end of the Potash Road, UT 279).

On the Green, boaters at low water need to watch for rocky areas at the mouth of Millard Canyon (33½ miles above the confluence, where a rock bar extends across the river) and at the mouth of Horse Canyon (14½ miles above the confluence, where a rock and gravel bar on the right leaves only a narrow channel on the left side). The trip from the town of Green River through Labyrinth and Stillwater canyons is 120 miles. Launch places include Green River State Park (Green River) and Mineral Canyon (52 miles above the con-

fluence; reached on a rough fair-weather road from UT 313).

No roads go to the confluence. Easiest return to civilization for nonmotorized craft is a pick-up by jet boat from Moab by Tex's Riverways or Tag-A-Long Tours (see "River Tours" in the Moab section). A far more difficult way out is hiking either of 2 trails just above the Cataract Canyon rapids to 4WD roads on the rim. Park rangers require that boaters above the confluence obtain a backcountry permit either in person from the Moab office or by mail (2 weeks in advance). River notes on boating the Green and Colorado are available on request from the Moab office. Belknap's *Canyonlands River Guide* has river logs and maps pointing out items of interest for the Green River below the town of Green River (UT) and all of the Colorado from the upper end of Westwater Canyon to Lake Powell.

## River Running
## Through Cataract Canyon

The Colorado River enters Cataract Canyon at the confluence and picks up speed. The rapids begin 4 miles downstream and extend

*the heart of Cataract Canyon*

for the next 14 miles to Lake Powell. The 26 or more rapids give a wild ride equal to the best in the Grand Canyon. The current zips along (up to 16 mph) and forms waves more than 7 feet high! When the excitement dies down, boaters have a 34-mile trip across Lake Powell to Hite Marina; most people either carry a motor or arrange for a power boat to pick them up. Because of the real hazards of running the rapids, the National Park Service requires boaters to have proper equipment and a permit. Most people go on a commercial trip in which everything has been taken care of (write the park for a list of boat companies). Private groups need to contact the Canyonlands River Unit far in advance for permit details at 125 W. 200 South, Moab, UT 84532; tel. 259-7164.

# ISLAND IN THE SKY DISTRICT

Panoramic views from the "Island" can be enjoyed from any point along the rim. You'll see much of the park and southeastern Utah. Short hiking trails lead to overlooks, Mesa Arch, Aztec Butte, Whale Rock, Upheaval Dome, and other features. Longer trails make steep, strenuous descents from the Island to the White Rim 4WD Trail below. Elevations on the Island average about 6,000 feet. *Bring water for all hiking, camping, and travel on Island in the Sky.* No services are available, except at the visitor center in emergencies (bottled water is sold).

## Visitor Center
Stop here for information about Island in the Sky and to see some exhibits. A $3/vehicle charge is made unless you have a receipt issued within the last 7 days from the Needles District of Canyonlands. Obtain a backcountry permit if making an overnight hike or planning to stay at campgrounds along the White Rim 4WD Trail (reservations by mail or in person are required for sites on the White Rim 4WD Trail). Open daily 8 a.m.-4:30 p.m. (may close noon-1 p.m. in winter); tel. 259-6577 (mobile phone). A bulletin board outside has area information. The visitor center is located just before crossing "The Neck" to Island in the

Sky. From Moab, go northwest 10 miles on US 191, turn left 15 miles on UT 313 to the junction for Dead Horse Point State Park, then continue straight 7 miles.

## Shafer Canyon Overlook
Continue 0.5 mile past the visitor center to this overlook on the left (just before crossing The Neck). Shafer Trail Viewpoint, across The Neck, provides another perspective 0.5 mile farther. The Neck is a narrow land bridge just wide enough for the road, and it's the only vehicle access to the 40-square-mile Island in the Sky. The overlooks have good views east down the canyon and the incredibly twisting **Shafer Trail Road.** Cattlemen Frank and John Schafer built the trail in the early 1900s to move stock to additional pastures (the "c" in their name was later dropped by mapmakers). The trail was upgraded to a jeep road during the 1950s so uranium prospectors could reach their claims at the base of the cliffs. Today the Shafer Trail Road connects the mesa top with the White Rim 4WD Trail and UT 279 (Potash Road) 1,200 feet and 4 miles below. High-clearance vehicles should be used on the Shafer, preferably with 4WD if you plan to climb up. Road conditions can vary considerably, so it's a good idea to first contact a ranger.

## Neck Spring Trail
The trail begins from the Shafer Canyon Overlook. A brochure should be available at the beginning. This moderately difficult hike follows a 5-mile loop down Taylor Canyon to Neck and Cabin springs, formerly used by ranchers, then climbs back to the Island in the Sky road at a second trailhead, ½ mile south of the start. Elevation change is 300 feet. Water at the springs supports maidenhair ferns and other water-loving plants. Also watch for birds and wildlife attracted to this spot. Bring water with you, as the springs aren't always suitable for drinking.

## Lathrop Trail
This is the only marked hiking route going all the way from Island in the Sky to the Colorado River. Trailhead is on the left, 1.3 miles past

The Neck. The first 2½ miles cross Gray's Pasture to the rim, then the route descends steeply 1,600 feet in the next 2½ miles to the White Rim 4WD Trail. Part of this section follows an old mining road past several abandoned mines, all relics of the uranium boom; don't enter the shafts as they're in danger of collapse and may contain poisonous gases. From the mining area, the route descends through a wash to the White Rim 4WD Trail, follows the road a short distance south, then goes down Lathrop Canyon Jeep Road to the Colorado River, another 4 miles with a descent of 500 feet. A primitive campground is at the river. Total distance for the strenuous hike is 9 miles one way with an elevation change of 2,100 feet. The trail has little shade and can be very hot.

## Mesa Arch Trail

This easy trail leads to an arch on the rim. The trailhead is on the left 5.5 miles from The Neck. On the way, the road crosses the grasslands and scattered juniper trees of Gray's Pasture. A trail brochure available at the start describes the ecology of the mesa. Hiking distance is only ½ mile roundtrip with an 80-foot elevation change. The arch, eroded from Navajo Sandstone, frames views of rock formations below and the La Sal Mountains in the distance.

## Murphy Point And Grand View Point

Go straight at the road junction just past the Mesa Arch Trailhead for these and other spectacular viewpoints. After 2.5 miles, a rough dirt road turns right 1.7 miles to Murphy Point. Hikers can take **Murphy Trail,** which begins off the road to the point, to the White Rim 4WD Trail. This strenuous route forks part way down; one branch follows Murphy Hogback (a ridge) to Murphy Campground on the 4WD road, and the other branch follows a wash to the road one mile south of the campground. A loop hike along both branches is 9 miles roundtrip with an elevation change of 1,100 feet.

Continue 2.5 miles on the main road past the Murphy Point turnoff to Grand View Picnic Area, a handy lunch stop. Two trails start here. **White Rim Overlook Trail** is an easy 1½-mile hike (roundtrip) east along a peninsula to an overlook of Monument Basin and beyond. **Gooseberry Trail** drops off the mesa and descends some extremely steep grades to the White Rim 4WD Trail just north of Gooseberry Campground; the strenuous trip is 2½ miles one way with an elevation change of 1,400 feet.

Continue one mile on the main road past the picnic area to Grand View Point, perhaps the most spectacular panorama from Island in the Sky. Monument Basin lies directly below, and countless canyons, the Colorado River, the Needles, and mountain ranges are in the distance. **Grand View Trail** continues past the end of the road for other vistas from the point, which is the southernmost tip of Island in the Sky. The easy hike is 1½ miles roundtrip.

## Green River Overlook
## And Willow Flat Campground

Return to the road junction, turn west ¼ mile, then turn south 1½ miles on an unpaved road to the overlook. Soda Springs Basin and a section of the Green River (deeply entrenched in Stillwater Canyon) can be seen below. The small campground is passed on the way to the overlook; it's open all year (no water or charge). Rangers occasionally present campfire programs here. Sites may fill in spring and autumn.

## Aztec Butte Trail

Trailhead is on the right, one mile northwest of the road junction. Aztec Butte is one of the few areas at Island in the Sky with Indian ruins; shortage of water prevented permanent settlement. An easy trail climbs 200 feet in ½ mile to the top of the butte for a good panorama of the Island.

## Whale Rock

Trailhead is on the right, 4.4 miles northwest of the road junction. An easy trail climbs this sandstone hump. Whale Rock is near the outer rim of Upheaval Dome. Distance is ½ mile roundtrip with an ascent of 100 feet.

## Upheaval Dome

Continue to the end of the road, 5.3 miles northwest of the road junction, for a look at this geological curiosity. There's also a small picnic area here. The easy **Crater View Trail** leads to overlooks on the rim of Upheaval Dome; the first viewpoint is ½ mile roundtrip, and the main viewpoint is one mile roundtrip. A fantastically deformed pile of rock lies below within a crater about 3 miles across and 1,200 feet deep. For many years, Upheaval Dome has kept geologists busy trying to figure out its origin. They once assumed that salt of the Paradox Formation pushed the rock layers upward to form the dome. Now, however, there is strong evidence that a meteorite impact caused the structure. The surrounding ring depression (caused by collapse) and the convergence of rock layers upward toward the center correspond precisely to known impact structures. Shatter cones and microscopic analysis also confirm an impact origin. When the meteorite struck, sometime in the last 150

million years, it formed a crater up to 5 miles across. Erosion removed some of the overlying rock, perhaps as much as a vertical mile. The underlying salt may have played a role in uplifting the central section.

Energetic hikers can reach Upheaval Dome from the parking area at the overlook or from White Rim 4WD Trail below. **Syncline Loop Trail** makes a strenuous 8-mile circuit completely around Upheaval Dome; elevation change is 1,200 feet. The trail crosses Upheaval Dome Canyon about halfway around from the overlook; walk east 1½ miles up the canyon to enter the crater itself. This is the only nontechnical route into the center of the dome. A hike around Upheaval Dome with a side trip to the crater totals 11 miles, best done as an overnight trip. Carry plenty of water for the entire trip; this dry country is usually very warm. The Green River is the only reliable source of water. From near Upheaval Campsite on White Rim 4WD Trail, you can hike 4 miles on **Upheaval Trail** through Upheaval Canyon to a junction with the Syncline Loop Trail, then another 1½ miles into the crater; elevation gain is about 600 feet.

## Alcove Spring Trail

Another hiking possibility in the area, leaves the road 1½ miles before the Upheaval Dome parking area and connects with White Rim 4WD Trail in Taylor Canyon. Total distance is 11 miles one way (5 miles on the trail in Trail Canyon and 6 miles on a jeep road in Taylor Canyon); elevation change is about 1,500 feet. Carry plenty of water—the strenuous trail is hot and dry.

## White Rim 4WD Trail

This driving adventure follows the White Rim below sheer cliffs of Island in the Sky. Travel along the winding road presents a constantly changing panorama of rock, canyons, river, and sky. Keep an eye out for desert bighorn sheep. You'll see all 3 levels of Island in the Sky District, from the high plateaus to the White Rim to the rivers. Only 4WD vehicles with high clearance can make the trip. The approximately 100 miles can be done in one

*contorted rock layers inside Upheaval Dome*

day, though this isn't recommended. Taking 2 or 3 days allows you to enjoy the scenery far better. Allow an extra day to travel all the road spurs. Primitive campgrounds along the way provide convenient stopping places. You'll need to obtain reservations and a backcountry permit for the White Rim campsites from park offices in Moab or Island in the Sky; this can be done only by mail or in person. Demand exceeds supply during the popular spring season, when you should make reservations as far in advance as possible. No services or developed water sources exist anywhere on the drive, so be sure to have plenty of fuel and water with some to spare. Access points are Shafer Trail Road (from Island in the Sky) and UT 279 (from Moab) on the east and Mineral Bottom Road on the west. To get a feel for this country, you can usually travel with a high-clearance 2WD vehicle to Musselman Arch on the White Rim via Shafer Trail Road or UT 279; you'll need 4WD beyond the arch. White Rim Sandstone forms the distinctive plateau crossed on the drive. A close look at the rock reveals ripple marks and crossbeds laid down near an ancient coastline. The plateau's east side is about 800 feet above the Colorado River. On the west side, the plateau meets the bank of the Green River.

## MAZE DISTRICT

Only adventurous and experienced travelers will want to visit this rugged land west of the Green and Colorado rivers. Vehicle access wasn't even possible until 1957, when mineral-exploration roads first entered what later became Canyonlands National Park. Today, you'll need a high-clearance 4WD vehicle, a horse, or your own two feet to get around. The National Park Service plans to keep this district in its remote and primitive condition. An airplane flight, recommended if you can't come overland, provides the only easy way to see the scenic features here. The names of the erosional forms are descriptive: Orange Cliffs, Golden Stairs, the Fins, Land of Standing Rocks, Lizard Rock, the Doll House, Chocolate Drops, the Maze, and Jasper Canyon. The many-fingered canyons of the Maze gave the district its name. Although not a true maze, these canyons give that impression.

### Ranger Station And Information

Glen Canyon National Recreation Area borders the Maze District on the west with scenic canyons, cliffs, rock formations, and overlooks of its own. The Hans Flat Ranger Station for the Maze District lies inside Glen Canyon N.R.A.; the station is open daily 8 a.m.-4:30 p.m.; tel. 259-6513 (mobile telephone; 8-9 a.m. is the best time to call). *There are no developed sources of water*. Hikers can obtain water from springs in some canyons (check with a ranger to find which are flowing) or from the rivers; purify all water before drinking. The Maze District has several primitive campsites. A backcountry permit is needed for these or for backpacking. You don't need a permit to camp in the Glen Canyon N.R.A. or on BLM land. The Trails Illustrated topo map of the Maze District describes and shows the few roads and trails here; some routes and springs are marked too. Agile hikers experienced in desert and canyon travel may want to take off on cross-country routes, which are either unmarked or lightly cairned. Extra care must be taken for preparation and travel in both Glen Canyon N.R.A. and the Maze. Always talk with the rangers beforehand to find out current conditions and to leave an itinerary. Unless the rangers know where to look for you in case of breakdown or accident, a rescue could take weeks!

Dirt roads to the Hans Flat Ranger Station and Maze District branch off from UT 24 (0.5 mile south of the Goblin Valley State Park turnoff), the town of Green River (take Airport Road and keep left at the fork 2.5 miles south of town), and UT 95 (take Flint Trail between the Dirty Devil and Hite bridges at Lake Powell). Easiest way in is the 59-mile road from UT 24. Flint Trail from UT 95 parallels Cataract Canyon; a short hike or drive to the rim provides views into the depths. All roads to the Maze District cross Glen Canyon National

Recreation Area. From Green River or UT 24, 2-wheel-drive vehicles with high clearance can travel to Hans Flat Ranger Station and other areas near but not actually in the Maze District.

# HORSESHOE CANYON UNIT

This canyon contains exceptional prehistoric rock art in a separate section of Canyonlands National Park. Ghostly life-size pictographs in the "Great Gallery" provide an intriguing look into the past. Archaeologists think that the images had religious importance, although the meaning of the figures remains unknown. The Barrier Canyon style of these drawings has been credited to an Archaic Indian Culture beginning at least 8,000 years ago and lasting until about A.D. 450. Horseshoe Canyon also contains rock art left by the subsequent Fremont and Anasazi Indians. The relation between the earlier and later prehistoric groups hasn't been determined.

## Visiting The Great Gallery

Horseshoe Canyon lies to the west of the Maze District. Two moderately difficult trails and a very rough jeep road lead down the canyon walls. In dry weather, cars with good clearance can be driven to a trailhead on the west rim. To reach this trailhead from UT 24, drive to a junction 0.5 mile south of Goblin Valley State Park turnoff, then turn east 30 miles on a dirt road (keep left at the Hans Flat Ranger Station/Horseshoe Canyon turnoff 25 miles in). Or, from the town of Green River, go south 47 miles on Airport Road (keep left at the road fork 2.5 miles south of town). A sign points the way to the trailhead, 1.2 miles south off the main drive. From the rim, the trail descends 800 feet in one mile on an old jeep road, now closed to vehicles. At the canyon bottom, turn right 2 miles upstream to the Great Gallery. The sandy canyon floor is mostly level; trees provide shade in some areas.

A 4WD road goes north 21 miles from Hans Flat Ranger Station and drops steeply into the canyon from the east side. The descent on this road is so rough that most people prefer to park on the rim and hike the last mile of road.

A vehicle barricade prevents driving right up to the rock art panel, but the 1½-mile walk is easy. A branch off the jeep road goes to the start of **Deadman's Trail** (1½ miles one way), which is less used and more difficult.

Look for other rock art along the canyon walls on the way to the Great Gallery. Take care not to touch any of the drawings; they're often very fragile as well as irreplaceable. (The oil from your hands will remove the paints.) Horseshoe Canyon also offers pleasant scenery and spring wildflowers. The canyon has 2 small camping areas, making it easier to explore beyond the main route. Carry plenty of water. Contact the Hans Flat Ranger Station or the Moab office for road and trail conditions (and backcountry permits if camping in the canyon).

*mysterious figures from the past . . .*
*Great Gallery detail*

## NEEDLES DISTRICT

The Needles showcase some of the finest rock sculptures in Canyonlands National Park. Spires, arches, or monoliths appear in almost any direction you look. Prehistoric ruins and rock art exist in greater variety and quantity than elsewhere in the park. Year-round springs and streams bring greenery to the desert. A paved road, several 4WD roads, and many hiking trails offer a variety of ways to explore the Needles.

### Needles Outpost
A general store just outside the park boundary offers groceries, ice, gas, propane, snack bar, campground ($8.48 tent or RV no hookups, $12.72 RV with water and sewer), showers, jeep tours, and scenic flights. Call or write ahead, if possible, to arrange for jeep tours and scenic flights; Box 1107, Monticello, UT 84535; tel. 259-2032 (mobile phone) or 259-8545. The season at Needles Outpost is mid-March to late October. Turnoff from UT 211 is one mile before the Needles Information Station.

### Information Station
The ranger station and a few exhibits are just inside the park. Stop here to find out about hiking, back roads, and other aspects of travel in the Needles. Backcountry permits, maps, brochures, and books are available. Open daily 8 a.m.-5 p.m.; tel. 259-6568 (mobile phone). A $3/vehicle charge is made unless you have a receipt issued within the last 7 days from Island in the Sky of Canyonlands. Outside office hours, get information and backcountry permits at the bulletin board next to the ranger station. To reach the Needles District, go 40 miles south from Moab (or 14 miles north of Monticello), turn west on UT 211, and continue 38 miles.

### Scenic Drive
The main road continues 6.5 miles past the ranger station to Big Spring Canyon Overlook. On the way, you can stop at several nature

trails, turn off on 4WD roads, or take short spur roads to trailheads and Squaw Flat Campground.

**Roadside Ruin** is on the left 0.4 mile past the ranger station. A ¼-mile loop trail goes near a well-preserved granary left by Anasazi Indians. A trail guide available at the start tells about the Anasazi and the local plants.

**Cave Spring Trail** introduces the geology and ecology of the park and goes to an old cowboy camp. Turn left 0.7 mile past the ranger station and follow signs about one mile to the trailhead. Pick up the brochure at the beginning. The 0.6-mile loop goes counterclockwise, crossing some slickrock; 2 ladders assist on the steep sections. If you want to visit just the camp and spring, walk 50 yards in the opposite direction from the trailhead (turn left). Cowboys used the cave as a line camp from the late 1800s until establishment of the park in 1964.

A road to **Squaw Flat Campground** and **Elephant Hill** turns left 2.7 miles past the ranger station. The campground, about 0.5 mile in from the main road, has water and a $6 fee from April to Sept.; it's open the rest of the year with no water or charge. (Water can be obtained year-round at a pumphouse near the ranger residences, about 1.5 miles from the campground.) Rangers present evening programs at the Campfire Circle on Loop A from spring through autumn. A picnic area is at the base of Elephant Hill, 3 miles past the campground turnoff. Hiking trails lead into wonderful rock formations and canyons from both the campground and picnic areas. Only experienced drivers in 4WD vehicles should continue past the picnic area up Elephant Hill.

**Pothole Point Nature Trail** is on the left of the main road, 5.0 miles past the ranger station. Highlights of this 0.6-mile loop hike are the many potholes dissolved in the Cedar Mesa Sandstone. A brochure illustrates the fairy shrimp, tadpole shrimp, horsehair worm, snail, and other adaptable creatures that spring to life when rains fill the potholes. You'll also enjoy fine views of distant buttes from the trail.

**Slickrock Trail** begins on the right 6.2 miles past the ranger station. The trail makes a loop of 2.4 miles roundtrip and takes you north to an overlook of the confluence of Big Spring and Little Spring canyons. Hiking is easy and offers good panoramas.

**Big Spring Canyon Overlook,** 6.5 miles past the ranger station, marks the end of the scenic drive but not of the scenery. The **Confluence Overlook Trail** begins here and winds west to an overlook of the Green and Colorado rivers (see below).

## Hiking

The Needles District has about 55 miles of backcountry trails. Many interconnect to provide all sorts of day and overnight trips. Cairns mark all of the trails; signs point the way at junctions. You can normally find water in Elephant Canyon and canyons to the east in spring and early summer, though the remaining water often becomes stagnant by midsummer. Treat water from all sources, including springs, before drinking. Chesler Park and other areas west of Elephant Canyon are very dry; you'll need to bring all water. Mosquitoes, gnats, and deer flies can be very pesky from late spring to midsummer, especially in the wetter places. Bring insect repellent then. To plan your trip, obtain the small hiking map available from the ranger station or Trails Illustrated's Needles District map.

## Confluence Overlook Trail

This trail goes west 5½ miles from Big Spring Canyon Overlook (at the end of the scenic drive) to a fine viewpoint overlooking the Green and Colorado rivers 1,000 feet below. You might see rafts in the water or bighorn sheep on the cliffs. The trail crosses Big Spring and Elephant canyons and follows a jeep road for a short distance. Higher points have good views of the Needles to the south. Except for a few short steep sections, this trail is level and fairly easy. A very early start is recommended in summer, as there's little shade. Carry water even if you don't plan to go all the way. This enchanting country has lured many a hiker beyond his original goal!

## Hiking Trails
### From Squaw Flat Trailhead

The main trailhead sits a short distance south of the campground and is reached by a separate signed road. You can also begin from a trailhead in the campground itself.

**Peekaboo Trail** winds southeast 5 miles (one way) over rugged terrain, including some steep sections of slickrock (best avoided when wet, icy, or snow covered). There's little shade; carry water. The trail follows Squaw Canyon, climbs over a pass to Lost Canyon, then crosses more slickrock before descend-

Chesler Park from its
southern edge
(near the Joint Trail)

ing to Peekaboo Campground on Salt Creek 4WD Road. Look for Anasazi ruins on the way and rock art at the campground. Peekaboo Spring, shown on some maps, was taken out by a rock slide. Options on this trail include a turnoff south through Squaw Canyon or Lost Canyon to make a loop of 8¾ miles or more.

**Squaw Canyon Trail** follows the canyon south for 3¾ miles one way. Intermittent water can often be found until late spring. You can take a connecting trail (Peekaboo, Lost Canyon, and Big Spring Canyon) or cross a slickrock pass to Elephant Canyon.

**Lost Canyon Trail,** 3¼ miles long one way, is reached via Peekaboo or Squaw Canyon trails and makes a loop with them. Water supports abundant vegetation; you may need to wade. Most of the way is in the wash bottom, except for a section of slickrock to Squaw Canyon.

**Big Spring Canyon Trail** crosses an outcrop of slickrock from the trailhead, then follows the canyon bottom to the head of the canyon, 3¾ miles one way. You can usually find intermittent water along the way except in summer. At canyon's end, a climb up steep slickrock (hazardous if covered by snow or ice) takes you to Squaw Canyon Trail and back to the trailhead for a good 7½-mile loop. Another possibility is to turn southwest to the head of Squaw Canyon, then hike over a slickrock saddle to Elephant Canyon for a 10¾-mile loop.

### Hiking Trails
### From Elephant Hill Trailhead

Drive west 3 miles past the campground turnoff to the picnic area and trailhead at the base of Elephant Hill. Sounds of racing engines and burning rubber can often be heard from above as vehicles attempt the difficult 4WD road that begins just past the picnic area. All of the following destinations can also be reached by trails from the Squaw Flat Trailhead, though distances will be slightly greater.

**Chesler Park** is a favorite hiking destination. A lovely desert meadow contrasts with the red and white spires that gave the Needles District its name. An old cowboy line camp is on the west side of the rock island in the center

of the park. Distance on **Chesler Park Trail** is about 6 miles roundtrip. The trail winds through sand and slickrock before ascending a small pass through the Needles to Chesler Park. Once inside, you can take **Chesler Park Loop Trail** (5 miles) completely around the park. The loop includes the unusual ½-mile **Joint Trail** that follows the bottom of a very narrow crack. Camping in Chesler Park is restricted to certain areas; check with a ranger.

**Druid Arch** reminds many people of the massive stone slabs at Stonehenge, popularly associated with the Druids, in southern England. The arch is an 11-mile roundtrip (15 miles if you start at Squaw Flat Trailhead). Follow the Chesler Park Trail 2 miles to Elephant Canyon, turn up the canyon 3¼ miles, then make a ¼-mile strenuous climb up loose rock to the arch. Upper Elephant Canyon has seasonal water but the narrow canyon is closed to camping.

**Lower Red Lake Canyon Trail** provides access to Cataract Canyon of the Colorado River. This is a long strenuous trip best suited for experienced hikers. Distance from the Elephant Hill Trailhead is 19 miles roundtrip; you'll be walking on 4WD roads and trails. Allow ample time. If you can drive Elephant Hill 4WD Road to the trail junction in Cyclone Canyon, the hike is only 8 miles roundtrip. The most difficult trail section is a steep talus slope that drops 700 feet in ½ mile into the lower canyon. Total elevation change is 1,000 feet. The canyon has little shade and lacks any water source above the river. Summer heat can make the trip grueling; temperatures tend to be 5-10° hotter than on other Needles trails. The river level drops between midsummer and autumn, allowing hikers to go along the shore both downstream to see the rapids and upstream to the confluence. Undertows and strong currents make the river dangerous to cross.

### Upper Salt Creek Trail

Several impressive arches and many inviting side canyons attract adventurous hikers to the extreme southeast corner of the park. The trail begins at the end of the 13.5-mile 4WD road up lower Salt Creek, then goes south 12 miles upcanyon to Beef Basin Road near Cathedral Butte, just outside the park boundary. The trail is nearly level except for a steep climb at the end. Water can usually be found. Some wading and bushwhacking are necessary.

**Four-wheel-drive Roads**
A back-road tour allows you to see beautiful canyon scenery, arches, and Indian rock art sites in the Needles District. Check with a ranger about special hazards before setting out. Also obtain a backcountry permit if you plan to use one of the campgrounds available along Salt Creek or in the area past Elephant Hill. Mountain bicyclists enjoy the challenge of going up Elephant Hill Road and the roads beyond. Colorado Overlook 4WD Road is good riding too, but Salt Creek and the other eastern canyons have too much loose sand.

**Salt Creek Canyon 4WD Road** begins near Cave Spring Trail, crosses sage flats for the next 2.5 miles, then heads deep into this spectacular canyon. Roundtrip distance, including a side trip to 150-foot-high Angel Arch, is about 30 miles. **Horse Canyon 4WD Road** turns off to the left shortly before the mouth of Salt Canyon. Roundtrip distance, including a side trip to Tower Ruin, is about 13 miles. Highlights of the 2 canyons include Angel Arch, Paul Bunyan's Potty, Tower Ruin, Peek-a-boo Springs pictographs, Castle Arch, and Fortress Arch. The canyons can easily be driven with 4WD vehicles. Usually Salt Canyon is closed due to quicksand after flash floods in summer or shelf ice in winter.

**Davis Canyon** and **Lavender Canyon** 4WD roads enter their canyons from UT 211, east of the park boundary. Both canyons contain arches and Indian sites and both are easily visited. Davis is about 20 miles roundtrip and Lavender is about 26 miles roundtrip.

**Colorado Overlook 4WD Road** begins beside the ranger station and follows Salt Creek to Lower Jump Overlook. Then it bounces across slickrock to a view of the Colorado River (upstream from the confluence). Driving is easy, though very rough the last 1.5 miles. Roundtrip distance is 14 miles.

**Elephant Hill 4WD Loop Road** begins 3 miles past the Squaw Flat Campground turn-

*Salt Creek's twisting canyon*

off. Only experienced drivers should attempt the extremely rough and steep climb up Elephant Hill. The loop is about 10 miles roundtrip. Connecting roads go to the Confluence Overlook Trailhead (viewpoint is one mile roundtrip on foot), the Joint Trailhead (Chesler Park is 2 miles roundtrip on foot), and several canyons. Some road sections on the loop are one way. The parallel canyons in this area are grabens caused by faulting where a layer of salt has shifted deep underground. In addition to Elephant Hill, several other difficult climbs must be negotiated. These roads can also be reached by a long route south of the park using Beef Basin Road from UT 211, about 60 miles one way. You'll enjoy spectacular vistas from the high country in the foothills of the Abajo Mountains. A *very* steep descent from Pappys Pasture into Bobbys Hole effectively makes this section one way; travel from Elephant Hill past Bobbys Hole is possible but much more difficult than going the other way.

*Newspaper Rock detail*

# UTAH'S SOUTHEASTERN CORNER

## NEWSPAPER ROCK STATE PARK

A profusion of petroglyphs depicts human figures, animals, birds, and abstract designs. These represent 2,000 years of human history during which archaic tribes and Anasazi, Fremont, Paiute, Navajo, and Anglo travelers have passed through Indian Creek Canyon. The patterns on the smooth sandstone rock face stand out clearly, thanks to a coating of dark desert varnish. Newspaper Rock lies just 150 feet off UT 211 on the way to the Needles District of Canyonlands National Park. A ¼-mile nature trail introduces you to the area's desert and riparian vegetation. Picnic areas, which can also be used for camping, lie along Indian Creek across the highway. The park is relatively undeveloped; no drinking water or charge. From US 191 between Moab and Monticello, turn west 12 miles on UT 211.

## CANYON RIMS RECREATION AREA

Viewpoints atop the high mesa east of Canyonlands National Park offer magnificent panoramas of the surrounding area. The BLM has provided 2 fenced overlooks, 2 campgrounds, and good access roads. Other overlooks and scenic spots can be reached on jeep roads or by hiking. Rock formations, canyons, slickrock, and rolling hills are features of the 20-mile-long mesa, shown on maps as Hatch Point. You have a good chance of seeing the graceful antelope-like pronghorn that thrive in this high-desert country. The turnoff for Canyon Rims is at Milepost 93 on US 191, located 32 miles south of Moab and 7 miles north of the UT 211 junction for the Needles District.

### Needles Overlook

Follow the paved road 22 miles west to its end (turn left at the junction 15 miles in). The BLM has a picnic area and interpretive exhibits here. A fence protects visitors from the sheer cliffs that drop off more than 1,000 feet. You can see much of Canyonlands National Park and southeastern Utah. Look south for Six-Shooter Peaks and the high country of the Abajo Mountains; southwest for the Needles (thousands of spires reaching for the heavens); west for the confluence area of the Green and Colorado rivers, the Maze District, the Orange Cliffs, and the Henry Mountains; northwest for the lazy bends of the Colorado River's canyon and the sheer-walled mesas of Island in the Sky and Dead Horse Point; north for the Book Cliffs; and northeast for the La Sal Mountains. The changing shadows and colors of the canyon country present a continuous show throughout the day.

### Anticline Overlook

Head west 15 miles on the paved road, then go straight (north) 17 miles on a good gravel road to the fenced overlook at road's end. Here you're standing 1,600 feet above the Colorado River. The sweeping panorama over the canyons, the river, and the twisted rocks of the Kane Creek Anticline is nearly as spectacular as that from Dead Horse Point, only 5½ miles west as the crow flies. Salt and other minerals of the Paradox Formation pushed up overlying rocks into the dome visible below. Downcutting by the Colorado River has revealed the twisted rock layers. The Moab Salt mine across the river to the north uses a solution technique to bring up potash from the Paradox Formation several thousand feet underground. Pumps then transfer the solution to the blue-tinted evaporation ponds. Look carefully on the northeast horizon to see an arch in the Windows Section of Arches National Park, 16 miles away.

You can reach **Pyramid Butte Overlook** by a gravel road that turns west off the main drive 2 miles before Anticline Overlook; the road goes around a rock monolith to viewpoints on the other side (1.3 miles roundtrip). Vehicles with 4WD can go west out to **Canyonlands Overlook** (17 miles roundtrip) on rough unmarked roads; the turnoff, which may not be

signed, is about 0.3 mile south of the Hatch Point Campground turnoff.

### Campgrounds

Each camping area has water (April to mid-Oct.), tables, grills, and outhouses; there's a small charge for overnight use. **Windwhistle Campground,** backed by cliffs to the south, has fine views to the north and a nature trail; follow the main road from US 191 for 6 miles and turn left. At **Hatch Point Campground,** in a pinyon-juniper woodland, you can enjoy views to the north; go 24 miles in on the paved and gravel roads toward Anticline Overlook, then turn right one mile.

### Trough Springs Trail

Hikers may want to follow this old livestock trail on the east side of Hatch Point. To reach the trailhead, turn east 0.6 mile on a dirt road 5 miles north of the Hatch Point Campground turnoff (or 4 miles south of Anticline Overlook). The trail begins from an abandoned well pad

*pronghorn* (Antilocapra americana)

and follows the canyon to its mouth at Kane Creek Road. The first 1/3 mile follows a jeep road, then cairns mark the way. Carry water. The moderately difficult hike is 5 miles round-trip and has an elevation change of 1,200 feet.

# MONTICELLO

The Mormon settlers who arrived in 1888 found the cool climate more suited to raising sheep and cattle than crops. Monticello (pronounced "mon-ti-SELL-o") lies at an elevation of 7,050 feet just east of the Abajo ("uh-BAH-hoe") Mountains. The small town is the seat of San Juan County (Utah's largest, at 5 million acres) and serves as a base for travelers to visit surrounding mountains and canyons, including the Needles District of Canyonlands National Park. Monticello is 54 miles south of Moab and 21 miles north of Blanding. Highway US 666 (Central) goes east from downtown to the Colorado border (17 miles) and Mesa Verde National Park (89 miles).

The **Monticello Museum** has exhibits of Anasazi artifacts, pioneer memorabilia, historic documents, and mineral specimens; open Mon. to Thurs. 2-8 p.m. and Fri. 2-6 p.m. from June 1 to Aug. 31; downstairs in the library building at the city park, 80 N. Main.

## Accommodations
(Summer rates shown; they drop at some places in winter.) **Canyonlands Motor Inn** is at 197 N. Main; tel. 587-2266; $29.96 s, $34.56 d, has a covered pool, jacuzzi, and sauna. **Navajo Trail Motel** is at 240 N. Main; tel. 587-2251; $28.10 s $30.25 d. **Triangle H Motel** is at 164 E. US 666; tel. 587-2274; starts at $34.56 s, $38.88 d. **Wayside Inn (Best Western)** is at 195 E. US 666; tel. 587-2261; $36.72 s, $39.96 d and up; has a pool. **The Grist Mill Inn** offers unique bed and breakfast accommodations in a restored flour mill; located at 64 S. 300 East; tel. 587-2597; $47.41 s, $56.03 d.

## Campgrounds
**Mountain View RV Park** is open May 1 to Oct. 31 at 632 N. Main; tel. 587-2974; $7.56 tent,

$10.80 w/hookups; has showers and laundry. **Westerner Trailer Park** is at 516 S. Main; tel. 587-2762; $7 tent or RV no hookups, $9 w/hookups; has showers; may close in winter. **Monticello/Canyonlands KOA** is open May 1 to Sept. 30; go 5 miles east on US 666, then 0.5 mile north; tel. 587-2884; $12.90 tent or RV no hookups, $16.66 w/hookups; has showers, store, and pool.

The U.S. Forest Service has 2 campgrounds located nearby on paved roads in the Abajos. **Dalton Springs** (elev. 8,400 ft.) has water early June to early Oct.; $5; go west 5.3 miles on 200 South. **Buckboard** (elev. 8,700 ft.) has water mid-June to early Oct.; $5; go west 6.5 miles on 200 South. Campgrounds may also be open off-season without water or fee.

## Food
**Chuck Wagon Restaurant** serves American food daily for breakfast, lunch, and dinner at 296 N. Main; tel. 587-2803. **Wagon Wheel Pizza** spins out pizza, sandwiches, and Mexican food; open daily (closed Sun. in winter) for lunch and dinner at 164 S. Main; tel. 587-2766. **Juniper Tree Restaurant** features steak, prime rib, roast beef, and other items; open daily for dinner at 133 E. US 666; tel. 587-2870. **Hoagies Restaurant** serves American food and pizza; open daily for breakfast, lunch, and dinner at 216 E. US 666; tel. 587-2550. **La Casita** has Mexican and American food; open Mon. to Sat. for lunch and dinner at 280 E. US 666; tel. 587-2959.

## Entertainment And Events
Watch movies at **The Movies,** 696 E. US 666; tel. 587-2535. **Annual events** include Pioneer Day (parade, softball, games, and food) on July 24, San Juan Amateur Golf Tourney and Mountain Cookout in early Aug., and San Juan County Fair (rodeo, exhibits, and dance) in August.

## Services And Recreation
The **post office** is at 197 S. Main; tel. 587-2294. **San Juan Hospital** provides medical care at 364 W. 100 North; tel. 587-2116. The **city park** has picnic areas and playground at

Main and US 666. A covered swimming pool (open in summer; tel. 587-2907), tennis courts, and ball fields are 3 blocks west of Main on Central. **San Juan Public Golf Course** has 9 holes, pro shop, and snack bar at 549 S. Main (south edge of town); tel. 587-2468. **Four Corners School of Outdoor Education** offers programs on the wildlife, geology, and archaeology of the Southwest; write for a brochure at East Route, Monticello, UT 84535; tel. 587-2859.

**Blue Mountain Ski Area** has 3 downhill runs (2 intermediate, one difficult) on the slopes of the Abajos. A poma tow takes skiers up the mountainside (900 vertical feet) for runs of 2,300-3,500 feet. Season lasts late Nov. to late Feb., snow permitting. Call the Travel Council about snow conditions, instruction, and rentals; tel. 587-3235. Head west 4.8 miles on 200 South, then turn left at the sign.

### Information

Visit the **San Juan Travel Council** for info about San Juan County towns and sights; regional books and maps are sold too; open Mon. to Fri. 8 a.m.-5 p.m.; located in the county courthouse at 117 S. Main (Box 490, Monticello, UT 84535); tel. 587-3235. Stop at the **National Park Service** office to learn about Canyonlands and Arches national parks and Natural Bridges National Monument; books and topo maps of southeastern Utah are sold; open Mon. to Fri. 8 a.m.-4:30 p.m.; 32 S. 100 East (one block east of Main on US 666) or write Box 40, Monticello, UT 84535; tel. 587-2737. The **Bureau of Land Management** (San Juan Resource Area) knows about Grand Gulch, Fish and Owl canyons, Dark Canyon, Arch Canyon, and many other fine hiking areas; they can also advise on backroad travel in San Juan County; books and maps are sold; open Mon. to Fri. 7:45 a.m.-4:30 p.m.; 435 N. Main (Box 7, Monticello, UT 84535); tel. 587-2141. The **Manti-LaSal National Forest** office has information about roads, camping, and hiking in the Abajo Range; their district (Monticello) includes the upper reaches of Dark Canyon; books and topo maps are sold; open Mon. to Fri. 8 a.m.-

noon and 12:30-4:30 p.m.; 496 E. US 666 (Box 820, Monticello, UT 84535); tel. 587-2041. The **public library** has general reading and an extensive collection of southeastern Utah history at 80 N. Main in the city park; open Mon. to Thurs. 2-9 p.m., Fri. 2-6 p.m., and Sat. 10 a.m.-2 p.m.; tel. 587-2281.

## VICINITY OF MONTICELLO

### Abajo Peak

The rounded Abajos, or "Blues" as they're sometimes called, actually rise higher than they seem to. Early Spanish explorers climbed the La Sals to the northeast and named these mountains "Abajo" (below). Intrusive volcanic rocks created the range in much the same way as they formed the Henry and La Sal mountains. Abajo Peak tops the range at 11,362 feet. Easiest way to the summit is by road; you'll need a high-clearance vehicle. Head west 0.8 mile on 200 South, then turn left about 12 miles on South Creek Road. Hikers can drive to the pass just northwest of Abajo Peak and head cross-country for about one mile to the top; to reach the pass, go west 5.5 miles on 200 South, then turn left 3.5 miles on Forest Route 079 up North Canyon. Another way to the summit is to hike along the ski lift and climb the ridge to the southwest. The Manti-LaSal forest map shows backroads and trails of the area. For more detail see the Trails Illustrated topo map of Dark Canyon and the Abajos. The U.S.G.S. maps are the 15-minute Monticello topo map for the Abajo Peak area and the 15-minute Mt. Linnaeus map for places farther west; the metric 1:100,000 Blanding map covers nearly all the range.

You can enjoy several scenic drives in the Abajos with a high-clearance vehicle. The range can be crossed to Blanding by heading west on 200 South, turning southwest on Forest Route 079 up North Canyon, then descending along Johnson Creek (about 37 miles total one way). A rougher, all-day drive branches west off Forest Route 079 to Elk Ridge and continues to UT 95 near Natural

Bridges National Monument. Cars with good clearance can often do these trips; ask at the U.S. Forest Service office in Monticello. Besides using the Blue Mountain Ski Area, winter visitors cross-country ski and go snowmobiling.

## BLANDING

The largest town in San Juan County, Blanding (pop. 3,800) is also a handy travelers' stop. The state park on the northwest edge of town provides an excellent introduction to the Anasazi Indians, who left behind many ruins in the Four Corners area. Pioneers began work on an irrigation system in 1897 to bring water from the Abajo Mountains to the rich soil of White Mesa. The first families arrived at the townsite, then known as Sidon, in 1905. Many of the Mormon farmers who followed had been driven from Mexico by political and religious intolerance or had lost their farms to floods at nearby Bluff. Residents apparently liked to change the name of their community. Originally known as Sidon, the town became Grayson, then Blanding. The story goes that in 1915 townsfolk jumped at the offer of a free library by Thomas W. Bicknell on the condition that they name their town after him. The town of Thurber in central Utah also wanted the library, so it was divided between the 2 communities; Thurber became Bicknell and Grayson became Blanding, the maiden name of Mrs. Bicknell.

*Anasazi cup*

## Edge Of The Cedars State Park

Prehistoric Anasazi Indians built at least 6 groups of pueblo structures between A.D. 700 and 1220 just outside present-day Blanding. The state museum features an excellent array of pottery, baskets, sandals, jewelry, and stone tools. The pottery collection on the second floor stands out for its rich variety of styles and decorative designs. Other displays illustrate Anasazi life and how archaeologists have learned about these ancient peoples through studies of stratigraphy, dendrochronology, and village layouts. The Special Exhibits room has changing exhibits related to the region and inhabitants. An observation tower in the museum provides panoramic views of the ruins outside and of mountains in 4 states; signs identify the features.

A short trail behind the museum leads past 6 clusters of ruins, each of which contains both rectangular rooms on the surface and circular depressions of underground kivas or pithouses. Only Complex 4 has been excavated and partly restored to give an idea of the village's appearance when the Anasazi lived here. You may enter the kiva by descending a ladder through the restored roof; the walls and interior features are original. The other 5 ruin groups haven't been restored and require some imagination. A large pit near Complex 4 is all that remains of a great kiva, a structure rarely seen this far north. Edge of the Cedars likely served as an important community center in its day.

The museum also has exhibits and artifacts of the people who followed the Anasazi—the Ute and Navajo Indians and the early Anglo pioneers. You may enter a Navajo hogan outside. Films and slide presentations, shown on request in the auditorium, illustrate Anasazi, Navajo, and pioneer cultures. There's often an art or photo exhibition in the auditorium, too. Books on the region's Indians and pioneer history are sold. Picnic tables outside provide a spot for having lunch. Edge of the Cedars is open daily 9 a.m.-6 p.m. from May 16 to Sept. 15, then daily 9 a.m.-5 p.m. the rest of the year; closed Thanksgiving Day, Christmas Day, New Year's Day, Civil Rights Day and

Presidents' Day; $1/person or $3/vehicle (whichever is less); tel. 678-2238. Head west on Center from downtown and follow signs one mile.

## PRACTICALITIES

### Accommodations

The **Gateway Motel (Best Western)** is at 88 E. Center; tel. 678-2278; $40.85 s, $45.15 d and up; has a pool. **Cliff Palace Motel** is at 132 S. Main; tel. 678-2264; $24.60 s, $28.40 d. **Prospector Motor Lodge** is at 591 S. Hwy. 191 (south edge of town); tel. 678-3231; $26.30 s, $31.70 d. **The Old Hotel Bed & Breakfast** features rooms in a Victorian house at 118 E. 300 South (turn east one block at Cedar Mesa Pottery); tel. 678-2388; $40 s, $47-55 d; closed in winter.

### Campgrounds

**KamPark** has showers and spaces on S. Hwy. 191 (south edge of town); tel. 678-2770; $7 tent, $10 RV no hookups, $12.50 w/hookups. **Devil's Canyon Campground** (elev. 7,100 ft.) in the Manti-LaSal National Forest has sites with water from early May to late Oct.; $6, no water or fee off season; a ¼-mile nature trail begins at the far end of the campground loop. Go north 8 miles on US 191, then west 1.3 miles on a paved road (turnoff is between Mileposts 60 and 61).

### Food

**Elk Ridge Restaurant** offers a varied American menu with a few Mexican items; open daily for breakfast, lunch, and dinner (except closed Sun. lunch) at 123 E. Center; tel. 678-9982. **Kenny's Restaurant** is an American cafe offering some Mexican dishes; open daily for breakfast, lunch, and dinner on N. Hwy. 191; tel. 678-9986. **Patio Drive-In, Mr. Bee's,** and **Pronto Deli** have fast food on N. Hwy. 191.

### Events and Services

A 3-day **Fourth of July Celebration** has fireworks, parade, horse events, meller-dramas, and a mudbog competition. Navajo and Ute Indians produce handpainted ceramics at **Cedar Mesa Pottery,** Main and 300 South; you can step in the adjacent factory on weekdays to watch the craftspeople at work; tel. 678-2241. **Blue Mountain Trading Post,** one mile south of town, has a large selection of high-quality Indian art and crafts; the adaptable Navajo produce much of the work—even the kachina dolls; tel. 678-2570. **Huck's Museum and Trading Post** has a large private collection of prehistoric Indian artifacts and a gift shop offering crafts by Navajo and other modern tribes; regional books are sold too; the museum costs $2 adult, $1 children; located in a log building on the south edge of town; tel. 678-2329/2946. **White Mesa Institute,** sponsored by the College of Eastern Utah, offers educational programs for youth and adults on Southwest archaeology, modern Indian tribes, pioneer history, wildlife, and geology; 639 W. 100 South (50-1), Blanding, UT 84511. The **post office** is at the corner of Main and 100 North; tel. 678-2627. **Blanding Clinic** provides medical services at 930 N. 400 West; tel. 678-2254; or contact the county hospital in Monticello; tel. 678-2830.

### Recreation

**Blanding Pool** and a tennis court are at 50 West and 200 South; tel. 678-2157. **Reservoir Park** (picnic area and playground) and the 9-hole **Blanding Golf Course** are north 3 miles on 300 West; the small reservoir has trout fishing. **Recapture Reservoir** offers boating and trout fishing 3 miles northeast of town; head northeast 1.3 miles on US 191, turn left (north) on a paved road between Mileposts 53 and 54 (just before the highway enters a road cut), then go 1.7 miles to the lake's southern shore; this road is the old highway and makes a good boat ramp where submerged. For access to the north and west sides of the reservoir, follow US 191 across the dam, continue 0.5 mile, then turn west on a gravel road. Fishermen can also turn in at either end of the dam to fish from the shore. No facilities are at the reservoir, though people sometimes camp (west end is best).

**Information And Tours**

Staff at the state park know about Blanding and can tell you of other Anasazi ruins in the area. The **public library** is at Main and 300 South; open Mon. to Sat.; tel. 678-2335.

Flights by **Scenic Aviation** go over spectacular country. Some destinations with costs per person (based on 2 or more) include: Comb Reef and nearby canyons (½ hour; $23), Canyonlands National Park (one hour; $45), Canyonlands N.P. and Lake Powell (1¾ hours; $80), Monument Valley (1¼ hours; $55), and Monument Valley, Rainbow Bridge, and San Juan River (1¾ hours; $80); tel. 678-3222 or (800) 888-6166. The airport is 3 miles south of town.

# HOVENWEEP NATIONAL MONUMENT

The Anasazi Indians built many impressive masonry buildings during their 350-year stay here. A drought beginning in A.D. 1274 and lasting 25 years probably caused their departure from this area. Also, several centuries of intensive farming, hunting, and woodcutting had already taken their toll on the land. Archaeologists believe the inhabitants retreated south sometime after 1277 to sites in northwestern New Mexico and northeastern Arizona. The Ute Indian word Hovenweep means "Deserted Valley," an appropriate name for the lonely high-desert country left behind. The Anasazi at Hovenweep had much in common with the Mesa Verde culture, though the Dakota Sandstone here doesn't form large alcoves suitable for cliff-dweller villages. Ruins at Hovenweep remain essentially unexcavated, awaiting some future archaeologist's trowel.

The Anasazi farmers had a keen interest in the seasons because of their need to know the best time for planting crops. Astronomical stations (alignments of walls, doorways, and tiny openings) allowed the sun priests to determine the equinoxes and solstices with an accuracy of one or 2 days. This precision also may have been necessary for a complex ceremonial calendar. Astronomical stations at Hovenweep have been discovered at Hovenweep Castle and Unit-Type House of Square Tower Ruins and at Cajon Ruins.

**Visitor Center And Campground**

Hovenweep National Monument protects 6 groups of villages left behind by the Anasazi. The sites lie near the Colorado border southeast of Blanding. Square Tower Ruins Unit, where the visitor center is located, has the greatest number of ruins and the most varied architecture. In fact, you can find all of the Hovenweep architectural styles here. The visitor center has a few exhibits on the Anasazi and photos of local wildlife. A ranger will answer your questions, provide brochures and handouts about various aspects of the monument, and give directions for visiting the other ruin groups. Related books can be purchased. Hours at the visitor center are 8 a.m.-5 p.m. year-round; the ruins stay open all the time. Mesa Verde National Park administers Hovenweep at Mesa Verde National Park, CO 81330; tel. (303) 529-4465. The campground, one mile from the visitor center, is open all year; from April to Oct. it has water, restrooms, and a $3 fee. The closest accommodations are at Blanding and Bluff in Utah and Cortez in Colorado. Nearest places for groceries and fuel are Hatch Trading Post (16 miles west in Utah) and Ismay Trading Post (14 miles southeast in Colorado). One approach from US 191 between Blanding and Bluff is to head east 9 miles on UT 262, continue straight 6 miles on a small paved road to Hatch Trading Post, then follow signs 16 miles. A good way in from Bluff is to go west 21 miles on the paved road to Montezuma Creek and Aneth, then follow signs north 20 miles. A scenic 58-mile route through Montezuma Canyon begins 5 miles south of Monticello and follows unpaved roads to Hatch and on to Hovenweep. From Colorado, take a partly paved road west 29 miles from US 666 (turnoff is 4 miles south of Cortez), then follow signs north 10 miles.

**Square Tower Ruins**

This extensive group of Anasazi towers and dwellings lines the rim and slopes of Little Ruin Canyon, a short walk from the visitor center.

Obtain a trail guide booklet from the ranger station; the booklet's map shows the several loop trails. You can take easy walks of less than ½ mile on the rim or combine all the trails for a loop of about 2 miles with some up and down sections in the canyon. The booklet has good descriptions of Anasazi life and architecture and of the plants growing along the trail. You'll see towers (D-shaped, square, oval, and round), cliff dwellings, surface dwellings, storehouses, kivas, and rock art. Take care not to disturb the fragile ruins. Keep an eye out for the prairie rattlesnake (a subspecies of the western rattlesnake), which is active at night in summer and during the day in spring and autumn. Please stay on the trail—don't climb ruin walls or walk on rubble mounds.

### Other Ruins

These are good to visit if you'd like to spend more time in the area. You'll need a map and directions from a ranger to find them, as they aren't signed. One group, the Goodman Point near Cortez (CO), has relatively little to see except unexcavated mounds.

**Holly Ruins** group is noted for its Great House, Holly Tower, and Tilted Tower. Most of Tilted Tower fell away after shifting of the boulder on which it sat. Great piles of rubble mark the sites of structures built on loose ground. Look for remnants of farming terraces in the canyon below the Great House. A hiking trail connects the campground at Square Tower Ruins with Holly Ruin; the route follows canyon bottoms and is about 8 miles roundtrip. Ask a ranger for a map and directions. Hikers could also continue to Horseshoe Ruins (one mile farther) and Hackberry Ruins (⅓ mile beyond Horseshoe). All of these lie just across the Colorado border and about 6 miles (one way) by road from the visitor center.

**Horseshoe** and **Hackberry** ruins are best reached by an easy trail (one mile roundtrip) off the road to Holly Ruins. Horseshoe House, built in a horseshoe shape similar to Sun Temple at Mesa Verde, has exceptionally good masonry work. Archaeologists haven't determined the purpose of the structure. An alcove in the canyon below contains a spring and small shelter. A round tower nearby on the rim has a strategic view. Hackberry House has only one room still intact. Rubble piles and wall remnants abound in the area. The spring under an alcove here still has a good flow and supports lush growths of hackberry and cottonwood trees along with smaller plants.

**Cutthroat Castle Ruins** were remote even in Anasazi times. The ruins lie along an intermittent stream rather than at the head of a canyon like most other Hovenweep sites. Cutthroat Castle is a large multistory structure with both straight and curved walls. Three round towers stand nearby. Look for wall fragments and circular depressions of kivas. High-clearance vehicles can go close to the ruins, about 11.5 miles (one way) from the visitor center. Visitors with cars can drive to a trailhead and then walk to the ruins (1½ miles roundtrip on foot).

**Cajon Ruins** are at the head of a little canyon on Cajon Mesa in the Navajo Reservation in Utah, about 9 miles southwest of the visitor center. The site has a commanding view across the San Juan Valley as far as Monument Valley. Buildings include a large multiroom structure, a round tower, and a tall square tower. An alcove just below has a spring and some rooms. Look for pictographs, petroglyphs, and grooves in rock (used for tool grinding). Farming terraces were located on the canyon's south side.

# BLUFF

The 1880 Hole-in-the-Rock Expedition arrived here after an epic journey by wagon train from Escalante. Too tired to go any farther, they chose this section of the San Juan River canyon in which to plant their fields and build new homes. They hoped that their presence here would secure the region for Mormon settlement and lead to conversion of the Indians. The settlers tried repeatedly to farm the fertile canyon soils, only to have the river wash their fields away. Most residents gave up and moved to more promising areas, but many of those who stayed prospered with large cattle herds. Today Bluff is a sleepy community of about 250 inhabitants. Take the signed "Bluff

*Tower at Cajon Ruins. Archaeologists recently removed the small ring of stones at upper left (reconstructed earlier this century) because the ring wasn't authentic.*

City Historic Loop" to see pioneer houses along the back streets. Many visitors also drive to the cemetery atop a small hill to read inscriptions and enjoy views of the valley (turn in beside Turquoise RV Park, turn left just past the Decker house, and follow the paved road to the top). Indians from the Navajo Reservation across the river occasionally have dance performances, horse races, rodeos, and other get-togethers in Bluff.

## Accommodations
**Recapture Lodge** offers rooms and kitchenettes ($25.80 s, $27.95 d and up), swimming pool, laundromat, and tours. Groups can reserve rooms in the 1898 Decker pioneer house. The owners know of Indian ruins and scenic places in the backcountry. They offer free slide shows in the evenings during the season and can suggest places to go. Or you

can take one of their organized naturalist tours to Monument Valley, Comb Ridge, Recapture Pocket, and other locations; $55 full day (minimum of 4 persons). Guided camping trips can also be arranged in the canyon country of southeastern Utah. Contact Recapture Lodge at Box 309, Bluff, UT 84512; tel. 672-2281. **Kokopelli Inn Motel** to the south has rooms at $26.88-45.15 s, $31.18-49.45 d (the higher rates apply in summer); tel. 672-2322/2221. **Mokee Motel** on the south edge of town has rooms for $26 s, $30 d; tel. 672-2217. **Bluff Bed & Breakfast** lies in a secluded canyon spot on the northeast edge of town; $53.75 s, $59.13 d; tel. 672-2220.

## Campgrounds
**K&C Store** has sites for tents ($4.30) and RVs ($8.60 no hookups, $12.90 w/hookups); no showers; tel. 672-2221. **Turquoise RV Park** offers sites for self-contained RVs, $8.48 w/hookups (no tents); tel. 672-2219. **Sand Island Recreation Area** is a primitive camping area along the San Juan River, 3 miles south of town; large cottonwood trees shade this pretty spot; no drinking water or charge; tenters need to watch for thorns in the grass. River runners often put in at the campground. You can see a panel of pictographs along the cliff ⅓ mile downstream of the camping area along a gravel road.

## Food And Shopping
**Cow Canyon Cafe** serves homemade dinners in an old trading post on the northeast edge of town; open Thurs. to Mon. from May to Oct.; the trading post is open all year with Indian crafts; tel. 672-2208. The **Sunbonnet Cafe** on the Bluff City Historic Loop has American and Indian foods, including Navajo tacos; open daily (summer only) for breakfast, lunch, and dinner. **Turquoise Restaurant** is a small cafe offering steaks, chops, Navajo tacos, sandwiches, and other items; open daily for breakfast, lunch, and dinner on the main highway. The **Dairy Cafe** has fast food. **Twin Rocks Trading Post** offers a good selection of high-quality Indian crafts, much of it produced locally by Navajo Indians; on the Bluff City Historic Loop.

**River Trips**
**Wild Rivers Expeditions** offers a variety of oar-powered raft and dory trips on the San Juan River. Day excursions to Mexican Hat cost $60 (motors may be used if water level is low). Other trips go from Bluff to Mexican Hat in 2-3 days ($248-362, with a minimum of 6 fares) and all the way to Lake Powell in 5-6 days ($632-718, with a minimum of 6 fares). Mexican Hat to Lake Powell takes 3-4 days ($415-481, with a minimum of 6 fares). The Montezuma Creek to Mexican Hat trip lasts 4 days and specializes in archaeological sites along the river ($470, with a minimum of 6). Boating through Cataract Canyon takes 5-8 days by oar-powered raft ($675-1075, with a minimum of 6). Office is on the main highway through town, or write Box 118, Bluff, UT 84512; tel. 672-2244 or (800) 422-7654 out of state. See "Mexican Hat" p. 407 for other river tours and "River Running on the San Juan" pp. 408-409 for a description of the river.

## VICINITY OF BLUFF

The canyon country of Cedar Mesa, Comb Ridge, and other nearby areas has beautiful scenery, Anasazi ruins, and abundant wildlife. Recapture Pocket has unusual rock formations (it's *west* of Recapture Creek, not east as some maps show). Local information should be obtained for backcountry trips.

**St. Christopher's Episcopal Mission**
Father Harold Lieber came to the Bluff area in 1943 and established this mission for the Navajo Indians. Relying on donations and volunteer help, he built a school, chapel, and other buildings. The current priest, Father Steven Plummer, is Navajo. Visitors are welcome to the pleasant tree-shaded grounds; go east 2 miles on the paved road from the northeast edge of Bluff.

**San Juan Footbridge**
**And 14-Window Ruin**
An easy walk of about 2 miles roundtrip crosses a suspension bridge over the San Juan River and follows roads to this Anasazi cliff dwelling. From Bluff, drive east 2 miles on the paved road to St. Christopher's Episcopal Mission, continue straight 1.3 miles, and turn right 0.5 mile on a dirt road (it may not be signed; keep right at a fork 0.1 mile in) to the footbridge. Walk across the bridge, follow dirt roads winding southeast about ½ mile to a road running beneath the cliffs, turn right (west) ½ mile, and look for the ruins in an alcove on the left. You can scramble up for a closer look. The walk passes farm lands on the Navajo Reservation; please resist the temptation to take shortcuts across the fields.

## WEST OF BLANDING TO NATURAL BRIDGES NATIONAL MONUMENT

Highway UT 95 turns west from US 191 4 miles south of Blanding and crosses Comb Ridge, Cedar Mesa, and many canyons. Follow UT 95 to Natural Bridges National Monument or continue on to Hite Marina at Lake Powell. UT 261 turns south along Cedar Mesa before twisting down the hairpin curves of the Moki Dugway north of Mexican Hat. UT 276 turns off for Halls Crossing Marina and the ferry across Lake Powell to Bullfrog Marina. Fill up with gas before venturing out on UT 95; you won't find any gas stations on the highway after turning off US 191 until Hanksville, 122 miles away. Hite and the other Lake Powell marinas do have gas and supplies, however.

Cedar Mesa and its canyons have an exceptionally large number of prehistoric Anasazi Indian sites. Several groups of ruins lie just off the highway. Hikers will discover many more. If you would like to explore the Cedar Mesa area, be sure to drop in at the **Kane Gulch Ranger Station,** located 4 miles south on UT 261 from UT 95; see p. 405. Bureau of Land Management (BLM) staff issue the free permits required to explore the Cedar Mesa backcountry; BLM people will also tell you about archaeological sites and their values, current hiking conditions, and locations of water.

## Butler Wash Ruins

Well-preserved pueblo ruins left by the Anasazi lie tucked under an overhang across the wash, 11 miles west on UT 95 (between Mileposts 111 and 112) from US 191. At the trailhead on the north side of the highway, follow cairns ½ mile through juniper and pinyon pine woodlands and across slickrock to the overlook.

**Butler Wash Road** turns south from the highway one mile east of the ruins turnoff; drivers with high-clearance vehicles can follow the winding road through a remote land of majestic rock formations to US 163 at a point 5 miles southwest of Bluff.

## Comb Ridge

Geologic forces have squeezed up the earth's crust in a long ridge running 80 miles south from the Abajo Mountains into Arizona. Sheer cliff faces plunge 800 feet into Comb Wash on the west side. Engineering the highway down these cliffs took considerable effort. A parking area near the top of the grade offers expansive panoramas across Comb Wash. The overlook is between Mileposts 108 and 109, 2.5 miles west of Butler Wash ruins. A jeep road runs south through Comb Wash to US 163 at a point about 8 miles southwest of Bluff.

In 1923, the West's last shoot-out between Indians and settlers took place in the Comb Ridge area. Conflicts between Ute Indians and ranchers had simmered for 57 years, with the white men taking the Indian's land and the Utes taking the white men's livestock. A group of renegade Utes under Chief Posey fled to this rugged area, knowing that the Blanding posse would have great difficulty in finding the few trails that existed then. The posse, however, caught up with the Indians, killing one of them. The disheartened Utes then surrendered. Old Posey, who had been shot earlier in Blanding, evaded capture only to die of his wounds about a week later, alone in a cave. The event drew national attention to the plight of the tribe, which was later given the White Mesa Indian Reservation 12 miles south of Blanding.

## Arch Canyon

This tributary canyon of Comb Wash has spectacular scenery and many Indian ruins. Much of the canyon can be seen on a day hike, but 2 or 3 days are needed to explore the upper reaches. The main streambeds usually have water (purify before drinking). To reach the trailhead, turn north 2.5 miles on a dirt road in Comb Wash (between Mileposts 107 and 108 of UT 95); go past a house and water tank, then park in a grove of cottonwood trees before a stream ford. This is also a good place to camp. The mouth of Arch Canyon lies just to the northwest (it's easy to miss!). Sign in at the register here. Look for an Indian ruin just up Arch Canyon on the right. More ruins lie tucked under alcoves farther upcanyon. From the trailhead (elev. 5,200 ft.), the canyon extends about 13 miles upstream into Elk Ridge and has several tributary canyons worth exploring. The first one is 2½ miles up on the right; it goes in 1½ miles to a ruin and spring. A second canyon on the right 6 miles up the main canyon also has a ruin and springs 1½ miles up. You'll reach Texas Canyon on the left 7½ miles up (elev. 5,600 ft.) in a grove of ponderosa pines; look across Arch Canyon from this junction to see a large arch. Texas Canyon goes back about 5 miles and has one fork. Continuing up Arch Canyon, you'll see a second arch on the right, then Butts Canyon on the right, 9 miles from the trailhead. From this point, Arch and Butts canyons each extend about 4 miles to their heads (elev. 7,500 ft.). Spring and autumn are the best times for hiking, though the upper reaches can be fine in summer too. In late spring and early summer, arm yourself with long pants and insect repellent against the deer flies. Most of the route follows the canyon bottoms; sometimes off-road vehicles travel the lower few miles. See the 15-minute Bears Ears and Brushy Basin Wash or the 1:100,000 Blanding topo maps; note that the highway was realigned after the Brushy Basin Wash map was published. The BLM offices at Kane Gulch or Monticello can advise on hiking.

## Arch Canyon Overlook

A road and short trail to the rim of Arch Canyon provide a beautiful view into the depths. Turn north 4 miles on Texas Flat Road (County 263) from UT 95 between Mileposts 102 and 103, park just before the road begins a steep climb, and walk east on an old jeep road about ¼ mile to the rim. This is a fine place for a picnic, although it has no facilities or guardrails. Texas Flat Road is dirt but OK when dry for cars with good clearance. Trucks can continue up the steep hill to other viewpoints of Arch and Texas canyons.

## Cave Towers

The Anasazi Indians constructed 7 circular towers of stone at the head of a small tributary of Mule Canyon. Parts of 3 towers still stand and you'll see remains of the other structures. Musical sounds of water rise from springs below the rim. These ruins aren't stabilized—be careful not to touch them or to let children get close. Turn south 0.3 mile from UT 95 on an unsigned dirt road 0.4 mile west of Milepost 103 (0.3 mile east of the Texas Flat Road junction) and go through 2 gates. Park before the road becomes too rough. Those in cars should walk the last ½ mile on the jeep road to the towers.

## Mule Canyon Ruin

Archaeologists have excavated and stabilized this Anasazi village on the gentle slope of Mule Canyon's South Fork. A stone kiva, circular tower, and 12-room structure can be seen, all originally connected by tunnels. Cave Towers (see above), 2 miles to the southeast, would have been visible from the top of the tower here. Signs describe the ruin and periods of Anasazi development. Turn north 0.3 mile on a paved road from UT 95 between Mileposts 101 and 102. Hikers can explore other Indian ruins in North and South forks of Mule Canyon; check with the Kane Gulch Ranger Station for advice and directions. You might see pieces of pottery and other artifacts in this area. Please leave *every* piece in place so future visitors can enjoy the discovery too. Federal laws also prohibit removal of artifacts.

# NATURAL BRIDGES NATIONAL MONUMENT

Streams in White Canyon and its tributaries cut deep canyons, then formed 3 impressive bridges. Silt-laden floodwaters sculpted the bridges by gouging tunnels between closely spaced loops in the meandering canyons. You can distinguish a natural bridge from an arch because the bridge spans a stream bed and was initially carved out of the rock by flowing water. These in the monument illustrate 3 different stages of development, from the massive, newly formed Kachina Bridge, to the middle-aged Sipapu Bridge, to the delicate and fragile span of Owachomo. All 3 natural bridges will continue to widen and eventually collapse under their own weight. A 9-mile scenic drive has overlooks of the picturesque bridges, Anasazi ruins, and the twisting canyons. You can follow short trails down from the rim to the base of each bridge or hike through all 3 bridges on an 8.6-mile trail loop. Paved highways allow easy access to the monument from 4 directions: from Blanding, drive 42 miles west on UT 95; from Hite Marina, drive 50 miles southeast on UT 95; from Halls Crossing Marina, drive 59 miles northeast on UT 263; or from Mexican Hat, drive 44 miles north via UT 261 (there's a 3-mile section of steep unpaved switchbacks). The National Park Service has a visitor center and a small campground.

## History

Ruins, artifacts, and rock art indicate a long Indian occupation by tribes ranging from archaic groups to the Anasazi. Many fine cliff dwellings built by the Anasazi still stand. In 1883, prospector Cass Hite passed on tales of the huge stone bridges that he had discovered on a trip up White Canyon. Adventurous travelers, including a 1904 *National Geographic* magazine expedition, visited this isolated region to marvel at the bridges. The public's desire for their protection led President Theodore Roosevelt to proclaim the area

a national monument in 1908. Federal admin-
istrators then changed the original bridge
names of "Edwin," "Augusta," and "Caroline"
to the Hopi names used today. Although the
Hopi never lived here, the Anasazi of White
Canyon very likely have descendants in the
modern Hopi villages in Arizona.

**Visitor Center**
From the signed junction on UT 95, drive in
4.5 miles on UT 275 to the visitor center (elev.
6,505 ft.). Monument Valley Overlook, 2 miles
in, has a panorama south across a vast ex-
panse of pinyon pine and juniper trees to
Monument Valley and distant mountains. A
slide show in the visitor center illustrates how
geologic forces and erosion created the canyons and natural bridges. Exhibits introduce
the Indians who once lived here, as well as the
geology, wildlife, and plants. Outside in front,
labels identify common plants of the monument. Rangers will answer your questions
about the monument and surrounding area.
You can purchase regional books, topo and
geologic maps, postcards, slides, and film.
Checklists of birds, other wildlife, and plants
are available on request. Hours at the visitor
center are daily 8 a.m.-4:30 p.m. all year,
except closed Thanksgiving, Christmas, New
Years, and Civil Rights Day. Admission is $3/
vehicle ($1 bicyclist or bus passenger). The
Bridge View Drive is always open during daylight hours except after heavy snow storms. A
winter visit can be very enjoyable; ice or mud
often close the steep Sipapu and Kachina
trails, but the short trail to Owachomo Bridge
usually stays open. Pets aren't allowed on the
trails or in the backcountry at any time. Address is Box 1, Natural Bridges, Lake Powell,
UT 84533; tel. 259-5174. Nearest accommodations and groceries are at Fry Canyon, 26
miles northwest of the visitor center on UT 95;
closest gas is 50 miles away at Hite.

**Photovoltaic Array**
Although inoperative at press time, a large
solar electric-power station sits across the
road from the visitor center. This demonstration system, the largest in the world when

constructed in 1980, had a quarter-million
solar cells spread over nearly an acre and
produced up to 100 kilowatts. Batteries, located elsewhere, stored a 2-day supply of
power. The monument lies far from the nearest power lines, and the solar cells provided
an alternative to continuous running of diesel-
powered generators.

**Campground**
Drive 0.3 mile past the visitor center and turn
right into the campground, set in a forest of
pinyon pine and juniper. Sites stay open all
year; no water or charge. Obtain water from a
faucet in front of the visitor center. Rangers
give talks several evenings each week during
the summer season. The campground is often
full, but you can easily drive to several parking
areas just outside the monument; their locations are shown on maps on the campground
and visitor center bulletin boards. RVs or
trailers more than 21 feet long will also have
to use these parking areas.

**Bridge View Drive**
The 9-mile drive begins its one-way loop just
past the campground. A booklet available at
the visitor center describes what you can see
at the numbered stops along the way and on
several short trails. A picnic area is between
Stops #5 and #6 (2.3 miles from the visitor
center). Allow about 1½ hours for a quick trip
around. To make all the stops and do a bit of
leisurely hiking will take most of a day. The
crossbedded sandstone of the bridges and
canyons is the 225-million-year-old Cedar
Mesa Formation.
   **Sipapu Bridge** viewpoint is at Stop #5, 2
miles from the visitor center. The Hopi name
refers to the gateway from which their ancestors entered this world from another world
below. Sipapu Bridge has reached its mature
or middle-aged stage of development. The
bridge is the largest in the monument and has
a span of 268 feet and a height of 220 feet.
Many people think Sipapu the most magnificent. Another view and a trail to the base of
Sipapu are at Stop #6, 0.8 mile farther. The
viewpoint is about halfway down on an easy

trail; allow ½ hour. A steeper and rougher trail branches off the viewpoint trail and winds down to the bottom of White Canyon, probably the best place to fully appreciate the bridge's size. Total roundtrip distance is 1.2 miles with an elevation change of 600 feet.

**Horse Collar Ruin,** built by the Anasazi, looks as though it has been abandoned only a few decades, not 800 years. A short trail leads to an overlook from Stop #7, 3.1 miles from the visitor center. The name comes from the shape of the doorway openings in 2 storage rooms. Hikers walking in the canyon between Sipapu and Kachina bridges can scramble up a steep rock slope to the site. Like all ancient ruins, these are very fragile and must not be touched or entered. Only with such care will future generations of visitors be able to admire the well-preserved structures. Other groups of Anasazi dwellings can be seen in and near the monument too; ask a ranger for directions.

**Kachina Bridge** viewpoint and trailhead are at Stop #9, 5.1 miles from the visitor center. The massive bridge has a span of 204 feet and a height of 210 feet. A trail, 1½ miles roundtrip, leads to the canyon bottom next to the bridge; elevation change is 650 feet. Look for pictographs near the base of the trail. Some of the figures resemble Hopi kachinas (spirits) and prompted the bridge's name. Armstrong Canyon joins White Canyon just downstream from the bridge; floods in each canyon abraded opposite sides of the rock fin that later became Kachina Bridge.

**Owachomo Bridge** viewpoint and trailhead are at Stop #10, 7.1 miles from the visitor center. An easy walk leads to Owachomo's base, ½ mile roundtrip with an elevation change of 180 feet. Graceful Owachomo spans 180 feet and is 106 feet high. Erosive forces have worn the venerable bridge to a thickness of only 9 feet. Unlike the other 2 bridges, Owachomo spans a smaller tributary stream instead of a major canyon. Two streams played a role in the bridge's formation. Floods coming down the larger Armstrong Canyon surged against a sandstone fin on one side while floods in Tuwa Canyon wore away the rock on the other side. Eventually a

hole formed, and waters flowing down Tuwa took the shorter route through the bridge. The name Owachomo means "flat-rock mound" in the Hopi language; a large rock outcrop nearby inspired the name. Before construction of the present road, a trail winding down the opposite side of Armstrong Canyon provided the only access for monument visitors. The trail, little used now, connects with UT 95.

**Sunset Point,** near the end of the loop drive, offers a good vantage point to enjoy the last rays of the sun if you're here late in the day. Distance is 9.1 miles from the visitor center.

### Hiking

A canyon hike through all 3 bridges can be the highlight of a visit to the monument. Unmaintained trails make an 8.6-mile loop in White and Armstrong canyons and cross a wooded plateau. The trip is easier if you start from

*Owachomo Bridge (from Armstrong Canyon)*

Sipapu and come out the relatively gentle grades at Owachomo. Most people take 5-6 hours for this moderately difficult hike. You can save 2½ miles by arranging a car shuttle between Sipapu and Owachomo trailheads. Another option is to go in or out on the Kachina Bridge Trail midway, cutting the hiking distance in about half. On nearing Owachomo Bridge from below, a small sign points out the trail which bypasses a deep pool. The canyons remain in their wild state; you'll need some hiking experience, proper footwear, canteen, compass, and map (the handout available at the visitor center is adequate). U.S.G.S. 15-minute and 7½-minute topo maps also cover this area. When hiking in the canyons, keep an eye out for natural arches and Indian writings. Please don't step on midget faded and Hopi rattlesnakes or other creatures. Be aware of flash-flood dangers, especially if you see big clouds billowing into the sky in an upstream direction. You don't need hiking permits, though it's a good idea to talk beforehand with a ranger to find out current conditions. Overnight camping within the monument is permitted only in the campground. Backpackers, however, can go up or down the canyons and camp outside the monument boundaries. Just be careful to choose high ground in case a flood comes rumbling through! Note that vehicles can't be parked overnight on the loop drive.

# VICINITY OF NATURAL BRIDGES NATIONAL MONUMENT

## Fry Canyon

The store here originally served uranium mining camps during the 1950s. Today the combination of store, cafe, motel, and campground offers the only services on UT 95 between Blanding and Hite Marina. The campground has sites for tents and RVs, $4 no hookups, $6 w/hookups; no showers. Rooms cost $29-45 s or d. Fry Canyon doesn't have a telephone. In winter, the cafe may close, but accommodations and store are usually still available. Two Anasazi ruins can be viewed nearby in Fry Canyon; a road goes to

an overlook of one ruin and a short trail goes to the other; ask for directions. Fry Canyon is 19 miles northwest of the Natural Bridges National Monument turnoff and 24 miles southeast of the Hite Marina turnoff.

## Dark Canyon

This magnificent canyon system lies about 15 air miles north of Natural Bridges National Monument. Dark Canyon, with its many tributaries, begins in the high country of Elk Ridge and extends west to Lake Powell in lower Cataract Canyon. Steep cliffs and the isolated location have protected the relatively pristine environment. The upper canyons tend to be wide with open areas and groves of Douglas fir and ponderosa pine. Farther downstream, the canyon walls close in and the desert trees of pinyon pine, juniper, and cottonwood take over. At its lower end, Dark Canyon has a year-round stream and deep plunge pools; cliffs tower more than 1,400 feet above the canyon floor. Springs and running water attract wildlife, including bighorn sheep, black bear, deer, mountain lion, coyote, bobcat, ringtail cat, raccoon, fox, and spotted skunk. Experienced hikers enjoy the solitude, wildlife, Anasazi ruins, and varied canyon scenery. Although it's possible to visit Dark Canyon on a day hike, you'll need several days to get a feel for this area. To explore the entire canyon and its major tributaries would take weeks! Hiking through the canyons is mostly easy, though strenuous scrambles are needed to bypass a few pour-offs and other obstacles. Elevations of Dark Canyon range from 8,200 feet at its upper end to 3,700 feet at Lake Powell. Hikers must be extra cautious and self-sufficient, because outside help can be days away. Check with people at the BLM or U.S. Forest Service offices before a trip. Topo maps are the 15-minute Mouth of Dark Canyon, Fable Valley, and Bears Ears maps or the 1:100,000 Hite Crossing and Blanding maps.

The upper half of the canyon system lies within Dark Canyon Wilderness, administered by the Manti-LaSal National Forest (Box 820, Monticello, UT 84535; tel. 587-2041). The Monticello office has information sheets on the dozen or so access trails to Dark Canyon and can advise on road conditions to the trailheads. A variety of loop hikes can be made using Woodenshoe, Peavine, Kigalia, and upper Dark canyons. Snow and mud usually block roads, all of which are unpaved, until early June. Spring through autumn are good hiking seasons in the higher country, though snowmelt sometimes causes spring flooding.

The lower half of Dark Canyon, currently designated a primitive area, lies mostly within BLM land; the area is a candidate for wilderness status. Trail notes describing hiking conditions, water sources, trailheads, and wilderness etiquette are available from BLM offices at Kane Gulch Ranger Station (trailhead for Grand Gulch) or Monticello (Box 7, Monticello, UT 84535; tel. 587-2141). Obtain a free permit from the BLM before visiting their lands. The **Sundance Trail** is the most popular entry to lower Dark Canyon. The start of the trail can be reached on dirt roads branching off UT 95 southeast of the Hite Marina turnoff; this approach can be used year-round in dry weather. Cairns mark the trail, which drops 1,200 feet in less than one mile on a steep talus slope. Boaters can reach the lower end of Dark Canyon in Glen Canyon National Recreation Area by going 14 miles up Lake Powell from Hite Marina. The lower canyon can be hiked year-round, with spring and autumn the best choices.

*mountain lion*
(Felis concolor)

## Grand Gulch Primitive Area

Within this twisting canyon system lie some of the most captivating scenery and largest concentrations of Anasazi ruins in all of southeastern Utah. The main canyon begins only about 6 miles southeast of Natural Bridges National Monument. From an elevation of 6,400 feet, Grand Gulch cuts deeply into Cedar Mesa on a tortuous path southwest to the San Juan River, dropping 2,700 feet in about 53 miles. Sheer cliffs, alcoves, pinnacles, Anasazi cliff dwellings, rock art sites, and a few natural bridges line Grand Gulch and its many tributaries. Canyon depths reach 600 feet. Nearly all of Grand Gulch has been cut out of Cedar Mesa Sandstone. The lower 1½ miles of canyon also reveal exposures of the older Cutler Formation (Halgaito Shale Member) and the Honaker Trail Formation. Wildlife to look for include mule deer, mountain lion, black bear, coyote, bobcat, fox, ringtail cat, spotted skunk, cottontail, white-tailed antelope squirrel, white-throated wood rat, Ord kangaroo rat, pinyon mouse, Great Basin gopher snake, Hopi rattlesnake, and midget faded rattlesnake. Some birds in the area are red-tailed hawk, great horned owl, mourning dove, titmouse, rock wren, and pinyon jay. Vegetation includes pinyon pine, juniper, cottonwood, Gambel oak, singleleaf ash, willow, sagebrush, blackbrush, rabbitbrush, prickly pear cactus, and flowering annuals. The Anasazi left behind hundreds of dwellings and thou sands of pictographs and petroglyphs. They arrived in Grand Gulch as early as A.D. 200, largely departed around 800 (perhaps because of drought), resettled the canyons about 1000, then left for good in the late 1200s. Mormon pioneers of the Hole-in-the-Rock Expedition named the canyon in 1880, but the exhausted group was in no mood to enjoy the scenery.

Kane Gulch and Bullet Canyon provide access to the upper end of Grand Gulch from the east side. A popular loop hike using these canyons is 23 miles long; you'll need a 7.5-mile car shuttle or you could hitch. Ask at the ranger station if a shuttle service is available. Collins Canyon, reached from Collins Spring Trailhead, leads into lower Grand Gulch from the west side. Hiking distance between Kane Gulch and Collins Spring trailheads is 38 miles one way. A car shuttle of about 29 miles (including 8 miles of dirt road) is needed. River runners can travel up the mouth from the San Juan River. The San Juan is 53 miles from Kane Gulch Trailhead and 19 miles from Collins Spring Trailhead. The lower third of Grand Gulch (below Collins Canyon) lacks the abundant Anasazi sites found in the middle and upper reaches and has few water sources.

The book *Wind in the Rock* by Ann Zwinger presents a personal account of the wonders of travel in Grand Gulch and nearby canyons. Spring and autumn are the choice times for hiking; summer is possible, though you'll want to sit out the midday heat. Winter snow makes some of the slickrock sections hazardous. Be sure to visit the BLM's Kane Gulch Ranger Station or Monticello office for a permit and information. The BLM map of Grand Gulch Primitive Area shows the topography, mileages for each section of canyon, and major points of interest; it's good for both planning a trip and using while hiking; U.S.G.S. maps cover the area with 1:100,000 and 7½- and 15-minute topo maps. Springs provide water in most parts of Grand Gulch but aren't always reliable, especially in summer; the BLM staff can give you an idea of what to expect. "Innocent vandalism" caused by visitors touching and climbing on the ruins and middens has caused serious damage. BLM staff will offer advice and literature on how to safely visit the ancient sites. Pot hunting has been another problem; report any suspicious behavior to the BLM. Grand Gulch is heavily used, so respect for ruins and for camping without leaving a trace become extra important.

## Kane Gulch Ranger Station
The BLM provides permits, archaeological information, current hiking conditions, literature, and sales of maps and books. The station is at Kane Gulch Trailhead, 4 miles south on UT 261 from UT 95; open daily from March 1 to the first Fri. in December. No telephone or water is available. Normally this is the best place for first-hand information. You can also visit the BLM office at 435 N. Main in Monti-

cello (Box 7, Monticello, UT 84535); tel. 587-2141; open year-round Mon. to Fri. 7:45 a.m.-4:30 p.m. Everyone visiting the Cedar Mesa backcountry should drop in for the required permit and to get the latest information. Note that groups of 10-15 people need to obtain permits beforehand from the ranger station or office; group size may not exceed 15. Help protect fragile desert soils by keeping all vehicles—including mountain bicycles—on established roads.

## Fish Creek And Owl Creek Loop Hike
Varied canyon scenery, year-round pools, Anasazi ruins, and a magnificent natural arch make this an excellent hike. Fish Creek and its tributary Owl Creek lie east of Grand Gulch on the other side of UT 261. A 1¾-mile trail atop Cedar Mesa connects upper arms of the 2 creeks to make a 15½-mile loop. From the trailhead (elev. 6,160 ft.), you'll be descending 1,400 feet to the junction of the 2 creeks. Opinions differ as to which direction to begin the loop, but either way is fine. Owl Creek might be the better choice for a day hike because it's closer to the trailhead and has the added attractions of easily accessible ruins just ½ mile away and Nevill's Arch 3½ miles farther (one way). Contact the Kane Gulch or Monticello BLM offices for trail notes and current trail and water conditions. Maps are essential for navigation, because it's easy to get off the route in some places. The BLM trail notes have a topo map, or you can use the 15-minute Bluff and Cedar Mesa topos. Camping places are easy to locate; just avoid washes. You can always find at least intermittent water in the upper parts of both creeks. The canyons have been carved in Cedar Mesa Sandstone, which forms many overhangs where the Anasazi Indians built cliff dwellings. Unfortunately, nearly all ruins sit high in the cliffs and can be hard to spot from the canyon bottoms (canyon depths average 500 feet). Binoculars come in handy for seeing the ruins, some of which are marked on the topo maps.

Turnoff for the trailhead is between Mileposts 27 and 28 of UT 261, one mile south of Kane Gulch Ranger Station. Head east 5.2

miles on San Juan County 253, passable by cars when dry, to a parking area at the site of an old drill hole. A sign points the way north 1½ miles to Fish Creek and southeast ¼ mile to Owl Creek. Cairns show the way into the canyons, then you just follow the creekbeds. The route into Fish Creek goes north 1½ miles across the mesa from the trailhead (watch closely for cairns—it's easy to miss the trail where it climbs out of a wash), makes a steep descent into an arm of Fish Creek, and follows Fish Creek downstream to the confluence with Owl Creek; total distance from the trailhead to this point is 9 miles one way. Turn right 2½ miles up Owl Creek, normally dry in this section, to Nevill's Arch. It's possible to rock-scramble up the slope to the window of the arch, where you'll enjoy fine views of the canyons and beyond. Owl Creek has water and becomes prettier and prettier as you head upstream. On the 4 miles from the arch to the trailhead, you'll need to circumvent 3 pour-offs: the first and second by going around to the right, the third by going to the left; look for the cairned routes. The first and second pour-offs have small waterfalls and idyllic pools. Above the third pour-off, you'll pass a well-preserved group of Anasazi ruins on the left. From here there's only a short but steep scramble to the rim, then ¼ mile across slickrock back to the trailhead.

### Slickhorn Canyon

Adventurous hikers enjoy the Indian ruins and impressive scenery in this rugged canyon south of Grand Gulch. Canyon depths along Slickhorn's 12-mile length range from about 300 feet in the northern reaches to 800 feet near the confluence with the San Juan River. Boulders, talus slopes, and pour-offs in the streambed hamper travel and discourage casual visitors. Allow about 4 days to explore Slickhorn Canyon and some of its tributaries. A more ambitious trip is to go down Slickhorn to the San Juan River, hike downstream along the shore to the mouth of Grand Gulch, then travel up to one of the Grand Gulch trailheads in a week or more of hiking. The BLM offices at Kane Gulch and Monticello have informa-tion sheets, trailhead information, and a map. The 15-minute Cedar Mesa topo map and the BLM'S Grand Gulch hiking map also cover this area. Several trailheads can be reached by turning west on an unpaved road from UT 261 opposite the signed Cigarette Springs Road, 9.4 miles south of the Kane Gulch Ranger Station.

### John's Canyon

This varied canyon lies southeast of Grand Gulch and Slickhorn canyons. A fingerlike net-work of deep narrow canyons in the upper drainages contrasts with a broad alluvial bot-tom downstream that's up to one mile wide. The main canyon is about 13 miles long and empties into the San Juan River. Canyon depths average about 1,000 feet. Experi-enced hikers will find the going relatively easy, as there are only a few boulder falls and small pour-offs in the upper canyons. High pour-offs in the lower canyon, however, effectively block access to the San Juan River. A map and information sheet available from the BLM of-fices have trailhead and spring information and a brief description of hiking in the canyon. Cliffs and overhangs on the rim in the north restrict access to only a few points; the BLM map shows one entry point, reached by a short dirt road off UT 261. In the south, a jeep road branches off UT 316 (the road to Goose-necks State Park), follows the rim of the San Juan River west, and then turns up into middle John's Canyon.

## MEXICAN HAT

Spectacular geology surrounds this tiny com-munity perched on the north bank of the San Juan River. Folded layers of red and gray rock stand out dramatically. Alhambra Rock, a jagged remnant of a volcano, marks the southern approach to Mexican Hat. Another rock, which looks just like an upside-down sombrero, gave Mexican Hat its name; you'll see this formation 2 miles north of town. The land has never proved good for much except its scenery. Farmers and ranchers thought it next to worthless. Stories of gold in the San

Juan River brought a frenzy of prospecting in 1892-93, but the mining proved mostly a bust. Oil, first struck by drillers in 1908, has brought mostly modest profits. The uranium mill across the river at Halchita gave a boost to the economy from 1956 until it closed in 1965. Mexican Hat now serves as a modest trade and tourism center. Monument Valley, Valley of the Gods Scenic Drive, Goosenecks State Park, and Grand Gulch Primitive Area lie only short drives away. The shore near town can be a busy place in summer as river runners on the San Juan put in, take out, or just stop for ice and beer.

### Practicalities
The **San Juan Inn** offers rooms ($45.15 s, $49.55 d), the **Olde Bridge Bar and Grill** (American, Mexican, and Navajo food daily for breakfast, lunch, and dinner), and the **San Juan Trading Post** (Indian crafts and gro-

*gold-mining operation at the Mexican Hat, 1890s*

ceries); located on a ledge overlooking the river near the highway bridge; tel. 683-2220. **Canyonlands Motel** offers basic rooms for $27.95 s, $32.25 d; closed in winter; tel. 683-2230. **Valle's Trading Post and RV Park,** open all year, has tent and RV sites w/hookups for $8 s, $9.50 d; the trading post offers Indian crafts, groceries, showers, vehicle storage, and car shuttles; tel. 683-2226. **Burch's Trading Post** has motel rooms ($33-38 s or d), RV park ($10 w/hookups), cafe with American and Navajo food (open daily for breakfast, lunch, and dinner; no breakfast in winter), ice cream parlor, Indian crafts, and groceries; tel. 683-2221. **Lee's Guest Ranch** in the Valley of the Gods north of town offers rustic accommodations, campground, meals, and horseback riding; ask at the El Sombrero; tel. 683-2222.

**El Sombrero** features Mexican food; open daily for lunch and dinner; tel. 683-2222. **Worldwide Explorations** runs half-day river trips on the San Juan from April to Sept.; meet at the San Juan Inn; $38 adult, $32.50 children; 2-6 day trips cost $190-550; tel. (800) 2PADDLE. The Conoco gas station (tel. 683-2221), San Juan Trading Post (tel. 683-2220), and Valle's Trading Post (tel. 683-2226) have car shuttle services for river runners.

## VICINITY OF MEXICAN HAT

### Valley Of The Gods
Great sandstone monoliths, delicate spires, and long rock fins rise from the broad valley. This strange red-rock landscape resembles better-known Monument Valley but is on a smaller scale. A 17-mile dirt road winds through the spectacular scenery. Cars can usually travel the road at low speeds if the weather is dry (washes are crossed). Allow 1-1½ hours for the drive. The east end of the road connects with US 163 at Milepost 29 (7.5 miles northeast of Mexican Hat or 15 miles southwest of Bluff); the west end connects with UT 261 just below the Moki Dugway switchbacks (4 miles north of Mexican Hat on US 163, then 6.6 miles northwest on UT 261).

## Goosenecks State Park

The San Juan River winds through a series of incredibly tight bends 1,000 feet below. So closely spaced are the bends that the river takes 6 miles to cover an air distance of only 1½ miles! The bends and exposed rock layers form exquisitely graceful curves. Geologists know the site as a classic example of entrenched meanders, caused by gradual uplift of a formerly level plain. Signs at the overlook explain the geologic history and identify the rock formations. Goosenecks State Park is an undeveloped area with a few tables and vault toilets as the only facilities. You could camp here; no water or charge. From the junction of US 163 and UT 261, 4 miles north of Mexican Hat, go one mile northwest on UT 261, then turn left 3 miles on UT 316 to its end.

## Muley Point Overlook

One of the great views in the Southwest lies just a short drive from Goosenecks State Park and more than 1,000 feet higher. Although the view of the Goosenecks below is less dramatic than at the state park, the 6,200-foot elevation provides a magnificent panorama across the Navajo Indian Reservation to Monument Valley and countless canyons and mountains. To get here, continue northwest 9 miles on UT 261 from the Goosenecks turnoff. At the top of the Moki Dugway switchbacks (an 1,100-foot climb with sharp curves and 5-10% grades), turn left (southwest) 5.3 miles on a gravel road to the point. The turnoff may not be signed.

## River Running On The San Juan

From the high San Juan Mountains in southern Colorado, this intriguing river wends its way into New Mexico, enters Utah near Four Corners, and twists through spectacular canyons before ending at Lake Powell. Sand waves spring up during flooding, usually in May and June. The waves can pop up out of flat water to heights of 3 feet and occasionally as much as 7 or 8 feet! Swift currents on the

*lazing down the lower San Juan River*

sandy bottom cause these harmless waves, which can migrate up or downstream before disappearing.

Below the town of Bluff, the muddy river picks up speed and dives deep within its canyon walls. Most boaters put in at Sand Island Campground near Bluff and take out at the town of Mexican Hat, 30 river miles downstream, or continue another 56 river miles through the Goosenecks to Clay Hills Crossing or Paiute Farms (not always accessible) on Lake Powell. Allow at least 4 days for the full trip, though more time will allow exploration of side canyons and visits to Anasazi sites. Rafts, kayaks, and canoes can be used. The season now usually lasts all year, due to the Navajo Reservoir upstream. Once, earlier this century, the river dried up completely! Many commercial river-running companies offer San Juan trips. If you go on your own, you should have river-running experience or be with someone who has. Private groups need to obtain permits from the BLM San Juan Resource Area office well in advance; Box 7, Monticello, UT 84535; tel. 587-2141. The book, *San Juan Canyons, A River Runner's Guide* by Don Baars and Gene Stevenson, has a river log with detailed maps, practical advice, and background. Some people also like to run the river between Montezuma Creek and Sand Island, a leisurely trip of 20 river miles. The solitude often makes up for the lack of scenery. It's easy to get a river permit for this section because no use limits or fees apply.

# MONUMENT VALLEY

Towering buttes, jagged pinnacles, and rippled sand dunes make this an otherworldly landscape. Changing colors and shifting shadows during the day add to the enchantment. Most of the natural monuments are remnants of sandstone eroded by wind and water. Agathla Peak and some lesser summits are roots of ancient volcanoes, whose dark rock contrasts with the pale yellow sandstone of the other formations. The valley lies at an elevation of 5,564 feet in the Upper Sonoran Life Zone; annual rainfall averages about 8½ inches.

In 1863-64, when Kit Carson was ravaging Canyon de Chelly in Arizona to round up the Navajo, Chief Hoskinini led his people to the safety and freedom of Monument Valley. Merrick Butte and Mitchell Mesa commemorate 2 miners who discovered rich silver deposits on their first trip to the valley in 1880. On their second trip both were killed, reportedly shot by Paiute Indians. Hollywood movies made the splendor of Monument Valley known to the outside world. *Stagecoach,* filmed here in 1938 and directed by John Ford, became the first in a series of westerns that has continued to the present. John Wayne and many other movie greats rode across these sands.

The Navajo have preserved the valley as a tribal park with a scenic drive, visitor center, and campground. From Mexican Hat, drive 22 miles southwest on US 163 and turn left 3.5 miles to the visitor center. From Kayenta, go 24 miles north on US 163 and turn right 3.5 miles.

## Visitor Center
Information desk, exhibits, and Indian crafts shop are open daily 7 a.m.-7 p.m. from May to Sept., then daily 8 a.m.-5 p.m. the rest of the year; tel. (801) 727-3287. Visitors pay a $2.50/person fee ($1 age 60 and over; under 6 free) collected on the entrance road.

## Monument Valley Drive
A 17-mile, self-guided scenic drive begins at the visitor center and loops through the heart of the valley. Overlooks provide sweeping views from different vantage points. The dirt road is normally OK for cautiously driven cars. Avoid stopping and becoming stuck in the loose sand that sometimes blows across the road. Allow 1½ hours for the drive, open the same hours as the visitor center. No hiking or driving off the signed route is allowed. Water and restrooms are available only at the visitor center.

## Valley Tours

Take one of the guided tour vehicles leaving daily year-round from the visitor center to visit a hogan, cliff dwelling, and petroglyphs in areas beyond the self-guided drive. The trips last 2½-3 hours and cost $15/person. Shorter trips of 1½ hours cost $12/person. Guided horseback riding costs $15 for 1½ hours; longer day and overnight trips can be arranged too; March to Nov. from the visitor center. If you'd like to hike in Monument Valley, you must hire a guide; hiking tours of 2 hours to a day or more can be arranged at the visitor center.

## Accommodations

**Mitten View Campground** near the visitor center costs $10; hot showers are available at an extra charge. Season is early March to mid-October. Tenters should be prepared for winds in this exposed location. Goulding's Lodge (see below) has the nearest motel, restaurant, and store. Motels are also found at Mexican Hat and Bluff in Utah and Kayenta in Arizona.

## Goulding's Lodge And Trading Post

Harry Goulding and his wife Mike opened the trading post in 1923. It's located 2 miles west of the US 163 Monument Valley turnoff, just north of the Utah-Arizona border. **Goulding's Museum,** in the old trading post building, displays prehistoric and modern Indian artifacts, movie photos, and memorabilia of the Goulding family; open daily except in winter. Motel rooms start at $83.85 s or d in summer, less off-season; guests can use a small indoor pool. A gift shop sells souvenirs, books, and high-quality Indian crafts. The nearby store has groceries and gas pumps. Monument Valley tours operate year-round; $23 half day, $43 full day with a 6-person minimum; children under 12 go at half price. The lodge and store stay open all year, though the restaurant, museum, and gift shop close in winter. For accommodation and tour info, write Box 1, Monument Valley, UT 84536; tel. (801) 727-3231. **Monument Valley KOA Campground** offers tent and RV sites a short drive west; rates are $11.71 tent, $12.84 RV no hookups,

$18.19 w/hookups; has showers and store; open April 1 to Nov. 1; tel. (801) 727-3280. The Seventh-day Adventist Church runs a hospital and mission nearby.

# FOUR CORNERS MONUMENT

An inlaid concrete slab marks the point where Utah, Colorado, New Mexico, and Arizona meet. It's the only spot in the United States where you can put your finger on 4 states at once. Over 2,000 people a day are said to stop at the marker in the summer season. Average stay? Seven to ten minutes. On the other hand, 5 national parks and 18 national monuments are within a radius of 150 miles from this point! Indians, mostly Navajo with perhaps some Ute and Pueblo, sell crafts and refreshments. Navajo Parks and Recreation collects a $1/vehicle fee ($.50 motorcycle) during the tourist season.

# KAYENTA

The "Gateway to Monument Valley" is a town of 3,400 in a bleak, windswept valley in Arizona. Its name is loosely derived from the Navajo name *Teehindeeh,* meaning "Bog hole," as there were once shallow lakes here. Kayenta is a handy stop for travelers, with 2 good motels and several restaurants.

## Accommodations

**Wetherill Inn** is in the center of town on US 163, one mile north of US 160. It was named after John Wetherill, an early trader and rancher of the region who discovered Betatakin, Mesa Verde, and other major Anasazi sites; rooms cost $62 s, $68 d in summer; tel. (602) 697-3231. The **Holiday Inn,** on US 160 at the turnoff for Kayenta, has rooms ($89 s, $98 d in summer), restaurant, gift shop, and pool; tel. (602) 697-3221 or (800) HOLIDAY. The **Coin-Op Laundry** in town has tent and RV spaces at $8.75 w/hookups; showers are also available for noncampers; tel. (602) 697-8282/3400.

### Food
The **Holiday Inn's** restaurant has good Navajo tacos and standard American fare; open daily for breakfast, lunch, and dinner. **El Capitan Cafe** is nearby on the other side of the highway; open daily for breakfast, lunch, and dinner. **La Fiesta Cafe** serves Mexican and American food; open Mon. to Fri. and sometimes Sat. for lunch and dinner; located on US 163 between the Kayenta turnoff and town. **Golden Sands Cafe,** next door to Wetherill Inn, offers American food daily for breakfast, lunch, and dinner. **Mikey's Pizza** next to the Teehindeeh Shopping Center dishes out pizza. Buy groceries at the supermarket in the shopping center or at the **Kayenta Trading Post** (behind the Wetherill Inn).

### Shopping And Services
Look for Indian crafts at both motels, Kayenta Trading Post, and Burch's Trading Company (near Wetherill Inn). Tours in 4WD vehicles to Monument Valley and surrounding country leave from both motels; costs start at about $24 half day or $40 full day with a minimum of 4 or 6 persons.

# PAGE

Before 1957, only sand and desert vegetation lay atop Manson Mesa in far northern Arizona where Page now sits, 130 miles north of Flagstaff (AZ) and 72 miles east of Kanab, Utah. In that year the U.S. Bureau of Reclamation decided to build a giant reservoir in Glen Canyon on the Colorado River. Glen Canyon Dam was to become one of the largest construction projects ever undertaken. The 710-foot-high structure would create a lake covering 250 square miles with a shoreline of nearly 2,000 miles. Workmen hastily set up prefabricated metal buildings for barracks, dining hall, and offices. Trailers rolled in, one serving as Page's first bank. The Bureau of Reclamation named the construction camp for John C. Page, who served as the bureau's first commissioner from 1937 to 1943.

The remote desert spot gradually turned into a modern town as schools, businesses, and churches appeared. Streets were named and grass and trees planted, and Page took on the appearance of American suburbia. The town still has a new and clean look. Though small (pop. 7,000), it's the largest community close to Lake Powell, and offers travelers a good selection of places to stay and eat. Wedged between Glen Canyon National Recreation Area to the north, the Arizona Strip to the west, and the Navajo Reservation to the east and south, Page makes a useful base for visiting all these areas. The townsite (elev. 4,300 feet) overlooks Lake Powell and Glen Canyon Dam; the large Wahweap Resort and Marina are just 6 miles away. Unless you take a commercial flight in, you'll need your own

*prehistoric ruins on the brink of Glen Canyon*

transport to get here. (Note: all telephone numbers below for Page and Wahweap Marina have the Arizona 602 prefix.)

**Powell Museum**

The collection honors scientist and explorer John Wesley Powell. In 1869 he led the first expedition down the Green and Colorado River gorges, then ran the rivers a second time in 1871-72. It was Powell who named the most splendid section the "Grand Canyon." Old drawings and photographs illustrate his life and voyages. Fossil and mineral displays interpret the thick geologic section revealed by canyons of the Colorado River. Other exhibits contain pottery, baskets, weapons, tools of Southwestern Indian tribes, and memorabilia of early pioneers and the founding of Page. Related videos are shown on request. Travel info, tours (river, lake, jeep, and flight), and regional books are available. Summer hours (June to Sept.) are Sun. 10 a.m.-6 p.m. and Mon.-Sat. 8 a.m.-6 p.m.; May and Oct. hours are Mon. to Sat. 8 a.m.-5 p.m.; March, April, and Nov. hours are Mon. to Fri. 9 a.m.-5 p.m.; closed in winter; tel. 645-9496. The museum is in downtown at the corner of Lake Powell Blvd. and N. Navajo Drive.

### Diné Bí Keyah Museum
### (Big Lake Trading Post)
This small collection of prehistoric and modern Indian artifacts is on the second floor; open

---

## PAGE

1. Glen Canyon Golf & Country Club
2. McDonald's
3. Holiday Inn
4. Inn at Lake Powell; Page/Lake Powell Chamber of Commerce
5. Weston Lamplighter Motel
6. Glen Canyon Steakhouse
7. Ken's Old West Restaurant
8. Page Hospital
9. Page Boy Motel
10. public library
11. Blue Water Adventures
12. Powell Museum
13. Bella Napoli
14. Zapata's Mexican Restaurant
15. Lakeview Shopping Center
16. Stromboli's Pizza
17. Starlite Restaurant; Pleasure Bound Bookstore; Wilderness River Adventures; Mesa Theatre
18. post office
19. Page Plaza
20. Empire House Motel; Desert Lake Motel; Yen Jing Restaurant
21. Page Memorial Park
22. Page High School
23. tennis courts
24. Page-Lake Powell Campground
25. Big Lake Trading Post

---

daily 6 a.m.-12:30 a.m.; free admission; tel. 645-2404. Big Lake Trading Post is 1.3 miles southeast on AZ 98; Indian crafts, groceries, and fishing supplies are sold.

## PRACTICALITIES

### Accommodations
All of Page's motels lie on or near Lake Powell Blvd., a 3¼-mile business loop designated US 89L that branches off the main highway. The summer rates listed here drop substantially in winter. **Desert Lake Motel** is at 121 S. Lake Powell Blvd.; $43.40-54.25 s, $48.83-59.68 d; tel. 645-2488. **Empire House Motel** has a coffee shop and swimming pool at 100 S. Lake Powell Blvd.; $45.57 s, $48.83 d; tel. 645-2406. **Comfort Lodge** is at 75 S. 8th Pl.; $48.83 s, $54.25 d; tel. 645-2858. **Page Boy Motel** has a swimming pool at 150 N. Lake Powell Blvd.; $30.38 s, $36.89 d; tel. 645-2416. The **Weston Lamplighter Motel** (Best Western) also offers a swimming pool at 201 N. Lake Powell Blvd.; $60.76 s, $66.19 d; tel. 645-2451. **Holiday Inn** features a swimming pool, restaurant, and views over Lake Powell from 287 N. Lake Powell Blvd.; $85.72 s, $92.23 d; tel. 645-8851 or (800) HOLIDAY. The **Inn at Lake Powell** has fine views, swimming pool, and an adjacent restaurant at 716 Rim View Dr. and Lake Powell Blvd. (across from Holiday Inn); $60.76-73.78 s, $67.27-81.38 d; tel. 645-2466.

### Campgrounds
**Page-Lake Powell Campground** offers sites with showers for tents and RVs, $14.11 no hookups, $17.36 w/hookups; located one mile southeast on AZ 98; tel. 645-3374. Other campgrounds, an RV park, and motels are in the Wahweap area (see "Lake Powell" below).

### Food And Entertainment
**Glen Canyon Steak House** serves American food daily for breakfast, lunch, and dinner; specialties include steaks, seafood, ribs, and chicken; live country-rock bands perform evenings Tues. to Sun.; 201 N. Lake Powell Blvd.; tel. 645-3363. **Ken's Old West Restaurant**

has steak, prime rib, and seafood; open daily for dinner; country-western bands provide music Tues. to Sat.; 718 Vista Ave. (across from Glen Canyon Steak House); tel. 645-5160. **Family Tree Restaurant** in the Holiday Inn offers a varied menu and is open daily for breakfast, lunch, and dinner; 287 N. Lake Powell Blvd.; tel. 645-8851.

Stop for Chinese food at **Yen Jing** (open Mon. to Fri. for lunch and daily for dinner; 125 S. Lake Powell Blvd.; tel. 645-3244); **Starlite** (open daily except Sun. for breakfast, lunch, and dinner; 46 S. Lake Powell Blvd.; tel. 645-3620); and **Dynasty** (open daily for breakfast, lunch, and dinner; 716 Rimview Dr. next to Inn at Lake Powell; tel. 645-8113). **Zapata's Mexican Restaurant** is open daily except Sun. for lunch and dinner; 615 N. Navajo Dr.; tel. 645-9006. Pizza, spaghetti, and other Italian fare are served by: **Strombolli's Pizza** (open daily for lunch and dinner; 711 N. Navajo Dr.; tel. 645-2605) and **Bella Napoli** (open daily except Sun. for dinner in spring, then daily for dinner until mid-autumn; closed in winter; 810 N. Navajo Dr.; tel. 645-2706). Catch movies at **Mesa Theatre**, 42 S. Lake Powell Blvd.; tel. 645-9565.

### Events

For more information about Lake Powell's events, contact Lake Powell Resorts and Marinas; tel. (800) 528-6154 (278-8888 in greater Phoenix). To learn about other events, contact Page/Lake Powell Chamber of Commerce; tel. 645-2741.

**January:** Hole-in-Rock Commemoration on Lake Powell celebrates the 1880 crossing of the Colorado River by Mormon pioneers; historic programs and tours take place at Wahweap and Bullfrog marinas. Striper Derby continues at Lake Powell (see November, below). **February:** Striper Derby continues at Lake Powell. **March:** Hot Air Balloon Regatta flies over the Page area. **April:** Bullfrog Open awards prizes for the biggest largemouth bass. **May:** Four-H Horse Show. Page Open Rodeo. **June:** Big Lake Trading Post sponsors an Indian Market with crafts and dancing on the last weekend. **July:** Fourth of July

celebration with food, games, and fireworks at Page Memorial Park. Pioneer Day Parade on third weekend. **August:** Halls Crossing-Bullfrog Swim is an early morning swimming race between the two marinas. **September:** Northern Arizona Fall Roundup Rodeo. Rod Run (show of custom and antique cars). Lake Powell Triathlon takes place at Bullfrog Marina. **November:** Fishermen compete for the biggest striped bass in the Striper Derby, lasting through Feb. at Lake Powell. Bullfrog's Festival of Lights Parade. **December:** Here Comes Santa Parade in Page and Wahweap Festival of Lights Parade on Lake Powell. Striper Derby continues at Lake Powell.

### Services And Recreation

**Post office** is at 615 Elm St.; tel. 645-2571. **Page Hospital** is at the corner of Vista Ave. and N. Navajo Dr.; tel. 645-2424. In **emergencies** (police, fire, medical), dial 911.

Page High School has an indoor **swimming pool** (open all year) near the corner of S. Lake Powell Blvd. and AZ 98; tel. 645-8801. Play **tennis** at the courts on S. Lake Powell Blvd. (Church Row). **Glen Canyon Golf and Country Club** has a 9-hole golf course west of town on US 89; tel. 645-2715.

### Information

**Page/Lake Powell Chamber of Commerce** has information about the sights and services of the area; staff also book lake and river tours and scenic flights; open daily Mon.-Fri. 8 a.m.-6 p.m. in summer and daily 8 a.m.-5 p.m. the rest of the year; located at the Inn at Lake Powell, 716 Rim View Dr. (Box 727, Page, AZ 86040); tel. 645-2741. The **public library** is open daily except Sun.; corner of 697 Vista Ave. and N. Lake Powell Blvd.; tel. 645-2231. **Pleasure Bound Bookstore** has regional titles and general reading at 48 S. Lake Powell Blvd. in Adkinson Mall; tel. 645-5333.

### Tours

**Lake Powell Overland Adventures** (tel. 645-5501/3155) and **Duck Tours** (tel. 645-2741/2955) offer back-road drives to Corkscrew (Antelope) Canyon and other destinations in the area. **Wilderness River Adventures** offers half-day raft trips down the Colorado River from just below Glen Canyon Dam to Lees Ferry, 15 miles of smooth-flowing water; $31.75 adult, $21.15 children under 12; the trips leave daily May to Sept. and can be arranged (6 person minimum) the rest of the year, weather permitting; Grand Canyon raft trips of 3-12 days are offered too; 50 S. Lake Powell Blvd. in Lakeview Shopping Center; (Box 717, Page, AZ 86040); tel. 645-3279 (800-528-6154 outside Arizona). **Blue Water Adventures** runs a scuba dive shop and leads snorkeling and scuba trips on Lake Powell; 697 N. Navajo Dr.; tel. 645-3087. **Lake Powell Air Service's** long list of "flight-seeing" trips includes Lake Powell and Rainbow Bridge (one-half hour, $47), Grand Canyon (1½ hours, $110), Monument Valley (1½ hours, $105; $135 w/ground tour), and Bryce Canyon (1½ hours, $105); a 2-person minimum applies to most tours; children 12 and under get 30% off; scenic flights to Phoenix, Las Vegas, Salt Lake City, and Grand Junction can also be arranged; tel. 645-2494. Boat tours to Rainbow Bridge and other destinations leave from the nearby Wahweap Marina; see "Lake Powell" below.

**Transport**
No bus service at press time. Wahweap Lodge and most area motels will provide transportation for guests to and from the airport. Rent cars at the airport from **Avis** (tel. 645-2494) or **Budget** (tel. 645-3977). From Page's airport on the east edge of town, **Sky West Airlines** flies once or twice daily (one-way fares) to Flagstaff ($75), Phoenix ($116), St. George ($73), Salt Lake City ($122), Las Vegas ($114), and other destinations; ask about roundtrip and discount fares; tel. 645-9200 or (800) 453-9417.

*Ord's kangaroo rat*
(Dipodomys ordii)

# GLEN CANYON
# NATIONAL RECREATION AREA

This vast recreation area covers 1.25 million acres, most of which spreads northeast into Utah. Lake Powell stands out as the centerpiece, surrounded by beautiful canyon country. Just a handful of roads approach the lake, so you'll need to do some boating or hiking to explore this unique land of water and rock. The recreation area also includes a beautiful remnant of Glen Canyon in a 15-mile section of the Colorado River from Glen Canyon Dam to Lees Ferry.

## LAKE POWELL

Conservationists deplored the loss of remote and beautiful Glen Canyon of the Colorado River beneath Lake Powell. Today, we have only words, pictures, and memories to remind us of its wonders. On the other hand, the 186-mile-long lake now provides easy access for many people to an area most had not even known existed. Lake Powell is the second largest man-made lake within the United States. Only Lake Mead, farther downstream, has a greater water-storage capacity. Lake Powell, however, has three times more shoreline—1,960 miles—and holds enough water to cover the state of Pennsylvania a foot deep! Bays and coves offer nearly limitless opportunities for exploration by boaters. Only the lower part—Glen Canyon Dam, Wahweap Resort and Marina, Antelope and Navajo canyons, and the lower parts of Labyrinth, Face, and West canyons—extends into Arizona. The elevation of the surface fluctuates from 3,640 to 3,700 feet. The Carl Hayden Visitor Center, perched beside the dam, has tours of the dam, related exhibits, and an information desk for all the Glen Canyon National Recreation Area.

### Climate

Summer, when temperatures rise into the 90s and 100s F, is the busiest season for swimming, boating, and water-skiing. Visits during the rest of the year can be enjoyable too, though activities shift more to sightseeing, fishing, and hiking. Spring and autumn are the best times to enjoy the backcountry. Winter temperatures drop to highs in the 40s and 50s, with freezing nights and the possibility of snow. Lake surface temperatures range from a comfortable 80° in Aug. to a chilly 45° in January. Chinook winds can blow day and night for periods from Feb. to May. Thunderstorms in late summer bring strong, gusting winds with widely scattered rain showers. Annual precipitation averages about 7 inches.

### Geology, Flora, And Fauna

The colorful rock formations that rise above the lake's surface tell a story of ancient deserts, oceans, and rivers. Uplift of the Colorado Plateau beginning about 60 million years ago started a cycle of erosion that has carved canyons and created delicately balanced rocks and graceful natural arches and bridges.

The desert comes right to the edge of the water, because fluctuating lake levels prevent plant growth along the shore. Common plants of this high-desert country are prickly pear and hedgehog cacti, rabbitbrush, sand sagebrush, blackbrush, cliffrose, mariposa and sego lilies, globemallow, Indian paintbrush, evening primrose, penstemon, and Indian rice grass. Pinyon pine and juniper trees grow on the high plateaus. Springs and permanent streams support sandbar willow, tamarisk, cattail, willow, and cottonwood. Look for hanging gardens of maidenhair fern, columbine, and other water-loving plants in small alcoves high on the sandstone walls.

Most animals are secretive and nocturnal; you're more likely to see them in early morning or in the evening. Local mammals include pronghorn, mule deer, mountain lion, coyote, red and gray foxes, ringtail cat, spotted and striped skunks, bobcat, badger, river otter, beaver, prairie dog, Ord kangaroo rat, black-tailed jack rabbit, several species of squirrels and chipmunks, and many species of mice and bats. Some lizards you might see sunning on a rock are collared, side-blotched, desert horned, and chuckwalla. Snake species include common kingsnake, gopher, striped whipsnake, western rattlesnake, and western diamondback rattlesnake. Birds stopping by on their migrations include American avocet, Canada goose, and teal. Others, such as blue heron, snowy egret, and bald eagle, come for the winter. Birds you might spot any time of the year are American merganser, mallard, canyon wren, pinyon jay, common raven, red-tailed and Swainson's hawks, great horned and long-eared owls, peregrine and prairie falcons, and golden eagle.

### Recreation At Lake Powell

If you don't have your own craft, Wahweap and other marinas will rent a boat for fishing, skiing, or houseboating. Boat tours visit Rainbow Bridge (the world's largest natural bridge) and other destinations from Wahweap, Bullfrog, and Halls Crossing marinas. Sailboats find the steadiest breezes in Wahweap, Padre, Halls, and Bullfrog bays, where spring winds average 15-20 knots. Kayaks and canoes can be used in the more protected areas. All boaters need to be alert for ap-proaching storms that can bring wind gusts up to 60 mph. Waves on open expanses of the lake are sometimes steeper than ocean waves and can exceed 6 feet from trough to crest. Marinas and book stores sell navigation maps of Lake Powell. You'll need an Arizona fishing license for the southern 5 miles of lake and a Utah license for the rest of Lake Powell. Licenses and information can be obtained from marinas on the water or sporting goods stores in Page. Fishermen catch largemouth, smallmouth, and striped bass, northern and walleye pike, catfish, crappie, and carp. Smaller fish include bluegill, perch, and sunfish. Wahweap has a swimming beach (no lifeguards), and boaters can find their own remote spots. Scuba divers step underwater to swim with the sizable bass. Hikers have a choice of easy daytrips or long wilderness backpack treks. The canyons of the Escalante (see pp. 322-327) rate among America's premier hiking areas. Other good hiking areas within or adjacent to Glen Canyon N.R.A. include Rainbow Bridge National Monument (see pp. 421-422), Paria Canyon (pp. 308-309), Dark Canyon (pp. 403-404), and Grand Gulch (pp. 404-405). National Park Service staff at the Carl Hayden Visitor Center can suggest trips and supply trail descriptions. Several guidebooks to Lake Powell have detailed hiking, camping, and boating informa-

*skimming the waters of Lake Powell*

tion. Most of the canyon country near Lake Powell remains wild and little explored—hiking possibilities are limitless! Be sure to carry plenty of water.

## GLEN CANYON DAM

Construction workers labored from 1956 to 1964 to build this giant concrete structure. It stands 710 feet high above bedrock, and its top measures 1,560 feet across. Thickness ranges from 300 feet at the base to just 25 feet at the top. As part of the Upper Colorado River Storage Project, the dam provides water storage (its main purpose), hydroelectricity, flood control, and recreation on Lake Powell. Eight giant turbine generators churn out a total of 1,150,000 kilowatts at 13,800 volts. Vertigo sufferers shouldn't look down when driving across Glen Canyon Bridge, just downstream of the dam; cold, green waters of the Colorado River glide 700 feet below.

### Carl Hayden Visitor Center
Photos, paintings, movies, and slide presentations in the Visitor Center show features of Glen Canyon National Recreation Area, including Lake Powell and construction of the dam. A giant relief map helps to visualize the rugged terrain surrounding the lake; look closely and you'll spot Rainbow Bridge. Guided tours inside the dam and generating room depart daily every hour 7:30 a.m.-4:30 p.m. in the warmer months. You can take a self-guided tour daily year-round; entry closes one hour before visitor center closes. National Park Service staff operate an information desk where you can find out about boating, fishing, camping, and hiking in the immense Glen Canyon National Recreation Area (or write Box 1507, Page, AZ 86040); tel. 645-2511 or 645-2471. The Glen Canyon Natural History Association has a variety of regional books for sale next to the information desk. A Navajo rug exhibit illustrates the many different patterns used. Souvenirs, snacks, and postcards can be purchased at a gift shop in the visitor center building. The Carl Hayden Visitor Center is

open daily about 7 a.m.-7 p.m. in summer and 8:30 a.m.-5 p.m. the rest of the year. Tours, exhibits, and movies are free. In summer, you can attend a campfire program several nights a week at nearby Wahweap Campground amphitheater.

## MARINAS

The **National Park Service** provides public boat ramps, campgrounds, and ranger offices at most of the marinas. Rangers know current boating and back-road conditions, primitive camping areas, and good places to explore. **Lake Powell Resorts & Marinas** operates marina services, boat rentals, boat tours, accommodations, RV parks, and restaurants; contact them for information and reservations (strongly recommended in summer) at 2916 N. 35th Ave., Suite 8, Phoenix, AZ 85017-5261; tel. (800) 528-6154 (278-8888 in greater Phoenix). To make reservations 7 days or less in advance, contact each marina or resort directly. All the marinas stay open year-round; you can avoid crowds and peak prices by coming in autumn, winter, or spring. Private or chartered aircraft can fly to Page Airport and airstrips near Bullfrog and Halls Crossing marinas.

### Wahweap
The name means "Bitter Water" in the Ute Indian language. Wahweap Lodge and Marina, Lake Powell's biggest, offers complete boaters' services and rentals, guided fishing trips, deluxe accommodations, an RV park, and fine dining. Wahweap is 7 miles northwest of Page, 5 miles beyond the Visitor Center. **Wahweap Lodge** offers several types of rooms starting at $74.91 s, $83.87 d in summer (May 15 to Oct. 15); $56.18 s, $63.04 d in spring and autumn; and $44.84 s, $50.11 d in winter (Nov. 1 to March 31). Guests enjoy lake views, restaurants, and, in summer, live entertainment and dancing. Contact Lake Powell Resorts & Marinas for reservations at 2916 N. 35th Ave., Suite 8, Phoenix, AZ 85017-5261; tel. (800) 528-6154 (278-8888 in greater Phoenix). Wahweap Lodge & Marina

can also be reached at Box 1597, Page, AZ 86040; tel. 645-2433. **Lake Powell Motel** has less expensive rooms nearby at Wahweap Junction (4 miles northwest of Glen Canyon Dam on US 89); $50.38 s, $55.92 d in summer; $37.72 s, $41.94 d in spring and autumn; and $30.33 s, $33.76 d in winter; call 645-2477 or contact Lake Powell Resorts & Marinas for reservations.

An **RV park** with coin showers and laundry costs $16.62 w/hookups ($10 in winter). **Wahweap Campground** is operated first-come, first-served by the National Park Service; sites have drinking water but no showers or hookups; $6; campers may use the showers and laundry facilities at the RV park. Primitive camping (no water or fee) is available at **Lone Rock** in Utah, 6 miles northwest of Wahweap off US 89. Boaters may also camp along the lakeshore, but not within one mile of developed areas. A free picnic area and fish-cleaning station are located just west of Wahweap Lodge. Public boat ramps are located adjacent to the lodge and at State Line, one mile northwest of the lodge. During summer (June 1 to Sept. 30), you can obtain recreation information from the **Wahweap Ranger Station** near the picnic area; at other times see the staff at Carl Hayden Visitor Center.

The marina offers six **lake tours,** ranging from an hour-long paddle-wheel cruise around Wahweap Bay ($7.75 adult, $5.35 children) to an all-day trip to Rainbow Bridge, 50 miles away ($54 adult, $27 children). Half-day trips to Rainbow Bridge cost $42 adult, $21 children. **Boat rentals** include a 16-foot skiff with 25-h.p. motor ($55.39/day), an 18-

foot powerboat with 120-h.p. motor ($155.61/day), and several sizes of houseboats starting at $664.65 for three nights. Fishing gear and water-skis can be rented too. Rental and some tour rates drop as much as 40% off-season.

**Dangling Rope**
This floating marina lies 42 miles uplake from Glen Canyon Dam. The only access is by boat. Services include a ranger station, store, minor boat repairs, gas dock, and sanitary pump-out station. A dangling rope left behind in a nearby canyon, perhaps by uranium prospectors, prompted the name. The dock for Rainbow Bridge is 10 miles farther uplake in Bridge Canyon, a tributary of Forbidding Canyon.

**San Juan**
No marinas existed on the San Juan Arm of the lake at press time. Boats can be hand launched at **Clay Hills Crossing** at the upper end of the San Juan Arm. An unpaved road branches 11 miles southwest from UT 276 (road to Halls Crossing) to the lake; don't attempt the road after rains. River runners on the San Juan often take out here; no facilities are provided.

**Halls Crossing-Bullfrog Ferry**
The *John Atlantic Burr* ferry can accommodate vehicles of all sizes and passengers for the short 20-minute crossing between these marinas. Halls Crossing and Bullfrog marinas lie on opposite sides of Lake Powell about 95 lake miles from Glen Canyon Dam, roughly

*channel catfish*
(Ictalurus punctatus)

midway up the length of the lake. Sections of paved Highway UT 276 connect each marina with UT 95. The ferry's daily schedule has six roundtrips from May 15 to Sept. 15, then four roundtrips the rest of the year; no reservations needed. You can pick up a schedule from the marinas. Service is suspended for a brief time annually, usually in Nov., for maintenance; signs at the UT 276 turnoffs will warn you when the ferry is closed.

## Halls Crossing

In 1880, Charles Hall built the ferry used by the Hole-in-the-Rock pioneers, who crossed the river to begin settlement in southeast Utah. The approach roads were so bad, however, that he moved the ferry 35 miles upstream to present-day Halls Crossing in the following year. Business continued to be slow, and Hall quit running the ferry in 1884.

Arriving at Halls Crossing by road, you'll first reach a small store offering **housekeeping units** (trailers: $77.40 d in summer, $58.05 d in spring and autumn, and $46.49 d in winter), an **RV park** ($16.93 w/hookups in summer, $10.21 w/hookups in winter), and gas pumps; the store may close in winter, but services are still available (ask at the trailer office next door). Coin-operated showers and laundry at the RV park are also open to the public. The separate National Park Service **campground,** just beyond and to the left, has sites with a good view of the lake, drinking water, and restrooms; $6. Continue 0.5 mile on the main road to the boat ramp and **Halls Crossing Marina.** The marina has a larger store (groceries and fishing and boating supplies), tours to Rainbow Bridge, a boat rental office (fishing, ski, and houseboat), gas dock, slips, and storage. The **ranger station** is nearby, though rangers are usually out on patrol; look for their vehicle in the area if the office is closed. Contact Lake Powell Resorts & Marinas for accommodation, boat rental, and tour reservations at 2916 N. 35th Ave., Suite 8, Phoenix, AZ 85017-5261; tel. (800) 528-6154 (278-8888 in greater Phoenix); the marina can also be reached at Hwy. 276, Lake Powell, UT 84533; tel. (801) 684-2261.

Stabilized Anasazi ruins at **Defiance House** in Forgotten Canyon make a good boating destination 12 miles uplake; a sign marks the beginning of the trail to the ruins. You can also take 2½-hour boat tours to Defiance House from Bullfrog Marina.

## Bullfrog

Before the days of Lake Powell, Bullfrog Rapids gave boaters a fast and bumpy ride. Bullfrog Marina now rivals Wahweap in its extensive visitor facilities. If driving in from either the ferry or the highway, you'll first see a large campground on the left; sites have drinking water and restrooms; $6. Continue on the main road to a junction; a service station here offers repairs and supplies. Continue straight at the junction for a picnic area and the boat ramp; turn right at the service station for Defiance House Lodge and Restaurant, Trailer Village, Bullfrog Painted Hills RV Park, Lily Pad (snack bar), and Bullfrog Marina. Formerly located near the boat ramp, the ranger station/visitor center and the Bullfrog Clinic will move to a new site opposite the Uplake District office, north on the highway in 1991.The **ranger station/visitor center** is open daily 8 a.m.-4:30 p.m. in summer and intermittently the rest of the year; tel. (801) 684-2243. The **clinic** is open mid-May to mid-Oct. and can be reached at tel. (801) 684-2288.

**Defiance House Lodge** offers luxury accommodations (rates are similar to Wahweap's) and the **Anasazi Restaurant** (open daily for breakfast, lunch, and dinner). The front desk at the lodge also handles **housekeeping units** (trailers) and an **RV park** (both located nearby with rates similar to those at Halls Crossing) and **tours** to Rainbow Bridge and Defiance House. Showers, laundry, convenience store, and post office are at **Trailer Village.** The RV park also has showers. Ask rangers for directions to primitive camping areas with vehicle access elsewhere along Bullfrog Bay.

All-day **Rainbow Bridge tours** usually leave daily from April 15 to Oct. 1 and stop on request to pick up passengers at Halls Crossing Marina; (may have a passenger minimum; $54 adult, $27 children). **Defiance House tours** leave on request during the same season (may have a passenger minimum; $17.25 adult, $12 children). **Bullfrog Marina** has a store, rentals (fishing, ski, and houseboat), gas dock, slips, and storage. Contact Lake Powell Resorts & Marinas for accommodation, boat rental, and tour reservations at 2916 N. 35th Ave., Suite 8, Phoenix, AZ 85017-5261; tel. (800) 528-6154 (278-8888 in greater Phoenix); Bullfrog Resort & Marina can also be reached at Box 4055-Bullfrog, Lake Powell, UT 84533; tel. (801) 684-2233.

**Ticaboo Lodge,** 12 miles north of Bullfrog Marina on UT 276, has accommodations for $49.05 s, $54.5 d; tel. 788-2110; closed Oct. 1 to April 1. Ticaboo is a tiny uranium mining camp currently in the doldrums. The mill (visible from the highway) and the mine were shut down at press time.

### Hite

In 1883, Cass Hite came to Glen Canyon in search of gold. He found some at a place later named "Hite City" and set off a small gold rush. Cass and a few of his relatives operated a small store and post office, the only services for many miles. Travelers wishing to cross the Colorado River here had the difficult task of swimming their animals across. Arthur Chaffin, a later resident, put through the first road and opened a ferry service in 1946. The Chaffin Ferry served uranium prospectors and adventurous motorists until the lake backed up to the spot in 1964. A steel bridge now spans the Colorado River far upstream. Cass Hite's store and the ferry site are underwater about 5 miles downlake from Hite Marina.

The uppermost marina on Lake Powell, Hite lies 141 lake miles from Glen Canyon Dam. From here boats can continue uplake to the mouth of Dark Canyon in Cataract Canyon at low water (Sheep Canyon in very low water) or into Canyonlands National Park at high water. Hite tends to be quieter than the other marinas and is favored by some fishermen and families. Turnoff for the marina is from UT 95 between Hanksville and Blanding. On the way in, you'll find a small **store** with gas pumps, **housekeeping units** (trailers; same rates as at Halls Crossing), and a primitive **campground** (no drinking water; free). Primitive camping is also available nearby off UT 95 at Dirty Devil, Farley Canyon, White Canyon, Blue Notch, and other locations. **Hite Marina,** at the end of the access road, has a small store, gas dock, boat rentals (fishing, ski, and houseboat), slips, and storage. Hikers can make arrangements with the marina to be dropped off or picked up at Dark Canyon. A **ranger station** is occasionally open; look for the ranger's vehicle at other times. Contact Lake Powell Resorts & Marinas for accommodation and boat reservations at 2916 N. 35th Ave., Suite 8, Phoenix, AZ 85017-5261; tel. (800) 528-6154 (278-8888 in greater Phoenix). Hite Marina can also be contacted at Box 501, Lake Powell, UT 84533; tel. (801) 684-2278

## RAINBOW BRIDGE NATIONAL MONUMENT

The bridge forms a graceful span 290 feet high and 275 feet wide; the Capitol building in Washington, D.C., would fit neatly underneath. Easiest way to Rainbow Bridge is by boat tour on Lake Powell from Wahweap, Bullfrog, or Halls Crossing marinas.

The more adventurous can hike to the bridge from near Navajo Mountain Trading Post (just north across the Utah-Arizona border on the east side of Navajo Mountain) or from the Rainbow Lodge ruins (just south of the Utah-Arizona border on the west side of Navajo Mountain). Rugged trails from each of these points wind through highly scenic canyons, meet in Bridge Canyon, then continue 2 miles to the bridge. Hiking either trail or doing a loop with both (car shuttle needed) is 26-28 miles roundtrip. Hikers must be experienced and self-sufficient on these trails, which cross a wilderness. Because the trails are unmaintained and poorly marked, bring a Navajo Mountain (Utah) 15-minute topo map.

No camping is allowed at Rainbow Bridge and no supplies are available; the marina and National Park Service ranger station are 10

*Rainbow Bridge*

miles away *by water only*. Best times to go are April to early June, Sept., and October. Winter cold and snow discourage visits, and summer is hot and brings hazardous flash floods. "Hiking to Rainbow Bridge" trail notes are available from the National Park Service, Glen Canyon N.R.A., Box 1507, Page, AZ 86040; tel. (602) 645-2511/2471. Obtain the required tribal hiking permit ($5 one person, $10 group of 2-10, $20 group of 11 or more) and camping permit ($1/person per night) by mail (allow 2 weeks) from Navajo Parks Dept., Box 308, Window Rock, AZ 86515; tel. (602) 871-6645. You can also get these permits in person from the tribal office building in Window Rock or the Cameron Visitor Center (junction of US 89 and AZ 64 near the Grand Canyon); both offices are open Mon. to Fri. about 8 a.m.-5 p.m.; the Cameron office is also open weekends from April to September.

The only road access to the Navajo Moun-tain area is Indian Route 16 from AZ 98 between Page and Kayenta in Arizona. To reach the east trailhead, go north 32 miles on Indian Route 16 past Inscription House Trading Post to a road fork, then turn right 6 miles to Navajo Mountain Trading Post (tours, gas, supplies, and info usually available). Continue on the main road 6.5 miles (go straight at the 4-way junction) to an earthen dam. Keep straight across the dam, take the left fork after 0.5 mile, then go 1.6 miles to Cha Canyon trailhead at the end of the road. The west trailhead is reached by going north 32 miles on Indian Route 16 and turning left about 6 miles at the road fork to the Rainbow Lodge ruins. Because Navajo Mountain is sacred to the Navajo, permission to climb it is needed from Navajo Parks Department. Guided hikes and horseback rides to Rainbow Bridge and Navajo Mountain can be arranged through Navajo Mountain Trading Post (Tonalea, AZ 86044).

# BOOKLIST

## DESCRIPTION AND TRAVEL

Abbey, Edward. "Slickrock." *Sierra Club Bulletin,* July-Aug. 1971; page 12. Conflicts of wilderness values with politics and business interests.

Aitchison, Stewart. *Utah Wildlands.* Utah Geographic Series, Inc. no. 3, 1987; 110 pages; $17.95. Text and beautiful color photos reveal some of the wonders in Utah's backcountry. The author also presents thoughts on the value of wilderness and proposals by various groups for and against new wilderness areas.

Barnes, F.A. *Canyon Country Camping.* Wasatch Publishers, Inc., 1978; 96 pages; $2.50. The best of southeastern Utah's canyon country lies away from towns and other developments. This handy guide provides practical tips for finding a place to camp. Includes listings of public campgrounds and a chapter devoted to primitive camping.

Barnes, F.A. *Canyon Country Exploring.* Wasatch Publishers, Inc., 1978; 64 pages; $1.95. Introduction to the beautiful canyon country of southeastern Utah and how you can see it. Includes tips on travel by car, off-road vehicle, horseback, foot, powerboat, raft, canoe or kayak, air, and commercial tours.

Barnes, F.A. *Canyon Country Off-Road Vehicle Trails: Arches & La Sals.* Wasatch Publishers, Inc., 1978; 96 pages; $4.50. Backcountry driving guide to Arches National Park area north of Moab, and the La Sal Mountains southeast of Moab. You'll also want the accompanying *Arches & La Sals Areas Off-Road Vehicle Trail Map* ($3).

Barnes, F.A. *Canyon Country Off-Road Vehicle Trails: Canyon Rims & Needles Areas.* Wasatch Publishers, Inc., 1978; 96 pages; $4.50. Backcountry driving guide to Canyonlands National Park's Needles District and other canyon areas southwest of Moab. You'll also want the accompanying *Canyon Rims & Needles Areas Off-Road Vehicle Trail Map* ($3).

Barnes, F.A. *Canyon Country Off-Road Vehicle Trails: Island Area.* Wasatch Publishers, Inc., 1978; 96 pages; $4. Backcountry driving guide to the back roads of Canyonlands National Park's Island in the Sky District area west of Moab. You'll also want the *Island Area Off-Road Vehicle Trail Map* ($3).

Barnes, F.A. *Utah Canyon Country.* Utah Geographic Series, Inc. no. 1, 1986; 120 pages; $17.95. Stunning color photos illustrate this book about the land, people, and natural history of southern Utah. The text also describes parks, monuments, and practicalities of travel in this fascinating region.

Bezy, John. *Bryce Canyon: The Story Behind the Scenery.* KC Publications, 1980; 48 pages; $5.95. Large color photos illustrate Bryce's creation, wonderful erosion forms, winter scenery, history, wildlife, and flora.

Bickers, Jack. *Canyon Country Off-Road Vehicle Trails: Maze Area.* Canyon Country Publications, 1988; 81 pages; $4.50. This guide will help you explore the remote western section of Canyonlands National Park and adjacent Glen Canyon N.R.A. lands. You'll also want the *Canyon Country Off-Road Vehicle Trail Map–Maze Area* ($3).

Bickers, Jack. *The Labyrinth Rims: 60 Accesses to Green River Overlooks.* 4-WD Trailguide Publications, 1989; 80 pages; $4. Maps and descriptions lead you to more than 60 overlooks of this deep, meandering canyon between the town of Green River and the confluence with the Colorado River.

Càrr, Stephen L. *The Historical Guide to Utah Ghost Towns.* Western Epics, 1986; 174 pages; $9.95. Excellent book about Utah's fading ghosts. The historic photos, well-written text, good directions, and maps will add to the pleasure of back-road travel.

Casey, Robert L. *A Journey to the High Southwest.* Pacific Search Press, 1983; 401 pages; $14.95. Introduction, history, and travel in southern Utah and adjacent Arizona, New Mexico, and Colorado.

Dunham, Dick, and Vivian Dunham. *Flaming Gorge Country: The Story of Daggett County, Utah.* Eastwood Printing and Publishing Co., 1978; 384 pages; $4.95. Tales and history of northeastern Utah.

Eardley, A.J., and James W. Schaack. *Zion: The Story Behind the Scenery.* KC Publications, 1971; 48 pages; $5.95. Large color photos illustrate descriptions of Zion's rock layers, canyons, prehistoric peoples, settlers, and ecology.

Gwynn, J. Wallace, ed. *Great Salt Lake: A Scientific, Historical, and Economic Overview.* Utah Geological and Mineral Survey Bulletin no. 116, June 1980; 400 pages; $20. Comprehensive and well-illustrated articles on the lake's geological and historical past and its present life forms, chemistry, industries, and recreation.

Hagood, Allen. *Dinosaur: The Story Behind the Scenery.* KC Publications, 1986; 32 pages; $5.95. Introduction to the dinosaurs, fossil excavation, geology, and canyons of Dinosaur National Monument in northeastern Utah.

Hirsch, Bob, and Stan Jones. *Fishin' Lake Powell.* Sun Country Publications; 96 pages; $8.50. Helpful advice on where and how to catch Lake Powell's gamefish.

Hoefer, Hans, et al. *American Southwest.* APA Insight Guides, 1984; 305 pages; $16.95. Outstanding color photography illustrates this travel guide of southern Utah and adjacent states. Many authors have contributed to the fine text.

Hoefer, Hans, et al. *The Rockies.* APA Insight Guides, 1985; 384 pages; $16.95. Impressive color photography illustrates this travel guide about the land, people, and history of the Rockies. Only the far north of Utah receives coverage, but this book provides good onward travel info for Wyoming and Colorado.

Hoffman, John F. *Arches National Park: An Illustrated Guide.* Western Recreational Publications, 1985; 128 pages; $9.95. Fine drawings and beautiful color photos illustrate descriptions of history, geology, flora, fauna, and touring the park.

Holdman, Floyd, and Nelson Wadsworth. *Utah.* Skyline Press, 1984. Eighty-eight color photos show the state's beauty and character in the towns, farms, mountains, and deserts.

Ingalls, Huntley. "We Climbed Utah's Skyscraper Rock." *National Geographic,* Nov. 1962; page 705. Difficult first ascent of Titan Tower—the highest of the Fisher Towers near Moab.

James, George Wharton. *Utah, The Land of Blossoming Valleys.* The Page Company, 1922; 371 pages. Old-fashioned but comprehensive guidebook about Utah's prehistory, settlement, railways, Mormon religion, Salt Lake City, art, farming, mining, geology, national forests, canyons, natural bridges, and birds.

Jones, Stan. *Boating and Exploring Map: Lake Powell and Its 96 Canyons.* Sun Country Publications, 1985; $3.50. Information-packed map showing natural features, marinas, Indian sites, hiking trails, and 4WD tracks. Map text describes points of interest, navigation, history, fishing, and wildlife.

Kelsey, Michael R. *Boater's Guide to Lake Powell*. Kelsey Publishing, 1989; 288 pages; $10.95. Explore the hundreds of canyons accessible by boat. This handy guide covers boating, hiking, camping, geology, archaeology, and history. Uses metric system.

Klinck, Richard E. *Land of Room Enough and Time Enough*. Peregrine Smith Books, 1984; 136 pages; $10.95. The land, legends, and peoples of Monument Valley.

Kluckhohn, Clyde. *Beyond the Rainbow*. Christopher Publishing House, 1933; 271 pages. Tales of travel from 1926 to 1929 in the still-wild country of Rainbow Bridge and among the Navajo in southeastern Utah and adjacent Arizona.

Lohman, S.W. *The Geologic Story of Arches National Park*. U.S. Geological Survey Bulletin no. 1393, 1975; 113 pages. This well-illustrated guidebook summarizes geologic history and explains how forces have created the many rock arches.

McCarry, Charles. *The Great Southwest*. National Geographic, 1980; 199 pages. Fantastic color photography with text about history and travels in the region, including the canyon and plateau country of southern Utah.

McClenahan, Owen. *Utah's Scenic San Rafael*. Self-published (Box 892, Castle Dale, UT 84513), 1986; 128 pages; $8.95. The author, a local "desert rat," takes you on driving tours through the scenic San Rafael region of east-central Utah. About half the trips can be done by car; the others need high clearance or 4WD.

Porter, Eliot. *The Place No One Knew: Glen Canyon on the Colorado*. Sierra Club, 1963; 170 pages. Beautiful color photos show a world now lost to the waters of Lake Powell. Thoughtful quotations from many individuals accompany the illustrations.

Roylance, Ward J. *Seeing Capitol Reef National Park*. Wasatch Publishers, 1979; 112 pages. Handy guide introduces the park's history, geology, climate, and life. Road logs and hiking trail descriptions aid exploration.

Roylance, Ward J. *Utah: A Guide to the State*. Utah: A Guide to the State Foundation, 1982; 779 pages; $22.50. An updated version of the book published by the W.P.A. Writers Program in 1941. Much of the original material and format have been preserved. The comprehensive introduction of Utah's people and history is followed by 11 tours of the state. A paperback version containing only the tours is also sold (507 pages; $9.95).

Sierra Club. *Desert Southwest: The Sierra Club Guides to the National Parks*. Random House, 1984; 352 pages; $17.95. Beautiful color photos illustrate the wildlife and scenic beauties of Utah's 5 national parks. The other parks described are Mesa Verde in Colorado, Grand Canyon and Petrified Forest in Arizona, Carlsbad Caverns in New Mexico, and Guadalupe Mountains and Big Bend in Texas. The text tells of the history, geology, wildlife, and flora. Maps and trail descriptions show hiking possibilities.

Stegner, Wallace, ed. *This is Dinosaur: Echo Park Country and its Magic Rivers*. Roberts Rinehart, Inc., 1985; 93 pages; $8.95. Essays on this rugged land—its geology, dinosaurs, wildlife, Indians, explorers, river running, and visiting Dinosaur National Monument.

Thompson, George A. *Some Dreams Die: Utah's Ghost Towns and Lost Treasures*. Dream Garden Press, 1982; 194 pages; $12.95. Treasure tales and historic photos make this an entertaining book. Historical inaccuracies and poor directions are weak points.

Till, Tom. *Utah: Magnificent Wilderness*. Westcliff Publishers, Inc., 1989; 112 pages; $14.95. Outstanding color photos by Tom Till and thoughtful quotations by Wallace Stegner grace this large-format book. You can also see one of Till's photos on the cover of *Utah Handbook,* 2nd edition!

Utah Division of Wildlife Resources. *Lakes of the High Uintas*. A series of 10 booklets available from Utah Division of Wildlife Resources (1596 W. North Temple, Salt Lake City, UT 84116), 1981-1985; 14-45 pages each; $1 each plus postage. Fishermen headed for the Uintas will find these detailed lake descriptions very useful. Also has practical advice on camping, hiking, and horse travel.

Utah Writers' Program of the Work Projects Administration. *Utah: A Guide to the State*. Hastings House, 1941; 595 pages. This classic guidebook to Utah still makes good reading. A lengthy introduction followed by detailed descriptions of towns and natural features provide a rich historical background. The book offers a look at Utah before the postwar industrialization. Libraries usually have a copy. Much of the material has been incorporated in the 1982 guide of the same name by Ward J. Roylance.

West, Linda, and Dan Chure. *Dinosaur: The Dinosaur National Monument Quarry*. Dinosaur Nature Assn., 1984; 40 pages; $4.95. A well-illustrated book about the difficulties and triumphs of early quarry digging and current work. Explains about dinosaurs and how they lived.

Wharton, Tom. *Utah! A Family Travel Guide*. Wasatch Publishers, Inc., 1987; 224 pages; $8.50. How to enjoy Utah's great outdoors with the kids. Also suggests museums, parks, and ski areas that the younger set will like. The well-illustrated guide contains many clever bits of wisdom.

Wilson, Ted. *Utah's Wasatch Front*. Utah Geographic Series, Inc. no. 4, 1987; 118 pages; $17.95. Beautiful color photos join with the wide-ranging text in portraying the cities, mountains, Great Salt Lake, and vigorous people of this region in northern Utah. The author served as Salt Lake City's mayor for 10 years prior to writing this book.

Vreeland, Robert H. *Nature's Bridges and Arches, Volume 2: Arches National Park, Utah*. Self-published, 1977; 124 pages; $2.50.

Fifty-four natural arches and windows of Arches Natural Park have photos and descriptions. Twenty-two other formations receive brief mentions.

Yandell, Michael D., ed. *Bryce Canyon & Zion National Parks*. National Parkways, 1972; 64 pages; $3.95. Introductions and information for seeing the parks by road and trail. Large color photos.

Zwinger, Ann. *Wind in the Rock: The Canyonlands of Southeastern Utah*. University of Arizona Press, 1986; 258 pages; $9.50. Well-written accounts of hiking in the Grand Gulch and nearby canyons. The author tells of the area's history, archaeology, wildlife, and plants.

## HIKING, BICYCLING, SKIING, AND CLIMBING

Barnes, F.A. *Canyon Country Hiking and Natural History*. Wasatch Publishers, Inc., 1977; 176 pages; $5. Introduction to the delights of hiking amongst the canyons and mountains in southeastern Utah.

Barnes, F.A., and Tom Kuehne. *Canyon Country Mountain Biking*. Canyon Country Publications, 1988; 145 pages; $8. Authors tell how to get the most out of bicycling the canyon country of southeast Utah. Trail descriptions take you through Arches and Canyonlands national parks, La Sal Mountains, and Canyon Rims.

Barnes, F.A. *Canyon Country Slickrock Hiking and Biking*. Canyon Country Publications, 1990; 289 pages; $12. "An illustrated guide to a completely different kind of hiking and mountain biking in the canyon country of southeastern Utah." A good introduction, areas to explore, personal anecdotes, and many b/w photos make this book fun to read and use.

Barnes, F.A. *Hiking the Historic Route of the 1859 Macomb Expedition*. Canyon Country Publications, 1989; 49 pages; $4. Captain John Macomb led the first expedition to explore and write about what's now Canyonlands National Park. Adventurous hikers can retrace part of Macomb's route, thanks to the descriptions, maps, and photos of this little guide.

Bjornstad, Eric. *Desert Rock: A Climber's Guide to the Canyon Country of the Southwest American Desert.* Chockstone Press, Inc., 1988; 464 pages; $25. Climbing routes on the towers, spires, buttes, and cliffs of the Four Corners region. Most of the book is devoted to Utah, including Canyonlands and Arches national parks, Fisher towers, Castle Valley, and Navajo lands.

Coello, Dennis. *Bicycle Touring in Utah.* Dream Garden Press, 1984; 118 pages; 11.95. Experience the beauty and varied landscapes of Utah on a bicycle. Tour descriptions and a section on getting started show the way.

Coello, Dennis. *The Mountain Bike Manual.* Dream Garden Press, 1985; 125 pages. Pedal away from the crowds and pavement with this book. Introduction explains how to choose and maintain a mountain bicycle. You'll also learn how to pack and plan for long-distance tours.

Davis, Mel. *High Uinta Trails.* Wasatch Publishers, Inc., 1974; 132 pages; $3.50. Guide to hiking, backpacking, camping, and fishing in the High Uintas Wilderness of northeastern Utah.

Gilson, Dale. *Alta Canyon Guidebook.* Redwood Coast Printers, 1977; 106 pages. A pocket-size guide to the hiking, rock climbing, and skiing near Alta (southeast of Salt Lake City). Nearly half the book is devoted to the area's history, wildlife, and plants.

Hall, David. *The Hiker's Guide to Utah.* Falcon Press Publishing Co., Inc., 1982; 212 pages; $9.95. Good selection of 60 trips within Utah. The day and overnight hikes range from easy to difficult. An introduction will help you get started hiking.

Kals, W.S. *Land Navigation Handbook.* Sierra Club Books, 1983; 230 pages; $9.95. This handy pocket guide will enable you to confidently explore Utah's extensive backcountry. Not only are details on using map and compass covered, but other methods such as altimeter navigation and using the sun and stars are explained.

Kelner, Alexis, and David Hanscom. *Wasatch Tours.* Wasatch Publishers, Inc., 1976; 222 pages; $6.50. A guide to about 100 cross-country ski tours near Salt Lake City.

Kelsey, Michael R. *Canyon Hiking Guide to the Colorado Plateau.* Kelsey Publishing, 1986; 256 pages; $9.95. Perhaps the best guide to hiking in southeastern Utah's canyon country. Geologic cross sections show the formations you'll be walking through. The book has descriptions and maps for 64 trips in Utah, 38 hikes in adjacent Arizona, 13 in Colorado, and 2 in New Mexico. The author is ahead of his time in using just the metric system, but the book is otherwise easy to follow.

Kelsey, Michael R. *Hiking and Exploring Utah's Henry Mountains and Robbers Roost.* Kelsey Publishing, 1987; 224 pages; $8.95. You'll find adventure and scenic beauty in this little-known region of high mountains and rugged canyons. Descriptions and maps cover 37 destinations. The book provides an excellent background of the region's history, mining, geology, and wildlife. Fascinating stories relate the escapades of Butch Cassidy. Uses metric system.

Kelsey, Michael R. *Hiking Utah's San Rafael Swell.* Kelsey Publishing, 1986; 144 pages; $8.95. Motorists driving across I-70 in east-central Utah get just a glimpse at the massive rock fold called the San Rafael Swell. This book presents the area's fascinating history and shows the way to hidden canyons with 30 hikes. Good maps and geologic cross sections. Uses metric system.

Kelsey, Michael R. *Utah Mountaineering Guide, and the Best Canyon Hikes.* Kelsey Publishing Co., 1986; 192 pages; $8.95. This guide points the way to Utah's highest peaks. The 74 hikes include some canyon treks in southern Utah. In the back are sections on old heliograph stations, Utah climates, bristlecone pines, geologic cross sections, and prehistoric Indians. Uses metric system.

Lambrechtse, Rudi. *Hiking the Escalante.* Wasatch Publishers, Inc., 1985; 189 pages; $7.50. "A wilderness guide to an exciting land of buttes, arches, alcoves, amphitheaters and deep canyons." Introduction to history, geology, and natural history of the Escalante region in southern Utah. Contains descriptions and trailhead info for 42 hiking destinations. The hikes vary from easy outings suitable for children to a highly challenging 4-day backpack trek.

Patterson, Thomas H. *Provo Area: Wasatch Hiking Map.* University of Utah Press, 1984; $5. Color topo map of trails on Mt. Timpanogos, Provo Peak, and Mt. Nebo.

Patterson, Thomas H. *Salt Lake City Area: Wasatch Hiking Map.* University of Utah Press, 1983; $5. Color topo map of trails southeast of Salt Lake City. Trails start from Mill, Big Cottonwood, and Little Cottonwood canyons.

Paxman, Shirley, Monroe Paxman, Gayle Taylor, and Weldon Taylor. *Utah Valley Trails.* Wasatch Publishers, Inc., 1978; 71 pages; $2.50. Handy hiking guide to mountains and canyons in the Provo area. Includes Timpanogos Peak, Provo Canyon, South Fork Provo Canyon, Hobble Creek Canyon, and Payson Canyon.

Ringholz, Raye Carleson. *Park City Trails.* Wasatch Publishers, Inc., 1984; 104 pages; $6.50. Hikes and cross-country ski tours in the mountains and canyons surrounding this old mining town. Includes a walking tour of Park City.

Schimpf, Ann, and Scot Datwyler. *Cache Tours.* Wasatch Publishers, Inc., 1977; 64 pages; $2.50. Thirty cross-country ski tours near Logan in northern Utah. Tour descriptions give distance, elevation change, and type of terrain; difficulties range from beginner to advanced.

Shelton, Peter. *The Insider's Guide to the Best Skiing in Utah.* Western Eye Press, Box 917, Telluride, CO 81435; 1989; 191 pages; $9.95. Good background and ski information.

Utesch, Peggy. *The Utah-Colorado Mountain Bike Trail System, Route I—Moab to Loma: Kokopelli's Trail.* Canyon Country Publications, 1990; 81 pages; $5. Learn about desert bicycling, then take off with the detailed descriptions of this well-illustrated guide. The 130-mile trail twists over spectacular terrain between Moab, Utah, and Loma, Colorado.

Wasatch Mountain Club and Betty Bottcher. *Wasatch Trails: Volume One.* Wasatch Mountain Club, 1973; 77 pages; $2. Pocket-sized guide to trails in the Wasatch Range southeast of Salt Lake City. Includes Parley's, Mill Creek, Big Cottonwood, and Little Cottonwood canyons.

Wasatch Mountain Club and Daniel Geery. *Wasatch Trails: Volume Two.* Wasatch Mountain Club, 1977; 112 pages; $2.50. This guide contains more difficult trails and routes in the Wasatch Range southeast of Salt Lake City. Many of these hikes link together for multi-day trips.

Waterman, Laura, and Guy Waterman. *Backwoods Ethics: Environmental Concerns for Hikers and Campers.* Stone Wall Press, 1979; 175 pages. Thoughtful commentaries on how the hiker can visit the wilderness with the least impact. Case histories dramatize need to protect the environment.

Williams, Brooke. *Utah Ski Country.* Utah Geographic Series, Inc. no. 2, 1986; 126 pages; $17.95. Incredible color photos illustrate the resorts, backcountry, and skiers surrounded by Utah's "Greatest Snow on Earth."

Wood, John. *Cache Trails*. Wasatch Publishers, Inc., 1987; 78 pages; $3.50. Hiking trails in the mountains of northern Utah near Logan.

Veranth, John. *Hiking the Wasatch*. Wasatch Mountain Club and Wasatch Publishers, Inc., 1989; 202 pages; $9.95. Introduction and description of major trails and routes in the central Wasatch, near Salt Lake City.

## RIVER RUNNING

Abbey, Edward. *Down the River*. E.P. Dutton, 1982; 242 pages; $7.95. Abbey's love for the wilderness comes through in thoughtful descriptions of travels along rivers through deserts of the West.

Aitchison, Stewart. *A Naturalist's San Juan River Guide*. Pruett Publishing Co., 1983; 57 pages; $10.95 (waterproof). Handy guidebook with topo maps and practical suggestions for a trip through the canyons of the San Juan River in southeastern Utah. Includes illustrations and background on geology, archaeology, history, flora, and fauna.

Anderson, Fletcher, and Ann Hopkinson. *Rivers of the Southwest: A Boater's Guide to the Rivers of Colorado, New Mexico, Arizona, and Utah*. Pruett Publishing Co., 1987; 139 pages; $16.95. Find out about running both the famous and the rarely traveled rivers of the region. Descriptions, photos, and maps tell what it's like. Ratings, suitable boats, and camping conditions tell what's needed.

Baars, Don, and Gene Stevenson. *San Juan Canyons: A River Runner's Guide*. Canon Publishers Ltd., 1986; 64 pages; $10.95 (waterproof). Probably the best guide to the San Juan. Text and detailed maps take you from Bluff to Clay Hills.

Belknap, Bill, and Buzz Belknap. *Canyonlands River Guide*. Westwater Books, 1974; 63 pages; $8.95 ($12.95 waterproof). Topo maps show the river and points of interest along the Green and Colorado rivers in southeastern Utah. Includes the Green through Labyrinth and Stillwater canyons, and the Colorado through Westwater and Cataract canyons to Lake Powell. Notes and photos provide a historical background.

Evans, Laura, and Buzz Belknap. *Desolation River Guide*. Westwater Books, 1974; 56 pages; $8.95 ($12.95 waterproof). Topo maps show the canyons and points of interest along the Green River through Desolation and Gray canyons. This 200-mile stretch connects Dinosaur National Monument and Green River, Utah. Notes and photos relate the river's history, Indians, geology, and wildlife.

Evans, Laura, and Buzz Belknap. *Dinosaur River Guide*. Westwater Books, 1973; 64 pages; $8.95 ($12.95 waterproof). Topo maps show the canyons and points of interest along the Green and Yampa rivers in Dinosaur National Monument of northeastern Utah and adjacent Colorado. Includes Lodore, Whirlpool, and Split Mountain canyons of the Green River. Notes and photos provide a historical background.

Goldwater, Barry M. *Delightful Journey: Down the Green & Colorado Rivers*. Arizona Historical Foundation, 1970; 209 pages; $16. Fewer than 100 persons had run the entire Grand Canyon in 1940, when Goldwater joined a 47-day, 1,463-mile expedition from Green River, Wyoming, to Lake Mead in Arizona.

Hayes, Philip T., and George C. Simmons. *River Runner's Guide to Dinosaur National Monument and Vicinity, With Emphasis on Geologic Features*. Powell Society, 1973; 78 pages; $3. This river guide covers the Green and Yampa rivers in Dinosaur National Monument in northeastern Utah and adjacent Colorado. The Green River log goes from below Flaming Gorge Reservoir to Ouray, Utah; the Yampa River log runs from Deerlodge Park to Echo Park.

Huser, Vern. *Canyon Country Paddles*. Wasatch Publishers, Inc., 1978; 96 pages; $2.50.

Introduction to river running in southeastern Utah by kayak, canoe, and raft. Has brief river descriptions of the Colorado, Green, San Juan, Muddy Creek, Dolores, Escalante, and Dirty Devil.

Mutschler, Felix E. *River Runners' Guide to the Canyons of the Green and Colorado Rivers, With Emphasis on Geologic Features; Volume 4.* Powell Society, 1972; 85 pages; $3. Guide to running the Green River from Ouray, Utah, to the town of Green River, passing through Desolation and Gray canyons.

Mutschler, Felix E. *River Runners' Guide to Canyonlands National Park and Vicinity, With Emphasis on Geologic Features.* Powell Society, 1977; 99 pages; $3. This guide covers the Green River from Green River, Utah, through Labyrinth and Stillwater canyons, and the Colorado River from Moab through Cataract Canyon to Lake Powell.

Nichols, Gary. *River Runners' Guide to Utah and Adjacent Areas.* University of Utah Press, 1986; 168 pages; $14.95. A comprehensive guidebook to running Utah's many rivers—the little-known ones as well as the popular Green and Colorado. Maps, photos, safety info, and difficulty ratings let you know the excitement and hazards of what you're getting into.

Stephens, Hal G., and Eugene M. Shoemaker. *In the Footsteps of John Wesley Powell: An Album of Comparative Photographs of the Green and Colorado Rivers, 1871-72 and 1968.* Johnson Books and the Powell Society, 1987; 286 pages; $34.95. Fascinating photo album of identical river views taken nearly 100 years apart. Photos show how little—and how much—the forces of erosion, plants, and man have changed the Green and Colorado river canyons. The text describes geologic features for each of the 110 pairs of photos. Maps show locations of camera stations.

Tejada-Flores, Lito. *Wildwater: the Sierra Club Guide to Kayaking and Whitewater Boating.* Sierra Club Books, 1978; 329 pages; $8.95. Comprehensive introduction to river running: choosing boats and equipment, river tech-

niques, safety, practical advice on trip planning, overview of river possibilities in the U.S., and history of whitewater boating.

Zwinger, Ann. *Run, River, Run: A Naturalist's Journey Down One of the Great Rivers of the American West.* Harper & Row, 1975; 317 pages; $10.95. An excellent description of the author's experiences along the Green River from its source in the Wind River Range of Wyoming to the Colorado River in southeastern Utah. The author weaves geology, Indian ruins, plants, wildlife, and her personal feelings into the text and drawings.

## HISTORY

Alexander, Thomas G., and James B. Allen. *Mormons & Gentiles: A History of Salt Lake City.* Pruett Publishing Co., 1984; 360 pages; $19.95. A detailed account of Salt Lake City's unique history.

Arrington, Leonard J. *Great Basin Kingdom: An Economic History of the Latter-day Saints.* Harvard University Press, 1958; 534 pages. More than just a book about numbers, you'll find a wealth of information on Mormon history and organization between the founding of the church in 1830 and the adjustments to mainstream America by 1900.

Burton, Richard F. *The City of the Saints and Across the Rocky Mountains to California.* First published in 1861; reprinted in 1963 by Alfred A. Knopf. Burton's lively writing style, broad scholarly background, and curiosity put you amidst the Mormon promised land in its early years. Meet the pioneers and other colorful characters of the Old West, learn about the savage Indian tribes, and experience the dust and mosquitos of 19th C. travel.

Colbert, Edwin H. *The Great Dinosaur Hunters and Their Discoveries.* Dover Publications, 1984; 283 pages; $8.95. Discovery of the "terrible lizards" in England during the 1820s and the worldwide fossil searches that followed. Includes early digging in what's now Dinosaur National Monument. Many photos and drawings illustrate the lively text.

Conrotto, Eugene L. "America's Last Indian War." *Desert Magazine,* March 1961; page 32. An uprising of the Ute Indians in 1923 near Blanding.

Crampton, C. Gregory. *Land of Living Rock.* Alfred A. Knopf, Inc., 1972; 267 pages; $19.95. Story of the geology, early explorers, Indians, and settlers in the high plateaus in Arizona, Utah, and Nevada. Well illustrated with color and b/w photos, maps, and diagrams.

Crampton, C. Gregory. *Standing Up Country.* Alfred A. Knopf, Inc., 1964; 191 pages; $12.75. Illustrated historical account of the people who came to the canyon lands of Utah and Arizona—the Indians, explorers, outlaws, miners, settlers, and scientists.

Dellenbaugh, Frederick S. *A Canyon Voyage: The Narrative of the Second Powell Expedition.* Reprinted by The University of Arizona Press, 1984; 277 pages; $9.95. Well-written account of John Wesley Powell's second expedition down the Green and Colorado rivers, 1871-72. The members took the first Grand Canyon photographs and obtained much valuable scientific knowledge.

Gillmor, Frances, and Louisa Wetherill. *Traders to the Navajo.* University of New Mexico Press, 1983; 265 pages; $7.95. The Wetherill brothers began a trading operation in the Monument Valley region during the late 1800s and were among the first white men to explore this scenic land. Authors relate tales of lost mines, early travelers, and the Navajo people.

Lester, Margaret D. *Brigham Street.* Utah State Historical Society, 1979; 263 pages; $34. Though currently known as "South Temple Street," this broad thoroughfare took the prophet's name in the city's early decades. Church leaders, including Brigham Young, built their homes along this street close to the temple, while wealthy businessmen constructed fine mansions farther east. This illustrated volume tells the stories of many of the notable citizens who settled along the

street, said to be the most beautiful between Denver and San Francisco.

McCormick, John S. *Salt Lake City: The Gathering Place.* Windsor Publications, Inc., 1980; 130 pages. Historic photos and drawings help tell the story of Salt Lake City. The text begins with Mormon leaders searching for their Zion, then relates the good times and bad as the pioneer settlement grew into a modern city. An excellent introduction to Salt Lake City's history.

Miller, David E. *Hole-in-the-Rock.* University of Utah Press, 1959; 229 pages. Detailed account of pioneers struggling to build a 200-mile wagon road to the remote southeastern corner of Utah in 1879-80. A group of about 250 men, women, and children in 80 wagons navigated some of the West's most rugged country to become the first white settlers in San Juan County.

Morgan, Dale L. *The Great Salt Lake.* University of New Mexico Press, 1973 (first published in 1947); 432 pages. Unusual, almost poetic history of what the author calls the mountain sea. Mountain men, explorers, and Mormon settlers march through the pages. Dale Morgan also served as the principal editor for the 1941 *Utah: A Guide to the State.*

Mortensen, A.R., ed. "Utah's Dixie...The Cotton Mission." *Utah Historical Quarterly,* July, 1961 (vol. 29, no. 3); 302 pages. Stories of the pioneers in the southwestern corner of Utah, known as Dixie.

Notarianni, Philip F. *Faith, Hope, and Prosperity: The Tintic Mining District.* Tintic Historical Society, 1982; 190 pages; $19.95. Fascinating picture book of Eureka and other early mining communities. Hundreds of photos reveal life of the miners and their families.

Peterson, Charles S. *Utah, a Bicentennial History.* W.W. Norton & Co., 1977; 213 pages; $7.95. Good popular history of Utah's exploration, Mormon settlements, economic changes, and politics through to modern times.

Poll, Richard D., ed. *Utah's History.* Brigham Young University Press, 1978; 757 pages; $15.95. Comprehensive account beginning with the prehistoric peoples, then through the eras of Spanish, fur traders, government surveyors, Mormon colonization, modern Indian tribes, statehood, and present-day Utah. Maps, charts, and notes on the physical setting add to an understanding of this unusual state.

Powell, John Wesley. *The Exploration of the Colorado River and its Canyons.* Dover Publications, reprinted 1961 (first published in 1895); 400 pages; $6.95. Powell's 1869 expedition down the Green and Colorado rivers. His was the first group to navigate through the Grand Canyon. A description of the 1879 Uinta Expedition is included too.

Reay, Lee. *Incredible Passage Through the Hole-in-the-Rock.* Meadow Lane Publications, 1980; 128 pages; $7.95. Story of the determined Mormon pioneers who crossed extremely rugged canyon country to settle in Bluff in southeastern Utah. Includes descriptions of pioneer life and Indians.

Smart, William B. *Old Utah Trails.* Utah Geographic Series, Inc. no. 5, 1988; 136 pages; $17.95. Join the early explorers of the West on their treks across this vast land. Quotations, maps, and beautiful color photos rekindle their experiences.

Stansbury, Howard. *Exploration and Survey of the Valley of the Great Salt Lake of Utah, Including a Reconnaissance of a New Route Through the Rocky Mountains.* Robert Armstrong, Public Printer, 1853; 495 pages. (Reprinted in shorter form by Ann Arbor University Microfilms, Inc., 1966.) In this report of an early U.S. Army surveying expedition to Utah, Stansbury describes the Indians, geography, climate, pioneer travelers, Mormon settlements, and difficulties experienced on the way.

*Utah Historical Quarterly.* Utah State Historical Society, published quarterly. Book reviews and stories from Utah's past.

# ARCHAEOLOGY

Ambler, J. Richard. *The Anasazi: Prehistoric Peoples of the Four Corners Region.* Museum of Northern Arizona, 1977; 50 pages; $6.95. Concise overview of this now-vanished pueblo tribe.

Lister, Robert, and Florence Lister. *Those Who Came Before.* University of Arizona Press, 1983; 184 pages; $12.95. A well-illustrated guide to the history, artifacts, and ruins of prehistoric Southwest Indians. The author also describes parks and monuments containing archaeological sites.

McGregor, John C. *Southwestern Archaeology.* University of Illinois Press, 1982; 511 pages; $16.95. Curious why archaeologists like their work and how it's done? This book presents motivations and techniques of the scientists. It also describes cultures and artifacts from the earliest known peoples to recent times in a readable and useful form.

Mays, Buddy. *Ancient Cities of the Southwest: A Practical Guide to the Prehistoric Ruins of Arizona, New Mexico, Utah, and Colorado.* Chronicle Books, 1982; 132 pages; $7.95. A handy guide to visiting places of the Anasazi and other departed tribes.

Noble, David Grant. *Ancient Ruins of the Southwest.* Northland Press, 1981; 156 pages; $10.95. Well-illustrated guide to prehistoric ruins of Utah, Arizona, New Mexico, and Colorado. Contains practical info on getting to sites, nearby campgrounds, and services.

Oppelt, Norman T. *Guide to Prehistoric Ruins of the Southwest.* Pruett Publishing Co., 1981; 208 pages; $10.95. Introduction to ancient cultures with descriptions of more than 200 sites in southeastern Utah and adjacent states.

Smith, Gary, and Michael E. Long. "Utah Rock Art: Wilderness Louvre." *National Geographic,* Jan. 1980; page 97. A photo essay.

Stokes, William Michael, and William Lee Stokes. *Messages on Stone.* Starstone Publishing Co., 1980; 57 pages; $2.50. Collection of petroglyphs and pictographs divided into related groups. Book presents ideas on how the rock art can be interpreted.

## UTAH INDIANS OF TODAY

Dedera, Don. *Navajo Rugs: How to Find, Evaluate, Buy and Care for Them.* Northland Press, 1975; 114 pages; $8.95. Dedera gives the history of Navajo weaving, illustrates how it's done, shows regional styles, and offers practical advice on purchasing.

Dyk, Walter (recorded by). *Son of Old Man Hat, A Navajo Autobiography.* University of Nebraska Press, 1967 (1938 original copyright); 378 pages; $9.95. A Navajo relates growing up in the late 1800s. He was born during his family's return from 4 years of internment at Fort Sumner, New Mexico.

Gilpin, Laura. *The Enduring Navajo.* University of Texas Press, 1968; 505 pages; $37.50. Excellent book about the Navajo, their homes, land, ceremonies, crafts, tribal government, and the trading posts.

Locke, Raymond F. *The Book of the Navajo.* Mankind Publishing, 1976; 464 pages; $4.95. Navajo legends, art, and history from early to modern times.

Looney, Ralph. "The Navajos." *National Geographic,* Dec. 1972; page 740. The Navajo people and how they've balanced their traditions with life in 20th C. America.

Luckert, Karl W. *Coyoteway: A Navajo Holyway Healing Ceremonial.* The University of Arizona Press and Museum of Northern Arizona Press, 1979; 243 pages; $13.95. A rare look at an important Navajo ceremony. The event requires 9 days and involves chanting, fire making, sandpainting, and other rituals. Photos and translations of chants reveal some of the intricate Navajo beliefs.

Zolbrod, Paul G. *Diné bahane': The Navajo Creation Story.* University of New Mexico Press, 1984; 431 pages; $22.50. Deities, people, and animals come to life in this translation of Navajo mythology.

## NATURAL SCIENCES

Arnberger, Leslie P., and Jeanne R. Janish. *Flowers of the Southwest Mountains.* Southwest Parks and Monuments Assn., 1982; 139 pages; $9.95. Coverage includes common flowers and trees of southern Utah's high country above 7,000 feet.

Baars, Donald L. *The Colorado Plateau: A Geologic History.* University of New Mexico Press, 1983; 279 pages; $13.95. Written for the layman, this book takes you on a tour of the Four Corners area geology from the ancient twisted rocks at the bottom of the Grand Canyon to the fiery volcanism and icy glaciations of the Pleistocene Epoch.

Barnes, F.A. *Canyon Country Geology for the Layman and Rockhound.* Wasatch Publishers, Inc., 1978; 157 pages; $5. Geologic history and a guide to rockhounding. Emphasis is on southeastern Utah and adjacent Arizona.

Craighead, John J. (and others). *A Field Guide to Rocky Mountain Wildflowers.* Houghton Mifflin Co., 1963; 275 pages; $9.95. Handy guide takes in Utah's high country. A plant key and detailed descriptions make identification easy. Illustrated with line drawings and color photos.

Dodge, Natt N. *100 Roadside Wildflowers of Southwest Uplands in Natural Color.* Southwest Parks and Monuments Assn., 1980; 64 pages; $4.95. Introduction with a brief description and color photo for those flowers usually found in southern Utah above 4,500 feet.

Dodge, Natt, N. *Poisonous Dwellers of the Desert.* Southwest Parks and Monuments

Assn., 1981; 40 pages. Creatures to watch out for: poisonous insects, snakes, and the Gila monster. Advice is given on bite treatment and insecticides. Some nonvenomous animals often mistakenly thought poisonous are listed too.

Doolittle, Jerome. *Canyons and Mesas.* Time-Life Books (American Wilderness Series), 1974; 184 pages. Text and photos give a feel for the ruggedly beautiful country of southern Utah and adjacent states.

Elmore, Francis H., and Jeanne R. Janish. *Shrubs and Trees of the Southwest Uplands.* Southwest Parks and Monuments Assn., 1976; 214 pages; $9.95. Color-coded pages help locate plants and trees above 4,500 feet (from the pinyon-juniper belt to treeline).

Halfpenny, James, and Elizabeth Biesiot. *A Field Guide: Mammal Tracking in Western America.* Johnson Books, 1986; 163 pages; $12.95. No need to guess what animal passed by. This well-illustrated guide shows how to read trails of large and small wildlife. More determined detectives can study the scatology chapter.

Hamilton, Wayne L. *The Sculpturing of Zion; With Road Guide to the Geology of Zion National Park.* Zion Natural History Assn., 1984; 132 pages; $12.95. Outstanding book explaining geologic forces and history. Clear graphs, drawings, and beautiful color photography illustrate the nontechnical text.

Haywood, C. Lynn, et al. *Birds of Utah.* BYU Great Basin Naturalist memoirs, 1976; 229 pages; $10. Introduction tells of bird habitats, conservation, and early observations. Descriptions tell where and when sighted. Illustrated with color and b/w photos.

Haywood, C. Lynn. *The High Uintas: Utah's Land of Lake and Forest.* Monte L. Bean Life Science Museum, 1983; 101 pages; $6.95. This book will help you enjoy your travels in the Uintas. Introduction to the geology, plant life, birds, and animals of Utah's loftiest lands. Well illustrated with color and b/w photos.

Lanner, Ronald M., and Christine Rasmuss. *Trees of the Great Basin: A Natural History.* University of Nevada Press, 1984; 215 pages; $19.95. Thoughtful and informative descriptions of 47 trees native to mountains of Nevada and western Utah. Author's enthusiasm for trees and their life cycles really comes across. Many of these trees occur in other parts of Utah too. The book has a color photo section.

Lindquist, Robert C. *The Geology of Bryce Canyon National Park.* Bryce Canyon Natural History Assn., 1977; 52 pages; $1.99. A well-illustrated, nontechnical account of Bryce's geologic history and formation of the colorful erosional features.

McKee, Edwin D. *Ancient Landscapes of the Grand Canyon Region.* Northland Press, 1982; 52 pages; $3. Brief account of geologic forces creating Zion, Bryce, and the Grand Canyon.

MacMahon, James A. *Deserts.* Alfred A. Knopf, The Audubon Society Nature Guides, 1985; 638 pages; $15.95. Comprehensive naturalist's guide to the Great Basin Desert, Colorado Plateau semidesert, and other arid regions of the West. Many color photos help identify the birds, mammals, fish, insects, reptiles, amphibians, and flora.

Nelson, Ruth, and Tom Blaue. *Plants of Zion National Park: Wildflowers, Trees, Shrubs, and Ferns.* Zion Natural History Assn., 1976; 333 pages; $9.95. Introduction to Zion's plants, habitats, and blooming seasons. A key, grouped according to families, aids identification. Many b/w drawings and color photos.

Olin, George, and Dale Thompson. *Mammals of the Southwest Deserts.* Southwest Parks and Monuments Assn., 1982; 97 pages; $5.95. Well illustrated with b/w and color drawings.

Patraw, Pauline M., and Jeanne R. Janish. *Flowers of the Southwest Mesas.* Southwest Parks and Monuments Assn., 1977; 112 pages; $9.95. Flowers and trees of the Upper

Sonoran Zone (pinyon-juniper belt) are illustrated and described.

Shaw, Richard J. *Wildflowers of the Wasatch and Uinta Mountains.* Wheelwright Press, 1983; 61 pages; $4.95. Compact guide with a color photo for each of the flowers described.

Sigler, William F., and Robert Rush Miller. *Fishes of Utah.* Utah State Dept. of Fish and Game, 1963; 203 pages. A handy guide for the fisherman who wants the inside story of his favorite fish. The book introduces Utah fishing and provides descriptions, illustrations, and life histories for many species. Available from Utah Division of Wildlife Resources, 1596 W. North Temple, Salt Lake City, UT 84116.

Stokes, William L. *Geology of Utah.* Utah Museum of Natural History Occasional Paper no. 6, 1986; 309 pages; $12. A comprehensive overview of Utah's geologic history, rock layers, fossils, and landscapes.

Stokes, William L. *Scenes of the Plateau Lands and How They Came to Be.* Starstone Publishing Co., 1969; 66 pages; $7.95. How mesas, canyons, volcanos, and other geologic features were formed.

Sweet, Muriel. *Common Edible and Useful Plants of the West.* Naturegraph Publishers, 1976; 64 pages. Nontechnical descriptions of plants and trees that have food, medicinal, and other uses. Most of these were first discovered by Indians and used later by pioneer settlers.

Taylor, Ronald J. *Rocky Mountain Wildflowers.* Mountaineers, 1986; 96 pages; $5.95. Pocket-sized guide to high-country flowers, each with a description and color photo.

Welsh, Stanley L., and Bill Ratcliffe. *Flowers of the Canyon Country.* Canyonlands Natural History Assn., 1986; 85 pages; $9.95. Beautiful color photography makes this book a pleasure to use while traveling in southern Utah. Each flower has a photo and nontechnical description.

Whitney, Stephen. *Western Forests.* Alfred A. Knopf, The Audubon Society Nature Guides, 1985; 670 pages; $16.95. Comprehensive guide to the woodlands, Rocky Mountain montane forests, and subalpine forests of Utah and other western states. The hundreds of color photos aid identification of wildflowers, trees, birds, mammals, reptiles, amphibians, and insects.

## ONWARD TRAVEL

Castleman, Deke. *Nevada Handbook.* Moon Publications, 1989; 302 pages; $10.95. A lively guide to the cities, ghost towns, deserts, and mountains. Learn the inside story of the gambling centers and many other facets of this unusual state, the "Wildest in the West."

Metzger, Stephen. *New Mexico Handbook.* Moon Publications, 1989; 351 pages; $11.95. Magical landscapes, ancient Indian villages, and thriving art centers are just a few of the attractions here. This handy guide will help you get the most from your visit.

Weir, Bill. *Arizona Traveler's Handbook.* Moon Publications, 1990; 505 pages; $13.95. If you like the *Utah Handbook,* you'll enjoy using this one too! It's the most comprehensive guide to the Grand Canyon State's scenic wonders, cities, towns, history, outdoor recreation, and practicalities.

## REFERENCE

Greer, Deon C. *Atlas of Utah.* Weber State College and Brigham Young University Press, 1981; 300 pages; $29.95. A comprehensive atlas of the state with excellent color maps. Good overview of Utah's geography, climate, geology, flora and fauna, history, social institutions, government, economy, and recreation.

Perry, John, and Jane Greverus Perry. *The Sierra Club Guide to the Natural Areas of Colorado and Utah.* Sierra Club Books, 1985; 317 pages; $9.95. A reference source with addresses, recreation possibilities, plant and animal checklists, and road directions for 189 different areas.

# THE GREAT WESTERN TRAIL

As its name implies, the Great Western Trail will traverse some of the West's most spectacular country. When completed, the approximately 350-mile length of the Utah section will link through trails in Arizona and Idaho with trails in New Mexico, Wyoming, and Montana. Planners envision a trail system stretching all the way from Mexico to Canada. Separate parallel trails will provide for bicycles, horses, and motorized vehicles as well as hikers. About 90% of the system can use existing roads and trails. Note that some trail sections are open for vehicles and pets, and some aren't. Obtain the latest trail info from the respective agencies below.

THE GREAT WESTERN TRAIL

The southernmost trail section in Utah follows washes and canyons across land administered by the Bureau of Land Management; elevations drop as low as 4,800 feet here. The Dixie National Forest section skirts the west edge of Bryce Canyon National Park and continues across high plateaus to Boulder Top, where it reaches elevations above 11,000 feet. Fishlake National Forest has more fine alpine country and expansive views from Thousand Lake Mountain, Windstorm Peak, and UM Plateau areas. In the Manti-LaSal National Forest, the trail ascends the lofty Wasatch Plateau and extends for 75 miles through rolling meadows and forest country. Uinta National Forest features lush forests beneath jagged peaks of the Wasatch Range's Mt. Timpanogos and Lone Peak. The ups and downs of the Wasatch Range continue as the trail winds through the Wasatch-Cache National Forest high above Salt Lake

City and the Great Salt Lake. The northern-most trail section in Utah climbs into the Bear River Range and meets the Idaho border near Beaver Mountain.

The **Great Western Trail Association** needs volunteers for trail construction and maintenance. If you'd like to help, contact the Association at Box 1428, Provo, UT 84602.

Cedar District Office
Bureau of Land Management
176 East DL Sargent Dr.
Cedar City, UT 84720
Tel. (801) 586-2401

Dixie National Forest
Box 580
82 N. 100 East
Cedar City, UT 84720
Tel. (801) 865-3700

Fishlake National Forest
115 E. 900 North
Richfield, UT 84701
Tel. (801) 896-4491

Manti-LaSal National Forest
599 West Price River Dr.
Price, UT 84501
Tel. (801) 637-2817

Uinta National Forest
Box 1428
88 W. 100 North
Provo, UT 84602
Tel. (801) 377-5780

Wasatch-Cache National Forest
8230 Federal Bldg.
125 S. State St.
Salt Lake City, UT 84138
Tel. (801) 524-5034

# INDEX

Bold-faced page numbers offer the primary reference.
*Italicized* page numbers indicate an illustration.
See the front matter for LIST OF MAPS and LIST OF CHARTS.

# ABOUT THE AUTHOR

Back in school, Bill Weir always figured that he'd settle down to a career job and live happily ever after. Then he "discovered" traveling. After graduating with a B.A. degree in physics from Berea College in 1972, Bill wound up as an electronic technician in Columbus, Ohio. But the very short vacation times just weren't enough for the trips he dreamed of. So in 1976 he took off with his trusty bicycle "Bessie" and rode across the United States from Virginia to Oregon with Bikecentennial '76. The following year he did an even longer bicycle trip—from Alaska to Baja California. Then the ultimate journey—a bicycle cruise around the world! That lasted from 1980 to 1984, with most of the time spent in the South Pacific and Asia. Naturally Bill used Moon's excellent *South Pacific Handbook* and *Indonesia Handbook*. Correspondence with the authors led to some text and photo contributions for their books and the idea of doing a guidebook of his own. From New Delhi in India, Bill returned to his home base of Flagstaff, Arizona, and set to work researching and writing the *Arizona Traveler's Handbook*. The immense project took 1½ years of writing and nearly another year of production.

As soon as the writing of the Arizona book came to an end, Bill headed north across the Grand Canyon to the Beehive State. The *Utah Handbook* turned out to be a big challenge, too, though the rewards of travel there matched his efforts. With Utah "out the door" to the printer, Bill did a 40-day trek in the Mount Everest area of Nepal, before hurrying back to rewrite a major new edition of Arizona. Hardly had he completed that task, when Utah beckoned once again! Now, 3,000 miles and what seems like a thousand phone calls later, *Utah Handbook*, Second Edition, is ready for you.

Still free and single, Bill's major interests continue to be writing, 35-mm and video photography, and travel. The diverse worlds of the American West and Asia remain his favorites.

*Author showing off Beech C-45 "Expeditor" at Hill AFB Museum*

## Moon Handbooks—The Ideal Traveling Companions

Open a Moon Handbook and you're opening your eyes and heart to the world. Thoughtful, sensitive, and provocative, Moon Handbooks encourage an intimate understanding of a region, from its culture and history to essential practicalities. Fun to read and packed with valuable information on accommodations, dining, recreation, plus indispensable travel tips, detailed maps, charts, illustrations, photos, glossaries, and indexes, Moon Handbooks are ideal traveling companions: informative, entertaining, and highly practical.

TO ORDER BY PHONE: (800) 345-5473 • Monday-Friday • 9 a.m.-5 p.m. PST

# The Pacific/Asia Series

**BALI HANDBOOK**  by Bill Dalton
Detailed travel information on the most famous island in the world. 12 color pages, 29 b/w photos, 68 illustrations, 42 maps, 7 charts, glossary, booklist, index. 428 pages.  **$12.95**

**INDONESIA HANDBOOK**  by Bill Dalton
This one-volume encyclopedia explores island by island the many facets of this sprawling, kaleidoscopic island nation. 30 b/w photos, 143 illustrations, 250 maps, 17 charts, booklist, extensive Indonesian vocabulary, index. 1,050 pages.  **$17.95**

**SOUTH KOREA HANDBOOK**  by Robert Nilsen
Whether you're visiting on business or searching for adventure, *South Korea Handbook* is an invaluable companion. 8 color pages, 78 b/w photos, 93 illustrations, 109 maps, 10 charts, Korean glossary with useful notes on speaking and reading the language, booklist, index. 548 pages.  **$14.95**

**SOUTHEAST ASIA HANDBOOK**  by Carl Parkes
Helps the enlightened traveler discover the real Southeast Asia. 16 color pages, 75 b/w photos, 11 illustrations, 169 maps, 140 charts, vocabularies and suggested reading, index. 873 pages. **$16.95**

**PHILIPPINES HANDBOOK** by Peter Harper and Evelyn Peplow
Crammed with detailed information, Philippines Handbook equips the escapist, hedonist or business traveler with a thorough introduction to the Philippines' colorful history, landscapes and culture. Color and b/w photos, illustrations, maps, charts, booklist, index. 400 pages. $12.95

**HAWAII HANDBOOK** by J.D. Bisignani
Winner of the 1989 Hawaii Visitors Bureau's Best Guide Book Award and the Grand Award for Excellence in Travel Journalism, this guide takes you beyond the glitz and high-priced hype and leads you to a genuine Hawaiian experience. 12 color pages, 86 b/w photos, 132 illustrations, 86 maps, 44 graphs and charts, Hawaiian and pidgin glossaries, appendix, booklist, index. 879 pages.  $15.95

**KAUAI HANDBOOK** by J.D. Bisignani
*Kauai Handbook* is the perfect antidote to the workaday world. 8 color pages, 36 b/w photos, 48 illustrations, 19 maps, 10 tables and charts, Hawaiian and pidgin glossaries, booklist, index. 236 pages.  $9.95

**MAUI HANDBOOK: Including Molokai and Lanai** by J.D. Bisignani
"No fool-'round" advice on accommodations, eateries, and recreation, plus a comprehensive introduction to island ways, geography, and history. 8 color pages, 60 b/w photos, 72 illustrations, 34 maps, 19 charts, booklist, glossary, index. 350 pages.  $10.95

**OAHU HANDBOOK** by J.D. Bisignani
A handy guide to Honolulu, renowned surfing beaches, and Oahu's countless other diversions. Color and b/w photos, illustrations, 18 maps, charts, booklist, glossary, index. 354 pages. $11.95

**BIG ISLAND OF HAWAII HANDBOOK** by J.D. Bisignani
An entertaining yet informative text packed with insider tips on accommodations, dining, sports and outdoor activities, natural attractions, and must-see sights. Color and b/w photos, illustrations, 20 maps, charts, booklist, glossary, index. 347 pages.  $11.95

**SOUTH PACIFIC HANDBOOK** by David Stanley
The original comprehensive guide to the 16 territories in the South Pacific. 20 color pages, 195 b/w photos, 121 illustrations, 35 charts, 138 maps, booklist, glossary, index. 740 pages. $15.95

**MICRONESIA HANDBOOK:**
**Guide to the Caroline, Gilbert, Mariana, and Marshall Islands** by David Stanley
*Micronesia Handbook* guides you on a real Pacific adventure all your own. 8 color pages, 77 b/w photos, 68 illustrations, 69 maps, 18 tables and charts, index. 287 pages.  $9.95

**FIJI ISLANDS HANDBOOK** by David Stanley
The first and still the best source of information on travel around this 322-island archipelago. 8 color pages, 35 b/w photos, 78 illustrations, 26 maps, 3 charts, Fijian glossary, booklist, index. 198 pages.  $8.95

**TAHITI-POLYNESIA HANDBOOK** by David Stanley
All five French-Polynesian archipelagoes are covered in this comprehensive guide by Oceania's best-known travel writer. 12 color pages, 45 b/w photos, 64 illustrations, 33 maps, 7 charts, booklist, glossary, index. 225 pages.  $9.95

**NEW ZEALAND HANDBOOK** by Jane King
Introduces you to the people, places, history, and culture of this extraordinary land. 8 color pages, 99 b/w photos, 146 illustrations, 82 maps, booklist, index. 546 pages. **$14.95**

**BLUEPRINT FOR PARADISE: How to Live on a Tropic Island** by Ross Norgrove
This one-of-a-kind guide has everything you need to know about moving to and living comfortably on a tropical island. 8 color pages, 40 b/w photos, 3 maps, 14 charts, appendices, index. 212 pages. **$14.95**

# The Americas Series

**NORTHERN CALIFORNIA HANDBOOK** by Kim Weir
An outstanding companion for imaginative travel in the territory north of the Tehachapis. 12 color pages, b/w photos, 69 maps, illustrations, booklist, index. 759 pages. **$16.95**

**NEVADA HANDBOOK** by Deke Castleman
*Nevada Handbook* puts the Silver State into perspective and makes it manageable and affordable. 34 b/w photos, 43 illustrations, 37 maps, 17 charts, booklist, index. Approx. 400 pages. **$12.95**

**NEW MEXICO HANDBOOK** by Stephen Metzger
A close-up and complete look at every aspect of this wondrous state. 8 color pages, 85 b/w photos, 63 illustrations, 50 maps, 10 charts, booklist, index. 350 pages. **$11.95**

**TEXAS HANDBOOK** by Joe Cummings
Seasoned travel writer Joe Cummings brings an insider's perspective to his home state. 12 color pages, b/w photos, maps, illustrations, charts, booklist, index. 483 pages. **$11.95**

**ARIZONA TRAVELER'S HANDBOOK** by Bill Weir
This meticulously researched guide contains everything necessary to make Arizona accessible and enjoyable. 8 color pages, 194 b/w photos, 74 illustrations, 53 maps, 6 charts, booklist, index. 505 pages. **$13.95**

**UTAH HANDBOOK** by Bill Weir
Weir gives you all the carefully researched facts and background to make your visit a success. 8 color pages, 102 b/w photos, 61 illustrations, 30 maps, 9 charts, booklist, index. 452 pages. **$12.95**

**ALASKA-YUKON HANDBOOK** by Deke Castleman, Don Pitcher, and David Stanley
Get the inside story, with plenty of well-seasoned advice to help you cover more miles on less money. 8 color pages, 26 b/w photos, 92 illustrations, 90 maps, 6 charts, booklist, glossary, index. 384 pages. **$11.95**

**WASHINGTON HANDBOOK** by Dianne J. Boulerice Lyons
Covers sights, shopping, services, transportation, and outdoor recreation, with complete listings for restaurants and accommodations. 8 color pages, 92 b/w photos, 24 illustrations, 81 maps, 8 charts, booklist, index. 400 pages. **$12.95**

**OREGON HANDBOOK** by Stuart Warren and Ted Long Ishikawa
Brimming with travel practicalities and insider views on Oregon's history, culture, arts, and activities. Color and b/w photos, illustrations, 28 maps, charts, booklist, index. Approx. 400 pages. **$12.95**

**WYOMING HANDBOOK** by Don Pitcher
All you need to know to open the doors to this wide and wild state. Color and b/w photos, illustrations, over 70 maps, charts, booklist, index. Approx. 500 pages. **$12.95**

**BRITISH COLUMBIA HANDBOOK** by Jane King
With an emphasis on outdoor adventures, this guide covers mainland British Columbia, Vancouver Island, the Queen Charlotte Islands, and the Canadian Rockies. 8 color pages, 56 b/w photos, 45 illustrations, 66 maps, 4 charts, booklist, index. 381 pages. **$11.95**

**GUIDE TO CATALINA and California's Channel Islands** by Chicki Mallan
A complete guide to these remarkable islands, from the windy solitude of the Channel Islands National Marine Sanctuary to bustling Avalon. 8 color pages, 105 b/w photos, 65 illustrations, 40 maps, 32 charts, booklist, index. 262 pages. **$9.95**

**YUCATAN HANDBOOK** by Chicki Mallan
All the information you'll need to guide you into every corner of this exotic land. 8 color pages, 154 b/w photos, 55 illustrations, 57 maps, 70 charts, appendix, booklist, Mayan and Spanish glossaries, index. 391 pages. **$12.95**

**CANCUN HANDBOOK and Mexico's Caribbean Coast** by Chicki Mallan
Covers the city's luxury scene as well as more modest attractions, plus many side trips to unspoiled beaches and Mayan ruins. Color and b/w photos, illustrations, over 30 maps, Spanish glossary, booklist, index. 257 pages. **$9.95**

**BELIZE HANDBOOK** by Chicki Mallan
Complete with detailed maps, practical information, and an overview of the area's flamboyant history, culture, and geographical features, *Belize Handbook* is the only comprehensive guide of its kind to this spectacular region. Color and b/w photos, illustrations, maps, booklist, index. 212 pages. **$11.95**

# The International Series

**EGYPT HANDBOOK** by Kathy Hansen
An invaluable resource for intelligent travel in Egypt. 8 color pages, 20 b/w photos, 150 illustrations, 80 detailed maps and plans to museums and archaeological sites, Arabic glossary, booklist, index. 510 pages. **$14.95**

**PAKISTAN HANDBOOK** by Isobel Shaw
For armchair travelers and trekkers alike, the most detailed and authoritative guide to Pakistan ever published. 28 color pages, 86 maps, appendices, Urdu glossary, booklist, index. 478 pages. **$15.95**

**MOSCOW-LENINGRAD HANDBOOK** by Masha Nordbye
Provides the visitor with an extensive introduction to the history, culture and people of these two great cities, as well as practical information on where to stay, eat, and shop. Color and b/w photos, illustrations, maps, charts, booklist, index. Approx. 250 pages. **$12.95**

# IMPORTANT ORDERING INFORMATION

**TO ORDER BY PHONE:** (800) 345-5473 · Monday-Friday · 9 a.m.-5 p.m. PST

**PRICES:** All prices are subject to change. We always ship the most current edition. We will let you know if there is a price increase on the book you ordered.

**SHIPPING & HANDLING OPTIONS:**
1) Domestic UPS or USPS 1st class (allow 10 working days for delivery):
   $3.50 for the 1st item, 50 cents for each additional item.

**Exceptions:**
- **Moonbelt** shipping is $1.50 for one, 50 cents for each additional belt.
- Add $2.00 for same-day handling.
2) UPS 2nd Day Air or Printed Airmail requires a special quote.
3) International Surface Bookrate (8-12 weeks delivery):
   $3.00 for the 1st item, $1.00 for each additional item.

**FOREIGN ORDERS:** All orders which originate outside the U.S.A. must be paid for with either an International Money Order or a check in U.S. currency drawn on a major U.S. bank based in the U.S.A.

**TELEPHONE ORDERS:** We accept Visa or MasterCard payments. Minimum order is US$15.00. Call in your order: 1 (800) 345-5473. 9 a.m.-5 p.m. Pacific Standard Time.

**MOONBELTS.** A new concept in moneybelts. Made of heavy-duty Cordura nylon, the Moonbelt offers maximum protection for your money and important papers. This pouch, designed for all-weather comfort, slips under your shirt or waistband, rendering it virtually undetectable and inaccessible to pickpockets. Many thoughtful features: 1-inch-wide nylon webbing, heavy-duty zipper, and a 1-inch high-test quick-release buckle. No more fumbling around for the strap or repeated adjustments, this handy plastic buckle opens and closes with a touch, but won't come undone until you want it to. Accommodates traveler's checks, passport, cash, photos. Size 5 x 9 inches. Available in black only. **$8.95**

# ORDER FORM

**FOR FASTER SERVICE ORDER BY PHONE: (800) 345-5473 · 9 a.m.-5 p.m. PST**
**(See important ordering information on preceding page)**

Name:_____Date:_____

Street:_____

City:_____

State or Country:_____Zip Code:_____

Daytime Phone:_____

| Quantity | Title | Price |
|----------|-------|-------|
|          |       |       |
|          |       |       |
|          |       |       |
|          |       |       |
|          |       |       |
|          |       |       |
|          |       |       |

|  | | |
|---|---|---|
| Taxable Total | | |
| Sales Tax (6.25%) for California Residents | | |
| Shipping & Handling | | |
| **TOTAL** | | |

Ship to: ☐ address above   ☐ other_____

_____

_____

Make checks payable to:
**Moon Publications, Inc., 722 Wall Street, Chico, California 95928, U.S.A.**
We Accept Visa and MasterCard
To Order: Call in your Visa or MasterCard number, or send a written order with your Visa or
MasterCard number and expiration date clearly written.

**Card Number:**   ☐ **Visa**   ☐ **MasterCard**

☐☐☐☐  ☐☐☐☐  ☐☐☐☐  ☐☐☐☐

expiration date:_____

**Exact Name on Card:** ☐ same as above

☐ other_____

signature_____

# WHERE TO BUY THIS BOOK

**Bookstores and Libraries:**
Moon Publications Handbooks are sold worldwide. Please write our Sales Manager for a list of wholesalers and distributors in your area that stock our travel handbooks.

**Travelers:**
We would like to have Moon Publications handbooks available throughout the world. Please ask your bookstore to write or call us for ordering information. If your bookstore will not order our guides for you, please write or call for a free catalog.

**MOON PUBLICATIONS INC.**
**722 WALL STREET**
**CHICO, CA 95928 U.S.A.**
**tel: (800) 345-5473**
**fax: (916) 345-6751**